PL/I Programming

Joan K. Hughes

John Wiley & Sons

New York   London   Sydney   Toronto

Library of Congress Cataloging in Publication Data:

Hughes, Joan Kirkby
  PL/I programming.

  Bibliography: p. 677
  1. PL/I (Computer program language). I. Title.

QA76.73.P25H83   001.6'424   72–7399
ISBN 0-471-42032-8

Printed in the United States of America

10 9 8 7 6 5 4 3 2 1

This book is dedicated to

D. Michael Tucker
IBM Systems Engineering Manager, Riverside, California

David G. Goldsmith
IBM Marketing Manager, Seattle, Washington

Lily Claus
IBM Executive Secretary, Los Angeles, California

Bonnie Gee
Consultant, Los Angeles, California

Preface

To the Reader

When something becomes part of a culture's humor, it seems that it is deeply entrenched in that culture. The subject of computers has found its way into our humor as shown in the following cartoon which pokes some gentle fun at programming:

THE WIZARD OF ID   BY PARKER AND HART

Programming—whether it becomes a career for you or not—can be fun. It's like playing a game (but is considerably more challenging than Tic Tac Toe)—a game for which you can get paid. Personally, I find an excitement about working in the field of computers because

1. it teaches you to think logically, and
2. it allows you to creatively solve problems that have never been solved by man before.

PL/I is a powerful language that can be used to solve both business and scientific problems. In this text, I have tried to present the PL/I language in as simple and logical a manner as possible. But, in addition, I have also tried to avoid weaknesses I have found in some college books I had to read. For example, the answers to the *checkpoint questions* are indeed in *that* chapter. A comprehensive *index* is pro-

Cartoon used by permission of John Hart and Field Enterprises, Inc.

vided so that you should be able to quickly reference a technical point or locate the answer to a question. If you are new to the field of computers, you will find the *glossary* in Appendix G most helpful in looking up the definitions of new terms. The suggested lab problems at the end of each chapter reinforce the technical material presented in that chapter. Many of the lab problems have been "field tested" in the programming classes I have taught at the IBM Los Angeles Education Center. My appreciation goes to not only my students in IBM classes but also to my students in Pierce College (Woodland Hills, California) evening classes for their assistance and feedback.

To the Instructor

PL/I is so comprehensive that a 1000 page book could be written and still, some things would be left unsaid. I have spent months wrestling with which topics to include and how to organize those topics.

I decided to present *List-Directed I/O* in Chapter 1 so that your students could—after reading only the first chapter of this book—actually code a complete (although simple) PL/I program that would compile and execute. And, of course, getting the students involved in *doing* at an early stage of a class gets their attention, their interest, and their commitment to the subject. (Either that, or they drop the course.) The material is organized on a "need to know" basis. *Stream I/O* is presented before *record I/O* because it appears to me that is the way it is taught in so many colleges today. Arrays are presented when the iterative DO is presented ; structures are discussed in the chapter dealing with record I/O because we do not need to use structures until we program using the RECORD form of I/O. There are well-defined lab problems at the end of each chapter. For some of the problems, flowcharts are provided if the student wishes to use them. Lab problems include suggested test data (thereby saving you time in making up representative sample test data) and sample output for the students to check their solutions against. Lab problems are carefully designed to reinforce the material presented in each chapter. The chapters are modular and self-contained to a large degree. The result is that you could teach according to your own sequence of topics and assign reading that is not in the sequence of this book. For example, there would be little loss of continuity, if any, if you wanted to teach record I/O before stream I/O :

Record I/O first :   Chapters 1, 2, 3, 4, 8
Stream I/O first :   Chapters 1, 2, 3, 4, 5

Chapter 6 (*Built-in Functions*) and Chapter 7 (*How to Write Sub-routines and Functions*) can be assigned any time after Chapters 1, 2, and 3 have been read. Chapter 11 deals with a most interesting aspect of PL/I—dynamic storage allocation. This chapter assumes only that the reader knows about subroutines (Chapter 7 material).

If you are teaching trimester or quarterly courses, chances are that you would not have time for the material presented in Chapter 10 (*Indexed and Regional File Programming Concepts*). I always felt remiss about leaving out this important topic in some of the college classes I have taught, because I know from my industry experience with IBM just how important direct access device programming really is—particularly now with the trend into *data base* and *data communications*.

Appendix A will undoubtedly be a valuable reference for you as an instructor. It contains a list of PL/I keywords and examples of their use.

I wish to extend my appreciation to Professor Richard Conway for permission to use his material on Cornell University's own PL/I compiler—called PL/C. (See Appendix C and Appendix A, in that order.) Also, I wish to express appreciation to two members of his staff in the Department of Computer Science at Cornell—Steven Worona and Mark Bodenstein—who reviewed, for technical accuracy, the PL/C entries in the comparison charts in Appendix A. My thanks also go to the Wiley staff: Gene Davenport, Editor; Bernard Scheier, Manager, Palo Alto Production; Elodie Sabankaya, Designer; Phyllis Niklas, Copy Editor; Linda Riffle, Editorial Supervisor; and Tom Wolf, Production Assistant.

There is a Teacher's Manual accompanying this text. I have included sample solutions to the lab problems, as well as some teaching notes and visual aids that might be useful to you in teaching PL/I. Having taught hundreds of students the PL/I language, I have so many thoughts on the problems (and joys) of teaching PL/I that space here does not permit a full treatment. Feel free to contact me personally (Joan K. Hughes c/o John Wiley & Sons, Inc., 605 Third Ave., New York, N.Y. 10016) if you have any questions on PL/I or the teaching of PL/I.

Joan K. Hughes

Contents

xii   Contents

chapter 1

Getting
Started

A new programming language, in fact, NPL—for New Programming Language—was one of its early names, has been added to the array of computer programming languages in use today. PL/I (note that Roman numeral I is always used) is a programming language that meets the needs of both scientific and commercial programmers, affords a flexibility heretofore available only to assembler language programmers, and takes advantage of new computer architecture developments.

Because PL/I incorporates many facilities, its richness has permitted use in a wide variety of applications. "At Yale University, where more than ten high-level languages are available, it is used in place of assembly language to write the utility programs that support the operating system. It is also used by musicologists and linguists for complex character manipulations that can only be accomplished with difficulty in other languages. Bell Telephone Laboratories used PL/I to process tapes recorded with a variety of non-standard word lengths. At MIT's Project MAC, the GE 645 operating system is written in a subset of PL/I. Corporations such as Union Carbide, Eastman Kodak, and General Motors do a significant amount of their programming in PL/I. This ranges from engineering graphics to accounts receivable applications."†

PL/I was developed (the first preliminary report is dated 1964) jointly by IBM and representatives of two customer groups—SHARE, a scientific users' organization, and GUIDE, its commercial counterpart. The objective of the working committee was to synthesize into one language the best features of the many existing languages, to incorporate the latest theoretical advances in language design, and to build into the new language features allowing control of the contemporary hardware configurations (for example, multiprocessors, real-time access devices, and direct access storage units).

†L. Frampton, "How Does PL/I Compare with Its Forebears?" *Computer Decisions*, May 1970.

2

The most important forerunners of PL/I are

1. FORTRAN—arrays and scientific features
2. ALGOL—particularly the block structure
3. COBOL—structures and direct access storage maintenance

Major computer manufacturers such as CDC (Control Data Corporation) and Burroughs have announced their PL/I compilers. However, at the time of publication of this text, the majority of PL/I compilers have been produced by IBM. Some of these compilers are listed in Figure 1.1. Each of the listed language compilers is designed to run under a specific *operating system.* Although these implementations of PL/I have a great deal of similarity with respect to the language capabilities, there are a number of small details or restrictions that set them apart from each other. Wherever possible, these differences will be noted in the summaries following each chapter. PL/I D will be referenced in the text as being the *subset language,* while the other IBM compilers above are referred to as having *full language* capabilities.

There are also a number of PL/I compilers provided by IBM for use with a computer terminal. A terminal (which in many cases resembles an electric typewriter) is attached via telephone lines to a computer so that information entered through the keyboard may be processed by the computer. Some of the IBM PL/I terminal languages are listed below.

Computer terminal languages
DOS ITF PL/I
OS ITF PL/I
TSO ITF PL/I
TSS PL/I F
CALL 360

The meanings of the above abbreviations include the following:

DOS	Disk Operating System
OS	Operating System
ITF	Interactive Terminal Facility
TSO	Time-Sharing Option
TSS	Time-Sharing System

Appendix B contains a bibliography of IBM reference manuals related to PL/I programming including the above terminal languages.

Language compiler	IBM computer	Operating system	IBM reference manual number
PL/I D	S/360, Model 25 and higher, or S/370	Disk Operating System (DOS) or Tape Operating System (TOS)	GC28–8202
PL/I F	S/360, typically Model 40 and higher, or S/370	Operating System (OS)	GC28–8201
DOS PL/I Optimizing Compiler	S/360 or S/370	Disk Operating System (DOS)	SC33–0005
OS PL/I Checkout and Optimizing Compilers	S/360 or S/370	Operating System (OS)	SC33–0009

FIGURE 1.1 IBM PL/I compilers.

PL/I Program Stages

Programming begins when you decide on a method for solving a particular problem. This is the *creative* part of programming. The subsequent steps are more mechanical. After arriving at a method of solution (during which time you may have drawn a *flowchart* to depict your logic), you write the PL/I statements on coding sheets—any general-purpose 80-column coding sheets will do. If you are a student learning PL/I, you will probably have to punch your own program or perhaps key it into the computer through a typewriter terminal. Assuming the program is punched into cards, the *source program* deck is then taken to the computer for *compilation.* Compilation is a translation process. A PL/I *compiler* is a program that will take your source statements and translate them into the language the computer "understands." This language is in *binary* and often is referred to as *machine language.* The machine language equivalent of your PL/I program is called the *object program.* The object program is always placed (by the PL/I compiler) on some *external storage* medium, such as cards, magnetic tape, or disk—most often on disk.

Figure 1.2 depicts the steps involved in compiling and executing a PL/I program. It shows the *source program* as being punched into cards. These cards are read and translated by the PL/I compiler into a machine language program, which we previously termed an *object program.* The *linkage editor* has the job of preparing an executable program in the format required by main storage. The linkage editor takes the object program from an external storage medium and combines it with other programs or subprograms which the object program requires to execute properly. These other programs or subprograms are typically catalogued in libraries stored on tape or disk. *Core image program* or *load module* is typical of the name given to program output from the linkage editor. Although load modules are customarily retained on a disk or magnetic tape for future or repeated use, the programs must be brought into main storage before they can be executed.

All of the various system programs, such as the PL/I compiler or the linkage editor, are executed only when instructions are given to execute them. These instructions are referred to as JCL, for *Job Control Language.* Some of the statements that make up the JCL must "surround" your PL/I source program to cause it to be compiled and executed. The format that job control statements take depends on the operating system you are using (e.g., DOS or OS). Because JCL

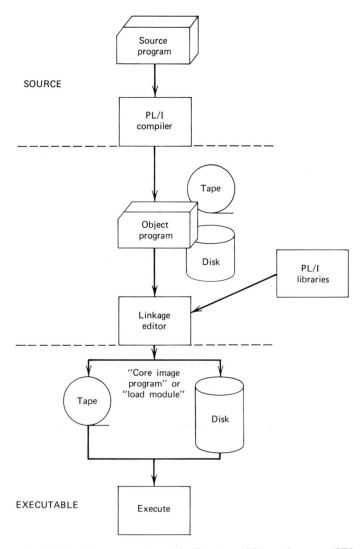

FIGURE 1.2   Program stages in System/360 or System/370.

can be a study in itself and because it is independent of programming languages, job control statements are not covered in this text.

Writing a PL/I Program

As an introduction to PL/I programming, let us examine a small program that will find the grade-point average of five examination marks. Assume the numeric grades are 100, 90, 80, 70, and 90. These grades can be punched into 80-column cards—say, one numeric grade per card. The program we are about to look at will read (input) these five values, find the sum of the numeric grades, and divide the sum by five to give the grade-point average (mean). The mean will then be printed.

It is good programming practice to begin your PL/I programs with a *comment.* For example:

/* PROGRAM TO CALCULATE GRADE POINT AVERAGE */

As you can see, a PL/I comment begins with /* and ends with */. Comments, which have no effect on the execution of a program, generally may appear anywhere in a PL/I program. In fact, comments may be embedded within a PL/I statement wherever blanks are allowed. Comments are not considered to be PL/I statements; thus, the first PL/I *statement* in the program is the PROCEDURE statement:

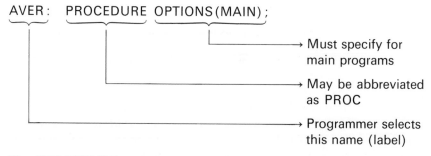

AVER :   PROCEDURE OPTIONS(MAIN) ;

→ Must specify for main programs

→ May be abbreviated as PROC

→ Programmer selects this name (label)

The PROCEDURE statement must always be labeled. In the example, AVER is termed a *label.* A label is separated from the rest of the PL/I statement with a colon (:). The label may be a combination of alphabetic and numeric characters, but the first character of the name or label must be alphabetic. The PROCEDURE statement is not executable. It is simply a way of telling the compiler that this statement marks the beginning of the block of PL/I statements. A distinction is made here

8   PL/I Programming

between *main* procedures and *subprogram* procedures, which, while different, also begin with a PROCEDURE statement but without the OPTIONS(MAIN). For example:

SUBRT: PROCEDURE;

(Subprogram procedures are covered in detail in Chapter 7.) Following the PROCEDURE OPTIONS(MAIN) statement, the statement to input the data (examination marks) should be specified. This could be accomplished with the statement

GET LIST(A,B,C,D,E);

Notice how all PL/I statements are ended with a semicolon (;). When the GET statement above is executed, the five values (100,90,80,70,90) punched in cards will be read into the computer and assigned correspondingly to the *variables* named A, B, C, D, and E. Thus, A will contain the value 100, B the value 90, C the value 80, and so on. Variables are names which represent data or are names to which data may be assigned.

The next programming step would be to calculate the grade-point average. This could be accomplished by the following *assignment statement*:

MEAN = (A+B+C+D+E)/5;

Expression

Arithmetic assignment statement

The sum of A, B, C, D, and E is computed first because all arithmetic operations specified within parentheses are performed before arithmetic operations that appear outside the parentheses in an expression. The slash (/) indicates a divide operation. Thus, the sum is divided by 5. The quotient is placed in the variable named MEAN. The equal sign (=) is referred to as the *assignment symbol* because it denotes the assignment statement. The assignment statement does not necessarily represent equality. The assignment statement can be verbally stated as, "Assign the value of the expression on the right of the assignment symbol (=) to the variable on the left of the assignment symbol."

The final step in this sample program is that of printing the results. This could be accomplished with the following statement:

PUT LIST('AVERAGE IS',MEAN);

This statement generates output to a system printer, generally a line printer. The printout would look like this:

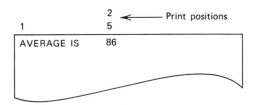

Why print position 1 and then 25? Data printed with a PUT LIST statement are automatically aligned on predetermined *tab positions*. These positions are 1, 25, 49, 73, 97, and 121. (It is possible that in some installations, these predetermined tab positions have been altered and thus may not match the positions stated above.) In the PUT LIST statement, two data items were output:

1. The literal 'AVERAGE IS'
2. The contents of the variable called MEAN

Notice how the literal was surrounded with single quotation marks in the PUT LIST statement; however, on output, the single quote marks are removed before the literal is printed. This literal is a character-string constant. A *constant* is an arithmetic data item or string data item that does not have a name and whose value cannot change. Other types of PL/I constants will be discussed later. The constant 5 in the assignment statement previously introduced is an example of an arithmetic data item. String constants are surrounded by single quote marks; arithmetic constants are not surrounded by any punctuation marks.

Logically, our grade-point average program is finished. A RETURN statement could be specified to indicate the logical point at which the program should terminate execution. It would be coded:

RETURN;   /* LOGICAL END */

Following the RETURN statement, an END statement must be specified which indicates the *physical end* of our program. For example:

END;   /* PHYSICAL END */

If a RETURN statement is to be immediately followed by an END statement in your program, then the RETURN statement may be omitted, for the END statement may be used to mark both the logical and physical end of a procedure block. (*Procedure block* and *program* are being used here as synonyms; however, a program actually consists of one or more procedure blocks.) The END statement may, optionally, contain the label of the procedure it is ending. For example:

    END AVER;

The label affixed to the PROCEDURE
OPTIONS(MAIN) statement

Here, then, is the complete program:

```
/* PROGRAM TO CALCULATE GRADE POINT AVERAGE */
AVER:   PROCEDURE OPTIONS(MAIN);
        GET LIST(A,B,C,D,E);
        MEAN=(A+B+C+D+E)/5;
        PUT LIST('AVERAGE IS',MEAN);
        END;
```

Default Attributes

Data names (variables) beginning with the letters I through N may represent whole numbers only—that is, integers. Thus, MEAN may contain only the integer portion of an arithmetic result. For the input data suggested, the result after summation and division is 86.0. However, if the input values had been, for example, 100, 90, 80, 70, 94, then a mixed number (a number composed of an integer and a fraction) of 86.8 would be the result of the arithmetic operations. If the value 86.8 is assigned to MEAN, only the integer portion of the number is retained. In this case, the .8 would be dropped.

Of course, having variable names which represent only whole numbers can work to our advantage. Suppose it is desired to give the grade-point average as a whole number, but rounded off. That is, if the average's fraction is .5 or more, round up to the next whole number so that a calculated average of 86.8 would be 87 on the printout. This could be accomplished by the statement:

$$MEAN = (A+B+C+D+E)/5+.5;$$

The expression $(A+B+C+D+E)/5+.5$ will be computed in such a manner that intermediate results allow for mixed numbers to be retained. When the result is assigned to MEAN, the fractional part is then *truncated* (dropped). Variables that begin with the letters A through H, O through Z, or the symbols @, #, $ are assumed to have the attributes FLOAT DECIMAL. An *attribute* is a descriptive property associated with a name. FLOAT DECIMAL data are represented inside the computer in a floating-point format. It is not important that you know how this data looks inside the computer, but you should know how to interpret floating-point notation in the printed form which is explained as follows (where X represents any decimal digit):

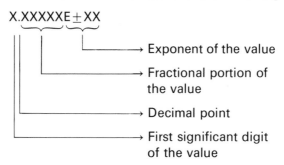

$$X.XXXXXE \pm XX$$

→ Exponent of the value

→ Fractional portion of the value

→ Decimal point

→ First significant digit of the value

Assume the following assignment statement had been coded:

$$AVERAGE = (A + B + C + D + E)/5 ;$$

If the result is 86, the grade-point average is printed in the following form:

8.60000E + 01

→ Think of E + 01 as the multiplier 10^1 (since 10^1 is equal to 10, multiply 8.6 by 10 to give result of 86.)

In the above example, the E + 01 *floats* the decimal point to the right 01 places so that AVERAGE will equal 86.

If the average were 86.8, then this would be printed:

8.68000E + 01

Thus, through the FLOAT DECIMAL variables it is possible to retain and print out mixed numbers. However, for business programming, this scientific notation is not desirable, because the floating-point format—though understood by the mathematician—is not acceptable to the accountant. The solution to the problem lies in giving the PL/I programmer the facility to specify other attributes for his data.

When variables begin with the letters I through N (or A through H, etc.), we have seen that certain attributes are assumed. These assumptions by the PL/I compiler are said to be *default* attributes. A default is an alternative attribute or option assumed when none has been specified.

The DECLARE Statement

If a programmer does not want the default attributes to apply to his variables, then the desired attributes may be specified through the DECLARE statement. For example, assume we would like to print the grade-point average to the nearest tenth of a point:

AVERAGE IS   86.8

When it is desired to work with mixed numbers but not in the floating-point format, declare your data to have the FIXED DECIMAL attributes:

DECLARE MEAN FIXED DECIMAL(4,1);

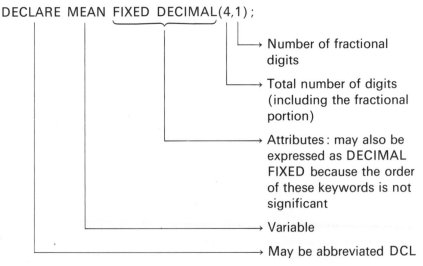

→ Number of fractional digits

→ Total number of digits (including the fractional portion)

→ Attributes: may also be expressed as DECIMAL FIXED because the order of these keywords is not significant

→ Variable

→ May be abbreviated DCL

In the above example, the total number of digits specified is four, to allow for the maximum grade-point average (i.e., 100.0). It is also possible to declare FIXED DECIMAL variables as representing whole numbers. For example:

DECLARE AVERAGE FIXED DECIMAL(3);
/* OR */
DECLARE AVERAGE FIXED DECIMAL(3,0);

In a DECLARE statement, if you specify only the attribute FIXED, the attribute DECIMAL will be assumed by default. However, if you specify only the attribute DECIMAL, the attribute FLOAT will be assumed by default. If you are programming business applications, then you should either use variables that begin with the letters I through N to represent data that are within the range of ±32,767 or declare variables to have the FIXED attribute.

Let us assume, then, that for this grade-point average program, we are including the following DECLARE statement:

DECLARE MEAN FIXED(4,1);

The variables A, B, C, D, and E could also be declared to have the FIXED DECIMAL attributes. For example:

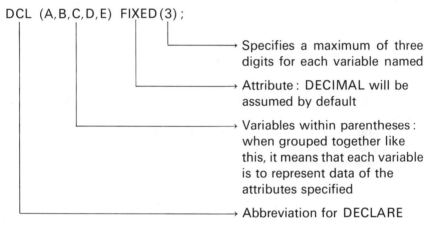

DCL (A,B,C,D,E) FIXED(3);

→ Specifies a maximum of three digits for each variable named

→ Attribute: DECIMAL will be assumed by default

→ Variables within parentheses: when grouped together like this, it means that each variable is to represent data of the attributes specified

→ Abbreviation for DECLARE

DECLARE statements may appear anywhere in a PL/I procedure. Typically, they are placed at the beginning of a procedure—perhaps immediately following the PROCEDURE statement. Here, then, is the program including the DECLARE statements:

```
/* PROGRAM TO CALCULATE GRADE POINT AVERAGE */
AVER:   PROCEDURE OPTIONS(MAIN);
        DCL MEAN FIXED(4,1);
        DCL (A,B,C,D,E) FIXED(3);
        GET LIST(A,B,C,D,E);
        MEAN = (A+B+C+D+E)/5;
        PUT LIST('AVERAGE IS',MEAN);
        END;
```

Identifiers

The general term *identifiers* is given to names of data (MEAN, A, B, C, D, and E in the grade-point average program), names of *procedures* (AVER in the same program), names of *files* (there were no defined or specified files in this program), labels of PL/I *statements* (only the PROCEDURE statement was labeled), and *keywords* (such as GET or PUT).

Keywords constitute the vocabulary that makes up the PL/I language. When keywords are used in proper context, they have a specific meaning. Appendix A provides a list of keywords available for various PL/I compilers.

An identifier for *data names* and *statement labels* may be from 1 to 31 alphabetic characters (A−Z, @,#,$), numeric digits (0−9), and break (_) characters,† providing that the first character is alphabetic. Some examples are

RATE_OF_PAY	$TWO
CONTINUE	LOOP_3
PERCENT	PIE_A_LA_MODE

Note that in PL/I, the characters @, #, and $ are considered to be alphabetic.

Names of *procedures* and *files* may be a maximum of six or seven characters long, depending on which PL/I compiler you are using. Some examples of procedure and file names are

PAYROL	CALC
CARDIN	PRINTR
P1	FILEA

Note that, generally, special characters such as the break character (_), or the # or @ may not be used in file names or procedure names even though they are allowed for other identifiers such as names of data.

	Number of characters allowed for procedure names or file names
Subset language	1 to 6
Full language	1 to 7

†The break character is the same as the typewriter underline character. It can be used within a data name, such as GROSS_PAY, to improve readability. A hyphen cannot be used because it would be treated as a minus sign.

Statement Format

PL/I is said to be free-form; that is, a statement may contain blanks as needed to improve readability of the source program. A PL/I statement may be continued across several cards. For example:

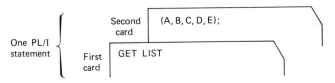

Or, one card may contain several PL/I statements. For example:

GET LIST(A, B, C, D, E); MEAN=(A+B+C+D+E)/5;

The reason that more than one statement may appear on a card is that a semicolon (;) terminates a PL/I statement. If a programmer inadvertently omits a semicolon at the end of a PL/I statement, thereby causing two statements to "run" together, the compiler may flag the combined statements as being in error. Sometimes the compiler can detect where the semicolon was to appear and insert one for you. Flagging of errors of this and other types is referred to as *compiler diagnostics.*

Because PL/I is free-form, no special coding sheets are required. Following is the generally accepted standard:

COLUMN 1	Reserved for use by the operating system
COLUMNS 2–72	May contain one or more PL/I statements or part of a statement
COLUMNS 73–80	May contain program identification name and/or a card sequence number; the compiler, however, does not check for consecutive order of sequence numbers

List-Directed I/O

List-Directed Input

List-directed data transmission is the first form of input/output discussed because it is easy to learn (thereby allowing you to start writing PL/I programs quickly), and, although it would not be used in production-type jobs, it can be a useful debugging or program checkout tool.

In the grade-point average program, the input statement

GET LIST(A,B,C,D,E) ;

caused data to be read from the system input device which is typically a card reader. For this type of input, each data value must be separated by a delimiter such as a blank. For example, the five values could have been punched into one card:

100 90 80 70 90

Because the data can be separated by one or more blanks, each value could have been punched on a separate card:

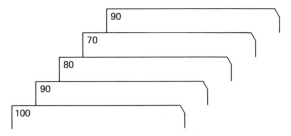

The input data could also have been separated by a comma and blanks. For example:

100, 90,80,70, 90

or by only a comma and no blanks. For example:

100,90,80,70,90

Notice that there is no comma following the last data item in the input *stream*. The term stream is used because in list-directed input or output data transmission, data are treated as one *continuous* stream of characters. In understanding this concept, it might be helpful to think of the data characters in an input stream as being on a conveyor belt.

A number of characters—perhaps decimal digits—will be "taken" off the conveyor belt and assigned to the appropriate variable by the GET LIST statement. Just how many digits are combined and assigned to one variable is determined by the blank or comma that separates each data item in the stream. Thus, characters are read (i.e., the conveyor belt is moved) until a blank or comma is encountered. That group of characters, then, would make up one data item. Assuming the data are punched in cards, when there are no more data on one card, then the next card would be input, and the "conveyor belt analogy" would continue. Another way of looking at the stream concept is to imagine taping all the cards in an input deck end-to-end:

As a further illustration of the stream concept, assume we have the following data card with the values from the grade-point average program punched in the following manner:

```
100 90 80 70 90
```

and we have written the statement

GET LIST(A,B,C);

Here, of course, A will take on the value of 100, B, the value of 90, and C, the value of 80. Now, assume the next statement in the PL/I program is

GET LIST(D,E);

The variable D will take on the value 70, and E, the value 90. A new card record is not read, because there are still some values contained on the first card. In other words, the card (or print line) is an *artificial boundary*, as seen by PL/I. Another way the five values from a single card could have been read is

GET LIST(A);
GET LIST(B);
GET LIST(C);
GET LIST(D);
GET LIST(E);

Although the above method is obviously inefficient, it does illustrate the use and flexibility of stream data transmission.

PL/I Constants Used in List-Directed I/O

Any type of PL/I constant may appear in the input stream for list-directed input. For example:

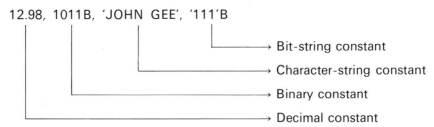

12.98, 1011B, 'JOHN GEE', '111'B

→ Bit-string constant

→ Character-string constant

→ Binary constant

→ Decimal constant

These and other types of PL/I constants may appear in the input stream. Let us consider some of them now.

Decimal fixed-point constants consist of one or more decimal digits and optionally, a decimal point. If no decimal point appears, then the data item is assumed to be an integer. Some examples are

$$3.1415 \qquad +52.98 \qquad -100 \qquad .0003$$

Decimal fixed-point constants are contrasted with *decimal floating-point constants,* which have the E-notation defined previously in this chapter. Some examples of decimal floating-point constants, along with their decimal fixed-point equivalents, are given below:

Decimal floating-point constant	Decimal fixed-point equivalent
12.E+05 or 12E5	1200000.
3141593E−6	3.141593
.1E−07	.00000001
−45E+11	−4500000000000.
84E	84

On S/360 or S/370, the range of decimal floating-point exponents is approximately 10^{-78} to 10^{+75} power.

A *string* is a sequence of characters or bits that is treated as a single data item. A *character-string* may include any character recognized by the computer system. Any blank included in a character-string is considered part of the data and is to be included in the count of the length of the string. When written in a program, character-string constants must be enclosed in single quote marks. Some examples are

> 'THE ROAD NOT TAKEN'
> 'DR. STRETCH, CHIROPRACTOR'
> '18215 BURBANK BLVD.'

If it is desired to represent an apostrophe within the character-string constant, it must be written as two single quotation marks with no intervening blanks. Consider the following constant:

> 'SHAKESPEARE''S HAMLET'

which will be stored inside the computer as

| S | H | A | K | E | S | P | E | A | R | E | ' | S | | H | A | M | L | E | T |

It is also possible to specify a *repetition factor* for string constants. This feature is useful when a *pattern* in the string data exists. For example, the character-string constant for the city of Walla Walla could be written

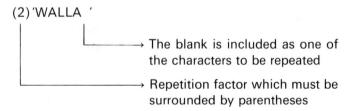

(2) 'WALLA '

⟶ The blank is included as one of the characters to be repeated

⟶ Repetition factor which must be surrounded by parentheses

and gives the following character-string with a length of 12:

| W | A | L | L | A | | W | A | L | L | A | |

If a character-string constant appears in the input stream and is to be read using a GET LIST statement, then the variable in the GET statement should have the attribute CHARACTER. The DECLARE statement must be used to specify a variable to have the CHARACTER attribute.

For example, to read 'WALLA WALLA', the following would be coded:

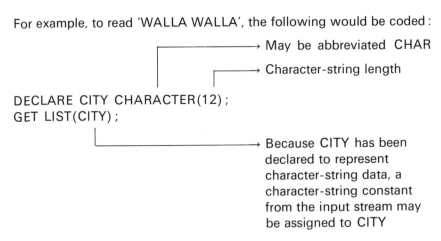

DECLARE CITY CHARACTER(12);
GET LIST(CITY);

→ May be abbreviated CHAR

→ Character-string length

→ Because CITY has been declared to represent character-string data, a character-string constant from the input stream may be assigned to CITY

Here is another example of the DECLARE statement and an assignment statement that assigns a character constant to the variable declared:

DCL NAME CHAR(20);
NAME = 'TOM ANDERSON';

T	O	M		A	N	D	E	R	S	O	N								

The name TOM ANDERSON is less than 20 characters, which is the length declared for NAME. In this case, unused positions of the variable will be padded on the right with blanks.

So far, we have been considering decimal data constants and character-string constants. Another type of data that we may work with in PL/I is binary data. (If you are not familiar with the binary number system, you may wish to consult Appendix D for an explanation.) First, the question must be raised, "Why use binary numbers in a PL/I program when it is difficult to 'think' in binary?" What is more, because we live in a *decimal world,* binary numbers will ultimately have to be translated to decimal to be meaningful. Another disadvantage of writing binary numbers is that it is difficult to represent binary fractions easily. (For example, try writing the binary equivalent for the decimal number 5.1.) The advantages of using binary data, however, are significant enough to override the disadvantages stated above. The advantages are these:

1. *Conserves space:* Generally, the binary method of representing data inside a computer requires the least amount of storage of any data format available.

On S/360 or S/370, the range of binary floating-point exponents is approximately 2^{-260} to 2^{+252} power.

If you have some previous knowledge about S/360 or S/370, then you know that there is only one form in which floating-point data are represented inside the computer, namely, floating hexadecimal. As we have seen, PL/I allows two forms of floating-point. The compiler will automatically convert these forms to the internal format (floating hexadecimal) for representation in main storage. Thus, in a PL/I program there are two forms of floating-point that may be coded, but both forms will appear in the same format inside the computer. The circumstances under which a scientific programmer might code binary floating-point constants rather than decimal floating-point constants are these:

1. The nature of the problem being solved dictates that binary is a more convenient form than decimal.
2. The programmer needs to express constants to the nearest bit rather than the nearest decimal digit.

A *bit-string* (*bit* is the abbreviation for *b*inary dig*it*) constant is written in a program as a series of binary digits enclosed in single quote marks and followed by the letter B. Bit-strings are valuable for general use as logical switches; they can be set to 1 or 0 as indicators that may be necessary later in the program for decision-making. Bit-strings are being increasingly used in information retrieval. Many "yes" or "no" answers can be recorded as a bit-string in a relatively small area. Here are some examples of bit-string constants:

```
'1'B
'11111010110001'B
(64)'0'B
```

The parenthesized number preceding the last example is a repetition factor which specifies that the following bit or bits are to be repeated the specified number of times. The example shown would result in a string of 64 binary zeros.

Do not confuse a bit-string with a binary fixed-point data item. Bit-strings are usually not used in calculations as binary fixed-point data may be. Instead, bit-strings may be used in a program to indicate whether or not certain conditions exist (yes or no, 1 or 0, true or false). Bit-strings can also be used as a compact method of describing characteristics. For example, assume a television and movie casting agency is using a computer to keep track of the thousands of Hollywood "bit-

2. *Saves execution time:* Less computer time is required to opera
    on binary data than is needed for decimal data. Thus, a progra
    operating on binary data will, in most cases, execute faster tha
    the equivalent program operating on decimal data.

Most PL/I programs will be written so that they operate on bot
binary and decimal data. Let us examine, then, the types of binai
constants that we may either input using GET LIST or express in
PL/I source program.

A *binary fixed-point* constant expresses a number using binai
notation. It is written as one or more binary digits followed by th
letter B. Here are some examples of binary fixed-point constants:

Constant	Decimal equivalent
10110B	22
11111B	31
−101B	−5
10000B	16

	Binary fixed-point constants
Subset language	Whole binary numbers only, e.g., 111B
Full language	Mixed binary numbers are allowed, e.g., 111.01B

Decimal floating-point constants were introduced previously in
this chapter. Usually, this type of data is used only by the scientific
programmer. In PL/I, it is also possible to express floating-point
constants in binary. Although this feature is not used too often, it
does provide a flexibility not generally available in high-level languages.

A *binary floating-point* constant consists of a field of binary
digits followed by the letter E, followed by a decimal integer exponent
followed by the letter B. The field of binary digits may contain a binary
point, and of course, a plus or minus sign. The exponent may be signed.
As with decimal data, the exponent indicates the displacement of the
binary point. For example:

Constant	Equivalent
11011E3B	$(11011000)_2 = (216)_{10}$
10110.1E0B	$(10110.1)_2 = (22.5)_{10}$
1011.E−3B	$(1.011)_2 = (1.75)_{10}$

part" actors (no pun intended) available for movie and television work. When the studio has determined its requirements for "extras," that request is sent to the casting agency. On what basis does the agency select the actors to fill this request? Or, when a request for a particular type of actor comes to the agency, how does the agency select from the thousands of possible actors the right person for the part? One method would be to describe the various talents (comedy, heavy dramatic) and characteristics (age, hair color, height) of the actors in terms of bit-strings, for example :

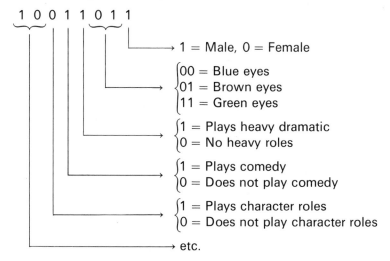

These bit-strings could be stored on tape or disk files. When a request for a certain type of actor is made, a bit-string of the desired characteristics is defined. Using this bit pattern as a guide, the files of bit-strings can be easily searched by a PL/I program for the person who most closely resembles the desired characteristics. You can see from the above example, how a lot of information about a person can be compacted into a small "space." Large companies, having computerized their personnel records, use the method of coding bit-strings to describe employees' capabilities and talents.

Here, then, is a summary of the PL/I constants we have just examined :

1.   Decimal fixed-point : 3.14159, −5280, 45.3
2.   Decimal floating-point : 12E5, +12.E+05, 84E, −76E+7, 3E−17
3.   Character-string : 'DR. SPITZ, DOG TRAINER', (2)'TOM '

4. Binary fixed-point: 10110B, 111B, −101B
5. Binary floating-point: 11011E3B, 10110.1E, −.11101E+02B
6. Bit-string: '1'B, '01011'B, (32)'0'B

These, and other types of constants may appear not only in the input stream for GET LIST but also in PL/I program statements. For example:

$$J = K + 1B;$$

                              → Add a *binary one* to K
                                   and assign it to J

List-Directed Output

Because PL/I constants may be data items in the PUT LIST statement, the statements,

PUT LIST(50,'ABC',123,127);
PUT LIST(23,86,87);

would give us this output:

	1	25	49	73	97	121 ← Tab positions
First line	50	ABC	123	127	23	
Second line	86	87				

In PUT LIST, the stream concept still applies. The data items specified for output will be printed beginning at predetermined tab positions. Notice how the first data item in the second PUT LIST statement was printed on the first line with data items from the first PUT LIST statement. From this you can see that a PUT statement does not necessarily cause data to be printed beginning on a new line. Output begins wherever that last output was ended. Notice that nothing was printed in tab position 121. This is because the line size for a PUT LIST is 120 positions. It has been shown that the tab positions are 1, 25, 49, 73, 97, and 121. How, then, does one output to a print position beyond 120 if the line size for PUT LIST is 120 maximum positions? The answer is that certain attributes or characteristics are assumed for the output file (e.g., the line printer) associated with the PUT LIST statement. One of these characteristics is that the line size is 120 positions. As will be seen later, it is possible to define a file whose line size is greater than 120 print positions, in which case tab position 121 would be used in the list-directed printed output (assuming the line printer has more than 120 print positions).

Constants, variables, or expressions may be specified as *data items* in a PUT LIST statement. For example:

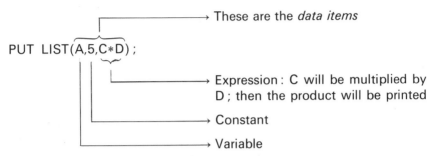

Assume it is desired to print one value on one line and a second value on the next line. This can be accomplished through the PAGE and/or SKIP options. The PAGE option causes the paper in the line printer to advance to the top of a new page. The SKIP option causes the paper in the line printer to be advanced the number of lines specified. If the number of lines is not explicitly stated, a SKIP(1) is assumed.

Whenever a PUT LIST is *first* executed in your program, there is an automatic skip to a new page on the line printer. Thereafter you must specify the *printer control options* as your program logic dictates. For example:

```
PUT PAGE LIST('ABC');      /* START A NEW PAGE */
PUT SKIP LIST(123);        /* SKIP ONE LINE BEFORE PRINT */
PUT SKIP(2) LIST(127);     /* SKIP TWO LINES BEFORE PRINT */
        └───────────→ Number of lines to skip
```

A SKIP(0) causes a suppression of the line feed. For example, suppose it is desired to print a heading on a new page and underline that heading (e.g., STANLEY P. SMERSCH & ASSOCIATES). These statements would accomplish it:

```
PUT PAGE LIST('STANLEY P. SMERSCH & ASSOCIATES');
PUT SKIP(0)LIST((31)'_');  /* A REPETITION FACTOR OF 31
    UNDERSCORE CHARACTERS IS SPECIFIED */
```

Since SKIP(0) prevents advancing of the paper in the printer, we simply go back to the beginning of the line on which the previous

information was printed. Using the break character in the second
PUT statement above causes the heading to be underlined.

	Maximum number of lines that may be skipped at any one time
Subset language	3
Full language	No maximum; however, you cannot skip beyond the end of a page

The LINE option may be used to indicate the line of the page on
which you would like information to be printed. For example:

PUT PAGE LINE(10) LIST(A,B,C);

This indicates that a new page should be started and that the values of
A, B, and C should be printed starting on line 10 of that new page.
It is also possible to write

PUT LINE(10) PAGE LIST(A,B,C);

The effect is the same as in the previous example. This is because
when PAGE and LINE are specified in the same PUT statement, there
is a hierarchy governing which option is exercised first. The order of
priority is PAGE first, then LINE.

The PAGE, SKIP, and LINE options may also appear by them-
selves. For example:

```
PUT PAGE;        /* START A NEW PAGE */
PUT SKIP(2);     /* SKIP TWO LINES */
PUT LINE(15);    /* SET CURRENT LINE COUNTER TO 15 */
```

In this example, there is a comment about the *current line counter.*
This is an internal counter provided by PL/I for keeping track of
vertical spacing on the line printer. Every time a line is printed during
the execution of your PL/I object program, the line counter is automatically incremented by one. When the value in the line counter
reaches a predetermined maximum, it is reset and the process begun
again for a new page. The maximum value for the line count is a system
standard which is defined at each computer installation or which may

be specified through a special option called PAGESIZE—this will be explained later.

In PL/I there is a special operation that facilitates manipulation of string data. The operation is called *concatenate.* It means "to join together" string (character or bit) data. As an illustration, assume that a heading is to be printed on a report that contains lines 80 characters long. The heading is

PAYROLL REGISTER

and it is desired to center the heading above the printout. This would be accomplished by having 32 leading blanks, followed by the literal data, followed by 32 trailing blanks. It would be coded:

PUT LIST((32)' '||'PAYROLL REGISTER'||(32)' ') ;

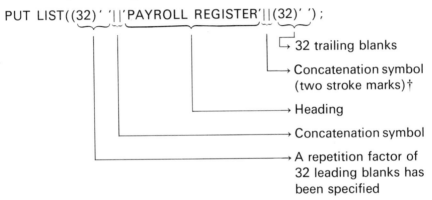

→ 32 trailing blanks

→ Concatenation symbol (two stroke marks)†

→ Heading

→ Concatenation symbol

→ A repetition factor of 32 leading blanks has been specified

Suppose it is desired to write the bit-string constant

11111111111111110000000000000000

where there are 16 ones and 16 zeros in one string. Using the repetition factor and the concatenation operator allows us to write the PL/I constant as follows:

(16)'1'B||(16)'0'B

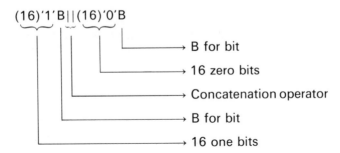

→ B for bit

→ 16 zero bits

→ Concatenation operator

→ B for bit

→ 16 one bits

†The stroke character is above the Y on a keypunch.

PL/I Language Components

Statement Format

PL/I statements take the general form

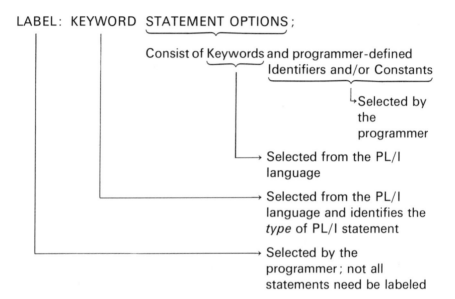

LABEL: KEYWORD STATEMENT OPTIONS;

Consist of Keywords and programmer-defined Identifiers and/or Constants

↳Selected by the programmer

→ Selected from the PL/I language

→ Selected from the PL/I language and identifies the *type* of PL/I statement

→ Selected by the programmer; not all statements need be labeled

For example:

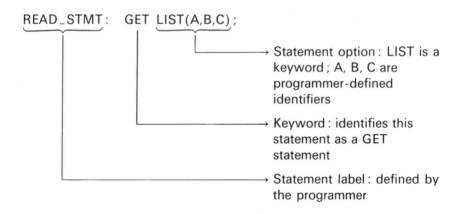

READ_STMT: GET LIST(A,B,C);

→ Statement option: LIST is a keyword; A, B, C are programmer-defined identifiers

→ Keyword: identifies this statement as a GET statement

→ Statement label: defined by the programmer

Character Sets

There are 60 characters in the PL/I language. They include:

Extended alphabet of 29 characters
$ @ # A B C D E F G H I J K L
M N O P Q R S T U V W X Y Z

Ten decimal digits
0 1 2 3 4 5 6 7 8 9

21 special characters

Blank	
Equal or assignment symbol	=
Plus sign	+
Minus sign	−
Asterisk or multiply symbol	*
Slash or divide symbol	/
Left parenthesis	(
Right parenthesis	)
Comma	,
Point or period	.
Single quotation mark or apostrophe	'
Percent symbol	%
Semicolon	;
Colon	:
"Not" symbol	¬
"And" symbol	&
"Or" symbol†	|
"Greater than" symbol	>
"Less than" symbol	<
Break character	_
Question mark	?

The question mark, at present, has no specific use in the language, even though it is included in the 60-character set.

Special characters may be combined to create other symbols; for example, $<=$ means "less than or equal to," $\neg =$ means "not equal to." The combination $**$ denotes exponentiation ($X**2$ means X^2, $X**3$ means X^3). Blanks are not permitted in such character

---

†The | symbol is called a *stroke character*.

combinations. For example,

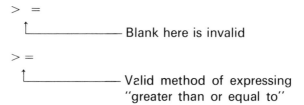

A special 48-character set is also available as an alternative to the 60-character set. This 48-character set is provided as a convenience to the programmer and would be used instead of the 60-character set if some of the special characters (> % ; : etc.) were not graphically available on the printer on which the source program is to be listed. Normally, a special print cartridge must be mounted on the printer in order for such characters as ; or : or # to be printed. The problem is that, even though the various print cartridges are interchangeable, some computer installations do not have a cartridge with all the required characters for PL/I. If the programmer writes programs using the punctuation from the 60-character set, but the line printer on which the source program is being listed does not have the proper characters, certain characters will not be printed. For example,

Note that it is not an "error" when the semicolon is not printed. It presents a problem to the programmer while debugging his PL/I program, for he will often have to resort to reading his source cards to verify that certain characters have indeed been punched.

Because certain symbols (e.g., > <) from the 60-character set are not available in the 48-character set, we must have a means to express such functions as "greater than" or "less than." Figure 1.3 illustrates how various punctuation marks and operations are expressed in each of the character sets. The small "b" in the 48-character set comparison operators indicates that a blank must appear at that place. Note that @, #, ?, and the break character (_) are not available in the 48-character set. When using the 48-character set, the special operators CAT, NE, NL, NG, GT, GE, LT, LE, NOT, OR, and AND are *reserved*

Explanation	60-character set	48-character set
Alphabetic letters	A through Z $ @ #	A through Z $ Not available Not available
Numeric digits	0123456789	0123456789

Punctuation
  Period
  Comma
  Single quote
  Parentheses
  Colon
  Semicolon
	.
	,
	'
	( )
	:
	;
		.
		,
		'
		( )
		. .
		, .

Arithmetic	+ − * / **	+ − * / **

Special
  Blank
  Break
  Percent
  Question mark
  Concatenation
  Equal
  Greater than
  Greater than or equal
  Less than
  Less than or equal
  Not less than
  Not greater than
  Not equal
  Not
  Or
  And
	
	_
	%
	?
	||
	=
	>
	> =
	<
	< =
	¬ <
	¬ >
	¬ =
	¬
	|
	&
		
		Not available
		/ /
		Not available
		bCATb
		=
		bGTb
		bGEb
		bLTb
		bLEb
		bNLb
		bNGb
		bNEb
		bNOTb
		bORb
		bANDb

FIGURE 1.3 Expressing punctuation and operations in 60- and 48-character sets.

keywords that must be surrounded by one or more blanks and cannot be used by the programmer for any other purpose. For example:

IF A LT B THEN Y=1;

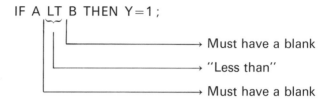

→ Must have a blank
→ "Less than"
→ Must have a blank

The following statement is invalid:

SUM = GE + VALUE;   /* INVALID IN 48 CHARACTER SET */

→ This is a reserved keyword when using the 48-character set; it can only be used to denote a logical operation

   All elements that make up a PL/I program are constructed from the character sets. On S/360 and S/370, a set of 256 characters has been defined. Included in this full set of characters but not in the 48- or 60-character set are such items as lowercase letters and additional mathematical symbols. In PL/I, character-strings and comments may contain any character from the full 256-character set. Appendix D contains a chart defining the full character set.

   In some compilers, to indicate which character set you wish to use in your PL/I program, a special statement, called the PROCESS statement, may be used. In this, a number of options may be specified, one of which is the character set you wish to use. If you specify that the 48-character set is to be used, you may still use any character from the 60-character set (except # @ _). The reverse, however, is not true; when specifying the 60-character set to mean >, <, =, etc., none of the 48 special symbols may be used. Thus, such keywords as LT, GT, or CAT may not be used to mean, respectively, *less than*, *greater than*, or *concatenate*; nor could the 48-character set symbol for a semicolon (,.) be specified.

   You should consult the appropriate Programmer's Guide for the PL/I implementation you are working with for a detailed description of the keywords that may appear in the PROCESS statement. A sample of the PROCESS statement specifying the 48-character option is shown in Figure 1.4.

PL/I D	* PROCESS 48C
PL/I F	* PROCESS ('CHAR48');
DOS PL/I Optimizing	* PROCESS CHARSET(48)
OS PL/I Optimizing	* PROCESS CHARSET(48)

FIGURE 1.4   PROCESS statement examples.
(In OS, the PARM parameter in the EXEC job control statement is used to specify CHAR48 or CHAR60 for the first procedure compiled. If more than one procedure is compiled at the same point in time, then the PROCESS statement is used for the subsequent procedures.)

SUMMARY

PL/I Program Stages: In this chapter, you were introduced to the stages of a PL/I program. The first stage is to decide on a method for solving a particular problem and, perhaps, draw a flowchart to depict your logic. Next, you write the PL/I statements on coding sheets. The statements are punched into cards, which are referred to as a source program deck. Compilation is the translation process in which the PL/I compiler reads your source statements and translates them into machine language. The machine language equivalent of your PL/I program is called the object program; this is placed on an external storage medium, such as cards, magnetic tape, or disk. The linkage editor is a program that prepares an executable program in the format required by main storage. Job Control Language statements must surround your PL/I source program to cause it to be compiled and executed.

PL/I Comments: A comment begins with /* and ends with */. Because the compiler takes the first card of your PL/I program and prints that information at the top of every page of output of the source listing, it is a good idea to have a comment heading your source program statements.

The PROCEDURE Statement: The PROCEDURE statement tells the compiler that this statement marks the beginning of the block of PL/I statements. There are two types of procedures: main procedures and subprogram procedures.

Identifiers: Names of data, procedures, files, labels of PL/I statements, and keywords are all given the general term identifiers. An identifier for data names and statement labels may be from one to 31 alphabetic characters (A–Z, @, #, $), numeric digits (0–9), and break (_) characters, providing that the first character is alphabetic. Names of procedures and files may be a maximum of six characters for the subset language and seven characters for the full language.

Statement Format: PL/I is said to be free-form; that is, a statement may contain blanks to improve readability of the source program. The general practice is to punch PL/I statements in columns 2 through 72 only.

Default Attributes: These are attributes assigned to identifiers when none has been explicitly declared. Variables that begin with A through H, O through Z, @, #, or $ default to the attributes DECIMAL FLOAT(6). (The 6 is the number of digits of precision.) Identifiers that begin with the letters I through N default to FIXED BINARY(15), where the 15 is the number of bits of precision. The attributes FIXED BINARY were not discussed in this chapter because, so far, we have only been concerned with declaring decimal data and character-strings. The I through N variables may be assigned decimal numbers even though their default attributes include BINARY. The decimal integer value that can be represented in 15 bits of precision must be within the range of $-32,768$ to $+32,767$.

The DECLARE Statement: This statement is used to define attributes for variables that represent data. Following are examples of the attributes introduced in this chapter:

```
DCL A FIXED DECIMAL(5) ;
DCL B FIXED(5,2) ;
DCL C CHARACTER(10) ;
DCL (D,E,F) CHAR(4) ;
```

List-Directed I/O: Input data may be separated by a comma or one or more blanks. The input data must be in the form of *valid* PL/I constants (e.g., 'ABC', 12.5, 1101B, 57E). Output is to tab positions 1, 25, 49, 73, 97, and 121. Examples are

```
GET LIST(A,B,C) ;
GET SKIP LIST(A,B,C) ;
PUT LIST(A*B) ;
PUT SKIP LIST(X,Y,Z) ;
PUT PAGE LIST('HEADING') ;
```

PAGE, SKIP, and LINE Options: The PAGE option causes the paper in the line printer to advance to the top of a new page. The SKIP option causes the paper in the line printer to be advanced the number of lines specified (e.g.,

PUT SKIP(2) ;). A SKIP(0) causes a suppression of the line feed. The LINE option may be used to indicate the line of the page on which you would like information to be printed (e.g., PUT PAGE LINE(10) ;). PAGE, SKIP, and LINE may not be specified in the same PUT statement for the subset language, but all three are allowed in the full language. The order of priority is PAGE first, then SKIP, then LINE.

Character Sets: There are 60 characters in the PL/I language. They include an extended alphabet of 29 characters, 10 decimal digits, and 21 special characters. Special characters may be combined to create other symbols. A special 48-character set is also available as an alternative to the 60-character set. This 48-character set would be used instead of the 60-character set if some of the special characters (> % ; : etc.) were not graphically available on the printer on which the source program is to be listed.

The END Statement: This statement is used to mark the physical end of a procedure and may also be used to logically end a procedure.

The Assignment Statement: This statement is denoted by the presence of the assignment symbol (=). The value of the expression on the right of the = is assigned (moved) to the variable on the left of the = symbol.

CHECKPOINT QUESTIONS

1. Distinguish between *source* and *object* programs.
2. Explain *compilation* and *execution.*
3. In what card columns may PL/I statements generally be punched?
4. What is the *linkage editor?*
5. What is a *keyword?*
6. What are the colon (:) and semicolon (;) punctuation marks used for in PL/I statement syntax?
7. (True or False) Only one PL/I statement may be punched in a card.
8. Why would a programmer want to write a program using the 48-character set instead of the 60-character set?
9. What characters other than A through Z are considered to be alphabetic in the 60-character set? the 48-character set?
10. What are *reserved words?* Give examples.

11. How do you specify which character set you would like to use in your PL/I program?

12. Write the following fixed-point decimal constants as floating-point decimal constants, where the floating constants are expressed as fractions:
    −15   7.6   0.00000098

13. Write the following literals as character-strings:

    WEEKLY ACTIVITY REPORT   (center heading on a 132 print position line)
    DUM DE DUM DUM
    PROGRAM'S RESULTS

14. Write DECLARE statements for the following:
    (*a*) A five-digit fixed decimal number with two fractions
    (*b*) A ten-position character-string
    (*c*) A seven-digit fixed decimal number (no fractions)

15. In list-directed input, how may data values in the input stream be separated?

16. When using list-directed output, how many tab positions are assigned by default on the printer?

17. How are comments indicated in a PL/I program?

18. Where may comments appear in a PL/I program?

19. Indicate the tab positions at which each of the data items would be printed when the following two statements are executed:

    PUT LIST(5,10,15);
    PUT LIST('THIS IS SOME FUN AND MARKS THE END OF JOB',
       '07/07/77');

20. Can we tell, from the following statements, just how many cards containing punched data will be read?

                    GET LIST(A,B,C,);
                    GET LIST(D,E);

21. What is string data?

22. Give the fixed-point decimal equivalent of the following floating-point numbers: .39E−07   .2678E+02   4.59E+00   7.23E+09

23. Given: A = 10.75; B = 2.9; C = 123.4. What will I, J, and K contain after the following statements are executed?

                    I=A;   J=B;   K=C;

24. If the programmer does not declare attributes for his variable names, what does the PL/I compiler do about it?

25. What are character-strings used for in programming?

26. What is an advantage of using bit-strings to describe an item or a person or event?

TERMS TO STUDY

"What is not fully understood
is not possessed."

GOETHE

In describing the elements of PL/I, a number of terms that were perhaps un-
familiar to you were used. You may wish to review the following words before
proceeding to the next chapter. Appendix G also provides a glossary of PL/I
terms.

assignment symbol	linkage editor
attribute	load module
binary	logical end
break character	machine language
compilation	object program
compiler	operating system
compiler diagnostic	OS
concatenate	physical end
constant	printer control options
core image program	procedure block
data item	program
data name	repetition factor
default	reserved keyword
DOS	60-character set
exponentiation	source program
external storage	stream
floating-point	string
flowchart	stroke character
48-character set	subset language
full language	tab position
identifier	truncate
JCL	variable
keyword	

PRACTICE PROBLEMS

Following are a few beginning programs you may wish to code and run on a computer. The emphasis in the first two problems is on using list-directed I/O and the DECLARE statement to define FIXED DECIMAL and CHARACTER data. The third problem uses floating-point data as well as fixed-point format. After coding the problems, punch them into cards. Be sure that the last statement in each program is an END statement. To compile and execute your programs, you will need *job control statements*. Consult your instructor or someone closely associated with the computer you will be using to assist you in the preparation of job control statements.

1. Write a program to read these data items from the input stream:

ITEM_DESCRIPTION	20 characters maximum
ITEM_NUMBER	6 characters (alphabetic and numeric)
PRICE	5-digit field with two decimals (XXX.XX)
QUANTITY	3-digit field (XXX)

Compute the extension (EXT) by multiplying PRICE by QUANTITY. Print results as shown in Figure 1.5. Suggested sample input might be

'WIDGIT','1234AB',4.95,13

DESCRIPTION	PART NUMBER	UNIT PRICE	QUANTITY	EXTENSION
WIDGIT	1234AB	4.95	13	64.35

END OF JOB -- YOUR NAME GOES HERE

FIGURE 1.5 Sample output format for Problem 1.

2. Punch your name and address into a card. Write a program to read this data and print an address label. For example, if the input is

'JOHN WILLIAM HUGHES','123 ELM ST.','ANYTOWN,SOMESTATE',91405

then output should be

> JOHN WILLIAM HUGHES
> 123 ELM ST.
> ANYTOWN, SOMESTATE
> 91405

3. Area of a Triangle

Problem Statement: Write a PL/I program to find the area of a triangle, given the base and height, where

$$\text{Area} = \frac{1}{2}\ \text{Base} \times \text{Height}$$

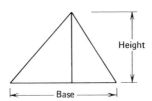

Also, find the area of a second triangle where only the lengths of the sides are known. The formula is

$$\text{Area} = \sqrt{S(S-A)(S-B)(S-C)}$$

where A, B, and C are the triangle's sides and

$$S = \frac{A+B+C}{2}$$

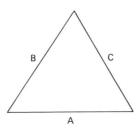

To find the square root of a value is to raise it to a half power. For example:

AREA = RESULT**.5;

└──────→ Double asterisks denote exponentiation

Purpose of the Problem: To code arithmetic calculations in floating-point but print fixed-point answers.

Input: Suggested input data might be:

Base	Height	A	B	C
10.0	14.5	10.0	15.5	20.0

Output: Assuming the above input values are used, output would be the results shown in Figure 1.6.

```
AREA OF TRIANGLE 1 IS     72.5

AREA OF TRIANGLE 2 IS     76.0
```

FIGURE 1.6   Sample output from Problem 3.

chapter 2

Writing

Programs

This chapter presents some PL/I statements you will need to use in writing meaningful and complete programs. These statements include:

Assignment statement
GO TO statement
IF statement
DECLARE statement

Before examining the above statements in detail, let us consider a problem that illustrates a need for these statements.

Assume it is desired to read 100 values and find the sum and the average of these values. Previously, when it was desired to read five values, it was accomplished with one input statement:

GET LIST(A,B,C,D,E) ;

However, the above approach would be a cumbersome method to use in the reading of 100 data items. Thus, another solution must be implemented. A method commonly used is to input one value at a time and accumulate that amount into a variable. When 100 values have been read and accumulated, then the average will be calculated. A flowchart that describes a method for solving the summation problem is given here.

Let us look at the PL/I statements needed to solve this problem. The first step, which may take several PL/I statements, is called an *initialization* step. Typically, in this step, variables are assigned predetermined values. For example:

SUM=0 ;
COUNTER=100 ;

It is necessary to assign SUM to a zero value before accumulating the data items into SUM. This initialization step is analogous to clearing an adding machine before attempting to find the sum of a new column of numbers. Assigning COUNTER to 100 establishes an identifier that indicates the number of times an instruction (or group of instructions) is to be repeated. Each time a data item is read, the value 1 will be

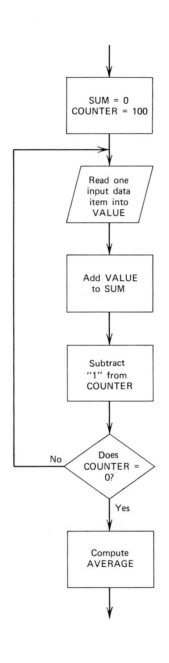

subtracted from COUNTER. When COUNTER is equal to zero, we know that the required number of data items has been processed.
The next step in this program is to read a data item,

$$READ: \quad GET \ LIST(VALUE);$$

and add that value to SUM:

$$SUM = SUM + VALUE;$$

Next, 1 is to be subtracted from COUNTER,

$$COUNTER = COUNTER - 1;$$

and COUNTER is to be tested for a nonzero condition to determine if more values are to be read from the input stream. This testing may be accomplished by the IF statement. For example:

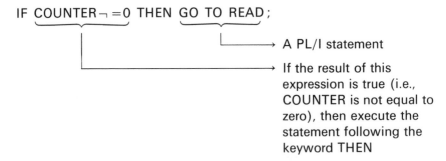

If the result of this expression is true (i.e., COUNTER is not equal to zero), then execute the statement following the keyword THEN

If the expression tested in the IF statement is not true, then go to the instruction immediately following the IF statement. The following instruction would be the statement that computes the average:

$$AVERAGE = SUM/100;$$

The result could then be printed or perhaps used in another computation in the program.
The repetitive processing of data is called a *loop*. There are three steps that must be performed in the programming of a loop:

1. *Initialize a counter:*   This is a programming step that sets up an identifier to indicate the number of times a segment of instruction is performed. For example:

$$COUNTER = 20;$$

2. *Modify counter:* After a specified sequence of instructions have been performed, it is necessary to modify the counter by "1," indicating that there has been one pass through the set of instructions. For example, if COUNTER has been set to 20, indicating the number of repetitions a program is to cycle through, then the following statement might be coded:

COUNTER = COUNTER − 1 ;

Notice that here a "countdown" technique is being used. If "1" is subtracted from COUNTER each time the program steps are performed, when the COUNTER reaches zero, we know that the required number of steps have been performed. Another way in which a loop could be programmed is to start the counter at a value of "1" and increment it each time through the sequence of statements. When the counter reaches the limit (e.g., 20), the loop is terminated.

3. *Test counter:* To determine if the maximum number of repetitions has been performed, the program must test the counter. If we are using the countdown technique, then the following statement might be used to test the counter:

IF COUNTER = 0 THEN GO TO PROGRAM_END ;

Or, if we are counting up from "1," this statement might be coded

IF COUNTER > 20 THEN GO TO PROGRAM_END ;

Figure 2.1 shows a flowchart that specifies the programming steps required to find the sum, average, high, and low values—given 20 input data items. The shaded flowchart symbols indicate the steps that accomplish or control the program loop. Figure 2.2 shows the PL/I programming solution to this flowchart. The statements in this program should look familiar to you. The GET LIST and PUT LIST statements were explained in Chapter 1. The assignment, GO TO, and IF statements are explained in detail in the following paragraphs. Notice the END statement in the program. It has a label following the word END. It is optional to place a label here; but, if you do, it *must* be the label identifier that appears on the PROCEDURE statement. Programmers often include the PROCEDURE label in the END statement for purposes of documentation. For example:

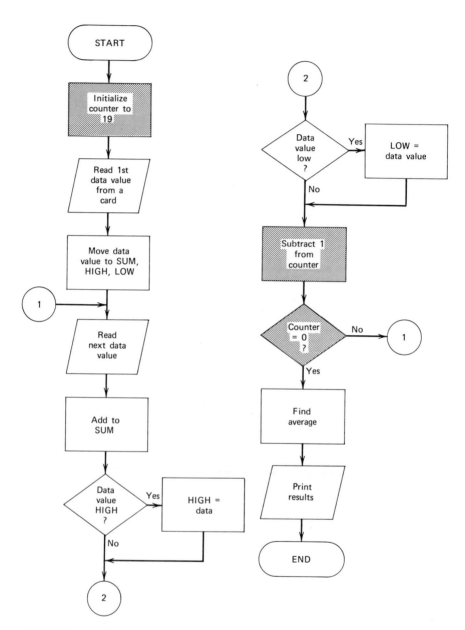

FIGURE 2.1 Flowchart to find sum, average, high, and low values.

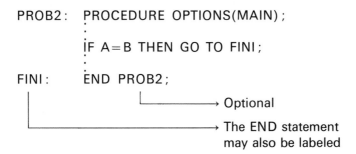

```
PROB2:   PROCEDURE OPTIONS(MAIN);
         .
         .
         IF A=B THEN GO TO FINI;
         .
         .
FINI:    END PROB2;
```

└─────────────→ Optional

└─────────────────────────→ The END statement
                              may also be labeled

Because the identifiers all begin with the letters I through N, it is assumed that the data the program is manipulating is in the form of integers only.

One thing to be sure to observe about this program is that the counter (ICTR) is initialized to 19 rather than 20, as you might have thought it should be. Actually, there are only 19 *repetitions* in the program because the *first* data value is read and assigned to SUM, IHIGH, and ILOW. That leaves 19 *values* to be read and accumulated into SUM, as well as compared with the contents of IHIGH and ILOW. Thus, ICTR is initialized to 19—the number of repetitions after the first data value is read and processed.

```
PROB2: PROCEDURE OPTIONS(MAIN);
         IDIVSR = 20;
         ICTR = 19;
         GET LIST (IVALUE);
         ISUM = IVALUE;
         IHIGH = IVALUE;
         ILOW = IVALUE;
LOOP:    GET LIST(IVALUE);
         ISUM = ISUM + IVALUE;
         IF IVALUE > IHIGH THEN IHIGH = IVALUE;
         IF IVALUE < ILOW THEN ILOW = IVALUE;
         ICTR = ICTR - 1;
         IF ICTR ¬= 0 THEN GO TO LOOP;
         IAVER = ISUM/IDIVSR;
         PUT PAGE LIST('SUM','AVERAGE','HIGH','LOW');
         PUT SKIP(2)LIST(ISUM,IAVER,IHIGH,ILOW);
         END PROB2;
```

FIGURE 2.2   PL/I program to find sum, average, high, and low of 20 values.

The Assignment Statement

You will be using this type of statement often because it specifies which arithmetic and logical operations should take place and/or causes data to be *moved* from one storage area to another.

Here is an example of an arithmetic assignment statement:

$$EXTENSION = PRICE*QTY;$$

In this type of PL/I statement, the system will compute the expression on the right side of the assignment symbol ($=$) and *assign* the result to the variable, EXTENSION on the left. The equal ($=$) sign in the arithmetic assignment statement means *replace the value of the variable on the left of the assignment symbol with the value of the expression on the right of the assignment symbol.* The arithmetic assignment statement is not an algebraic equation, although, in the above example, it looks like one. This is because the assignment symbol is identical to the equal sign. However,

$$N = N - 1;$$

is a valid arithmetic assignment statement. Clearly, in this example, the statement is not an equation.

Expressions specify a computation and appear to the right of the assignment symbol in an assignment statement. A *variable* is a term used to indicate a quantity that is referred to by name and a *constant* is an actual number. A name is classified as a variable because it can take on different values during the execution of a program, whereas a constant is restricted to one value. In PL/I when we want to compute new values, we combine variables and constants together into expressions. The actual arithmetic operations to be performed upon the data variables are indicated by operators and PL/I built-in functions.

Arithmetic Operations

The PL/I symbols for the five basic arithmetic operations are:

Symbol	Operation
**	Exponentiation
*	Multiplication
/	Division
+	Addition
−	Subtraction

Multiplication must always be indicated with the asterisk (∗) operator. Multiplication in PL/I cannot be implied as it can be in algebraic notation. For example, the expression

$$(a + b)(c + d)$$

would be written in PL/I as

$$(A+B)*(C+D) \qquad \text{or} \qquad MULTIPLY(A+B,C+D)$$

The second form shows the use of a built-in function, which we will come to later. Note, also, the use of capital letters in the expression. Only capital letters are used in PL/I statements.

Let us summarize some rules regarding arithmetic expressions:

Rule 1. The order in which arithmetic operations are performed is

1. *Exponentiation* (raising a number to a power, moving from right to left in an expression)
2. *Multiplication or division* (whichever appears first, moving from left to right in an expression)
3. *Addition or subtraction* (whichever appears first, moving from left to right in the expression)

Rule 2. Parentheses are also used in expressions to affect the order of arithmetic operations. They serve the same function as do parentheses and brackets in algebraic equations. *When parentheses are specified, the expression within the parentheses will be evaluated first, starting with the innermost pair of parentheses* and solving according to the hierarchy established previously in Rule 1.

It is important to understand how the use of parentheses can affect the order in which arithmetic operations are performed. For example, in the expression

$$A+B/C$$

the order of execution is:

1. Divide B by C
2. Add A to the quotient

However, if the expression

$$(A+B)/C$$

were given, the order of operations is:

1. Add A to B
2. Divide sum by C

In some cases, the use of parentheses does not change the order of arithmetic operations in an expression. For example:

$$A*B+C$$

is the same as

$$(A*B)+C$$

A good rule to follow is, when in doubt about the order of arithmetic operations, use parentheses. Specifying *extra* parentheses to clarify the order of operations—perhaps just for *documentation* purposes—is valid and does not affect the efficiency of the arithmetic expression.

Rule 3.   A *prefix operator* is an operator that precedes, and is associated with, a single operand. The prefix operators in PL/I are

¬	Not
+	Positive sign
−	Negative sign

Prefix operators are contrasted with *infix operators*, which specify a specific operation such as addition, subtraction, multiplication, etc. For example:

$$Y=X**-A;$$

→ Prefix operator (negative sign)

→ Infix operator (exponentiation)

In the above statement, X is raised to the $-A$ power. *When prefix operations are indicated in an expression, they are performed before infix operations.* The prefix operators do not have to be separated from the infix operators with parentheses as is the restriction in other high-level languages. For example, the PL/I statement

$$Y=X**-A;$$

would have to be written in other languages that contain a similar type of arithmetic statement as

$$Y=X**(-A)$$

Rule 4.   *Any expression or element may be raised to a power and the power may have either a positive or negative value.* For example:

$$X**2$$
$$(X+5)**3$$
$$X**-A$$

The exponent itself may be an expression:

$$X**(I+2)$$

Rule 5. *If two or more operators of the highest priority appear in the same expression, the order of priority of those operators is from right to left.* For example, prefix operations are performed on the same level as exponentiation (see Figure 2.3, below). In the expression

$$-A**2$$

the order of operations is:

1. Exponentiation
2. Prefix operation, negation

As a further example, in the expression

$$-A**-Y$$

the order of operations is:

1. Negation $(-Y)$
2. Exponentiation
3. Negation

The expression

$$A**B**C$$

is evaluated in PL/I as

$$A**(B**C)$$

Comparison Operations

The following operations are used to test (compare) two data items to determine the relationship that exists between them:

Symbols	Operation
GE or $>=$	Greater than or equal to
GT or $>$	Greater than
NE or $\neg=$	Not equal
$=$	Equal
LT or $<$	Less than
LE or $<=$	Less than or equal to
NL or $\neg<$	Not less than
NG or $\neg>$	Not greater than

Typically, the comparison operators listed above are used in an IF statement. For example:

IF A> = B THEN GO TO CONTINUE;

These operators may also be used in an assignment statement. Note the results assigned to the variable on the left of the assignment symbol in the following examples:

A = B = C;
⌣
└──────→ If B = C, then A will be assigned a value of 1
If B is not equal to C, then A will be assigned a value of 0

A = B > C;
└──────────→ A = 1 if B > C
A = 0 if B is not greater than C

Bit-String Operations

These operations involve either the establishing of true or false conditions regarding the relationship of expressions or the manipulation of bit-string data. The three bit-string operations in PL/I are:

Symbol	Operation
(¬)	NOT
(&)	AND
(|)	OR

As an illustration of the establishing of true or false conditions of expressions, consider the following example:

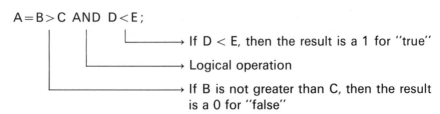

A = B > C AND D < E;
└──────────→ If D < E, then the result is a 1 for "true"
└──────────→ Logical operation
└──────────→ If B is not greater than C, then the result is a 0 for "false"

The identifier A will be set equal to a 1 if both expressions have a 1 generated as a result of a *comparison operation*. In all other cases, A in the above example will be set to zero.

There are four possible combinations of true/false conditions:

First expression	Second expression
True	True
True	False
False	True
False	False

Substituting a 1 for true and a 0 for false, the following tables define the result (either a 0 or a 1) for the AND and OR operations:

```
        AND                     OR
    1 & 1 → 1               1 | 1 → 1
    1 & 0 → 0               1 | 0 → 1
    0 & 1 → 0               0 | 1 → 1
    0 & 0 → 0               0 | 0 → 0
          └──→ Result             └──→ Result
```

The NOT operation simply yields a result of the opposite condition: if a bit is a 1, result is 0; if a bit is a 0, result is a 1. For example:

```
        /* ASSUME B = '1'B */
        A = ¬ B ;
         │    │ └──────────→ An operand
         │    └───────────→ NOT symbol
         └────────────────→ A = '0'B
```

Notice that there is only one operand with the NOT operation.

The ANDing or ORing of bit-string data is often referred to as a Boolean operation.† In either logical operation, two bit-strings are compared, one bit with one bit at a time. The result is a bit-string according to the rules illustrated above.

Using the AND operation on bit-strings is a way of "turning off" bits. In the following example, the resulting bit-string will contain a 1 bit whenever there is a corresponding 1 bit in *both* operands. (Sometimes the second operand is referred to as a *mask*.)

```
          1111010011111000 → First operand
    AND   0000100000001010 → Second operand (mask)
          ─────────────────
          0000000000001000 → Result
```

† It is said that the founding of Boolean algebra was marked when George Boole (1815–1864) wrote a treatise on "The Mathematical Analysis of Logic." Boole applied his algebra to sets and to sentences; its use in the foundation of mathematics and in switching circuits which led to the development of computers came later.

Using the OR operation is a way of "turning on" bits. Notice from the following example that the resulting bit-string will contain a 1 bit whenever there is either a 1 bit in the first or second operand or both.

$$1111000011110000 \rightarrow \text{First operand}$$

$$\text{OR} \quad \underline{0001001100110001} \rightarrow \text{Second operand (mask)}$$

$$1111001111110001 \rightarrow \text{Result}$$

Note also that if you are ANDing or ORing bit-strings of unequal length, the shorter string is automatically expanded with zeros to match the length of the longer string.

String Operation

There is only one string operation: concatenation (||). This operation may be specified for bit-strings or character-strings. It simply means that two strings are to be joined together to form one longer string. For example:

```
A = 'JOHN ';
B = 'SMITH';
C = A||B;        /* C=JOHN SMITH */
C = B||', '||A;  /* C=SMITH, JOHN */
D = '1100'B;
E = '0001'B;
F = D||E;        /* F=11000001 */
```

The various PL/I operations have been introduced. Because any number of operations may be specified in an expression, it is necessary to establish a *priority* in which these operations take place so that we may predict the results of expressions. The hierarchy of these operations is summarized in Figure 2.3.

Special Form of the Assignment Statement

A form of the assignment statement available only in the full language PL/I compilers is the statement where more than one identifier (variable name) may appear to the left of the assignment symbol. For example:

$$A, B, C = 0;$$

This statement causes A, B, and C each to be assigned a value of zero.

Levels	60-character set	48-character set
1	prefix +, prefix ¬, **, ¬	prefix +, prefix −, **, NOT
2	*, /	*, /
3	infix +, infix −	infix +, infix −
4	||	CAT
5	> =, >, ¬ =, =, <, < =, ¬ <, ¬ >	GE, GT, NE, =, LT, LE, NL, NG
6	&	AND
7	|	OR

FIGURE 2.3 Complete hierarchy of PL/I operations.

Any value or expression may appear to the right of the assignment symbol in this type of statement. For example :

$$W,X,Y,Z = I*J ;$$

The GO TO Statement

This statement causes a branch or transfer to a labeled PL/I statement. The statement is written :

GO TO LOOP ;

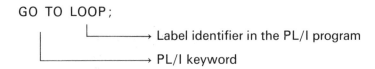

→ Label identifier in the PL/I program

→ PL/I keyword

It is only permissible to transfer to *executable* statements. For example, the DECLARE statement and the PROCEDURE statement are not executable statements; therefore you would not specify a branch to these statements.

The IF Statement

The IF statement is used in a PL/I program when a test or decision is to be made between alternatives. Comparison operators are used to specify the test to be made.

IF (with Transfer of Control)

In this statement type, if the result of evaluating the expression is true, a transfer or branch is made to another point in the program. For example :

IF A<0 THEN GO TO NEGATIVE ;

→ Transfer to a PL/I statement labeled NEGATIVE

IF (without Transfer of Control)

In this statement type, a single statement will appear as the action to be taken if the expression (condition) tested is true. For example:

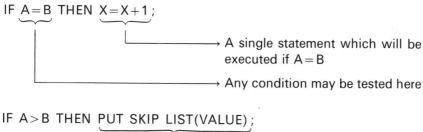

IF A=B THEN X=X+1;

→ A single statement which will be executed if A=B

→ Any condition may be tested here

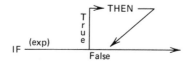

IF A>B THEN PUT SKIP LIST(VALUE);

→ Almost any PL/I statement may follow the THEN keyword

If the condition tested is true, the statement following the THEN keyword is executed before the program proceeds to the next sequential statement. If the condition tested is false, the statement following the THEN keyword is ignored and the program continues immediately with the next sequential statement. The following diagram represents this type of IF (where exp stands for expression):

IF (exp)
True
THEN
False

The Compound IF

This IF statement is called *compound* because it contains two PL/I statements. Its form includes the use of the keyword ELSE. Here is a logical diagram of the compound IF:

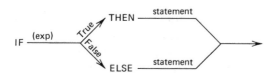

IF (exp)
True
THEN — statement
False
ELSE — statement

If the condition tested is true, we execute the statement following the THEN; if the condition tested is false, we perform the statement following the ELSE. For example:

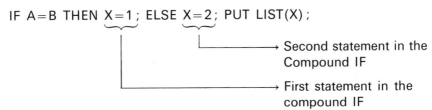

IF A=B THEN X=1; ELSE X=2; PUT LIST(X);

→ Second statement in the Compound IF

→ First statement in the compound IF

In this example, X will be set equal to 2 when A is not equal to B. It is important to understand that, if A is equal to B (in which case X will be set to 1), then the ELSE clause is ignored. The next sequential instruction here would be PUT LIST.

Nested IF Statements

There may be IF statements contained in either the THEN or ELSE clause of another IF statement. For example:

IF A=B THEN IF A=C THEN X=1; ELSE X=2; ELSE X=3;

To help clarify the pairing of the THEN and ELSE clauses, it would be more understandable to show the above statement in the following manner:

```
IF A=B
    THEN IF A=C
        THEN X=1;   /* A=B AND A=C */
        ELSE X=2;   /* A=B BUT A¬=C */
    ELSE X=3;   /* A¬=B */
```

A logical diagram of this nested IF statement would look like this:

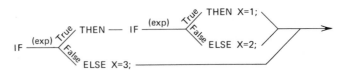

In a series of nested IF statements, each ELSE clause is paired with the closest IF that is not already paired, starting at the innermost level. The conditions in the IF are tested in the order in which they are written. As soon as a condition tested is false, the testing of subsequent conditions is stopped and the matching ELSE clause is executed. Control is then transferred out of the entire series of nested IF statements.

In the nest of IF statements, an associated ELSE clause may or may not appear for the outermost IF. But every nested IF must have an associated ELSE clause whenever any IF statement at the next outermost level requires an associated ELSE. For example:

```
 ┌IF
 │  THEN    ┌IF . . .
 │          │   THEN    ┌IF . . .
 │          │           │ THEN . . . ;
 │          │           └ELSE . . . ;
 │          │
 │          └ELSE    ┌IF
 │                   │ THEN . . . ;
 │                   └ELSE . . . ;
 │
 └ELSE . . . ;
```

The use of nested IF statements, at this point, may seem a bit complicated. However, let us look at an example where the use of nested IF statements actually simplifies our programming task. Assume a company is looking for prospective employees who, ideally, are 30 years of age or younger and who weigh less than or equal to 250 pounds. There are four possibilities or categories of people who could apply for the job. These options are summarized below:

≤ 30 yrs	≤ 30 yrs	> 30 yrs	> 30 yrs
≤ 250 lbs	> 250 lbs	≤ 250 lbs	> 250 lbs
Age OK	Age OK	Age not OK	Age not OK
Weight OK	Weight not OK	Weight OK	Weight not OK
"HIRE"	"DO NOT HIRE"	"CONSIDER"	"OVERAGE AND OVERWEIGHT"

Here are the nested IF statements to test for the four possible conditions:

```
IF AGE< =30
   THEN IF WEIGHT< =250
           THEN PUT LIST('HIRE'||NAME) ;
           ELSE PUT LIST('DO NOT HIRE'||NAME) ;
   ELSE IF WEIGHT< =250
           THEN PUT LIST('CONSIDER'||NAME) ;
           ELSE PUT LIST(NAME||'OVERAGE AND OVERWEIGHT') ;
```

A Null ELSE in Nested IF Statements

Earlier, a nested IF statement was shown which set X equal to 1, 2, or 3, depending on the condition tested. The statement was

```
IF A=B
   THEN IF A=C
           THEN X=1;
           ELSE X=2;
   ELSE X=3;
```

In other words:

```
Set X = 1 when A = B and A = C.
Set X = 2 when A = B but A ¬ = C.
Set X = 3 when A ¬ = B.
```

Now, let us assume that we would like to do the following:

```
Set X = 1 when A = B and A = C.
Set X = 3 when A ¬ = B.
```

However, for the condition of A = B but A ¬ = C, we do not want to alter X. This situation builds the case for the use of the *null ELSE*. The null ELSE is an ELSE with a null statement as its clause. The null statement is simply a semicolon. For example:

```
;
```

Or, it may be a semicolon with a label attached to it:

```
POINT:   ;
```

The null ELSE is, as its name implies, a nonoperative statement. It gives no direction to the computer. Rather, its effect is to supply the necessary ELSE clause to be associated with the innermost IF. Our example would be written as follows:

```
IF A=B
   THEN IF A=C
           THEN X=1;
           ELSE;   /* THIS IS A NULL ELSE */
   ELSE X=3;
```

Consider what would have happened had you omitted the null ELSE.

The statement would have been written

```
IF  A=B
    THEN  IF  A=C
          THEN  X=1 ;   /* A=B AND A=C */
          ELSE  X=3 ;   /* A=B BUT A¬=C */
```

Notice that for the condition under which we did not want to change X, X was erroneously set equal to 3.

These examples have illustrated the nesting of IF statements only to the second level. Deeper nesting is allowed and follows the same reasoning and rules.

The DO-Group in an IF Statement

The IF statement is designed to execute *one* statement following the THEN or ELSE clause. Sometimes, however, it is necessary to execute more than one statement following the THEN or ELSE. This can be accomplished through the use of a *DO-group.* The DO-group is simply a series of PL/I statements headed by the word DO and terminated by the keyword END. For example:

```
DO ;
X=1 ;
Y=2 ;
Z=3 ;
END ;
```

Placing the above DO-group in an IF statement gives us the necessary flexibility of being able to execute more than a single statement following a THEN or ELSE. The following example utilizes multiple DO-groups:

```
IF  A=B
    THEN  DO ;
          X=1 ; Y=2 ; Z=3 ;
          END ;
    ELSE  DO ;
          X=4 ; Y=5 ; Z=6 ;
          END ;
```

We have now encountered *two* uses of the END statement. You are already aware that END must be the very last statement in your PL/I source program. Yet, as you can see from the above example, the END may appear to be embedded in your PL/I program. However, the PL/I compiler can always tell by the context which END represents the *true* end of your program because each DO in the program has its own END.

Bit-String Operators in the IF Statement

The operators AND (&) and OR (|) can be useful in the IF statement to eliminate nested IF statements. For example, the nested IF statement,

IF A=B THEN IF C¬=D THEN GO TO POINT_5;

could also be written using the AND operation. For example:

IF A=B & C¬=D THEN GO TO POINT_5;

When the AND symbol (&) is specified, both the expression to the left and the expression to the right of the & symbol must be true for the statement following the THEN to be executed. If either expression is not true, the statement following the THEN is bypassed.

For a comparison expression containing the OR (|) operator, consider the following example:

IF A=B | C=D THEN GO TO LOC_1;

In this case, if *either* the expression to the left *or* the expression to the right of the OR symbol (|) is true, the statement following the THEN is executed. If both expressions are true, the system would still branch to the place called LOC_1 in the above example. The only condition that would keep the program from transferring to LOC_1 is if A is not equal to B and C is not equal to D.

The DECLARE Statement

If you are thoroughly familiar with the types of data (e.g., packed decimal, fixed-point binary, floating-point, EBCDIC) provided on a S/360 or S/370, continue with your reading of this section on the DECLARE statement. If not, turn to Appendix D for a discussion of the various data formats available on S/360 or S/370.

The DECLARE statement is needed in two instances :

1. When the programmer does not wish to use the data formats which are assigned by the compiler by default (i.e., I—N for fixed binary data or A—H and O—Z for floating-point data) or assigned by the programmer through the use of the DEFAULT statement.†
2. When information is to be supplied to the compiler that a variable represents a *data aggregate*.

DECLARE statements may appear anywhere following the PRO-CEDURE statement. It is common to find a number of DECLARE statements placed at the beginning of a PL/I program because it is logical to declare the attributes of the data before writing the instruc-tions which process that data and it is easier to find the DECLARE statements if you want to alter them later.

Base and Scale Attributes

Consider this example of a DECLARE statement :

DECLARE PRICE DECIMAL FIXED(5,2) ;

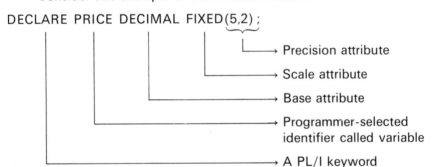

          → Precision attribute

          → Scale attribute

          → Base attribute

          → Programmer-selected identifier called variable

          → A PL/I keyword

A DECLARE statement always begins with the keyword DECLARE as its statement identifier. Its statement body contains one or more variables and a description of the characteristics of the value of each variable. The words used to describe the characteristics of data are called *attributes.* In the above DECLARE statement, the variable is PRICE. It is declared to have the *base attribute* DECIMAL, the *scale*

---

†The DEFAULT statement, which is available in the optimizing compilers, will be described later.

attribute FIXED, and the *precision attribute* (5,2). Another way in which the above statement could be written is

DCL PRICE FIXED DEC(5,2) ;

because most attributes may appear in any sequence, and abbreviations of some words are allowed. (The precision attribute must follow either the base or the scale attribute in the DECLARE statement.) Attributes are separated by one or more blanks.

When a variable has its attributes described in a DECLARE statement, it is said to be declared *explicitly*. When variable names begin with the letters I through N and are simply used in a program without appearing in a DECLARE statement, the FIXED scale attribute, the BINARY base attribute, and a precision attribute of (15, 0) are assumed, and that variable is said to be declared *implicitly*. Variables beginning with any alphabetic letter other than I through N and not described in a DECLARE statement or the DEFAULT statement are *implicitly* declared to have the attributes DECIMAL FLOAT(6).

One of the biggest problems for the beginning PL/I programmer is failing to realize that, if he does not declare the base, scale, and precision of data items, the compiler will assume certain attributes by default. Often, these *default* assumptions are not those which the programmer desired.

More than one variable name may be specified in a DECLARE statement. For example:

DECLARE INTEREST FIXED DECIMAL(3,3), PRINCIPAL FIXED
    DECIMAL(9,2) ;

> ↳ Blank is optional
>
> ↳ Must have a comma
> to separate each
> data item.

Thus, in the above example INTEREST and PRINCIPAL were both described in one DECLARE statement.

The Precision Attribute

The precision attribute specifies the number of significant digits of data and/or the decimal point alignment. The precision of a variable is either attributed by default or it is declared along with the base and/or scale, and it is never specified alone. It must follow either (or both) the base or scale in the declaration. For example :

DECLARE VALUE FIXED DECIMAL(7,2)

> Number of fractional digits

> Number of significant digits including the fractional digits

In the above example, VALUE may contain up to a *seven*-digit number of which *two* are fractional. Thus, its form may be stated as

XXXXX.XX

where X represents any decimal digit. If there are no fractional digits, then you may omit the comma and second digit of the precision attribute. For example :

DECLARE QUANTITY FIXED DECIMAL(5) ;

The above statement is equivalent to

DECLARE QUANTITY FIXED DECIMAL(5,0) ;

It was stated previously that the precision is never specified alone. Thus, using the above DECLARE as an example, had the FIXED scale and DECIMAL base attributes been omitted, the statement

DECLARE QUANTITY(5,0) ;

becomes an *invalid* precision declaration.

For floating-point data, declare only the number of significant digits. For example :

DCL PI FLOAT DECIMAL(6) ;
PI = 3.14159 ;

Do not specify fractions in the precision attribute for floating-point data. For example :

DCL PI FLOAT DECIMAL(6,5) ;

is invalid.

The Length Attribute

The word *precision* refers only to arithmetic data. In referring to string data, the term *length* is used. The length is the number of characters or bits a data item is to contain. For example:

DECLARE NAME CHARACTER (20);

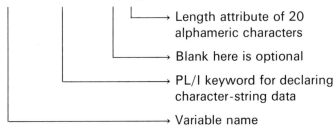

→ Length attribute of 20 alphameric characters

→ Blank here is optional

→ PL/I keyword for declaring character-string data

→ Variable name

The Mode Attribute

Mode specifies whether a variable has the REAL or COMPLEX attribute. If the mode is not declared, REAL is assumed. In the full language implementations of PL/I, either mode may be declared for variables. The following information is of value only to those who have the need to use complex quantities in their programming solutions of various problems. Thus, if the expression

$$8 + 2i$$

where i is

$$\sqrt{-1}$$

has no meaning to you, you will not miss anything by skipping to the next section of this chapter. In the *complex* mode, an arithmetic data item has two parts: (*a*) a real part, and (*b*) a signed imaginary part.

There are no complex constants in PL/I. A complex value is obtained by a real constant and an imaginary constant. An imaginary constant is written as a real constant of any type followed by the letter I. Here are some examples:

15I
7.14E10I
1101.001BI

Each of these is considered to have a real part of zero.

A complex value with a nonzero real part is represented in the following form:

$$[+\,|-]\ \text{Real constant}\ \{+\,|-\}\ \text{Imaginary constant}$$

Thus, a complex value could be written as

46+2I

The keyword attribute for declaring a complex variable is COMPLEX. For example:

> DCL A FLOAT DECIMAL(6) COMPLEX;

A complex variable may have any of the attributes valid for the different types of real arithmetic data. Each of the base, scale, and precision attributes applies to both fields.

The standard arithmetic operations are provided for complex data. For example:

```
DCL (X,Y,SUM,DIFF,PRODUCT,QUOTIENT,POWER)
   COMPLEX DECIMAL FLOAT(6);
GET LIST(X,Y);
SUM=X+Y;
DIFF=X-Y;
PRODUCT=X*Y;
QUOTIENT=X/Y;
POWER=X**3;
```

	COMPLEX variables allowed
Subset language	No
Full language	Yes

Factored Attributes

When the same base, scale, and precision could apply to more than one variable, then the attributes may be *factored*. Here is an example:

DECLARE (A, B, C) FIXED DECIMAL(7,3);

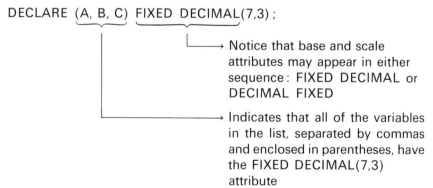

→ Notice that base and scale attributes may appear in either sequence: FIXED DECIMAL or DECIMAL FIXED

→ Indicates that all of the variables in the list, separated by commas and enclosed in parentheses, have the FIXED DECIMAL(7,3) attribute

The above example is equivalent to

DECLARE A FIXED DECIMAL(7,3), B FIXED DECIMAL(7,3),
C FIXED DECIMAL(7,3) ;

Here is an example of *nesting* of factored attributes :

DCL((A FIXED(5,2), B FLOAT(6), (C, D) FIXED(9,3))DECIMAL ;

In this statement, A is declared as FIXED DECIMAL(5,2) ; B is FLOAT
DECIMAL(6) ; and C and D are FIXED DECIMAL(9,3).

The INITIAL Attribute

In addition to declaring the base, scale, and precision of an
arithmetic variable or the length of a string, it is also possible to set that
variable to an initial value by adding the INITIAL attribute in the
DECLARE statement.

DECLARE AMT FIXED DECIMAL(7,2) INITIAL(24.50) ;

It is important to understand that the DECLARE statement is not
executable. Therefore, when the value of a variable is initialized through
the use of the INITIAL attribute (the assigning of 24.50 in the above
example), this is done once only and before any of the PL/I executable
statements in a *block†* are performed by the computer. Another method
for assigning values to a variable is to use the assignment statement.
For example :

AMT = 24.50 ;

Under certain circumstances, using the INITIAL attribute to initialize
a variable to a predetermined value can result in greater program
efficiency than if the assignment statement were used to initialize a
variable. To accomplish this efficiency, another attribute must be added
to the DECLARE statement. For example :

DCL AMT FIXED DECIMAL(7,2) INITIAL(24.50) STATIC ;

           ↳ A storage class to be explained in
             Chapter 11

Here are some examples of the use of the INITIAL attribute.
Note that the constant specified after the keyword INITIAL must be
enclosed in parentheses.

---

†There are two types of blocks in PL/I : procedure blocks and begin blocks. So far, you
have only been introduced to procedure blocks ; begin blocks will be covered later.

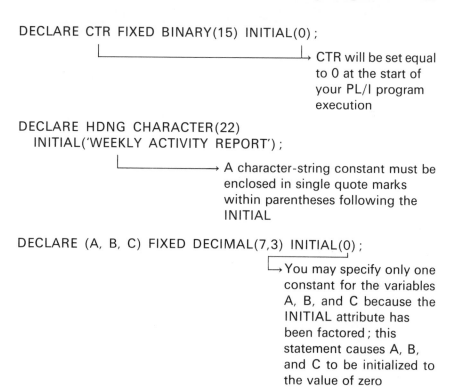

DECLARE CTR FIXED BINARY(15) INITIAL(0) ;

└──────────────────────────────┘→ CTR will be set equal to 0 at the start of your PL/I program execution

DECLARE HDNG CHARACTER(22)
INITIAL('WEEKLY ACTIVITY REPORT') ;

└──────────────────┘→ A character-string constant must be enclosed in single quote marks within parentheses following the INITIAL

DECLARE (A, B, C) FIXED DECIMAL(7,3) INITIAL(0) ;

└→ You may specify only one constant for the variables A, B, and C because the INITIAL attribute has been factored; this statement causes A, B, and C to be initialized to the value of zero

DECLARE (X,Y,Z) FLOAT DECIMAL(16) INITIAL(1,2,3) ;

└→ ILLEGAL: even though three variables are specified (X, Y, and Z), because they are *factored*, only one constant may be given following the keyword INITIAL

To accomplish the above type of initialization and still factor the common attributes, you must code:

DCL (X INIT(1), Y INIT(2), Z INIT(3)) FLOAT DECIMAL(16) ;

Note that expressions following the parentheses in the INITIAL attribute are *invalid* in all compilers except the optimizing compilers:

DECLARE VALUE FIXED DECIMAL INITIAL(7+5) ;
DECLARE AMT FIXED DECIMAL(5,2) INITIAL(I*2) ;
DECLARE MSSG CHAR(20) INITIAL('ERROR'||(15)'*') ;

As mentioned earlier, certain keywords may be abbreviated for the convenience of the programmer. For example:

DCL VALUE FIXED DEC(9) INIT(12345.) ;

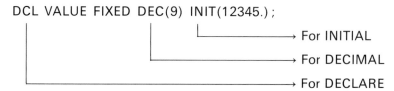

→ For INITIAL

→ For DECIMAL

→ For DECLARE

Partially Declared Identifiers

We have seen that characteristics of arithmetic data are normally described with three basic attributes: *base, scale,* and *precision.* It is possible to make a partial declaration of variables. To declare partially a variable name is to specify one of the following:

1. The base: DCL A DECIMAL, B BINARY;
2. The scale: DCL C FIXED, D FLOAT;
3. The base and precision: DCL AA DECIMAL(16), BB BINARY(53) ;
4. The scale and precision: DCL CC FIXED(9,2), DD FLOAT(16) ;

The chart in Figure 2.4 summarizes the defaults that will be taken for partially declared variables. To summarize some of the points implicit in the chart, note that when you specify only the base (BINARY

Declared attributes	Default attributes
DECIMAL FIXED	(5,0)
DECIMAL FLOAT	(6)
BINARY FIXED	(15,0)
BINARY FLOAT	(21)
DECIMAL	FLOAT(6)
BINARY	FLOAT(21)
FIXED	DECIMAL(5,0)
FLOAT	DECIMAL(6)
None—initial character I—N	BINARY FIXED(15)
None—all others	DECIMAL FLOAT(6)

FIGURE 2.4   Default attributes for partially declared identifiers.

or DECIMAL), the *scale* will default to FLOAT and the *precision* to 21 for BINARY or 6 for DECIMAL. In other words, when you write

DECLARE K9 DECIMAL;

it is equivalent to

DECLARE K9 DECIMAL FLOAT(6);

When you specify only the *scale* (FIXED or FLOAT), the *base* will default to DECIMAL. Thus, when you write

DECLARE A2 FIXED;

it is equivalent to

DECLARE A2 FIXED DECIMAL(5); /* OR */
DECLARE A2 FIXED DECIMAL(5,0);

Precision may not be specified alone.

PL/I Data Attributes

Because you may wish to reference the following section at a later time, for each data type, pertinent facts are concisely presented and examples of DECLARE statements are given. Also, you may wish to review the material in Appendix D before continuing in this chapter.

FIXED DECIMAL

S/360, S/370 Data Format Name: packed
Type of Data: coded arithmetic
Default Precision: 5 decimal digits (99999.)
Maximum Precision: 15 decimal digits (999,999,999,999,999.)
Examples:

```
DCL A FIXED DECIMAL, B DECIMAL FIXED, C FIXED, D FIXED(5),
   E FIXED(5,0), F FIXED DEC, G DEC FIXED;
   /* A,B,C,D,E,F, and G ARE EQUIVALENT */
DCL AMT FIXED(7) INITIAL(12345);   /* AMT=0012345. */
DCL PRINCIPAL FIXED(9,2) INIT(24.00);
DCL RATE FIXED(3,3) INIT(.045);
```

Note carefully in the following examples how a number will be altered to fit the declared precision (whether intended or not):

```
DCL HOURS FIXED(3,1) INIT(42.6);    /* HOURS=42.6 */
DCL HOURS FIXED(5,2) INIT(42.6);    /* HOURS=042.60 */
DCL HOURS FIXED(1,1) INIT(42.6);    /* HOURS=.6 */
DCL HOURS FIXED(3,2) INIT(42.6);    /* HOURS=2.60 */
DCL HOURS FIXED(7,4) INIT(42.6);    /* HOURS=042.6000 */
DCL HOURS FIXED(5,0) INIT(42.6);    /* HOURS=00042. */
```

A negative scale factor may also be specified for FIXED DECIMAL data. For example:

```
DCL A FIXED(3,-2);
```

⌐─────────→ The negative scale factor means, in this case, the assumed decimal point is two places to the rightmost digit (e.g., XXX00., where X is any decimal digit)

Comments: This is the type of data that commercial programmers most often use. The FIXED DECIMAL format provides the capability needed for monetary calculations. It is more efficient to declare the precision of fixed decimal data as an odd number (5, 7, 9, etc.) of digits. There are several terms in PL/I which refer to this data type:

FIXED,   FIXED DECIMAL,   or   DECIMAL FIXED

This format can be used to represent mixed numbers (e.g., 12.98), fractions (.035), or whole numbers (144).

┌─────────────────┐
│ **FIXED BINARY** │
└─────────────────┘

S/360, S/370 Data Format Name: fixed-point
Type of Data: coded arithmetic
Default Precision: 15 bits (equivalent to 32,767 in decimal)
Maximum Precision: 31 bits (equivalent to 2,147,483,647 in decimal)
Examples:

```
DCL A FIXED BINARY, AA BINARY FIXED, AAA FIXED BIN(15);
   /* THE ABOVE THREE ITEMS ARE EQUIVALENT */
DCL ICTR INITIAL(500);   /* ICTR=500 AND DEFAULTS TO
   FIXED BINARY */
```

```
DCL VALUE FIXED BIN(8) INITIAL(11110011B);   /* BINARY
    CONSTANT */
DCL EVENT FIXED BIN(31) INIT(-2147483647);   /* DECIMAL
    CONSTANT */
```

Comments: Notice from the examples above that either binary or decimal constants may be used to initialize FIXED BINARY variables. Generally, instructions that perform arithmetic operations on FIXED BINARY data have a faster execution time than instructions that operate on other data types. Thus, fixed-point binary data should be used whenever execution time of a program is a primary consideration. This does not apply, however, if you are going to be converting, repeatedly, binary data to characters for output.

Variables that begin with the letters I through N default to FIXED BINARY(15).

	FIXED BINARY	
	Number of bytes used	Type of data allowed
Subset language	4	Integers only
Full language	2 if precision <= 15 4 if precision > 15	Integers, fractions, or mixed numbers

FLOAT DECIMAL

S/360, S/370 Data Format Name: floating-point
Type of Data: coded arithmetic
Default Precision: 6 decimal digits
Maximum Precision: 16 decimal digits (33 in the OS PL/I Optimizing Compiler)
Range of Exponent: 10^{-78} to 10^{+75}
Examples:

```
DCL A FLOAT, B FLOAT DECIMAL, C DECIMAL FLOAT, D DECIMAL,
    E DEC, F DEC(6), G FLOAT DEC(6);
    /* A,B,C,D,E,F, AND G ARE EQUIVALENT */
```

DCL PI FLOAT(6) INITIAL(3.14159) ;   /* PI = 3.14159 */
DCL MILE FLOAT INIT(.528E + 04) ;   /* MILE = 5280. */
DCL LIGHT YEAR FLOAT INIT(6E + 12) ;
   / * LIGHT YEAR = 6,000,000,000,000 */

Comments: Because of the range of the exponent of floating-point data, scientific programmers find this data format useful for working with very large or very small numbers that do not require more than 16 digits of accuracy. Identifiers whose letters begin with anything other than I through N will default to FLOAT DECIMAL(6). Notice in the first DECLARE statement above, that a number of keywords may be used to specify this type of data. Notice, also, that fixed-point decimal constants (e.g., 3.14159) or floating-point decimal constants (e.g., 6E + 12) are used to initialize floating-point variables. Floating-point data is not suitable for commercial programs where dollars and cents accuracy is required.

FLOAT BINARY

S/360, S/370 Data Format Name: floating-point
Type of Data: coded arithmetic
Default Precision: 21 bits (1,048,576 in decimal)
Maximum Precision: 53 bits (109 in OS PL/I Optimizing Compiler)
Range of Exponent: 2^{-260} to 2^{+252}
Examples:

DCL A FLOAT BINARY, B BINARY FLOAT, C BINARY, D BIN(21),
   E FLOAT BIN, F FLOAT BIN(21) ;
   /* A,B,C,D,E, AND F ARE EQUIVALENT */
DCL ALPHA BINARY INIT(101101E5B) ;
   /* ALPHA = 10110100000 */
DCL BETA FLOAT BIN(53) INIT(1011E + 72) ;
DCL GAMMA BINARY FLOAT INIT(1111E − 06) ;

Comments: In main storage, there is no difference between the format of FLOAT DECIMAL data and FLOAT BINARY data. The difference exists externally for the convenience of the programmer. Usually, FLOAT BINARY data format is used in highly specialized areas such as where the programmer desires to *control* the number of bits of precision generated when decimal fractions are converted to binary fractions. To draw an analogy, we know that the decimal fraction 1/3 is a continuing fraction (.33333333333 on to infinity). Perhaps, for computation purposes, you only want to use the value .33. You are *controlling* the number of digits of precision by using two decimal digits to represent or approximate 1/3. The same situation can occur in working with binary data. For example, in its binary equivalent, the decimal number 1/10 will be a continuing fraction. If the programmer so desires, he may indicate the precision that 1/10 is to have for purposes of a specific computation. Just as we said that two decimal digits would be used to approximate 1/3, we could also say that, through the use of FLOAT BINARY(12), only 12 bits will be used to approximate the decimal fraction 1/10.

CHARACTER

S/360, S/370 Data Format Name: character
Type of Data: alphameric
Default Length: none
Maximum Length: varies with the compiler; see Summary at the end of this chapter
Examples:

```
DCL NAME CHARACTER(9) INITIAL('JOHN JINX');
```
NAME = | J | O | H | N | | J | I | N | X |
```
DCL NAME CHAR(10) INIT('JOHN JINX');
```
NAME = | J | O | H | N | | J | I | N | X | |
```
DCL NAME CHAR(8) INIT('JOHN JINX');
```
NAME = | J | O | H | N | | J | I | N |

Comments: Notice from the above examples how character-string data is padded with blanks on the right if the assigned character constant is *shorter* than the declared length of the character-string. If the character constant is *longer* than the declared length of the character-string, then truncation to the right of the data occurs. In the following example, notice the use of the repetition factor and concatenation to center the heading WEEKLY ACTIVITY REPORT in the middle of a 120 print position line. Only the leading 49 blanks had to be specified. To the right of the literal heading, blanks are automatically padded or filled in.

```
DCL PRINT_LINE CHAR(120);
PRINT LINE = (49)' '||'WEEKLY ACTIVITY REPORT';
```

In some levels of PL/I, although it is not recommended, you may do arithmetic on data having the CHARACTER attribute. In this case, the numeric characters are automatically converted to the coded arithmetic form FIXED DECIMAL.

	Arithmetic operations allowed on CHARACTER attribute data providing data contains valid arithmetic constants in character form
Subset language	No
Full language	Yes

It has been illustrated that when a smaller character-string is assigned to a larger character-string field, there is padding on the right with blanks. There may be some instances, however, when it is not desired to have this padding with blanks. A string value is not extended with blanks when it is assigned to a character-string variable that has the VARYING attribute. To illustrate:

DCL NAME CHAR(20) VARYING;

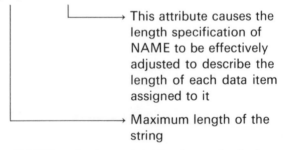

→ This attribute causes the length specification of NAME to be effectively adjusted to describe the length of each data item assigned to it

→ Maximum length of the string

In the above example, NAME so far has a length of zero (called a *null string*) because no character-string has been assigned to it. When the statement

NAME = 'MIKE TUCKER';

is executed, NAME will have a length of 11 because there are 11 characters in the character-string constant. If the statement

NAME = 'MIKE';

is specified, NAME now has a length of 4. If the statement

NAME = '   ';

which contains no characters, is assigned to NAME, the length be-comes zero again. Incidentally, the character-string constant ' ', or one with a repetition factor of zero, is referred to as a *null string* because it contains no character. The VARYING attribute may be specified for identifiers that have the CHARACTER or BIT attribute. Truncation will occur if the length of an assigned string exceeds the maximum length declared for the varying-length string variable. For example:

```
DCL X BIT(4) VARYING;
X='11001'B;   /* X='1100'B */
```

The rightmost bit in the string constant was truncated when assigned to X.

	VARYING attribute
Subset language	No
Full language	Yes

BIT

S/360, S/370 Data Format Name: none, as bits are packed to the nearest byte
Type of Data: logical
Default Length: none
Maximum Length: varies with the compiler; see Summary at the end of this chapter

Examples:

```
DCL ITEM BIT(9) INITIAL('111100001'B);
DCL PATTERN BIT(16) INIT((8)'10'B);
  /* PATTERN='1010101010101010'B */
DCL ITSY BIT(8) INIT('1111'B);   /* ITSY='11110000'B */
DCL SYMPTOMS BIT(4) INIT('0011100'B);
  /* SYMPTOMS='0011'B */
```

Comments: Notice from the examples above that bit-string con-stants are enclosed in single quote marks followed by a B. Also, note that bit-string data are assigned from left to right in the field as are character-string data. Thus, if a smaller bit-string is assigned to a larger field, there is padding on the right with zeros. If a bit-string is larger than the field to which it is being assigned, then the leftmost bits only (as many as will fit) are assigned. In other words, those on the right in bit-string data are truncated. Do not confuse a bit-string with a binary arithmetic data item. Bit-strings are usually not used in calculations. Instead, they may be used in a program to indicate whether or not certain conditions exist (yes or no, 1 or 0, true or false). Note this use of data with the BIT attribute. In the following example, the identifier SWITCH is being tested for a true or false condition:

```
DCL SWITCH BIT(1);
SWITCH = '1'B;
IF SWITCH THEN GO TO TRUE_COND;
```

SWITCH is an expression, of the type ultimately required in this position —BIT(1). The above IF statement accomplishes the same operation as if this statement had been coded:

```
IF SWITCH = '1'B THEN GO TO TRUE_COND;
```

LABEL

Besides arithmetic data and string data, a PL/I programmer can define and use statement-label data. We label PL/I statements which our program will reference. For example:

```
LOOP1:   GET LIST(A, B, C);
         IF A = 0 THEN GO TO EOJ;
         PUT LIST(A + B + C);
         GO TO LOOP1;
```

It is obvious from the context that LOOP1 is the label of a PL/I statement. Moreover, LOOP1 is a statement-label *constant*; i.e., its value will never change—LOOP1 will always be the label of the GET statement. PL/I also allows statement-label *variables*. A statement-label variable is a programmer-defined identifier which has been given the LABEL attribute in a DECLARE statement. For example:

```
DECLARE LBL LABEL INITIAL (LOOP1);
     .             /* LOOP1 MUST BE A LABEL ATTACHED TO
     .                A PL/I STATEMENT IN THIS PROGRAM; I.E., IT
     .                MUST BE A STATEMENT LABEL CONSTANT. */
```

```
LOOP1 :   GET LIST(A, B, C) ;
          .
          .
          .
          GO TO LBL;
                        /* PROGRAM CONTROL IS TRANSFERRED TO
                        THE VALUE OF LBL, CURRENTLY LOOP1 */
```

The above example illustrates a form of *indirect addressing*. Instead of directly addressing a location (that is, branching to a label in our program), we specify another location (in this case, it is named LBL) ; in that location is the name of the place to which our program should transfer. To use an analogy, assume that good ol' Joe invited some of the boys over for poker one Friday night. When Joe informed his wife of the poker party, she informed him she was having her bridge group over that same evening. The conflict was easily solved when good neighbor Sam said the poker party could be held at his house. Instead of calling his friends, Joe simply had them come to his house as originally planned. When they arrived, Joe gave them the directions to Sam's house. The idea here, of course, is that in this "human situation" the poker players went to one *location* (Joe's house) to pick up the *address* of where they ultimately were to go (Sam's house). Interestingly, the terms *address* and *location* are also programming terms because of their similarity in function.

A statement-label variable may assume many values during the execution of a program. For example :

```
          DCL LBL LABEL;
INPUT :   GET LIST(A,B,C) ;
          .
          .
          .
          IF A=1 THEN LBL=TYPE1 ;
          ELSE IF A=2 THEN LBL=TYPE2 ;
               ELSE LBL=TYPE3 ;
          GO TO LBL;

TYPE1 :   ——
TYPE2 :   ——
TYPE3 :   ——
```

Arithmetic Operations on Mixed Data Types

This section has dealt with the various data formats on S/360 and S/370 and the PL/I keywords that describe these formats. Before leaving the topic of data formats, one question must be raised and answered: "What happens when, for example, a FIXED DECIMAL value is to be added to a FIXED BINARY value?" A computer cannot do arithmetic operations on two values having unlike data formats. Likewise, logical operations cannot be performed on unlike string data. Therefore, when mixed data types appear in an arithmetic expression, the PL/I compiler automatically inserts the appropriate instructions to cause one of the data items to be converted to the data format of the other. The rules for conversion are these:

1. If the *base* of the data items differs, DECIMAL is converted to BINARY.
2. If the *scale* of the data items differs, FIXED is converted to FLOAT.
3. If CHARACTER and BIT are specified, then BIT is converted to CHARACTER.

Figure 2.5 illustrates these conversions.

The DEFAULT Statement

The DEFAULT statement, which is available in the two IBM PL/I optimizing compilers, is provided to enable the programmer to define default attributes for identifiers other than those to which PL/I would *normally* default. To put it another way, this statement is used to override the PL/I language default attributes; it consists of the keyword DEFAULT followed by one or more keyword options.

The RANGE Option

This option specifies the identifiers to which the associated default rules are to be applied. Following are some examples of this option in the DEFAULT statement:

DEFAULT RANGE (A:D) FIXED;

      └────→ Identifiers that begin with A through D will default to FIXED(5), 5 being the standard PL/I default precision for FIXED data

Values to be operated on	Conversion that takes place	Comments
DCL A FIXED DEC, B FLOAT DEC; Y = A + B;	A is converted to FLOAT DEC	Scale is different; thus, FIXED → FLOAT
DCL C FIXED DEC, D FIXED BIN; I = C*D;	C is converted to FIXED BIN	Base is different; thus, DECIMAL → BINARY
DCL E FIXED DEC, F FLOAT BIN; Z = E/F;	E is converted to FLOAT BIN	Both base and scale are different; thus, FIXED → FLOAT DECIMAL → BINARY
DCL G FIXED DEC, H FIXED DEC; R = G − H;	None	Base and scale are already the same

DCL K CHAR(13),
    I CHAR(5),
    J BIT(8)
K = I ‖ J;
	J is converted to
	CHARACTER(8)
		String data formats are different; thus,
		BIT → CHARACTER
		before concatenation is performed

FIGURE 2.5 Examples of data conversions that take place in mixed expressions.

DEFAULT RANGE (∗) FIXED;

                    └─────→ Asterisk specifies that all identifiers (names beginning with A through Z, @, $, #) will default to a FIXED DECIMAL data item with a precision of (5) digits

DEFAULT RANGE (PRO) FLOAT;

                    └─────→ All identifiers whose first three letters are PRO will default to FLOAT(6)

DEFAULT RANGE (A,C,R,T) FIXED BINARY;

                    └─────→ Identifiers that begin with either A, C, R, or T will default to FIXED BINARY with a precision of 15 bits

Note that in the above examples, which specify coded arithmetic attributes (e.g., FIXED, FLOAT, FIXED BINARY), precision may not be specified. The assumed precision in each case will be the standard PL/I default precision.

The VALUE Option

This option is used where it is desirable to specify the default precision of coded arithmetic data or the length of string data. For example:

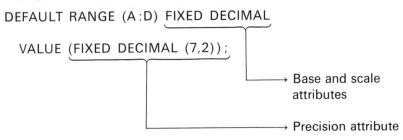

In this example, identifiers that begin with A through D will now default to FIXED DECIMAL with a precision of (7,2).

This option is also used to specify the length of character- and/or bit-strings. For example:

DEFAULT RANGE(C:E) CHARACTER VALUE (CHAR(20));

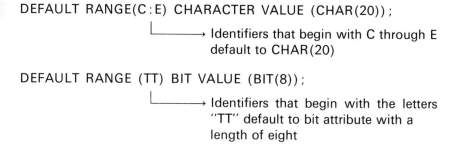

↦ Identifiers that begin with C through E default to CHAR(20)

DEFAULT RANGE (TT) BIT VALUE (BIT(8));

↦ Identifiers that begin with the letters "TT" default to bit attribute with a length of eight

If only the precision attribute is to be specified, thereby leaving the base and scale attributes to be assumed by default, then the following form of the DEFAULT statement may be used:

DEFAULT RANGE (A:D) VALUE (DECIMAL FLOAT(15));

If this DEFAULT statement appears in a program in which identifiers whose names begin with A through D would normally be declared by default, those identifiers will specifically default to DECIMAL FLOAT(15) rather than to the standard default of DECIMAL FLOAT(6).
In the statement

DEFAULT RANGE (∗) VALUE (FIXED BINARY(31),
    FIXED DECIMAL(15), FLOAT BINARY(53),
    FLOAT DECIMAL(15));

the asterisk (∗) refers to *all* identifiers; the attributes in parentheses following the keyword VALUE are the precisions that will apply if variables are partially declared (i.e., only as to base and scale attributes). Thus, if the statement

DECLARE A FIXED;

is encountered in the program, the identifier A will default to FIXED DECIMAL with a precision of 15 because FIXED DECIMAL(15) was specified in the VALUE option list. Or, as another example, if the statement

DCL B BINARY;

is encountered, the identifier B will default to BINARY FLOAT(53) because when BINARY is specified alone, the assumed scale is FLOAT, and the precision specified in the VALUE option list for FLOAT BINARY is 53. Notice what happens, however, when either a base or scale attribute is specified in the DEFAULT statement and an identifier is only partially declared:

DEFAULT RANGE (A:H) FIXED VALUE (FIXED BINARY(31), FIXED DECIMAL(15));

Assuming this DEFAULT statement, if we write

DECLARE A BINARY;

then the identifier A will default to FIXED BINARY(31). This is because only two data attributes were specified in the VALUE option list: FIXED BINARY and FIXED DECIMAL. By declaring A to be BINARY, the only attribute that could apply for purposes of adding the missing scale is the FIXED attribute. Thus, if we write

DECLARE B DECIMAL;

the identifier B will default to FIXED DECIMAL(15).

A program may not contain both a DEFAULT statement to establish default rules and another DEFAULT statement to modify these rules or restore the standard default rules for the same range.

	The DEFAULT statement
Subset language	Not available
Full language	Provided in the PL/I optimizing compilers but not in PL/I F

Case Study: Calculation of Stock Turnover Rate

To obtain a higher rate of return on capital invested, businesses are interested in maximizing sales while minimizing inventory. The ratio of sales to inventory can be determined by a simple formula, the results of which provide useful guidelines for inventory management. For example, if the ABC Company has determined that its stock turnover is once a year, but its closest competitor turns its stock over three times a year, then ABC is possibly carrying too large an inventory. Faster turnover of stock-on-hand might improve ABC's profits.

To find its stock turnover rate, the ABC Company determined the retail value of its inventory by month for the past 12 months to be the following:

Month	Value of inventory
January	$90,000
February	92,000
March	94,000
April	83,000
May	87,000
June	91,000
July	89,000
August	90,000
September	92,000
October	94,000
November	88,000
December	85,000

The company's gross retail sales (S) for this period were $523,000.

There are 12 inputs representing the retail inventory values for each month. The company's gross retail sales figure becomes additional input. The program shown in Figure 2.6 reads the retail sales figure

```
        /* CALCULATION OF STOCK TURNOVER RATE */
 1    STOCK:  PROCEDURE OPTIONS(MAIN);
 2            DECLARE S FIXED DECIMAL(9,2);   /*---S IS TOTAL
                                                    RETAIL SALES-------*/
 3            DECLARE A FIXED DECIMAL(9,2);   /*---A IS AVERAGE RETAIL
                                                    INVENTORY VALUE----*/
 4            DECLARE R FIXED DECIMAL(2,1);   /*---R IS RATE OF STOCK
                                                    TURNOVER-----------*/
 5            ICTR = 1;
 6            GET LIST(S);
 7    LOOP:   GET LIST(VALUE);                /*---VALUE IS MONTH'S
                                                    INVENTORY AMOUNT-----*/
 8            SUM = SUM + VALUE;
 9            ICTR = ICTR + 1;
10            IF ICTR <= 12 THEN GO TO LOOP;
11            A = SUM/12;                     /*---AVERAGE RETAIL VALUE-*/
12            R = S/A;                        /*---STOCK TURNOVER RATE--*/
13            PUT SKIP LIST('TOTAL RETAIL SALES',S);
14            PUT SKIP(2)LIST('AVERAGE RETAIL INVENTORY VALUE',A);
15            PUT SKIP(2)LIST('RATE OF STOCK TURNOVER FOR 12 MONTH '||
                      'PERIOD',R);
16            PUT PAGE LIST('END OF JOB');
17            END STOCK;
```

FIGURE 2.6   Calculation of stock turnover rate.

first and then the inventory values by month (thereby creating the need for a *loop* operation). The average monthly inventory value is found simply by adding the 12 months' values and then dividing by 12. Next, the rate of stock turnover is determined by the formula

$$R = \frac{S}{A}$$

where R is the rate of stock turnover, S is gross retail sales, and A is the average stock value. Desired output is

TOTAL GROSS RETAIL SALES	XXXXXX.00
AVERAGE RETAIL INVENTORY VALUE	XXXXXX.00
RATE OF STOCK TURNOVER FOR 12 MONTH PERIOD	X.X

Observations Regarding Figure 2.6

1. The PL/I *comments* are written in such a manner that they stand out on the page.
2. A comment precedes the PROCEDURE OPTIONS(MAIN) statement. This card will be printed as a heading on every page of the source program listing provided by the PL/I compiler.
3. The first output statement was PUT LIST. Because this is the first PUT LIST statement in the program, there will be an automatic advance to a new page when the statement is executed. Hence, it is not necessary to say PUT PAGE LIST. Had we done so, an extra sheet of printer paper would have been ejected and wasted.
4. The last PUT LIST statement of this case study printed an end-of-job message so there will be no question as to whether or not the job ran to successful completion. Notice that this message will print on a new page.
5. Because LIST I/O is being used, all of the data this program is to process could be punched on one input card. For example:

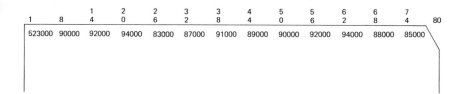

1	1 8	1 4	2 0	2 6	3 2	3 8	4 4	5 0	5 6	6 2	6 8	7 4	80
523000	90000	92000	94000	83000	87000	91000	89000	90000	92000	94000	88000	85000	

Figure 2.6 shows the printout from the PL/I compiler. Notice how the compiler inserted statement numbers to the left of each PL/I source statement. These numbers are used by the programmer as references when debugging a PL/I program. Although there are no diagnostics shown, the compiler does assist the programmer immeasurably by providing as many diagnostic messages as possible. In interpreting them, be aware that an error in one statement may cause several subsequent statements to be flagged as being in error. Yet, there may be nothing wrong with them. When the first error is corrected, the subsequent errors will automatically clear up. This is particularly true if you have an error in a DECLARE statement.

Actually, diagnostics may be generated at two different times:

1. When errors are detected during *compile time*
2. When errors are detected during *execution time* (also called *object time*)

Following your source program listing, compile-time diagnostics (describing errors found by the compiler) will be printed. Execution-time diagnostics (describing errors encountered while your program is in execution) may also be printed. For an explanation of how to interpret execution-time diagnostics, consult the appropriate programmer's guide for the PL/I implementation you are using. Typically, this topic will appear in the guide's index under the heading "object-time diagnostics." Figure 2.7 shows the computer output from the execution of this program. Results are for the values shown in observation number 5 above.

```
TOTAL GROSS RETAIL SALES                        523000.00

AVERAGE RETAIL INVENTORY VALUE                   89583.31

RATE OF STOCK TURNOVER FOR 12 MONTH PERIOD       5.8
```

FIGURE 2.7   Computer output from stock turnover rate program.

SUMMARY

A Program Loop: The repetitive processing of data is called a loop operation. Program loops have three steps:

1. Initialize a counter
2. Modify counter
3. Test counter

The Assignment Statement: You will be using this type of statement often because it specifies which arithmetic and logical operations should take place and/or causes data to be *moved* from one storage area to another. The assignment symbol ($=$) in the arithmetic assignment statement means "replace the value of the variable on the left of the equal sign with the value of the expression on the right of the assignment symbol." Expressions specify a computation and appear to the right of the assignment symbol in an assignment statement. A variable is a term used to indicate a quantity that is referred to by name, and a constant is an actual number. There are a number of operations that may be performed in expressions. They include:

1. *Arithmetic operations:* The order in which arithmetic operations are performed is (*a*) exponentiation (raising a number to a power, moving from right to left in an expression); (*b*) multiplication or division (whichever appears first, moving from left to right in an expression); (*c*) addition or subtraction (whichever appears first, moving from left to right in the expression). When parentheses are specified, the expression within the parentheses will be evaluated first, starting with the innermost pair of parentheses. A prefix operator is an operator that precedes, and is associated with, a single operand. The prefix operators in PL/I are $-$, $+$, and $\neg$. Consider the following valid PL/I statement:

$$Y = X * -W;$$

In the above example, the prefix ($-$) does not signify a subtraction operation; it simply means to find the negative (i.e., reverse the sign) of W. When prefix $+$ (positive) and prefix $-$ (negative) symbols are indicated in an arithmetic expression, they are performed before infix $+$ (addition) and infix $-$ (subtraction) are performed. Note that the prefix operators do not have to be separated from the infix operators with parentheses as is the restriction in other high-level languages. The expression A**B**C is evaluated by PL/I as A**(B**C), because each exponentiation operation is performed moving from right to left in the expression. A form of the assignment statement not available in the subset languages but available in full language compilers is the statement where more than one identifier (variable name) may appear to the left of the equals sign (e.g., A,B,C=0;). This statement causes A, B, and C each to be assigned a value of zero.

2. *Comparison operations:* These operations include:

Symbol	Operation
GE or $>=$	Greater than or equal to
GT or $>$	Greater than
NE or $\neg=$	Not equal
$=$	Equal
LT or $<$	Less than
LE or $<=$	Less than or equal to
NL or $\neg<$	Not less than
NG or $\neg>$	Not greater than

3. *Bit-string operations:*

AND	OR	NOT
$1 \& 1 \to 1$	$1 \mid 1 \to 1$	$\neg 0 \to 1$
$1 \& 0 \to 0$	$1 \mid 0 \to 1$	$\neg 1 \to 0$
$0 \& 1 \to 0$	$0 \mid 1 \to 1$	
$0 \& 0 \to 0$	$0 \mid 0 \to 0$	

The anding or oring of bit-string data is often referred to as a *Boolean operation.*

4. *String operation:* The concatenation operation may be specified for bit- or character-strings. It simply means to join two strings together to form one longer string, for example:

$$\text{'J'} \mid\mid \text{'.'} \to \text{J.}$$
$$\text{'110' B} \mid\mid \text{'11' B} \to 11011$$

Refer to Figure 2.3 for the complete hierarchy of PL/I operations.

The GO TO Statement: This statement causes a branch or transfer to a labeled PL/I statement (e.g., GO TO READ;).

The Null Statement: The null statement is simply a semicolon, or a semicolon with a label attached to it. It is an executable statement, but nothing happens.

The IF Statement: The IF statement is used in a PL/I program when a test or decision is to be made between alternatives.

1. *IF (with transfer of control):* In this statement, if the condition is true, a transfer or branch is made to another point in the program (e.g., IF CTR=0 THEN GO TO EOJ;).

2. *IF (without transfer of control):* In this statement, a single statement will appear as the action to be taken if the condition is true (e.g., IF X<0 THEN X=1;).

3. *The compound IF:* This IF statement is called compound because it contains two PL/I statements. Its form includes the use of the keyword ELSE. If the condition tested is true, the statement following the THEN is performed; if the condition tested is not true, the statement following the ELSE is performed (e.g., IF A=B THEN X=1; ELSE X=2;).

4. *Nested IF statements:* There may be IF statements contained in either the THEN or ELSE clause of another IF statement; for example:

```
IF A=B
THEN IF A=C
        THEN X=1;   /* A=B=C */
        ELSE X=2;   /* A=B but A¬=C */
ELSE X=3;   /* A¬=B */
```

5. *A null ELSE in nested IF statements:* The null ELSE is an ELSE with a null statement (recall the semicolon) as its clause. It is, as its name implies, a nonoperative statement. It gives no direction to the computer. Rather, its effect is to supply the necessary ELSE clause to be associated with the innermost IF; for example:

```
IF A=B
THEN IF A=C
        THEN X=1;
        ELSE;   /* THIS IS A NULL ELSE */
ELSE X=3;
```

6. *The DO-group in an IF statement:* The IF statement is designed to execute one statement following the THEN or ELSE clause. If it is desired to execute more than one statement following the THEN or the ELSE, a DO-group may be specified; for example:

```
IF A=B
    THEN DO;
            X=1; Y=2; Z=3;
            END;
    ELSE DO;
            X=4; Y=5; Z=6;
            END;
```

7. *Bit-string operators in the IF statement:* The operators AND (&) and OR (|) can be used in the IF statement to eliminate nested IF statements; for example, the nested IF statement

```
IF A=B THEN IF C¬=D THEN GO TO POINT_5;
```

could also be written using the comparison operator AND; for example:

```
IF A=B & C¬=D THEN GO TO POINT_5;
```

The DECLARE Statement: The DECLARE statement is needed when the programmer does not wish to use the data formats which are assigned by the compiler by default, or when information is to be supplied to the compiler to reserve storage for a number of data items. The words used to describe the characteristics of data are called attributes. Most attributes may appear in any sequence, and abbreviations of some words are allowed. Attributes are separated by one or more blanks in the DECLARE statement. Attributes covered include:

1. Base (DECIMAL or BINARY)
2. Scale (FIXED or FLOAT)
3. Precision (number of significant digits and/or decimal point alignment)
4. Length (number of characters or bits for string data)
5. Mode (REAL or COMPLEX)

When a variable has its attributes described in a DECLARE statement, it is said to be declared *explicitly*; when variable names are simply used in a program without appearing in a DECLARE statement, they are said to be declared *implicitly*. (One of the biggest problems for the beginning PL/I programmer is failing to realize that if he does not DECLARE the base, scale, and precision of data items, the compiler will assume certain attributes by default. Often these default assumptions are not those which the programmer desires.) The precision of a variable is either attributed by default or it is declared along with the base and/or scale, and it is never specified alone. Figure 2.8 summarizes the allowable lengths, precisions, and ranges for each type of data we may work with in PL/I.

Factored Attributes: When the same base, scale, and precision could apply to more than one variable, then the attributes may be factored; for example:

> DECLARE (A,B,C) FIXED;
> DCL (W FIXED, X FLOAT(6)) DECIMAL;

The INITIAL Attribute: In addition to declaring the base, scale, and precision of an arithmetic variable or the length of a string, it is also possible to set that variable to an initial value by adding the INITIAL attribute in the DECLARE statement; for example:

> DCL CTR FIXED(3) INITIAL(100);
> DECLARE NAME CHARACTER(15) INIT('PATTI WILLIAMS');

Partially Declared Identifiers: We have seen that characteristics of arithmetic data are normally described with three basic attributes: base, scale, and precision. It is possible to make a partial declaration of variables by specifying either:

1. Base
2. Scale
3. Base and precision
4. Scale and precision

	FIXED DECIMAL	FIXED BINARY	FLOAT DECIMAL	FLOAT BINARY	CHARACTER	BIT
Subset language	1 to 15 decimal digits	1 to 31 bits (whole numbers only)	10^{-78} to 10^{+75} 1 to 16 decimal digits	2^{-260} to 2^{+252} 1 to 53 bits	1 to 255 for variables 1 to 255 for constants	1 to 64 bits
Full language	1 to 15 decimal digits	1 to 31 bits (mixed numbers allowed)	10^{-78} to 10^{+75} 1 to 16 decimal digits[a]	2^{-260} to 2^{+252} 1 to 53 bits[b]	1 to 32767 for variables 1 to 1000 for constants	1 to 32767 bits for variables 1 to 8000 bits for constants

FIGURE 2.8   Summary of allowable precisions.

[a]For OS PL/I optimizing compiler, 33 decimal digits maximum.
[b]For OS PL/I optimizing compiler, 109 bits maximum.

When you specify only the base (BINARY or DECIMAL), the scale will default to FLOAT and the precision to 21 for BINARY or 6 for DECIMAL. When you specify only the scale (FIXED or FLOAT), the base will default to DECIMAL. The chart in Figure 2.4 summarizes the defaults taken for partially declared identifiers.

PL/I Data Attributes: Following are the data types provided in PL/I:

1. *FIXED DECIMAL:*   This is the type of data that commercial programmers most often use. It is more efficient to declare the precision of fixed decimal data as an odd number (5, 7, 9, etc.) of digits. This format can be used to represent mixed numbers (e.g., 12.98), fractions (.035), or whole numbers (144).
2. *FIXED BINARY:*   Identifiers beginning with I through N default to FIXED BINARY(15).
3. *FLOAT DECIMAL:*   Because of the range of the exponent of floating-point data, scientific programmers find this data format useful for working with very large or very small numbers. Identifiers whose letters begin with anything other than I through N will default to FLOAT DECIMAL(6). Floating-point data is not suitable for commercial programs where dollars and cents accuracy is required.
4. *FLOAT BINARY:*   There is no difference between the internal format of FLOAT DECIMAL data and FLOAT BINARY data. The difference exists externally for the convenience of the programmer in being able to declare precision in terms of bits.
5. *CHARACTER:*   Character-string data is padded with blanks on the right if the assigned character constant is shorter than the declared length of the character-string. If the character constant is longer than the declared length of the character-string, then truncation to the right of the data occurs. A string value is not extended with blanks when it is assigned to a character-string variable that has the VARYING attribute. In the full language level of PL/I, you may do arithmetic on data having the character attribute (although it is not recommended). In this case, the numeric characters are automatically converted to the coded arithmetic form FIXED DECIMAL.
6. *BIT:*   Bit-string data is assigned from left to right in the field as is character-string data. Thus, if a smaller bit-string is assigned to a larger field, there is padding on the right with zeros. If a bit-string is larger than the field to which it is being assigned, then the leftmost bits only (as many as will fit) are assigned. Bit-strings are usually not used in calculations. Instead, they may be used in a program to indicate whether or not certain conditions exist (yes or no, 1 or 0, true or false).
7. *LABEL:*   A statement-label variable is a programmer-defined identifier which has been given the LABEL attribute in a declare statement. A statement-label variable may assume many values (i.e., "labels" of PL/I statements) during the execution of a program.

Data Conversions: The rules for conversion are these:

1. If the base of the data items differs, DECIMAL is converted to BINARY.
2. If the scale of the data items differs, FIXED is converted to FLOAT.
3. If CHARACTER and BIT are specified, then BIT is converted to CHARACTER.

Following is a summary of the data conversions allowed:

	Arithmetic[a] to CHARACTER	CHARACTER to Arithmetic	Arithmetic to BIT	BIT to Arithmetic	CHARACTER to BIT	BIT to CHARACTER
Subset language	No	No	Yes[b]	Yes[b]	No	Yes
Full language	Yes	Yes	Yes	Yes	Yes	Yes

[a] Arithmetic refers to any coded arithmetic data item (FIXED, FLOAT, FIXED BINARY, etc.)
[b] The maximum number of bits allowed is 31.

CHECKPOINT QUESTIONS

1. What does the = symbol mean in an arithmetic assignment statement?
2. In the PL/I statement below,

$$Y = A + B/C;$$

identify the following:
(a) Operation symbol(s)
(b) Expression(s)
(c) Arithmetic assignment statement(s)
3. What function(s) do parentheses serve in arithmetic expressions?
4. Indicate the order in which arithmetic operations will be performed in the following expressions:
(a) A*X+B*X   (c) X**2/Y**2
(b) ((A*X)+B)*X   (d) −Y*B

5. (True or False)   The null statement is executable.

6. Write the IF statement to set X = 1 if A = B and X = 2 if A ¬ = B.

7. Write the nested IF statements to set X to the following:

X = 1	X = 2	X = 3	X = 4	
A = B	A = B	A ¬ = B	A ¬ = B	These are the conditions which
C = D	C ¬ = D	C ¬ = D	C = D	determine how X is to be set

8. What are the purposes of the END statement?

(To answer questions 9 through 12, you may need to reference Appendix D.)

9. Show how these values would be represented in bytes in the packed decimal format (use decimal notation):

    +123   +45,045   −9999   123.45

10. What is a PL/I term for packed data?

11. What is the largest decimal number that may be specified using the packed decimal data format on S/360 or S/360?

12. How many bytes does it take to represent 2,147,483,647 in fixed-point binary?_____ In packed decimal?_____

13. Which type of programmer, commercial or scientific, would be most likely to use data in the floating-point format?

14. Select the values that could be assigned to the short-form floating-point data format without losing *precision* of the value.

    .0000039   12,345,678.   1,000,000,000.   43.79

15. Where may DECLARE statements appear in your PL/I program?

16. What purpose(s) does the DECLARE statement serve?

17. Given that X and Y are DECIMAL FLOAT(6), must they be explicitly declared in a PL/I program?

18. Which data type provides for fastest execution time on arithmetic operations?

    (*a*)   FIXED DECIMAL   (*b*)   FIXED BINARY

19. Which takes more storage?

    (*a*)   DCL ALPHA FIXED(7)   (*b*)   DCL ALPHA FIXED(6)

20. Which is more efficient?

    (*a*)   K = K + 1 ;   (*b*)   K = K + 1B ;

21. Using the chart in Figure 2.4, what are the default attributes for the following partially declared identifiers?

(*a*)	DCL ALPHA;	(*f*)	DCL INPUT;
(*b*)	DCL HENRY FIXED;	(*g*)	DCL COST FIXED(5,2);
(*c*)	DCL LEAF FLOAT;	(*h*)	DCL PLUS FLOAT DECIMAL;
(*d*)	DCL HELP_IN BINARY;	(*i*)	DCL MASON BINARY FIXED;
(*e*)	DCL COUNT DECIMAL;	(*j*)	DCL DIXON FLOAT(6);

22. Using the chart in Figure 2.8, indicate which of the following examples are

96 PL/I Programming

valid and which are invalid in the subset language. Also, which are invalid in the full language?

(a) DCL GOOD FIXED(5);
(b) DCL SHIP FIXED(16);
(c) DCL LOLLIPOP FIXED BIN(31,2);
(d) DCL SHIRLEY FIXED BIN(32);
(e) DCL TEMPLE FLOAT(7,2);
(f) DCL BLACK CHARACTER(275);

23. What is the value that will be placed in each of the following identifiers?
(a) DCL A FIXED DECIMAL(5,2); A=12345;
(b) DCL B FIXED BINARY; B=32769;
(c) DCL C FIXED DECIMAL; C=43.76;
(d) DCL D FIXED BINARY; D=3.6;
(e) DECLARE ANAME BIT(8) INIT ('11'B);
(f) DECLARE BNAME BIT(3) INIT('11011'B);
(g) DECLARE CNAME BIT(10) INIT('111'B);

24. Given the following statements, to what point will the program transfer?

        DECLARE T_POINT LABEL INIT(CONT);
        GO TO T_POINT;

25. What happens when there is a transfer to the last physical END statement in a PL/I program?

26. What is the difference, internally, between FLOAT DECIMAL and FLOAT BINARY?

27. What will SONG contain given the following DECLARE?

        DECLARE SONG CHAR(12) INIT('MISSISSIPPI MUD');

28. How many bytes will the following bit-strings require?
(a) '11'B   (c) '110000111'B
(b) '11111001'B   (d) '0'B

29. In the following mixed-mode expressions, indicate the data conversion that takes place:
(a) DCL A FIXED BINARY, B FIXED DECIMAL; A=A+B;
(b) DCL A CHARACTER(3), B BIT(3); A=B;

30. Consider the following sequence of arithmetic assignment statements to be executed in the order they are written. After each statement has been executed, show the current values of the variables A, B, and C, assuming each was originally zero.

	A	B	C
A=5;			
B=-A;			
C=A/B-1;			
C=C+1;			
B=B*B+C;			

	A	B	C
A = A**2 − B ;			
B = B − C + A ;			
C = B*C ;			
B = B/2 ;			
A = C/B + 12 ;			

31. Match the following constants with their PL/I attributes:

(a) '011000'B		(1) FIXED DECIMAL(5,2)
(b) 01011101B		(2) FIXED BINARY(8)
(c) 01011101		(3) DECIMAL FLOAT(3)
(d) '5'		(4) CHARACTER(5)
(e) 34.5E2		(5) BINARY FLOAT(5)
(f) 101.11E3B		(6) DECIMAL FIXED(8)
(g) 101.11		(7) CHARACTER(1)
(h) 101.11B		(8) BINARY FIXED(5,2)
(i) 'ABCDE'		(9) BIT(6)
(j) 101.11E3		(10) DECIMAL FLOAT(5)
		(11) BIT(8)
		(12) NO-MATCH

TERMS TO STUDY

assignment symbol
base
bit-string operators
Boolean
byte
comparison operators
compile-time versus object-time
concatenation
counter
data aggregate
DO-group
exponent
expression
factored attributes
implicit versus explicit declaration
infix

initialize
length attribute
loop
mixed expression
mode attribute
null ELSE
null string
packed data
partially declared attributes
precision
prefix
range versus precision
scale
statement-label variable
truncate

PRACTICE PROBLEMS

1. Drill on the DECLARE Statement

Problem Statement: Write a series of declarations for the constants listed in the table given here. Print the values defined.

Purpose of the Problem: To gain practice in declaring various data types available in PL/I as well as use of the INITIAL attribute and various PL/I abbreviations (BIN,CHAR,DCL,DEF,INIT,PIC,PROC).

Input: There is no input from any device. Instead, declare identifiers to have the necessary attributes for the constants listed in the table.

Process: Assign the constants given in the table (using the INITIAL attribute) to the appropriate variable names you have selected (or you may use the names #1, #2, #3, etc.).

Name	Attribute	Constant	Comments
#1	CHARACTER	Love's a Four Letter Word	
#2	FIXED DECIMAL	1929	
#3	BIT "STRING"	0101010101010101	Specify a repetition factor in writing this constant
#4	FIXED DECIMAL	− 19,402.13	
#5	FIXED DECIMAL	000000212	
#6	CHARACTER	The Road Not Taken	
#7	FLOAT BINARY	1011E+12B	
#8	FIXED BINARY	− 35000	
#9	CHARACTER	436559005	
#10	FIXED BINARY	1111B	

NOTE: It is only possible to print (using PUT LIST) the decimal equivalent for the binary constants in items #7 and #10 above. Can you determine the decimal equivalents of these values?

Output: Print results using PUT LIST. A sample of the output is shown in Figure 2.9.

2. Inventory Audit Report

Problem Statement: Write a program to read five data cards where each card contains:

Part number (ITEM#)
Unit price (PRICE)
Quantity on hand (IQTY)

```
LOVE'S A FOUR LETTER WORD
      1929
'0101010101010101'B
   -19402.13
             212
THE ROAD NOT TAKEN
   4.505600E+04
      -35000
  436559005
            15
```

FIGURE 2.9 Sample
output from Problem 1.

Compute the extension (EXT) by multiplying PRICE∗IQTY. For each data card read, print a line using PUT LIST. Be sure to include the appropriate DECLARE statements for the ITEM# (as a character-string), PRICE, IQTY, and EXT of each variable.

Purpose of the Problem: To program a loop operation and perform arithmetic calculations.

Card Input: Use the data below. Each punched value should be separated by a blank in the input stream.

ITEM#	PRICE	IQTY
'1001'	20.00	030
'2104'	07.30	030
'4030'	01.05	150
'3035'	17.50	002
'2200'	01.45	010

Printer Output: Start output on a new page in the format shown in Figure 2.10.

Flowchart: See Figure 2.11.

3. Salesmen's Total Sales and Commission Report

Problem Statement: Write a program to total the sales for each of four sales-men for each day of a one-week period. Accumulate total sales for each sales-

```
        INVENTORY    AUDIT    REPORT

PART NUMBER      PRICE        QUANTITY        EXTENSION

    1001         20.00           30            600.00
    2104          7.30           30            219.00
    4030          1.05          150            157.50
    3035         17.50            2             35.00
    2200          1.45           10             14.50
```

FIGURE 2.10 Sample output from Problem 2.

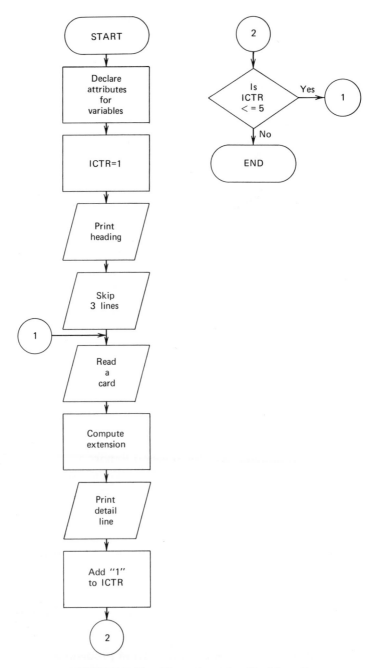

FIGURE 2.11   Flowchart for Problem 2.

man and compute a 10% commission. Print total sales and commission for each salesman.

Purpose of the Problem: To practice programming a loop within a loop (nested loops).

Card Input: See Figure 2.12.

```
100.25   75.40   137.50   263.20   179.45
200.15   157.34   257.30   236.05   45.80
152.20   510.00   136.25   435.06   50.45
251.15   150.00   263.52   255.04   87.60
```

FIGURE 2.12 Sample card data for Problem 3.

Printer Output: If the suggested input values are used, output should be as shown in Figure 2.13.

SALESMAN	TOTAL SALES	COMMISSION
1	755.80	75.58
2	896.64	89.66
3	1283.96	128.39
4	1007.31	100.73

FIGURE 2.13 Sample output from Problem 3.

Flowchart: A program flowchart is provided in Figure 2.14.

4. Sort Three Values

Problem Statement: Write a PL/I program to read three values using GET LIST. Sort (arrange) these values into ascending sequence and print them on the line printer using the PUT LINE ( ) LIST form of list-directed output.

Purpose of the Problem: To give you practice in using the IF statement and the DO-group; also to cause you to think about how the contents of variables may be exchanged (switched) in a program.

Card Input: It is suggested that you punch the values 4376, 752, 2040; one data item per card. You can then rearrange your input cards and execute your program two or three times in order to check out the logic in your program.

Printer Output: If the suggested input values are used, output should be as shown in Figure 2.15.

Hint on Getting Started: Notice in Figure 2.15 that the three input values are to be listed in a column starting with the second tab position (print position 25). This is easy to accomplish if, in your PUT LIST statement, you output a

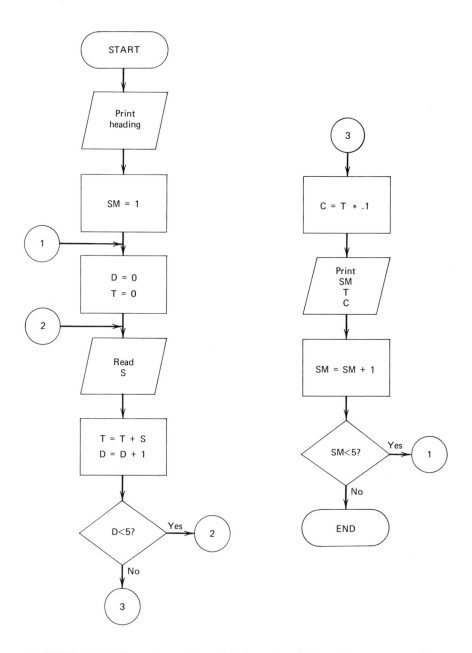

FIGURE 2.14 Flowchart for Problem 3: SM, salesman number; D, day; S, day's sales; T, total sales; C, commission.

```
ORDER OF INPUT VALUES        4376

                              752

                             2040

SORTED VALUES ARE:            752

                             2040

                             4376
```

FIGURE 2.15   Sample output from Problem 4.

character constant of a "blank" to the first tab position, for example:

PUT LIST('ORDER OF INPUT VALUES',K1);
PUT SKIP(2) LIST(' ',K2);
PUT SKIP(2) LIST(' ',K3);

└─────────────────────→ Causes a blank to be output at
                        first tab position on printer

Flowchart: A program flowchart is given in Figure 2.16.

5.   Using the Iterative Solution

An *iterative* solution, which might also be referred to as a "trial and error" approach, may be used in solving for an unknown quantity when there is no simple algebraic method for solution. For example, the equation

$$X^6 - X^4 = 650$$

is to be solved for X. In solving for X that will be accurate to four decimal places, the process will be time-consuming and subject to error. Thus, this is a perfect exercise for the computer. In a computer solution, we begin by converting the above equation to

$$X^6 - X^4 - 650 = 0$$

and then start with a trial value of X and evaluate the function $(X^6 - X^4 - 650)$. If the value is negative, try a larger X. When this process produces a positive value for the function, do the following:

1.   Decrease the trial X to its previous (negative producing) value;
2.   Reduce the increment to 1/10 its former size.
3.   Start the evaluation—increment process again.

When a satisfactory number of decimal places have been computed, stop the calculation and print the value of X. To produce four accurate decimal places, five should be computed. Thus, stop the iterative process when a positive result has been reached with the increment .00001. In calculating for various

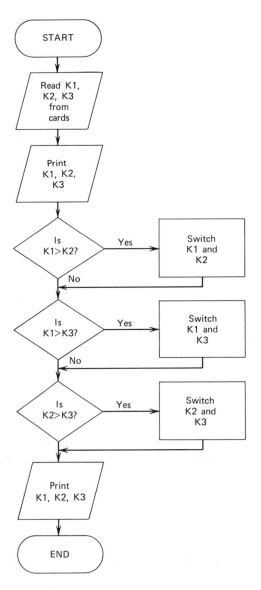

FIGURE 2.16   Program flowchart for Problem 4.

trial values, the table given here shows the progression of data in the solution of this problem. Most efficient use of the computer can be obtained by beginning with a reasonable initial value of X. Each problem must be examined separately.

X	X^6	X^4	$X^6 - X^4 - 650$
1.00000E+00	1.00000E+00	1.00000E+00	-6.50000E+02
2.00000E+00	6.40000E+01	1.60000E+01	-6.02000E+02
3.00000E+00	7.29000E+02	8.10000E+01	-2.00000E+00
4.00000E+00	4.09600E+03	2.56000E+02	3.19000E+03
3.10000E+00	8.87502E+02	9.23520E+01	1.45150E+02
3.01000E+00	7.43699E+02	8.20852E+01	1.16135E+01
3.00100E+00	7.30455E+02	8.11078E+01	-6.53076E-01
3.00200E+00	7.31916E+02	8.12159E+01	6.99463E-01
3.00110E+00	7.30598E+02	8.11184E+01	-5.20020E-01
3.00119E+00	7.30744E+02	8.11291E+01	-3.85498E-01
3.00129E+00	7.30888E+02	8.11398E+01	-2.51953E-01
⋮	⋮	⋮	⋮

In this case, a first approximation of X can be obtained as follows:

$$X^6 - X^4 = X^4(X^2 - 1) = 650$$
$$X^4(X + 1)(X - 1) = 650$$
$$X^6 \cong 650$$
$$X \cong (650)^{1/6} = 2.94 \qquad \therefore \text{ Start with } X = 3$$

Input: The program generates data, so there is no input of data in this exercise.
Output: Sample output might read as follows:

THE VALUE OF 'X' IN THE EQUATION(X**6−X**4=650) IS NN.NNNN

where N is any decimal digit. (The answer is 3.00148.)

6. Table of Time and Distance Traveled
Problem Statement: An object dropped from a height travels the distance (d) in feet (neglecting air resistance),

$$d = \frac{1}{2} at^2$$

where

$$a = 32.174 \text{ (ft/sec}^2; \text{ the gravitational constant)}$$
$$t = \text{time (sec)}$$

Write a program that will generate a table of distances for times of 1 sec, 2 sec, 3 sec, etc., up to and including 100 sec.
Purpose of the Problem: To program a loop operation as well as perform arithmetic operations including exponentiation.
Input: There is no input data to this program.

TIME IN SECONDS	DISTANCE TRAVELED
1	16
2	64
3	144
4	257
5	402
6	579
7	788
8	1029
9	1303
10	1608
11	1946
12	2316
13	2718
14	3153

97	151362
98	154499
99	157668
100	160869

FIGURE 2.17   Sample output for Problem 6.

Output: Suggested output format is shown in Figure 2.17.

7.   Find the Roots of a Quadratic Equation

Problem Statement: Write a PL/I program to find the roots of the quadratic equation of the general form

$$ax^2 + bx + c = 0$$

using the solution formula

$$\frac{-b \pm \sqrt{b^2 - 4ac}}{2a}$$

When the discriminant is negative, the roots are imaginary. In this case, the program should branch around the computation of the roots and print only a, b, and c and the message NO SOLUTION.

Purpose of the Problem: To note the necessity of providing for branching *out* (in this case, unconditionally) from each segment of a program entered as an alternative.

Input: Test this program using at least four sets of data. Suggested input:

A	B	C
− 23.12	00.0	274.2
3	2	4
1	− 1	− 6
− 1	2	− 2

A VALUE	B VALUE	C VALUE	ROOT1	ROOT2
-2.31200E+01	0.00000E+00	2.74200E+02	-3.44381E+00	3.44381E+00
3.00000E+00	2.00000E+00	4.00000E+00	NO SOLUTION	
1.00000E+00	-1.00000E+00	-6.00000E+00	3.00000E+00	-2.00000E+00
-1.00000E+00	2.00000E+00	-2.00000E+00	NO SOLUTION	

FIGURE 2.18   Sample output for Problem 7.

Output: Sample output is illustrated in Figure 2.18.

8. Find the Greatest Common Divisor

Problem Statement: Find the greatest common divisor of pairs of integers (A and B) that are read from punched cards. The greatest common divisor (gcd) is the largest integer that divides evenly into A and B. For example, 24 and 16 have common divisors of 2, 4, and 8; thus, the gcd is 8. (If the gcd is 1, the numbers are said to be "relatively prime" or "prime to each other." For example, 15 and 22 have only the value 1 as a common divisor.)

Purpose of the Problem: To use the IF statement to test the relationship between values and to code a program iteration.

Input: Read any number of pairs of values and find the gcd. When a pair of numbers are equal (e.g., 99, 99), terminate the program. Suggested input is

$$88 \quad 36 \quad 27 \quad 14 \quad 24 \quad 16 \quad 6 \quad 12 \quad 99 \quad 99$$

Processing: To find the gcd use the Euclidean algorithm given here: Let a and b represent the pair of values in question. Divide a by b, obtaining a quotient of q and a remainder of r_1, which is less than b and greater than or equal to zero. Thus,

$$a = bq_1 + r_1$$

When the remainder (r) is equal to zero, b is the gcd. If the remainder is not equal to zero, consider

$$b = r_1 q_2 + r_2$$

where

$$0 < r_2 < r_1$$

Should r_2 equal zero, r_1 is the gcd. Continuing in this manner, we obtain:

$$r_1 = r_2 q_3 + r_3$$
$$r_2 = r_3 q_4 + r_4$$
$$r_{n-2} = r_{n-1} q_n + r_n$$

where $0 < r_n < r_{n-1}$ and $r_n = 0$. Thus, r_{n-1} is the gcd of a and b.
    Example 1 :   Find the gcd of 88 and 36 :

$$88 = 36(2) + 16$$

Because $16 < 36$ and $16 \neq 0$, we shift left and proceed:

$$36 = 16(2) + 4$$

Because $4 \neq 0$, we again shift left and proceed:

$$16 = 4(4) + 0 \qquad r_2 = 4 \text{ (gcd)}$$

Because 0 has been reached, 4 is the gcd of 88 and 36.

Example 2: Find the gcd of 27 and 14:

$$
\begin{aligned}
27 &= 14(1) + 13 & 13 &\neq 0 \\
14 &= 13(1) + 1 & 1 &\neq 0 \\
13 &= 1(13) + 0 & r_2 &= 1 \text{ (gcd)}
\end{aligned}
$$

Thus, 1 is the gcd; 27 and 14 are relatively prime.

Output: Sample output is illustrated in Figure 2.19.

Flowchart: See Figure 2.20.

```
GREATEST COMMON DIVISOR OF THE FOLLOWING VALUES IS
      36                        8                              4


GREATEST COMMON DIVISOR OF THE FOLLOWING VALUES IS
      27                        14                             1


GREATEST COMMON DIVISOR OF THE FOLLOWING VALUES IS
      24                        16                             8


GREATEST COMMON DIVISOR OF THE FOLLOWING VALUES IS
      12                        6                              6
```

FIGURE 2.19   Sample output for Problem 8.

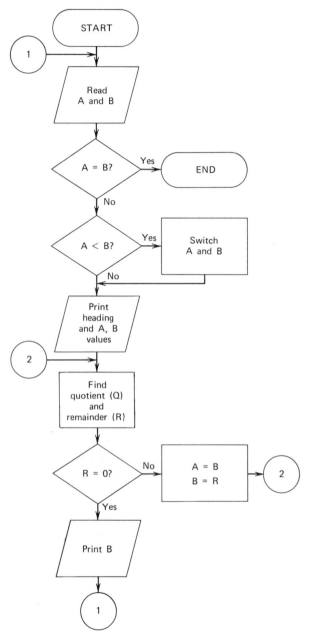

FIGURE 2.20   Suggested flowchart for Problem 8.

chapter 3

File Declarations, Conditions, and Pictures

At the beginning of this book, you were introduced to PL/I programming through the problem of finding the grade-point average for five examination marks. Here is that first program:

```
AVER:   PROCEDURE OPTIONS(MAIN);
        GET LIST(A,B,C,D,E);
        MEAN=(A+B+C+D+E)/5;
        PUT LIST('AVERAGE IS',MEAN);
        END;
```

Seldom would a program be written just to process one set of data as the above program does. Rather, a number of sets of values would be read and processed. Thus, a program loop would be constructed so as to process multiple sets of input data. Now, the question is—just how many sets of data are there? Typically, it is not known how many records (punched cards, in this case) there are to be processed each time a program is executed. For example, is the grade-point average program to calculate the mean score for 20 students? 30 students? 50 students? Because it is desirable to code a generalized program that could handle any number of students, there must be a way of determining when there are no more input data records. In IBM operating systems, the end of a card data deck is indicated by the following job control statement:

When the /* card is read by the system input routines, an end-of-file condition is raised signifying that no more GET statements to that file may be executed. One of two possible courses of action may now be taken:

1. *System action:*   The system immediately terminates the job with an abnormal ending error message unless this is over-ridden by programmer-defined action.
2. *Programmer-defined action:*   The PL/I programmer may specify the action to be taken when the end-of-file condition is detected. This is done with the statement

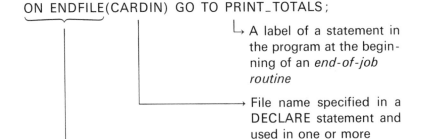

ON ENDFILE(CARDIN) GO TO PRINT_TOTALS;

↳ A label of a statement in the program at the beginning of an *end-of-job routine*

→ File name specified in a DECLARE statement and used in one or more statements

→ PL/I keywords specifying the ON statement and the ENDFILE condition

The ON statement need be executed only once in your program (unless program logic dictates otherwise), for once you have specified what action is to be taken when the end-of-file is detected, that information is "remembered." Special symbols other than /∗ are used to mark the end of a tape or disk file; thus, all files have a method for marking the physical end-of-file. The end-of-file condition is detected when you attempt to read the end-of-file marker. As illustrated above, the ON ENDFILE statement must contain the name of the file for which an end-of-file condition is to be tested and action taken.

A PL/I file is represented in the program by a file name which is declared to have the FILE attribute. For example:

DECLARE CARDIN FILE...

It is through the use of this name that we will access or create the data records which are stored on an external device such as cards, disk, or magnetic tape. The collection of records which we will think of as a file is called a *data set*. We must describe for PL/I the exact nature of the data set that we are to access through our file name. For example, we must specify the direction of data transmission (e.g., INPUT or OUTPUT); and we must specify the form of the records contained in the data set (are they all the same size? do their lengths vary?), the length of the records in the data set (How many bytes long are they?), and the location of the data set (is it on tape or disk? or, is it a card or printer data set?). Let us look at an example of a file declaration:

DCL CARDIN FILE INPUT STREAM ENVIRONMENT(F(80));

This declaration describes a file, to be called CARDIN in this program, whose data transmission direction is INPUT, and whose records shall be accessed only by the stream input keyword GET. In this case, the file specifications are being made in the DECLARE statement. In some operating systems (such as OS), however, many of the file attributes may be specified in job control statements and need not be specified in your program. Another place where file attributes may be specified is in the OPEN statement. For example:

OPEN FILE(CARDIN)INPUT;

Before our PL/I program can communicate with a data set, that file must be opened. (With stream I/O, the opening of files is automatic; therefore, it would not be necessary for you to include the OPEN statement in your program.) The opening of files is necessary because it is at that time that device readiness is checked (e.g., is the power on and is the device in a ready state?) and all attributes for the file are merged. In other words, some attributes may be specified in job control statements, others (but not the same ones) may be in the DECLARE statement, and still other attributes may be in the OPEN statement. It is at *open* time that attributes from these three sources are combined to form the description of the data set our program is going to communicate with.

The method in which you specify file attributes depends upon which implementation of PL/I you are using. In PL/I F and OS PL/I optimizing compilers, most of the information can be specified in job control statements. However, in PL/I D, and DOS PL/I optimizing compilers, the information is required in the DECLARE statement. The OS compilers recognize the various specifications unique to DOS/TOS PL/I compilers and issue a warning message that certain specifications are being ignored. This ensures a high degree of upward compatibility between compilers. In previous chapters, differences have been cited between the subset and full language implementations:

Subset	Full
PL/I D	DOS PL/I Optimizing Compiler
	PL/I F
	OS PL/I Optimizing Compiler

However, the specifications that would appear in the ENVIRONMENT attribute are related to the operating system, *not* the language implementation. The operating systems and some of the compilers that are provided are

DOS/TOS	**OS**
PL/I D	PL/I F
DOS PL/I Optimizing	OS PL/I Optimizing Compiler
Compiler	OS Checkout Compiler

Let us look below at an example of a declaration of a file which will be used to access card records from the IBM 2540 Card Reader. Notice that the ENVIRONMENT attribute's options are placed in parentheses following the keyword ENV (ENV is the abbreviation for ENVIRONMENT). Also, the options are to be separated from each other by a blank or other delimiter. The parentheses are delimiters, so the following example does not need a blank between the F(80) option and the MEDIUM option.

Here is an example of a declaration for a data set associated with a line printer:

```
DCL PRINTR FILE STREAM OUTPUT ENV(F(132)MEDIUM
    (SYSLST,1403)) ;
```

Most of the keywords in a file declaration may appear in any sequence. Comparing the PRINTR file declaration with CARDIN, you will see that the sequence of keywords has been altered (INPUT STREAM versus STREAM OUTPUT). Following are some points to keep in mind when declaring files under a specific operating system, using a particular PL/I implementation.

1. *The MEDIUM option:* For PL/I D and DOS optimizing compilers, this option must be specified. The MEDIUM option is used to specify a symbolic device name and the type of device on which the data set is stored or through which we will access the data. Within parentheses following the keyword MEDIUM, specify SYSIPT for card input and SYSLST for line printer output as the symbolic device name. The physical device numbers you specify are dependent upon the type of devices attached to the computer on which your PL/I program is to be run. Some of the more commonly used IBM devices are

    Card read/punch : 2540, 1442
    Card readers : 2520, 2501
    Line printers : 1403, 1443

116 PL/I Programming

DCL CARDIN FILE INPUT STREAM ENV(F(80)MEDIUM(SYSIPT,2540)) ;

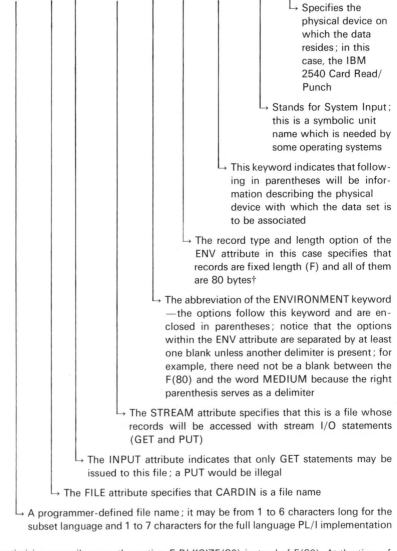

↳ Specifies the physical device on which the data resides; in this case, the IBM 2540 Card Read/Punch

↳ Stands for System Input; this is a symbolic unit name which is needed by some operating systems

↳ This keyword indicates that following in parentheses will be information describing the physical device with which the data set is to be associated

↳ The record type and length option of the ENV attribute in this case specifies that records are fixed length (F) and all of them are 80 bytes†

↳ The abbreviation of the ENVIRONMENT keyword —the options follow this keyword and are enclosed in parentheses; notice that the options within the ENV attribute are separated by at least one blank unless another delimiter is present; for example, there need not be a blank between the F(80) and the word MEDIUM because the right parenthesis serves as a delimiter

↳ The STREAM attribute specifies that this is a file whose records will be accessed with stream I/O statements (GET and PUT)

↳ The INPUT attribute indicates that only GET statements may be issued to this file; a PUT would be illegal

↳ The FILE attribute specifies that CARDIN is a file name

↳ A programmer-defined file name; it may be from 1 to 6 characters long for the subset language and 1 to 7 characters for the full language PL/I implementation

†The optimizing compilers use the option F BLKSIZE(80) instead of F(80). At the time of publication of this book, either F(80) or F BLKSIZE(80) could be specified for the full language implementations.

2. *The record form and record size option:*   The F in the ENVIRON-
   MENT section of the file declaration specifies the record type as
   being fixed length. For card input, the record type is always
   fixed and must always be 80 bytes long [e.g., F(80) or F
   BLKSIZE(80)]. For line printer output, the record type can be
   variable (V instead of F). However, for purposes of simplicity,
   we will limit our discussion in this chapter to fixed-length
   record types. The record length of a printer data set—that is,
   the number of printed positions on a line—may be any value
   as long as that value does not exceed the maximum number of
   print positions for the line printer that you are using. Typically,
   a line printer is either 120, 132, 144, or 150 print positions wide.
   Thus, F(132) might be the specification you would write in the
   ENVIRONMENT section of the file declaration statement.

The list-directed input statement where a file name is explicitly
specified takes this general form :

GET FILE(file name)LIST(data names) ;

Using the previous DECLARE statement for the CARDIN file, we could
specify the following :

GET FILE(CARDIN)LIST(A,B,C,D,E) ;

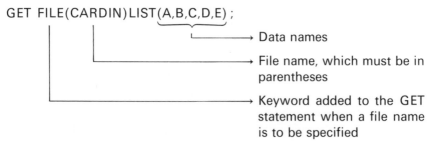

Data names

File name, which must be in parentheses

Keyword added to the GET statement when a file name is to be specified

Here is an example of a list-directed file declaration and output
statement for a line printer that has 120 print positions :

DCL PRINTR FILE OUTPUT STREAM PRINT ENV(F(121)
    MEDIUM(SYSLST,1403)) ;
PUT PAGE FILE(PRINTR)LIST(A,B,C,D) ;

The PRINT attribute is added to the file declaration statement for
stream files associated with a line printer so that the carriage control
options such as PAGE and LINE may be specified in the PUT statement.
(The PRINT attribute applies only to files with the STREAM and OUT-
PUT attributes.) It indicates that the file is eventually to be printed—

that is, the data associated with the file is to appear on printed pages, although it may first be written on some other medium. The PRINT attribute causes the initial byte of each record of the associated data set to be reserved for a printer control character. The printer control character is initialized through the use of such keywords as PAGE, SKIP, or LINE in your PUT statement. It was indicated that the line printer referenced in the above example has 120 print positions. Notice that the record size was specified as F(121)—one greater than the number of actual printing positions on a line. The extra position had to be added to the record size to provide the initial position necessary to contain the printer control character.

The following is an example of the DECLARE and PUT statements for operating on a STREAM I/O file having the PRINT attribute:

```
DCL PRINTR FILE OUTPUT STREAM PRINT ENV(F(133)
  MEDIUM(SYSLST,1403)) ;
DCL AREA CHAR(133) ;
PUT FILE(PRINTR)PAGE LIST(AREA) ;
```

Without the PRINT attribute, we have the following DECLARE and PUT:

```
DCL PRINTR FILE OUTPUT STREAM ENV(F(132)
  MEDIUM(SYSLST,1403)) ;
DCL AREA CHAR(132) ;
PUT FILE(PRINTR) LIST(AREA) ;
```

Notice that the record size—F(132)—is one less than that in the first example, because the first position of the output area will not be used for a carriage control character. However, there will be a space of one line before print because the record size—F(132)—and AREA—CHAR (132)—are the same length.

Stream files without the PRINT attribute may output to a printer *immediately*. Immediately, in this context, means from main storage to the printer. However, on medium- to large-scale systems, it is both possible and frequently desirable to output print data to an external storage device such as tape or disk. The data would be kept there for subsequent printing. When this is the case, it is necessary to precede each print record with the appropriate carriage control character (hence, PRINT must be specified) so that the program *dumping†* these records to the printer at a later time will know how to control

---

†Usually means the writing of data from one storage medium to another.

the carriage. The *dump program* need not be written in PL/I. In fact, there are standard *utility programs*‡ (typically supplied by the computer manufacturer) to print these records. These utility programs usually require that the first position of each print record contain a carriage control character.

Returning to the grade-point average program, let us look at the PL/I statements (including a file declaration) that accomplish the input and processing of an undetermined number of students' grades. The output will consist of printing each student's name and his grade-point average.

```
AVER:   PROCEDURE OPTIONS(MAIN) ;
        DCL NAME CHAR(20) ;
        DCL CARD FILE INPUT STREAM ENV(F(80)MEDIUM
          (SYSIPT,2501)) ;
        ON ENDFILE(CARD) GO TO EOJ;
LOOP:   GET FILE(CARD)LIST(NAME,A,B,C,D,E) ;
        MEAN = (A + B + C + D + E)/5;
        PUT SKIP(2)LIST(NAME,MEAN) ;
        GO TO LOOP;
EOJ:    END;
```

When file names are omitted from a GET or PUT, two file names are assumed: SYSIN for the standard input file and SYSPRINT for the output file. Thus, the statements

```
                GET  LIST(A,B,C) ;
                PUT  LIST(A,B,C) ;
```

are equivalent to

```
        GET  FILE(SYSIN)LIST(A,B,C) ;
        PUT  FILE(SYSPRINT)LIST(A,B,C) ;
```

These files need not be declared, as a standard set of attributes is applied automatically. (Note: the EXTERNAL attribute is explained later.) In addition to these attributes, the following options are default for the SYSPRINT file:

LINESIZE = 120 print positions
PAGESIZE = 60 lines per page

‡The name given to programs that facilitate (among other things) data transfer between I/O devices; for example, card-to-tape, card-to-printer, tape-to-tape, tape-to-disk, tape-to-printer, disk-to-printer.

	SYSIN	SYSPRINT
Subset language	STREAM, INPUT, EXTERNAL, F(80)	STREAM, OUTPUT, PRINT, EXTERNAL, F(121)
Full language	STREAM, INPUT EXTERNAL, F(80)	STREAM, OUTPUT, PRINT, EXTERNAL, V(121)[a]

[a] V stands for variable-length record as contrasted with F for fixed-length record. With V-type records, each record size may vary in length; however, no record may be larger than the stated maximum—in this case, 121.

In the subset language implementations, you may not use the file names SYSIN and SYSPRINT unless they are *explicitly* declared as files. For example:

DCL SYSIN FILE INPUT STREAM ENV(F(80)MEDIUM
(SYSIPT,2540));

Actually, SYSPRINT could not be used for a file name, because it is longer than six characters—the maximum allowed in the subset language.

	Methods for referencing the standard default files SYSIN and SYSPRINT
Subset language	GET LIST(...); PUT LIST(...);
Full language	GET FILE(SYSIN)LIST(...); PUT FILE(SYSPRINT)LIST(...);

In the full language, these two standard file names and their attributes do not have to be explicitly declared. Although there is really no advantage to coding

GET FILE(SYSIN)LIST(A,B,C);

instead of

GET LIST(A,B,C);

there is an advantage in being able to reference the SYSIN file in the ENDFILE statement. For example :

ON ENDFILE(SYSIN) GO TO WRAP_UP ;

Thus, we may take program-specified action to the end-of-file condition without having to explicitly declare the SYSIN file. This flexibility is not provided in the subset language.

Conditions

During the execution of a PL/I program, there are a number of conditions that could arise. A *condition* is an occurrence, within a PL/I program, that could cause a program interrupt. It may be the detection of an unexpected error or of an occurrence that is expected, but at an unpredictable time. There are a number of conditions that may occur during input or output operations. Some of these include :

ENDFILE   A condition indicating that the end of a given file has been reached
ENDPAGE   A condition indicating that the end of a page of printed output has been completed
TRANSMIT   A condition indicating that an input or output device did not transmit data correctly
RECORD   A condition indicating that the size of a record in a given file does not match the record size declared in the PL/I program

In addition to conditions related to I/O operations, there are conditions that may occur during arithmetic operations—for example, *overflow*, which indicates that a value has exceeded the maximum precision allowed by the computer hardware.

The ON Statement

The ON statement is used to specify action to be taken when any subsequent occurrence of a specified condition causes a program interrupt. ON statements may specify particular action for any of a number of different conditions. The ON statement takes the form

ON condition   on-unit;

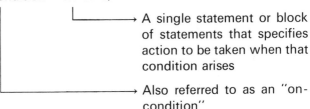

A single statement or block of statements that specifies action to be taken when that condition arises

Also referred to as an "on-condition"

For example:

ON ENDFILE(DETAIL) GO TO NEXT_MASTER;

This statement specifies that when an interrupt occurs as the result of trying to read beyond the end of the file named DETAIL, control is to be transferred to the statement labeled NEXT_MASTER.

When execution of an on-unit is successfully completed, control will normally return to the point of the interrupt or to a point immediately following it, depending upon the condition that caused the interrupt.

For all of the conditions, a standard system action exists as a part of PL/I, and if no ON statement is in force at the time an interrupt occurs, the standard system action will take place. For most conditions, the standard system action is to print a message and terminate execution.

There are a number of conditions that may be raised during I/O operations. These include:

ENDFILE(file name)
ENDPAGE(file name)
RECORD(file name)
TRANSMIT(file name)
CONVERSION
SIZE

In addition to conditions related to I/O operations, there are some conditions that may be raised during arithmetic operations. These include:

CONVERSION
FIXEDOVERFLOW
OVERFLOW
UNDERFLOW
ZERODIVIDE
SIZE

If you compare the names in the above list with the conditions that may occur during I/O operations, you will see that CONVERSION and SIZE are common to both lists. Following are descriptions of the arithmetic conditions and one of the I/O conditions. Discussion of the other I/O conditions will be deferred until later.

I/O Conditions

The ENDFILE Condition. The ENDFILE condition can be raised during a GET or READ operation; it is caused by an attempt to read the end-of-file delimiter of the file named in the GET or READ statement. After ENDFILE has been raised, no further GETs or READs should be executed for the file. One form of the ON statement for this condition is

        ON ENDFILE(CARDIN)GO TO END_RT;

Another form of this statement is

        ON ENDFILE(CARDIN) BEGIN;
                .
                .   Any block of coding
                .   may appear here
              END;

The begin block is described in detail later. It is being introduced here because it may be used in the full language. The begin block as shown above starts with the word BEGIN and ends with the word END (as does a DO-group). This block of coding is similar to a *subroutine.* One of the characteristics of a subroutine is that it has a universal entry and exit facility; that is, the subroutine may be entered from any point in another program (or the same program) and exited by returning control to the instruction following the one which called the sub-routine.

   In the above example, the begin block will be entered when the ENDFILE condition is detected for the CARDIN file. When the END statement is encountered, there is an automatic return to the statement following the READ or GET that caused the ENDFILE condition to be raised. Following is an example of a complete begin block:

    ON ENDFILE(SYSIN) BEGIN;
                    TOTAL=TOTAL+DETAIL;
                    PUT SKIP(3)LIST(TOTAL);
                    PUT PAGE LIST('NUMBER OF
                       CUSTOMERS PROCESSED',COUNT);
                    GO TO WRAP_UP;
                    END;

	Begin blocks allowed following an on-unit	Allowable PL/I statements following an on-unit
Subset language	No	GO TO statement Null statement
Full language	Yes	Any PL/I statement—typically, a begin block

Arithmetic Conditions

The CONVERSION Condition. The CONVERSION condition occurs whenever a conversion is attempted on character-string data containing characters which are invalid for the conversion being performed. This attempted conversion may be made internally or during a stream input operation.

Here is an example of when the CONVERSION condition would be raised during an internal operation:

```
DCL X BIT(4);
DCL Y CHAR(4) INIT('10AB');
X=Y;  /* CONVERSION CONDITION RAISED */
```

In the above example, the CONVERSION condition is raised because the character-string in Y contains a character other than a 0 or 1.

All conversions of character-string data are carried out character-by-character in a left-to-right sequence, and the condition occurs for the first illegal character. When such a character is encountered, an interrupt occurs (provided, of course, that CONVERSION has not been disabled), and the current action specification for the condition is executed. When CONVERSION occurs, the contents of the entire result field are undefined.

The FIXEDOVERFLOW Condition. The FIXEDOVERFLOW condition occurs when the length of the result of a fixed-point arithmetic operation exceeds N digits. For S/360 and S/370 implementations, N is 15 for decimal fixed-point values and 31 for binary fixed-point values.

```
DCL (A,B,C) FIXED DECIMAL(15) ;
A = 40000000 ;
B = 80000000 ;
C = A*B ;  /* FIXEDOVERFLOW CONDITION BECAUSE RESULT
   WILL BE LARGER THAN 15 DIGITS */
```

The OVERFLOW Condition. The OVERFLOW condition occurs when the magnitude of a floating-point number exceeds the permitted maximum. (For S/360 and S/370 implementations, the magnitude of a floating-point number or intermediate result must not be greater than approximately 10^{75} or 2^{252}. Compare this with UNDERFLOW.)

```
A = 55E71 ;
B = 23E11 ;
C = A*B ;  /* OVERFLOW CONDITION BECAUSE RESULTING
   EXPONENT IS GREATER THAN 10^75 */
```

The UNDERFLOW Condition. The UNDERFLOW condition occurs when the magnitude of a floating-point number is smaller than the permitted minimum. (For S/360 and S/370 implementations, the magnitude of a floating-point value may not be less than approximately 10^{-78} or 2^{-260}.)

```
A = 23E−71 ;
B = 3E−9 ;
C = A*B ;  /* UNDERFLOW CONDITION BECAUSE RESULTING
   EXPONENT IS LESS THAN 10^-78 */
```

The ZERODIVIDE Condition. The ZERODIVIDE condition occurs when an attempt is made to divide by zero. This condition is raised for both fixed-point and floating-point division.

```
A = 15 ;
B = 0 ;
C = A/B ;  /* ZERODIVIDE CONDITION */
```

The SIZE Condition. The SIZE condition occurs when high-order (i.e., leftmost) nonzero binary or decimal digits (also known as significant digits) are lost in an assignment operation (i.e., assignment to a variable or to an intermediate result) or in an input/output operation. This loss may result from a conversion involving different data types, bases, scales, or precisions. The SIZE condition differs from the FIXEDOVERFLOW condition in an important sense. We noted that FIXEDOVERFLOW occurs when the length of a calculated fixed-point value exceeds the maximum precision allowed. The SIZE condition, however, occurs when the value being assigned to a data item exceeds the declared (or default) size of the data item. The SIZE condition can occur on the assignment of a value regardless of whether or not the FIXEDOVERFLOW condition arose in the calculation of that value. The SIZE condition may also occur during stream input for the same reason.

The declared size is not necessarily the actual precision with which the item is held in storage; however, the limit for SIZE is the declared or default size, not the actual size in storage. For example, a fixed binary item of precision (20) will occupy a full word in storage, but SIZE is raised if a value whose size exceeds FIXED BINARY(20) is assigned to it.

Standard System Action Condition

In the absence of your program specifying an action to be taken when conditions are detected, a standard system action will take place. For most conditions, the standard system action is to print a message and then raise the ERROR condition. *The ERROR condition is raised as a result of the standard system action for any other on-unit.* Unless otherwise specified, when the ERROR condition is raised, the system action is to terminate the PL/I program and return control to the operating system.

Condition Prefixes

Some conditions are always *enabled* unless explicity *disabled.* When a condition is enabled, it means that, if the condition occurs, either programmer-defined action or system action will take place. Thus, when conditions are disabled, errors may go undetected. The I/O conditions are always enabled and may not be disabled. The following computational conditions are enabled unless the programmer specifies that they should be disabled:

> CONVERSION
> FIXEDOVERFLOW
> OVERFLOW
> UNDERFLOW
> ZERODIVIDE

The SIZE condition, conversely, is disabled unless enabled by the programmer.

Conditions are enabled or disabled through a *condition prefix* which is the name of one or more conditions separated by commas, enclosed in parentheses, and prefixed to a statement by a colon. The word NO preceding the condition name indicates that the condition is to be disabled. For example:

(NOFIXEDOVERFLOW) : CALC : SUM = A + B + C ;

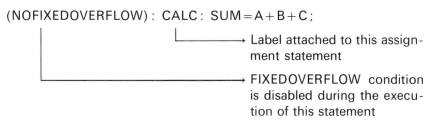

→ Label attached to this assignment statement

→ FIXEDOVERFLOW condition is disabled during the execution of this statement

Notice how the condition name precedes the statement's label. Of course, the label is optional. If it is desired to disable or enable a condition for the entire execution of a procedure, specify the condition prefix on a PROCEDURE statement. For example:

(SIZE,NOFIXEDOVERFLOW) : PROG1 : PROC OPTIONS(MAIN) ;

In the above example, the SIZE condition is enabled and the FIXED-OVERFLOW condition is disabled during the execution of the procedure labeled PROG1. Continuing with this example, assume it is later desired to disable the SIZE condition during the execution of a single statement. The following could be coded:

(NOSIZE) : Y = A*B/C ;

Even though some conditions may never be disabled, it does not mean that some action must take place for those conditions. It is possible to specify a *null* action for conditions that cannot be disabled. For example, the ENDPAGE condition is raised when the maximum number of specified lines has been printed on a page. Recall that the ENDPAGE condition may not be disabled. However, in some cases, it may be desired to continue printing beyond the end of a page because the printer paper is a continuous form. The following *null* form of this statement could be specified in your program:

ON ENDPAGE (SYSPRINT) ;

The null form of the ON statement simply indicates "no action should be taken for this on-unit." A null action may be specified for any of the exceptional conditions except CONVERSION, ENDFILE, and KEY. (The KEY condition will be covered in Chapter 10.)

The SIGNAL Statement

The programmer can simulate the occurrence of a condition through the use of the SIGNAL statement. Execution of the SIGNAL statement has the same effect as if the condition had actually occurred. If the signaled condition is not enabled, the SIGNAL statement is treated as a null statement. One of the uses of this statement is in program checkout to test the action of an on-unit and to determine that the correct program action is associated with the condition. The general form is

SIGNAL condition;

└─────────→ Any condition name may appear here

Pictures

In programming, we are often concerned not only with the *value* that data variables may have but also with the way data *looks*. As an example, let us consider a payroll program that computes earnings and prints a payroll check for each employee of a firm. In such a program, we would probably have a variable named NET_PAY into which we would place the amount each employee earned after all taxes and deductions were subtracted. NET_PAY would contain the amount for which the payroll check should be written. In a PL/I program, we might declare the variable to have the attributes FIXED DECIMAL(7,2). From a discussion of S/360 and S/370 data formats in Appendix D, we know that this is stored internally as packed decimal data, two digits per byte. A NET_PAY value of $1032.75 would appear in storage as

0 1	0 3	2 7	5 +

This form is readily acceptable *to the computer* for computation. However, it is not acceptable *to the printer*, because the printer prints one character per byte, whereas we have two digits per byte in our field named NET_PAY. Another objection that might be raised is that no *real* decimal point appears in the data, and we know that the stockholders of the firm would object if we printed the payroll checks with no decimal point in the amount field. (Employees would probably not complain.) The bank on which we write the payroll check probably would like the dollar amount of each check to be written in a specific form and would not be willing to cash a check that looked like this:

```
                       XYZ  COMPANY

   Pay to the order of        JOHN  JONES        0103275+

   1st Big Bank
   Anytown, USA
```

The bank would prefer to have the amount of the check printed with a decimal point in the proper location, separating the dollars from the cents, suppressing the printing of the leading zero, as well as supplying a dollar sign and commas.

So, we have a number of problems to solve in transferring the NET_PAY that we have computed into a form which is acceptable to the printer, the stockholders, the employees, and the bank. To solve our problems, we use the PICTURE attribute. The PICTURE attribute provides, as its name implies, a *picture* of the form we want the data in the variable with the PICTURE attribute to assume. At the same time, we do not want to *invalidate* the value of the data to be stored there. To illustrate what is meant by invalidation, recall from the example above that when each digit of our packed decimal field was converted into a character for printing, we produced a check written for the amount 0103275+. By doing this, we changed the *value* of the number from 1032.75 to 103275. We still want to be able to treat such a variable as an arithmetic quantity preserving the correct value. In the payroll NET_PAY problem, we would declare a new variable with the PICTURE attribute. For example:

    DCL NET_PAY_PRINT PICTURE '$ZZ,ZZZV.ZZ';

The picture of NET_PAY_PRINT is provided in the PICTURE attribute. The picture is made up of characters which have special meaning when they appear between the apostrophes following the keyword PICTURE. In the example above, the Z's indicate that we want a decimal digit (0–9) to appear in each position that a Z appears. If, however, that digit is a leading or nonsignificant zero, we want a blank to appear in the value of the variable. This action is called *zero suppression;* hence, the character Z is a means of specifying that action. The dollar sign, comma, and decimal point in our example are called *insertion characters*. With them we specify that we want to *insert* those characters into the value of our variable. The V character in our picture is used to specify the position of the implied decimal point. Our picture shows a total of seven Z's (each representing a digit), five of them to the left of the implied decimal point (V) and two of them to the right. (Do you recognize a precision of (7,2)?)

We would use the variable NET_PAY_PRINT in the printing of the value of each payroll check. But, before we can do this, we must place the value of NET_PAY into the pictured variable NET_PAY_PRINT. To accomplish this, we would use the assignment statement

NET_PAY_PRINT = NET_PAY ;

This statement tells the compiler to generate object program instructions and to place the *value* of NET_PAY (a packed decimal field) into the variable NET_PAY_PRINT, *and* when doing so to make the value *look like* the picture which is described in the PICTURE attribute of NET_PAY_PRINT. After such an assignment, the value of NET_PAY_PRINT in main storage would be the following:

$			1	,	0	3	2	.	7	5

This corresponds to our picture:

$ Z Z , Z Z Z $\overset{V}{.}$ Z Z

Notice that the V, which specifies where decimal alignment is to be performed, does not occupy a byte location, but merely serves to logically point out the separation of the fractional part of the value from the integer part. The decimal point does not cause alignment in a picture.

With the PICTURE attribute, we have solved the problems that were facing us. We have maintained the *value* of NET_PAY, but have represented that value in a form which is readily acceptable to the printer and to those people concerned with the check being printed.

This example illustrates a few of the many characters which can be used to specify the picture form we want our data to assume. In the following pages, many more *picture specification characters,* as the Z, comma, dollar sign, etc. are called, will be described and their uses explained. The example shows one use of the PICTURE attribute: to edit output data into a form acceptable for printing. There are a number of reasons for using PICTURE data:

1. To edit data.
2. To validate data.
3. To treat arithmetic quantities as character-strings.
4. To treat character-strings as arithmetic quantities.

The general form of the PICTURE attribute specification follows:

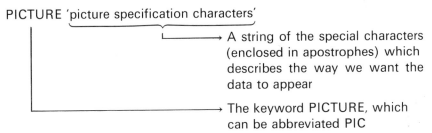

PICTURE 'picture specification characters'

⟶ A string of the special characters (enclosed in apostrophes) which describes the way we want the data to appear

⟶ The keyword PICTURE, which can be abbreviated PIC

There are two types of PICTURE attributes covered in this text: decimal pictures† and character-string pictures.

Decimal Pictures

The decimal picture specifies the form that an arithmetic value is to assume. It allows character insertion (e.g., the decimal point and comma in the example above), zero suppression (Z picture character), decimal point alignment (indicated by a V which stands for virtual point picture character), and signs (+, −, and the commercial debit and credit symbols—DB and CR). The decimal picture causes the data to be stored internally in character form—each digit, insertion character, and sign occupies one byte. Even though it has the appearance of a character-string, the data item declared with the PICTURE attribute retains the attributes necessary to qualify it as an arithmetic quantity; i.e., base, scale, and precision. The base and scale are *implicitly* DECIMAL and FIXED, respectively. (We never declare a variable to have both the PICTURE attribute and either DECIMAL and/or FIXED.) The precision is determined by the number of 9's and Z's in the picture and the location of the V picture character.

---

†In some PL/I manuals, you will see *decimal picture* referred to as *numeric character picture*. The trend is toward the use of the preferred term, decimal picture.

Here are some examples of simple picture declarations:

DCL (A, B) PICTURE '99999V99';

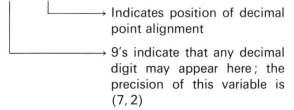

→ Indicates position of decimal point alignment

→ 9's indicate that any decimal digit may appear here; the precision of this variable is (7, 2)

In the above example, both A and B will occupy seven bytes of storage. The V or decimal alignment character does not require a byte of storage. Another way in which the above statement could have been written is

DCL (A, B) PICTURE '(5)9V99' INIT (0);

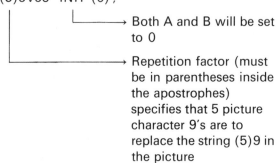

→ Both A and B will be set to 0

→ Repetition factor (must be in parentheses inside the apostrophes) specifies that 5 picture character 9's are to replace the string (5)9 in the picture

Decimal Picture Specification Characters

A number of characters may be used to describe numeric data in a picture. The basic picture specification characters include:

9   Indicates any decimal digit

V   Indicates the assumed location of a decimal point; it does not specify an actual decimal point character in the character representation of the data item, thus, no additional main storage is needed if a V appears in the picture; if no V is specified, then it is assumed that the decimal point is to the right of the number; a V may not appear more than once in a picture

S   Indicates that the sign of the value (+ if > 0 and − if < 0) is to appear in the character representation of the variable; the S picture specification may appear to the left or right of all digit positions in the picture

+ Indicates that a plus sign (+) is to appear in the character representation of the variable if the value is greater than or equal to zero and that a blank is to appear if the value is less than zero

− Indicates that a minus sign (−) is to appear in the character representation of the variable if the value is less than 0 and that a blank is to appear if the value is greater than or equal to zero

The chart in Figure 3.1 shows some picture examples using the above characters. Notice the numbers referring to comments. These comments explain the corresponding example.

Comment 1. The decimal point alignment of the picture and its data caused the two most significant digits of the constant to be truncated as follows:

Comment 2. The picture specified here indicated a fractional number only. Thus, when a whole number is assigned to a fractional number, the whole number is lost, but the corresponding picture will be set to zero.

Comment 3. In this example, realize that there is automatic decimal point alignment of the V in the picture with the decimal point in the constant:

$$\overset{|}{9}V\overset{|}{9}$$
$$1\overset{|}{2}3.4\overset{|}{5}$$

Comment 4. A negative constant was specified, but the picture did not include provision for a sign. The minus sign was dropped, making the value positive in main storage. Erroneously, only 9's were specified in the picture—no "S" for *sign* or "−" for possible negative values.

Comment 5. These two examples correct the previous example's problem—that of losing the negative sign.

Comment 6. When an S appears in the picture, a sign must precede or follow the numeric value; it cannot be embedded in the numeric value.

PICTURE specification	Number of bytes of main storage used	Coded arithmetic form (conversion occurs prior to arithmetic operation)	Input value placed in the corresponding picture	Internal decimal picture result	Comment number
99999	5	FIXED(5)	12345	12345∧	
99999V	5	FIXED(5)	12345	12345∧	
999V99	5	FIXED(5,2)	123.45	123∧45	1
999V99	5	FIXED(5,2)	12345	345∧00	2
V99999	5	FIXED(5,5)	12345	∧00000	
99999	5	FIXED(5)	123	00123∧	
999V99	5	FIXED(5,2)	123	123∧00	
9V9	2	FIXED(2,1)	123.45	3∧4	3
999V99	5	FIXED(5,2)	-123.45	123∧45	4
S999V99	6	FIXED(5,2)	-123.45	-123∧45	5
-999V99	6	FIXED(5,2)	-123.45	-123∧45	5
S999V99	6	FIXED(5,2)	+123.45	+123∧45	6
999V99S	6	FIXED(5,2)	-123.45	123∧45-	6
+999V99	6	FIXED(5,2)	+123.45	+123∧45	7

FIGURE 3.1 Examples of decimal pictures. (Note: In the fifth column, the ∧ indicates that the assumed decimal point is here. In the sixth column, the numbers given refer to numbered comments in the text.)

Comment 7.   Here, the value being placed in the picture may have a + sign or no sign.

Arithmetic Operations on Decimal Picture Data

When an arithmetic operation is specified for decimal picture data, the data will automatically be converted to the coded arithmetic form FIXED DECIMAL. For example, assume the program statements

DCL SUM PIC'9999', (A,B) PIC'999' ;
SUM = A + B ;

are coded. To add A to B and assign the results to SUM, the following steps are performed automatically :

1. Convert A from decimal picture to FIXED DECIMAL data format.
2. Convert B from decimal picture to FIXED DECIMAL data format.
3. Add A and B together.
4. Convert the results to numeric character form (PICTURE).
5. Place the results in the variable called SUM.

Editing Data for Printed Output

As we saw in the introduction to this chapter, we frequently have the need to edit data in order to improve its readability. For example, instead of printing the value

45326985.76

we might *edit* the data by inserting a dollar sign and commas so that the output would look like this :

$45,326,985.76

There are a number of characters that may appear in pictures for the purpose of editing data. The data declared with pictures that contain these "editing" characters can be used in calculations, but it is very inefficient to do so and it should be avoided. Editing characters are actually stored internally in the specified positions of the data item. The editing characters are considered to be part of the character-string value but not part of the variable's arithmetic value.

Data items with the PICTURE attribute to be used as output (i.e., to a printer or a punched card) usually receive their values via an assignment statement. Values are normally developed during a program's execution using a coded arithmetic data type. When final results are obtained, the values are assigned to pictured data variables for printing and/or punching. A wide variety of output editing is required in many applications. To meet these requirements, a large number of picture specification characters can be used to create the properly edited fields for output. Let us discuss the functions of the more commonly used editing characters.

THE Z PICTURE CHARACTER—ZERO SUPPRESSION

The Z may be used to cause the suppression of leading zeros in the data field, replacing the nonsignificant zeros with blanks. Figure 3.2 shows some examples of how PICTURE with the Z character will cause zeros to be suppressed (that is, replaced with blanks) in the character representation of the data variable.

PICTURE specification	Value to be assigned to variable	Internal character representation
ZZZZ9	100	bb100
ZZZZ9	0	bbbb0
ZZZZZ	0	bbbbb
ZZZV99	123	12300
ZZZVZZ	1234	23400
ZZZVZZ	.01	bbbb1
ZZZV99	0	bbb00
Z9999	0	b0000
ZZZVZ9	ILLEGAL PICTURE—if a Z appears to the right of the V character, then *all* digits to the right must be specified as Z	
ZZ9ZZ	INVALID PICTURE—all Z characters must appear to the left of all 9's	

FIGURE 3.2 Pictures illustrating zero suppression.

If a value is to have leading blanks as well as a sign, then the "S" PICTURE character may be used. For example:

DCL A PIC'SZZZ9';

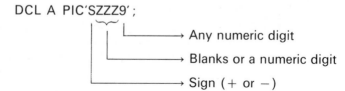

→ Any numeric digit

→ Blanks or a numeric digit

→ Sign (+ or −)

In the above example, a sign will always appear in the leftmost position of the character-string representation.

THE DECIMAL POINT (.)

The decimal point is an *insertion character,* meaning that the decimal point will be inserted in the output field in the position where it appears in the picture specification. For example:

```
DCL PRICE PIC'999V.99' INIT(12.34);
PUT LIST(PRICE);   /* 012.34 WILL BE PRINTED */
```

Note that if the PICTURE is specified without the decimal point, the output will appear as follows:

```
DCL UNIT_COST PIC'999V99' INIT(12.34);
PUT LIST(UNIT_COST);   /* 01234 WILL BE PRINTED */
```

Do not think of the decimal point as causing alignment; only the V accomplishes this function. Consider the following:

```
DCL VALUE PIC'999.99' INIT(12.34);
PUT LIST(VALUE);   /* 000.12 IS PRINTED */
```

Because the V accomplishes the function of alignment and the decimal point the function of inserting a physical indication of this alignment, we normally specify the V and the decimal point in adjacent positions in our picture specification.

In the above example, no V is specified, thus the implied decimal point is to the right of the number. When the constant 12.34 is aligned with the implied V, we have this undesirable result:

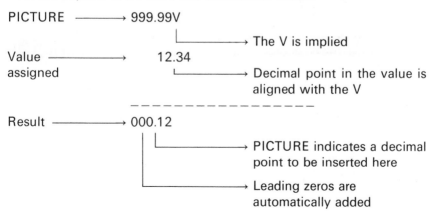

The usual case is to place the V to the left of the decimal point in a picture specification, although it may appear to the right of the decimal point:

```
DCL PRICE PIC'999.V99' INIT(12.34) ;
PUT LIST (PRICE) ;   /* 012.34 IS PRINTED */
```

In this example, the output is the same as if the V had appeared to the left of the decimal point. However, in other cases, the position of the V in relationship to the decimal point is most significant. To illustrate, let us look at what happens when zero suppression is specified in a PICTURE containing a V and a decimal point (small "b" represents a blank):

```
DCL A PIC'ZZZV.99' INIT(.05) ;
PUT LIST(A) ;   /* bbb.05 IS PRINTED */
DCL B PIC'ZZZ.V99' INIT(.05) ;
PUT LIST(B) ;   /* bbbb05 IS PRINTED */
```

The rule to be derived from the above example is this: When the V is to the left of the decimal point, the V may be thought of as "guarding" the decimal point; hence, if leading zeros are to be suppressed, the decimal point will not be replaced with a blank. However, if the V is to the right of the decimal point in the picture and leading zeros are to be suppressed, the decimal point will be replaced by a blank whenever the integer portion of the number is zero. We may conclude that the V ought *normally* to be located to the left of the decimal point in the picture.

THE COMMA (,)

The comma is another *insertion character*. It will be inserted in the output field in the position corresponding to its location in the PICTURE. For example:

```
DCL BIG_VALUE PIC'999,999V.99' INIT(104056.98) ;
PUT LIST(BIG_VALUE) ;   /* 104,056.98 IS PRINTED */
```

If zero suppression is specified, the comma is inserted only when a significant digit appears to the left of the comma; otherwise, the comma is replaced with a blank, as the following example illustrates:

```
DCL AMT PIC'ZZZ,ZZZV.99';
AMT=450.75;
PUT LIST(AMT);   /* bbbb450.75 IS OUTPUT */
AMT=1450.75;
PUT LIST(AMT);   /* bb1,450.75 IS OUTPUT */
AMT=0;
PUT LIST(AMT);   /* bbbbbbb.00 IS OUTPUT */
```

THE BLANK (B)

The blank is another *insertion character.* It is used to insert blanks to the right of a value on output. (Of course, to obtain blanks on the left of the value, the Z picture character may be used.) Here are some examples:

```
DCL A PIC'999V.99BBB';
DCL B PIC'Z,ZZZV.99(7)B';
```

In the subset language, the B picture character may only appear to the right of a decimal picture. The following example is valid only in the full language implementations:

```
DCL D PIC'99B99B99';
```

	B insertion character
Subset language	May appear only to the right of a decimal picture
Full language	May be embedded in the decimal picture

THE DOLLAR SIGN ($)

The $ character is a *drifting character.* It specifies a currency symbol in the character representation of numeric data. This character may be used in either a *static* or *drifting* manner. The static use of the $ specifies that a currency symbol will always appear in the position fixed by its location in the picture. In the drifting form, there are multiple adjacent occurrences of the character. A drifting dollar sign specifies that leading zeros are to be suppressed and that the rightmost suppressed zero will be replaced with the $ symbol. Here are some examples:

```
DCL A PIC'$999V.99' INIT(12.34) ;
PUT LIST (A) ;   /* $012.34 IS PRINTED */
DCL B PIC'$$$$V.99' INIT(12.34) ;
PUT LIST (B) ;   /* b$12.34 IS PRINTED */
DCL C PIC'$$,$$$V.99(5)B' INIT(1024.76) ;
PUT LIST (C) ;   /* $1,024.76bbbbb IS OUTPUT */
DCL D PIC'$Z,ZZZV.99' INIT(12.34) ;
PUT LIST (D) ;   /* $bbb12.34 IS OUTPUT */
```

THE SIGN CHARACTERS (S, +, −)

These editing characters may also be either drifting or static. The following examples should be self-explanatory:

```
DCL A PIC'S999' INIT(12) ;
PUT LIST (A) ;   /* +012 IS OUTPUT */
DCL B PIC'SSS9' INIT(12) ;
PUT LIST (B) ;   /* b+12 IS OUTPUT */
DCL C PIC '9999S' INIT(1234) ;
PUT LIST(C) ;   /* 1234+ IS OUTPUT */
DCL D PIC'−−−9'INIT(−12) ;
PUT LIST (D) ;   /* b−12 IS OUTPUT */
D = +12 ;
PUT LIST (D) ;   /* bb12 IS OUTPUT */
DCL E PIC'+99' INIT(144) ;   /* ERROR */
PUT LIST (E) ;   /* +44 IS PRINTED */
DCL F PIC'999V.99S' INIT(−123.45) ;
PUT LIST(F) ;   /* 123.45− IS OUTPUT */
```

In the full language implementations of PL/I, the minus sign may also be treated as a hyphen and thus appear more than once in a picture or embedded within a picture. For example, the following picture might be coded for the editing of a Social Security number:

```
DCL SS_# PIC'999−99−9999' ;
```

	Hyphen allowed in other than the leftmost position of a picture
Subset language	No
Full language	Yes

THE ASTERISK (∗)

The asterisk is a fill character and is used in much the same way as the Z. The "asterisk fill" capability is useful in applications that require check protection. For example, in using a computer to print checks or statements indicating amounts paid, it is desirable to precede the dollar and cents amounts with leading asterisks so as to preclude any tampering with or modification of those amounts. The asterisk *cannot* appear with the picture character Z, nor can it appear to the right of a 9 or any drifting character. Here are some examples:

```
DCL PAY PIC'*****9V.99' INIT(104.75) ;
PUT LIST (PAY) ;   /* ***104.75 IS PRINTED */
DCL AMT_PAID PIC'*****V.**' INIT (843.50) ;
PUT LIST (AMT_PAID) ;   /* **843.50 IS OUTPUT */
AMT_PAID = .75 ;   /* SEE PICTURE DECLARED ABOVE */
PUT LIST (AMT_PAID) ;   /* *****.75 IS OUTPUT */
DCL PAYS PIC'$***V.99' INIT(4.75) ;
PUT LIST (PAYS) ;   /* $**4.75 IS OUTPUT */
DCL QTY PIC'***' INIT(123) ;
PUT LIST(QTY) ;   /* 123 IS OUTPUT */
```

CREDIT (CR) AND DEBIT (DB) CHARACTERS

The paired characters CR and/or DB specify the sign of numeric fields. They are used most often on business report forms (e.g., billing, invoicing).

CR   Indicates that the associated positions will contain the letters CR *if* the value of the data is negative, otherwise, the positions will contain two blanks; the characters CR can only appear to the right of *all* digit positions in a PICTURE

DB   Is used in the same fashion as the CR, except that the letters
DB appear in the associated print positions if the value is
negative

```
DCL D PIC '99V.99CR' INIT(−12.34) ;
PUT LIST(D) ;   /* 12.34CR IS PRINTED */
DCL E PIC '99V.99DBBBBB' INIT(−12.34) ;
PUT LIST(E) ;   /* 12.34DBbbbb IS PRINTED */
DCL F PIC 'S999V.99CR' ;   /* INVALID PICTURE BECAUSE
   BOTH 'S' and 'CR' ARE SPECIFIED */
DCL G PIC '99V.99CR' INIT (+12.34) ;
PUT LIST(G) ;   /* 12.34bb IS PRINTED */
```

Both DB and CR will appear in the edited field of *negative* values.
However, there are some business applications where either a "debit"
or "credit" applies to a positive value. For example, if you have a
savings account, your account is *debited* each time a withdrawal is
made and *credited* each time a deposit is made; for example:

$$
\begin{array}{r}
500.00 \ \text{CR} \\
120.00 \ \text{DB} \\
35.00 \ \text{DB} \\
100.00 \ \text{DB} \\
75.00 \ \text{CR}
\end{array}
$$

Assume it is desired to print the above list with the CR and DB designations. Assume, also, that the source data we are about to edit will be
preceded with a minus sign if the value is a debit amount; otherwise,
the value is assumed to be positive and, therefore, a credit amount.
Thus, the input stream would appear as

```
500     −120.00     −35.00     −100.00     75.00
```

The following programming example illustrates a technique that
might be used to list the above values with the CR and DB designations,
even though some of the input values are positive. Notice that AMT is
converted to a negative value by subtracting it from zero. Then, when
AMT is edited into the AMT_CR field, the picture characters CR will be
included in the edited result.

```
              DCL AMT FIXED(7,2);
              DCL AMT_CR PIC'ZZ,ZZZV.99CR';
              DCL AMT_DB PIC'ZZ,ZZZV.99DB';
     GET:     GET LIST (AMT);
              IF AMT>0 THEN DO;
                    AMT=0-AMT;
                    AMT_CR=AMT;
                    PUT SKIP LIST (AMT_CR);
                    END;
              ELSE DO;
                    AMT_DB=AMT;
                    PUT SKIP LIST (AMT_DB);
                    END;
              GO TO GET;
```

Overpunch Signs

In business data processing, sometimes numeric values punched in a card have an *overpunch* for sign representation. An overpunch is simply a 12-punch for a + sign or an 11-punch for a − sign over one of the digits in a predetermined column of a multidigit field. The use of overpunches has the advantage of minimizing the number of card columns required to represent signed numeric data. Thus, for example, the value of −154 could be represented in only three card columns because the sign (−) can be punched over the units position (i.e., the 4). Figure 3.3 shows this as its first example.

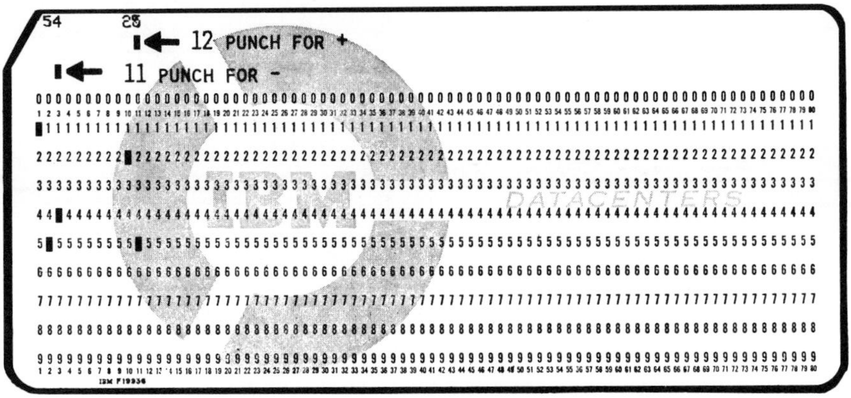

FIGURE 3.3   Overpunches in numeric fields.

The following special characters are used in a PICTURE to indicate an overpunch in the units position of a numeric field:

T   Indicates that the associated position will contain a digit over-punched with the sign of the data

I   Indicates that the associated position will contain a digit over-punched with a 12-punch (representing +) if the value is zero or positive; otherwise, it will contain only the digit with no overpunching, indicating the value is negative

R   Indicates that the associated position will contain a digit over-punched with an 11-punch (representing −) if the value is negative; otherwise, it will contain the digit with no over-punching, indicating the value is positive or zero

The picture characters T, I, and R cannot be used with any other sign characters (i.e., S, −, and +) in the same PICTURE. Only one over-punch may appear in a fixed-point number. Figure 3.4 shows some examples of pictures with these overpunch characters and the results when data is assigned to these pictures.

	Overpunch
Subset language	May appear only in the units position of the numeric field
Full language	May appear in any digit position of the numeric field

Character-String Pictures

Another type of PICTURE attribute is the character-string picture specification. Its form is like decimal pictures, except that the characters which make up the picture specification are A, X, and 9. Furthermore, the data item declared with the character-string picture *does not* have the arithmetic attributes of base, scale, and precision, but does have the character-string *length* attribute.

PICTURE specification	Number of bytes of core used	Coded arithmetic form (conversion occurs prior to arithmetic operation)	Value assigned to the corresponding picture	Internal decimal picture result	Coded arithmetic value when used in a calculation
999V9T	5	FIXED(5,2)	+123.45	1234E	+12345
999V9T	5	FIXED(5,2)	−123.45	1234N	−12345
999I	4	FIXED(4)	+1234	123D	+1234
999I	4	FIXED(4)	1234	1234	−1234
99R	3	FIXED(3)	123	123	+123
99R	3	FIXED(3)	−123	12L	−123

FIGURE 3.4 Pictures illustrating overpunched digits.

The actions performed by the picture specification characters for character-string pictures are as follows:

A   Specifies that the associated position of the picture may contain the alphabetic characters A through Z or a blank; this picture specification character is not available in the subset language

X   Specifies that the associated position of the picture may contain *any* character

9   Specifies that the associated position of the picture may contain only the digits 0 through 9 or blank

Some examples of character-string pictures are shown in Figure 3.5, where "b" represents a blank.

The comma and decimal point insertion characters may not be specified in a character-string picture; however, the B insertion character may be specified. For example:

DCL OUTPUT_FIELD PIC'BBBXXXXX';

In the subset language, the minus sign may only appear in a decimal picture. In the full language, the minus sign may appear in character-string pictures for use as hyphens. For example:

DCL SOCIAL_SECURITY_NO PIC'XXX–XX–XXXX';

	Allows the A PICTURE character?	Allows X and 9 in the same PICTURE? (e.g., PIC'XX999')	Minus sign allowed in character-string
Subset language	No	No	No
Full language	Yes	Yes	Yes

The character-string PICTURE attribute is used primarily in data validation rather than in output editing. If you are programming using full language PL/I, then the following example is applicable: Assume an inventory item is identified by a part number which consists of

Source attributes	Source data in constant form	PICTURE specification	Character-string value
CHAR(4)	'ABCD'	AAAA	ABCD
CHAR(4)	'ABCD'	XXXX	ABCD
CHAR(5)	'ABCDb'	AAAAAA	ABCDbb
CHAR(5)	'12Q21'	99A99	12Q21
CHAR(5)	'#B123'	XA999	#B123
CHAR(5)	'12bbb'	99XXX	12bbb
CHAR(5)	'12AB9'	99AAA	INVALID
CHAR(5)	'AB123'	AAA99	INVALID
CHAR(5)	'L26.7'	A99X9	L26.7

FIGURE 3.5   Examples of character-string pictures.

alphabetic and numeric characters such as

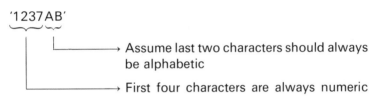

'1237AB'

⟶ Assume last two characters should always be alphabetic

⟶ First four characters are always numeric

On input, this part number could be *validated* by reading it into a picture that contains A and 9 picture specifications. For example:

```
DCL PART_NUM PIC '9999AA';
DCL ITEM CHAR(6);
GET LIST (ITEM, ETC);
PART_NUM = ITEM;
```

When ITEM is assigned to PART_NUM, data validation occurs. If the part number consists of four leading digits followed by two alphabetic characters, we know that the part number is in the correct form. Of course, we do not know if it is an actual part number in our inventory without doing further checking.

If the number is incorrectly punched as

'123ABC'

and read into ITEM, the CONVERSION condition is raised when ITEM is assigned to PART_NUM. The raising of this condition means that an error has occurred. In this example, it would be a data validation error. Here is a programming example illustrating its use:

```
/* THIS EXAMPLE APPLIES TO FULL LANGUAGE
   IMPLEMENTATIONS */

TEST:    PROC OPTIONS (MAIN);
         DCL PART_NUM PIC '9999AA';
         DCL ITEM CHAR(6);
         ON ENDFILE(SYSIN) GO TO EOJ;
         ON CONVERSION GO TO ERROR;
GET:     GET LIST (ITEM);
         PART_NUM=ITEM;
         PUT LIST (ITEM);
         GO TO GET;
ERROR:   PUT LIST ('INVALID PART NUMBER:', ITEM);
         GO TO GET;
EOJ:     END;
```

The DEFINED Attribute

The DEFINED attribute is a very useful feature of PL/I. How it works will be introduced here, but the many uses of this attribute will be illustrated throughout the remainder of this book. The DEFINED attribute allows you to equate two or more different names to the same storage area. In addition, one of the names being declared may represent either all or part of the same storage as that assigned to the other. For example, the statements

```
DECLARE NAME CHAR(20) INITIAL('JAMES WILEY RHOADES');
DECLARE FIRST CHAR(5) DEFINED NAME;
```

would produce the following storage layout:

```
 J |A|M|E|S|  |W| I |L|E|Y|  |R|H|O|A|D|E|S|
 _____/
     FIRST
 _____/
                   NAME
```

In this example, NAME and FIRST occupy the same storage area. However, FIRST will be equated only to the five leftmost characters (i.e., it will be left justified in the NAME field) of the string inasmuch as FIRST has a length attribute of five. NAME is considered to be the *base identifier*; this is the variable name to which other variable names are equated or "defined." The PL/I term for this function is *overlay defining.* You may only specify the INITIAL attribute for the base identifier. Also, the base identifier must be equal to or greater than any of the other variables that are overlay defined on it. Finally, more than one item may be overlay defined on a base identifier. For example:

```
DCL A CHAR(8),
      B PIC'ZZ9V.99CR' DEFINED A,
      C PIC'9,999V.99' DEFINED A;
```

Here is an ILLEGAL example of overlay defining:

```
DCL A CHAR(8);
DCL B PIC'ZZ9V.99CR' DEF A;
DCL C PIC'9,999V.99' DEF B;   /* ILLEGAL */
```

In this case, B can overlay define A, but C cannot overlay define B. The base identifier cannot have the DEFINED attribute. To accomplish what was intended in the illegal statement, we can code

```
DCL C PIC '9,999V.99' DEF A;
```

Following is a list of possible base identifiers and the type of items that may be overlay defined on them.

Base identifier	Defined item
A coded arithmetic variable	A coded arithmetic variable of the *same* base, scale, and precision
A label variable	A label variable
String variable	String variable
PICTURE attribute or CHARACTER attribute variable	PICTURE or CHARACTER attribute variable

The POSITION Attribute

The POSITION attribute may be specified in overlay defining of bit- and character-strings. For example:

```
DECLARE LIST CHARACTER (40),
        A_LIST CHARACTER (10) DEFINED LIST,
        B_LIST CHARACTER (20) DEFINED LIST POSITION (21),
        C_LIST CHARACTER (10) DEFINED LIST POSITION (11);
```

In this example of overlay defining, A_LIST refers to the first ten characters of LIST, B_LIST refers to the twenty-first through fortieth characters of LIST, and C_LIST refers to the eleventh through twentieth characters of LIST.

	POSITION attribute
Subset language	No
Full language	Yes

Case Study: Daily Cash Report

This case study illustrates a number of PL/I features described in Chapter 2 and in this chapter. These features include

> Declaring coded arithmetic data
> Factoring of attributes
> The INITIAL attribute
> The DEFINED attribute
> Editing of output data using PICTURE

Problem Description

Following each day of business, a savings and loan company summarizes the transactions which occurred during the day. The purposes of the summary are the following:

1. To determine if the transactions balance; i.e., have any clerical mistakes been made during the day?
2. To provide a breakdown of the total amount on hand at the end of the day into cash on hand and checks on hand.
3. To calculate the source of cash to be available for the next day's business.
4. To calculate the amount to be deposited in the company's bank account.

This savings and loan company, by policy, always begins each day with $60,000.00 in cash. This figure becomes the data item named

CASH_FUND in our program. It is given the initial value of $60,000.00 and is never changed. Other input data to the program include:

MORTGAGE_RECEIPTS	The amount received during the day in payment of mortgage loans
SAVINGS_RECEIPTS	The amount received during the day from customers' deposits into their accounts
CASH_PAID	The amount paid to customers who withdraw from their savings accounts
CASH_ON_HAND	The total amount of cash on hand at the end of the day, including the initial $60,000.00
CHECKS_ON_HAND	The total amount of checks on hand at the end of the day

To provide the necessary information for the summary, certain values must be computed. These are

TOTAL_RECEIPTS	MORTGAGE_RECEIPTS + SAVINGS_RECEIPTS
TOTAL_ON_HAND	CASH_ON_HAND + CHECKS_ON_HAND
RECONCILIATION	To determine if an error has been made in the handling of cash during the day, we must take into account the amount we started with at the beginning of the day (CASH_FUND), the amount of cash the company paid out during the day (CASH_PAID), the total receipts for the day from mortgage payments and savings (TOTAL_RECEIPTS), and the total dollar amount in cash and checks on hand at the end of the day (TOTAL_ON_HAND). If we start with the TOTAL_ON_HAND at the end of the day and subtract from it the amount we started the day with (CASH_FUND), we should derive the net effect of the day's business on the company. (It may be either negative or positive.) Next, if we subtract the CASH_PAID during the day from the TOTAL_RECEIPTS, we should also find the net effect of the day's business on the company. By comparing these two numbers, we can determine whether an error has been made and, if so, if it was in a

152 PL/I Programming

customer's favor or in the company's favor. An easy way to do this is to subtract one number from the other, storing the result in the data item named RECONCILIATION. For example:

RECONCILIATION = (TOTAL_ON_HAND −
CASH_FUND) − (TOTAL_RECEIPTS −
CASH_PAID);

If RECONCILIATION is negative, then there is cash *shortage* (an error in a customer's favor); if it is positive, then there is a cash *overage* (an error in the company's favor); and if it is equal to zero, then daily cash *balances*. The desired output for this information is a print line in one of these formats:

SHORTAGE $50.00
                    (if RECONCILIATION < 0)

or

OVERAGE $33.50
                    (if RECONCILIATION > 0)

or

DAILY CASH RECONCILES
                    (if RECONCILIATION = 0)

Notice that a numeric value is to be printed only if a shortage or overage occurs, not if daily cash reconciles.

REIMBURSEMENT   If the CASH_ON_HAND is less than $60,000.00, then the cash fund must be reimbursed to meet the company policy figure of $60,000.00 in cash. This data item is the amount of the reimbursement.

DEPOSIT   All of the checks received during the day must be deposited, as well as any cash in excess of the CASH_FUND minimum of $60,000.00. Therefore, this figure will be either CHECKS_ON_HAND or, if CASH_ON_HAND > CASH_FUND, then CHECKS_ON_HAND + (CASH_ON_HAND − CASH_FUND).

Figure 3.6 shows a summary of the desired output; a general flowchart depicting program logic is shown in Figure 3.7.

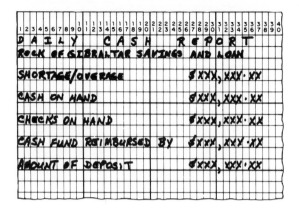

FIGURE 3.6 Output format for daily cash report case study.

Programming Techniques Used in Case Study

Figure 3.8 shows a compiled program listing. Following is an explanation of the statements in the program.

Source Statement 2. Notice the factoring of attributes where all the declared variables have the same attribute.

Source Statement 3. Notice the use of the INITIAL attribute to assign $60,000 to the identifier called CASH_FUND.

Source Statement 4. When the first output statement for a STREAM file to the printer is issued, there is an automatic skip to a new page. This PUT LIST statement causes the first line of the report to be printed.

Source Statement 6. Input data is read. Sample data could be punched into one card as follows:

15000.00   8050.00   5000.00   55000.00   23000.00

Source Statements 7–9. TOTAL_RECEIPTS, TOTAL_ON_HAND, and RECONCILIATION are calculated.

Source Statements 10–17. The test, using IF's with DO-groups, is made to determine if CASH_ON_HAND is greater than or less than $60,000. The DEPOSIT and REIMBURSEMENT are determined by the CASH_ON_HAND figure.

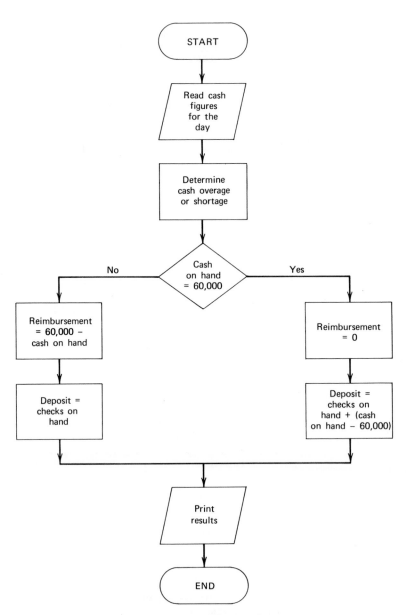

FIGURE 3.7   General flowchart for daily cash report.

```
        /* DAILY CASH REPORT -- CASE STUDY */
1     CASH:    PROC OPTIONS(MAIN);
2              DCL (MORTGAGE_RECEIPTS,SAVINGS_RECEIPTS,CASH_PAID,
                    CASH_ON_HAND,CHECKS_ON_HAND,TOTAL_RECEIPTS,
                    TOTAL_ON_HAND,RECONCILIATION,DEPOSIT,REIMBURSEMENT)
                    FIXED(9,2);
3              DCL CASH_FUND FIXED (9,2) INIT (60000);
4              PUT LIST ('D A I L Y    C A S H    R E P O R T');
5              PUT SKIP LIST ('ROCK OF GIBRALTER SAVINGS AND LOAN');
6              GET LIST (MORTGAGE_RECEIPTS,SAVINGS_RECEIPTS,
                    CASH_PAID,CASH_ON_HAND,CHECKS_ON_HAND);
7              TOTAL_RECEIPTS = MORTGAGE_RECEIPTS + SAVINGS_RECEIPTS;
8              TOTAL_ON_HAND = CASH_ON_HAND + CHECKS_ON_HAND;
9              RECONCILIATION =(TOTAL_ON_HAND - CASH_FUND)
                             -(TOTAL_RECEIPTS - CASH_PAID);
10             IF CASH_ON_HAND < CASH_FUND THEN DO;
11                  REIMBURSEMENT = CASH_FUND - CASH_ON_HAND;
12                  DEPOSIT = CHECKS_ON_HAND;
13                  END;
14             ELSE DO;
15                  REIMBURSEMENT = 0;
16                  DEPOSIT = CHECKS_ON_HAND + (CASH_ON_HAND-CASH_FUND);
17                  END;
        /* EDIT DATA FOR OUTPUT */
18             DCL OUTPUT PIC'$$$$,$$9V.99', HEADING CHAR (21);
19             DCL OUT CHAR (11) DEFINED OUTPUT;
20             OUTPUT = RECONCILIATION;
21             IF RECONCILIATION < 0 THEN HEADING = 'SHORTAGE';
22             ELSE IF RECONCILIATION > 0 THEN HEADING = 'OVERAGE';
23             ELSE DO; HEADING = 'DAILY CASH RECONCILES'; OUT=' '; END;
27             PUT SKIP(3) LIST (HEADING,OUTPUT);
28             OUTPUT = CASH_ON_HAND;
29             PUT SKIP(2) LIST ('CASH ON HAND',OUTPUT);
30             OUTPUT = CHECKS_ON_HAND;
31             PUT SKIP(2) LIST ('CHECKS ON HAND',OUTPUT);
32             OUTPUT = REIMBURSEMENT;
33             PUT SKIP(2) LIST ('CASH FUND REIMBURSED BY',OUTPUT);
34             OUTPUT = DEPOSIT;
35             PUT SKIP(2) LIST ('AMOUNT OF DEPOSIT',OUTPUT);
36             END;
```

FIGURE 3.8   Daily cash report program listing.

Source Statement 18.   The identifier OUTPUT is declared with editing characters which include the floating dollar sign and automatic zero suppressing, comma insert, and decimal point insert. Each value that is to be printed will be "edited" when the value is assigned to OUTPUT. The HEADING is declared for the purpose of assigning to it the first detail line of literal output (e.g., either OVERAGE, SHORTAGE, or DAILY CASH RECONCILES).

Source Statement 19.   A character-string of 11 positions is overlay defined on the picture called OUTPUT. The length of 11 characters was selected because OUTPUT is 11 bytes long; i.e.,

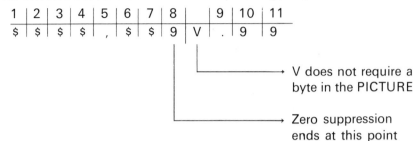

1	2	3	4	5	6	7	8		9	10	11
$	$	$	$	,	$	$	9	V	.	9	9

V does not require a byte in the PICTURE

Zero suppression ends at this point

The reason for using define overlay in this program is explained in the paragraph describing source statements 23–27.

Source Statements 20–22. RECONCILIATION is edited by assigning it to OUTPUT. If RECONCILIATION is negative, then first detail line of print is to be the literal SHORTAGE followed by amount of shortage. If RECONCILIATION is positive, then first detail line is to be the literal OVERAGE followed by the amount of overage.

Source Statements 23–27. If RECONCILIATION is zero, then first detail line is to be the literal DAILY CASH RECONCILES followed by blanks in the amount field of the report. Statement 27 consists of printing HEADING followed by OUTPUT. There is one case, however, when OUTPUT should contain blanks—when daily cash reconciles. OUTPUT is a picture depicting a numeric field. Hence, only digits 0 through 9 may be assigned to this picture. It is not possible to assign blanks *directly* to the identifier called OUTPUT, because a blank is not a numeric character. The solution to the problem is to use define overlay on OUTPUT to give that area of main storage the CHARACTER attribute as well as the PICTURE attribute. Statement 25 is

OUT = ' ' ;

The above statement is valid because OUT has the CHARACTER attribute. The statement causes, in effect, OUTPUT to be cleared to blanks. Thus, when the statement

PUT SKIP(3) LIST(HEADING,OUTPUT) ;

is encountered in the program, blanks will be printed following HEADING.

Source Statements 28–36. These statements accomplish the assigning of the calculated results to OUTPUT for purposes of editing the data. Each remaining detail line is printed by a separate PUT SKIP LIST statement. The program is logically ended when the END statement is encountered.

SUMMARY

File Declarations: A PL/I file is represented in the program by the file name which is declared to have the FILE attribute. It is through the use of this name that we will access or create the data records which are stored on an external device such as a disk or tape or cards. The collection of records is called a data set. The ENVIRONMENT attribute of the DECLARE statement describes the physical environment of the data set. The MEDIUM option is used in the DOS/TOS operating system to specify a symbolic device name and the type of device on which the data set is stored or through which we will access the data. Within parentheses following the keyword MEDIUM, specify SYSIPT for card input and SYSLST for line printer output as the symbolic device name. The physical device numbers you specify are dependent upon the type of devices attached to the computer on which your PL/I program is to be run. The F in the ENVIRONMENT section of the file declaration specifies the record type as being fixed length.

Standard PL/I File Names: The identifiers SYSIN and SYSPRINT are the file names for the standard input and output files, respectively. The statements

```
GET LIST(A, B, C);
PUT LIST(A, B, C);
```

are equivalent to

```
GET FILE(SYSIN) LIST(A, B, C);
PUT FILE (SYSPRINT) LIST(A, B, C);
```

These files need not be declared, because a standard set of attributes is applied automatically. In subset languages, you may not use these file names unless they are explicitly declared as files. However, when you write

```
GET LIST(A, B, C);
PUT LIST(A, B, C);
```

the attributes of the SYSIN and SYSPRINT files are assumed for the GET and PUT operations, respectively.

Conditions: The ON statement is used to specify the action to be taken when an exceptional condition arises. An exceptional condition is the occurrence of an unexpected event or an expected event at an unpredictable time. In the absence of your program specifying an action to be taken, when these exceptional conditions are detected, a standard system action will take place. For most conditions, the standard system action is to print a message and then raise the ERROR condition which usually results in termination of your PL/I program. Some conditions are always enabled unless explicitly disabled. When a condition is enabled, it means that, if the condition occurs, either programmer-defined action or system action will take place. Thus, when conditions are disabled, errors may go undetected. The I/O conditions are always enabled and may not be disabled. Conditions are enabled through a condition prefix which is the name of one or more conditions separated by commas, enclosed in parentheses, and prefixed to a statement by a colon. The word NO preceding the condition name indicates that the condition is to be disabled. Through the use of the SIGNAL statement, the programmer may simulate the occurrence of any of the exceptional conditions. Execution of the SIGNAL statement has the same effect as if the condition had actually occurred. (See Figure 3.9.)

The PICTURE Attribute: This attribute provides a picture of the form we want the data in the variable with the PICTURE attribute to assume. There are a number of reasons for using PICTURE:

1. To edit data.
2. To validate data.
3. To treat arithmetic quantities as character-strings.
4. To treat character-strings as arithmetic quantities.

Decimal Picture: This type of picture specifies the form that an arithmetic value is to assume. The base and scale are implicitly DECIMAL and FIXED, respectively. The precision is determined by the number of 9's and Z's in the picture and the location of the V picture character.

Decimal Picture Specification Characters: The basic picture specification characters include 9, V, S, +, −.

Arithmetic Operations on Decimal Picture Data: In order for an arithmetic operation on decimal picture data to take place, the data must be converted to the coded arithmetic form FIXED DECIMAL.

Editing Data for Printed Output: Data items with the PICTURE attribute to be used as output usually receive their values via an assignment statement. Values are normally developed during a program's execution using coded arithmetic data type. When final results are obtained, the values are assigned to data variables for printing and/or punching.

Specifying Overpunched Signs with the PICTURE Attribute: In business data processing, sometimes numeric values punched in a card have an overpunch for sign representation. An overpunch is a 12-punch for a + sign or an 11-punch for a − sign over one of the digits in a predetermined column of a multidigit field. The use of overpunches has the advantage of minimizing the number of card columns required to represent signed numeric data.

Character-String Picture: The characters which make up this type of picture are A, X, and 9. The data item declared with the character-string picture does not have the arithmetic attributes of base, scale, and precision, but does have the character-string length attribute. Figure 3.10 shows the picture specification characters covered in this chapter.

Character-String
- X   Position may contain any character
- A   Position may contain any alphabetic character[1]
- 9   Position may contain any decimal digit or blank[1]

Digit and point specifiers
- 9   Any decimal digit
- V   Assumed decimal point and subfield delimiter

Zero suppression characters
- Z   Digit or blank
- *   Digit or

Static or drifting characters[2]
- $ Digit, $, or blank
- S   Digit, $\pm$ sign, or blank
- +   Digit, +, or blank
- −   Digit, −, or blank

Insertion characters
- ,   If zero suppression and no digit, a blank will appear
- .   Decimal point
- B   Blank

Credit, debit, and overpunched signs
- CR   CR if field < 0
- DB   DB if field < 0
- T   Digit will be overpunched by sign
- I   Digit will be overpunched by + if field $> = 0$[1]
- R   Digit will be overpunched by − if field < 0

FIGURE 3.10   Picture specification characters. (1: Not available in subset language. 2: These are also zero suppression characters.)

Type of condition	ON-condition	Normally enabled/disabled	Cause	What the programmer should do or result	Normal return to (if null on-unit is used)	Standard system action
Input/output	ENDFILE (file name)	Enabled (cannot be disabled)	An attempt to read past the file delimiter of the file named in the GET or READ statement	Not attempt to READ or GET again from file; CLOSE the file	Null on-unit cannot be specified	ERROR condition
	ENDPAGE (file name)	Enabled (cannot be disabled)	PUT statement resulting in an attempt to start a new line beyond the limit specified for the current page	Write a required footing (or total lines) and skip to another page	(1) Resulting from data transmission: current line (2) Resulting from LINE or SKIP option: action specified by option is ignored	New page started
Standard system action	ERROR	Enabled (cannot be disabled)	(1) Another ON-condition for which it is the standard system action (2) An error for which there is no ON-condition	Dependent upon requirements of installation	Control returned to the operating system control program	Message printed and control returned to operating system control program (execution terminated)
Computational conditions	CONVERSION	Enabled (cannot be disabled)	Illegal conversion attempt on character-string data internally or on input/output operation	Undefined	Null on-unit cannot be specified	ERROR condition

Condition	Normal status	Cause	Value of result	Point of resumption	Standard system action
FIXEDOVERFLOW	Enabled (can be disabled)	Result of arithmetic fixed-point operation that exceeds maximum precision allowed (15 for decimal, 31 for binary)	Undefined	The point logically following the point of the interrupt	ERROR condition
OVERFLOW	Enabled (can be disabled)	Magnitude of a floating-point number greater than permitted maximum	Undefined	The point logically following the point of the interrupt	ERROR condition
SIZE	Disabled (can be enabled)	Nonzero high-order binary or decimal digits are lost in an assignment operation (i.e., assignment to a variable or an intermediate result) or in an input/output operation	Undefined	The point logically following the point of the interrupt	ERROR condition
UNDERFLOW	Enabled (can be disabled)	Magnitude of a floating-point number smaller than allowable minimum	Invalid floating-point value set to 0	The point logically following the point of the interrupt	Message printed and execution continues
ZERODIVIDE	Enabled (can be disabled)	Attempt to divide by zero	Undefined	The point logically following the point of the interrupt	ERROR condition

FIGURE 3.9

The DEFINED Attribute: This attribute allows you to equate two or more different names to the same storage area. In addition, one of the names being declared may represent either all or part of the same storage as that assigned to the other. The base identifier is the variable name to which other variable names are equated or "defined." The PL/I term for this function is overlay defining. Only the base identifier may be initialized if the INITIAL attribute is specified. The base identifier must be equal to or greater than (in length) any of the other variables that are overlay defined on it.

The POSITION Attribute: This attribute may be specified in overlay defining of bit- and character-strings. It allows you to specify a position within a string on which another variable may be overlay defined. Not available in the subset language.

CHECKPOINT QUESTIONS

1. When an end-of-file mark is encountered, what are the two possible courses of action that may be taken?
2. In which PL/I compilers referenced in this text must the MEDIUM option be included? In which compilers should it be excluded?
3. (True or False) File names may be the same length as any other PL/I identifier—1 to 31 characters long.
4. For the optimizing compilers, how would the record form
$$F(80)$$
be specified?
5. What does the PRINT attribute accomplish in a file declaration statement?
6. In which language implementation (subset or full) is the following statement valid?
ON ENDPAGE(SYSPRINT) GO TO HDNG_RT;
7. What are the default attributes for the SYSIN file?
8. What is the ON statement used for?
9. Under what conditions is the ERROR condition raised?
10. What does the *condition prefix* accomplish?
11. What does the *null* form of the ON statement indicate?
12. How can the programmer simulate the occurrence on an ON condition?
13. Distinguish between FIXEDOVERFLOW and SIZE.

14. How many bytes of storage will each of the following identifiers require?
    (a) DECLARE PRICE PICTURE '999V99';
    (b) DECLARE QUANTITY PICTURE '9999';
    (c) DECLARE BACK_ORDERED PICTURE 'S999999';
    (d) DECLARE AMT PIC 'SSSSV99';
    (e) DECLARE FLD PICTURE '(5)X(7)9';

15. Each time that a decimal picture is to be used in a calculation, what conversion takes place?

16. Give the numeric results after the following identifiers are initialized:
    (a) DCL GROSS_PAY PIC '9999V99' INIT (550);
    (b) DCL REORDER_QTY PIC '999' INIT (1000);
    (c) DCL HOURS_WORKED PIC '99' INIT (40.75);
    (d) DCL INTEREST_DUE PIC '999V99' INIT (3.4567);

17. What are the uses of the PICTURE attribute?

18. Given the following DECLARE, what would the *output* values look like?
    DECLARE AVALUE PICTURE 'ZZZ99';
    (a) AVALUE = 12345;
    (b) AVALUE = 123;
    (c) AVALUE = 0;

19. What is *overlay defining*? Why use it?

20. Are the following assignment statements valid in the subset language, given the following DECLARE statement?
    DCL A PIC'99999', B CHAR(5);
    (a) A = B;
    (b) B = A;

21. Write the PICTURE that will cause the value 123.45 to be output with three leading blanks and four trailing blanks (i.e., bbb123.45bbbb—where b stands for blank).

22. What is an overpunch? Why is it used?

TERMS TO STUDY

base identifier
byte
coded arithmetic data
condition prefix
data set

decimal picture
decimal point alignment
disabled
drifting character
dump program

editing	overpunch
enabled	static character
file	system action
insertion character	utility program
null on-unit	zero suppression
on-unit	11-punch
overlay defining	12-punch

PRACTICE PROBLEMS

1. Drill Using the PICTURE Attribute

Problem Statement: Write a series of declarations for the constants listed below. Print the values defined.

Purpose of the Problem: To gain practice in declaring various data types using the PICTURE attribute.

Input: Read the following data items into variables that contain the PICTURE attribute describing the data items.

Input PL/I constant	Comments
5123.45	Insert comma (i.e., 5,123.45) on output
'THE QUICK BROWN FOX'	
'123AB'	
−23.75	
000212	Suppress leading zeros
2048.95	Include a drifting dollar sign on output
00123.45	Include asterisk insertion (i.e., **123.45)
0678.90	Insert a drifting + sign (i.e., +678.90)
−1950430.75	Insert commas and drifting dollar sign and CR symbol separated from the value by a blank (i.e., $1,950,430.75 CR)
00.33	Print this value two ways using zero suppression (i.e., .33 and 33)

Output: See Figure 3.11.

2. Price List

Problem Statement: Compute a table of prices for handy reference. Calculate price of one item, two items, three items, all the way up to 100 items for a unit price called PRICE.

```
5,123.45
THE QUICK BROWN FOX
123AB
-23.75
    212
$2048.95
**123.45
  +678.90
$1,950,430.75 CR
   .33
   33
```

FIGURE 3.11   Problem 1 sample output using suggested test data.

Purpose of the Problem: To gain experience in programming a "loop" operation as well as to do some editing of output data (e.g., zero suppression and
comma insert).

Card Input: Suggested test data are

                        1234   15.25

Printer Output: See Figure 3.12.

3.   Extending Prices

Problem Statement: Write a program to read data cards for a part number
(ITEM), unit price (PRICE), and quantity (IQTY). Compute the *extension* by
multiplying PRICE*IQTY. For each data card read, print a *detail line* which

```
PRICE TABLE FOR ITEM #        1234

QUANTITY                      PRICE


   1                          15.25
   2                          30.50
   3                          45.75
   4                          61.00
   5                          76.25
   6                          91.50
   7                         106.75


  96                       1,464.00
  97                       1,479.25
  98                       1,494.50
  99                       1,509.75
 100                       1,525.00
```

**FIGURE 3.12   Problem 2 sample output using
suggested test data.**

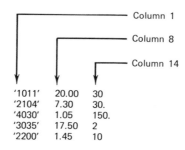

FIGURE 3.13   Problem 3 suggested test data.

consists of ITEM, PRICE, IQTY, and EXTENSION. Also, keep a "running total" of the extensions. When the end-of-file condition is detected, compute TAX by multiplying TOTAL by 5%, add TAX to TOTAL to give amount due (AMT), and print TOTAL, TAX, and AMT.

Purpose of the Problem: To declare PL/I coded arithmetic data as well as pictures for editing purposes and to use the ON statement.

Card Input: Suggested test data are shown in Figure 3.13.

Printer Output: If you use the suggested input data, your output to the line printer should be like that shown in Figure 3.14.

Flowchart: See Figure 3.15.

Programming Hint: Notice from Figure 3.14. that when the total lines are to be printed, each of the three lines starts with the literal constant (e.g., "TOTAL")

PART NUMBER	PRICE	QUANTITY	EXTENSION
1001	20.00	30	600.00
2104	7.30	30	219.00
4030	1.05	150	157.50
3035	17.50	2	35.00
2200	1.45	10	14.50
		TOTAL	1026.00
		TAX	51.30
		AMOUNT DUE	$1,077.30

FIGURE 3.14   Problem 3 sample output using suggested test data.

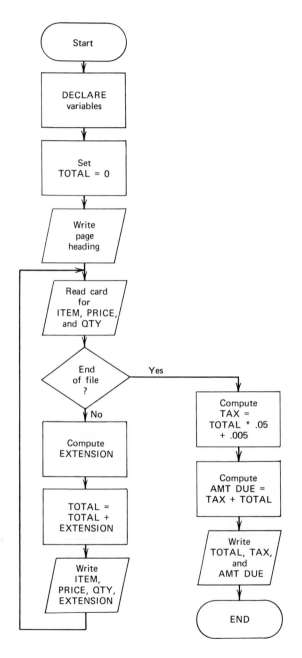

FIGURE 3.15 Flowchart for Problem 3.

beginning at the third tab position (print position 49). This can be accomplished by the following:

PUT SKIP LIST(' ', ' ', 'TOTAL',TOTAL)

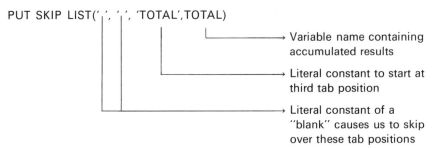

→ Variable name containing accumulated results

→ Literal constant to start at third tab position

→ Literal constant of a "blank" causes us to skip over these tab positions

4. Powers of Two Table

Problem Statement: Write a program to generate a powers of two table where the output values range from 2^0 to 2^{30}.

Purpose of the Problem: To use exponentiation, to program a loop, and to edit data using the PICTURE attribute.

Input: There is no input for this problem, as the program generates the results.

Output: See Figure 3.16. for suggested printer layout.

5. Fibonacci Numbers

Problem Statement: Leonardo of Pisa, who is also called Leonardo Fibonacci, originated the following sequence of numbers in the year 1202:

$$0, 1, 1, 2, 3, 5, 8, 13, 21, 34, \ldots$$

In this sequence, each number is the sum of the preceding two and is denoted by F_n (F for Fibonacci and n for number). Formally, this sequence is defined as

$$F_0 = 0$$
$$F_1 = 1$$
$$F_{n+2} = F_{n+1} + F_n$$

where

$$N \geq 0$$

Write a program to print out the first 55 terms of a Fibonacci sequence.

Purpose of the Problem: This is a good computer exercise in addition, as the hand method of calculation makes the solution impractical. Fibonacci wrote, "It is possible to do [the addition] in this order for an infinite number of months."

Input: There is no input data, as the program will generate the sequence.

Output: Sample output is shown in Figure 3.17.

```
2 TO THE N-TH POWER              N

                  1              0
                  2              1
                  4              2
                  8              3
                 16              4
                 32              5
                 64              6
                128              7
                256              8
                512              9
              1,024             10
              2,048             11
              4,096             12
              8,192             13
             16,384             14
             32,768             15
             65,536             16
            131,072             17
            262,144             18
            524,288             19
          1,048,576             20
          2,097,152             21
          4,194,304             22
          8,388,608             23
         16,777,216             24
         33,554,432             25
         67,108,864             26
        134,217,728             27
        268,435,456             28
        536,870,912             29
      1,073,741,824             30
```

**FIGURE 3.16 Sample output for
Problem 4.**

FIBONACCI SEQUENCE OF NUMBERS

0	1	1	2	3
5	8	13	21	34
55	89	144	233	377
610	987	1597	2584	4181
6765	10946	17711	28657	46368
75025	121393	196418	317811	514229
832040	1346269	2178309	3524578	5702887
9227465	14930352	24157817	39088169	63245986
102334155	165580141	267914296	433494437	701408733
1134903170	1836311903	2971215073	4807526976	7778742049
12586269025	20365011074	32951280099	53316291173	86267571272

FIGURE 3.17   Sample output for Problem 5.

chapter 4

DO's and

Dimensions

$\mathbf{P}$L/I has the facilities for arranging data in collections that can be referred to by a single name. There are two types of *data aggregates* in PL/I: arrays and structures. Structures will be covered in a later chapter. In this chapter, we will look at arrays in detail and examine some PL/I statements that are used to manipulate arrays.

Arrays

An *array* is a table of data items in which each item has the same attribute as every other item in the array. An array has storage reserved for it by means of a DECLARE statement. For example:

DECLARE TEMPERATURES(365)FIXED(4,1);

In the above DECLARE statement, TEMPERATURES is the name of the array. It is declared with four attributes:

1. (365) is the number of elements in the array
2. DECIMAL is the base attribute of all its elements
3. FIXED is the scale attribute of all its elements
4. (4,1) is the precision attribute of all its elements

As you can see, the attribute defining the number of elements in an array is placed immediately after the name of the array in the DECLARE statement. A precision attribute, if written, must always follow a base or scale attribute; thus, you can tell, by its position in the DECLARE statement, whether an attribute is a precision attribute or whether it defines the number of elements in an array.

Bounds

In declaring the size of an array, a *bound* is specified. In the example,

DCL TEMPERATURES(365)FIXED(4,1);

172

the number 365 specifies the *upper* bound of the array. The *lower* bound in this example is assumed to be 1.

In the full language, it is possible to specify both a lower and an upper bound. For example:

DCL TABLE (0:11) FIXED;

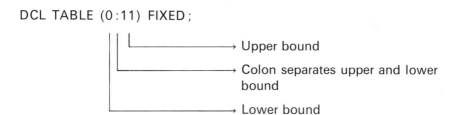

→ Upper bound

→ Colon separates upper and lower bound

→ Lower bound

The *extent* is 12 because there are 12 elements between 0 and 11.

It is also possible in the full language to specify a negative value for bounds. For example:

DCL GRAPH (−5:+5);

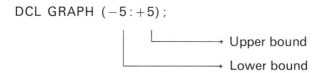

→ Upper bound

→ Lower bound

Thus, the array GRAPH might be thought of as follows:

−5 −4 −3 −2 −1 0 +1 +2 +3 +4 +5

Graph

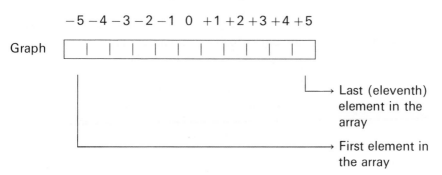

→ Last (eleventh) element in the array

→ First element in the array

Here is another example of specifying upper and lower bounds with the array *pictured* in a vertical manner (note the use of the INITIAL attribute):

DCL LIST(−2:6) INIT(91,20,82,11,73,48,19,16,70) ;

List		
(−2)	91
(−1)	20
(0)	82
(1)	11
(2)	73
(3)	48
(4)	19
(5)	16
(6)	70

	Specifying the bound of an array
Subset language	May not specify lower bound—it is always assumed to be 1; bounds must be expressed as decimal integer constants
Full language	If upper bound only is specified, then lower bound is assumed to be 1, or both an upper and lower bound may be declared; bounds can be constants, variables, expressions, or asterisks

Dimensions

The number of sets of upper and lower bounds specifies the number of dimensions in an array. For example, 12 data items could be arranged in two groups of six items each. The array could be declared,

DCL TABLE(6,2) FIXED ;

→ Second dimension

→ First dimension

and could be thought of as a two-dimensional table. For example :

	Column 1	Column 2
Row 1		
Row 2		
Row 3		
Row 4		
Row 5		
Row 6		

In referring to two-dimensional arrays, sometimes the terms *rows* and *columns* are used. These terms, however, are not used to describe parts of arrays that have more than two dimensions.

Here is an example of declaring a two-dimensional array in which the upper and lower bounds are explicitly declared :

DCL AXIS($-3:3,-4:4$)INIT((63)0) ;

Axis	−4	−3	−2	−1	0	1	2	3	4
−3	0	0	0	0	0	0	0	0	0
−2	0	0	0	0	0	0	0	0	0
−1	0	0	0	0	0	0	0	0	0
0	0	0	0	0	0	0	0	0	0
1	0	0	0	0	0	0	0	0	0
2	0	0	0	0	0	0	0	0	0
3	0	0	0	0	0	0	0	0	0

There are 63 elements in the AXIS array. Notice how the INITIAL attribute specified an iteration factor of 63 in a pair of parentheses preceding the 0 constant. This causes all elements of the AXIS array to be initialized to zero. Had the statement

DCL AXIS($-3:3,-4:4$)INIT(0) ;

been declared, only the first position (upper leftmost corner of the array) would be initialized to zero.

A three-dimensional array could also be declared. For example, assume it is desired to store statistical data on the urban and rural population of each state in the United States for ten decades. The statement declaring such an array could be written

DCL POPULATION(2,50,10) ;

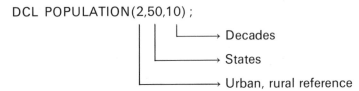

→ Decades

→ States

→ Urban, rural reference

In some PL/I implementations, more than three dimensions may be specified.

	Generally, the number of dimensions allowed
Subset language	3
Full language	15

Subscripting

We reference an element of an array by means of a *subscript*. For example :

T=TEMPERATURES(2) ;

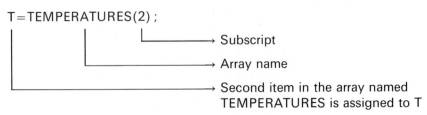

→ Subscript

→ Array name

→ Second item in the array named TEMPERATURES is assigned to T

Assume that a two-dimensional table of salesmen's commission rates is to be defined for three products a company sells. A salesman's commission rate depends on the quantity he sells. For example:

Quantity sold	Commission rate for item		
	#1	#2	#3
1–50	0.01	0.01	0.02
51–100	0.02	0.015	0.025
101–500	0.025	0.022	0.03
501–999	0.03	0.031	0.035
1000 or more	0.032	0.035	0.04

To declare this table we would write

DCL COMMISSIONS(5,3) FIXED(3,3) ;

where the table could be pictured as follows:

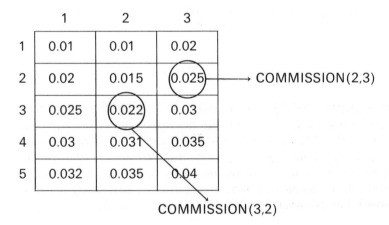

In the above example, row 1 contains the commission rates for 1–50 units sold; row 2 contains rates for 51–100 units sold; row 3 for 101–500 units sold, etc. Column 1 corresponds to item #1, column 2 to item #2, and column 3 to item #3. To retrieve the salesman's commission rate if he sold 450 units of item #1, we could code

RATE=PRICE*QTY*COMMISSION(3,1) ;

Variable Subscripts. Subscripts need not be constants, as illustrated above, but also may be variables. For example:

K=3;
T=TEMPERATURE(K);

                └──────→ Because K was assigned a value of 3, it
                               will be the third element of
                               TEMPERATURES that is assigned to T

Here are some other examples of retrieving values from the COMMISSION array (note the use of variable subscripts):

J=3;
RATE=PRICE*QTY*COMMISSION(J,1);
   /* COMMISSION(3,1) IS BEING REFERENCED */

K=2;
RATE=PRICE*QTY*COMMISSION(J,K);
   /* COMMISSION(3,2) IS BEING REFERENCED */

The following example is invalid because the value assigned to K is outside the declared range of the COMMISSION array:

K=7;
RATE=PRICE*QTY*COMMISSION(1,K);

SUBSCRIPTRANGE Condition. In the full language compilers, referencing a location outside the bounds of the array will cause the SUBSCRIPTRANGE condition to be raised if the condition is enabled. Because this condition is always disabled unless the programmer enables the on-unit, it will be necessary to enable the condition. This is done in the same way that other on-units previously discussed are enabled. For example:

(SUBSCRIPTRANGE): RATE=PRICE*QTY*COMMISSION(1,K);

Or, to enable the condition for the entire procedure, prefix the keyword SUBSCRIPTRANGE to the PROCEDURE statement. For example:

(SUBSCRIPTRANGE): PROG: PROCEDURE OPTIONS(MAIN);

The abbreviation for SUBSCRIPTRANGE is SUBRG. To specify the action to be taken should the SUBSCRIPTRANGE condition be raised, you might code

```
ON SUBSCRIPTRANGE GO TO ERROR;   /* OR */
ON SUBSCRIPTRANGE BEGIN;
                         .
                         .
                         .
                       END;
```

If your program does not specify action to be taken for the SUBSCRIPT-RANGE condition, then *system action* is taken (providing the condition occurs and is enabled). The system action is to print an error message and then raise the ERROR condition. The ERROR condition terminates your job unless you have specified otherwise (e.g., ON ERROR GO TO CONTINUE;). The SUBSCRIPTRANGE condition is a useful debugging tool, for it is during the program checkout phase that you are most likely to inadvertently specify a subscript that references a nonexistent position of an array.

	SUBSCRIPTRANGE condition available
Subset language	No
Full language	Yes

In those compilers for which SUBSCRIPTRANGE is not available, extra care must be taken by the programmer to guard against referencing a position outside of the declared array. This is particularly true if the programmer is specifying the array as a receiving field. For example:

```
DCL  TABLE(5);
K=50;
TABLE(K)=0;
```

In this case, zero will be assigned TABLE(50), which is not part of the declared array. Typically, any position outside of an array could still be part of your program; hence, the value assigned destroys perhaps part of an instruction or another data item. Often, this kind of destruction causes a program to "hang-up." The computer may simply "stop" and the programmer has no clues as to "what went wrong."

Subscript Expressions. In addition to constants and variables, *any* valid PL/I arithmetic expression may be specified as a subscript. For example:

$$T = TEMPERATURES(\underbrace{J - 1 + K})\,;$$

$\longrightarrow$ Subscript expression

Subscripted Subscripts. Subscript expressions may include subscripted items resulting in nested subscripts. For example:

```
DCL  X(5)  INIT(10,20,30,40,50) ;
DCL  Y(3)  INIT(3,2,1) ;
I = 3 ;
Z = X(Y(I)) ;
```

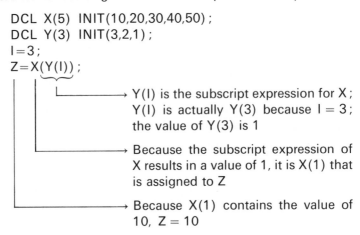

$\longrightarrow$ Y(I) is the subscript expression for X; Y(I) is actually Y(3) because I = 3; the value of Y(3) is 1

$\longrightarrow$ Because the subscript expression of X results in a value of 1, it is X(1) that is assigned to Z

$\longrightarrow$ Because X(1) contains the value of 10, Z = 10

A case where nested subscripts are extremely useful is illustrated in Problem 3 at the end of this chapter.

Cross Sections of Arrays

So far we have seen that a subscript is an element expression specifying a location within a dimension of an array. A subscript may also be an asterisk, in which case it specifies the entire extent of the dimension. This extent is referred to as a *cross section* of an array.

A subscripted name containing asterisk subscripts represents not a single data element, but rather a larger part of the array. For example, assume PERCENT has been declared as follows:

DCL PERCENT(3,4) ;

PERCENT(*,1) refers to all of the elements in the first column of the array. It specifies the cross section consisting of PERCENT (1,1), PERCENT(2,1), and PERCENT(3,1). PERCENT(2,*) refers to all of the data items in the second row of the array [i.e., PERCENT(2,1), PERCENT(2,2), PERCENT(2,3), and PERCENT(2,4)].

As an illustration of how cross sections of arrays may be useful in manipulating data, the following arrays are declared:

DCL PERCENT(3,4), PRICE(3), TOTALS(3);

Assume the arrays pictured below have been assigned the values shown in the various elements.

Percent	(1)	(2)	(3)	(4)		Price	Totals
(1)	0.04	0.02	0.04	0.03	(1)	4.00	
(2)	0.06	0.03	0.05	0.04	(2)	2.50	
(3)	0.05	0.03	0.06	0.05	(3)	3.60	

←———— Salesman ————→

The PERCENT array represents commission rates various salesmen receive for three different items they sell. To find the commission paid to salesman 4 for selling a single unit of each of the three items, the following could be coded:

TOTALS=PERCENT(*,4)*PRICE;

Each element in the fourth column of the PERCENT array is multiplied by the corresponding element of the PRICE array, and the product is assigned to the corresponding element of the TOTAL array. Note that a cross section of an array is considered to be an *array expression;* thus, any other array appearing in an arithmetic operation with the cross section must have the same bounds and dimension as the cross section.

	Cross sections of arrays
Subset language	No
Full language	Yes

I/O Operations and Arrays

In the absence of explicit element specifications, data items are read into arrays starting with the lowest numbered subscripted element and finishing with the highest subscripted element. For example:

```
DCL TEMP(20) PIC'999V9';
GET LIST(TEMP);
```

Columns 1–4 will be read into TEMP(1), columns 5–8 into TEMP(2), and so on, to columns 77–80, which are placed in TEMP(20).

If a multi-dimensional array is specified, then *the right-hand subscript varies most rapidly*. For example, if the array

```
DCL AMT(20,4) CHAR(1);
GET LIST(AMT);
```

is defined, data is read into the AMT array elements in this order:

```
AMT(1,1)
AMT(1,2)
AMT(1,3)
AMT(1,4)
AMT(2,1)
AMT(2,2)
AMT(2,3)
AMT(2,4)
AMT(3,1)
      .
      .
      .
AMT(20,3)
AMT(20,4)
```

Data items are assigned to an array in *row major order;* that is, with the rightmost subscript varying most rapidly. Here is an example for a three-dimensional array:

```
DCL TABLE(2,3,4);
GET LIST(TABLE);
```

└──────────→ As many data items are read as necessary to fill the entire array

To determine the number of elements in the above array, simply multiply each bound by the next: 2*3*4=24 elements. Elements of this array will be filled in the following order:

TABLE(1,1,1) ← First position filled
TABLE(1,1,2)
TABLE(1,1,3)
TABLE(1,1,4)
TABLE(1,2,1)
TABLE(1,2,2)
TABLE(1,2,3)
TABLE(1,2,4)
TABLE(1,3,1)
TABLE(1,3,2)
TABLE(1,3,3)
TABLE(1,3,4)
TABLE(2,1,1)
TABLE(2,1,2)
TABLE(2,1,3)
TABLE(2,1,4)
TABLE(2,2,1)
TABLE(2,2,2)
TABLE(2,2,3)
TABLE(2,2,4)
TABLE(2,3,1)
TABLE(2,3,2)
TABLE(2,3,3)
TABLE(2,3,4)

The INITIAL Attribute for Arrays

Here are some examples of the INITIAL attribute applied to the declaration of arrays:

DCL A(50) FIXED INITIAL(0);

       └──────→ Value to be placed into
           first element of the array

Only the first element, A(1), will be initialized to a value of zero. If it is desired to initialize the entire array to zeros, then an iteration factor must be specified.

DCL A(50) FIXED INITIAL((50)0) ;

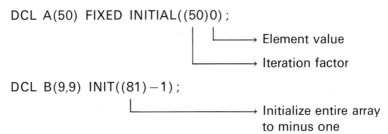

       → Element value

       → Iteration factor

DCL B(9,9) INIT((81) −1) ;

       → Initialize entire array
         to minus one

  Here are some general rules for using the INITIAL attribute to initialize arrays :

1. Only one constant value may be specified for an element variable. More than one value may be given for an array.
2. Constant values specified for an array are assigned to successive elements of the array in the order where the right-hand subscript varies most rapidly. The example

    DECLARE A(2,2) INITIAL(1,2,3,4) ;

results in the following :

	A	(1)	(2)
A(1,1) ← 1			
A(1,2) ← 2	(1)	1	2
A(2,1) ← 3 or			
A(2,2) ← 4	(2)	3	4

If too many constant values are specified for an array, excess ones are ignored ; if not enough are specified, the remainder of the array is not initialized.

3. Each item in the list may be a constant or an iteration specification. The iteration specification has one of the following general forms :

    (iteration factor)   constant
    (iteration factor)   (item [,item] . . .)

The iteration factor must be a decimal integer constant equal to or greater than one.

4. If only one parenthesized decimal integer constant precedes a string initial value, it is interpreted as a repetition factor for the

string. If two appear, the first is taken to be an initialization iteration factor, and the second, a string repetition factor. For example:

DCL TABLE(10) CHAR(2) INIT((2)'A');

causes the *first* element of the array TABLE to be initialized to the character-string value AA because (2) 'A' is equivalent to 'AA'. Should it be desired to initialize the first *two* elements of TABLE, then the following statement would be specified:

DCL TABLE(10) CHAR(2)
  INIT((2) (2)'A');

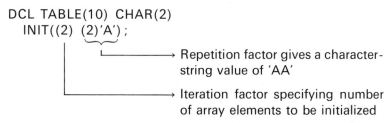

→ Repetition factor gives a character-string value of 'AA'

→ Iteration factor specifying number of array elements to be initialized

5. If it is desired to skip certain elements of an array during initialization, an asterisk may be specified to indicate the skip. For example:

DCL A(3) INIT(10,*,30);

Here, A(1) will be initialized to 10, A(3) will be initialized to 30, and A(2) will not be initialized.

Array Assignment

There are two types of move operations that may be specified for arrays: scalar-to-array and array-to-array.

Scalar-to-Array. In this type of array assignment, an entire array is assigned a single (scalar) value. For example:

DCL MONTHS(12) FIXED(4,1);
MONTHS=0;

Each element in the MONTHS array will be set to zero. To assign a value to a single element of the array, a subscript must be specified. For example:

MONTHS(5) = 72.6;

Array-to-Array. In this case, one array may be moved (assigned) to another array, providing the arrays have identical bounds. For example:

```
DCL A(5,5), B(5,5);
A=0;  /* SCALAR-TO-ARRAY ASSIGNMENT */
B=A;  /* ARRAY-TO-ARRAY ASSIGNMENT */
```

Array Expressions

An array expression is an expression whose evaluation yields an array result. All operations performed on arrays are performed on an element-by-element basis. All arrays referred to in an array expression must have identical bounds.

Prefix Operators and Arrays.   When a prefix operator is specified for an array, the result is an array of identical bounds in which each element is the result of the operation having been performed. For example:

If A is the array

1	3	−5
4	−2	−7
6	12	13

then −A is the array

−1	−3	5
−4	2	7
−6	−12	−13

Infix Operators and Arrays.   When an infix operator is specified for an array and a scalar variable, the result is an array of identical bounds in which each element is the result of the infix operation having been performed. For example:

If A is the array

5	10	15
20	25	30

then A*5 is the array

25	50	75
100	125	150

Here is another example:

If A is the array

1	2	3
4	5	6

then A+2 is the array

3	4	5
6	7	8

All operations on the array are performed on an element-by-element basis in an order in which the rightmost subscript varies most rapidly. To illustrate the effect of this order of operations, assume

A is

1	2	3
4	5	6

If the statement

$$A = A*A(1,2);$$

is specified, the result is the following array:

A is

2	4	12
16	20	24

Note that the original value for A(1,2), which is 2, is used in evaluation for only the first two elements of A. Since the result of the expression is assigned to A, changing the value of A, the new value of A(1,2) is used for all subsequent operations. The first two elements are multiplied by 2, the original value of A; all other elements are multiplied by 4, the new value of A(1,2).

When an infix operator is specified for two arrays, both arrays must have the same number of dimensions and identical bounds. The result is an array with dimensions and bounds identical to those of the original arrays; the operation is performed upon the corresponding elements of the two original arrays.

If A is the array

2	4	3
6	1	7
4	8	2

and if B is the array

1	5	7
8	3	4
6	3	1

then A+B is the array

3	9	10
14	4	11
10	11	3

and A*B is the array

2	20	21
48	3	28
24	24	2

Data Conversion in Array Expressions. The examples in this discussion of array expressions have shown only single arithmetic operations. The rules for combining operations and for data conversion of operands are the same as those for element operations.

Arrays and the LABEL Attribute

Usually, arrays are used to manipulate arithmetic data or perhaps character- or bit-strings. However, it is also possible to declare an array to have the LABEL attribute, in which case each element of the array may contain a label. For example:

```
        DCL X(4) LABEL INITIAL(READ,WRITE,CALC,ERROR);
READ:   GET LIST(A,B);
        IF A=0 THEN GO TO X(1);
          ELSE IF A>B THEN GO TO X(2);
          ELSE IF A<B THEN GO TO X(3);
          ELSE GO TO X(4);
WRITE:  PUT SKIP LIST(A,B);
        GO TO READ;
CALC:   Y=A*B/100;
        PUT SKIP LIST(A,B,Y);
        GO TO READ;
ERROR:  PUT SKIP LIST('ERROR', A,B);
        GO TO READ;
          .
          .
          .
```

Here is another capability of the LABEL attribute and arrays available only in the full language.

```
        DCL L(4) LABEL;
          .
          .
          .
        I=3;
        GO TO L(I);
```

Notice that the L array was not initialized. Instead, the subscripted array names may be the actual labels of PL/I statements. For example:

L(1): M = N + 1;
.
.
.
L(2): M = N − 2;
.
.
.
L(3): M = N*2;
.
.
L(4): M = N/2;

└─────────────→ The system builds into the L array the
                addresses of these subscripted labels

	Allows subscripted labels to be affixed to a statement [e.g., L(1): M = N + 1;]
Subset language	No
Full language	Yes

Array Manipulation Built-in Functions

Built-in functions are subroutines that extend the basic facilities of the PL/I language. These small programs are called *built-in* because they are standard with the PL/I language and have the attribute BUILTIN. The built-in functions we are going to examine here are those functions that facilitate the manipulation of array data.

Two of the array built-in functions (ANY and ALL) require bit-string arguments. All other array functions require floating-point data format arguments. For example:

TOTAL=SUM (ARRAY);

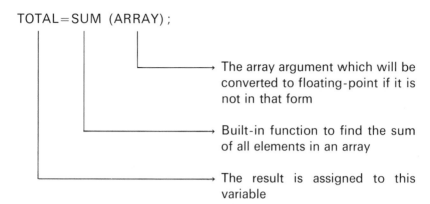

→ The array argument which will be converted to floating-point if it is not in that form

→ Built-in function to find the sum of all elements in an array

→ The result is assigned to this variable

All of the functions require array name arguments and return, as a result, a single value. Because only a single value is returned from these functions, a function reference to any array function is an *element expression* as contrasted with an *array expression*, which has been previously discussed.

The SUM Built-in Function. This function finds the sum of all the elements in an array. For example:

DCL GRADE(5) FIXED(2) INIT(90,85,76,93,81);
AVERAGE=SUM(GRADE)/5;

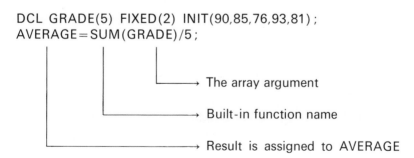

→ The array argument

→ Built-in function name

→ Result is assigned to AVERAGE

A word of caution is given to the commercial programmer. Recall that the arguments to these built-in functions will be converted to floating-point (if they are not in that form) before the function is invoked. The results of calculations performed on floating-point data may not be accurate to the degree that you would like. For example, assume the following values are to be summed:

$$
\begin{array}{r}
43.10 \\
57.38 \\
\underline{9.10} \\
109.58
\end{array}
$$

However, if the following had been coded:

```
DCL TABLE(3) FIXED(5,2);
DCL TOTAL FIXED(7,2);
GET LIST (TABLE);
/* ASSUME TABLE (1)=43.10
          TABLE (2)=57.38
          TABLE (3)=9.10 */
TOTAL=SUM (TABLE);
```

with the above set of values which will be converted to floating-point for the SUM function, TOTAL would contain the value 109.57. This result is not correct—it is a penny off. The problem, of course, is in decimal–binary conversion and back, and has nothing to do with the adequacy of the programming of the conversion routines. To obtain the correct answer, it would be necessary to code the following:

```
TOTAL=SUM(TABLE)+.005;
```

The .005 rounds off the intermediate floating-point result to give the correct answer—in this case, 109.58. The best solution in this type of problem is to stay in decimal; and if this is done, then the SUM function cannot be used.

The PROD Built-in Function. This function finds the product of all the elements of an array. For example:

```
DCL ALIST(5) INIT(1,2,3,4,5);
PRODUCT=PROD(ALIST);
```

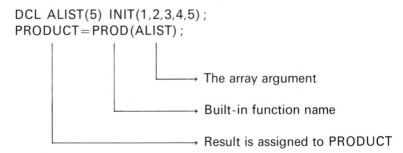

→ The array argument

→ Built-in function name

→ Result is assigned to PRODUCT

The statement invoking the PROD function is equivalent to the following arithmetic operation :

PRODUCT = ALIST(1) * ALIST(2) * ALIST(3) * ALIST(4) * ALIST(5) ;

The computation is always carried out in floating-point arithmetic.

The POLY Built-in Function. This function is used to form a polynomial expansion in floating-point from two arguments. For example, assume the GRADE array has been declared and initialized to the following values:

Grade (1) | 90
(2) | 85
(3) | 76
(4) | 93
(5) | 81

Then, if the statements

X = 10.5 ;
ANSWER = POLY(GRADE,X) ;

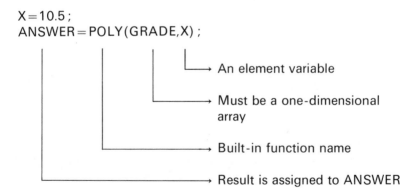

An element variable

Must be a one-dimensional array

Built-in function name

Result is assigned to ANSWER

are coded, the following arithmetic operations are performed:

$$90 + 85X + 76X^2 + 93X^3 + 81X^4$$

The values, 90, 85, etc., are the values contained in the GRADE array, and X is a constant value defined in the second argument of the

POLY function. The result, then, may be expressed as

$$\sum_{j=0}^{n-m} a(m + j) * x ** j$$

where

a is the first argument (a one-dimensional array)
x is the second argument
m is the lower bound of the a array
n is the upper bound of the a array

It is also permissible to specify the second argument, x, as a one-dimensional array. In that case, the value returned by the POLY function is defined as

$$a(m) + \sum_{j=1}^{n-m} \left[a(m + j) * \prod_{i=0}^{j-1} x(p + i) \right]$$

where a, x, m, and n are the same as defined above and p represents the lower bound of the second argument.

The ALL Built-in Function.   This function is used to test all bits of a given bit-string array. If *all* bits in the same position within each element are '1'B's, then the result is a '1'B; otherwise, the result is a '0'B. You may recognize this operation as being the same in logic as the rules of the Boolean AND operation. Here is an example:

```
DCL BIT_ARRAY(4) BIT(6);
DCL RESULT BIT(6);
RESULT=ALL(BIT_ARRAY);
```

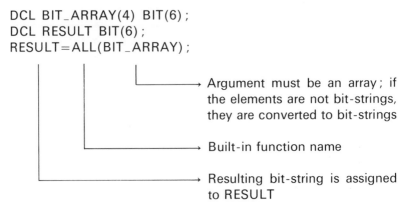

Argument must be an array; if the elements are not bit-strings, they are converted to bit-strings

Built-in function name

Resulting bit-string is assigned to RESULT

Assume that the BIT_ARRAY elements have been initialized to the following bit-string configurations:

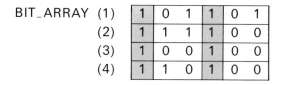

RESULT
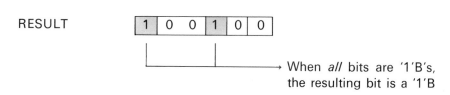

→ When *all* bits are '1'B's, the resulting bit is a '1'B

The ANY Built-in Function. This function is used to test the bits of a given bit-string array. If *any* bits in the same position of the elements of an array is a '1'B, then the result is a '1'B; otherwise, the result is '0'B. You may recognize this operation as being the same in logic as the Boolean OR operation. Here is an example:

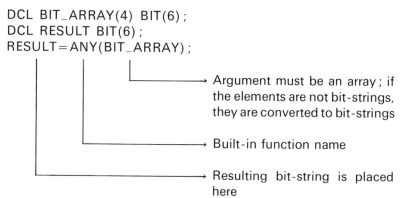

```
DCL BIT_ARRAY(4) BIT(6);
DCL RESULT BIT(6);
RESULT = ANY(BIT_ARRAY);
```

→ Argument must be an array; if the elements are not bit-strings, they are converted to bit-strings

→ Built-in function name

→ Resulting bit-string is placed here

Assume that the BIT_ARRAY elements have been initialized to the following bit-string configurations:

BIT_ARRAY (1)   1   0   1   1   0   1
          (2)   1   1   1   1   0   0
          (3)   1   0   0   1   0   0
          (4)   1   1   0   1   0   0

RESULT

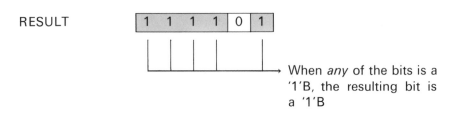

When *any* of the bits is a '1'B, the resulting bit is a '1'B

Manipulating Array Data (the DO-Loop)

Assume that the temperature for each day of a given year has been punched into a card. It is desired to input these values and find the mean (average) temperature for the year. The statements to accomplish this are simple. First, we begin by declaring an array to contain the year's daily temperatures as well as a single variable to contain the mean:

DCL TEMPERATURES(365) FIXED(4,1);
DCL AVERAGE_TEMPERATURE FIXED(4,1);

Next, it would be necessary to read the values into the array. This can be accomplished with the following GET LIST statement:

GET LIST(TEMPERATURES);

Notice that only the array name is specified in parentheses following the keywords GET LIST. In this case, data items will be read from the input stream until the entire array has been filled with data or an end-of-file condition is detected. Here, it would not be desirable to have an end-of-file condition detected before the entire array was set equal to the daily temperatures for the year. The next step is to find the average yearly temperature. This is easily accomplished through the use of the SUM built-in function:

AVERAGE_TEMPERATURE=SUM(TEMPERATURES)/365;

The above problem becomes a bit more complex if it is desired to write a generalized program that takes into account the number of days in leap year (366) as well as the number of days in a non-leap year (365). To do this, our program must first determine the number of days in the year for which the average temperature is to be found. Assume that YR is an identifier containing the year for which the mean is to be found. Leap years are those years whose dates are evenly divisible by four [i.e., 1972, 1976, 1980, etc.—except for century years (i.e., 2000 is not a leap year)]. Thus, if any given year is divided by 4 and there is no remainder from the division, we know that the year is a leap year. There is a built-in function that facilitates the testing of a remainder after a divide operation. The function is called MOD (for modulo). For example:

Y=MOD(YR,4);

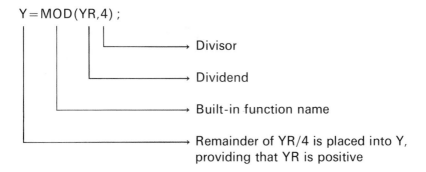

→ Divisor

→ Dividend

→ Built-in function name

→ Remainder of YR/4 is placed into Y, providing that YR is positive

The purpose of the MOD function is not to obtain a remainder, but to return the smallest positive number that must be subtracted from the first argument in order to make it exactly divisible by the second argument. This means that if the first argument is positive, the returned value is the remainder resulting from a division of the first argument by the second. If the first argument is negative, the returned value is the modular equivalent of the remainder. For example, MOD(-29,6) returns the value 1:

$$\begin{array}{r} -4 \\ 6\overline{\smash{\big)}-29} \\ -24 \\ \hline -5 \end{array} \quad \text{Remainder}$$

then,

6 − 5 = +1

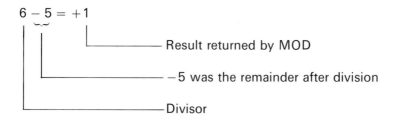

Result returned by MOD

−5 was the remainder after division

Divisor

To determine the number of days in the year, then, we could code the following statements :

```
IF MOD(YR,4)=0 THEN LIMIT=1 ;
                ELSE LIMIT=0 ;
NO_DAYS=365+LIMIT ;
```

However, as the solution to this problem is developed, you will see that we need to have the variable LIMIT contain the number of days in February. Thus, the following coding will be used :

```
IF MOD(YR,4)=0 THEN LIMIT=29 ;
                ELSE LIMIT=28 ;
NO_DAYS=337+LIMIT ;
```

(The constant 337 was selected because that is the number of days in the months of the year excluding February.) It will be necessary to declare the TEMPERATURES array with enough elements to include the extra day in leap year. For example :

```
DCL TEMPERATURES(366) FIXED(4,1) ;
```

If we wish to read temperatures into this array using the statement

```
GET LIST(TEMPERATURES) ;
```

366 values will be taken from the input stream and assigned to the corresponding elements of the array. A total of 366 values will be read, because that is the declared length of the TEMPERATURES array. However, for a non-leap year, we would only want to read 365 values. The problem, then, is how do we write a program that will input 365 values on one occasion and 366 values on another occasion? The *iterative DO statement* provides a simple solution. There are three general forms of the DO statement :

	Example	Comment
Type 1	DO ; . . . END ;	This DO-group is noniterative; generally, it is executed only once
Type 2	DO WHILE(expression) ; . . . END ;	Used to specify repetitive execution of the statements within the group
Type 3	DO i TO j BY k WHILE(expression) ; . . . END ;	Used to specify repetitive execution of the statements within the group

The DO-Group—Noniterative

Type 1 has already been explained in Chapter 2. Recall that this DO-group is to be treated logically as a single statement. It is used in an IF statement to specify a group of statements to be executed in the THEN clause or the ELSE clause.

The DO WHILE

Type 2 is the DO WHILE statement. It specifies that the instructions contained between the DO and its corresponding END are to be executed repetitively as long as the expression following the WHILE is true. For example, in controlling the number of temperatures to be summed, we could code the following (recall that NO_DAYS has previously been set to either 365 or 366, depending on whether or not we are reading data for a leap year) :

```
I=1;
TOTAL=0;
DO WHILE (I<=NO_DAYS);
TOTAL=TOTAL+TEMPERATURES(I);
I=I+1;
END;
AVERAGE_TEMPERATURE=TOTAL/NO_DAYS;
```

The statements contained in the DO-group will be executed a repetitive number of times; they will be executed as long as "I" is less than or equal to the limit found in NO_DAYS. The expression following the WHILE is tested *before* any statements in the DO-group are executed. Thus, it is possible that the statements following a DO WHILE and terminated with an END may never be executed. This would occur when the expression tested is false. When using the DO WHILE, a program must always provide, in some way, for the modification of the expression following the WHILE, so that eventually the expression is no longer true. Do you see what would happen had the statement

$$I=I+1;$$

not been included in the above example? It is obvious that the program would be caught in an interminable loop. One solution to the problem could be to use this form of the DO WHILE:

```
DO I=1 BY 1 WHILE(I<=NO_DAYS);
```

Here is another example of the DO WHILE:

```
DCL SWITCH BIT(1) INIT('1'B);
DO WHILE(SWITCH);
```
```
.
.           └──────→ As long as SWITCH is true (i.e.,
.                    ='1'B), the DO-group will be
END;                 repetitively executed
```

The DO-Group—Iterative

The format of the type 3 DO solves our problem of reading data using GET LIST where the number of input values may be either 365 or 366. Here is one solution:

```
DO I=1 TO NO_DAYS;
GET LIST(TEMPERATURES(I));
END;
```

Before continuing with the calculation of the average temperature problem, let us pause to consider the DO statement in more detail. Note the terminology used to describe various parts of the iterative DO:

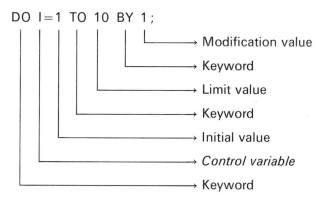

The iterative DO statement performs the following steps in the sequence listed:

1. *Initialize the control variable:* This variable (I, in the above example) will be set equal to the initial value (1, as specified above). Greater program efficiency results if you select a FIXED BINARY identifier for your variable. You may not modify this variable inside the DO-loop, although it is permitted to reference it on the right side of the assignment symbol.
2. *Test control variable:* If the control variable is less than or equal to the limit value, execute the sequence of statements that follow the DO; otherwise, transfer to the statement following the END statement that terminates the DO.
3. *Execute statements following the DO:* The statements headed by the DO and terminated by the END are executed.
4. *Modify control variable:* The modification value is added to the control variable. Using the example above, the constant 1 is added to the contents of I. After the modification of the control variable, return to step 2.

Consider the value of the *control variable* each time through the loop. For example, in the statement

DO K=1 TO 100 BY 5;

the first time through the loop, K will be equal to 1. The second time through the loop, K will be equal to 6. Recall that the modification value, in this case 5, is to be added to the control variable (5 + 1 = 6). The third time through the loop, K will be equal to 11. The last time through the loop, K will be equal to 96. When the modification value of 5 is added to K, K becomes 101. Then, when the test on the control variable is performed, the DO-loop is terminated, because K is greater than the limit value.

The preceding explanation of the steps performed in a DO-loop apply when the modification value is positive. It is also possible to specify a negative modification value, in which case a "count down" operation is in effect. For example, in the loop

DO K=60 TO 1 BY −1;
.
.
.
END;

the steps performed would be the following:

1. Initialize K to 60.
2. Test K: If the control variable is greater than or equal to the limit value, execute statements that follow the DO; otherwise, transfer to the statement following the END. (In the above example, when the loop is terminated, K will be equal to 0.)
3. Execute statements following the DO.
4. When END is encountered, modify K by −1. Then, return to step 2.

So far, you have been introduced to this form of the DO:

DO I=1 TO 100 BY 1;

Notice in the following variation of the above DO statement that the *BY* 1 and the *TO* 100 have been reversed:

DO I=1 BY 1 TO 100;

Also, if the modification value is a 1, it is not necessary to specify it. For example, the statement

$$DO \ I=1 \ TO \ 100;$$
.
.
.
$$END;$$

accomplishes the same number of iterations as if

$$DO \ I=1 \ TO \ 100 \ BY \ 1;$$
.
.
.
$$END;$$

had been coded. Or, the limit value may be omitted from the DO. For example:

$$DO \ I=1 \ BY \ 1;$$
.
.
.
$$END;$$

In the above, the termination of the DO-group must be accomplished by other coding within the DO, as there is no comparison made with a limit value. However, if there is no other coding to terminate the DO, the control variable will eventually be increased to the point where an overflow (FIXEDOVERFLOW or OVERFLOW) condition is raised.

In a DO, the initial value, the limit value, and the modification value may be specified in the form of constants, variables, or expressions. In addition, these values may be whole numbers, fractions, or mixed numbers, and they may be positive or negative. Here are some examples:

```
DO I=K*2 TO K*5 BY J−4;
DO A=.1 TO 1 BY .1;
DO B=1.5 TO 10 BY .025;
DO J=5 TO −5 BY −1;
```

Here is another variation of the DO—it makes use of the *multiple specification:*

DO ICNT=1 TO 10, 21 TO 30, 41 TO 50;
.
              ↑
. |——————— Implied DO ICNT = 21 to 30 ;
.

END ;

In this example, the loop would be executed 30 times. ICNT goes from 1 to 10; then ICNT is initialized to 21 and goes to 30; finally, ICNT is set to 41 and goes to 50 in the loop. Upon exit from the loop, ICNT would contain the value of 51. Note that it is not necessary to specify any numeric sequence or pattern in this form of the DO. For example:

DO K=1 TO 5, 8 TO 18 BY 2, 50 TO 55, 40 TO 44;
.
.
.

END ;

Another form of the DO is shown below :

DO J=1,8,9,11,6,13 ;
.
.
.

END ;

The statements in the above DO-loop will be executed a total of six times. The first time through the loop, J will be a 1; the second time, J will be an 8; the third time J will be a 9; etc. Upon exit from the loop J will be a 13.

    It is also possible to include the WHILE option with the iterative DO we have been examining. For example :

DO K=1 TO 10 WHILE(X>100) ;
.
.
.

END ;

As in the case of the iterative DO, the expression following the WHILE is tested *before* statements following the DO are performed. If the expression is true, the DO-loop will be executed. If X remains greater than 100, the loop will be performed a maximum of ten times. However, if the expression is false, in this example, when $X <= 100$, then there is a transfer to the statement following the END statement.

In the following example, the DO specifies that the group is to be executed at least ten times, and then (providing that A is equal to B) once more :

$$DO \ I=1 \ TO \ 10, \ 11 \ WHILE(A=B) ;$$
$$.$$
$$.$$
$$.$$
$$END ;$$

If "BY 0" were inserted after the 11,

$$DO \ I=1 \ TO \ 10, \ 11 \ BY \ 0 \ WHILE(A=B) ;$$
$$.$$
$$.$$
$$.$$
$$END ;$$

then execution would continue with I set to 11 as long as A remained equal to B. Note that a comma separates the two specifications. A succeeding specification is considered only after the preceding specification has been satisfied.

Nested DO-Groups

DO-groups may be nested within other DO-groups. For example :

$$DO \ I=1 \ TO \ 99 ;$$
$$DO \ J=I+1 \ TO \ 100 ;$$
$$.$$
$$.$$
$$.$$
$$. \quad END ;$$
$$.$$
$$.$$
$$END ;$$

All statements in the range of the inner DO must be within the range of the outer DO. This arrangement of DO-groups is referred to as *nested*

DO-groups and takes the following form (brackets are used to indicate the range of the DO-groups) :

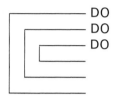

The following configuration is not valid :

It is possible to transfer out of a DO-group before the maximum number of iterations have been performed. However, the rules of the PL/I language are that it is not permitted to transfer to a statement in an iterative DO-group.

For an example of nested DO-groups, let us return to the problem of calculating the average temperature for the year. Recall that all temperatures for the year are in the TEMPERATURES array. TEMPERA-TURES(1) through TEMPERATURES(31) contain the daily temperatures for the month of January; TEMPERATURES(32) through either TEMPERATURES(59) for non-leap year or TEMPERATURES(60) for a leap year contain the daily values for the month of February; and so on. Assume it is desired not only to find the average yearly temperature but also to calculate the average *monthly* temperature. The average temperature for each month is to be placed into a 12-element array called MONTHS. Recall, also, that it was the MOD function that established the number of days in February. For example :

IF MOD(YR,4) = 0 THEN LIMIT = 29; ELSE LIMIT = 28;

The identifier LIMIT contains the number of days in February. Now let us look at the nested DO-groups needed to calculate average monthly temperatures :

```
            J = 1 ;
            M = 1 ;
OUTER :    DO K = 31,LIMIT,31,30,31,30,31,31,30,31,30,31 ;
            TOTAL = 0 ;
```

```
INNER:              DO L=M TO K+M−1;
                    TOTAL=TEMPERATURES(L)+TOTAL;
                    END INNER;
             MONTHS(J)=TOTAL/K;
             J=J+1;
             M=L;
             END OUTER;
```

The variable J is used to identify the month for which the average temperature is being calculated. Thus, J will start at 1 and go to 12. The variable M is used to identify the julian day†. It will start at 1 and go up to 365 or 366.

The *outer DO* statement consists of 12 specifications; each specification represents the number of days in each month beginning with January. The DO-group will be executed 12 times, because 12 specifications are listed. The variable TOTAL is used to accumulate each month's temperatures.

The *inner DO*-group sums the temperatures for a given month. (Note the expression specified for the limit value in the inner DO.) When all the values for a given month have been accumulated, there is a transfer out of the inner DO. The transfer is to the statement in the outer DO that calculates the average monthly temperature and assigns that value to the corresponding position of the MONTHS array [e.g., MONTHS(1) contains the January average temperature, MONTHS(2) contains the February average temperature, etc.]. The variable J is then incremented to point to the next month for which the mean is to be found. The variable M is set equal to L, where L is pointing to the next sequential numbered day in the year. When the

END OUTER;

statement is encountered, K is set equal to the next specification in the DO, and there is a transfer to the statement

TOTAL=0;

The nested DO-groups are concluded when the mean has been found for each of the 12 months in the year.

Figure 4.1 summarizes the allowable forms of the DO statement.

---

†Julian day numbers are the days of the year numbered consecutively; e.g., julian day "32" would be February 1.

from	TO	BY	WHILE	Example	Explanation
O	O	O	O	DO :	Merely delimits a group
O	O	O	W	DO WHILE (X>0) ;	Do-group performed only if WHILE is true
O	All other combinations with the *from* omitted are invalid				
W	W	W	W	DO I=1 TO N BY 2 WHILE (X>0) ;	If the WHILE is true, repeat DO-group a maximum of N/2 times
W	W	W	O assumed to be true	DO I=1 TO N BY 2 ;	Without the WHILE specified, it is implied to be true; hence, repeat DO-group a maximum of N/2 times
W	W	O assumed to be 1	O assumed to be true	DO I=1 TO N ;	Repeat DO-group a maximum of N times; example implies: DO I=1 TO N BY 1 ;

W	O assumed to be the same as from value	O assumed to be 1	O assumed to be true	DO I=2 ;	Execute DO-group once; the example implies the following DO: DO I=2 TO 2 BY 1 WHILE(0=0) ;
W	O	W	W	DO I=2 BY 2 WHILE (X>0) ;	Repeat DO-group as long as WHILE is true; DO is stopped by "not-true" WHILE
W	O	W	O assumed to be true	DO I=2 BY 2 ;	The DO is stopped only by other coding
W	O assumed from value	O assumed to be 1	W	DO I=2 WHILE (X>0) ;	DO once if WHILE is true; example implies DO I=2 TO 2 BY 1 WHILE (X>0) ;
W	W	O assumed to be 1	W	DO I=1 TO N WHILE (X>0) ;	If the WHILE is true, repeat DO-group a maximum of N times

FIGURE 4.1 Allowable forms of the DO statement. (Key: W = written; O = not written.)

The term FROM used in the chart refers to the initial value assigned to the control variable; i.e.,

> DO I=1 TO 50 BY 2 WHILE(A=1);

The word *from* in Figure 4.1 refers to the starting value

The Repetitive Specification of a Data Item

In stream I/O, data list elements may contain a repetitive specification which is similar to the iterative DO. For example:

> GET LIST((TEMPERATURES(I) DO I=1 TO NO_DAYS));

Each repetitive specification must be enclosed in parentheses

Even if the repetitive specification is the only element in the data list, this outer set of parentheses is required

In the case of the repetitive specification of a data item, an END statement is not used to terminate the DO in the data list.

Repetitive specifications may be nested; that is, an element of a repetitive specification can itself be a repetitive specification. Each DO portion must be delimited on the right with a right parenthesis, with its matching parenthesis added to the beginning of the entire repetitive specification. For example:

> GET LIST(((A(I,J) DO I=1 TO 5) DO J=3 TO 7));

When DO portions are nested, the rightmost DO is at the outer level. Thus, the above GET statement is equivalent to

> DO J=3 TO 7;
>   DO I=1 TO 5;
>   GET LIST(A(I,J));
>   END;
> END;

Here is an example of several data list items containing repetitive specifications:

> GET LIST((A(I)DO I=1 TO 50),(B(J),C(J)DO J=1 TO 12));

Returning to the calculation of temperatures problem, Figure 4.2 shows a flowchart for a program that will read daily temperatures for a given year and calculate the average yearly temperature. You have already seen segments of the program given in Figure 4.3; the entire program is shown to tie together those segments that were explained in this chapter. The topics illustrated in the program include:

1. Array manipulation
2. Nested DO-groups
3. DO in STREAM I/O
4. Initialization of arrays in a DECLARE
5. MOD and SUM built-in functions

Comments About the Program

Before studying the following comments, examine the program shown in Figure 4.3. Some of the statements should be familiar to you, so they will not be explained.

Statement 5. The SUM built-in function is used to total all values in the TEMPERATURES array. It is necessary to initialize the 366th element of this array to a zero value because on non-leap year, only the first 365 elements will contain meaningful data. If we do not initialize the 366th element, the value in TEMPERATURES(366) is unpredictable.

Statement 10. The variable K is used as an index variable in statement 19. Normally, we would implicitly or explicitly declare index variables to have the FIXED BINARY(15) attributes, for that is the most efficient method. However, because K will subsequently be used in an arithmetic operation (see statement 24), K was declared to have the FIXED DECIMAL attributes. This avoids, in statement 24, having a mixed data type of arithmetic operation. (See Chapter 2 for a review of mixed data type operations.)

Statements 11–14. The year for which the subsequent temperature data applies is read. Then the MOD function is invoked to determine if YEAR is a leap year. Finally, NO_DAYS is set equal to the number of days in YEAR.

Statements 15–16. The GET LIST statement reads values into the TEMPERATURES array, and the AVERAGE_TEMPERATURE is computed.

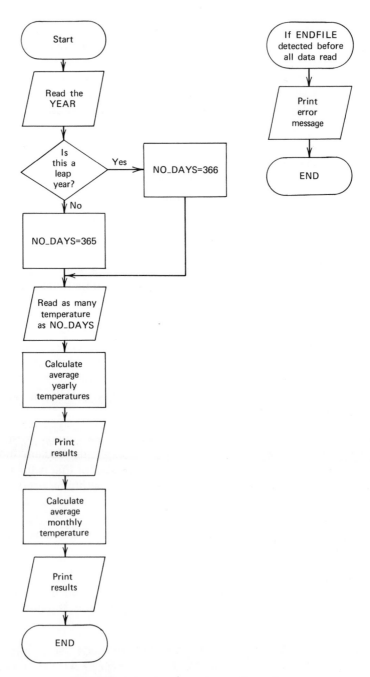

FIGURE 4.2 Temperatures flowchart.

```
 1   TEMPS:     PROC OPTIONS(MAIN);
 2              DCL CARDIN FILE INPUT STREAM ENV (F(80)MEDIUM(SYSIPT,2540));
 3              ON ENDFILE(CARDIN) GO TO ABEND;
 4              DCL TEMPERATURES(366) FIXED(4,1);
 5              TEMPERATURES( 366) = 0;
 6              DCL MONTHS(12) FIXED(4,1);
 7              DCL AVERAGE_TEMPERATURE FIXED(4,1);
 8              DCL TOTAL FIXED(6,1);
 9              DCL YEAR FIXED(4);
10              DCL K FIXED(3);
11              GET FILE(CARDIN)LIST(YEAR);
12              IF MOD(YEAR,4) = 0 THEN LIMIT=29; ELSE LIMIT =28;
14              NO_DAYS = 337 + LIMIT;
15              GET FILE(CARDIN)LIST((TEMPERATURES(I) DO I=1 TO NO_DAYS));
16              AVERAGE_TEMPERATURE = SUM(TEMPERATURES) / NO_DAYS +.05;
17              J = 1;
18              M = 1;
19   OUTER:     DO K=31,LIMIT,31,30,31,30,31,31,30,31,30,31;
20              TOTAL = 0;
21   INNER:         DO L = M TO K+M-1;
22                  TOTAL = TEMPERATURES(L) + TOTAL;
23                  END INNER;
24              MONTHS(J) = TOTAL / K;
25              J = J + 1;
26              M = L;
27              END OUTER;
28              PUT LIST('JANUARY','FEBRUARY','MARCH','APRIL');
29              PUT SKIP LIST((MONTHS(I) DO I=1 TO 4));
30              PUT SKIP(2)LIST('MAY','JUNE','JULY','AUGUST');
31              PUT SKIP LIST((MONTHS(I) DO I=5 TO 8));
32              PUT SKIP(2)LIST('SEPTEMBER','OCTOBER','NOVEMBER','DECEMBER');
33              PUT SKIP LIST((MONTHS(I) DO I=9 TO 12));
34              PUT LINE(13)LIST('AVERAGE YEARLY TEMPERATURE IS');
35              PUT SKIP(2)LIST (AVERAGE_TEMPERATURE);
36              RETURN;
37   ABEND:     PUT LIST('LESS THAN 365 TEMPERATURES WERE INPUT');
38   FINI:      END;
```

FIGURE 4.3   Sample program to calculate average temperatures.

Statements 17–27. This sequence of statements was explained in this chapter under the heading "Nested DO-Groups." All the temperatures for a given month are accumulated into the variable TOTAL. Upon exit from the inner DO, TOTAL is divided by K, where K is the number of days in a given month. In statement 10, K was declared to have the FIXED attribute. Had K been allowed to default to FIXED BINARY(15), and then been divided into TOTAL, which has the attributes FIXED DECIMAL (6, 1), the accuracy of the average monthly temperature would have been affected. For example, the average monthly temperature (calculated on a desk calculator) would be a value of 64.4; in PL/I where K is FIXED BINARY(15), TOTAL is FIXED DECIMAL(6, 1), and TOTAL is divided by K, the quotient would be 64.3. This error in accuracy is due to the mixed data types in arithmetic operations. Recall that when FIXED BINARY data is combined in arithmetic expressions with FIXED DECIMAL, the DECIMAL base will be converted to BINARY. Thus, TOTAL will be converted to FIXED BINARY. In the conversion, the fractional portion of TOTAL may only be an approximation of the decimal fraction (e.g., .1 in decimal can only be approximated in binary; the binary equivalent in this case will never be exactly equal to the decimal fraction). This approximation of the fractions affects the accuracy of the result. The solution to this problem is to avoid mixed data types in the same arithmetic expression. Hence, K and TOTAL were declared as FIXED DECIMAL, and we will obtain the accurate answer when the statement

$$MONTHS(J) = TOTAL/K;$$

is executed.

Statement 36. The RETURN statement causes the program to be terminated. The statement

$$GO\ TO\ FINI;$$

could appear in place of the RETURN. Either statement accomplishes the same function. RETURN indicates to "return to the *calling program.*" (The calling program in this case is the operating system.) The END, when it is encountered as the logical end of the program, also accomplishes a "return to the calling program" operation.

Statement 37. In the event that less than 365 temperatures are specified in the input stream, the ENDFILE statement specifies a transfer to this "abnormal ending" routine. Thus, an error message will be printed and the program terminated.

Figure 4.4 shows the sample output from the temperatures calculation program. Upon closer inspection of this output, you may be wondering why the numeric values are not "lined-up" or left-justified under the month's name. That is, the output is this:

$$JANUARY$$
$$65.4$$

not this:

$$JANUARY$$
$$65.4$$

The reason for the indentation of the temperatures under their respective headings has to do with the rules for *data conversion*. The output

JANUARY	FEBRUARY	MARCH	APRIL
60.9	57.4	55.0	63.3
MAY	JUNE	JULY	AUGUST
72.9	79.3	90.5	91.2
SEPTEMBER	OCTOBER	NOVEMBER	DECEMBER
85.6	75.3	65.8	66.0

AVERAGE YEARLY TEMPERATURE IS

72.0

FIGURE 4.4   Output from sample program to find average temperatures.

temperatures have the attributes FIXED DECIMAL (4, 1). The rule for converting FIXED DECIMAL data to a character-string is this:

Character-string length = Precision of decimal value +3

The constant of 3 was selected to allow room for the following:

1.   A leading blank
2.   A minus sign, if value is negative; otherwise, a blank for a positive value
3.   A decimal point, if the value is a mixed number

Thus, in Figure 4.4, we see the numeric data printed as character-strings of length 7. To illustrate:

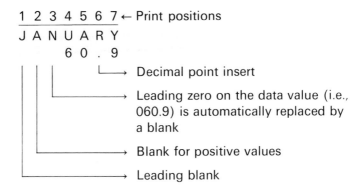

1 2 3 4 5 6 7 ← Print positions

J A N U A R Y

6 0 . 9

└─→ Decimal point insert

└─→ Leading zero on the data value (i.e., 060.9) is automatically replaced by a blank

└─→ Blank for positive values

└─→ Leading blank

Case Study

> "Now," said Rabbit, "this is a Search and I've organized it—"
> "Done what to it?" said Pooh.
> "Organized it. Which means—well, it's what you do to a
> Search when you don't all look in the same place at once."

from *The House at Pooh Corner*
by A. A. Milne

The *binary search technique* is a method that may be used for locating data in a table. As an illustration, assume that two tables are stored on a direct access device. These tables consist of codes and corresponding premiums. For example:

Codes		Premiums	
(1)	107	(1)	25.90
(2)	137	(2)	35.16
(3)	243	(3)	14.75
(4)	375	(4)	47.35
(5)	491	(5)	5.23
(6)	503	(6)	15.34
(7)	620	(7)	4.10
(8)	745	(8)	5.95
(9)	847	(9)	13.46
Codes (10)	960	Premiums (10)	10.57

In an insurance application, each code in the table identifies a specific type of coverage offered by the insurer. The corresponding premium is the cost that the insured must pay for that coverage. Typically, the tables in which the codes and premiums are stored are fairly large, although only ten items are shown here for purposes of simplicity.

Assume that both tables (Codes and Premiums) are read into main storage from the direct access device in the initialization phase of the program. The codes in the table called "Codes" are referred to as the *table arguments*. These codes are in ascending sequence.

Assume that it has been determined that several coverages are to be included in a given insurance policy for a customer. Codes indicating the types of coverage desired, along with the customer name, are punched into a card; e.g.,

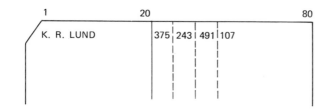

These card codes (a maximum of 20 per customer) are referred to as the *search arguments*. The program reads each search argument from the card and "searches" the codes table for an equal code. When equality is found, the corresponding premium should be added to a total. When all premiums have been summed up for a given customer, the customer's name and total premiums due are printed. If a card contains an invalid code (one not in the table), an error message is printed and the card record is bypassed. The term *table function* is often associated with table look-up techniques. The table function in this case is the retrieval of the corresponding premium and the accumulation of premiums to give a total for each customer. Because the purpose of this case study is to illustrate the binary search technique, the program keeps to a minimum the processing and formatting of output.

One method for locating a code in the codes table is to take the search argument and compare it with each table argument, beginning at the top of the table and sequentially continuing down the table until either an equal compare occurs or the end of the table is reached. Because the search arguments (card codes) are in random order, each new search through the codes table must begin at the top of the table. If the codes table contains 500 table arguments, the sequential method of comparing is time-consuming. If the table arguments are sequentially organized, as they are in the codes table, another way to locate the desired code is to use the *binary search* method. In a binary search, the technique is to take the search argument and compare it with the middle table argument. For example, if there are 500 table arguments, the search argument is to be compared with the 250th table argument. If the search argument is greater than the table argument, we know that the corresponding code for the search argument must lie within the second half of the table. This method allows us to eliminate searching half of the table with just *one* compare. Of course,

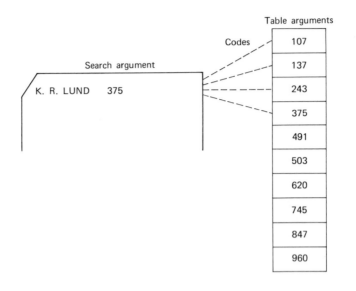

for this method to work, the table arguments must be sorted into ascending sequence. The binary search method is so named because the technique is to divide each remaining portion of the table in half and compare the search argument with the table argument until an equal compare occurs or the last compare has been made. What is so striking about this method is that after two compares, three-fourths of the table has been eliminated from the search.

Figure 4.5 illustrates a generalized algorithm for a binary search. To see the logic of the algorithm, it is suggested that you select a search argument and work through the flowchart using the ten-element codes table illustrated in the introduction of this case study. Figure 4.6 illustrates a solution to the insurance premium calculation program.

Comments About the Case Study

Statements 4–9. The single variables and arrays are declared. The array CODES will contain the table arguments and the array PREM will contain the corresponding insurance premiums. The array CCODE has been dimensioned for 20 elements, thereby allowing for up to 20 codes to be specified per customer.

Statements 10–12. The table arguments and premiums are initialized with data from input cards.

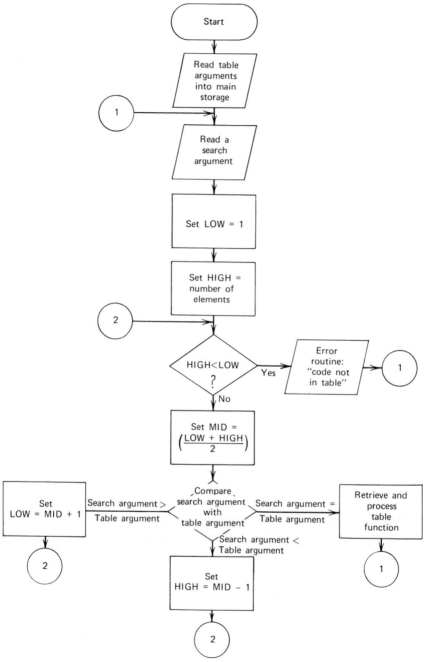

FIGURE 4.5 Algorithm for binary search.

```
1    CASE:    PROC OPTIONS(MAIN);
2             DCL CARD FILE INPUT STREAM ENV(F(80)MEDIUM(SYSIPT,2540));
3             ON ENDFILE(CARD)GO TO EOJ;
4             DCL NAME CHAR(20);
5             DCL CCODE(20) FIXED(3);
6             DCL (MID,HIGH,LOW) FIXED(3);
7             DCL TOTAL FIXED(5,2);
8             DCL CODES(10) FIXED(3);
9             DCL PREM(10) FIXED(5,2);
10               DO J = 1 TO 10;
11               GET FILE(CARD)LIST(CODES(J),PREM(J));
12               END;
13   P1:      GET FILE(CARD)LIST(NAME,CCODE);
14            TOTAL = 0;
15            DO J = 1 TO 20;
16            IF CCODE(J)=0 & TOTAL -=0 THEN GO TO PRINT;
17            IF CCODE(J)=0 & TOTAL=0 THEN GO TO P1;
18                LOW = 1;
19                HIGH = 10;
20   P2:          IF HIGH < LOW THEN DO;
21                   PUT SKIP LIST('UNABLE TO FIND CODE IN TABLE FOR');
22                   PUT SKIP LIST(CUSTOMER_RECORD);
23                   GO TO P1;
24                   END;
25                MID = (LOW + HIGH)/2;
26                IF CCODE(J) > CODES(MID) THEN DO;
27                   LOW = MID +1;
28                   GO TO P2;
29                   END;
30                IF CCODE(J) < CODES(MID) THEN DO;
31                   HIGH = MID - 1;
32                   GO TO P2;
33                   END;
                  /* RETRIEVE DATA & PROCESS */
34                TOTAL = TOTAL + PREM(MID);
35                END;
36   PRINT:   PUT SKIP LIST(NAME,TOTAL);
37            GO TO P1;
38   EOJ:     END;
```

FIGURE 4.6   Solution for table look-up using binary
search technique.

Statement 13.   A customer card is read. It contains the customer's
name and up to 20 codes indicating type of insurance coverage.

Statement 14.   TOTAL is set to zero. The premiums due for each
type of coverage are accumulated into TOTAL.

Statement 15.   A DO-loop is established to process a maximum of
20 codes.

Statement 16.   When a code in the card is zero, it means that there
are no more search arguments in the input record. If TOTAL is nonzero,
then it is time to print the customer's name and total amount due in
premiums.

Statement 17.   Should a search argument be zero and the TOTAL is zero, then this card record is probably in error. It is simply by-passed. In standard applications, however, it would be advisable to print an exception message whenever a record is by-passed, because its format does not match the expected format.

Statements 18–19.   LOW and HIGH are initialized.

Statements 20–24.   The relationship of HIGH to LOW is tested. Should HIGH be less than LOW, then there was no corresponding table argument for the specified search argument. In this case, an error message is printed and there is a branch to the place in the program (P1) where another card record is to be read.

Statement 25.   The midpoint of the argument table is calculated.

Statements 26–33.   The search argument is compared with the table argument. The HIGH or the LOW point indicator is adjusted, depending on the relationship between the search argument and the table argument.

Statement 34.   Should the search argument match the table argument, then the data is to be retrieved from the PREM array and processed. The "processing" consists of simply accumulating the premium into TOTAL.

Statement 35.   This END statement terminates the DO in statement 15.

Statements 36–37.   The customer's name and total amount due is printed, and then control is returned to statement 13.

Statement 38.   The program is terminated when the end-of-file condition is encountered.

SUMMARY

Arrays: An array is a table of data items in which each item has the same attribute as every other item in the array. An array has storage reserved for it by means of a DECLARE statement.

Bounds: In declaring the size of an array, a bound is specified. All arrays have upper and lower bounds. When a single bound is specified, it is the upper bound. The lower bound would then be assumed to be 1.

Dimensions: The number of sets of upper and lower bounds specifies the number of dimensions in an array. In referring to two-dimensional arrays, sometimes the terms rows and columns are used. Maximum number of dimensions allowed in subset language is 3; in full language, 15.

Subscripting: We reference an element of an array by means of a subscript which appears in parentheses following an array name in an expression; e.g., TABLE(7) refers to the seventh element in the array called TABLE. Subscripts may be constants, variables, expressions, or subscripted subscripts; e.g., TABLE(J(K)).

SUBSCRIPTRANGE Condition: In the full language PL/I compilers, referencing a location outside the bounds of the array will cause the SUBSCRIPT-RANGE condition to be raised if the condition is enabled. Because this condition is initially disabled, it will be necessary to enable the condition in your program. The SUBSCRIPTRANGE condition is a useful debugging tool, for it is during the program checkout phase that you are most likely to inadvertently specify a subscript that references a nonexistent position of an array.

Cross Sections of Arrays: In the full language, a subscript may also be an asterisk, in which case, it specifies the entire extent of the dimension. This extent is referred to as a cross section of an array. A subscripted name containing asterisk subscripts represents not a single data element, but, rather, a larger part of the array; e.g., PERCENT(*,1) refers to all of the elements in the first column of the array called PERCENT.

I/O Operations and Arrays: In the absence of explicit element addressing, data items are read into arrays starting with the lowest numbered subscripted element and finishing with the highest subscripted element. If a multidimensional array is specified in an I/O statement, the right-hand subscript varies most rapidly.

Array Assignments: There are two types of move operations that may be specified for arrays—scalar-to-array and array-to-array:

1. *Scalar-to-array:* In this type of array assignment, an entire array is assigned a single value.
2. *Array-to-array:* In this case, one array may be assigned to another array, providing the arrays have identical bounds.

Array Expressions: An array expression is a single array variable or an expression that includes at least one array operand. Array expressions may also include operators (both prefix and infix), element variables, and constants. Evaluation of an array expression yields an array result. All operations performed on arrays are performed on an element-by-element basis. All arrays referred to in an array expression must have identical bounds.

Arrays and the LABEL Attribute: Usually, arrays are used to manipulate arithmetic data or perhaps character- or bit-strings. However, it is also possible to declare an array to have the LABEL attribute, in which case, each element of the array may contain a label.

Array Manipulation Built-in Functions: All of these functions require array name arguments, and they return, as a result, a single value. Because only a single value is returned from these functions, a function reference to any array function is considered an element expression, as contrasted with an array expression. The array manipulation built-in functions include:

1. *The SUM built-in function:* This function finds the sum of all elements in an array.
2. *The PROD built-in function:* This function finds the product of all the elements of an array. Not available in the subset language.
3. *The POLY built-in function:* This function is used to form a polynomial expansion from two arguments.
4. *The ALL built-in function:* This function is used to test all bits of a given bit-string array. If all bits in the same position within each element are '1'B's, then the result is a '1'B; otherwise, the result is a '0'B.
5. *The ANY built-in function:* This function is used to test the bits of a given bit-string array. If any in the same position of the elements of an array is a '1'B, then the result is a '1'B; otherwise, the result is '0'B.

The DO Statement: There are three general forms of the DO statement:

1. *The DO-group—noniterative:* Specifies that the DO-group is to be treated logically as a single statement. It is most often used in an IF statement to specify a group of statements to be executed in the THEN or ELSE clause.
2. *The DO WHILE:* Specifies that the instructions contained between the DO and its corresponding END are to be executed repetitively as long as the expression following the WHILE is true.
3. *The DO-group—iterative:* Specifies that instructions contained between the DO and its corresponding END are to be executed repetitively until the index variable is greater than the limit value; e.g., DO K=1 to 100; when K=101, loop is terminated. Review Figure 4.1 for a summary of the various formats of the DO statement.

The Repetitive Specification of a Data Item: In stream I/O, data list elements may contain a repetitive specification which is similar to the iterative DO: e.g.,

GET LIST((TABLE(K) DO K=5 TO 10));

Nested DO-Groups: DO-groups may be nested within other DO-groups. All statements in the range of the inner DO must be within the range of the outer DO. It is possible to transfer out of a DO-group before the maximum number of iterations have been performed. However, the rules of the PL/I language are that it is not permitted to transfer to a statement in an iterative DO-group.

CHECKPOINT QUESTIONS

1. In a DECLARE statement, how can you tell whether an attribute is a precision attribute or whether it defines the number of elements in an array?

2. In reference to an array, what are *bounds*?

3. When a *lower bound* is not specified in an array declaration, what is it assumed to be?

4. (True or False) A *one-dimensional* array would appear differently in main storage from the way a *two-dimensional* array of the same number of elements would appear.

5. How do you reference individual elements of an array?

6. Under what circumstances will the SUBSCRIPTRANGE condition be raised?

7. What will C contain when the following assignment statements are executed?

    ```
    DCL A(3) FIXED BINARY INIT(55,56,57);
    DCL B(5) FIXED BINARY INIT(3,3,2,2,1);
    K=2;
    C=A(B(K));
    ```

8. Given the statement
    ```
    DECLARE X(10);
    ```
    which of the following statements are equivalent?
    (a) GET LIST(X);
    (b) GET LIST((X(K) DO K=1 TO 10));
    (c) DO K=1 TO 10;
         GET LIST(K);
         END;

9. Given the declaration and input statement,
    ```
    DECLARE TIC(3,3);
    GET LIST(TIC);
    ```
    what will TIC(2,3) contain if the input stream consists of these values (in the order shown, reading from left to right):
    ```
    1, 2, 3, 4, 5, 6, 7, 8, 9
    ```

10. (True or False) The following statement causes all elements of the array to be initialized to zero:
    ```
    DCL A(100) INIT(0);
    ```

11. Write the DECLARE statement to initialize all 20 elements of an array called CODE. Each element is to be five characters long and contain the alphameric characters

    99999

    Use the INITIAL attribute.

12. Write the DECLARE statement to initialize to zero only the first and last elements of a five-element, one-dimensional array. Use the INITIAL attribute.

13. Is the following assignment statement valid? Why or why not?

    DCL A(6), B(2,3) ;
    GET LIST(A) ;
    B = A ;

14. Array built-in functions perform arithmetic operations on what type of arguments (e.g., fixed-point, floating-point, character-string, bit-string, etc.)?

15. Identify the array built-in functions that operate on bit-strings.

16. What are the four steps performed automatically in an iterative DO?

17. Given the following iterative DO, what will K be equal to upon exit from the loop?

    DO K=1 TO 50 BY 2 ;
    .
    .
    .
    END ;

18. In which of the following PL/I statement types may a *repetitive specification* appear?
    (a) Assignment statement
    (b) DECLARE statement
    (c) Stream I/O statements (GET and PUT)
    (d) Iterative DO statement

19. What value would K contain after each of the following program segments had been executed?

    (a) J=3 ;   (b) J=3 ;
         K=4 ;   L=10 ;
         DO M=1 to J ;   K=2 ;
         K=K+M ;   DO M=J to L ;
         END ;   K=K+M ;
                                        IF K<250 THEN GO TO OUT ;
                                        END ;
                                        OUT: PUT LIST(K) ;

TERMS TO STUDY

array
array expression
bound
control variable
cross section
data aggregate
dimension
element
iteration factor

iterative DO
multiple specification
nested DO
repetition factor
repetitive specification
row major order
subscript
subscripted subscript

PRACTICE PROBLEMS

1.   Removing Blanks from Character Data

Problem Statement: Read data cards; remove any blanks from these character-strings that may be imbedded within the data by "squeezing up" the data. For example, if input data is

'NOW IS THE TIME'

then, compacted data would be

NOWISTHETIME

Print compacted message.

Purpose of the Problem: To gain experience using arrays and the DO i TO j and/or DO WHILE statements.

Input: Make up your own data for this problem.

Output: Should be the compacted message with no imbedded blanks.

Programming Hint: Because you are to read character-strings from the input stream, it will be necessary to use the DEFINED attribute so that you may operate on individual characters within the string. That is, it will be necessary for you to define overlay an array—whose attributes are CHARACTER(I)—on the input character-string. Assume character-strings will have a maximum length of 75.

| 72 | −31 | 63 | 2 | −41 | 31 | 99 | −99 | 0 | 5 |

FIGURE 4.7   Suggested input data for Problem 2.

2.   Sorting an Array of Numbers

Problem Statement: Read ten numbers into an array. Sort the numbers into ascending sequence, i.e., so that the smallest number is in the first element of the array and the highest number is in the last element of the array. Print the numbers after you have sorted them.

Purpose of the Problem: To gain experience in the manipulation of arrays and subscripts within DO-loops.

Input Data: Ten numbers in a card in random sequence. Suggested input is shown in Figure 4.7.

Output Layout Description: See Figure 4.8.

Flowchart: See Figure 4.9. The sorting technique used here is called a "bubble sort." The numbers in the array are "flip-flopped" whenever any two adjacent numbers are not in the proper sequence. The solution calls for searching through the array until a complete pass can be made without making a single exchange. When this occurs, the numbers will be in sequence.

```
SORTED NUMBERS
        −99
        −41
        −31
          0
          2
          5
         31
         63
         72
         99
```

FIGURE 4.8   Problem 2 sample output using suggested test data.

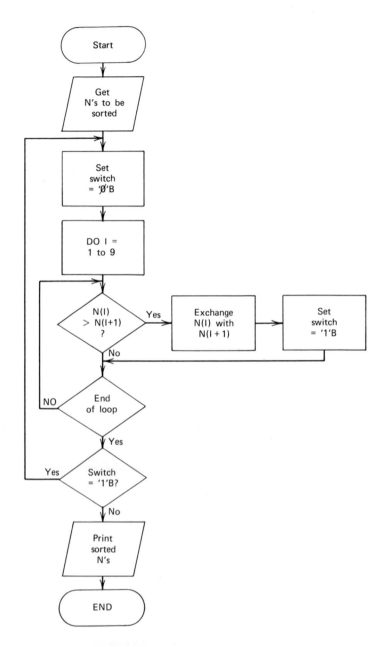

FIGURE 4.9   Flowchart for Problem 2.

3. Tag Sorting of Character-Strings

Problem Statement: Read ten character-strings into an array. Using the "tag sorting" method (described below), sort the character-strings into ascending alphameric sequence. Print the character-strings in alphabetic sequence.

Purpose of the Problem: To gain experience in the use of arrays, subscripts, and DO-loops. This problem demonstrates the use of a subscripted subscript. It also shows the value of the tag sort method of sequencing.

Input Data: Ten character-strings, each 50 characters maximum in length. Each string occupies one card image in the input stream and is in the form acceptable to list-directed I/O, i.e., is enclosed in quotes. The strings are in random alphameric sequence in the input stream. Make up your own data for this problem.

Output Layout Description: Use list-directed output, printing names in a column.

Flowchart: Use the flowchart for Problem 2.

Tag Sorting Description: Refer to Problem 2 concerning the exchange method of sorting. The technique employed in that exercise "flip-flopped" the numbers within the array whenever any two adjacent numbers were not in the proper sequence. It continued to do this until a complete pass could be made through the array without making a single exchange. At that point, the numbers were in sequence. The exchange sorting technique involves a great deal of *data movement*, because we physically change the location of the data in the array we are sorting. In Problem 2, the cost of moving the numbers around was not too great because each number occupied a small amount of main storage. However, in this problem we are sorting long strings of data. The cost of data movement here would be much greater. And, of course, the longer the strings to be sorted, the greater that cost. Another method of sorting, called *tag sorting*, will help us eliminate much of the data movement.

In this approach, we will declare two arrays. The first array will contain the data (character-strings) to be sorted. For example:

DCL STRINGS(10) CHARACTER (50);

The second array will contain the subscripts of the first array:

DCL SUBSC(10)FIXED BINARY(15);

The second array should be initialized at the beginning of the program to contain the numbers 1–10 in the first through tenth elements. A picture of the arrays before sorting might help.

	STRINGS Array containing data to be sorted	SUBSC Array containing subscripts STRINGS	
STRINGS(1)	WINEGARDEN, R	1	SUBSC(1)
STRINGS(2)	QUIGLEY, W	2	SUBSC(2)
STRINGS(3)	CLAUS, L	3	SUBSC(3)
STRINGS(4)	KRISE, V	4	SUBSC(4)
STRINGS(5)	DEMPSEY, D	5	SUBSC(5)
STRINGS(6)	BENCKE, P	6	SUBSC(6)
STRINGS(7)	GEE, J	7	SUBSC(7)
STRINGS(8)	EINSTEIN, A	8	SUBSC(8)
STRINGS(9)	CHAMBERS, M	9	SUBSC(9)
STRINGS(10)	RUNDLE, A	10	SUBSC(10)

Now we are ready to begin sorting. Notice that the subscript array acts as a list of pointers into the data array. In tag sorting, we must always use the subscript array in accessing the data in the data array. We do this by nesting subscripts. Nested subscripts are also referred to as *subscripted subscripts*. An example of this is

$$STRINGS (SUBSC (I))$$

The element of STRINGS to which this refers is that element whose subscript is found in the Ith element of SUBSC!

Tag sorting now merely becomes an exchange sort where we compare the elements in the data array, but when an exchange is required, we exchange not the data but the subscripts. The coding would look something like this:

```
IF STRINGS(SUBSCR(I)) > STRINGS(SUBSC(I+1)) THEN DO;
TEMP = SUBSC(I);
SUBSC(I) = SUBSC(I+1);
SUBSC(I+1) = TEMP;
SW = '1'B;
END;
```

Notice that the data in the array named STRINGS is never moved, only the subscripts are moved.

After one comparing pass through the data array, the two arrays would look like this:

	STRINGS	SUBSC	
(1)	WINEGARDEN, R	2	(1)
(2)	QUIGLEY, W	3	(2)
(3)	CLAUS, L	4	(3)
(4)	KRISE, V	5	(4)
(5)	DEMPSEY, D	6	(5)
(6)	BENCKE, P	7	(6)
(7)	GEE, J	8	(7)
(8)	EINSTEIN, A	9	(8)
(9)	CHAMBERS, M	10	(9)
(10)	RUNDLE, A	1	(10)

Just as in exchange sorting, you must keep making passes through the data array (always referenced through the subscript array) until no exchanges are required. At that point, the data is still not in sequence (because we did not move the data). However, the subscript array contains the subscripts of the data in the right sequence.

The two arrays, after sorting, look like this:

	STRINGS			SUBSC	
(1)	WINEGARDEN, R			6	(1)
(2)	QUIGLEY, W			9	(2)
(3)	CLAUS, L			3	(3)
(4)	KRISE, V			5	(4)
(5)	DEMPSEY, D			8	(5)
(6)	BENCKE, P			7	(6)
(7)	GEE, J			4	(7)
(8)	EINSTEIN, A			2	(8)
(9)	CHAMBERS, M			10	(9)
(10)	RUNDLE, A			1	(10)

The data can now be printed in sequence using *nested subscripts*.

4. Dollar Bill Change

Problem Statement: Write a program to calculate the number of different ways a dollar bill can be broken into change (e.g., 1 × 50¢, 1 × 25¢, 25 × 1¢ is one way; 2 × 25¢, 2 × 10¢, 6 × 5¢ is another). Print the answer.

Purpose of the Problem: To write a program using *five* nested DO-loops, one of which will be a DO WHILE statement.

Input: There is no input to this problem, as the program will generate the data.

Output: Print the answer (which is 292) using PUT LIST.

5. Theory of Organizational Relationships

Problem Statement: The complexities of managing people may be described in terms of mathematical formulas.† As the number of people a manager must manage increases, so does the possible number of basic relationships increase.

†Reference: *A FORTRAN Primer with Business Administration Exercises,* C20-1605, IBM, 1964.

As will be seen, from the computer output of this problem, added numbers of subordinates illustrates the geometric increase in the complexities of managing people. Three types of subordinate—manager relationships may be identified as :

1. *Direct single:* The manager relates directly and individually with his immediate subordinates. The number of relationships is equal to the number of subordinates, n. Thus,

$$\text{SUBORDINATES} = n$$

2. *Direct group:* The manager interacts with each possible combination of subordinates. For example, if A as the manager has three subordinates, B, C, and D, the direct group relationships are

B with C	B with D
C with B	C with D
D with B	D with C

B with C and D
C with B and D
D with B and C

The number of direct group relationships with n subordinates is defined with the following formula :

$$\text{GROUP} = n(2^n/2 - 1)$$

3. *Cross:* Subordinates relate with each other. For example, subordinates B, C, and D can relate to each other in these ways :

B to C	B to D
C to B	C to D
D to B	D to C

The number of cross relationships may be stated as follows :

$$\text{CROSS} = n(n - 1)$$

From the above analysis, the formula to yield the total number of possible relationships with n subordinates is :

$$\text{TOTAL} = n(2^n/2 + n - 1)$$

Write a PL/I program that will first input the number of different subordinate values. Then read as many n's as indicated. For each value of n, compute the number of relationships in each category described above (i.e., SUBORDINATES, GROUP, CROSS) plus TOTAL. Print a table showing the number of subordinates and the number of relationships for each type.

Purpose of the Problem: To use arrays, referencing the elements by subscripts, to use the iterative DO statement, and to use the repetitive specification in GET and PUT statements.

Input: Suggested input might be

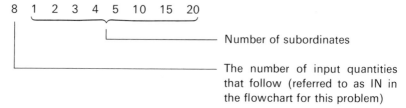

Output: Sample output is shown in Figure 4.10.

Flowchart: See Figure 4.11.

6. Compute Standard Deviation

Problem Statement: Write a program to compute the arithmetic mean ($\overline{X}$) and standard deviation (S_x) of a maximum of 100 data items stored in an array. Use the formulas

$$\overline{X} = \frac{\Sigma X}{n}$$

$$S_x = \sqrt{\frac{\Sigma X^2}{n} - \overline{X}^2}$$

where n is the number of data items. (Note, in the second formula, that the numerator under the radical is the sum of squares, not the square of a sum.)

Purpose of the Problem: To manipulate array data in a mathematical type of program.

Input: Make up your own data for this problem.

Output: Print the standard deviation using list-directed output. Sample output might be in this form:

STANDARD DEVIATION IS   3.90459E+02

RELATIONSHIPS WITH VARIABLE NUMBER OF SUBORDINATES

NUMBER OF SUBORDINATES	CROSS RELATIONSHIPS	GROUP RELATIONSHIPS	TOTAL
1	0	0	1
2	2	2	6
3	6	9	18
4	12	28	44
5	20	75	100
10	90	5110	5210
15	210	245745	245970
20	380	10485740	10486140

FIGURE 4.10   Sample output for Problem 5.

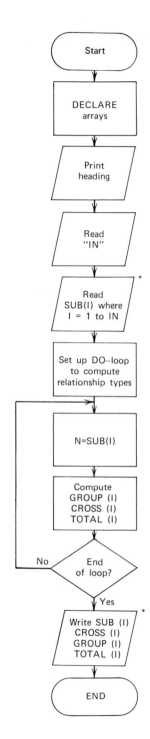

FIGURE 4.11
Flowchart for Problem 5. (For steps marked with an asterisk, use repetitive specification in the GET or PUT statements.)

7. Prime Number Generation

Problem Statement: A prime number is a number that is not divisible by any number other than itself and the number 1. All prime numbers other than the number 2 are odd; but all odd numbers are not prime numbers. Write a program to determine the numbers that are prime between 1 and 100 and print them out.

Purpose of the Problem: To program nested DO-loops in a mathematical type of problem that also makes use of integer divide as a means of determining whether a divisor goes into a dividend without a remainder; i.e.,

$$\text{Divisor } \overline{)\text{Dividend}} \quad \text{Quotient and Remainder} = 0$$

Input: There is no input, as the program will generate the data.

Processing: The fact that prime numbers are odd suggests that only odd numbers should be tested for possible prime values; this cuts the computation time. Further time-saving results by restricting the divisors to previously proved prime numbers, because even numbers will not divide into odd numbers and odd numbers that are not prime are divisible by one or more prime numbers. This, then, becomes the logic of the program. The only other problem is to devise a method for determining whether a divisor goes into a dividend without

PRIME NUMBERS BETWEEN 1 AND 100

1
2
3
5
7
11
13
17
19
23
29
31
37
41
43
47
53
59
61
67
71
73
79
83
89
97

FIGURE 4.12 Sample output for Problem 7.

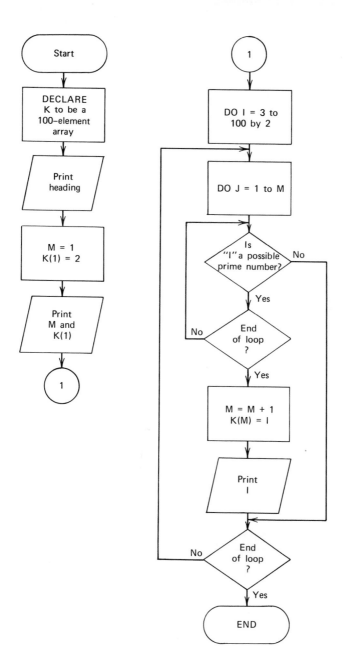

FIGURE 4.13   Flowchart for Problem 7.

a remainder. One method is to divide whole numbers by whole numbers and then multiply the quotient by the divisor. If a value divides without a remainder, the dividend is recovered after multiplication. For example:

$$N = I*K;$$
$$IF \ N*K = I \ THEN \ GO \ TO \ NO\_REMAINDER;$$

If the number divides with a remainder, a number smaller than the dividend results—indicating that the number is a possible prime number.

Output: See Figure 4.12 for sample output format.

Flowchart: See Figure 4.13 for suggested program logic.

chapter 5

Stream I/O

In stream I/O, all input and output data are considered to be in the form of a continuous stream of characters. In stream input, characters from the input stream are converted to the internal attributes of the identifiers specified in the GET statement. On output, coded arithmetic data is automatically converted back to character form before the output takes place.

You have already been introduced to one of the forms of stream I/O: list-directed. This chapter will discuss the remaining forms: edit-directed and data-directed. The DISPLAY/REPLY statement will also be covered.

Edit-Directed I/O

Introduction

Each form of stream I/O offers the PL/I programmer certain advantages and disadvantages. Advantages of list-directed I/O are that it is easy to code and it is a useful debugging tool. A disadvantage of GET LIST is that the data items must be PL/I constants separated by blanks or commas and, hence, more space is usually required to represent the data on the input medium than in other types of stream input.

A disadvantage of PUT LIST for printed output is that data may be printed beginning only at predetermined "tab positions" on the printer. There is, therefore, little flexibility in the formatting of data to provide a meaningful and esthetically pleasing report.

Edit-directed I/O eliminates some disadvantages of list-directed I/O. Edit-directed I/O is not as easy to code, but you will find that it provides for considerable efficiency in the representation of input data and offers a great deal of flexibility in the formatting of output data.

240

Assume that the input data below is to be read using list-directed input. The card data would have to be punched as follows :†

EMPLOYEE NUMBER		NAME		RATE OF PAY	HRS WKD	DEDUC- TIONS	
1	1 8 9 0		2 3 3 9 0 1	3 3 3 5 6 7	4 4 0 1	4 4 4 2 7	
'435928'		' DAVID P. GOLDSMITH '		1 0.55	41.3	103.21	

In this example, a minimum of 47 card columns would be needed to represent the data that would be read using the following GET LIST statement:

GET LIST(EMP#,NAME,RATE,HOURS,DEDUCTIONS);

Using edit-directed input, the number of card columns needed to represent the above data can be reduced significantly because no blanks are needed to separate the data items in the input stream and no punctuation marks are needed to indicate the type of input data (e.g., single quotation marks surrounding character data or a decimal point indicating the true decimal value). The data to be input using GET EDIT could be punched as follows:

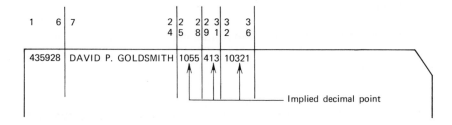

As can be seen, only 36 columns are needed to represent the payroll information for edit-directed input, as compared to 47 columns for list-directed input. However, with no punctuation marks or delimiters in the input stream to indicate the characteristics of the various data

†Recall that data items for list-directed input must be PL/I constants. Hence, the character-strings must be surrounded by single quotation marks.

fields, it will be necessary for the GET EDIT statement to provide this information through a *format list*. Here is one form of this statement :

GET EDIT (data list) (format list) ;

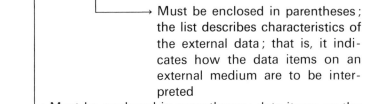

→ Must be enclosed in parentheses ; the list describes characteristics of the external data ; that is, it indicates how the data items on an external medium are to be interpreted

↳ Must be enclosed in parentheses ; data items on the external medium are converted to the attributes of the data list identifiers and placed at the locations of those identifiers

↳ Indicates edit-directed data transmission

To input the card data illustrated, the following statement could be coded :

GET EDIT (EMP#,NAME,RATE,HOURS,DEDUCTIONS)

(COLUMN (1),A(6),A(20),F(4,2),F(3,1),F(5,2)) ;

The *data list* consists of EMP#, NAME, RATE, HOURS, DEDUCTIONS. The *format list* consists of the items COLUMN(1), A(6), A(20), etc. The arrows in the above example point to the format item corresponding to each data item. These format items describe the appearance of data on an external medium. The COLUMN(1) format item indicates that input begins at column one or position one of the external storage medium. The A format item describes alphameric data, and the F format item describes fixed-point numeric data. The numbers in parentheses following the A and F specifications describe the width of the input field. Thus, six characters will be taken from the input stream and assigned to EMP# ;† 20 characters will be assigned to NAME ; four digits, of which two are fractions, will be assigned to RATE ; and so on. Notice that we have not yet declared the attributes

---

†EMP#, in this case, is being treated as an alphameric field rather than a fixed-point numeric field, because fixed numeric fields are generally used to identify data that will be used in calculations. However, it would also be correct to specify an F format item for the employee number (EMP#).

of EMP#, NAME, RATE, etc. It is important to understand that external data formats do not have to match the data declarations which describe the way data will appear in main storage. Let us look at a sample DECLARE statement for these data items:

```
DCL EMP# CHAR(6),
    NAME CHAR(25),
    RATE FIXED(4,2),
    HOURS FIXED(3,1),
    DEDUCTIONS FIXED(5,2) ;
```

Notice that NAME is declared to be a character-string of length 25 in main storage, whereas only 20 characters were taken from the input stream and assigned to NAME. Because NAME has a length attribute of 25, there will be padding on the right of the field with blanks. Other fields in the above DECLARE, such as RATE or HOURS, have precision attributes that match the width specifications of their corresponding format items. But, remember, it is not necessary that they match.

Format items may be divided into three categories:

1. *Data format items:* These are items describing the format of the external data. These items describe whether data in the stream are characters or arithmetic values in character form and how long they are. In the above format list, the A specifies *alphameric* data (hence, CHARACTER data), and the F indicates arithmetic values in the *fixed-point* notation (as contrasted with floating-point notation which is an E format item).
2. *Control format items:* These are items describing page control, line control, and spacing operations. In the above format list, COLUMN(1) is a control format item.
3. *Remote format item:* This item indicates that one or more data format items and/or control format items are located *remotely* from the GET or PUT EDIT statement in a FORMAT statement. Here is an illustration of this type, which will be discussed in greater detail later:

```
GET EDIT(EMP#,NAME,RATE,HOURS,DEDUCTIONS) (R(RFMT)) ;

RFMT:   FORMAT(COLUMN(1),A(5),A(20),F(4,2),F(3,1),F(5,2)) ;
```

The remote format item, R(label), is useful when the same format list or parts of a list apply to more than one GET or PUT EDIT statement. Using the R format item would eliminate redundant coding in the specification of identical format items.

Syntax Rules

The paragraphs below explain the way in which GET EDIT and PUT EDIT work.

All Data List Items Have Corresponding Format Items. In the statement

GET EDIT(A,B) (F(5), F(6,2)) ;

the format item F(5) specifies that five columns in the input stream are to be interpreted as a fixed decimal constant, its value to be assigned to the variable A. The value of the fixed decimal constant in the next six columns in the input stream is to be assigned to B. The item F(6,2) further specifies that, of the six positions, two represent the fractional part of the value. If the characters in the input stream were 123456, then the value 1234.56 would be assigned to B. With this specification, it is also permissible to have the decimal point appear with the data in the input stream. For example, the specification for 123.4 would be F(5,1), where the width (5) includes the decimal point. If the data value in the input stream has a decimal point specified that does not match the format description, the decimal point in the stream overrides the GET EDIT format item. For example, if

DCL A FIXED(8,3) ;
GET EDIT(A) (F(8)) ;

is coded and the input value is 12.34, then A will be given the value of 12.34.

If There Are More Format Items than Data Items, the Extra Format Items Are Ignored. For example:

GET EDIT(A, B) (F(4), F(5), F(6)) ;

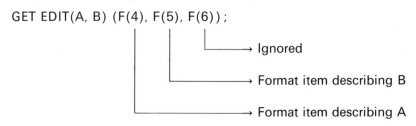

If There Are Less Format Items than Data Items, There Is a Return to the Beginning of the Format List. For example:

GET LIST(A, B, C) (F(4), F(5)) ;

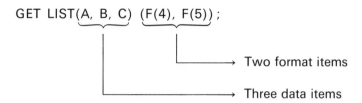

→ Two format items

→ Three data items

Here, the first format item will be used again to describe a remaining data list item. Thus, in the above example,

> F(4) describes A's external data
> F(5) describes B's external data
> F(4) describes C's external data

The Data List Item Need Not Have the Same Width Specification as the Corresponding Format Item. In the example

> DCL NAME CHAR(25) ;
> GET EDIT(NAME) (A(20)) ;

20 characters are taken from the input stream and assigned to NAME. Because NAME has a length attribute of 25, there will be padding on the right with blanks before assigning the value to NAME. Here is an example for an arithmetic data item:

> DCL RATE FIXED(5, 2) ;
> GET EDIT(RATE) (F(4, 2)) ;

Four characters are taken from the input stream, *converted* to the internal attributes of FIXED DECIMAL(5,2), and assigned to RATE.

I/O Continues Until the Data List Is Exhausted. Because stream I/O continues until all data items have been read or written, it is possible to handle more than one record with just one GET or PUT statement. For example:

> DCL A CHAR(70), B CHAR(40) ;
> GET EDIT(A,B) (A(70),A(40)) ;

The following picture illustrates how the data from two cards will be assigned to A and B :

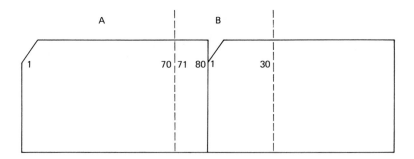

Suppose it is desired to take the first 70 columns of the first card and assign them to A, as above, but to take columns 1–40 of the second card and assign them to B. To accomplish this, the COLUMN control format item could be specified. For example :

```
DCL A CHAR(70), B CHAR(40) ;
GET EDIT(A, B) (COLUMN(1),A(70),COLUMN(1),A(40)) ;
```

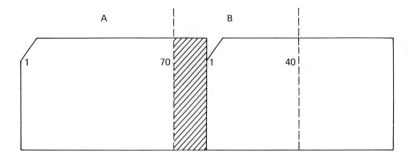

In some implementations of PL/I,† the COLUMN control format item is not available. To accomplish the above *spacing* between cards, however, the X control format item, which is available in all implementa-

---

†M-20 PL/I.

tions of PL/I, could be specified. Here is an example:

```
DCL A CHAR(70), B CHAR(40);
GET EDIT(A, B) (A)70), X(10), A(40));
```

→ On input, 10 columns are to be
spaced over and ignored

→ Control format item to signify
horizontal spacing

Format items

Assume it is desired to read the first 40 columns of ten cards and list the cards on the printer. How would this be accomplished using GET and PUT EDIT? The following coding is proposed as a solution:

```
DCL CARD_DATA CHAR(40);
DO I=1 TO 10;
GET EDIT(CARD_DATA) (COLUMN(1),A(40));
PUT EDIT(CARD_DATA) (COLUMN(1), A(40));
END;
```

Notice that COLUMN may be used for both an input and output control format item. On output to a printer, COLUMN refers to print position.

Data List Items May Be Names of Data Aggregates. The edit-directed examples you have seen so far have shown only single data elements in the data list. It is possible, however, to specify the name of an array as a list item. For example:

DCL TABLE(100) ;
GET EDIT(TABLE) (COLUMN(1), F(6, 2)) ;

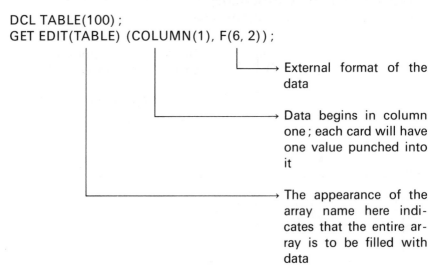

→ External format of the data

→ Data begins in column one; each card will have one value punched into it

→ The appearance of the array name here indicates that the entire array is to be filled with data

TABLE is an array representing 100 data items. The format list has one control item and one data specification: COLUMN(1) and F(6,2), respectively. The first data item read—TABLE(1)—exhausts the format list. For the second input value, there is a return to the beginning of the format list. Thus, for each new value read, input begins with column one. If we wished to read only part of the above array, a DO-group would be included in the following manner:

GET EDIT((TABLE(K) DO K=1 TO 50)) (COLUMN(1), F(6, 2)) ;

Note the required parentheses in the above statement. Each repetitive specification must be enclosed in parentheses. If a repetitive specification is the only element in a data list, two sets of outer parentheses are required because the data list must have one set of parentheses and the repetitive specification must have another.

If a multidimensional array is specified without a DO-group to qualify the order and/or number of items to be processed, then the rightmost subscript varies most rapidly. For example, the PUT statement for the TT array

DCL TT(81,9) ;
PUT EDIT(TT) (F (10)) ;

causes data to be output in the following order :·

TT(1,1), TT(1,2), TT(1,3), TT(1,4), . . . , TT(81,8), TT(81,9)

Several nested DO's may be specified in a GET or PUT statement. When DO portions are nested, the rightmost DO is at the outer level of nesting. For example :

```
DCL TT(81, 9) ;
GET EDIT(((TT(I, J) DO I=1 TO 81)DO J=1 TO 9)) (F(10)) ;
```

Note the three sets of parentheses, in addition to the set used to delimit the subscript. The outermost set is the set required by the data list; the next is that required by the outer repetitive specification. The third set of parentheses is that required by the inner repetitive specification. This statement is equivalent to the following nested DO-groups :

```
      DO J=1 TO 9;
          DO I=1 TO 81;
          GET EDIT(TT(I, J)) (F(10)) ;
          END;
      END;
```

Values are given to the elements of the array TT in the following order :

TT(1, 1), TT(2, 1), TT(3, 1), TT(4, 1), ..., TT(80, 9), TT(81, 9)

If, within the data list of a GET statement, a variable is assigned a value, this *new* value is used if the variable appears in a later reference in the data list. For example :

GET EDIT(N, (X(I) DO I=1 TO N)) (COLUMN(1), F(4, 2)) ;

When this statement is executed, a new value is assigned to N. Next, elements in the X array are assigned values in the order of X(1), X(2), ..., X(N).

All elements of an array have the same attributes. However, it may be possible that data read into an array may have varying external data formats. For example, assume that half of an array shall be filled with data in the external form of F(3) and the other half in the form of F(4).

Here are the statements to accomplish this:

```
DCL TABLE(50);
GET EDIT(TABLE) (25 F(3),25 F(4));
```

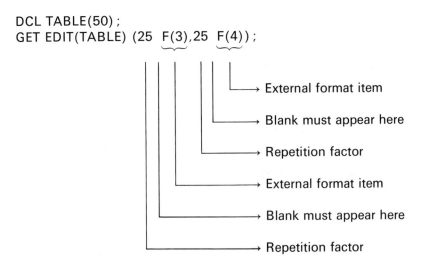

→ External format item

→ Blank must appear here

→ Repetition factor

→ External format item

→ Blank must appear here

→ Repetition factor

Input Data Items May Be Pseudo-Variables. The SUBSTR built-in function is used to manipulate smaller parts of string data (i.e., SUB STRings). For example, to extract the last five characters of a 20-position character-string called TITLE, the following would be coded:

```
S = SUBSTR(TITLE,15,5);
```

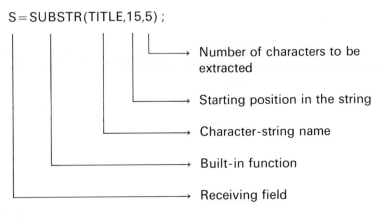

→ Number of characters to be extracted

→ Starting position in the string

→ Character-string name

→ Built-in function

→ Receiving field

SUBSTR may also be a *pseudo-variable*. Pseudo-variables are built-in functions that may be designated as a receiving field. For example:

SUBSTR(N1,1,3) = SUBSTR(N2,5,3) ;

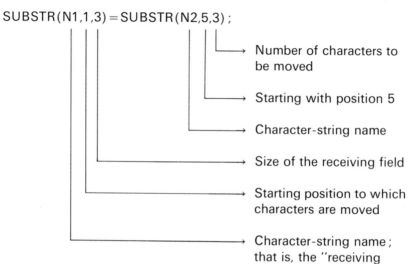

→ Number of characters to be moved

→ Starting with position 5

→ Character-string name

→ Size of the receiving field

→ Starting position to which characters are moved

→ Character-string name; that is, the "receiving field"

Pseudo-variables (e.g., SUBSTR) may appear on the left side of an assignment symbol or in a GET statement. For example:

```
DCL NAME_FIELD CHAR(35) ;
GET EDIT(SUBSTR(NAME_FIELD,5,20))(A(20)) ;
```

Twenty characters from the input stream will be assigned to NAME_FIELD, beginning with position five of the character-string.
    Here is another example:

```
GET EDIT(K,SUBSTR(NAME_FIELD,K,4))(F(2),A(4)) ;
```

When this statement is executed, a new value is assigned to K. That value is then used as an argument in the SUBSTR pseudo-variable. For example, if the input stream consisted of the digits 28, then that value is assigned to K. The SUBSTR pseudo-variable in effect, therefore, has the parameters

SUBSTR(NAME_FIELD,28,4)

→ Value assigned to K in the GET statement

Suppose an error had been made in the punching of the data; assume the digits 28 had been transposed so that the input stream begins with the digits 82. Consider the effect when the GET statement is now executed:

GET EDIT(K,SUBSTR(NAME_FIELD,K,4))(F(2),A(4));

Because K now has a value of 82, the parameters in the SUBSTR pseudo-variable become

SUBSTR(NAME_FIELD,82,4)

       └──→ Starting position of NAME_FIELD to which data is to be assigned

However, NAME_FIELD was declared to have a maximum length of 35 characters. Clearly, there is no position 82 in the character-string, and thus, the above situation is in error. In the full language, the condition called STRINGRANGE is raised. This condition is raised when there is a reference to a position outside the length of the character- (or bit-) string. This condition, by default, is disabled. Thus, if you anticipate the STRINGRANGE condition to be raised, you must enable the condition; e.g.,

(STRINGRANGE)PROG1 : PROC OPTIONS(MAIN) ;

       └──────→ Enabled for entire procedure's execution

In your program, you might code

ON STRINGRANGE BEGIN ;

.

.

.

END ;
/* OR */ ON STRINGRANGE GO TO ERROR ;

In the subset language, where STRINGRANGE is not available, extra care must be taken by the programmer to guard against referencing a position outside the string length. Typically, any position outside the string data area could still be part of your program; hence, the value assigned to that outside position destroys, perhaps, part of an instruction or another data item. Often, this kind of destruction causes a program to "hang up" and the programmer has no clues as to "what went wrong."

	STRINGRANGE condition
Subset language	No
Full language	Yes

Output Data Items May Be Built-in Functions. When included as a data item in a PUT statement, the specified built-in function is invoked and the value it returns is output. For example:

PUT EDIT(DATE) (P'XX/XX/XX') ;

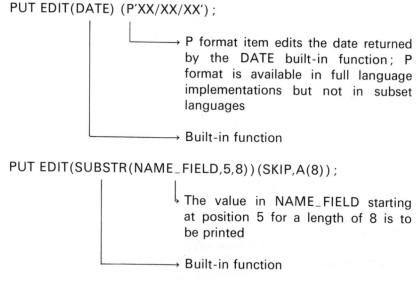

→ P format item edits the date returned by the DATE built-in function; P format is available in full language implementations but not in subset languages

→ Built-in function

PUT EDIT(SUBSTR(NAME_FIELD,5,8)) (SKIP,A(8)) ;

↳ The value in NAME_FIELD starting at position 5 for a length of 8 is to be printed

→ Built-in function

Output Data Items May Be PL/I Constants. This capability is particularly useful for the printing of literal data; i.e., character-string constants.

PUT EDIT('WEEKLY ACTIVITY REPORT') (PAGE, COLUMN(40),A) ;

Data Items May Consist of Element Expressions. Operational expressions may be specified in the data list of a PUT statement. For example:

PUT EDIT(A*3, B + C/D) (F(10), F(8, 2)) ;

Such expressions may not involve arrays or structures in the subset languages.

More than One Data List and Corresponding Format List May Be Specified. Here is another variation of the edit-directed I/O statements:

GET EDIT(data list) (format list) (data list) (format list) . . . ;

You may specify as many pairs of data lists and format lists as you wish. This format is useful when there are a lot of data items to be specified and it is desired to keep the format item *closer* to the specified data item so as to improve readability of the program by clarifying which format items belong to which data items. For example:

PUT EDIT (A,B,C) (PAGE,F(12),F(15,3),A)
(D,E,F) (B(10),F(5,2),COLUMN (60),A)
(G,H) (LINE(5),F(8),A(22)) ;

Subset Language Restrictions

Arithmetic data items may have only the format items F (fixed-point) or E (floating-point) specified. For example, the statements

DCL HOURS FIXED(3) ;
GET EDIT(HOURS) (A(3)) ; /* INVALID IN SUBSET LANGUAGE
IMPLEMENTATIONS */

are invalid, because the A format item may be specified for data that has the CHARACTER attribute only. The following data types may be input or output using the F or E format item specifications:

FIXED BINARY
FIXED DECIMAL
FLOAT BINARY
FLOAT DECIMAL

Remember, E and F describe external data formats. It is possible, for example, to read a value according to an E format item and have that value converted to the internal form of FIXED BINARY or FIXED DECIMAL. The reverse is true for the F format item; data may be input according to the F format item and converted to FLOAT BINARY or FLOAT DECIMAL, as well as, of course, FIXED BINARY and FIXED DECIMAL.

Another format item is the B (for bit-string data). Here is an example:

```
DCL STRING1 BIT(16);
GET EDIT(STRING1)(B(10));
```

The format item B(10) specifies that ten characters are to be taken from the input stream, converted to a bit-string, and then assigned to STRING1. Because STRING1 is longer than the input length, the six rightmost bits of STRING1 will be filled with zeros. The characters in the stream must be composed of 1's and 0's or a CONVERSION error will occur. In

```
DCL STRING BIT(10);
GET EDIT(STRING) (B(16));
```

sixteen characters will be taken from the input stream, but only the ten leftmost characters from the input stream will be converted and assigned to STRING.
In

```
DCL VALUE FIXED BINARY(31);
GET EDIT (VALUE) (B(31)); /* INVALID IN SUBSET LANGUAGE
                                    IMPLEMENTATIONS */
```

the GET EDIT is invalid, because VALUE is an arithmetic data item, and thus, it may only be described with the F or E format item.

Writing Headings

To see the flexibility that edit-directed output provides us in the writing of headings on printed output, assume the following literal data is to be printed:

Assume that the date in the above heading has been read into the following character-strings:

```
DCL(MM,DD,YY) CHAR(2);
```

Our program may manipulate the month, day, and year through the names MM, DD, and YY, respectively. To output the Payroll Register heading, we may begin by coding the following statement:

PUT EDIT('PAYROLL REGISTER - - WEEK ENDING') (PAGE, A(31));

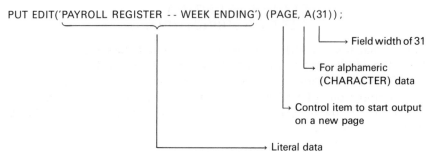

→ Field width of 31

→ For alphameric (CHARACTER) data

→ Control item to start output on a new page

→ Literal data

On output, however, it is not necessary to specify the field width following the A format item if the field width is to be the same length as the data item. Thus, the above statement could be shortened by coding

PUT EDIT('PAYROLL REGISTER - - WEEK ENDING') (PAGE,A);

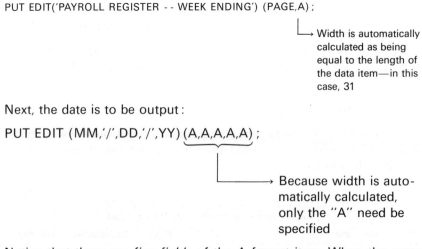

→ Width is automatically calculated as being equal to the length of the data item—in this case, 31

Next, the date is to be output:

PUT EDIT (MM,'/',DD,'/',YY) (A,A,A,A,A);

→ Because width is automatically calculated, only the "A" need be specified

Notice that there are *five fields* of the A format item. When the same format item is to be repeated a number of times, a repetition factor may be specified. Thus, the above statement could be coded

PUT EDIT(MM,'/',DD,'/',YY) (5 A);

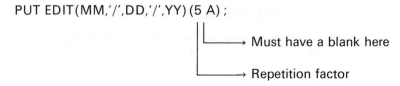

→ Must have a blank here

→ Repetition factor

In full language implementations, the repetition factor may be specified in parentheses; e.g.,

PUT EDIT (...) (COLUMN(5), (10)A(12)) ;

└─────────→ Repetition factor in parentheses

and it may be an expression as well; e.g.,

K = 10;
PUT EDIT (...) (SKIP, (K)A(10)) ;

└─→ Repetition factor may be any expression

Returning to the Payroll Register headings, we see that the next line of output could be coded

PUT EDIT('EMPLOYEE NO. NAME','RATE HOURS DEDUCTIONS
    NET PAY') (SKIP(2), A, COLUMN(40),A) ;

A SKIP(2) causes one blank line of output. The first literal will be output, automatically beginning in print position one, because of the SKIP to a new line. The second literal ('RATE HOURS DEDUCTIONS NET PAY') will be output beginning in print position 40, which was indicated by the COLUMN (40) format item.

The above explanation separated parts of the output into several PUT EDIT statements so that various points could be illustrated more simply. However, to code the output of these two heading lines in a PL/I program, only one statement need be written:

PUT EDIT('PAYROLL REGISTER—WEEK ENDING',
    MM,'/',DD,'/',YY,'EMPLOYEE NO. NAME',
    'RATE   HOURS   DEDUCTIONS   NET PAY')
    (PAGE, 6 A, SKIP(2),A,COLUMN(40),A) ;

Or, here is another way in which the above statement may be coded:

PUT EDIT('PAYROLL REGISTER—WEEK ENDING',
    MM,'/',DD,'/',YY,'EMPLOYEE NO. NAME',
    'RATE   HOURS   DEDUCTIONS   NET PAY')
    (PAGE, 6 A, SKIP(2),A,X(21),A) ;

└─→ In effect, the spacing of 21
    positions causes the next
    data item to be output
    beginning at print position
    40 [i.e., COLUMN (40)]

Note that commas are always used to separate the data list items and the format items. Thus, blanks separating these items would be used only if it is desired to improve readability of the GET or PUT. Of course, remember that a blank is required between the repetition factor and the format item to which it applies. A blank is not required following the repetition factor in the format list if there is another punctuation mark separating the repetition factor from the format items to which it applies. For example, assume data is to be output where the format consists of F(5), F(3, 1), F(5), F(3, 1), F(5), F(3, 1). As you can see, there are three pairs of (F(5), F(3, 1)) format items. The following statement would accomplish the output of data items according to this pattern of format items:

PUT EDIT(A,B,C,D,E,F)(PAGE, 3(F(5), F(3, 1)));

> The left parenthesis serves as the delimiter between the repetition factor and the format items to which it applies; hence no blank is needed

> Repetition factor

File Declarations

The declaration of files was introduced in Chapter 3. Here is a list of some of the attributes and options that may appear in your DECLARE statement for stream files:

Attributes/options	Comment
FILE	Optional
STREAM	Default if not specified
INPUT/OUTPUT	OUTPUT is default if file has PRINT attribute
PRINT	See explanation in following paragraphs
ENVIRONMENT	ENV is the abbreviation
MEDIUM	Use only in DOS/TOS
SYSIPT	System input device†
SYSLST	System output device†
SYSPCH	System punch device†
F(blocksize)	Fixed-length record
F BLKSIZE(n)	Fixed-length record for the optimizing compilers

†These keywords follow the MEDIUM option and apply only to PL/I D and DOS PL/I optimizing compilers.

Some examples of stream file declarations include

```
DCL CARDIN FILE STREAM INPUT ENV(F(80)MEDIUM
     (SYSIPT,2501)); /* A PL/I D EXAMPLE */
DCL PUNCH  FILE STREAM OUTPUT ENV(F BLKSIZE(80)
     MEDIUM(SYSPCH,2540)); /* A DOS PL/ OPTIMIZING
                 COMPILER EXAMPLE */
DCL PRINTR FILE STREAM PRINT OUTPUT ENV(F(133));
                 /* A PL/I F EXAMPLE */
DCL TAPE FILE OUTPUT STREAM ENV(F BLKSIZE(800));
     /* An OS PL/I OPTIMIZING COMPILER EXAMPLE */
```

Note that keywords may appear in any sequence in the DECLARE statement.

The place where attributes are specified may depend on the operating system you are using. For PL/I D, and DOS PL/I optimizing compilers, all attributes should be specified in the DECLARE statement. However, in PL/I F and OS PL/I optimizing compilers, the file attributes may be specified in job control statements, the OPEN statement, or the DECLARE statement.

The PRINT Attribute. When a file has this attribute, the first position of the output area is reserved for a carriage control character. For example, if you wish to output a 60-position print line, the following file declaration might be coded:

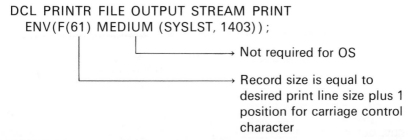

```
DCL PRINTR FILE OUTPUT STREAM PRINT
     ENV(F(61) MEDIUM (SYSLST, 1403));
```

⟶ Not required for OS

⟶ Record size is equal to desired print line size plus 1 position for carriage control character

The carriage control character is placed into the first position of the output area through the use of control format items or control options; e.g.,

PUT FILE (PRINTR)EDIT(A,B,C)(PAGE, 3 F(10));

⟶ This *format item* causes the first position of the output area to be initialized to the code that causes an advance to a new page

PUT FILE(PRINTR)PAGE EDIT(A,B,C)(3 F(10)) ;

         └────────────→ This *control option* accom-
               plishes the same function as
               the format item does

PAGE and LINE may be specified only for stream files that have the PRINT attribute. COLUMN and SKIP, which can be used to accomplish carriage control operations, may be specified for either PRINT or non-PRINT files.

The OPEN/CLOSE Statements

   Stream files are automatically opened when the first GET or PUT to that file is issued. In the case of a file with the PRINT attribute, there is an automatic advance to a new page for the first PUT to that file. The reason for using the OPEN statement is so that additional file attributes and/or options may be specified. The options are PAGESIZE and LINESIZE. They may only appear in an OPEN statement—never in a file DECLARE statement. To illustrate :

OPEN FILE(PRINTR)PAGESIZE(50) ;

           └─→ Specifies number of lines to be
             output per page of print ; if
             PAGESIZE is not specified, the
             default is 60

   The following option is available in the full language implementations, but not the subset PL/I :

OPEN FILE(PRINTR) LINESIZE(120) ;

           └─→ Specifies number of print positions
             per printed line ; if this option is
             used, it is not necessary to specify
             a record size [e.g., F(133)] in the
             file declaration

	Some attributes and options that may be specified in the OPEN statement
Subset language	PAGESIZE
Full language	STREAM or RECORD LINESIZE INPUT or OUTPUT PAGESIZE PRINT

Here are some examples:

```
OPEN FILE(PRINTR) PRINT OUTPUT STREAM PAGESIZE(45)
        LINESIZE(133); /* FULL LANGUAGE */
OPEN FILE(CARDIN) STREAM OUTPUT; /* FULL LANGUAGE */
OPEN FILE(PRINTR) PAGESIZE(55); /* OK FOR SUBSET
        LANGUAGE */
```

Options and/or attributes in the OPEN statement may be specified in any sequence.

Only the file name is specified in the CLOSE statement (no options or attributes). For example:

```
CLOSE FILE(TAPE);
```

If a stream file is not explicitly closed by the CLOSE statement, it will automatically be closed when the PL/I program is logically terminated. However, should your program abnormally terminate (e.g., through an error condition such as the CONVERSION on-unit), files will not be closed. This presents a problem to the programmer if he is in the process of creating a tape or disk file, because no end-of-file mark is written unless the file is closed. Thus, if a program is creating a tape or disk file and the program is abnormally terminated, the programmer will have to correct the error in his program and create the file again.

Data Format Items

A(w). On input, a string of length w characters is read into a variable. If the variable's declared length attribute is greater than w characters, blanks are padded on the right; if the length is less than w characters, input data will be truncated on the right. On output, the data item is left-justified in the field and, if necessary, padded on the right with blanks.

A. Allowed for output only; the length of the character-string variable is the value of the declared character-string length. Character-strings enclosed in apostrophes may also be included as data list items. They are handled in the same manner as are character-string variables.

Internal data	Format specification	Output result
ABC12	A	ABC12
ABC12	A(3)	ABC
ABC12	A(7)	ABC12bb

	A format item
Subset language	The data item corresponding to the A format item must have the CHARACTER attribute
Full language	The above restriction does not apply to the full language implementations

B(w). On input, a string of length w characters is read into a variable having the BIT attribute. If the variable's declared length attribute is greater than w characters, 0's are padded on the right; if the length is less than w characters, input data will be truncated on the right. On output, a bit-string is converted to a character-string of 0's and 1's and left-justified in the output field. The bit-string data is padded with blanks on the right if the bit-string is shorter than w.

B. Allowed for output only; the length of the bit-string variable is the value of the declared bit-string length.

Internal value	Format specification	Output result
1101	B	1101
1101	B(4)	1101
1101	B(3)	110
1101	B(6)	1101bb

	B format item
Subset language	The data item corresponding to the B format must have the BIT attribute
Full language	The above restriction does not apply to the full language implementations

C. Complex variables are specified in one of two forms:

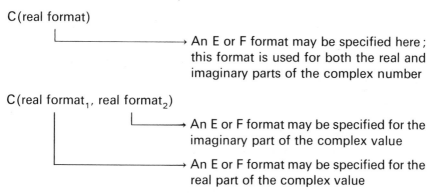

C(real format)

└──────────────→ An E or F format may be specified here; this format is used for both the real and imaginary parts of the complex number

C(real format$_1$, real format$_2$)

└─────→ An E or F format may be specified for the imaginary part of the complex value

└────────────→ An E or F format may be specified for the real part of the complex value

E(w, d). The input stream contains data in floating-point notation (e.g., .57E + 13). On input, if no decimal point is punched, the format specification d represents the number of fractional decimal places. The letter w represents the total number of characters including the decimal point (if punched), signs, and the designation E. If a blank field is input under the E specification, the CONVERSION condition is raised.

On output, the exponent always requires four characters, E ± xx, and the number is printed with d fractional decimal places. The sign, blank or minus, of the number precedes the decimal point. The number is right-justified in the field of w characters. It is not necessary to include a space, for the sign if the number is positive.

The number of significant digits output will be equal to 1 plus d. For example, if 175.36E + 05 is the internal value and the output format specification is E(10,2), then the output result will be bbl.75E + 07. This is because out of a field width (w) of ten, two positions (d) will be fractional digits. The number of significant digits will be three (d + 1). Thus, only the leftmost three digits of the value (175.36E + 05) will appear in the output stream. To illustrate :

bbl.75E+07

If the value 175.36E+05 is output according to the specification E(15, 5), the result is

bbbb0.17536E+08

If it is desired to print five digits of significance where more than *one* integer digit is to appear in the output value, the E(w, d, s) format may be specified.

E(w, d, s). On input, the s is ignored. The decimal point is assumed to be d digits from the right of the fraction ; if a decimal point is punched, the actual decimal point overrides the d specification.

On output, s indicates the number of significant digits to be output to the left of the decimal point. If s is not specified [i.e., E(w,d)], the number of significant digits to the left of the decimal point will default to 1.

Internal value	Format specification	Output result
175.36E+05	E(12, 2, 5)	bb175.36E+05
175.36E+05	E(12, 0. 5)	bb17536E+03
175.36E+05	E(12, 5, 5)	bb.17536E+08

	E format item
Subset language	The data item corresponding to the E format item must be in arithmetic coded form (FIXED BINARY, FIXED DECIMAL, FLOAT BINARY, FLOAT DECIMAL)
Full language	The above restriction does not apply to full language implementations

F(w). The input or output field consists of w characters containing a fixed-point decimal value. On input, if no decimal point is punched, the number is assumed to be an integer. A minus sign precedes a negative number. For positive values, a + sign is optional.

On output, the data is punched or printed as an integer and no decimal point will appear. For negative values, a minus sign will appear to the left of the value; for positive values, a blank will appear. There is automatic zero suppression to the left of the number.

Internal value	Format specification	Output result
123	F(3)	123
−123	F(3)	SIZE error
−123	F(4)	−123
123	F(5)	bb123

If w is not large enough to contain the output value, the SIZE error condition is raised, and the results of the output field are undefined.

F(w, d). On input, if no decimal point is specified, it is assumed that there are d decimal places to the right of the field. For example, if the input stream contains the digit characters 1234 and the format item F(4,2) is specified, input value becomes 12.34. If a decimal is actually punched, its position overrides the d specification.

On output, a decimal point is punched or printed if the d specification is greater than zero. If w is not large enough to contain the output value, then asterisks will appear in the output field, and the SIZE condition is raised. Notice in the fourth example in the table that if fewer fractional digits are output than the data item contains, the fraction is rounded off.

Internal value	Format specification	Output
123.45	F(4,0)	b123
123.45	F(6,2)	123.45
123.45	F(7,3)	123.450
123.45	F(6,1)	b123.5
123.45	F(5,2)	SIZE error

F(w,d,p). The designation p is a scaling factor; it must always be written with a sign. It effectively multiplies the value of the data item in the stream by 10 raised to the power of the value of p. Thus, if p is positive, the number is treated as though the decimal point appeared p positions to the right of its given position. If p is negative, the number is treated as though the decimal point appeared p positions to the left of its given position. The given position of the decimal point is that indicated either by an actual point, if it appears, or d, in the absence of an actual point.

Value in the input stream	Format specification	Resulting internal value
12345.67	F(10, 2, -2)	123.4567
12345.67	F(10, 2, $+2$)	1234567
1234567	F(10, 2, $+1$)	12345670

Internal value	Format specification	Resulting output
12345	F(6, 2, -2)	123.45
.12345	F(6, 2, $+3$)	123.45

	F format item
Subset language	The data item corresponding to the F format item must be in arithmetic coded form (FIXED BINARY, FIXED DECIMAL, FLOAT BINARY, FLOAT DECIMAL)
Full language	The above restriction does not apply to full language implementations

P('picture specification'). This format item is available only in full language compilers. The *'picture specification'* consists of any character allowed in the PICTURE declaration (see Chapter 3).

On input, the picture specification describes the form of the data item expected in the data stream and, in the case of a numeric picture item, how its arithmetic value is to be interpreted. Note that the picture specification should accurately describe the data in the input stream, including characters represented by editing characters. If the indicated character does not appear in the stream, the CONVERSION condition is raised.

On output, the value of the associated element in the data list is edited to the form specified by the picture specification before it is written into the data stream.

Input value	Format specification	Resulting internal value
bb15	P'ZZZ9'	0015
1234	P'99V99'	12̬34
AB123	P'AA999'	AB123
AB123	P'99999'	CONVERSION error

Internal value	Format specification	Resulting output
12.34	P'$$$$V.99'	$12.34
−12.34	P'S999V.99'	−012.34
2112.34	P'$$,$$$V.99CR'	$2, 112.34
−2112.34	P'$$,$$$V.99CR'	$2, 112.34CR
15	P'ZZZ9'	bb15
0	P'ZZZ9'	bbb0
12.34	P'****V.99'	**12.34

Simulating P Format in the Subset Language. The need for P format most often arises when it is desired to *edit* data (i.e., insert dollar sign, comma, CR symbol, etc.). In previous chapters, you have seen how to accomplish editing—typically, by assigning data to identifiers that contain PICTURE editing characters. For example:

```
DCL PRICE PIC'$$$,$$$V.99';
PRICE=1050.78;   /* PRICE=$1,050.78 */
```

In the subset language implementations of PL/I, we have a problem because it is not permitted to output (using edit-directed I/O) directly from a PICTURE that contains insertion characters (i.e., $, *, CR, DB, etc.). Thus, the following PUT EDIT (assuming the above DECLARE and assignment statements apply) would be invalid:

```
PUT EDIT(PRICE) (A(10));
```

└──────→ A format items apply only to data that has the CHARACTER attribute; in this example, even though PRICE appears in main storage in character format, the attribute of PRICE is PICTURE (do you see the subtle distinction?)

The following examples, however, do not violate the rule in the subset language that you may not output directly from a picture that contains insertion characters:

```
DCL A PIC'999V99' INIT(12.34);
DCL B PIC'XXXX' INIT('ABCD');
PUT EDIT(A,B)(F(6,2),A(5));
/* ON OUTPUT, A=b12.34 AND B=ABCDb */
```

There are two methods that may be used for printing from a PICTURE identifier with editing characters. The first method is perhaps the easiest to understand. A built-in function called CHAR is provided in PL/I. This function converts its argument to a character-string. For example:

```
DCL PRICE PIC'$$$,$$$V.99';
PRICE = 1050.78;
PUT EDIT(CHAR(PRICE))(COLUMN(40),A(10));
```

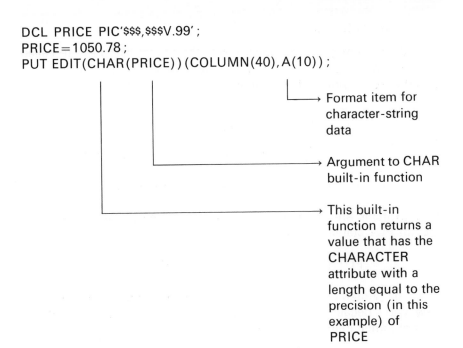

→ Format item for character-string data

→ Argument to CHAR built-in function

→ This built-in function returns a value that has the CHARACTER attribute with a length equal to the precision (in this example) of PRICE

The other method for simulating P format is to use overlay defining. This method is more efficient than the method of invoking the CHAR built-in function each time a PICTURE value is to be treated as a character-string. For example:

```
DCL PRICE PIC'$$$,$$$V.99';
DCL PR CHAR(10)DEFINED PRICE;
PRICE = 1050.78;  /* EDIT DATA */
PUT EDIT (PR) (COLUMN(40), A(10));
```

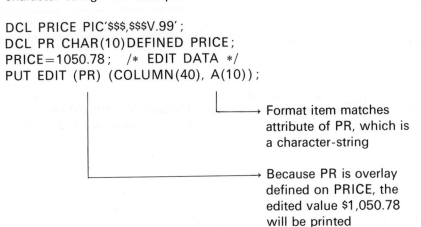

→ Format item matches attribute of PR, which is a character-string

→ Because PR is overlay defined on PRICE, the edited value $1,050.78 will be printed

Control Items

When control items appear inside the format list, they are called *control format items*; if they appear outside the format list, they are called *control options*. For example:

PUT SKIP EDIT(A,B) (SKIP(3),F(7,2));

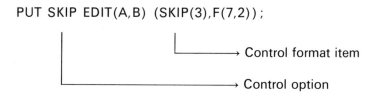

→ Control format item

→ Control option

Control items are performed in the order in which they appear in a GET or PUT statement. For example:

PUT PAGE EDIT(A,B)(F(5),PAGE,F(7,2));

A will be printed on a new page and B will be printed on the following new page because of the position in the format list of the PAGE control format item. In this example,

PUT PAGE EDIT (A,B)(F(5), F(7,2));

is equivalent to

PUT EDIT(A,B)(PAGE, F(5), F(7,2));

A control item has no effect unless it is encountered before the data list is exhausted. For example:

PUT EDIT(A) (F(8),SKIP);

→ This control item will be ignored, because the data list was satisfied by the format item F(8)

COLUMN(n). On input, this format item positions the input stream to the nth byte or card column of the record. On output, it positions the output stream to the nth byte in the record or the nth print position on the line printer. In the full language implementations, the abbreviation COL may be used in place of COLUMN.

LINE(n). Used for output only, this format item specifies that the next data item is to be printed on the nth line on a page of a PRINT file. LINE may be specified only for stream files that have the PRINT attribute. If the specified line has already been passed on the current page, or if the specified line is beyond the limits set by the PAGESIZE option of the OPEN statement (or by default), the ENDPAGE condition is raised. ENDPAGE is raised only once per page; consequently, printing can be continued beyond the specified PAGESIZE after the ENDPAGE condition has been raised the first time. If the response to the on-unit does not start a new page, the current line number may increase indefinitely.

It would not be logical to specify a line number that is negative or zero [i.e., LINE(−3) or LINE(0)]; however, if a negative or zero value is specified, PL/I will substitute LINE(1) for the illogical specification.

PAGE. According to the rules of the PL/I language, PAGE may only be specified for stream files that have the PRINT attribute. PAGE causes a skip to the first print line of the next page.

SKIP. On input, SKIP means to start or continue reading at the beginning of the next logical record. On output, its meaning is summarized below:

Format item	Action taken
SKIP(0)	Suppresses line feed
SKIP or SKIP(1)	Starts printing on the next line
SKIP (expression)	Causes "expression minus 1" lines to be left blank before printing on the next line; in subset language, a maximum of SKIP(3) may be specified

X(w). On input, w characters are ignored. On output, w blanks are inserted into the stream.

Remote Format Item

The R format item allows a FORMAT statement to replace this specification. For example:

PUT EDIT(A,B,C) (R(OUT1));

                          └──→ A label constant or an element label variable that has as its value the statement label of a FORMAT statement; the FORMAT statement includes a format list that is taken to replace the format item; the statement label may not be subscripted

OUT1 : FORMAT(PAGE,F(5,2),SKIP,2 F(8));

                    └──────────→ A FORMAT statement may not contain an R format item

If the GET or PUT statement is the single statement of an on-unit, e.g.,

ON ENDPAGE(PRINTR)
    PUT FILE(PRINTR)EDIT('HEADING') (PAGE,A);

then the input or output statement may not contain a remote format item.

A remote format item may be combined with other format items. For example:

      GET EDIT(A,B,C,D,E,F) (F(1),R(INP),A(7),R(INP));
INP : FORMAT(F(5),E(15,2));

In the above example, the data items and their corresponding format specifications are

A	F(1)
B	F(5)
C	E(15,2)
D	A(7)
E	F(5)
F	E(15,2)

The STRING Option

The STRING option may appear in a GET or PUT statement in place of the FILE option. For example, instead of

GET FILE (INPUT) EDIT (A,B,C) (F(5),F(6),F(7)) ;

the statement

GET STRING(DATA)EDIT (A,B,C) (F(5),F(6),F(7)) ;

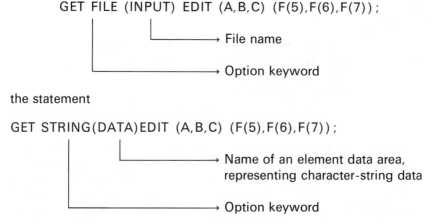

→ Name of an element data area, representing character-string data

→ Option keyword

may be specified. The STRING option causes internal data movement; it does not cause an I/O operation. It offers another method for effecting data movement, the assignment statement being the most common.

In addition, it offers a method for causing the conversion of character-type data to a coded arithmetic form; this feature is particularly useful in the subset language, as it provides a fairly straightforward method for converting character data to arithmetic form.

The following example illustrates a character-string-to-character-string data movement. Assume that NAME is a string of 36 characters and that FIRST, MIDDLE, and LAST are string variables:

```
GET STRING (NAME) EDIT
(FIRST, MIDDLE, LAST)
(A(15),A(1),A(20)) ;
```

This statement specifies that the first 15 characters of NAME are to be assigned to FIRST, the next character to MIDDLE, and the remaining 20 characters to LAST.

The PUT statement with the STRING option in the following example specifies the reverse operation:

```
PUT STRING (NAME) EDIT
(FIRST, MIDDLE, LAST)
(A(15), A(1), A(20) ;
```

This statement specifies that the values of FIRST, MIDDLE, and LAST are to be concatenated (in that order) and assigned to the string variable NAME.

In addition, the STRING option may be used to effect character-string-to-arithmetic or arithmetic-to-character-string conversion. For example:

```
DCL NAME CHAR(20), EMP# CHAR(7);
DCL HOURS FIXED(3,1), RATE(4,2);
DCL RECORD CHAR(80);
PUT STRING(RECORD) EDIT
    (NAME, EMP#, HOURS*RATE)
    (A(20), A(7), F(8));
```

This statement specifies that the character-string value of NAME is to be assigned to the first (leftmost) 20 character positions of the string named RECORD, and that the character-string value of EMP# is to be assigned to the next seven character positions of RECORD. The value of HOURS is then multiplied by the value of RATE, and the product is to be handled like F format output and assigned to the next eight character positions of RECORD.

Sometimes records of different formats appear in the same file. Each record, then, would carry with it an indication of its format in the form of a code. For example:

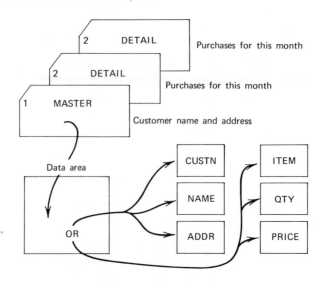

The STRING option facilitates manipulation of these differing card formats in the same file. For example:

```
DCL CARD CHAR(80) ;
GET EDIT(CARD)(A(80)) ;
IF   SUBSTR(CARD,1,1) = '1' THEN
     GET STRING(CARD)EDIT
     (CUSTN,NAME,ADDR)
     (X(1),A(6),X(3),2 A(20)) ;
IF   SUBSTR(CARD,1,1) = '2' THEN
     GET STRING(CARD)EDIT
     (ITEM, QTY, PRICE)
     (X(1),A(8),F(3),F(7,2)) ;
```

Note that print option format items (e.g., COLUMN, SKIP, etc.) may not be specified in the STRING option of a GET or PUT.

Conditions

There are a number of exceptional conditions that may occur during stream I/O; ENDFILE, ENDPAGE, CONVERSION, SIZE, TRANSMIT, and ERROR. Some of the conditions were introduced in Chapter 3. Here is additional information on three of these conditions.

The CONVERSION Condition. This on-unit is raised if any alphameric characters appear within a field of data that is to be a numeric field. For example, a blank is an alphameric character that will cause the CONVERSION condition to be raised if it is embedded within a numeric field. Thus, the data

input by the statement

```
GET EDIT(VALUE) (COLUMN(1),F(5)) ;
```

will cause the CONVERSION condition to be raised. However, a blank (but *not* any other alphameric character) may appear before a numeric value, in which case the leading blank is interpreted to be a leading zero on input. For example, given the data field

and the edit-directed statement

GET EDIT(VALUE) (COLUMN(1),F(5)) ;

will cause the identifier VALUE to be set to 05798. If a blank follows a numeric field, e.g.,

it is ignored. Thus, if the above data field were input with the statement

GET EDIT(VALUE) (COLUMN(1),F(5)) ;

then VALUE would contain 5798. If the entire field is blank, it is interpreted as zero.

The SIZE Condition. This on-unit may be raised during output if the width specification for a FIXED BINARY or a FIXED DECIMAL number is not large enough to contain the total value. For example, if

VALUE = −123 ;

and it is output using the specification

PUT EDIT(VALUE) (F(3)) ;

the SIZE condition will be raised, providing it has been enabled. To print the above negative value, a minimum field width of four must be specified. According to the rules of the PL/I language, the results of the output field are *undefined*. In some compilers, the output field is filled with asterisks; in other compilers, high-order truncation occurs, and that value will be output; in still other compilers, blanks may appear. It varies with the compiler you are using.

The ENDPAGE Condition. The ENDPAGE condition is raised when a PUT statement results in an attempt to start a new line beyond the limit specified for PAGESIZE. This limit can be specified by the PAGESIZE option in an OPEN statement. If PAGESIZE has not been specified, an installation-defined system limit applies. The attempt to exceed the limit may be made during data transmission (including any format items specified in the PUT statement) by the LINE option, or by the SKIP option. ENDPAGE is raised only once per page. When the ENDPAGE condition is raised, the standard system action is to skip to a new page and continue executing.

PL/I maintains a *current line counter* which is incremented by 1 each time a new line is printed. When this line counter exceeds the maximum number specified by the PAGESIZE option (or the default) the ENDPAGE condition is raised. Thus, at this point, the current line counter is one greater than the maximum page size value.

After ENDPAGE has been raised, a new page may be started in either of the following ways:

1. Execution of a PAGE option or a PAGE format item.
2. Execution of a LINE option or a LINE format item specifying a line number less than or equal to the current line number.

When either of these occurs, a new page is started in the same way that it is when a PAGE option is executed; i.e., ENDPAGE is not raised and the current line is set to 1. If a new page is not started, the current line number may increase indefinitely. When ENDPAGE is raised, it is possible to continue writing on the same page.

In the full language, a begin block may follow the ENDPAGE keyword. For example:

        ON ENDPAGE (PRINTR) BEGIN;
                        .
                        .
                        .
                    END;

This begin block is treated like a subroutine in that the block is entered when the ENDPAGE condition is raised and returns to the place in the program immediately following the point of interruption. In the subset language, only a GO TO or a null statement may follow the on-unit. Thus, if a group of statements is to be logically performed, it will be necessary for the program to handle the branching "into" and "out of" the group of statements. In Figure 5.1, an 80/80 list program is coded two ways: one for full language implementations and the other for subset implementations. Studying the subset program solution first will give you an appreciation of some of the features of the full language PL/I capabilities (e.g., default files, begin blocks, LINESIZE). The 80/80 list program copies a card file onto a line printer, printing 45 lines per page. Notice how the statement,

SIGNAL ENDPAGE(PRINTR) ;

was used to cause a heading to be printed on the *first* page of output. The loop operation consists of reading cards and printing on the printer. In this program, the ENDPAGE condition will be detected *before* the PUT FILE statement is executed for the forty-sixth time. In the HDNG routine in the subset example, it is necessary—after printing the heading and incrementing the page counter—to return control to

```
          /* 80/80 LIST FOR FULL LANGUAGE IMPLEMENTATIONS */
       1  LIST:     PROC OPTIONS(MAIN);
       2            DCL DATA CHAR(80);
F      3            DCL PAGE_NO FIXED(2)INIT(1);
U      4            ON ENDPAGE(SYSPRINT) BEGIN;
L      5               PUT EDIT('80/80 LISTING -- PAGE',PAGE_NO)
L                           (PAGE,COL(25),A,F(3));
       6               PUT SKIP(2);
L      7               PAGE_NO = PAGE_NO + 1;
A      8               END;
N      9            OPEN FILE(SYSPRINT) PAGESIZE(45) LINESIZE(80);
G     10            ON ENDFILE(SYSIN) GO TO EOJ;
U     11            SIGNAL ENDPAGE(SYSPRINT);
A     12  LOOP:     GET EDIT(DATA)(A(80));
G     13            PUT EDIT(DATA)(A);
E     14            GO TO LOOP;
      15  EOJ:      END;

          /* 80/80 LIST FOR SUBSET IMPLEMENTATIONS        */
       1  LIST:     PROC OPTIONS(MAIN);
       2            DCL PAGENO FIXED(2) INIT(1);
S      3            DCL CARDIN FILE INPUT STREAM ENV(F(80)MEDIUM(SYSIPT,2540));
U      4            DCL PRINTR FILE OUTPUT STREAM PRINT
B                        ENV(F(81)MEDIUM(SYSLST,1403));
S      5            DCL DATA CHAR(80);
E      6            ON ENDFILE(CARDIN) GO TO EOJ;
T      7            ON ENDPAGE(PRINTR) GO TO HDNG;
       8            OPEN FILE(PRINTR) PAGESIZE(45);
L      9            SIGNAL ENDPAGE(PRINTR);
A     10  LOOP:     GET FILE(CARDIN)EDIT(DATA)(COLUMN(1),A(80));
N     11  PUT:      PUT FILE(PRINTR)EDIT(DATA)(SKIP,A);
G     12            GO TO LOOP;
U     13  HDNG:     PUT FILE(PRINTR)EDIT('80/80 LISTING -- PAGE ',PAGENO)
A                        (PAGE,COLUMN(25),A,F(3));
G     14            PUT FILE(PRINTR)SKIP(2);
E     15            PAGENO = PAGENO + 1;
      16            GO TO PUT;
      17  EOJ:      END;
```

FIGURE 5.1   An 80/80 list program coded two ways.

the PUT statement so that the forty-sixth detail line is printed. Then, of course, the program continues until ENDFILE condition occurs.

A Built-in Function for PRINT files

There is a built-in function that is available in the full language called LINENO, which finds the current line number for a file having the PRINT attribute and returns that number to the point of invocation. For example:

I = LINENO(PRINTR);

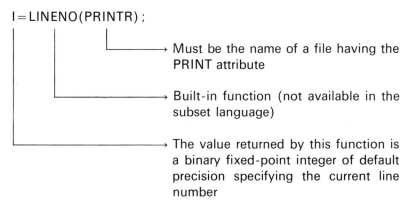

→ Must be the name of a file having the PRINT attribute

→ Built-in function (not available in the subset language)

→ The value returned by this function is a binary fixed-point integer of default precision specifying the current line number

	LINENO built-in function
Subset language	No
Full language	Yes

Data-Directed I/O

This form of stream I/O is available in the full language implementations only. Data-directed I/O gives the programmer the flexibility of transmitting self-identifying data. This means that each data item in the input stream is in the form of an assignment statement that specifies both the value and the variable to which it is to be assigned. For example, the input stream could contain the following assignment statements:

$$A = 12.3, \quad B = 57, \quad C = \text{'ABCDEF'}, \quad D = \text{'1110'B};$$

Notice that the values are in the form of valid constants. Statements are separated by a comma and/or one or more blanks; a semicolon ends each group of items to be accessed by a single GET statement. Here is an example of a data-directed statement for the input of the above items:

GET DATA (A, B, C, D);

All names in the stream should appear in the data list; however, the order of the names need not be the same. Thus, the GET statement could have been written

GET DATA (C, B, A, D);

Also, the data list may include names that do not appear in the stream; e.g.,

GET DATA (A, B, C, D, E);

In this case, E is not altered by the input operation. However, it is an error if there is an identifier in the input stream but not in the data list. For example, C and D are in the input stream but not in the data list:

GET DATA (A, B);   /* ERROR */

This error raises the NAME condition, which may be handled in your program in the same manner as with other on-units; for example:

ON NAME (SYSIN) BEGIN;

.
.
.

END;

It is possible (and not contradictory) to omit entirely data list names in the GET statement; for example:

GET DATA;

In this case, the names in the stream may be any names known at the point of the GET statement. A data list in the GET statement is optional, because the semicolon determines the number of items to be obtained from the stream. If the data list includes the name of an array, subscripted references to that array may appear in the stream although subscripted names cannot appear in the data list. The entire array need not appear in the stream; only those elements that actually appear in the stream will be assigned. For example, the following could be coded:

```
DCL TABLE(50) FIXED(5, 2);
GET DATA(TABLE);
```

where the input stream consists of the following assignment statements:

```
TABLE(3) = 7.95, TABLE(4) = 8.43, TABLE(7) = 50;
```

Although the data list has only the name of the array, the associated input stream may contain values for individual elements of the array. In this case, three elements are assigned; the remainder of the array is unchanged. The maximum number of elements permitted in a list for data-directed input is 320.

On output, each data item is placed in the stream in the form of assignment statements separated by blanks. The last item output by each PUT statement is followed by a semicolon. Leading zeros of arithmetic data are suppressed. The character representation of each value reflects the attributes of the variable, except for fixed-point binary and floating-point binary data which appear as values expressed in fixed-point decimal notation.

For PRINT files, data items are automatically aligned on preset tab positions described for list-directed I/O. For example, given the statements,

```
DCL (A, B) FIXED INIT(0);
DCL C FIXED BIN INIT(175);
PUT DATA (A, B, C);
```

output would be to the default file SYSPRINT in the format

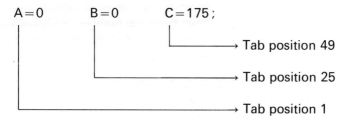

The data list may be an element, array, or structure variable, or a repetitive specification involving any of these elements or further repetitive specifications. Subscripted names can appear. In addition, any of the printer spacing options described for list-directed I/O may be specified for data-directed I/O; e.g.,

> PUT PAGE DATA (A, B, C);
> PUT SKIP(3) DATA (A, B, C);
> PUT LINE(5) DATA (A, B, C);

It is also possible to specify

> PUT DATA;

in which case, all variables known to the program at the point of the PUT statement will be output. This feature is a powerful debugging tool.

There is a built-in function that may be particularly useful to you when using the form of GET DATA where no data list is specified. The function is called COUNT; it determines the number of data items that were transmitted during the last GET or PUT operation on a given file and returns the result to the point of invocation. For example:

> DCL INPUT FILE INPUT STREAM;
> GET FILE (INPUT) DATA;
> I = COUNT (INPUT);

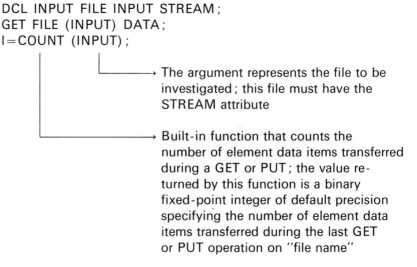

The argument represents the file to be investigated; this file must have the STREAM attribute

Built-in function that counts the number of element data items transferred during a GET or PUT; the value returned by this function is a binary fixed-point integer of default precision specifying the number of element data items transferred during the last GET or PUT operation on "file name"

If a begin block or another procedure is entered during a GET or PUT operation, and within that begin block or procedure a GET or PUT is executed for the same file, the value of COUNT is reset for the new operation and is not restored when the original GET or PUT is continued.

The DISPLAY/REPLY Statement

The DISPLAY statement is available in all compilers; it facilitates machine operation communication with the PL/I program in execution. The basic format is

DISPLAY('SAMPLE MESSAGE GOES HERE');

> └──────→ Must be a CHARACTER variable or constant or expression

The REPLY option allows the operator to reply. For example:

DCL RESPONSE CHAR(3);
DISPLAY('IS EXCEPTION TAPE MOUNTED? TYPE YES OR NO')
    REPLY(RESPONSE);

In the above example, when the operator enters either the words YES or NO, his reply will be placed into the program variable, RESPONSE. Execution of the program is suspended until the operator has entered his reply. For this reason, it is not good practice to overuse this type of man/machine communication in a program. Typically, if the DISPLAY statement is used, it is used without the REPLY option.

	Maximum number of characters allowed	
	DISPLAY	REPLY
Subset language	80	255
Full language	72	72

In the full language, there is an option that may be specified in the DISPLAY/REPLY statement that will, to a degree, override the suspension of program execution until the operator has entered his reply. For example:

```
DCL RESPONSE (CHAR(3);
DISPLAY('IS EXCEPTION TAPE MOUNTED? TYPE YES OR NO')
    REPLY (RESPONSE) EVENT (E1);
    .
    .
    .
WAIT(E1);
```

⎿ ⟶ Program execution will not continue unless the "event" is complete; the "event" in this case would be complete when the operator signals "end-of-message input"

The variable E1 is contextually declared (by its appearance in an EVENT option) to have the EVENT attribute. Conversion between event variables and other data types is not possible.

	EVENT attribute
Subset Language	No
Full Language	Yes

It is possible to enter messages through the console typewriter in either capital or lowercase letters. It would provide an added flexibility to our program if we allowed either capital or lowercase messages to be entered. It is easy to incorporate this flexibility into our program once it is understood how capital and lowercase letters are represented in bytes of main storage. Appendix D shows a *complete* list of the binary representations of alphameric data; a few samples are shown below:

```
A = 11000001   B = 11000010   J = 11010001   Z = 11101001
a = 10000001   b = 10000010   j = 10010001   z = 10101001
```

From an observation of these bit patterns, you can see that the only difference between capital letter and its lowercase counterpart is that the second bit from the left is a "1" for capital letters and a "0" for lowercase letters. Thus, if the operator enters a lowercase message into our program via the console typewriter, all our program has to do to convert lowercase to capital letters is to insert a 1 bit into the second position of each byte.

The OR (|) operation in PL/I is generally used to test logical relationships of data. For example:

IF A = B | C = D THEN GO TO CALC;

└─────────────→ If either A = B *or* C = D, the statement following the THEN is executed

However, when the OR operation is applied to bit-strings, it has a different function, for it may be used to *modify* bit-string data according to the following rules:

$$1 \mid 1 \rightarrow 1$$
$$1 \mid 0 \rightarrow 1$$
$$0 \mid 1 \rightarrow 1$$
$$0 \mid 0 \rightarrow 0$$

Thus, if we had the first operand shown below ORed to the second operand, which is sometimes referred to as a *mask*, note the results:

```
       10000001     → Bit code for "a"
OR     01000000     → Mask
       _____

       11000001     → Result from an OR operation
```

The result, of course, is the bit code for capital letter "A." Suppose the same *mask* is to be ORed to the bit code for a capital "A":

```
       11000001     → Bit code for "A"
OR     01000000     → Mask
       _____

       11000001     → Result from an OR operation
```

Here, the result is still a capital "A." Thus, ORing the mask shown above to either capital or lowercase letters will always yield capital letters.

For our program to change lowercase to capital letters, it will be necessary to manipulate the alphameric character as a bit-string for purposes of merging in the 1 bit in the second position of the byte. To do this, we need to invoke the UNSPEC built-in function. This function allows you to *unspecify* any data item so that it will be treated as a bit-string. Its general format is

UNSPEC (K) ;

        └──────→ The argument that is to be treated as a bit-string without conversion taking place

      Assume it is desired to have the operator enter a maximum eight-character reply. For example :

DCL RESPONSE CHAR(8) ;
DISPLAY ('ENTER CANCEL OR CONTINUE') REPLY (RESPONSE) ;

The following statement would be written to change lowercase into capital letters. Of course, if capital letters already appear in RESPONSE, the ORing of a bit in the second position of each byte will not alter that bit pattern.

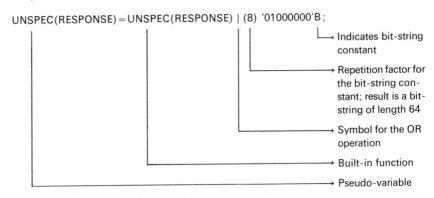

UNSPEC(RESPONSE) = UNSPEC(RESPONSE) | (8) '01000000'B ;

        └→ Indicates bit-string constant

        → Repetition factor for the bit-string constant; result is a bit-string of length 64

        → Symbol for the OR operation

        → Built-in function

        → Pseudo-variable

      Pseudo-variables are built-in functions that may be specified as receiving fields. It was necessary to use UNSPEC on the right side of the assignment symbol to treat RESPONSE as a bit-string for purposes of ORing a 1 bit into the second position from the left in each of the characters in the message. UNSPEC on the left of the assignment symbol causes the receiving field, which is RESPONSE, to be treated as a bit-string with no conversion. This is necessary in order to assign the bit-string on the right of the assignment symbol to the variable on the left. Had the variable on the left been a character-string, e.g.,

RESPONSE = UNSPEC(RESPONSE) | (8) '01000000'B ;

        → Bit-string expression

        → Character-string

then the rules for PL/I assignments of different data types specify that the bit-string is to be *converted* to characters. Recall that RESPONSE has previously been declared as CHAR(8). Because of the use of the UNSPEC function, RESPONSE now becomes a bit-string; on the right side of the assignment symbol in the above example, it has a bit length of 64 (8 characters = 64 bits). For example:

$$11000011 \ldots\ldots\ldots\ldots 11000101 \text{ (64 bits)}$$

In converting bits to characters, only the leftmost eight bits of this string would be converted to characters when placed into a variable with the CHARACTER attribute. Thus, if the above bit-string were assigned to RESPONSE (without the use of the UNSPEC pseudo-variable), which has the CHARACTER attribute, RESPONSE would contain the characters 11000011 rather than the word 'CONTINUE'.

Case Study: Sales History Bar Charts

This case study illustrates a number of facilities of edit-directed I/O—repetitive specifications, SKIP, COLUMN, remote format items (R), nested format lists, and the STRING option of the GET statement. The program is designed to produce a series of bar charts graphically depicting the net sales of each item produced by the Acme Company in the last three years. The net sales figure for each item is to be displayed by month as a horizontal bar across the page, with each print position representing 1000 units sold. Figure 5.2 illustrates this bar chart.

Data for this graph is punched into cards. There are two types of cards:

1. *Order records:* These contain the gross orders for a particular item for each month of a given year. The letter O punched in column 79 identifies this card type.
2. *Cancellation records:* These contain cancellations for the corresponding item. The letter C punched in column 79 identifies this card type.

(It is more common to use digits 1 and 2 to represent card types and it is more common to punch these values in column 80—rather than 79—however, the formats described above were selected to illustrate some edit-directed I/O coding techniques.)

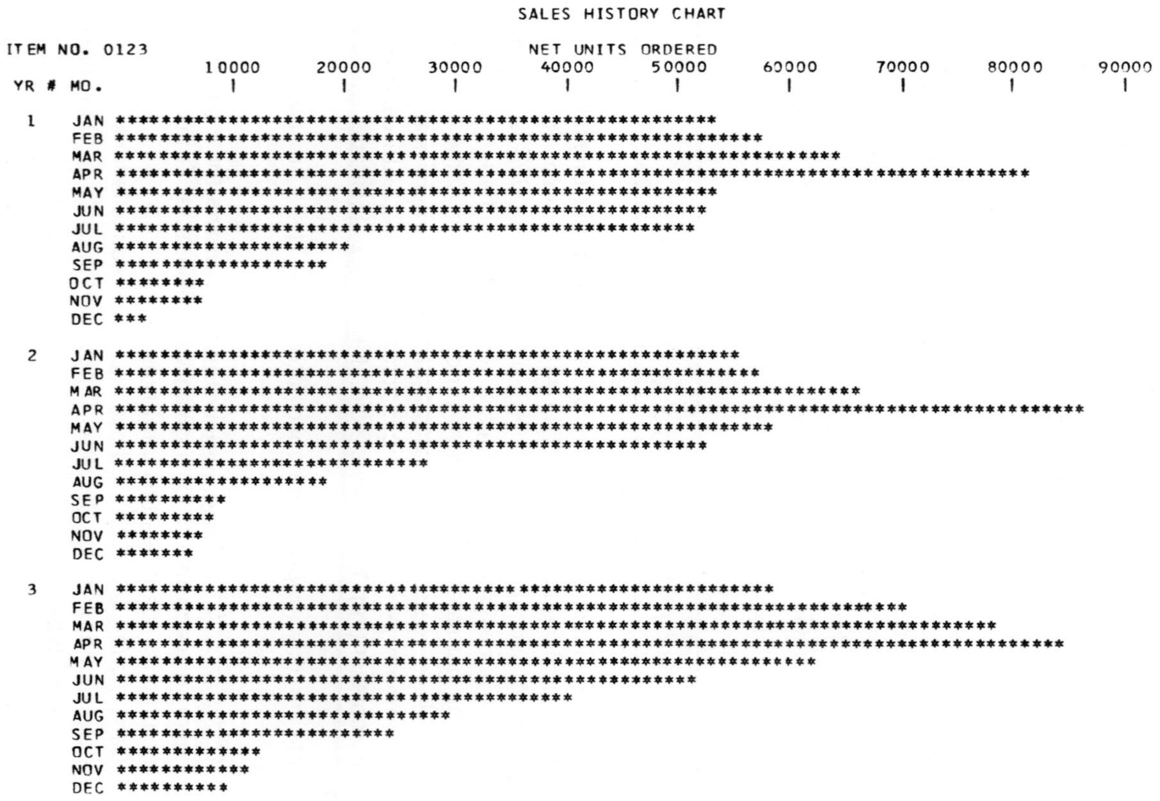

FIGURE 5.2   Bar chart for Acme sales history.

Figure 5.3 shows the record layout for each type of input card. Notice that an item number is punched in positions one through four of each card; however, four columns are then used to represent quantity ordered for each of twelve months, whereas, only three columns are used for quantity cancelled for each of twelve months. Typically, identical field widths (four columns, in this case) for quantity ordered and quantity cancelled would be selected in the design of these record layouts. However, having two different card formats in the input stream will illustrate the need for using the GET STRING option of edit-directed I/O. The net sales figures per month are determined by subtracting quantity cancelled from quantity ordered.

Because it is desired to compare sales history for the past three years, there will be up to six records per item—one order record and one cancellation record for each of three years. Assume the cards are arranged in ascending sequence by item number; thus, all six records for a given item will be together in the file. However, the six records may be in any order. The cards could also have been sorted into sequence by year within item number. This has been intentionally avoided for this case study to illustrate how the same thing may be accomplished by program logic. For this reason, columns 77 and 78 of the input cards have been used to designate the year to which the order or cancellation record applies (e.g., year "1" or year "2" or year "3"). A flowchart is given in Figure 5.4, and the source program is shown in Figure 5.5. The following is an explanation of the PL/I statements in the program.

Statement 2. The variables declared in this statement include ITEM and NEXT_ITEM. These two variables are used for comparing the item numbers read from cards. The current item number is assigned to NEXT_ITEM on input. This is then compared with the old item number found in ITEM. As long as ITEM and NEXT_ITEM are equal, we know that we are still reading orders and cancellations for the same item. When NEXT_ITEM is not equal to (i.e., greater than) ITEM, we may then assume that all records have been read for a particular item and that it is time to print the bar chart for that item. Later in the program NEXT_ITEM will be assigned to ITEM, now becoming the old item number against which the next item number will be compared.

Statement 4. A remote format statement is specified because there are two GET statements (7 and 12) that each require the same format list.

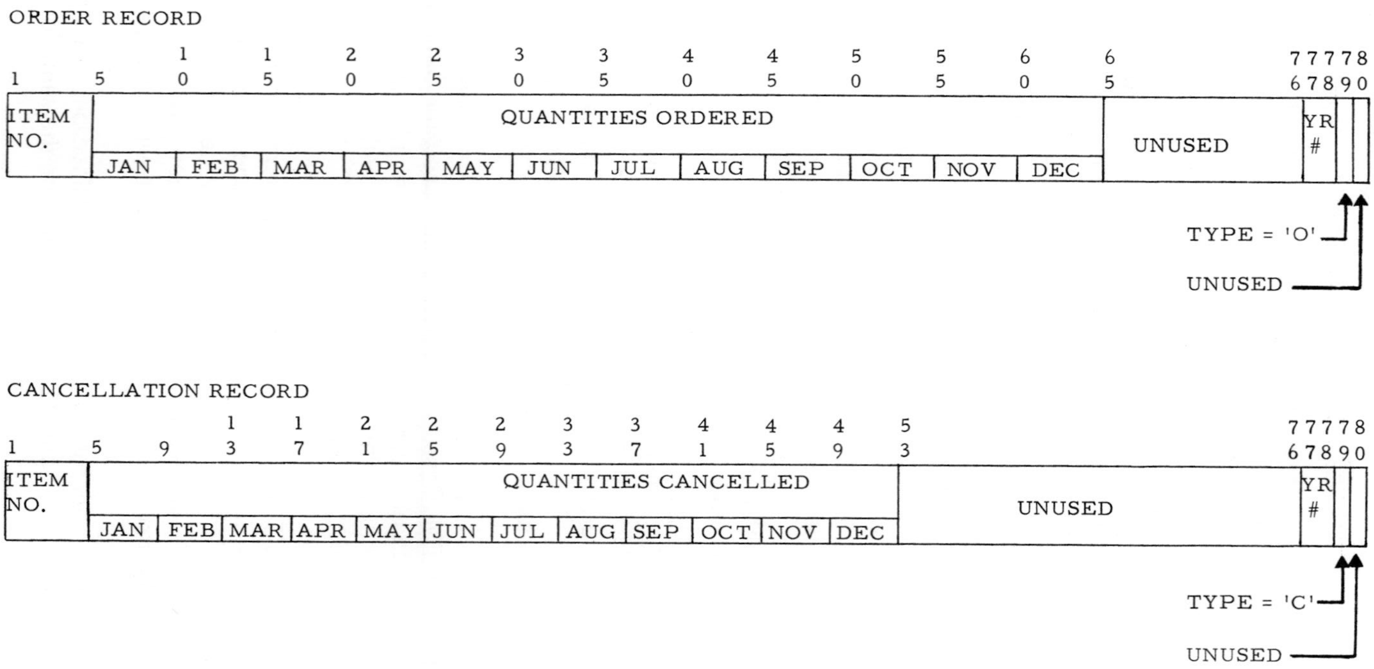

ORDER RECORD

```
 1      1     1     2     2     3     3     4     4     5     5     6     6      77778
 5      0     5     0     5     0     5     0     5     0     5     0     5      67890
┌──────┬─────────────────────────────────────────────────────────────┬──────┬──────┐
│ITEM  │                  QUANTITIES ORDERED                          │      │ YR # │
│NO.   ├───┬───┬───┬───┬───┬───┬───┬───┬───┬───┬───┬───┤    UNUSED    │      │      │
│      │JAN│FEB│MAR│APR│MAY│JUN│JUL│AUG│SEP│OCT│NOV│DEC│              │      │      │
└──────┴───┴───┴───┴───┴───┴───┴───┴───┴───┴───┴───┴───┴──────────────┴──────┴──────┘
```

TYPE = 'O'

UNUSED

CANCELLATION RECORD

```
 1      1     1     2     2     3     3     4     4     5                77778
 5      0     5     0     5     0     5     0     5     3                67890
┌──────┬─────────────────────────────────────────────┬───────────────┬──────┐
│ITEM  │          QUANTITIES CANCELLED                │               │ YR # │
│NO.   ├───┬───┬───┬───┬───┬───┬───┬───┬───┬───┬───┬───┤    UNUSED     │      │
│      │JAN│FEB│MAR│APR│MAY│JUN│JUL│AUG│SEP│OCT│NOV│DEC│               │      │
└──────┴───┴───┴───┴───┴───┴───┴───┴───┴───┴───┴───┴───┴───────────────┴──────┘
```

TYPE = 'C'

UNUSED

FIGURE 5.3 Layout of order and cancellation records.

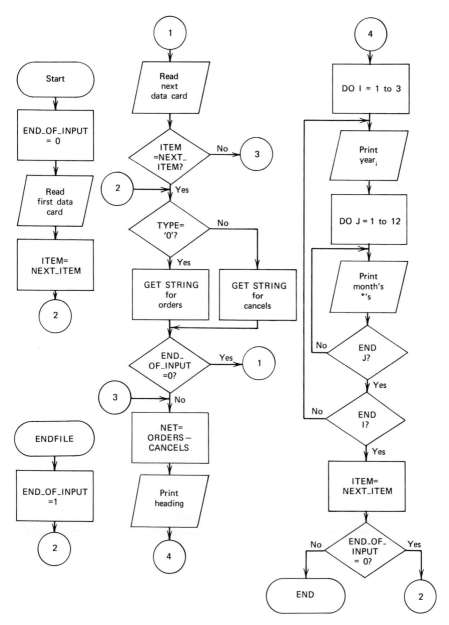

FIGURE 5.4   Flowchart for sales history chart.

292 PL/I Programming

```
1    SALES:   PROC OPTIONS(MAIN);
2             DCL (ITEM,NEXT_ITEM) CHAR(4), TYPE CHAR(1),
                  YR FIXED BINARY(15), FIELDS CHAR(60),
                  END_OF_INPUT BIT (1) INIT ('0'B),
                  (ORDERS,CANCELS,NET)(12,3) DECIMAL FIXED(5) INIT((36)0),
                  MO(12) CHAR(3) INIT('JAN','FEB','MAR','APR','MAY','JUN',
                                      'JUL','AUG','SEP','OCT','NOV','DEC');
3             DCL LIMIT FIXED;
4    REM:     FORMAT(A(4),A(60),X(12),F(2),A(1));
5             DCL CARDN FILE INPUT STREAM ENV(F(80)MEDIUM(SYSIPT,2540));
6             ON ENDFILE(CARDN) GO TO END;
7             GET FILE(CARDN) EDIT(NEXT_ITEM,FIELDS,YR,TYPE)(R(REM));
8             ITEM = NEXT_ITEM;
9             GO TO SKIP;
10   END:     END_OF_INPUT = '1'B;
11            GO TO SKIP;
12   AGAIN:   GET FILE(CARDN) EDIT(NEXT_ITEM,FIELDS,YR,TYPE)(SKIP,R(REM));
13            IF ITEM = NEXT_ITEM THEN DO;
14   SKIP:        IF TYPE = '0'
                  THEN GET STRING(FIELDS) EDIT
                       ((ORDERS(I,YR) DO I = 1 TO 12))(F(5));
15                ELSE GET STRING(FIELDS) EDIT
                       ((CANCELS(I,YR) DO I = 1 TO 12))(F(4));
16            IF ¬END_OF_INPUT THEN GO TO AGAIN;
17            END;
18            NET = ORDERS - CANCELS;
19            PUT EDIT('SALES HISTORY CHART')(PAGE,CCLUMN(47),A)
                  ('ITEM NO. ',ITEM,'NET UNITS ORDERED')
                  (SKIP(2), 2 A,COLUMN(48),A)
                  ((I,'0000' DO I = 1 TO 10))
                  (SKIP,COLUMN(18), 10 (F(2),A,X(4)))
                  ('YR # MO.',('|' DO I = 1 TO 10))
                  (SKIP,COLUMN(2),A,COLUMN(21), 10 A(10));
20            DO I = 1 TO 3;
21            PUT EDIT(I)(SKIP(2),F(3));
22            DO J = 1 TO 12;
23                PUT EDIT (MO(J))(COLUMN(7),A(4));
24                LIMIT = NET(J,I)/1000 + .5;
25                DO K = 1 TO LIMIT;
26                PUT EDIT('*')(A);
27                END;
28            END;
29            END;
30            ITEM = NEXT_ITEM;
31            IF ¬END_OF_INPUT THEN GO TO SKIP;
32   FINI:    END SALES;
```

FIGURE 5.5 Case study program: sales history bar charts.

Statement 5. The card input file is defined. Because STREAM is the default attribute for files, it need not be specified in this file declaration.

Statement 6. This statement specifies the action to be taken when the ENDFILE condition is raised.

Statement 7. This statement reads the first card. There are no control format items [e.g., SKIP, COLUMN(1), etc.] in this statement because reading will automatically begin with column one of the first input card.

Statement 12. This statement reads all subsequent cards. Notice that a control format item now had to be specified because of the nature of stream input. The SKIP causes reading to begin with the first column of the next record. Had SKIP been omitted from this GET statement, a logical error would result. This is because the card type is punched in column 79. Thus, column 79 is the last column "taken" from the input stream. Without the SKIP, input for the second GET statement would begin in column 80. Clearly, this is an error, because data for each new record read with a GET begin in column one.

Statements 14 and 15. These statements test for card type and, based on whether each is an ORDERS or CANCELS card, the appropriate GET STRING statement is executed. This option is useful in this case study because there are two different card formats in the input stream. All cards are read with the GET EDIT statement and then reread (i.e., reformatted) with the GET STRING option once the card type has been determined.

Statement 16. This statement tests the end-of-input-file indicator set by the program when the ENDFILE condition is raised. Because END_OF_INPUT has the BIT attribute, it may be tested with the NOT (¬) bit-string operator. Recall that a '1'B is a "true" condition. By testing for the "not true" condition, this IF statement is specifying that, "should END_OF_INPUT contain a '0'B, then go to AGAIN; else go to the next statement.

Statement 18. Array arithmetic is used to determine net sales.

Statement 19. Several heading lines are output with this one PUT EDIT statement. Notice this variation of the PUT statement; a data list is followed by a format list, and then another data list is followed by another format list, and so on.

Statement 20. This DO statement establishes the loop operation to output three years of sales history.

Statement 21. This PUT statement causes the year designation (e.g., 1, 2, or 3) to be printed.

Statement 22. This DO statement establishes the loop operation for the printing of the horizontal bar representing sales figures for each month of each year.

Statement 23. The alphameric designation for a given month is output.

Statement 24.   The net sales figures are scaled down because each asterisk on printer output represents 1000 units sold. Thus, if 60,000 units were sold, then 60 asterisks will appear on one line. The number of asterisks for output is assigned to the variable called LIMIT. The +.5 is used to round off the sales figure to the nearest dollar.

Statements 25–27.   These statements cause one line of asterisks to be printed. The number of asterisks printed is determined by the value in LIMIT.

Statements 28–29.   These end the other DO's specified.

Statement 30.   The current item number (NEXT_ITEM) is saved in the variable (ITEM) that held the old item number.

Statement 31.   This statement tests the END_OF_INPUT indicator. By testing for the "not true" condition, this IF statement is specifying that, "should END_OF_INPUT contain a '0'B, then go to SKIP; else go to FINI."

SUMMARY

Edit-Directed I/O Eliminates Some Disadvantages of List-Directed I/O: It provides for considerable efficiency in the representation of input data and offers a great deal of flexibility in the formatting of output data. The general form of edit-directed I/O statements is

GET EDIT(data items)(format items);

The following points should be remembered when using the GET EDIT and PUT EDIT statements:

1. All data list items have corresponding format items. There are three types:
   (a) *Data format items:*   These are items describing the format of the external data.
   (b) *Control format items:*   These are items describing page control, line control, and spacing operations.
   (c) *Remote format item:*   This item indicates that one or more data format items and/or control format items are located remotely from the GET or PUT EDIT statement in a FORMAT statement.

2. If there are more format items than data items, the extra format items are ignored.
3. The data list item need not have the same width specification as the corresponding format item.
4. Input continues until all data items have been read.
5. Data list items may be names of data aggregates. It is possible to specify the name of an array as a list item. If an array is specified without a DO-group to qualify the order and/or number of items to be processed, the rightmost subscript varies most rapidly from the lowest to the highest value. If a repetitive specification (DO) appears in a data list, the repetitive specification must have a separate set of parentheses. In addition, the data list must have one set of parentheses.
6. Input data items may be pseudo-variables. Pseudo-variables are built-in functions that may be designated as receiving fields; hence, pseudo-variables may appear on the left side of an equal sign or in a GET statement. Typically, the SUBSTR pseudo-variable might be used.
7. Output data items may be built-in functions.
8. Output data items may be PL/I constants. This capability is particularly useful for the printing of literal data (i.e., character-string constants that constitute headings).
9. Data items may consist of element expressions. Operational expressions may be specified in the data list of a PUT statement. Such expressions may not involve arrays in the subset languages.
10. There are subset language restrictions. The data list item must match the format item with respect to data type. Arithmetic data items may have only the format items F (fixed-point) or E (floating-point) specified. CHARACTER data may only be described by the A format item and BIT data by the B format item.

Format Items: Figure 5.6 lists the various format items and the language levels in which they are available. In full language implementations, it is permissible to specify expressions for w, d, and s. In the subset languages, only constants may be specified. If a SIZE error occurs during output controlled by an F or E format item, the results of the output field are undefined.

Simulating P Format: The need for using P format most often arises when it is desired to edit data. In the subset language, it is not permitted to output from a PICTURE that contains insertion characters. There are two methods that may be used for printing from a PICTURE identifier with editing characters:

1. Invoke the CHAR built-in function in the data list.
2. Use overlay defining of a character-string on a PICTURE.

	Subset	Full
Data formats		
A(w)	X	X
B(w)	X	X
C(real format item[, real format item])	N/A	X
E(w, d[, s])	X	X
F(w[, d[, p]])	X	X
P'picture specification'	N/A	X
Control formats		
COLUMN(n)	X	X
LINE(n)	X	X
PAGE	X	X
SKIP[(n)]	X	X
X(w)	X	X
Remote format		
R(label)	X	X

FIGURE 5.6   Format items available in subset and full language implementations. [Key: N/A, not available; [ ], optional; w, width; d, decimals (fractional digits); s, significant digits; p, decimal point scale factor; n, number.]

The STRING Option: This option may appear in a GET or PUT statement in place of the FILE option. For example:

GET STRING(DATA)EDIT(X,Y,Z) (B(5),2 F(9,2));

The STRING option causes internal data movement. In the subset language implementations, it may be used to convert character data to coded arithmetic data, which is just about the only way this data conversion may be effected. (Of course, in full language implementations, the conversion of character data to coded arithmetic data may be accomplished through the assignment statement.) The STRING option also facilitates manipulation of differing record formats in the same file.

Data-Directed I/O: This form of stream I/O is available in full language implementations. Data-directed I/O provides the facility for transmitting self-identifying data. Each data item in the input stream is in the form of an assignment statement that specifies both the value and the variable to which it is to be assigned. The input values are in the form of valid PL/I constants. Input items are separated by a comma and/or one or more blanks; a semicolon ends each group of items to be accessed by a single GET statement. The NAME condition will be raised if the input stream contains an identifier not in the data list unless the data list is omitted entirely.

The DISPLAY/REPLY Statement: The DISPLAY statement facilitates machine operator communication while the PL/I program is in execution. The REPLY option allows the operator to respond to a displayed message.

Summary of I/O Statements: The types of stream I/O available in the subset and full languages are shown in the table.

	Data-directed	List-directed	Edit-directed
Subset language	No	Yes	Yes
Full language	Yes	Yes	Yes

CHECKPOINT QUESTIONS

1. Under what circumstances would the remote format item be useful?
2. Given the following statement, what is the format item that applies to C?

   GET EDIT(A,B,C) (F(4),F(5)) ;
3. Is this valid?

   GET EDIT(A,B) (SKIP,F(2),F(3),F(4)) ;
4. How many lines will be skipped, given the following statement:

   PUT EDIT(A,B,C) (SKIP(1),3 F(5,2),SKIP(2)) ;
5. (True or False) An external data item need not agree in precision with the corresponding internal data item.
6. What are the control format items that may be specified to effect printed output so as to begin on a new line?
7. Which of the following may be specified for files that do not have the PRINT attribute?

   (a) PAGE

   (b) SKIP

   (c) COLUMN

   (d) LINE

8. (True or False) Stream files must be *explicitly* opened.

9. What does the PAGESIZE option in the OPEN statement accomplish?

10. Given the input value 12.34 and the statements,

    DCL VALUE FIXED(4);
    GET EDIT(VALUE) (F(5,2));

    what will VALUE contain?

11. Given the following statements, what value will be output?

    DCL VALUE FIXED(5,3);
    VALUE=12.347;
    PUT EDIT(VALUE) (F(5,2));

12. Given the following statements,

    DCL AMT FIXED(7,2);
    AMT=1024.57;

    write the PUT EDIT statement to accomplish output in this form:

    $1,024.57

    (Note: If you are using the subset language, the programming solution must also include another DECLARE and assignment statement.)

13. Write the PUT EDIT statement to print the following heading; be sure to include the underline.

    WEEKLY ACTIVITY REPORT

14. Distinguish between *control format item* and *control option*.

    PUT PAGE EDIT(A,B,C) (SKIP(3),F(5));

15. (True or False) A FORMAT statement may contain an R format item.

16. Given the following statement, what will A, B, and C contain after input where the input stream is this? (Note: b = blank.)

    b123bbbbbb12b34
    GET EDIT(A,B,C) (F(5));

17. Is this statement valid? Why or why not?

    DISPLAY('DATA ERROR ON TIME CARD FOR EMP. NO.',EMP#);

18. What alphabetic character will be contained in X after the following statements are executed? (Consider yourself "superbright" if you get the correct answer.)

    DCL X CHAR(1) INIT('A');
    UNSPEC(X)=UNSPEC(X) | '0011'B;

19. Given the following internal data and corresponding format specifications, how will the output appear? Show any blanks which may be output with the data. Indicate any errors that may occur (e.g., SIZE condition or asterisk * in output).

	Internal data	Format specification
(a)	123	F(3)
(b)	123	F(3,0)
(c)	123.45	F(6,2)
(d)	123.45	F(6,1)
(e)	123.45	F(5,2)
(f)	ABC12	A(8)
(g)	ABC12	A
(h)	ABC12	A(3)
(i)	110010	B(8)
(j)	110010	B(2)
(k)	123	F(2)
(l)	12.345	F(5,2)

20. Write the format item(s) which would be used in a GET EDIT statement to input the following values to the corresponding variable; 'b' is a blank column; '$\wedge$' is an assumed decimal point. What value will each variable have after the GET statement is executed?

	Variable name	Data value in input stream
(a)	FIELD_1 DECIMAL FIXED (7,2)	00123$\wedge$675
(b)	FIELD_2 DECIMAL FIXED (6,0)	0017.38
(c)	FIELD_3 BINARY FIXED (31)	bbbbbbb
(d)	FIELD_4 BINARY FIXED (15)	bbbbb23.7
(e)	FIELD_5 DECIMAL FLOAT (6)	123.4E1
(f)	FIELD_6 CHAR (5)	ABCDEF
(g)	FIELD_7 DECIMAL FLOAT (6)	00123$\wedge$88
(h)	FIELD_8 DECIMAL FLOAT (6)	008.310bb
(i)	FIELD_9 DECIMAL FIXED (7,4)	bb.16753
(j)	FIELD_10 BINARY FLOAT (21)	27$\wedge$58A
(k)	FIELD_11 DECIMAL FIXED (7,2)	03$\wedge$461E2
(l)	FIELD_12 BIT (5)	1011101
(m)	FIELD_13 BIT (7)	0064
(n)	FIELD_14 CHAR (11)	03$\wedge$461E2
(o)	FIELD_15 CHAR (3)	bbbbb
(p)	FIELD_16 DECIMAL FIXED (3)	10175$\wedge$00
(q)	FIELD_17 BINARY FIXED (31)	A2345$\wedge$67
(r)	FIELD_18 BINARY FLOAT (21)	276.4201
(s)	FIELD_19 DECIMAL FIXED (7,7)	384.747
(t)	FIELD_20 BIT (16)	32767

21. Given the following fields and their associated values, describe the output values if they were placed on file SYSPRINT with a PUT EDIT command using the associated format items. Show any blanks which may be output with the data. (This question is only applicable to full language implementations.)

Field	Value	Format item
(a) FIELD_1 FIXED BINARY (31)	1239	F(7,2)
		E(14,5,7)
		A(14)
		P'9999V99'
		P'999V.99T'
(b) FIELD_2 FIXED DECIMAL (7,3)	123.456	F(7,2)
		F(10,3)
		E(13,5,6)
		E(13,5,7)
		P'ZZZV99.999'
(c) FIELD_3 DECIMAL FLOAT (6)	−463.72E+5	F(15,2)
		E(14,7,8)
		F(7,2)
		P'(10)ZV.(4)9T'
		A(20)
(d) FIELD_4 CHAR(4)	'ABC5'	A(5)
		A(2)
		P'XXXX'
		P'AAA9'

TERMS TO STUDY

control format item
data-directed I/O
data list
edit-directed I/O
external data

format list
remote format item
STRINGRANGE
UNSPEC

PRACTICE PROBLEMS

1. Sequencing a PL/I Source Deck

Problem Definition: Write a program that will place a five-character alphabetic program name in columns 73–77 and a sequence number in columns 78–80 of a PL/I source program deck.

Purpose of the Problem: To gain experience in declaring stream files for the card reader and card punch; to use the DISPLAY/REPLY statement.

Input: If a console typewriter is available, use the DISPLAY/REPLY statement for the purpose of entering the parameters (program name and beginning sequence number). Otherwise, punch these parameters into a card and make this card the first data your program reads. For the source program input, use any debugged PL/I program you have on hand.

Processing: The beginning sequence number must be incremented. If you wish, one additional input parameter may be an incremental value. If this is specified, then the sequence number is to be incremented by the value of that parameter.

Output: Punch a copy of each source card read (including, of course, the added program name and sequence number), and list each card on the line printer.

Note: For subset language programmers using the DISPLAY/REPLY statement, it will be necessary to use the DEFINED attribute for the sequence number. For example:

```
DISPLAY('ENTER 3-DIGIT SEQUENCE NUMBER')
    REPLY (SEQ);
```
└────────────→ Must have the CHARACTER attribute

```
DCL SEQ CHAR(3) DEF SQ;
DCL SQ PIC'999';
```
└────────────→ The decimal picture field is required so that
                arithmetic may be performed on the sequence
                number; e.g., $SQ = SQ + 1$;

The above restriction applies to the subset languages where it is not permitted to do arithmetic on data having the CHARACTER attribute. In the full language implementations, arithmetic of CHARACTER data is permitted.

2. Printing Address Labels—"One-Up"

Problem Definition: Assume an organization has punched its members' names and addresses into cards. Write a program to prepare labels for attachment to envelopes.

Purpose of the Problem: To gain practice using the GET STRING and edit-directed I/O statements.

Input: There are two card formats in the input stream, as shown. Make up your own data for this problem, but be sure to specify at least 12 names and addresses.

Processing: Check that the member's number in columns 2–7 is the same for card 1 and card 2. Also, check column 1 to ensure that the cards are in the

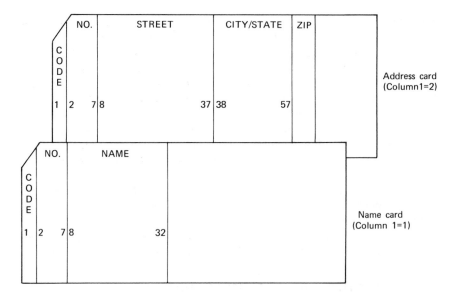

sequence 1, 2, 1, 2, 1, 2, etc. If the cards are out of sequence or the member's number in card 1 does not match that in card 2, print an error message and terminate the job.

Output: Print each member's name and address in the format shown.

```
NAME
STREET ADDRESS
CITY, STATE
                    ZIP
```

Skip three lines between labels.

3. Printing Address Labels—"Three-Up"

This is a variation of the previous problem. Instead of printing one label at a time, print three labels at a time, side-by-side. See Figure 5.7 for the desired layout. Inasmuch as less than three labels may be printed for the last group, you will probably find it advisable to maintain a program counter that tests for the number of labels available to be printed in each subsequent group of output.

4. Computation of an Interest Table

Problem Statement: Compute the value of loans in amounts of $1,000, $2,000, $3,000, and so on up to $10,000, at interest rates varying from 1% to 10% incrementing by 1%, for periods ranging from 1 year to 10 years in yearly increments. Interest is to be compounded annually. Keep all values in a three-dimensional array. Print results when all calculations are complete.

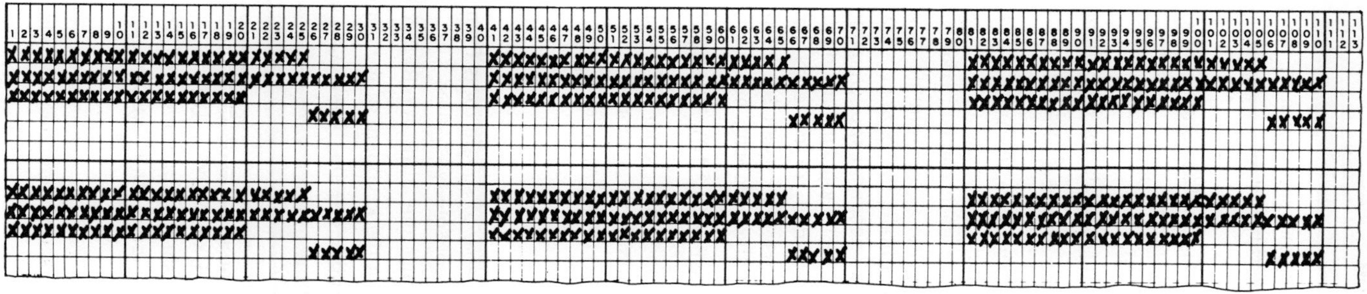

FIGURE 5.7 Desired printer layout for address labels—"three-up."

Purpose of the Problem: To gain experience in the use of arrays and their manipulation with DO-loops and indexes.

No Input Is Required

Desired Printer Layout: See Figure 5.8. Start a new page with each table; thus, there will be ten pages of output.

Sample Output: See Figure 5.9.

Suggestion: Use the following formula for computing the value of the loan.

$$V = P * (1 + I) ** N$$

where V is the value of the loan, P is the principal amount, I is the interest rate (1% = 0.01), N is the number of years the loan is outstanding.

After your program has set each element of the three-dimensional array to the values of the loan using the above formula, it will be necessary to *half adjust* the results in order to obtain the correct answers. This half adjust is necessary because the formula specifies exponentiation. When exponentiation is specified, the calculation will be handled in floating-point. Normally, floating-point operations should be avoided for currency calculations, because the result is an approximation rather than exact to the penny. However, in this problem, declare your array in the following manner:

$$DCL\ VALUE(10,10,10)\ FIXED(9,2)\ ;$$

Compute the interest table, and then, after all calculations are completed, include the following array arithmetic statement:

$$VALUE = VALUE + .5\ ;$$

Now, results will be accurate.

5. Table of Square Roots

Problem Statement: Print a table of square roots from N_1 to N_2, where these parameters are input from the console typewriter.

Purpose of the Problem: To use the DISPLAY/REPLY facility of PL/I.

Input: Data is to be read from the keyboard of the console typewriter.

Output: Print the square roots on the typewriter. Include an appropriate heading.

6. Analytic Geometry

Problem Statement: Write a program to describe the loci of the homogeneous equations of the form $AX^2 + BXY + CY^2 + DX + EY + F = 0$, where the coefficients A, B, C, D, E, and F are rational numbers. (The degenerate cases and those in which the locus is a point or imaginary are not considered in this program.)

Purpose of the Problem: To code a mathematics-oriented program where use of the remote format list saves redundant coding.

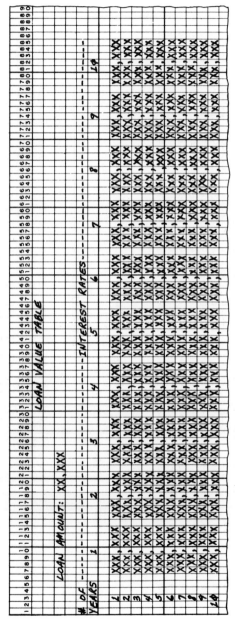

FIGURE 5.8   Desired printer layout for Problem 4.

LOAN VALUE TABLE

LOAN AMOUNT: 1,000

# OF YEARS	------------------------------INTEREST RATES------------------------------									
	1	2	3	4	5	6	7	8	9	10
1	1,010	1,020	1,030	1,040	1,050	1,060	1,070	1,080	1,090	1,100
2	1,020	1,040	1,061	1,082	1,102	1,124	1,145	1,166	1,188	1,210
3	1,030	1,061	1,093	1,125	1,158	1,191	1,225	1,260	1,295	1,331
4	1,041	1,082	1,126	1,170	1,216	1,262	1,311	1,360	1,412	1,464
5	1,051	1,104	1,159	1,217	1,276	1,338	1,403	1,469	1,539	1,611
6	1,062	1,126	1,194	1,265	1,340	1,419	1,501	1,587	1,677	1,772
7	1,072	1,149	1,230	1,316	1,407	1,504	1,606	1,714	1,828	1,949
8	1,083	1,172	1,267	1,369	1,477	1,594	1,718	1,851	1,993	2,144
9	1,094	1,195	1,305	1,423	1,551	1,689	1,838	1,999	2,172	2,358
10	1,105	1,219	1,344	1,480	1,629	1,791	1,967	2,159	2,367	2,594

LOAN VALUE TABLE

LOAN AMOUNT: 10,000

# OF YEARS	------------------------------INTEREST RATES------------------------------									
	1	2	3	4	5	6	7	8	9	10
1	10,100	10,200	10,300	10,400	10,500	10,600	10,700	10,800	10,900	11,000
2	10,201	10,404	10,609	10,816	11,025	11,236	11,449	11,664	11,881	12,100
3	10,303	10,612	10,927	11,249	11,576	11,910	12,250	12,597	12,950	13,310
4	10,406	10,824	11,255	11,699	12,155	12,625	13,108	13,605	14,116	14,641
5	10,510	11,041	11,593	12,167	12,763	13,382	14,026	14,693	15,386	16,105
6	10,615	11,262	11,941	12,653	13,401	14,185	15,007	15,869	16,771	17,716
7	10,721	11,487	12,299	13,159	14,071	15,036	16,058	17,138	18,280	19,487
8	10,829	11,717	12,668	13,686	14,775	15,938	17,182	18,509	19,926	21,436
9	10,937	11,951	13,048	14,233	15,513	16,895	18,385	19,990	21,719	23,579
10	11,046	12,190	13,439	14,802	16,289	17,908	19,672	21,589	23,674	25,937

FIGURE 5.9   Sample output for Problem 4. (Note: only first and last tables are shown.)

```
.0000X**2=     .0000XY=     .0000Y**2+    1.0000X=    2.0000Y+    3.0000=0    NOT QUAD
2.0000X**2=   5.0000XY=    3.0000Y**2+    1.0000X=    2.0000Y+    3.0000=0    HYPERBOLA
2.0000X**2=   4.0000XY=    2.0000Y**2+    1.0000X=    2.0000Y+    3.0000=0    PARABOLA
3.0000X**2=    .0000XY=    3.0000Y**2+    1.0000X=    2.0000Y+    3.0000=0    CIRCLE
2.0000X**2=    .0000XY=    3.0000Y**2+    1.0000X=    2.0000Y+    3.0000=0    ELLIPSE
2.0000X**2=    .0000XY=    4.0000Y**2+    1.0000X=    2.0000Y+    3.0000=0    ELLIPSE
```

FIGURE 5.10 Sample output for Problem 6.

Input: Each input record contains the values A, B, C, D, E, and F in that order. Suggested test data might be:

A	B	C	D	E
0	0	1	2	3
5	3	1	2	3
4	2	1	2	3
0	3	1	2	3
0	3	1	2	3
0	4	1	2	3

Output: Print the equation of the curve and its name: "Parabola," "Hyperbola," "Ellipse," "Circle," or "Not Quad." Sample output is shown in Figure 5.10.

Flowchart: See Figure 5.11.

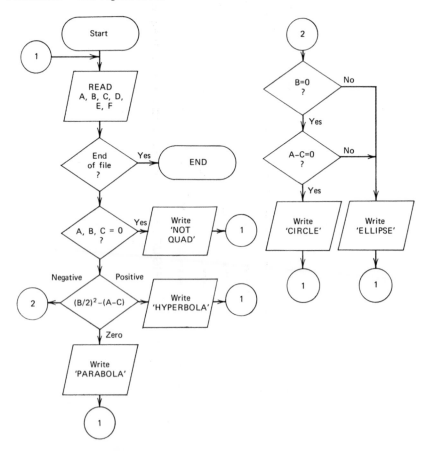

FIGURE 5.11   Flowchart for Problem 6.

chapter 6

Built-in

Functions

A *function* produces a new value for each value or set of values it receives. Graphically, the function of producing square roots can be pictured as follows:

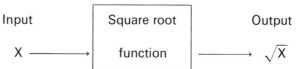

Input | Square root function | Output
X ⟶ | | ⟶ $\sqrt{X}$

Some functions require more than one input value in order to produce an output value. The motion of an airplane can be described by a complicated function requiring basically four input values:

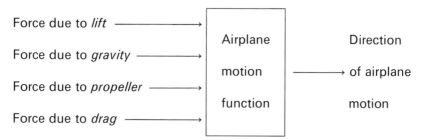

Force due to *lift* ⟶
Force due to *gravity* ⟶
Force due to *propeller* ⟶
Force due to *drag* ⟶

Airplane motion function ⟶ Direction of airplane motion

Functions, regardless of the number of input values, which are called *arguments*, always produce a single value. A *built-in function* is a function that is supplied as a part of the PL/I language. Functions for which there are general uses are provided as a feature of the PL/I language. Built-in functions are given the attribute BUILTIN.

We invoke a PL/I function by using its name. For example, SQRT is the name of the PL/I built-in function that performs the action of computing square roots. Arguments (the values to be input to a function) are specified by a value or a list of the argument values separated by commas and enclosed in parentheses following the function name.

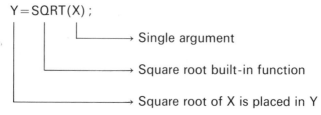

Y = SQRT(X);

⟶ Single argument
⟶ Square root built-in function
⟶ Square root of X is placed in Y

310

A reference to a PL/I built-in function will cause that function to be performed on the argument values, resulting in the function value. The value *returned by* the function logically replaces the function reference in any expression. Most functions require arguments. However, some functions return a value which is independent of everything else in the program and, hence, do not require an argument. An example is the DATE function. When we use a function requiring no arguments, it is a good idea (indeed, it is required with some compilers) to explicitly declare that name as having the attribute BUILTIN. For example:

DECLARE DATE BUILTIN;

The reason for this is that, because a reference to such a function looks so much like a variable, it is preferred to state explicitly that we always want DATE to stand for the value returned by the BUILTIN function.

Function references (i.e., the values returned by functions) can be used as arguments to other functions. For example:

Y=SUBSTR(DATE,1,2);

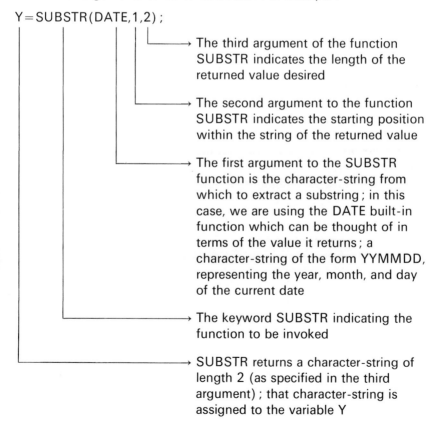

→ The third argument of the function SUBSTR indicates the length of the returned value desired

→ The second argument to the function SUBSTR indicates the starting position within the string of the returned value

→ The first argument to the SUBSTR function is the character-string from which to extract a substring; in this case, we are using the DATE built-in function which can be thought of in terms of the value it returns; a character-string of the form YYMMDD, representing the year, month, and day of the current date

→ The keyword SUBSTR indicating the function to be invoked

→ SUBSTR returns a character-string of length 2 (as specified in the third argument); that character-string is assigned to the variable Y

Note that for almost all functions the position of the arguments is critical. For example, the first argument to the function SUBSTR must be the name of the string from which we want to extract a substring. SUBSTR(DATE,1,2) is *not* equivalent to SUBSTR(1,2,DATE).

Pseudo-variables

A pseudo-variable is a built-in function name appearing to the left of the assignment symbol as if it were a variable. Several built-in function names may be used as pseudo-variables. For example, SUBSTR, when used as a built-in function, returns a string which is a substring of the first argument to the function. When used as a function, SUBSTR represents the value of the substring. SUBSTR may also be used as a pseudo-variable if, for example, we want to *store* a value in the substring of another string. In other words, we want to designate a part of a string as the *receiving field* in an assignment statement. For example:

```
DECLARE D CHAR(14)INIT('DATE: 03/14/77');
        /*CHANGE MONTH 03 TO MONTH 12 */
SUBSTR (D,7,2)='12';
```

By using SUBSTR in this manner, we designated a substring of the variable D to be the receiving field of an assignment statement. SUBSTR is not a function when we use it in this way; it is called a *pseudo-variable*.

The PL/I built-in functions that can be used as pseudo-variables are SUBSTR, UNSPEC, STRING, ONCHAR, and ONSOURCE. Pseudo-variables allow us to use the definition of the function to designate *target* variables specified by the function rules.

Built-in functions fall into the following categories:

> Arithmetic
> Mathematical
> String handling
> Array manipulation (covered in Chapter 4)
> Miscellaneous

Arithmetic Built-in Functions

These functions facilitate the manipulation of arithmetic data. They are useful in testing a value, determining a given relationship of several values, or modifying a given value.

The arguments of arithmetic built-in functions may be expressions or array names. If an argument is an array name, the value returned by the built-in function is an array of the same dimension and bounds as the argument, the function having been performed once for each element of the array.

All values returned by the arithmetic built-in functions are in coded arithmetic form (e.g., FIXED DECIMAL, FIXED BINARY, FLOAT DECIMAL, FLOAT BINARY). The arguments of these functions should also be in that form; otherwise, before the function is invoked, they will be converted to coded arithmetic form according to the rules of data conversion.†

ABS

This function finds the absolute value of a given quantity. The argument may be a single value, an expression, or an array.

Examples

```
DCL (X,Y) DECIMAL FIXED(5,3);
X = 3.714;
Y = ABS(X);        /* Y NOW IS +3.714 */
X = -7.479;
Y = ABS(X);        /* Y NOW IS +7.479 */
DCL A(3) FIXED INIT(-3,5,-7);
A = ABS(A);        /* A(1) NOW IS +3
                      A(2) STILL IS +5
                      A(3) NOW IS +7  */
```

CEIL

This function finds the *smallest* integer that is greater than or equal to a given value. For example, if the argument is 7.4, the ceiling of that value would be 8.

Examples

```
DCL (X,Y) FIXED DECIMAL(3,2);
X = 3.32;
Y = CEIL(X);       /* Y NOW IS 4.00   */
X = 6.00;
Y = CEIL(X);       /* Y NOW IS 6.00   */
X = -3.32;
Y = CEIL(X);       /* Y NOW IS -3.00  */
```

†See Appendix C for data conversion rules.

FLOOR

This function is the opposite of the CEIL function. FLOOR finds the *largest* integer that does not exceed a given value. For example, if the argument is 7.4, the *floor* of that value would be 7.

Examples

```
DCL (X,Y) FIXED(3,2);
X = 3.32;
Y = FLOOR(X);    /* Y NOW IS 3.00    */
X = -3.32;
Y = FLOOR(X);    /* Y NOW IS -4.00   */
X = 5.00;
Y = FLOOR(X);    /* Y NOW IS 5.00    */
```

MIN

This function finds the smallest value from a given set of two or more arguments. The arguments may be single values or expressions, but they may not be arrays.

Examples

```
DCL (W,X,Y,Z) FIXED DECIMAL(7,2);
X = 127.4;
Y = 32.84;
Z = -6.24;
W = MIN(X,Y,Z); /* W NOW IS -6.24   */
DCL (A,B,C) FIXED;
A = 2;
B = 5;
C = MIN(A,B);    /* C NOW IS 2       */
C = MIN(A*-2,B);:/* C NOW IS -4      */
```

If the arguments are of mixed characteristics, they will be converted to the highest characteristic according to the rules for data conversion. Any sequence of arguments is allowed. The returned value from MIN is in the form of the highest characteristic of all the arguments that were specified. For example :

```
DCL A FIXED DECIMAL INIT(5) ;
DCL B FLOAT DECIMAL INIT(4) ;
DCL C FIXED BINARY ;
C = MIN(A,B) ;
```

⟶ This argument is converted to FLOAT DECIMAL (the highest characteristic) and then compared with B

⟶ Result returned will be 4 in the form FLOAT DECIMAL (again, the highest characteristic)

⟶ Results will be converted to FIXED BINARY, the attributes declared for C

MAX

The opposite of MIN, this function finds the largest value from a set of two or more arguments. The arguments may be single values or expressions, but may not be array names. At least two arguments must be specified. If the arguments are of mixed characteristics, they will be converted to the highest characteristic according to the rules for data conversion. Arguments may be listed in any sequence.

Examples

```
DCL (W,X,Y,Z) DECIMAL FIXED(7,2);
X = 424.23;
Y = -3117.74;
Z = 1007.98;
W = MAX(X,Y,Z); /* W NOW IS 1007.98 */
DCL (A,B,C,D) FIXED;
A = 2;
B = 5;
C = -47;
D = MAX(12*A,B,C); /* D NOW IS 24   */
```

ROUND

This function rounds a given value at a specified digit and pads spare digit positions with zeros. For example, if the argument is 8.77

and it is desired to round to the first fractional digit, the result would be 8.80. There are two arguments to this function:

ROUND(m,n)

→ Second argument

→ First argument

First Argument. This is the value to be rounded. It must be a coded arithmetic or decimal picture data item. It may be an element expression or array name representing the value (or values, in the case of an array). If the value to be rounded is negative, its *absolute* value is rounded, but its sign remains unchanged.

Second Argument

1. *Subset language:* This must be a decimal integer constant specifying the fractional digit position to the right of the decimal point at which the first argument is to be rounded. For example:

```
DCL PRIN FIXED DECIMAL(6,4);
PRIN = 24.8693;
PRIN = ROUND(PRIN,2); /* PRIN NOW IS 24.8700 */
```

2. *Full language:* The constant specifying the digit at which the argument is to be rounded may be unsigned or signed. The second argument, which is called "n," specifies the digit at which the value is to be rounded. If n is positive, rounding occurs at the nth digit to the right of the decimal (or binary) point in the first argument; if n is zero, rounding occurs at the first digit to the left of the decimal (or binary) point in the first argument; if n is negative, rounding occurs at the (nth + 1) digit to the left of the decimal (or binary) point in the first argument. For example:

```
DCL (X,Y) DECIMAL FIXED (7,4);
X = 123.7261;
Y = ROUND(X,3); /* Y NOW IS 123.7260 */
Y = ROUND(X,2); /* Y NOW IS 123.7300 */
Y = ROUND(X,1); /* Y NOW IS 123.7000 */
Y = ROUND(X,0); /* Y NOW IS 124.0000 */
X = -123.7261;
Y = ROUND(X,2); /* Y NOW IS -123.7300 */
Y = ROUND(X,0); /* Y NOW IS -124.0000 */
Y = ROUND(X,-1);/* Y NOW IS -120.0000 */
X = 9.9999;
Y = ROUND(X,0); /* Y NOW IS 10.0000 */
```

Generally, only fixed-point values would be rounded using the ROUND function. Floating-point values, for practical purposes, would not be rounded using this function. (The usual practice is to round floating-point values just before output. Recall that this rounding is automatically done in stream output.) Should the first argument to the ROUND function be in floating-point format, the second argument of ROUND is ignored, and the rightmost bit in the internal floating-point representation of the expression's value is set to 1 if it is 0. If the rightmost bit is 1, it is left unchanged. If the first argument is a character- or bit-string, the returned value is the same string unmodified.

TRUNC

This function changes the fractional part of an argument to zero.

Examples

```
DCL (X,Y) DECIMAL FIXED(3,2);
X = 3.32;
Y = TRUNC(X);    /* Y NOW IS 3.00 */
X = -3.32;
Y = TRUNC(X);    /* Y NOW IS -3.00 */
```

MOD

This function extracts the remainder resulting from the division of the first argument by the second argument. The value returned is the smallest number that must be subtracted from the first argument in order to make it exactly divisible by the second argument. This means that if the first argument is positive, the returned value is the remainder resulting from a division of the first argument by the second. For example, MOD(29,6) returns the value 5:

$$6 \overline{)\ 29}$$
$$\begin{array}{r} 4 \\ 6 \overline{)\ 29} \\ 25 \\ \hline +5 \ \text{Remainder} \end{array}$$

If the first argument is negative, the returned value is the modular equivalent of this remainder. Thus, MOD(−29,6) will return the value 1:

$$\begin{array}{r} -\ 4 \\ 6 \overline{)\ -29} \\ -24 \\ \hline -\ 5 \ \text{Remainder} \end{array}$$

Then, 6 − 5 = +1

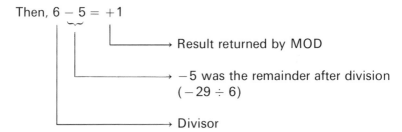

→ Result returned by MOD

→ −5 was the remainder after division (−29 ÷ 6)

→ Divisor

   When the MOD function is used with fixed arguments of different scale factors, the results may be truncated, in which case the SIZE condition will be raised (if enabled). If SIZE is disabled, no error message will be printed, and the result is undefined. If the value of the second argument is zero, the ZERODIVIDE condition is raised.

Examples

```
DCL (X,Y,Z) DECIMAL FIXED(5,0);
X = 34;
Y = 8;
Z = MOD(X,Y);    /* Z NOW IS 2 */
X = -34;
Z = MOD(X,Y);    /* Z NOW IS 6 */
Z = MOD(29,6);   /* Z = 5 */
Z = MOD(-29,6);  /* Z = 1 */
Y = 0;
Z = MOD(X,Y);    /* RAISES ZERODIVIDE
                    CONDITION       */
```

SIGN

This function determines whether a value is positive, negative, or zero. It returns a fixed-point binary value of default precision (15) according to the following rules:

1. If X is greater than 0, the returned value is 1.
2. If X is equal to zero, the returned value is 0.
3. If X is less than zero, the returned value is −1.

Examples

```
DCL X DECIMAL FIXED(4);
DCL I BINARY FIXED(15);
X = 123;
I = SIGN(X);     /* I NOW IS 1  */
X = -175;
I = SIGN(X);     /* I NOW IS -1 */
X = 0;
I = SIGN(X);     /* I NOW IS 0  */
```

Arithmetic Functions to Override Conversion Rules

The primary reason for the following arithmetic functions being provided in the PL/I language is to override the rules of the language concerning the conversion of data items with different bases, scales, and precisions. Consult Appendix C for details of the language specifications on data conversions.

ADD

This function finds the sum of two values. It is provided so that the programmer may control the precision of the result of an add operation. The function reference is described as follows:

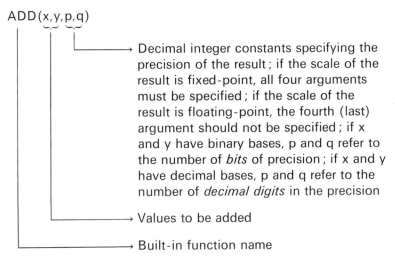

ADD(x,y,p,q)

→ Decimal integer constants specifying the precision of the result; if the scale of the result is fixed-point, all four arguments must be specified; if the scale of the result is floating-point, the fourth (last) argument should not be specified; if x and y have binary bases, p and q refer to the number of *bits* of precision; if x and y have decimal bases, p and q refer to the number of *decimal digits* in the precision

→ Values to be added

→ Built-in function name

Example

```
DCL A FIXED BINARY(31)   INIT(67108862);

DCL B FIXED DECIMAL(8,6) INIT(13.031875);

DCL C FIXED BINARY(31)   INIT (0);
C = A + B;               /* FIXEDOVERFLOW  */
C = ADD(A,B,31,0);       /* C = 67108875   */
```

In the above example, it is desired to add A and B together and assign the result to C, where

$$A = 67108862$$
$$B = 00000013.031875$$
$$C = 67108875.$$

Note that it is intended for the fractional part of the sum to be truncated when it is assigned to C. The declared precision of C is large enough to contain the sum. However, when A and B are added together, FIXED-OVERFLOW occurs. If you turn to Appendix C, Figure C.1, you will see a chart describing the results of addition and subtraction operations where the operands have differing bases and scales. The first operand in the above example has the attributes FIXED BINARY(31). The second operand has the attributes FIXED DECIMAL(8,6). In Figure C.1, the information in the first row, third column, pertains to the add operation with which we are concerned. That information is as follows:

BINARY FIXED(p,q)

$p = 1 + MAX(p_1 - q_1, r - s) + MAX(q_1, s)$

$q = MAX(q_1, s)$

where

$r = 1 + p_2 * 3.32$

$s = q_2 * 3.32$

The above equations describe the rules by which precision will be computed when unlike data types are to be operated on. So that you may see why FIXEDOVERFLOW occurred in the above example, the equations are worked out where the precisions of the variables A and B are substituted for the symbols p_1, q_1, p_2, q_2 :

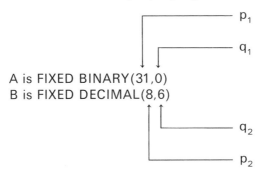

A is FIXED BINARY(31,0)
B is FIXED DECIMAL(8,6)

The resulting precision is called p and the resulting number of fractional digits is called q. Recall that when operating arithmetically on two operands, where one of the operands has the decimal base and the other the binary base, the decimal base data item is to be converted to the binary base before the arithmetic operation can be performed. First, we will compute r and s :

$r = 1 + P_2 * 3.32$ $s = q_2 * 3.32$

$\therefore r = 1 + 8 * 3.32$ $\therefore s = 6 * 3.32$

$\therefore r = 29.88$ $\therefore s = 19.92$

The constant 3.32 is used because it takes approximately 3.32 bits to represent a decimal digit in binary. Continuing with how the precision of differing data types is arrived at, we see that p (the precision) is calculated as follows :

$p = 1 + MAX(p_1 - q_1, r - s) + MAX(q_1, s)$

$\therefore p = 1 + MAX(31 - 0, 29.88 - 19.92) + MAX(0, 19.92)$

$\therefore p = 1 + 31 + 19.92$

$\therefore p = 51.92$

The precision needed in this case is computed as being 51.92 bits, which will be rounded to 52 bits. However, the precision of the result can never exceed implementation-defined maximums (e.g., 31 for FIXED BINARY, 15 for FIXED DECIMAL, 53 for FLOAT BINARY, 16 for FLOAT DECIMAL in S/360 and S/370). Because the precision in the above example (52 bits) clearly exceeds the maximum allowed for FIXED BINARY data, the FIXEDOVERFLOW condition will occur. The solution, then, is to use the ADD built-in function which allows the programmer to define the precision to be used throughout the addition operation (31,0).

To control the precision of two operands in a subtraction operation, simply reverse the sign of one of the arguments and invoke the ADD function. For example, if it is desired to subtract B from A, where both operands are positive, then the following statement could be coded to accomplish subtraction:

$$C = ADD(A, -B, 31, 0);$$

DIVIDE

This function divides the first argument by the second argument and returns the quotient. It is provided so the programmer may control the precision of the result of a divide operation. The arguments are described as follows:

DIVIDE(x, y, p, q)

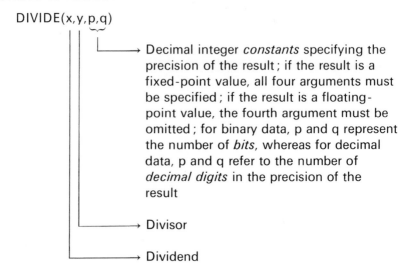

→ Decimal integer *constants* specifying the precision of the result; if the result is a fixed-point value, all four arguments must be specified; if the result is a floating-point value, the fourth argument must be omitted; for binary data, p and q represent the number of *bits*, whereas for decimal data, p and q refer to the number of *decimal digits* in the precision of the result

→ Divisor

→ Dividend

Example

```
DCL (X,Y) DECIMAL FIXED(7,0);
DCL Z DECIMAL FIXED(15,15);
X = 1;
Y = 3;
Z = X/Y;                  /* Z IS .333333330000000
                             BECAUSE OF PRECISION
                             OF INTERMEDIATE RESULT */
Z = DIVIDE(X,Y,15,15); /* Z IS .333333333333333  */
```

MULTIPLY

This function finds the product of two arguments. The precision of the results is determined by the third and fourth arguments. The arguments are described as follows:

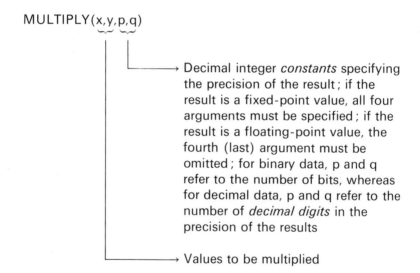

MULTIPLY(x,y,p,q)

→ Decimal integer *constants* specifying the precision of the result; if the result is a fixed-point value, all four arguments must be specified; if the result is a floating-point value, the fourth (last) argument must be omitted; for binary data, p and q refer to the number of bits, whereas for decimal data, p and q refer to the number of *decimal digits* in the precision of the results

→ Values to be multiplied

Example

```
DCL (X,Y,Z) DECIMAL FIXED(10,9);
X = 1.0;
Y = 1.0;
Z = X * Y;        /* FIXEDOVERFLOW CONDITION
                     RAISED BECAUSE OF PRECISION
                     OF INTERMEDIATE RESULT        */
Z = MULTIPLY(X,Y,10,9); /* Z NOW IS 1.000000000 */
```

BINARY

This function converts a decimal value to the binary base:

BINARY(x,p,q)

→ Decimal integer *constants* specifying the precision of the binary result; the arguments p and q refer to the number of *binary digits* desired in the precision; the precision of a fixed-point result is (p,q); the precision of a floating-point result is (p); if both p and q are omitted, the precision of the result is determined according to the rules given for base conversion; for floating-point arguments, q must be omitted

→ Represents the decimal value to be converted to binary base

Example

```
DCL X FIXED DECIMAL(1,1);
DCL I FIXED BINARY(8,8);
X = .1;
I = X;       /* I HAS A VALUE OF .0625 BECAUSE
                OF BASE CONVERSION RULES         */
I = BINARY(X,8,8); /* I NOW IS .09765625         */
             /* NOTE: I CAN NEVER BE EXACTLY .1 */
```

DECIMAL

This function converts a binary value to the decimal base:

DECIMAL (i,p,q)

→ Decimal integer *constants* specifying the precision of the decimal result; the precision of a fixed-point result is (p,q); the precision of a floating-point result is (p); if both p and q are omitted, the precision of the result is determined according to the rules given for base conversion; for floating-point arguments, q must be omitted

→ Represents the binary value to be converted to a decimal base

Example

```
DCL I FIXED BINARY(15);
DCL X FIXED DECIMAL(3,1);
I = 1;
X = I * .1; /* X IS NOW 0.00 BECAUSE OF
                PRECISION OF INTERMEDIATE RESULT  */
X = DECIMAL(I,3,1) * .1; /* X IS NOW 00.1          */
```

FIXED

This function converts a floating-point value to the fixed-point scale:

FIXED(x,p,q)

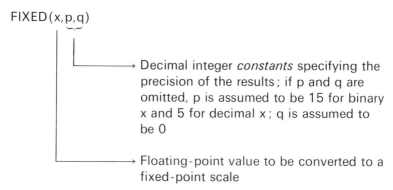

→ Decimal integer *constants* specifying the precision of the results; if p and q are omitted, p is assumed to be 15 for binary x and 5 for decimal x; q is assumed to be 0

→ Floating-point value to be converted to a fixed-point scale

Example

```
DCL X FLOAT DECIMAL(6);
DCL SUBRT ENTRY;
/*'SUBRT'EXPECTS A FIXED(7,2) ARGUMENT */
/* HENCE'FIXED'MUST BE INVOKED TO CAUSE
   THE NECESSARY DATA CONVERSION        */
CALL SUBRT(FIXED(X,7,2));
```

FLOAT

This function converts a fixed-point value to a floating-point scale:

FLOAT (i,p)

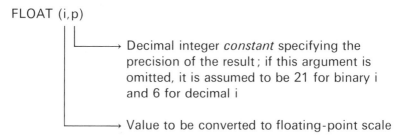

→ Decimal integer *constant* specifying the precision of the result; if this argument is omitted, it is assumed to be 21 for binary i and 6 for decimal i

→ Value to be converted to floating-point scale

Example

```
DCL I FIXED BINARY(15);
DCL SUBRT ENTRY;
/* 'SUBRT' EXPECTS A FLOATING-POINT ARGUMENT */
/* HENCE 'FLOAT' MUST BE INVOKED TO CAUSE
   THE NECESSARY DATA CONVERSION              */
CALL SUBRT(FLOAT(I,21));
```

PRECISION

This function converts a given value to the specified precision. It is used for right truncation and may not be used for left truncation:

PRECISION(x,p,q)

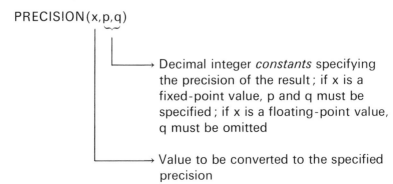

→ Decimal integer *constants* specifying the precision of the result; if x is a fixed-point value, p and q must be specified; if x is a floating-point value, q must be omitted

→ Value to be converted to the specified precision

Example

```
CCL X DECIMAL FIXED(10,5);
X = 1374 + 1/3; /* FIXEDOVERFLOW CONDITION RAISED
                   BECAUSE OF PRECISION OF
                   INTERMEDIATE RESULT              */
X = 1374 + PRECISION(1/3,10,5);
                /* X IS NOW 1374.33333             */
```

Mathematical Built-in Functions

Mathematical functions are provided for the scientific programmer. They are listed in Figure 6.1. The functions operate on arguments in the floating-point scale. If an argument is not in floating-point, it will automatically be converted to floating-point before the function is invoked.

Function reference	Value returned	Error conditions
ATAN(x)	arctan(x) in radians $-(pi/2) < $ ATAN(x) $ < (pi/2)$	
ATAN(x,y)	arctan (x/y) in radians	Error if x = 0 and y = 0
ATAND(x)	arctan(x) in degrees $-90 < $ ATAND(x) $ < 90$	
ATAND(x,y)	arctan (x/y) in degrees	Error if x = 0 and y = 0
ATANH(x)	$\tanh^{-1}(x)$	Error if ABS(x) $\geq$ 1
COS(x) x in radians	cos(x)	
COSD(x) x in degrees	cos(x)	
COSH(x)	cosh(x)	
ERF(x)	$\dfrac{2}{\sqrt{\pi}} \displaystyle\int_{0}^{x} e^{-t^2}\, dt$	
ERFC(x)	$1 - $ ERF(x)	
EXP(x)	e	
LOG(x)	log(x)	Error if x $\leq$ 0
LOG10(x)	$\log_1(x)$	Error if x $\leq$ 0
LOG2(x)	$\log_2(x)$	Error if x $\leq$ 0
SIN(x) x in radians	sine(x)	
SIND(x) x in degrees	sine(x)	
SINH(x)	sinh(x)	
SQRT(x)	$\sqrt{x}$	Error if x < 0
TAN(x) x in radians	tan(x)	
TAND(x) x in degrees	tan(x)	
TANH(x)	tanh(x)	

FIGURE 6.1   Mathematical built-in functions.

An argument to a mathematical built-in function may be a single value, an expression, or an array name. If an argument is an array name, the value returned by the built-in function is an array of the same dimensions and bounds as the argument, the function having been performed once for each element of the array. Thus, for example, an array argument passed to the cosine function, COS, results in an array, each element of which is the cosine of the corresponding element in the array argument. The mathematical functions shown in Figure 6.1 include an explanation of what they accomplish. For some functions, error conditions result if invalid arguments are specified (e.g., a negative argument to the square root function). In general, an error message with an identification code as to the nature of the error will be printed and the program terminated.

String Handling Built-in Functions

These functions are used for manipulating bit- or character-string data. In general, data with the BIT, CHARACTER, or PICTURE attributes are specified as arguments to the string handling built-in functions.

BIT

This function converts a coded arithmetic data item or character-string to a bit-string. The argument may be a single value, an expression, or an array name. The length of the resulting bit-string is determined according to the type of conversion rules (Appendix C), when only one argument is supplied. For example:

$$I = BIT(X);$$

It is also possible to supply two arguments to the BIT function, in which case the second argument is a decimal integer *constant* specifying the length of the resulting bit-string. For example:

$$I = BIT(X,15);$$

Examples

```
DCL I FIXED BINARY(4);
DCL C CHARACTER(5);
I = 15;     /* I NOW CONTAINS 1111B *
/* NOW IT IS DESIRED TO MOVE I TO C
   SO THAT C WILL CONTAIN '1111 '
C = BIT(I);    /* C NOW CONTAINS '1111 ' */
C = BIT(I,5); /* C NOW CONTAINS '11110' */
```

BOOL

This function is used to manipulate bit-strings. It provides a unique flexibility to the PL/I programmer in that it allows the programmer to define the answer he would like to have as the result of a logical operation on two bit-strings. The logical operation is referred to as a *Boolean operation*, hence the name of this built-in function, BOOL. The AND and OR Boolean operations have been introduced previously. There are other Boolean functions for which there are no specific PL/I keywords. One of these is the exclusive OR operation. Following are the four bit combinations and their respective results for this operation:

$$0 \quad \text{EOR} \quad 0 \rightarrow 0$$
$$0 \quad \text{EOR} \quad 1 \rightarrow 1$$
$$1 \quad \text{EOR} \quad 0 \rightarrow 1$$
$$1 \quad \text{EOR} \quad 1 \rightarrow 0$$

In the exclusive OR operation, we obtain a 1 bit when either but *not* both of the bits is a 1. If a 1 bit is exclusive ORed with a 1 bit, or a 0 bit with a 0 bit, then the result is a 0 bit. One method for accomplishing the exclusive OR function in PL/I is to code an expression that uses the AND, OR, and NOT operations in such a way as to accomplish exclusive OR. For example:

```
DCL (B1,B2,B3) BIT(5) ;
B1 = '10011'B ;
B2 = '11010'B ;
B3 = (B1 | B2)&(¬(B1 & B2)) ;
```

Here, B1 is exclusive ORed with B2, and B3 is now equal to '01001'B. As you can see, this method is somewhat complex. Another method that you might use to accomplish the exclusive OR function is to invoke the BOOL built-in function. For example :

B3 = BOOL (B1,B2,'0110'B) ;

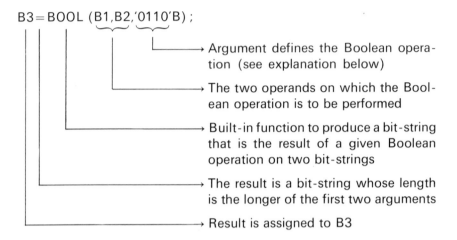

Argument defines the Boolean operation (see explanation below)

The two operands on which the Boolean operation is to be performed

Built-in function to produce a bit-string that is the result of a given Boolean operation on two bit-strings

The result is a bit-string whose length is the longer of the first two arguments

Result is assigned to B3

First and Second Arguments. Arguments B1 and B2 represent the two bit-strings upon which the Boolean operation specified by the third argument is to be performed ; these arguments can be bit-string, character-string, or arithmetic element expressions or array names. If B1 and B2 are not bit-strings, they are converted to bit-strings. If B1 and B2 differ in length, the shorter string is extended with zeros on the right to match the length of the longer string.

Third Argument. This argument defines the Boolean operation. It is a bit-string that is selected (determined) by the programmer. The left-most bit in the string argument defines the result you would like when a 0 is logically operated on with a 0 ; the second leftmost bit defines the result of a 0 operand and a 1 operand ; the third bit (third from the left) defines the result of a 1 operand and a 0 operand ; and finally, the fourth bit defines the result of a 1 operand and a 1 operand.

The third argument in the BOOL function can be a bit-string, character-string, arithmetic coded item, expression, or array name. It is converted to a bit-string of length 4. There are 16 possible bit combinations and thus 16 possible Boolean operations. In summary, then, it needs to be emphasized that the third argument of the BOOL function defines what happens on a bit-for-bit basis in each corresponding pair of bits of the first two arguments.

To illustrate the way in which any logical operation may be specified with the BOOL function, assume two 15-bit strings have been declared and initialized:

DCL (A,B) BIT(15);
A = '111001000010l001'B;
B = '100l011001111000'B;

Now, it is desired to perform a logical NAND operation on the above two operands (A and B). (A NAND operation is a ─AND operation in which the resulting bits after an AND operation are simply reversed; thus, 1's become 0's and vice versa.) The truth table for the NAND operation would be the following:

0 NAND 0 → 1
0 NAND 1 → 1
1 NAND 0 → 1
1 NAND 1 → 0

The BOOL function to accomplish the NAND operation would be coded as follows:

C = BOOL(A,B,'1110'B);

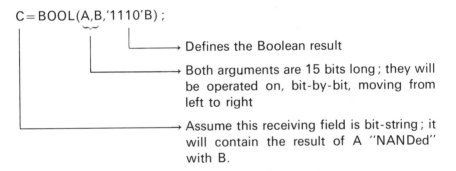

→ Defines the Boolean result

→ Both arguments are 15 bits long; they will be operated on, bit-by-bit, moving from left to right

→ Assume this receiving field is bit-string; it will contain the result of A "NANDed" with B.

Example

```
DCL (B1,B2,B3) BIT(5);
B1 = '10011'B;
B2 = '11010'B;
B3 = (B1 | B2) & (¬(B1 & B2));
         /* B1 IS EXCLUSIVE OR'D WITH B2
            AND B3 IS NOW '01001'B          */
B3 = BOOL(B1,B2,'0110'B);
         /* B3 IS NOW '01001'B              */
B3 = ¬(B1 & B2);           /* B3 = '01101'B */
B3 = BOOL(B1,B2,'1110'B); /* B3 = '01101'B */
```

CHAR

This function converts a given value to a character-string.

Subset Language. The argument may be a CHARACTER, PICTURE, or BIT attribute single value, expression, or array argument. The CHAR function is most useful in the subset language for simulating "P format" (see Chapter 5, page 269). For example:

```
DCL X PIC'$$$,$$$V.99';
X = 1002.34;
PUT EDIT (CHAR(X))(A);
```

Full Language. The argument may be CHARACTER, PICTURE, BIT, or any coded arithmetic (e.g., FIXED DECIMAL) data item. Expressions or arrays are allowed.

In both the subset and full language implementations, there is another form of the CHAR function in which two arguments may be specified. The function reference is described as follows:

CHAR (x,n)

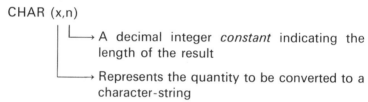

A decimal integer *constant* indicating the length of the result

Represents the quantity to be converted to a character-string

LENGTH

This function finds the length of a given bit- or character-string. It is useful in full language implementations of PL/I to determine the length of string data items that have the VARYING attribute. The argument, however, need not represent a character- or bit-string. If it does not, it is converted before the function is invoked to a character-string, if the argument has the decimal base, or a bit-string, if the argument has a binary base. The LENGTH function returns the result of the attributes FIXED BINARY(15). [*Note:* This function is not provided in the subset language.]

Examples

```
DCL NAME CHAR(30) VARYING;
NAME = 'D.M. TUCKER';
I = LENGTH(NAME);        /* I = 11   */
```

SUBSTR

This function extracts a substring of user-defined length from a given bit- or character-string and returns the substring to the point of invocation. The arguments are described as follows:

SUBSTR(x,i,j)

> → Specifies the length of the substring to be extracted (*subset language*, may only be a decimal constant; *full language*, may be a constant, a variable, or an expression, or may be omitted entirely)

> → Specifies the starting point of the substring

> → Represents the string from which a substring will be extracted; this argument can be a binary coded arithmetic, bit-string, character-string, or decimal character data item, expression, or array name; if this argument has a binary base, it is converted to a bit-string before the function is invoked

For a programming example of this built-in function, see Chapter 5, page 275. SUBSTR may also be a pseudo-variable. This means that the function name may be designated as a receiving field. This facility is also illustrated in Chapter 5, page 251.

Example

```
DCL (M,N)CHAR(10);
M = 'MONOLITHIC';
N = SUBSTR(M,1,4);          /* N ='MONO        '  */
N = SUBSTR(M||'S',8,4);     /* N ='HICS         '  */
SUBSTR(M,4,6)=SUBSTR(M,7,2); /* ASSUMING  M=MONOLITHIC,
                               M NOW EQUALS 'MONTH      '  */
GET EDIT(SUBSTR(M,6,5))(A(5)); /* ASSUMING M=MONTH AND INPUT
                               IS "--JAN" THEN M=MONTH--JAN */
```

UNSPEC

This function returns a bit-string that is the internal representation of a given value. In other words, through this function it is possible to examine the bit configuration of a data item.

The argument may be an arithmetic, character-string, or pointer value; it cannot be a bit-string. An array name may be specified as an argument.

The length of the resulting bit-string depends upon the attributes of the argument. For example, a FIXED BINARY(31) data item would return a length of 32, because there are four bytes (32 bits) in this type of data item. The length of a FIXED DECIMAL data item of precision (p,q) is defined as $8*FLOOR((p+2)/2)$. For short-form floating-point data items, the length returned is 32 bits; for long-form floating-point, the length returned is 64 bits. For an application of when this function would be useful, see Chapter 5, page 285.

INDEX

This function searches a string for a specified bit or character configuration. If the configuration is found, the starting location of the leftmost configuration within the string is returned. If the configuration does not exist, the value returned will be zero. The result returned has the attributes BINARY FIXED(15). The arguments to INDEX are described as follows:

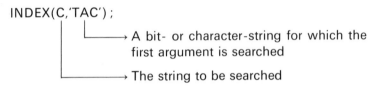

INDEX(C,'TAC');

→ A bit- or character-string for which the first argument is searched

→ The string to be searched

These arguments may be bit-string, character-string, binary coded arithmetic, decimal picture, or array names. If neither argument is a bit-string, or if only one argument is a bit-string, both arguments are converted to character-strings. If both arguments are bit-strings, no conversion is performed. Binary coded arithmetic arguments are converted to bit-string; decimal picture arguments are converted to character-string before the above conversions are performed.

Examples

```
DCL C CHARACTER(40);
C ='THE DOG CHASED THE TAC'; /* 'CAT' IS MISSPELLED */
J = INDEX(C,'TAC');
SUBSTR(C,J,3) = 'CAT';        /* C NOW CONTAINS THE
                                 CORRECT SPELLING OF CAT*/

C ='CONSTELLATION';
J = INDEX(C,'E');             /* J = 6   */
J = INDEX(C,'L');             /* J = 7   */
J = INDEX(C,'P');             /* J = 0   */
```

STRING

This function concatenates all the elements in an array of a structure† into a single character- or bit-string element. Thus, if it is desired to concatenate a number of elementary items found in a

†Structures are explained in Chapter 8.

structure or array, it would be easier to code the STRING function than to code the concatenation operation a number of times. STRING may also be used as a pseudo-variable.

Examples

```
DCL 1 STRUCTURE,
       2 A CHAR(5) INIT('ABCDE'),
       2 B CHAR(3) INIT('123'),
       2 C CHAR(7) INIT('XYZXYZX');
CCL S CHAR(15);
S = STRUCTURE;
       /* ILLEGAL MOVE                      */
S = STRING(STRUCTURE);
       /* S = 'ABCDE123XYZXYZX'             */
STRUCTURE = S;
       /* STRUCTURE.A = 'ABCDE'             */
       /* STRUCTURE.B = 'ABC '              */
       /* STRUCTURE.C = 'ABCDE12'           */
STRING(STRUCTURE) = S;
       /* STRUCTURE.A = 'ABCDE'             */
       /* STRUCTURE.B = '123'               */
       /* STRUCTURE.C = 'XYZXYZX'           */
```

REPEAT

This function takes a given string value and forms a new string consisting of the string value concatenated with itself a specified number of times. The arguments are described as follows:

REPEAT(m,n);

└─→ Must be a decimal integer *constant* greater than zero representing the number of times that the first argument is to be concatenated with itself

└─→ Represents a character- or bit-string from which the new string will be formed; this argument can be a binary coded arithmetic, bit-string, character-string, or numeric character element expression or array name; if an argument other than a bit- or character-string is specified, it is converted before the function is invoked, to a bit- or character-string

└─→ Concatenates the first argument with itself n times, where n is the second argument

Examples

```
DCL CITY CHARACTER(12);
CITY = (2)'WALLA ';        /* CITY = 'WALLA WALLA ' */
CITY = REPEAT('WALLA ',2); /* CITY = 'WALLA WALLA ' */
DCL B BIT(3), A BIT(15);
B = '101'B;
A = REPEAT(B,5);           /* A = '101101101101101'B */
```

TRANSLATE

This function substitutes one character with another character or one bit with another bit. There are three arguments to this function:

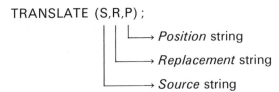

TRANSLATE (S,R,P);

→ *Position* string

→ *Replacement* string

→ *Source* string

To illustrate the translation that takes place, the following example is given:

```
DCL (S,T) CHAR(5);
DCL (R,P) CHAR(1);
S = '+1234';
R = '+';
P = ' ';
```

→ If a '+' sign appears in the source string, replace it with a blank

When the TRANSLATE function is invoked, e.g.,

T = TRANSLATE (S,P,R);

if S = '+1234', then T = '1234'.

The *replacement* and *position* strings may contain as many characters as it is desired to have substituted. For example:

```
R = '- + ';
P = '#  0';
```

→ Replace blanks with zeros

→ Replace plus signs with blanks

→ Replace minus signs with pound signs

[*Note:* This function is not available in the subset language.]

Example

```
DCL (S,T) CHAR(10);
DCL (P,R) CHAR(1);
P = ' ';
R = '0';
S = '  12  34';
T = TRANSLATE(S,R,P);        /* T = '0012003400'  */
```

VERIFY

This function examines two strings to verify that each character or bit in the first string is represented in the second string, returning a fixed binary value of 0 if this is the case; otherwise, the value returned is the position of the first character in the first string that is not represented in the second string.

Examples

```
DCL STR CHAR(5);
DCL DIGITS CHAR(10)INIT('0123456789');
STR = '01234';
I = VERIFY(STR,DIGITS);      /* I = 0 */
STR = '123.4';
I = VERIFY(STR,DIGITS);      /* I = 4 */
STR = '973  ';
I = VERIFY(STR,DIGITS);      /* I = 1 */
```

DATE and TIME

These functions find the current date and time. When these functions are used, they should be explicitly declared to have the BUILTIN attribute. For example:

DECLARE (DATE, TIME) BUILTIN;

Here are explanations of each function:

D = DATE;

→ Returns the current date in the form YYMMDD, where YY is year, MM is month, DD is day

→ The value returned is a character-string of length six

→ Must be an element character-string; incorrect results will be given if D is a structure†

†Structures are explained in Chapter 8.

T=TIME;

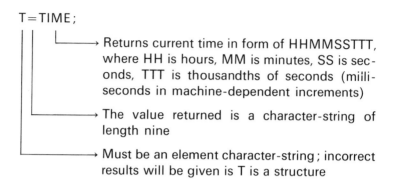

→ Returns current time in form of HHMMSSTTT, where HH is hours, MM is minutes, SS is seconds, TTT is thousandths of seconds (milliseconds in machine-dependent increments)

→ The value returned is a character-string of length nine

→ Must be an element character-string; incorrect results will be given is T is a structure

A Suggested Approach to Generalized Debugging

"By proper use of the aids provided in PL/I and by the full level implementations, almost all debugging can be done at the source level, without resorting to listings of the generated object code or hexadecimal storage dumps. Moreover, after encountering an error which might normally require abnormal termination, the programmer can choose to continue execution of the program at a programmer-specified point in the program, or, in some cases following the point of interruption. By doing so, several different errors might be detected in a single test run, thus improving the profitability of each run and helping to shorten program development time, especially in installations where program test turn-arounds are eight hours or more."†

Following is a description of built-in functions that facilitate program debugging in the full language implementations of PL/I.

ONCHAR and ONSOURCE

ONCHAR and ONSOURCE are pseudo-variables as well as built-in functions. As built-in functions, ONCHAR and ONSOURCE return the character and source fields, respectively, containing the character that caused the CONVERSION condition to be raised. As pseudo-variables, ONCHAR and ONSOURCE may be used to modify the data in the source field that caused the CONVERSION condition.

---

†Excerpted from a paper entitled "Debugging in PL/I" by D. M. Tucker, IBM Corporation.

CHAR = ONCHAR;

└──────→ Extracts the character that caused the CONVERSION condition to be raised; it can be used in an on-unit for the CONVERSION condition or in an ERROR on-unit as result of a conversion error; if it is used out of context, it returns a blank; the value returned by this function is a character-string of length 1, containing the character that caused the CONVERSION condition to be raised

SOURCE = ONSOURCE;

└──────→ Extracts the contents of the field that was being processed when a CON-VERSION condition was raised; this function can be used in the on-unit for a CONVERSION condition or in an on-unit for an ERROR condition; when used out of context, a null string is returned; the value returned by this function is a varying-length character-string giving the contents of the field being processed when CONVERSION was raised

Example: The following example illustrates the use of ONSOURCE and ONCHAR, both as built-in functions and as pseudo-variables:

```
DCL FIELD CHAR(5),
    CHAR CHAR(1),
    SOURCE CHAR(20) VARYING,
    NUM FIXED(5);
FIELD = '123X4';
/* ON UNIT ENTERED UPON CONVERSION ERROR */
ON CONVERSION BEGIN;
    CHAR = ONCHAR;       /* CHAR IS 'X'       */
    SOURCE = ONSOURCE;   /* SOURCE IS '123X4' */
    ONCHAR = 0;          /* FIELD IS '12304'  */
    ONSOURCE = '00000';  /* FIELD IS '00000'  */
    END;
NUM = FIELD;             /* CONVERSION ERROR */
```

ONCODE

The ONCODE built-in function may be used in any on-unit to determine the type of interrupt that caused the on-unit to become active. ONCODE returns a binary integer of default precision. This "code" defines the type of interrupt that caused the entry into the current active on-unit. The codes are given in the appropriate programmer's guide for the PL/I compiler you are using. If ONCODE is used out of context, a value of 0 is returned.

ONLOC

Whenever an on-condition is raised, the ONLOC built-in function may be used in the on-unit for that condition to determine the entry point to the procedure in which that condition was raised. ONLOC may be used in any on-unit.

A Generalized Error Handling Program

Following is a suggested program (for full language implementations) to handle possible errors that cause an on-unit to be raised.

```
(SIZE, STRINGRANGE, SUBSCRIPTRANGE):
PROG: PROC OPTIONS(MAIN);
ON CONVERSION BEGIN;
    PUT SKIP LIST (ONCODE, ONCHAR, ONSOURCE,
    ONFILE);
    ONCHAR='0';
    END;
ON SIZE PUT SKIP LIST (ONCODE, ONLOC);
ON OVERFLOW PUT SKIP LIST(ONCODE, ONLOC);
ON UNDERFLOW PUT SKIP LIST (ONCODE, ONLOC);
ON ZERODIVIDE PUT SKIP LIST (ONCODE, ONLOC);
ON STRINGRANGE PUT SKIP LIST (ONCODE, ONLOC);
ON SUBSCRIPTRANGE PUT SKIP LIST (ONCODE, ONLOC);
ON FIXEDOVERFLOW PUT SKIP LIST (ONCODE, ONLOC);
ON ERROR BEGIN;
    PUT SKIP LIST (ONCODE, ONLOC, ONFILE, ONKEY);
    GO TO RESTART_LABEL;
    END;
```

If the preceding PL/I statements were included in the PL/I program immediately following the PROCEDURE statement defining the external OPTIONS(MAIN) block, all computational errors would be intercepted and noted on SYSPRINT. Execution would continue at the point of interruption. (Note that the conditions SIZE, SUB-SCRIPTRANGE and STRINGRANGE must be enabled by a condition prefix preceding the PROCEDURE statement.) All other errors would be intercepted by the ERROR on-unit. Of course, any ON statement for any of the above conditions which are subsequently executed would override the preceding on-unit.

SUMMARY

Built-in functions are supplied as part of the PL/I language. Functions are invoked by reference, and their arguments are supplied in a list, separated by commas, enclosed in parentheses following the name. For example:

INITIAL = SUBSTR(NAME,2,1);

→ Arguments

→ Built-in function

For those functions requiring *no* arguments, the function name should be declared to have the BUILTIN attribute. For example:

DCL DATE BUILTIN;
TODAY = DATE;

Functions may be used as arguments to other functions. The position of arguments is critical; arguments must be provided in the order stated for each function. A *pseudo-variable* is a built-in function name appearing to the left of the assignment symbol as if it were a variable. The built-in functions that can be used as pseudo-variables are SUBSTR, UNSPEC, STRING, ONCHAR, ONSOURCE.

The array manipulation built-in functions were covered in Chapter 4. Following is a brief description of each function covered in this chapter. In addition, you may wish to consult Appendix A for examples of a few additional built-in functions not presented in this chapter.

Arithmetic Built-in Functions

ABS: Finds the absolute value of a given quantity
CEIL: Finds the smallest integer that is greater than or equal to a given value
FLOOR: Finds the largest integer that does not exceed a given value
MIN: Finds the smallest value from a given set of two or more arguments; arguments may not be arrays
MAX: Finds the largest value from a set of two or more arguments; arguments may not be arrays
ROUND: Rounds a value at a specified digit and pads spare digit positions with zeros
TRUNC: Changes the fractional part of an argument to zero
MOD   Returns the smallest number that must be subtracted from the first argument in order to make it exactly divisible by the second argument
SIGN: Determines whether a value is positive, negative, or zero

Arithmetic Functions to Override Conversion Rules

ADD: Finds the sum of two values where the programmer controls the precision of the results
DIVIDE: Finds the quotient where the programmer controls the precision of the results
MULTIPLY: Finds the product where the programmer controls the precision of the results
BINARY: Converts a decimal value to the binary base
DECIMAL: Converts a binary value to the decimal base
FIXED: Converts a floating-point value to the fixed-point scale
FLOAT: Converts a fixed-point value to a floating-point scale
PRECISION: Converts a given value to the specified precision; it is used for right truncation

Mathematical Built-in Functions: See Figure 6.1 for a summary of these functions.

String Handling Built-in Functions

BIT: Converts a coded arithmetic data item or character-string to a bit-string
BOOL: Allows the programmer to define any one of 15 Boolean or logical operations to be carried out on two bit-strings
CHAR: Converts a given value to a character-string
LENGTH: Finds the length of a given bit- or character-string
SUBSTR: Extracts a substring of user-defined length from a given bit- or character-string
UNSPEC: Returns a bit-string that is the internal representation of a given value
INDEX: Searches for a string for a specified bit or character configuration

STRING :   Concatenates all the elements in an array or structure into a single character- or bit-string element

REPEAT :   Takes a given string value and forms a new string consisting of the string value concatenated with itself a specified number of times

TRANSLATE :   Substitutes one character with another character or one bit with another bit

VERIFY :   Examines two strings to verify that each character or bit in the first string is represented in the second string

DATE :   Finds the current date, assuming the date was entered into the system correctly for that day

TIME :   Finds the current time, assuming the correct time had been entered into the system

Built-in Functions to Facilitate Debugging

ONCHAR :   Returns the character that caused the conversion condition to be raised

ONSOURCE :   Returns the source field that caused the conversion condition to be raised

ONCODE :   Returns a value that defines the type of interrupt that caused the entry into the current active on-unit

ONLOC :   Returns the name of the procedure in which a given condition was raised

CHECKPOINT QUESTIONS

1. What will X contain after the following statements are executed?

$$Y = 18 ;$$
$$X = ABS(5 - Y/2) ;$$

2. What precision will SUM have given the following?

$$SUM = ADD(A, B, 7, 3) ;$$

3. What is accomplished by the following statements?

(a) A = BINARY(B,7,2) ;   (c)   A = DECIMAL(B,5,2) ;

(b) A = FLOAT(FX,6) ;   (d)   A = FIXED(FL,2) ;

4. What will A contain after each of the following functions are invoked?

$$B = 5.7 ;$$
$$A = CEIL(B) ;$$
$$A = FLOOR(B) ;$$

5. What will I contain when the following statements are executed?

```
ALPHA = 'ABCDEFGHI';
I = INDEX(ALPHA,'DEF');
```

6. What will I contain when the following statements are executed?

```
DCL NAME CHAR(20) VARYING;
NAME = 'FREDDIE';
I = LENGTH(NAME);
```

7. Given the following statements, what will A contain after each function is executed?

```
X = 5; Y = 17; Z = -3;
A = MIN(X,Y,Z);
A = MAX(X,Y,Z,50);
```

8. What will A contain?

```
A = MOD(27,5);
```

9. What will B contain after the following statements are executed?

```
DCL B CHAR(6);
B = 'ABCDEF';
SUBSTR(B,1,3) = SUBSTR(B,4,3);
```

10. Given the following statements, what will K contain?

```
DECLARE K BIT(5);
IVALUE = 19;
K = UNSPEC(IVALUE);
```

TERMS TO STUDY

argument	function
built-in	pseudo-variable
ceiling (as an arithmetic term)	truncate
floor (as an arithmetic term)	

PRACTICE PROBLEMS

1. States Grouped by Letter

Problem Statement: Write a program to list the 50 states grouped by letter.

Purpose of the Problem: To manipulate alphameric data using the SUBSTR built-in function.

Input: Input consists of the 50 states in alphabetical order. Use edit-directed input to read the data.

Output: See Figure 6.2 for desired output.

```
AL ABAMA
AL ASKA
AR IZONA
ARKANSAS

CALIFORNIA
COLORADO
CONNECTICUT

DELAWARE

FLORIDA
     .
     .
     .
```

**FIGURE 6.2 Sample
output for Problem 1**

2. Determining Frequency of Occurrence

Problem Statement: Write a program that will determine the frequency of occurrence of the word "NO" in a group of sentences punched in cards.

Purpose of the Problem: To use some of the character-string manipulation built-in functions (e.g., INDEX, SUBSTR).

Input: To test your program, punch the following four sentences:
THERE IS NOTHING SO STIMULATING AS NEW KNOWLEDGE.
NO MAN'S KNOWLEDGE CAN GO BEYOND HIS EXPERIENCE.
YES! NO!

Output: Print the number of times that NO (as a separate word) appears. For example:

"NO" APPEARS 2 TIMES.

└──────────→ Your program calculates this value

3. The Indian Problem

Problem Definition: In 1627, Peter Minuit bought Manhattan Island from the Indians for approximately $24.00. Had the Indians deposited this amount in a bank savings account to be compounded annually at $3\frac{1}{2}$% interest, how much would they be worth today?

Purpose of the Problem: To use the P format item in PUT EDIT if you are using the full language or either optimizer; *or* to simulate the P format item if you are using the subset language; also, to use the ROUND, MOD, and TIME built-in functions, the remote format specification, and ENDPAGE condition.

346 PL/I Programming

Input: There is no input to this problem, as the initial principal of $24.00 and interest of $3\frac{1}{2}$% may be specified as program constants.

Processing: Compound interest for each full year beginning with 1627 and ending with the last full year. For example, if the current year is 1977, then compound interest up to and including 1976. In addition, check the accumulated principal for such time as it exceeds one million dollars. On output, print asterisks by the year in which the principal became equal to or greater than the one million dollar figure. (As a matter of "interest," you may wish to try running this program *without* using the ROUND built-in function and compare the final results with the program's output when ROUND *was* used.) It is suggested that you draw a program flowchart before beginning to code this problem. Use the TIME built-in function to calculate running time of the program. Print the elapsed time on a time page following the report of interest earned.

Output: See Figure 6.3. Specify page size as 55 lines, and print headings on every page of output.

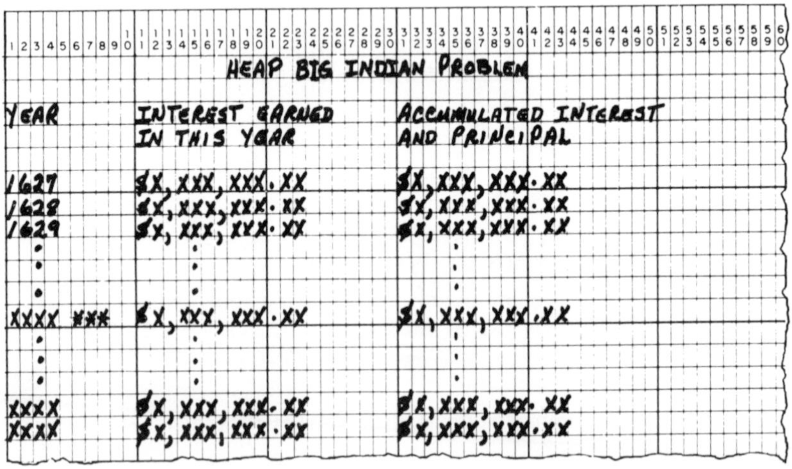

FIGURE 6.3   Suggested printer layout for Problem 3.

4.   Square Root Algorithm

Problem Statement: Write a program to compute the square root using the Newton–Raphson method. Also, invoke the SQRT built-in function, providing as an argument the input value for which you just computed your own square root. Print this result so that you may compare the accuracy of your solution with that of the built-in function.

Purpose of the Problem: To use several of the mathematical built-in functions (SQRT and ABS) as well as inspect the approximation method of finding square root.

Input: Make provisions in your program to read *any* number of input values for which the square root is to be computed.

Output: For each input value, two results will be printed:

1. The result you programmed.
2. The result from the SQRT built-in function.

Flowchart: See Figure 6.4.

5. Generating a Mathematical Table

Problem Statement: Write a program to print a table of X, sine X, cosine X, and tangent X for values of X in degrees that range from 1.0 to 2.0 in increments of 0.1. Compare the printed results with a published mathematical table.

Purpose of the Problem: To use some of the mathematical built-in functions and observe the accuracy of their results.

Input: There is no input, as the program will generate the data.

Output:

DEGREE/MINUTE	SINE	COSINE	TANGENT	COTANGENT
X.X	.XXXXX	.XXXXX	.XXXXX	XX.XXX
X.X	.XXXXX	.XXXXX	.XXXXX	XX.XXX
X.X	.XXXXX	.XXXXX	.XXXXX	XX.XXX

6. Potpourri

Problem Statement: As a means of using a number of built-in functions, code the following exercises:

(a) Given the statements,

```
DCL X1(8) FIXED(3,1);
DCL X(8) FIXED(3,1) INIT(-55.5,-41.6,-19.0,-4.3,0,6.9,16,33.2);
```

write the statements necessary to find the *ceiling* and *floor* of each value in X array; store results in X1. Print results.

(b) Truncate the values in array X and place in X1. Print the truncated array.

(c) An array is declared as follows:

```
DCL X_SIGN FIXED(1)
DCL X_SIGN(8) FIXED(1);
```

Set each element of the array to a -1 for the corresponding negative values in the X array in part a above; set corresponding elements of X_SIGN to zero, for zero values of X; and set elements of X_SIGN to +1 for positive values of X. Print results.

(d) Given the statements,

$$A=1; \quad B=7; \quad C=13; \quad D=-21;$$

invoke the built-in functions necessary to find the largest and the smallest value in the list of scalars. Print results.

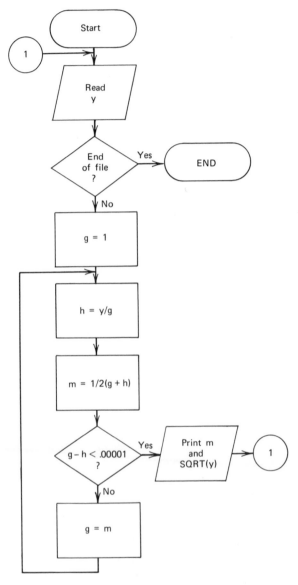

FIGURE 6.4 Flowchart of Newton–Raphson square root method. [Key: y = argument, g (for guess), m = midpoint, h = any positive number.]

(e) Given the statements,

$$A = 32.5;$$
$$I = 15;$$

print A and I as bit-strings.

(f) Use the BOOL built-in function to perform a NOR ($\neg$OR) operation on the following bit-strings:

```
1  1  0  0  1  1  1  0
1  0  0  1  0  1  1  0
```
———————————
```
0  0  1  0  0  0  0  1
```
⟶ This should be the result printed

Input: There is no input data to this problem, as all data is generated by the program.

Output: Sample output is shown in Figure 6.5.

```
X ARRAY
-55.5    -41.6    -19.0    -4.3       .0      6.9      16.0     32.2

CEILING OF X
-55.0    -41.0    -19.0    -4.0       .0      7.0      16.0     33.0

FLOOR OF X
-56.0    -42.0    -19.0    -5.0       .0      6.0      16.0     32.0

X TRUNCATED
-55.0    -41.0    -19.0    -4.0       .0      6.0      16.0     32.0

X_SIGN ARRAY
 -1.0     -1.0     -1.0    -1.0       .0      1.0       1.0      1.0

MIN IS -21

MAX IS   13

NUMERIC VALUE          BIT-STRING
  -32.0                000000000100000
    15                 000000000001111

     11001110
NOR  10010110
     00100001
```

FIGURE 6.5 Sample output from Problem 6.

chapter 7

How to Write

Subroutines

and Functions

Frequently a programmer finds that he must perform the same series of instructions at several points in a program. A good example of this is found in most report writing programs. The heading of a report may have to be printed whenever one of several conditions occurs. For example, the heading lines must be printed when the end of a page is encountered or whenever the end of a major reporting group is reached (i.e., at the end of a department or division) or, of course, at the beginning of the program's execution to cause the heading to appear

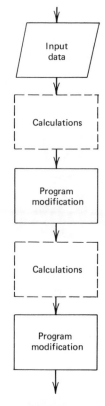

FIGURE 7.1

on the first page. In most programs, this requirement of executing the same sequence of statements at several points does arise.

As another example, assume that a series of calculations are needed at several points within a program. This program's execution sequence is illustrated in Figure 7.1. However, a more efficient program sequence is shown in Figure 7.2. In this example, each time the calculations are to be performed, there is a transfer from the main sequence of statements to the block of instructions that carries out the calculations. After the calculations are performed, there is a return to the main sequence of statements. The main program modifies data and then transfers again to the block of statements that performs the calculations.

PL/I provides several methods of optimizing the use of main storage by allowing the programmer to have one copy of the common statements which can be executed *out-of-line*. In other words, the programmer, when it is desired to execute a common sequence of instructions, can cause execution to transfer to a single copy of the instructions and upon completing them return to the instruction following the transfer.

The block of statements which is used from several points in the program is commonly referred to as a *subprogram*. A *reference* or

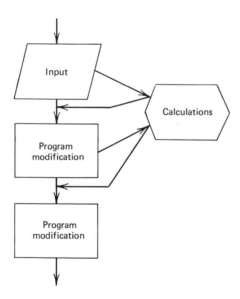

FIGURE 7.2

call to a subprogram, which causes the transfer to the common statements, has the same effect as if the statements were written at the point in the program where the reference or call were made. When writing a program, the programmer should try to design the program in such a way that all of the functions to be performed are organized into logical units or building blocks. By using the facilities of PL/I, the programmer need write only statements which CALL these logical units of code. This method of coding is called *modular programming*. A program then takes on the following form:

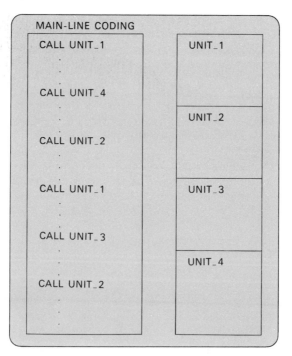

As each logical unit of code is required by the main-line routine, a CALL is made to that subprogram to perform the necessary function. After completing the process, the subprogram will return to the statement following the CALL to continue execution of the main-line program.

The data that a subprogram manipulates is usually determined at the time each reference is made to a subprogram. A subprogram is written in a generalized manner to handle any particular set of values which is *passed* to it by the statement which invokes the subprogram.

The values which are passed are called *arguments*. The subprogram execution is then determined by the values of these arguments. In the subprogram, the values become *parameters* to the subprogram. The subprogram performs its calculations upon the parameters which are now associated with the particular arguments passed to it. Graphically, this can be shown as:

MAIN-LINE PROGRAM

```
.
.
.
CALL SUBPGM (ARG1,ARG2) ;            SUBPGM (PARM1,PARM2)
.
.                                     .
.                                    Data referred to as PARM1
CALL SUBPGM (ARG3,ARG4)               and PARM2 in the sub-
.                                     program
.                                     .
```

PARM1 and PARM2 are names which are associated with the particular arguments of each CALL. In the first CALL, the arguments ARG1 and ARG2 are associated with PARM1 and PARM2. Any operations performed on PARM1 and PARM2 in the subprogram are as if they were performed on ARG1 and ARG2. In the second CALL, ARG3 and ARG4 are passed. During the second execution of the SUBPRG subprogram, any references to PARM1 and PARM2 actually are references to ARG3 and ARG4. Thus, SUBPGM is a generalized routine which performs a logically related set of operations on different values which are determined by the working main-line program.

In summary, a subprogram is a block of statements written only once, but it may be referred to often. Each *reference* or *call* to a subprogram has the same effect as if the statements were written at the point in the program where the reference or call were made. The program that calls or references a subprogram is called the *invoking procedure*. The invoking procedure could be a *main* procedure or it could be another subprogram procedure. The subprogram procedure is termed the *invoked procedure* when it is called or referenced by another procedure.

Sometimes subprograms are referred to in the general sense as *subroutines*. However, in PL/I, the term subprogram is preferable to subroutine, because there are two types of subprograms—one of which is called a *subroutine procedure*. The other type is called a *function procedure*. The subroutine and function procedures explained in this chapter are, typically, compiled separately from the main procedure. It is possible, however, to have subprograms embedded within a main procedure or other subprogram procedure. For example:

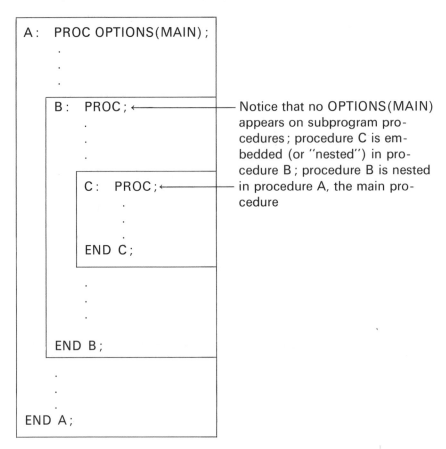

```
A:   PROC OPTIONS(MAIN);
     .
     .
     .

     B:   PROC;  ←────────────  Notice that no OPTIONS(MAIN)
          .                     appears on subprogram pro-
          .                     cedures; procedure C is em-
          .                     bedded (or "nested") in pro-
                                cedure B; procedure B is nested
          C:   PROC;  ←──────   in procedure A, the main pro-
               .                cedure
               .
               .
          END C;


          .
          .
          .

     END B;

     .
     .
     .

END A;
```

An explanation of why a programmer might choose to embed a PROCEDURE within another PROCEDURE is given in Chapter 11.

In this chapter, we shall be concerned with subprograms that are compiled separately from the main procedure or other subprogram procedures.

There are several advantages to using modular programming techniques:

1. *Saves main storage:* The sequence of coding that is to be used several times throughout a given program need appear only once in main storage with the calling program.
2. *Saves coding effort:* Where subprograms are separately compiled, these programs, once written, may be saved either in card form, on a direct access device, or on tape. Subprograms on a direct access device or tape are cataloged by the subprogram's name. They may be easily retrieved from these storage media and added to your main program by the linkage editor. (See Chapter 1 for a review of the linkage editor's function.)
3. *Reduces possibilities of programming and keypunching errors:* A subprogram, once checked out, can be used with a reasonable degree of certainty that the correct answer will be given. This allows the programmer to concentrate on checking out the main sequence of his program statements.
4. *Reduces programming time:* Programming tasks can be divided among several programmers, thus shortening the total programming elapsed time.

Subprogram Names

Subroutine or function procedures that are separately compiled from the invoking procedure are *external procedures*. Thus, the length of these names is limited by the rules that apply to other external names: for subset language implementations, subprogram names may be a maximum of six characters; for full language implementations, subprogram names may be a maximum of seven characters.

Functions versus Subroutines

A function is a procedure that returns a *single* value to the invoking procedure. A function is invoked in the same manner that PL/I built-in functions are referenced. For example, you would invoke a function procedure whose label is CALC and has two arguments in the following manner:

Z=CALC(X,Y);

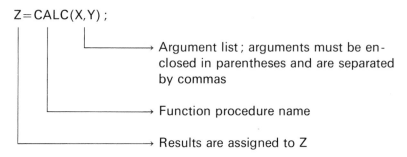

→ Argument list; arguments must be enclosed in parentheses and are separated
by commas

→ Function procedure name

→ Results are assigned to Z

Or you might wish to reference CALC in an IF statement:

IF CALC(X,Y)<0 THEN GO TO ERROR;

By contrast, a subroutine cannot return a value to the point of invocation. The value of arguments, in certain cases, may be modified by the subroutine (or function) and in this way results are effectively returned to the invoking program. A subroutine is invoked by a CALL statement:

CALL SUBRT(X,Y,Z);

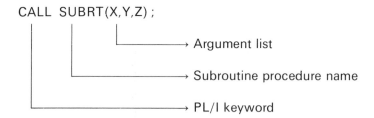

→ Argument list

→ Subroutine procedure name

→ PL/I keyword

Functions should not be invoked by a CALL, nor should subroutines be invoked by a function reference.

It is important to understand that a function is written to compute a single value which is returned to the point of invocation. The value returned may not be an array or a structure. A subroutine, on the other hand, may return none, one, or many results to the invoking procedure through the modification of arguments in the subroutine CALL. A subroutine can alter an argument and thereby "return" an array or structure value. Thus, you would code a function when your program needs a single value to replace the function reference. Use a subroutine when no results are to be returned to the invoking procedure; e.g., code a subroutine to prepare headings for printed output. Or, code a subroutine when results are to be placed in arrays or structures, or more than one value is to be returned to the invoking procedure.

Arguments and Parameters

Arguments passed to an invoked procedure must be accepted by that procedure. This is done by the explicit declaration of one or more *parameters* in a parenthesized list in the PROCEDURE statement of the invoked procedure. For example:

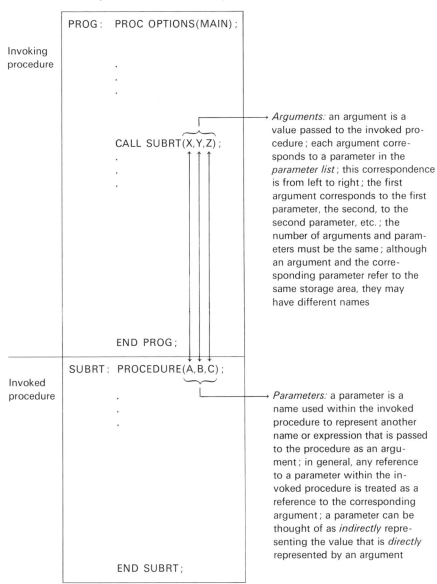

Invoking procedure

```
PROG:   PROC OPTIONS(MAIN);
        .
        .
        .
        CALL SUBRT(X,Y,Z);
        .
        .
        .
        END PROG;
```

Arguments: an argument is a value passed to the invoked procedure; each argument corresponds to a parameter in the *parameter list*; this correspondence is from left to right; the first argument corresponds to the first parameter, the second, to the second parameter, etc.; the number of arguments and parameters must be the same; although an argument and the corresponding parameter refer to the same storage area, they may have different names

Invoked procedure

```
SUBRT:  PROCEDURE(A,B,C);
        .
        .
        .
        END SUBRT;
```

Parameters: a parameter is a name used within the invoked procedure to represent another name or expression that is passed to the procedure as an argument; in general, any reference to a parameter within the invoked procedure is treated as a reference to the corresponding argument; a parameter can be thought of as *indirectly* representing the value that is *directly* represented by an argument

The attributes of a parameter and its corresponding argument must be the same. If the attributes of an argument are not consistent with those of its corresponding parameter, an error will probably result, as no conversion is automatically performed. Here is an example of the coding steps necessary to provide consistent attributes for arguments and their corresponding parameters:

Invoking procedure	```
	PROG: PROC OPTIONS(MAIN);
	    DCL (X, Y) FIXED(7,2),Z FIXED(8,2);
	    GET LIST(X,Y);
	    CALL SUBRT(X,Y,Z);
	    PUT LIST('RESULT IS', Z);
	    END PROG;
	``

Invoked procedure	```
	SUBRT: PROC(A,B,C);
	    DCL (A,B) FIXED(7,2), C FIXED(8,2);
	    C=A+B;
	    END SUBRT;
	``

In the invoking procedure, the arguments X and Y are declared to have the FIXED(7,2) attribute. In the invoked procedure, the corresponding parameters A and B are also declared to have the FIXED(7,2) attributes. The argument Z and the parameter C are given the FIXED(8,2) attributes. The above example illustrates a very simple, but complete, subroutine procedure. The subroutine adds two values together and returns the sum through one of the subroutine's parameters, C. Any change of value specified for a parameter in the invoked procedure actually is a change in the value of the argument in the invoking procedure. Such changes remain in effect when control is returned to the invoking procedure. Thus, in the above example, when the invoking procedure prints the value of Z, it is the sum of X and Y that is output.

Figure 7.3 summarizes the types of arguments and parameters allowed in the subset and full language implementations.

Dummy Arguments

In this discussion of arguments and parameters, it is important to understand that the name of an argument, not its value, is passed

	Arguments	
	May be	May not be
Subset language	Variable Constant Expression Array Major structure Minor structure Entry name File name Label	Based variable (ex- plained in Chapter 11) Built-in function Array expression Structure expression (see Chapter 8)
Full language	In general, an argument and its corre- sponding parameter may be any data type	

FIGURE 7.3   Argument and parameter types.

to a subroutine or function. However, there are times when an argument has no name. A constant, for example, has no name; nor does
an operational expression. As an illustration, the following arguments
might be specified when invoking SUBRT:

CALL SUBRT(7.5,X-Y,Z) ;

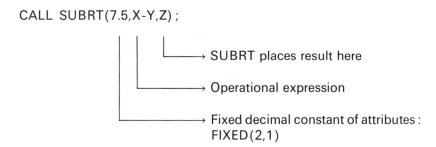

Because the first two arguments to SUBRT do not have names,
it will be necessary for the compiler to select a name for the constant
7.5 and a name for the results of the arithmetic operation X − Y. For

example:

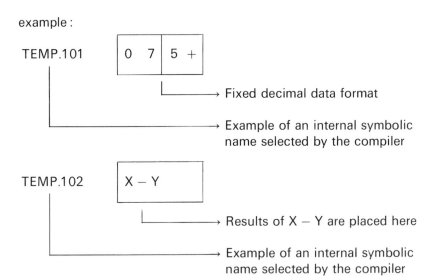

TEMP.101 [0 7 5 +]

→ Fixed decimal data format

→ Example of an internal symbolic name selected by the compiler

TEMP.102 [X − Y]

→ Results of X − Y are placed here

→ Example of an internal symbolic name selected by the compiler

Internal names are called *dummy arguments*. They are not accessible to the PL/I programmer, but the programmer should be aware of their existence. If we substitute the internal names for the constant and the expression in the above CALL, we have the following statement:

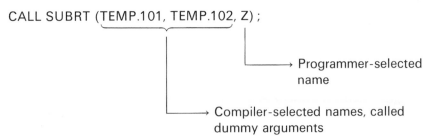

CALL SUBRT (TEMP.101, TEMP.102, Z);

→ Programmer-selected name

→ Compiler-selected names, called dummy arguments

Of course, you could not code the above statement, because internal names are not available to the PL/I programmer.

Recall the statement:

CALL SUBRT(7.5,X−Y,Z);

Recall, also, that in SUBRT, the first and second parameters had the attributes FIXED(7,2). We know that an argument must agree precisely with its corresponding parameter in terms of attributes. Above, we saw that a dummy argument was created for the constant 7.5. When a dummy argument is created for an argument that is a constant, the attributes of the dummy argument will be those indicated by the constant. Thus, 7.5 will have the attributes FIXED(2,1). These attributes do not correspond to the attributes of the first parameter of SUBRT. This is an error, and incorrect results will be produced by SUBRT. One way to avoid the error is to declare an identifier to have the proper attributes and assign the constant to that identifier. For example:

```
DCL ARG1 FIXED(7,2);
ARG1= 7.5;
CALL SUBRT(ARG1, X−Y,Z);
```

Note, also, that argument expressions could cause the same kind of inconsistent attributes problem raised by specifying argument constants. This is because of the PL/I language rules governing arithmetic operations and conversion of data types. (See Appendix C for these rules.) When in doubt about the attributes of results from an expression, it would be wise to assign the results to an identifier having the desired attributes. For example:

```
DCL (ARG1,ARG2)FIXED(7,2);
ARG1 =7.5;
ARG2 =X−Y;
CALL SUBRT(ARG1,ARG2,Z);
```

Another method for ensuring consistent attributes and parameters is to use the ENTRY attribute.

The ENTRY Attribute

The general form of the ENTRY attribute is

DCL identifier ENTRY(parameter attribute, parameter attribute...);

The keyword ENTRY may also be specified without attribute lists. For example:

DCL SUBRT ENTRY;

Generally, in subset language implementations, the above statement must be included for all external subprograms referenced in the invoking procedure. It is necessary to declare a subprogram to have the ENTRY attribute in full language implementations if the identifier is not otherwise recognizable as an entry name; that is, if it is not explicitly or contextually declared to be an entry name in one of the following ways :

1. By its appearance as a label of a PROCEDURE or ENTRY statement (explicit declaration) embedded within the invoking procedure.
2. By its appearance immediately following the keyword CALL contextual declaration).
3. By its appearance as the function name in a function reference that contains an argument list (contextual declaration).

In the full language implementations, an additional facility is given to the ENTRY attribute that allows you to direct the compiler to generate coding to convert one or more arguments to conform to the attributes of the corresponding parameters, should arguments and their corresponding parameters have different attributes.

As an example of how the ENTRY attribute would be used to cause the conversion of arguments to match the attributes of their corresponding parameters, assume we are still working with the subroutine called SUBRT, where its first two parameters must be FIXED(7,2) and the third parameter must be FIXED (8,2) ; i.e.,

```
SUBRT:   PROC (A, B, C)
         DCL (A, B) FIXED(7,2), C FIXED(8,2) ;
         C = A + B ;
         END SUBRT ;
```

In the program that invokes SUBRT, assume that the first two arguments appear in floating-point format; the third argument has the same attribute as the third parameter. Here is a segment of coding from the invoking procedure :

```
DCL (X,Y)FLOAT, Z FIXED(8,2) ;
GET LIST(X,Y) ;
CALL SUBRT(X,Y,Z) ;
```

The above example will cause an error, because X and Y do not have the same attributes as their corresponding parameters. However, explicit declaration of SUBRT as an ENTRY solves this problem:

DCL SUBRT ENTRY
  (FIXED(7,2),FIXED(7,2),FIXED(8,2));

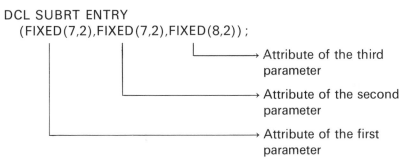

→ Attribute of the third
  parameter

→ Attribute of the second
  parameter

→ Attribute of the first
  parameter

The above declaration tells the compiler that SUBRT is an entry name that has three parameters, as indicated by the attribute list in parentheses. If there is no need to specify the attributes for a particular parameter, attributes do not have to be specified, but the parameter's place must be kept by a comma. For example, the third argument in the calling sequence matches the attributes of the third parameter. Thus, the following DECLARE statement would suffice:

DCL SUBRT ENTRY
  (FIXED(7,2),FIXED(7,2),,);

└─→ Because the attributes of the third
      parameter are not stated, no
      assumptions are made and no
      conversions are performed

Here is an example of the invoking procedure using the ENTRY attribute to direct the compiler to convert arguments to match the attributes of their corresponding parameters:

```
PROG:   PROC OPTIONS(MAIN);
        DCL SUBRT ENTRY(FIXED(7,2),FIXED(7,2),,);
        DCL (X, Y) FLOAT, Z FIXED(8,2);
        GET LIST(X, Y);
        CALL SUBRT(X, Y, Z);
        PUT LIST ('RESULT IS', Z);
        END PROG;
```

Continuing with this example, assume that in the invoking procedure we have been using, X, Y, and Z have the FLOAT attribute. The same subroutine procedure, SUBRT, is to be invoked. Thus, in the invoking procedure, the following statements could be written:

```
DCL (X, Y, Z) FLOAT(6);
DCL SUBRT ENTRY(FIXED(7,2),FIXED(7,2),FIXED(8,2));
GET LIST(X, Y, Z);
CALL SUBRT(X, Y, Z);
```

→ Before calling SUBRT, Z will be converted from FLOAT(6) to FIXED (8,2)

→ Y will be converted from FLOAT(6) to FIXED(7,2)

→ X will be converted from FLOAT(6) to FIXED(7,2)

Assume that the statement

```
GET LIST(X,Y,Z);
```

causes the values 1.2, 3.45, and 67.89 to be assigned to the identifiers X, Y, and Z, respectively. The program's storage locations would contain the following:

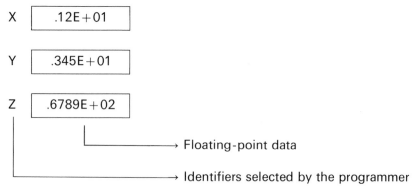

X $.12E+01$

Y $.345E+01$

Z $.6789E+02$

→ Floating-point data

→ Identifiers selected by the programmer

When the subroutine SUBRT is invoked, compiler-generated coding causes X and Y to be converted to FIXED(7,2) and Z to be converted to FIXED(8,2). The converted values (i.e., the FIXED DECIMAL equivalents of the DECIMAL FLOAT data) are not placed into the identifiers X, Y, or Z, but rather into new locations selected by the compiler. Internal symbolic names will be assigned to represent the new locations. For example:

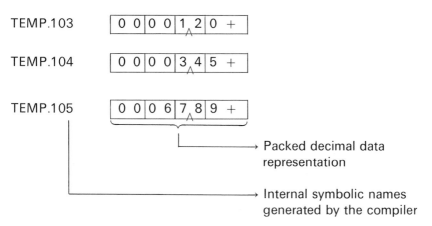

TEMP.103 | 0 | 0 | 0 0 | 1 ‚2 | 0 | + |

TEMP.104 | 0 | 0 | 0 0 | 3 ‚4 | 5 | + |

TEMP.105 | 0 | 0 | 0 6 | 7 ‚8 | 9 | + |

→ Packed decimal data representation

→ Internal symbolic names generated by the compiler

As previously stated, internal names are dummy arguments. To illustrate:

Original arguments (converted to →)   **Dummy arguments**

X | .12E+01 | TEMP. 103 | 00 | 00 | 12 | 0+ |

Y | .345E+01 | TEMP. 104 | 00 | 00 | 34 | 5+ |

Z | .6789E+02 | TEMP. 105 | 00 | 00 | 46 | 5+ |

Recall that SUBRT specifies the statement

$$C = A + B;$$

In the original example of arguments being associated with parameters, we saw that A indirectly represented X, B indirectly represented Y, and C indirectly represented Z. However, in the case of dummy arguments, A (in the above example) indirectly represents dummy argument TEMP. 103, B indirectly represents dummy argument TEMP. 104, and C indirectly represents dummy argument TEMP. 105. In the subroutine, A is added to B. Using the data illustrated above, the sum would be 4.65. The sum is assigned to C, which is associated with the dummy argument TEMP. 105. Thus, it is the dummy argument that is modified to contain the result rather than the original argument's location. When the invoking procedure executes the statement

$$PUT \ LIST \ ('RESULT \ IS', Z);$$

368 PL/I Programming

the original floating-point value of Z (that is, 67.89) will be output, not the result contained in the dummy argument. To avoid this error, if a subroutine is to modify a parameter, make sure an actual argument (*not* a dummy argument) of the identical attributes is passed to the subprogram.

A dummy argument is always created in the following cases:

1. If an argument is constant.
2. If an argument is an expression involving operators.
3. If an argument is an expression in parentheses.
4. If an argument is a variable whose data attributes are different from the data attributes declared for the parameter in an entry name attribute specification appearing in the invoking block.
5. If an argument is itself a function reference containing arguments.

In all other cases, the argument name is passed directly. The parameter becomes identical with the passed argument; thus, changes to the value of a parameter will be reflected in the value of the original argument only if a dummy argument is not passed.

The ENTRY Statement

The keyword ENTRY is a PL/I statement as well as an attribute. When it appears in a DECLARE statement, it describes the attributes of parameters and/or defines an identifier to be a subprogram name. When used as a statement, the keyword defines an alternate entry point in a procedure. For example:

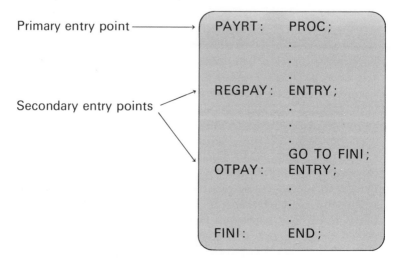

Primary entry point ⟶ PAYRT: PROC;

Secondary entry points — REGPAY: ENTRY;

GO TO FINI;
OTPAY: ENTRY;

FINI: END;

Following is an example of how calls to the above multiple entry points might be coded:

```
IF HRS_WORKED< =40
      THEN CALL REGPAY;
IF HRS_WORKED> =40
      THEN CALL OTPAY;
```

In addition, the ENTRY statement may be used to provide an alternate parameter list to which arguments may be passed, corresponding to that entry point. For example:

```
PAYRT:    PROC;
             .
             .
             .
REGPAY:   ENTRY (REG_HRS,RATE);
             .
             .
             .
          RETURN;
OTPAY:    ENTRY (OT_HRS,RATE,BONUS);
             .
             .
             .
FINI:     END;
```

Multiple entry points—that is, alternate entry points—may be specified for both subroutines and functions.

Subroutines

When a subroutine is called, the arguments of the invoking statement are associated with the parameters of the entry point and control is then passed to that entry point. The subroutine is thus activated and execution begins.

A subroutine may be terminated in several ways: One method of subroutine return is when control reaches the final END statement of the subroutine. For example:

```
SUBRT:   PROC (A,B,C);
             .
             .
             .

         END;
```

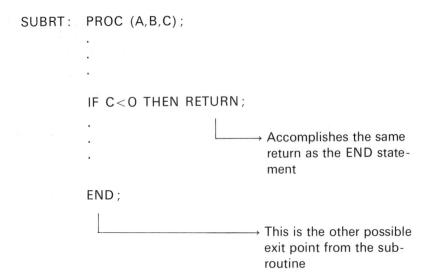

→ Execution of this statement causes control to be returned to the first executable statement logically following the CALL statement to this subroutine

Another way in which a subroutine may be terminated is through the use of the RETURN statement. For example:

```
SUBRT:   PROC (A,B,C);
             .
             .
             .

         IF C<O THEN RETURN;
             .
             .
             .

         END;
```

→ Accomplishes the same return as the END statement

→ This is the other possible exit point from the subroutine

A subroutine may also be terminated with a GO TO statement.

For example :

```
PROG:     PROC OPTIONS(MAIN);
              .
              .
              .
          CALL SUBRT(X,Y,Z,LBL);
          PUT LIST('RESULT IS',Z);
          GO TO END;
LBL:      PUT LIST('ERROR IN ARGUMENT LIST');
END:      END PROG;

SUBRT:    PROC(X,Y,Z,ERROR);
          DCL ERROR LABEL;
          Z=X+Y;
          IF Z=0 THEN GO TO ERROR;
          END;
```

In this example, it was possible for the subroutine to return to one of two possible points in the invoking procedure, depending on whether or not an error condition existed. Note that the parameter ERROR must be given the LABEL attribute in the subroutine. This, of course, is because the subroutine is compiled separately from the invoking procedure and there would be no way for the compiler to determine that ERROR represented a label in another program unless it is explicitly declared in the subroutine.

A STOP or EXIT statement encountered in a subroutine abnormally terminates execution of that subroutine and of the entire program associated with the procedure that invoked it.

Functions

When a function is invoked, the arguments of the invoking statement are associated with the parameters of the entry point, and control is then passed to that entry point. The function is thus activated and execution begins.

The RETURN statement is used to terminate a function. Its use in a function differs somewhat from its use in a subroutine; in a function, not only does it return control, but it also returns the value to the point of invocation. For example:

RETURN (element-expression) ;

⎣⎯⎯⎯⎯⎯→ The value returned to the invoking procedure; it must be a single value

The RETURN statement, then, can accomplish the return of a single value to the calling program. It would also be possible to return additional values from a function subprogram by assigning them as output arguments in the same manner explained for subroutine subprograms.

We have seen how the programmer must be concerned with the attributes of arguments and those of the matching parameters. When writing a function, an additional consideration is that of the attributes of the value returned by the function. If the attributes of the value returned by the function are different from those expected by the invoking procedure, errors will result. As an example, consider the following function procedure:

CALC: PROC(A,B,C) ;
        RETURN(A+B+C) ;
        END ;

When the above function is invoked, e.g.,

W=CALC(X,Y,Z) ;

the sum of the three arguments is calculated by CALC, and the result is returned to the point of invocation. The compiler must know the attributes of the result returned by a function so that the proper conversion instructions may be generated for the purpose of converting the result to the data format of the variable on the left of the equals sign. The attributes of returned values may be declared in two ways:

1. They may be declared by default according to the first letter of the function name. For example, if the function name begins with the letters A through H or O through Z, then the result will be DECIMAL FLOAT(6), because that is the default attribute of identifiers beginning with those letters. Function names beginning with the letters I through N return a result

with the attributes FIXED BINARY(15). Thus, in invoking a function such as CALC, the following rules apply:

W = CALC (X,Y,Z);

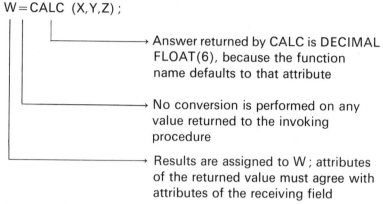

→ Answer returned by CALC is DECIMAL FLOAT(6), because the function name defaults to that attribute

→ No conversion is performed on any value returned to the invoking procedure

→ Results are assigned to W; attributes of the returned value must agree with attributes of the receiving field

2. Because the default attributes for function names do not allow us to return a result that is FIXED DECIMAL or FLOAT DECIMAL(16), for example, we must have another method of specifying the attributes of a returned value. This is accomplished through the RETURNS keyword. The general form is

RETURNS(attribute list)

This keyword will appear in both the invoking procedure and the invoked procedure. To illustrate, assume that CALC is to return a FIXED DECIMAL(7) result. The function procedure would be written as follows:

```
CALC:   PROC(A,B,C) RETURNS(FIXED DECIMAL(7));
        RETURN(A+B+C);
        END;
```

The RETURNS keyword, when specified in a PROCEDURE or ENTRY statement, is referred to as *The RETURNS option*. In the above example, the value returned by CALC will have the attributes FIXED and DECIMAL. The invoking procedure must also specify that CALC is returning a FIXED DECIMAL value of the same precision because these attributes differ from the attributes determined from the first letter of the function name. The *RETURNS attribute*, specified in a DECLARE statement for an entry name, indicates the attributes of the value returned by

that function. For example, the following procedure invokes
the CALC function:

```
PROG:   PROC OPTIONS(MAIN);
        DCL CALC RETURNS(FIXED DECIMAL(7));
        DCL SUM FIXED DECIMAL(7);
        GET LIST(A,B,C);
        SUM=CALC(A,B,C);
        PUT LIST('SUM IS',SUM);
        END PROG;
```

The RETURNS attribute also specifies, by implication, the
ENTRY attribute for the name.

The EXTERNAL Attribute

So far, we have been looking at subroutines and functions where
there are argument lists associated with parameter lists. There is another
method for making data names known in more than one separately
compiled procedure. It is the EXTERNAL attribute that specifies a
name to be known in other procedures containing an EXTERNAL
declaration of the same name. For example, assume a subroutine
procedure is coded to find the sum of a 200-element array whose
attributes are FIXED DECIMAL. Here is that subroutine:

```
ADDSUM:   PROC;
          DCL ARRAY(200) FIXED EXTERNAL;
          DCL SUM FIXED(7) EXTERNAL;
          SUM=0;
          DO K=1 TO 200;
          SUM=SUM+ARRAY(K);
          END;
          END ADDSUM;
```

Notice that there is no parameter list in the PROCEDURE statement.
Also, ARRAY and SUM are given the EXTERNAL attribute, which

indicates that these exact names and attributes should be declared in another procedure (the invoking procedure). For example:

```
PROG:    PROC OPTIONS(MAIN)
         DCL ARRAY(200) FIXED EXTERNAL;
         DCL SUM FIXED(7) EXTERNAL;
         GET LIST(ARRAY);
         CALL ADDSUM;
         PUT LIST ('RESULTS ARE', SUM);
         END PROG;
```

The important thing to understand here is that when identifiers are given the EXTERNAL attribute, it means that the identifiers may be known *by name* in other separately compiled procedures. It is imperative that the exact attributes be declared for these EXTERNAL names in all procedures; otherwise, errors will result. Note that some data a subprogram manipulates may be EXTERNAL and other data may be passed as arguments.

Identifiers that have the EXTERNAL attribute must be limited to six characters for the subset language and seven characters for the full language implementations. Consider the following examples:

```
DCL PAY FIXED(7,2) EXTERNAL;
DCL ZIP_CODE CHAR(5) EXTERNAL;   /* INVALID:
   IDENTIFIER IS TOO LONG */
```

In the full language, EXTERNAL may be abbreviated as EXT.

Two Programming Examples

A Subroutine Procedure

Figure 7.4 illustrates a subroutine procedure that will calculate the julian date, if given an argument in the form YYMMDD.† To CALL

†Here, YY stands for year; MM for month; DD for day.

```
 1              JULIAN: PROC(DATE,DAY);
 2                      DCL DATE PIC'(6)9',DAY PIC'ZZ9';
 3                      DCL (YY,MM) PIC'99';
 4                      DCL DAYS_TABLE(12) FIXED(3)INIT(31,28,31,30,31,30,
                                   31,31,30,31,30,31);
 5                      YY = SUBSTR(DATE,1,2);
 6                      MM = SUBSTR(DATE,3,2);
 7                      DAY = SUBSTR(DATE,5,2);
 8                      IF MOD(YY,4)=0 & YY¬=2000 THEN DAYS_TABLE(2)=29;
 9                      DO K = 1 TO MM - 1;
10                      DAY = DAY + DAYS_TABLE(K);
11                      END;
12                      END JULIAN;
```

FIGURE 7.4   A subroutine procedure.

this subroutine, the following statements would be coded:

```
DCL DATE BUILTIN, JULIAN ENTRY;
DCL DAY PIC'ZZ9', D CHAR(6);
D=DATE;   /* INVOKE DATE FUNCTION */
CALL JULIAN (D, DAY);
```

→ The julian date is placed into this argument by the subroutine called JULIAN; the attribute of DAY is to be PIC'ZZ9'

→ The first argument is to be a six-position character-string that gives the date in the form of YYMMDD

Below is a description of the statements in the subroutine in Figure 7.4.

Statement 1.   Following the keyword PROC, the parameters are specified within parentheses. These parameters will be associated with the arguments passed from the calling program. Notice that the parameter DATE refers to a six-position character-string, not the built-in function. This is because the DATE function will actually be invoked before JULIAN is called. What is stored in the first parameter of JULIAN is the result returned from the DATE built-in function.

Statement 2.   The parameter attributes are defined.

Statements 3–4.   Year, month, and day are declared, and the number of days in each month are assigned to an array.

Statements 5–7.   The substring built-in function is used to retrieve the year, month, and day from the longer string called DATE.

Statement 8.   The second month of the year is set equal to 29 days if YY is a leap year.

Statements 9–11.   DAY is modified to contain the results of the calculation that gives the julian date.

Statement 12.   When this statement is encountered during execution of the JULIAN procedure, it causes a return to the calling program.

A Function Procedure

Figure 7.5 illustrates a function procedure that will convert 24-hour clock time (e.g., 1740 hours) to AM or PM time (e.g., 5:40 PM). There are no arguments passed to this function procedure. The result from this function, which is called TIMEX, will be in the form of a character-string of length eight,

HH:MM AM   or   HH:MM PM   or
HH:MM N   or   HH:MM M

where HH stands for hours, MM stands for minutes, N stands for noon,

```
1          TIMEX:   PROCEDURE RETURNS(CHAR(8));
2                   DCL T PIC'(9)9',(HH,MM)PIC'Z9';
3                   DCL TIME BUILTIN, R CHAR(8)INIT('   :  ');
4                   T = TIME; /* INVOKE TIME BUILTIN FUNCTION */
5                   HH=SUBSTR(T,1,2);
6                   MM = SUBSTR(T,3,2);
7                   IF HH > 0  & HH < 12 THEN DO;
8                        SUBSTR(R,7,2) = 'AM';
9                        GO TO EXIT;
10                       END;
11                  IF HH > 12 & HH < 24 THEN DO;
12                       SUBSTR(R,7,2) = 'PM';
13                       HH = HH - 12;
14                       GO TO EXIT;
15                       END;
16                  IF HH = 0 | HH = 24 THEN DO;
17                       IF MM = 0 THEN SUBSTR(R,7,2)='M';
18                       ELSE SUBSTR(R,7,2) = 'AM';
19                       HH = 12;
20                       GO TO EXIT;
21                       END;
22                  IF  HH = 12 THEN IF MM = 0 THEN SUBSTR(R,7,2)='N';
23                                   ELSE SUBSTR(R,7,2) = 'PM';
24         EXIT:    SUBSTR(R,1,2) = HH;
25                  SUBSTR(R,4,2) = MM;
26                  RETURN(R);
27                  END;
```

FIGURE 7.5   A function procedure.

and M stands for midnight. To invoke this function, the following statements would be coded:

```
DCL TIMEX RETURNS(CHAR(8));
DCL T CHAR(8);
T=TIMEX;
```

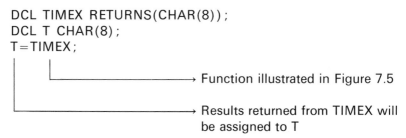

→ Function illustrated in Figure 7.5

→ Results returned from TIMEX will be assigned to T

Below is a description of the statements in the function procedure.

Statement 1. The PROCEDURE statement specifies the attributes of the result returned by this function through the RETURNS option.

Statement 2. Receiving field for time is declared.

Statements 3–4. TIME is declared as a built-in function and invoked. Result is hours and minutes. The seconds and thousandths of seconds also returned by TIME are ignored by this subprogram.

Statements 5–6. Hours and minutes are extracted from T.

Statements 7–23. These statements test the hours value so that the 24 hour time format returned by the TIME built-in function may be converted to the morning and afternoon time designation.

Statements 24–25. Hours and minutes are moved to the output area containing the results.

Statement 26. This statement causes a return to the invoking procedure, with the results specified in parentheses following the keyword RETURN.

SUMMARY

Functions versus Subroutines: A function is a procedure that returns a single value to the invoking procedure. By contrast, a subroutine cannot return a value to the point of invocation. The value of arguments, in certain cases, may be modified by the subroutine, and in this way results are effectively returned to the invoking program. A function is written to compute a single value which is returned to the point of invocation. The value returned may not be an array or a structure. A subroutine may return none, one, or many results to the invoking procedure through the modification of arguments in the sub-routine call.

Arguments and Parameters: Arguments passed to an invoked procedure must be accepted by that procedure. This is done by the explicit declaration of one or more parameters in a parenthesized list in the PROCEDURE statement of the invoked procedure. The attributes of a parameter and its corresponding argument must be the same. If the attributes of an argument are not consistent with those of its corresponding parameter, an error will probably result.

	Maximum number of arguments allowed in one subroutine CALL or function reference
Subset language	12
Full language	64

It is important to understand that the name of an argument, not its value, is passed to a subroutine or function. There are times when an argument has no name. A constant, for example, has no name; nor does an operational expression. *Internal names* are given to constants or expressions and are called *dummy arguments*.

The ENTRY Attribute: It is necessary to declare a subprogram to have the ENTRY attribute, if the identifier is not otherwise recognizable as an entry name; e.g.,

```
DCL SUB2 ENTRY;
CALL SUB1 (SUB2,A,B);
```

Following is a summary of the allowable forms of the ENTRY attribute. Generally, in the subset language implementations, you will get a diagnostic message if you call a procedure but fail to declare its name as having the ENTRY attribute.

	Allowable forms of the ENTRY attribute
Subset language	DCL name ENTRY; /* MUST BE SPECIFIED */
Full language	DCL name ENTRY; /* OPTIONAL */ DCL name ENTRY (parameter attribute,parameter attribute . . .);

In full language compilers, the ENTRY attribute allows you to direct the compiler to generate coding to convert one or more arguments to conform to the attributes of the. corresponding parameters, should arguments and their corresponding parameters have different attributes.

The ENTRY Statement: This statement defines an alternate entry point in a procedure; e.g.,

```
        A :   PROC;
              .
              .
              .
        A1:   ENTRY;
              .
              .
              .
              END;
```

Subroutines: A subroutine may be terminated in several ways:

1. When control reaches the final END statement of the subroutine.
2. Through the use of the RETURN statement.
3. By terminating with a GO TO statement.
4. By a STOP statement—this abnormally terminates execution of that subroutine and of the entire program associated with the procedure that invoked it.

Functions: The RETURN statement is used to terminate a function. Its use in a function differs somewhat from its use in a subroutine; in a function, not only does it return control, but it also returns the value to the point of invocation; e.g.,

    RETURN(element-expression);
           └──────────────→ The value returned to the invoking
                            procedure; it must be a single value

The RETURNS Attribute: The attributes of returned values may be declared in two ways:

1. They may be declared by default according to the first letter of the function name. If the function name begins with the letters A through H or O through Z, then the result will be DECIMAL FLOAT(6). Function names beginning with the letters I through N return a result with the attributes FIXED BINARY(15).
2. Because the default attributes for function names do not allow us to return a result that is FIXED DECIMAL or FLOAT DECIMAL(16), for example, the RETURNS keyword may define the attributes of a returned value.

The RETURNS attribute also specifies, by implication, the ENTRY attribute for the name. The RETURNS attribute is specified in the *invoking* procedure.

The RETURNS Option: This keyword is specified in a PROCEDURE statement of function procedures when it is desired to override the default attributes of the entry name. The RETURNS option is specified in the *invoked* procedure.

The EXTERNAL Attribute: This attribute specifies that a name is known in other procedures containing an EXTERNAL declaration of the same name. When identifiers are given the EXTERNAL attribute, it means that the identifiers may be known in other separately compiled procedures. It is imperative that the exact attributes (and names) be declared for these EXTERNAL names in all procedures; otherwise, errors will result.

CHECKPOINT QUESTIONS

1. What is the difference between an argument and a parameter?
2. How many values may be returned by
   (a) a function?
   (b) a subroutine?
3. Is this valid? Why or why not?

```
                     .
                     .
                     .
              CALL SUBRT(I,J,K);
   SUBRT:    PROCEDURE(A,B,C);
                     .
                     .
                     .
```

4. Given the following statement and explanation, what DECLARE statement must be added in order to compile without diagnostics?

   CALL ASUB(X,Y,SUBRT);

   → Name of a subroutine being passed as an argument

   → Two floating-point arguments

5. What attribute causes the conversion of arguments to match the attributes of their corresponding parameters?
6. What value will appear in B after the S procedure is invoked? (Be careful, this tests your understanding of dummy arguments.)

```
DCL S ENTRY(FIXED,FIXED(10));
A=5;
B=10;
CALL S(A,B);
```

```
S:   PROCEDURE(X,Y);
     DCL X FIXED,Y FIXED(10);
     Y=X*Y;
     END;
```

7. What does the ENTRY statement accomplish?
8. What happens if a STOP or EXIT statement is encountered in a subroutine?
9. What is the difference between the RETURNS *attribute* and the RETURNS *option*?
10. Is this valid? Why or why not?

```
DCL (A,B) EXTERNAL;          SUB:  PROCEDURE(Z);
A=10;                              DCL (A,B) EXT;
B=5;                               Z=A/B;
CALL SUB(C);                       END;
```

TERMS TO STUDY

argument
call
dummy argument
external procedure
internal name
invoked procedure

invoking procedure
modular programming
multiple entries
parameter
reference
subprogram

PRACTICE PROBLEMS

1. Convert Time

Write a subroutine procedure to convert thousandths of hours (TTT) to seconds (SS). To invoke this procedure, the following CALL would be coded:

CALL CTIME ((TIME), RES);

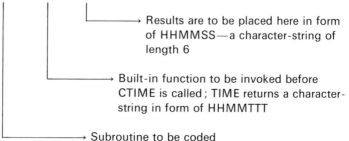

Results are to be placed here in form of HHMMSS—a character-string of length 6

Built-in function to be invoked before CTIME is called; TIME returns a character-string in form of HHMMTTT

Subroutine to be coded

2. Convert Julian Date

Given the julian date as an argument, write a function procedure to return the corresponding month and day. The function reference to invoke this procedure would be coded:

```
DCL DTE RETURNS(CHAR(4));
DCL X CHAR (4);
X=DTE (YEAR, JULIAN_DAY);
```

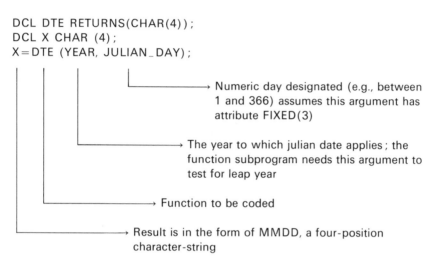

→ Numeric day designated (e.g., between 1 and 366) assumes this argument has attribute FIXED(3)

→ The year to which julian date applies; the function subprogram needs this argument to test for leap year

→ Function to be coded

→ Result is in the form of MMDD, a four-position character-string

3. Count Characters

Given an argument of 30 characters maximum, write a function procedure to determine the number of characters in a surname. The surname will be left-justified in the argument field padded on the right with blanks. To invoke this procedure, the following would be coded:

```
DCL CNT RETURNS (FIXED(2));
DCL X FIXED(2);
X=CNT(SURNAME);
```

→ A character-string of length 30

→ Function to be coded

→ Number of characters in argument is to be assigned to X

4. Count Bits

Given a bit-string of length 64, write a function procedure to count the number of "one" bits in the string and return this count to the point of invocation. The calling sequence is:

```
DCL ARG BIT(64);
DCL COUNT FIXED(2);
DCL CTBITS RETURNS (FIXED(2));
COUNT = CTBITS (ARG);
```

```
                                      ────────────→ Bit-string of length 64

                               ───────────→ Function to be coded

                        ─────────────→ Number of "1" bits found in the argument
```

5. Edit Data

Given a FIXED DECIMAL Social Security number, write a function procedure to edit this number by inserting hyphens. Result is to be a character-string in the form XXX-XX-XXXX. The calling sequence would be coded:

```
DCL EDITSS RETURNS (CHAR(11));
DCL SS_# CHAR(11);
DCL NO FIXED(9);
SS_# = EDITSS (NO);
```

```
                          ────────────→ Social Security number argument in the
                                          FIXED DECIMAL form XXXXXXXXX

                   ───────────→ Function to be coded

             ────────────→ Result is to be CHAR(11) with hyphens inserted;
                             e.g., XXX-XX-XXXX
```

This function would be most useful in the subset language implementations of PL/I, because the insertion of hyphens requires manipulation of subfields in the character-string. In the full language implementations, the following picture is valid to accomplish the hyphen insertion:

```
                    DCL SOC_SEC PIC'999-99-9999';
```

6. Search Tax Table

Write a function procedure to determine the tax amount due for a given taxable income. The calling sequence for this function follows:

```
DCL TAXAMT RETURNS (FIXED(7,2));
DCL ADJ_GROSS FIXED(9,2);   /* TAXABLE INCOME */
DCL TAX FIXED(7,2);
TAX=TAXAMT (ADJ_GROSS,N);
```

→ N = 1 for separate return
N = 2 for joint return
N = 3 for head of household return

→ Taxable income

→ Function to be coded

→ Result, whose attribute is FIXED(7,2), is placed here

In determining the tax amount due, use the following table in your function procedure:

If the taxable income is	Separate		Joint		Head of household	
0		14%		14%		14%
$500	70	15%	$70	14%	$70	14%
$1000	$145	16%	$140	15%	$140	16%
$1500	$225	17%	$215	15%	$220	16%
$2000	$310	19%	$290	16%	$300	18%
$3000	$500	19%	$450	17%	$480	18%
$4000	$690	22%	$620	19%	$660	20%
$6000	$1130	25%	$1000	19%	$1060	22%
$8000	$1630	28%	$1380	22%	$1500	25%
$10000	$2190	32%	$1820	22%	$2000	27%

→ Percent by which to multiply the amount over the taxable income figure in the leftmost column; for example, if taxable income is $1700, then TAX = 225. + .17 * (1700 − 1500)

→ The amount of tax due if the taxable income is the figure in the leftmost column; for example, if the taxable income is $2000, then tax is $310; however, if taxable income is between $2001 and $2999, then tax is $310 plus 19% of anything over $2000

7. Compute Sine

The sine of an angle may be obtained from the series

$$\sin x = x - \frac{x^3}{3!} + \frac{x^5}{5!} - \frac{x^7}{7!} + \frac{x^9}{9!} - \cdots$$

where x is measured in radians. Write a function subprogram called SINE to compute the sine of a radian argument using the first five terms of this series. You may wish to use the subprogram in Problem 13 in this subprogram. Both the argument and the result have the attributes DECIMAL FLOAT(6).

8. Find MAX and MIN

Write a subroutine procedure to find the smallest and largest values in an array whose size is indicated by an argument. The calling sequence is:

CALL MAXMIN (ARRAY, NSIZE, MAX, MIN);

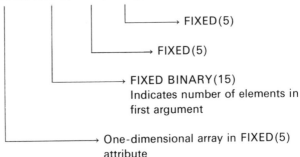

$\longrightarrow$ FIXED(5)

$\longrightarrow$ FIXED(5)

$\longrightarrow$ FIXED BINARY(15)
Indicates number of elements in first argument

$\longrightarrow$ One-dimensional array in FIXED(5) attribute

9. Reverse Array Elements

Write a subroutine procedure to reverse the elements of a 100-element array. For example, an array consists of the numbers 501−600 in elements 1−100, respectively; then the returned array should have the numbers 600 back to 501 in elements 1−100, respectively.

10. Calculate Volume of a Vessel

Write a function procedure to calculate the volume of water that may be contained in a child's wading pool where the diameter and height are floating-point arguments to the function. To invoke this procedure, the following function reference may be coded:

POOL=VOLUME (DIAMETER, HEIGHT);

$\longrightarrow$ Floating-point arguments, in inches

$\longrightarrow$ Function to be coded

$\longrightarrow$ Floating-point result

The formula for finding the volume (in gallons) of a circular vessel is

$$\text{Volume} = \frac{\pi r^2 h}{231}$$

where π is 3.14159, r is radius, h is height.

11. Find n! by Actual Multiplication

Write a function subprogram that will compute n!, where n is a DECIMAL FLOAT(6) argument to the subprogram:

$$n! = 1 \times 2 \times 3 \times 4 \times \cdots \times n$$

The subprogram should return a DECIMAL FLOAT(16) result. If the computed factorial causes the OVERFLOW condition to be raised, return a value of zero to the calling program.

12. Find n! by Forsyth's Approximation

Write a function subprogram that will compute n!, where n is a DECIMAL FLOAT(6) argument to the subprogram. Forsyth's approximation for n! is

$$n! = \sqrt{2\pi} \left\{ \frac{\sqrt{n^2 + n + 1/6}}{e} \right\}^{n+1/2}$$

The subprogram should return a DECIMAL FLOAT(16) result. If the computed factorial causes the OVERFLOW condition, return a zero result to the calling program. (*Note:* You may wish to code both methods for computing n! and then write a "driver program" that will call each of these subroutines and then print the results, organizing output so that the results from each subroutine may be compared.

13. Find Length of Triangle Side

The law of cosines says that

$$a^2 = b^2 + c^2 - 2bc(\cos A)$$

where a, b, c are the lengths of the sides of a triangle and A is the angle opposite side a. Write a function subprogram to find the length a for a triangle, given the argument b and c in feet and A in radians. The arguments, parameters, and

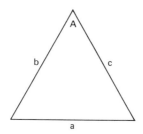

the result returned by the function should have the attributes DECIMAL FLOAT(6) or DECIMAL FLOAT(16).

14. Matrix Multiply

Write a subroutine subprogram called MATMPY which will multiply two matrices, each of which is a two-dimensional array of the same bounds. The calling sequence is:

```
DCL BOUND FIXED BINARY(15);
CALL MATMPY(A,B,C,BOUND);
```

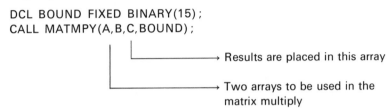

→ Results are placed in this array

→ Two arrays to be used in the matrix multiply

The first three arguments have the attributes DECIMAL FLOAT(6). As an illustration of how a matrix multiply works, assume two matrices, A and B, are 10 × 10 arrays. The product of two matrices is formed by multiplying each number in a row by a number in a column and adding the products, repeating for all combinations of rows and columns. In formula form it is

$$c_{ij} = \sum_{k=1}^{10} (a_{ik})(b_{kj}) \qquad \text{for all combinations of i and j}$$

or, for example:

$$c_{1,1} = a_{1,1}b_{1,1} + a_{1,2}b_{2,1} + a_{1,3}b_{3,1} + a_{1,4}b_{4,1} + \cdots + a_{1,10}b_{10,1}$$
$$c_{1,2} = a_{1,1}b_{1,2} + a_{1,2}b_{2,2} + a_{1,3}b_{3,2} + a_{1,4}b_{4,2} + \cdots + a_{1,10}b_{10,2}$$

$$c_{1,10} = a_{1,1}b_{1,10} + a_{1,2}b_{2,10} + a_{1,3}b_{3,10} + a_{1,4}b_{4,10} + \cdots + a_{1,10}b_{10,10}$$
$$c_{2,1} = a_{2,1}b_{1,1} + a_{2,2}b_{2,1} + a_{2,3}b_{3,1} + a_{2,4}b_{4,1} + \cdots + a_{2,10}b_{10,1} \cdots$$

In other words, any ijth element of the c matrix is composed of ten products added together, the products being corresponding elements of the ith row of the a matrix and the jth column of the b matrix multiplied together. Notice that the examples above show that the first subscript of the a matrix always agrees with first subscript of the desired c element, while the second subscript of the b matrix always agrees with the second subscript of the c element. The column subscript of a and the row subscript of b are always the same, also. Thus, this problem can be handled with three nested DO-loops, the innermost of which controls the summation.

chapter 8

Introduction

to Record I/O

and Structures

There are two types of data transmission in PL/I: stream and record. Stream data transmission has already been covered, and we saw that the keywords GET and PUT were always specified for this type of I/O. For the record I/O, the keywords READ and WRITE are used. When a READ or WRITE statement is given in PL/I, an *entire record* is read or written. An example would be reading an entire 80-column card; no more than one card can be read with one READ statement (recall that this is not the case with the GET statement). Or, when a WRITE statement is executed, if the output is to a line printer, then one line is printed; no more than one line of output (i.e., a record) may be written with one WRITE statement. Or, suppose a magnetic tape file contains employee payroll records that are 280 characters long; then a READ or WRITE statement would accomplish input or output for 280 characters at a time—that is, one employee's payroll record of 280 bytes in length. By contrast, with stream data transmission, *less than, more than,* or *one* record may be processed with *one* GET or PUT statement.

Record versus Stream

In stream data transmission, input consists of a stream of characters representing numeric constants or string constants. In stream input mode, PL/I scans the input stream and converts the data in the stream into the data type of the matching element in the *data list* of the GET statement. For example:

```
DECLARE A DECIMAL FLOAT(6),
        B CHARACTER(10),
        C FIXED DECIMAL(7,2),
        D BINARY FIXED(31);
GET LIST (A, B, C, D);
```

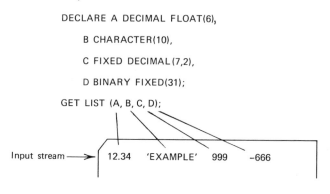

Input stream ——▶ | 12.34   'EXAMPLE'   999   –666

390

Notice the attributes of the *constants* in the input stream. The constant 12.34 is a FIXED DECIMAL(4,2) constant. 'EXAMPLE' is a character-string constant of length seven; i.e., CHAR(7). The remaining two constants are both FIXED DECIMAL(3). None of the items in the stream have exactly the same attributes as the matching items in the data list of the GET statement. It is one of the functions of the GET statement to convert these dissimilar forms in the stream to the proper base, scale, and precision (or proper length in the case of strings) and assign the resulting value to the corresponding item in the data list. On output, using a PUT statement, the reverse occurs. A major function of the PUT statement is to convert data list items which are stored in the internal coded form to a character representation which will be suitable for printing.

Record I/O does not perform this conversion. A READ statement merely transfers a complete record of data into a main storage location; it does not scan the data; it does not verify its validity, nor does it perform any conversions.

Because record I/O does not perform all the same functions that stream I/O does, we must be particularly careful to observe an important convention. Primarily, we must describe the data that we wish to input from the external storage device in exactly the same form that it appears on the external device. For example, on magnetic tape we have a record consisting of two fields. Assume that each field represents a dollars and cents quantity, in tens of thousands of dollars. The record might look like this:

First number   Second number

1	3	4	2	7	3	3	+	3	2	5	7	2	4	9	−

Notice that the fields are stored in the internal coded form that is called packed decimal in S/360 or S/370 terms. The numbers each occupy four bytes of external storage. When reading this record into main storage using record I/O, we merely state to PL/I where we want the record placed. We must ensure that there is enough main storage starting at that location to contain the record and, most importantly, that the attributes of the data items located where the record is to be placed match exactly the attributes of the data in the record. In the example above, both numbers are in the internal coded form of FIXED DECIMAL(7,2). We must declare two variables, A and B, in our program with exactly those attributes. However, if we declared A and B to be FIXED DECIMAL(9,2), an extra byte of storage would be reserved for each variable. When the record was read from the file into the space provided by A and B, the signs of the data would not be in the low order digit positions of A and B, nor would the first digit of the second number be located in the first position of the field named B. Let us look at a picture of this situation.

Assume that A and B are declared (erroneously) FIXED DECIMAL(9,2). The lowercase d represents a digit position and the S the sign of the value. If we now read the record shown above into the space in main memory using record input, it would appear in main storage as

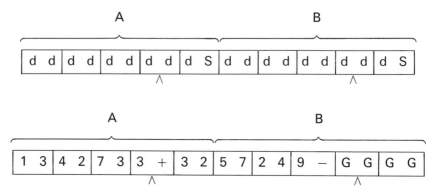

The capital G in the picture represents *garbage*—unusable data. But that is not the only problem we face due to our mistake. Notice the value in the sign position of the variable A. It is a digit two, the second digit of the second number we had stored on our file. The digit two is an invalid sign. Should we ever attempt to use this data in our program, we will encounter an error condition. Record I/O did not check the values it was placing in the variables A and B for validity, nor did it convert any data from one type to another. It simply placed the record in main storage as is. You might ask, "Why would anyone choose to use record I/O rather than stream I/O?" The answer is that, because it has relatively little processing to perform, record I/O is usually faster than stream I/O. If many different types of data conversions take place during stream I/O, then stream may not only be slower than record, but it may also require more main storage than record I/O.† In some cases, however, record I/O is the only form that may be used to

†In future implementations of PL/I, the differences in speed and main storage requirements between record and stream I/O may be negligible.

communicate with a data set. For example, direct access devices may contain files that are organized according to the *indexed sequential* method or the *direct* or *random* method. These types of data set organizations, which will be explained in Chapter 10, may only be accessed by record I/O statements.

Figure 8.1 illustrates the difference between record and stream I/O with respect to when data conversions take place. The broken-line box enclosed the first two steps of stream input to illustrate that both steps are accomplished by the stream input operation. The same is true for stream output.

This chapter will explain the record I/O statements in PL/I. The programming techniques illustrated facilitate *report writing*. Because you have learned to use edit-directed statements for card and printer

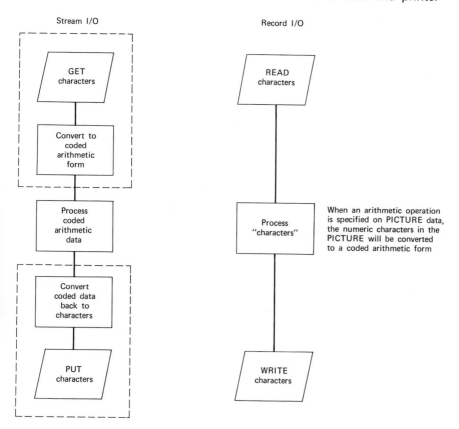

FIGURE 8.1 Comparison of conversions to coded arithmetic form.

programs, you may feel that programming these devices is more cumbersome using record I/O. If you have a COBOL background, however, record I/O will be more familiar to you.

Record I/O

The following are examples of record I/O statements:

READ FILE (CARDIN) INTO (CARD_AREA);

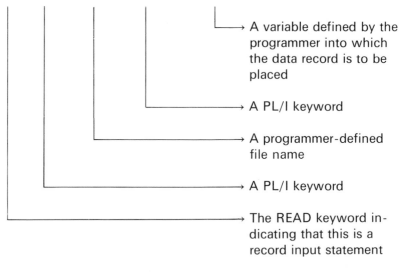

A variable defined by the programmer into which the data record is to be placed

A PL/I keyword

A programmer-defined file name

A PL/I keyword

The READ keyword indicating that this is a record input statement

WRITE FILE (PRINTR) FROM (PRINT_AREA);

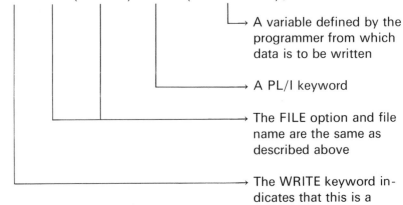

A variable defined by the programmer from which data is to be written

A PL/I keyword

The FILE option and file name are the same as described above

The WRITE keyword indicates that this is a record output statement

The file names CARDIN and PRINTR are programmer-defined identifiers. An introduction to the declaration of stream files has been given earlier in this text. The only difference between the previous file declarations and the file declarations for record-type files is that the keyword RECORD will replace the keyword STREAM. Here are some examples for the various compilers:

PL/I D	DCL CARDIN FILE INPUT RECORD ENV(F(80) MEDIUM(SYSIPT,2540));
DOS PL/I optimizing	DCL CARDIN FILE INPUT RECORD ENV(F BLKSIZE (80) MEDIUM(SYSIPT, 2540));
PL/I F	DCL CARDIN FILE INPUT RECORD ENV(F(80));
OS PL/I optimizing	DCL CARDIN FILE INPUT RECORD ENV(F BLKSIZE(80));

An 80/80 List Program

Assume it is desired to read a card which contains character information, and to print that card image on the printer. This operation is often referred to as an 80/80 list. Returning to the READ statement, let us look again at the I/O area specification:

READ FILE (CARDIN) INTO (CARD_AREA);

$\qquad\qquad\qquad\qquad$└──→ Name of an area that has the CHARACTER or PICTURE attribute if card data are being input

In record I/O there is no conversion of external characters to an internal data format. Thus, the area into which card data is read must have CHARACTER or PICTURE attributes. For example:

DCL CARD_AREA CHAR(80);

The length of input areas must be exactly the same as the length specified in the ENVIRONMENT section of the file declaration statement; this rule also applies to an output area and its corresponding output file, because we are using only fixed-length records.

In our program so far, to read one card and print it on a line printer, we would have the following statements:

```
DCL CARDIN FILE INPUT RECORD ENV(F(80)MEDIUM(SYSIPT,
    2540));
DCL PRINTR FILE OUTPUT RECORD ENV(F(80)MEDIUM(SYSLST,
    1403));
DCL CARD_AREA CHARACTER(80);
READ FILE (CARDIN) INTO (CARD_AREA);
WRITE FILE (PRINTR) FROM (CARD_AREA);
```

In the READ statement, blanks between FILE and (CARDIN) and INTO and (CARD_AREA) are optional, because the parentheses serve as delimiters. The same is true of the options specified in the ENVIRONMENT section of the file declarations and the WRITE statement.

There is one other step that must be added to our program for listing cards—that of opening the files. The statements would be written

```
        OPEN FILE(CARDIN);
        OPEN FILE(PRINTR);
```

Several files may be opened with *one* OPEN statement. For example:

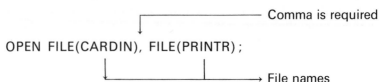

```
OPEN FILE(CARDIN), FILE(PRINTR);
```

All files must be opened *before* a READ or WRITE to these files is executed. There are several things that happen when files are opened; these are described here.

Attributes Are Merged.   As you will see later, there are some file attributes that may be specified in one of several places. For example, the INPUT attribute may be written in the file DECLARE statement or it may appear in the OPEN statement. Or, in an OS environment, many attributes may be specified in a job control card and never appear in the PL/I program. Thus, when the file is opened, the attributes from these various sources are located and combined to form the description that applies to the file we are opening.

Labels Are Checked. If you are communicating with disk or tape data sets, *data set labels* are also checked at OPEN time. When a tape or DASD data set is created, a label is defined through job control statements. This label contains the name by which the data set is identified to the operating system and is not to be confused with the file name you select in your file declaration statement.

Device Readiness Is Checked. An I/O device may not be in a *ready* state for several reasons: Perhaps the operator failed to press the START button that readies a device or perhaps there is no power supplied to the device. Typically, an error message is displayed on the operator's console when device failure is noted at OPEN time.

	Opening of files
Subset language	RECORD files must be explicitly opened; STREAM files are automatically opened the first time a GET or PUT to that file is issued
Full language	Both RECORD and STREAM files are automatically opened the first time a READ, WRITE, GET, or PUT to that file is issued

When files are closed, through the CLOSE statement, the file name is dissociated from the data set. The CLOSE is optional, because, when a PL/I program ends, all files are automatically closed. In the case of an output file on magnetic tape, an end-of-file tape mark is written and the tape is rewound. In the case of creating a file on a direct access device, an end-of-file mark is recorded.

Returning to the 80/80 list program, we see that Figure 8.2 shows a flowchart and the corresponding PL/I statements to list cards on a line printer. This flowchart could serve as a generalized approach to the programming steps that you would be coding when using record I/O.

If the program were now to be executed, the output would begin wherever the line printer stopped after the last job was run. There is a possibility that our output would appear on the same page as the output

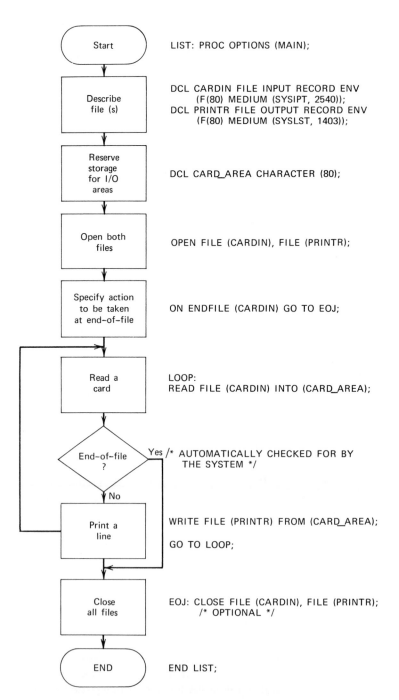

FIGURE 8.2 Sample program flowchart for record I/O.

from the job run just prior to the list program. Also, if there were more than 60 cards to be listed (assuming single spacing), the card image data would be printed on the perforation of the paper. These two problems occur because the list program did not make provisions for printing a certain number of lines per page, nor did it give the *equivalent* record I/O command for the PUT PAGE statement that accomplishes skipping to a new page on stream files. (*Note:* PUT PAGE causes an advance to a new page for *stream* files associated with a line printer. Thus, PUT PAGE should not be used to accomplish carriage control options for *record* files associated with a line printer.)

Carriage Control in Record I/O

One method for handling page overflow in record I/O is for the programmer to keep track in his program of the number of lines that are being printed on a page. Each time a WRITE is issued for a printer file, a *program counter* would be incremented by one. When the program counter reaches the maximum number established for the desired output page size, then the program gives the "command" to the printer to skip to a new page.

To accomplish carriage control for record I/O, we will append an extra character to the beginning of each record. In that character, we will place a code specifying the action we want performed; e.g., skip to a new page, skip two lines, etc. A keyword must be added to the ENVIRONMENT section of the file declaration to notify PL/I that these carriage control characters are being used in the program and that the I/O routines are to interpret the first character of each record accordingly. Two different sets of carriage control characters may be used in PL/I. The choice is made by specifying in the ENV attribute either the keyword CTLASA† or the keyword CTL360. If either of these keywords is used, it means that the first character of the output area will be the carriage control character. It is the programmer's responsibility to place a meaningful character in this position. Figure 8.3 gives the character codes that can be used with the CTLASA option. The character codes for CTL360 are given in Figure 8.4. The difference between CTLASA and CTL360 is that when CTLASA is specified, the carriage control operation will take place *before* the print operation, whereas, if CTL360 is specified, the carriage control operation will take place *after* the print operation.

†CTL stands for *control* and ASA refers to the American Standards Association, which has now changed its name to ANSI—American National Standards Institute.

400 PL/I Programming

Which option, CTLASA or CTL360, should you select? Generally, CTL360 carriage control is faster than CTLASA. However, the beginning programmer may find it easier to program carriage control options that take place *before* the print operation (CTLASA). The codes for CTL360 are usually specified using the BIT attribute.

Character code	Resulting carriage control operation
(blank)	Space one line before printing
0	Space two lines before printing
-	Space three lines before printing
+	Suppress space before printing
1	Skip to channel 1 before printing
2	Skip to channel 2 before printing
3	Skip to channel 3 before printing
4	Skip to channel 4 before printing
5	Skip to channel 5 before printing
6	Skip to channel 6 before printing
7	Skip to channel 7 before printing
8	Skip to channel 8 before printing
9	Skip to channel 9 before printing
A	Skip to channel 10 before printing
B	Skip to channel 11 before printing
C	Skip to channel 12 before printing
V	Select stacker 1
W	Select stacker 2

FIGURE 8.3 Carriage control characters that can be used with CTLASA option.

Figure 8.5 shows a modified version of the list program to provide for printing 55 lines per page. Some comments follow.

Statement 2. Notice that the CARDIN and PRINTR files are declared in one DECLARE statement. Also notice that the keyword CTLASA has been added to the ENVIRONMENT section of the file declaration. The record size has been changed from F(80) to F(81). Because we are using CTLASA, an extra position must be added to the record size to allow for the placement of the carriage control character.

Statements 3–4. These two statements were punched into the

Eight-bit code	Function
00000001	Write (no automatic space)
00001001	Write and space 1 line after printing
00010001	Write and space 2 lines after printing
00011001	Write and space 3 lines after printing
10001001	Write and skip to channel 1 after printing
10010001	Write and skip to channel 2 after printing
10011001	Write and skip to channel 3 after printing
10100001	Write and skip to channel 4 after printing
10101001	Write and skip to channel 5 after printing
10110001	Write and skip to channel 6 after printing
10111001	Write and skip to channel 7 after printing
11000001	Write and skip to channel 8 after printing
11001001	Write and skip to channel 9 after printing
11010001	Write and skip to channel 10 after printing
11011001	Write and skip to channel 11 after printing
11100001	Write and skip to channel 12 after printing
00001011	Space 1 line immediately
00010011	Space 2 lines immediately
00011011	Space 3 lines immediately
10001011	Skip to channel 1 immediately
10010011	Skip to channel 2 immediately
10011011	Skip to channel 3 immediately
10100011	Skip to channel 4 immediately
10101011	Skip to channel 5 immediately
10110011	Skip to channel 6 immediately
10111011	Skip to channel 7 immediately
11000011	Skip to channel 8 immediately
11001011	Skip to channel 9 immediately
11010011	Skip to channel 10 immediately
11011011	Skip to channel 11 immediately
11100011	Skip to channel 12 immediately

Stacker selection on 1442

10000001	Select into stacker 1
11000001	Select into stacker 2

Pocket selection on 2540

00000001	Select into pocket 1
01000001	Select into pocket 2
10000001	Select into pocket 3

Stacker selection on 2520

00000001	Select into stacker 1
01000001	Select into stacker 2

FIGURE 8.4 Bit combinations that can be used with CTL360 for printer control and stacker selection.

```
1     LIST: PROC OPTIONS(MAIN);
2           DCL CARDIN FILE INPUT RECORD ENV(F(80)MEDIUM(SYSIPT,2540)),
            PRINTR FILE OUTPUT RECORD ENV(F(133)CTLASA MEDIUM(SYSLST,1403));
3           DCL CARD_AREA CHAR(80);  DCL PRINT_AREA CHAR(133);
5           OPEN FILE(CARDIN), FILE(PRINTR);  ON ENDFILE(CARDIN) GO TO EOJ;
7           LINE_CT=55;
8     LOOP: READ FILE (CARDIN) INTO (CARD_AREA);
9           LINE_CT=LINE_CT+1;
10          IF LINE_CT > 55 THEN DO;
11                              LINE_CT=0;
12                              PRINT_AREA='1'||CARD_AREA;
13                              END;
14                     ELSE PRINT_AREA=' '||CARD_AREA;
15          WRITE FILE(PRINTR) FROM (PRINT_AREA);
16          GO TO LOOP;
17    EOJ:  END;
```

FIGURE 8.5   Program to list cards using record I/O and carriage control option—CTLASA.

same source card. The declaration of a PRINT_AREA is a new statement. It had to be added because the output area is now a different length than the input area.

Statement 7. This is a new statement. It initially sets LINE_CT equal to 55—the maximum number of lines we wanted to print on a page. Initializing LINE_CT to this value causes the program, later on, to skip to a new page *before* the first card is to be printed. If we did not skip to a new page at the beginning of our program output, the printed output would have started wherever the line printer paper was last positioned. Usually, there is printing on that page, so the new data in our program would appear with previous printout from some other program.

Statement 9. The line counter is incremented here.

Statements 10–14. The IF statement tests the line counter. If the line counter is greater than 55, it is the time to reset it to zero and put a character of '1' in the first position of the print area. The '1' specifies that we want to skip to channel 1 before printing the line. Channel 1 corresponds with the punch in the carriage tape that is lined up with the first print line on a page. Notice how the carriage control character was concatenated to CARD_AREA so that the two fields could be moved as a single string into the PRINT_AREA. If the line count has not reached the maximum, then control is transferred to the ELSE statement in the IF statement. A blank (' '), which is also concatenated to CARD_AREA, is a carriage control character to space one line before printing.

A Programming Example

Introduction to Structures

In the discussion of the 80/80 list program, it was stated that the I/O area must have the CHARACTER or PICTURE attribute because input was from cards. Thus, declaring a character-string having a length of 80 met our needs for simply reading cards and listing them. More frequently, we are interested in manipulating fields within a card. To illustrate, assume that a college bookstore has ordered a number of books to add to its inventory for the coming semester. In a few cases, the books ordered are not on-hand in the publisher's warehouse, although in most cases the orders can readily be filled. The bookstore keeps a record of which orders are outstanding by punching a card for each title ordered. The card layout is described in Figure 8.6. Our task is to write a program to generate a report showing, among other things, the number of books that are back ordered and the amount due for books delivered.

Columns	Description
1–5	Catalog number: a five-digit field
6–9	Author number: a four-digit field
10–13	Quantity ordered: a four-digit field
14–17	Quantity delivered: a four-digit field
18–23	Unused at this time
24–27	Unit price: a four-digit field with an assumed decimal point between the second and third digits
28–47	Title: an alphameric description
48–58	Author: an alphameric description
59–68	Publisher: an alphameric description
69–80	Unused at this time

FIGURE 8.6

There are eight items of data on each card, as well as the two unused fields (columns 18–23 and 69–80). We could declare those data items with the following DECLARE statement:

```
DCL   CATALOG_NO PIC'(5)9',
      AUTHOR_NO CHAR(4),
      QTY_ORDERED PIC'9999',
      QTY_DELIVERED PIC'9999',
      PRICE PIC'99V99',
      TITLE CHAR(20),
      AUTHOR_NAME CHAR(11),
      PUBLISHER CHAR(10) ;
```

If we add up the total number of bytes declared in the above statement, we will find that there are only 62 characters accounted for in the card. The missing 18 characters are in the two areas of the card which are unused. However, we must have an 80-byte area into which we can read the card file, because the physical record is 80 columns long. Therefore, we must insert into our declaration, between QTY_DELIV-ERED and PRICE, a variable—call it UNUSED—which has the attribute CHAR(6), and we must append a declaration for a variable—call it REST_OF_RECORD—with the attribute CHAR(12). Now we have a total of 80 characters declared—just the right size for a card image.

Unfortunately, we are still not out of the woods with our data declaration. A problem which is not so obvious is still facing us. When we declare independent variables, as in our DECLARE statement above, no guarantee is made by PL/I concerning the physical *location* of the variables in main storage, except that space *somewhere* will be assigned by the compiler for those variables. In other words, there is no guarantee that the variable named AUTHOR_NO will immediately follow the variable CATALOG_NO, or that REST_OF_RECORD will be the last 12 bytes of an 80-byte area. Yet, we know from our previous discussions on record I/O that we must provide a contiguous area equal in length to the record size, because a READ statement simply places the 80 bytes of the card into main storage starting at the location specified in the INTO option. But, with the above declaration, we cannot be sure that these data variables are in storage *relative to one another*. That last phrase is most important. We do not care *where* the variables are in main storage as long as they are contiguous and in the proper sequence relative to one another. To accomplish this, we must use a new type of data called a structure.

A *structure* is a collection of data items whose locations relative to one another are critical. Usually, the data items which appear in a structure have a logical relationship to each other. To describe the card layout in Figure 8.6, the following structure could be coded:

```
DCL 1 CARD_REC,
        2 CATALOG_NO PIC'(5)9',
        2 AUTHOR_NO CHAR(4),
        2 QTY_ORDERED PIC'9999',
        2 QTY_DELIVERED PIC'9999',
        2 UNUSED CHAR(6),
        2 PRICE PIC'99V99',
        2 TITLE CHAR(20),
        2 AUTHOR_NAME CHAR(11),
        2 PUBLISHER CHAR(10),
        2 REST_OF_RECORD CHAR(12);
```

In this example of a structure, the individual items were declared with PICTURE and CHARACTER attributes and were preceded with the digit 2. This digit is referred to as a *level number*. All of the items are grouped together under the structure name of CARD_REC, which has a level number of 1. Major structure names always have a level number of 1. Any number greater than 1 may be used for subdivisions of the structure. Thus, in the above example, although we specified a level number of 2 for all the fields within CARD_REC, we could have selected the value 3 or 5 or 66—just as long as it is greater than 1. All of the data items are at the same logical level and are each a part of CARD_REC. The 80 bytes declared in this structure are made up of contiguous fields in the sequence in which they are declared. That is, the first five bytes of the structure make up the CATALOG_NO, the next four bytes make up the AUTHOR_NO, the next four bytes make up the QTY_ORDERED, and so on.

To read data into the CARD_REC structure, the following record input statement could be coded:

```
READ FILE(CARDIN)INTO(CARD_REC);
```

In a READ or WRITE statement, only the major structure name may be specified.

Not only are structures used for describing input data, but they are also used for formatting and editing output data. Continuing with our bookstore example, we stated that after a card had been read, the quantity back ordered and the amount due for books delivered were to be computed and printed. The computations are

$$BACK = QTY\_ORDERED - QTY\_DELIVERED;$$
$$AMT = PRICE*QTY\_DELIVERED;$$

The layout of the report showing the calculated results, as well as the title and catalog number, is shown in Figure 8.7. At the top of this figure are two heading lines. To declare the character-string literals that establish these headings, we could code

```
DCL HEADING CHAR(60);
HEADING='1CATALOG NO.'||(11)' '||'TITLE'||(9)' '||' BACK ORD.'
  ||'AMT. DUE FOR';
```

In the above assignment statement, the "1" in the front of the literal CATALOG is the carriage control character. The '1' causes a skip to a new page before the heading is printed, yet the '1' will not be printed. The printer layout in Figure 8.7 shows that 59 print positions will be used for this report. However, it was necessary to declare a character-string of length 60 to allow for the insertion of the carriage control character. Notice also in the above assignment statement how blanks were concatenated between each word in the heading. To print the second line of the heading, we can designate that literal constant in the following way:

```
HEADING=(48)' '||'BOOKS DELV''D';
```

There are 47 leading blanks on the printer layout in Figure 8.7. Because a blank is the carriage control character to skip one line, 48

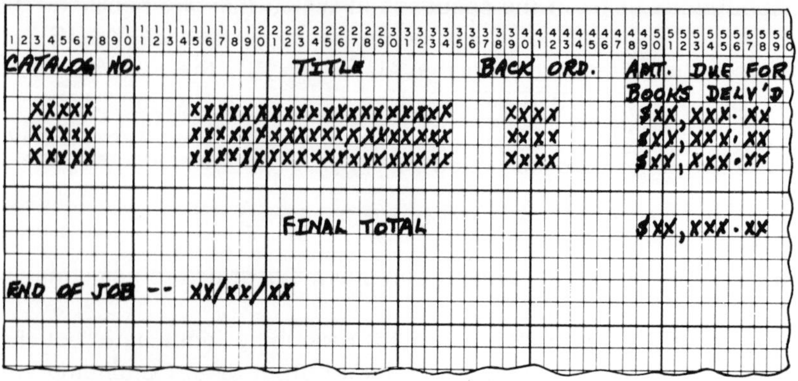

FIGURE 8.7   Printer layout form for book status report.

leading blanks were specified in the character-string literal. Notice that an apostrophe is to be inserted in the output heading. To do this, a double apostrophe must be specified in the character-string constant, but only one apostrophe will actually print. The other apostrophes are those used to surround or delineate the literal.

A structure is also needed to describe the detail line format.

```
DCL 1 OUTPUT_AREA,
        2 CARRIAGE_CONTROL CHAR(3),        /*  3 CHAR'S */
        2 CATALOG_# PIC '(5)9(7)B',        /* 12 CHAR'S */
        2 BOOK_TITLE CHAR(24),             /* 24 CHAR'S */
        2 BACK_ORDERED PIC '(3)Z9(6)B',    /* 10 CHAR'S */
        2 AMT_DUE PIC '$$$,$$$V.99B';      /* 11 CHAR'S */
```

An explanation of each elementary item in the above structure follows.

CARRIAGE_CONTROL CHAR(3).   Only one character needs to be reserved for the carriage control feature. Two more characters were added to this field to provide two blanks preceding the catalog number (see the printer layout in Figure 8.7). Later on, we will discuss the entire program that prints this report. In this program the following statement will initialize the carriage control character. If a shorter character-string is assigned to a longer character-string, there is padding on the right with blanks; for example:

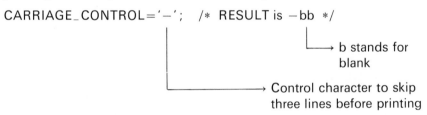

```
CARRIAGE_CONTROL='-';   /* RESULT is -bb */
```

b stands for blank

Control character to skip three lines before printing

CATALOG_# PIC '(5)9(7)B'.   In this picture a repetition factor of five 9's is specified, followed by seven blanks. Again, from Figure 8.7, notice how there are seven blanks following the catalog number. Using the B (for blank) in the picture is one method of specifying trailing blanks.

BOOK_TITLE CHAR(24).   This field will have assigned to it the 20-character title that was read from cards. Because the title is to be followed by four blanks, the character-string length was specified as 24.

BACK_ORDERED PIC '(3)Z9(6)B'.   This field is ten positions in length: 3 Z's, a 9, and 6 B's. As you can see, this field has zero suppression and trailing blanks specified. Thus, if a value of 23 is assigned to this PICTURE, this is the resulting character-string: bb23bbbbbb.

AMT_DUE PIC '$$$,$$$V.99B'. Floating dollar sign and comma and decimal point insertion are specified in this PICTURE. This PICTURE had to be followed by a blank (B) to bring the total number of characters in the entire structure up to 60, because the first heading line was 60 characters long and we are using only fixed-length records. Inasmuch as all print areas for a file with fixed-length records must be the same length, we must make all records equal in length to the longest.

For our sample program, we will use the following statement:

DCL PRINTR FILE OUTPUT RECORD ENV(CTLASA F(60)
        MEDIUM(SYSLST,1403));

Because there are two heading lines to be printed, the following output statement will appear *twice* in the program:

WRITE FILE(PRINTR)FROM(HEADING);

Built-in Functions

The functions we are going to examine here are those needed to generate the sample report in the bookstore application.

The DATE Built-in Function. In the last line of the report shown in Figure 8.7, the literal END OF JOB is to be printed followed by the date. The current date is recorded in the computer each day that it is started up, usually by the operator. Then, any program wishing to retrieve this value may do so. In PL/I, the method used is to invoke the DATE built-in function. The DATE function returns to the calling program (that is, your program) a string of six characters in the form of YYMMDD.

The SUBSTR Built-in Function. This function manipulates *substrings* of data; thus, the abbreviation SUBSTR. The string data may have the CHARACTER, BIT, or PICTURE attribute. The format of this function is

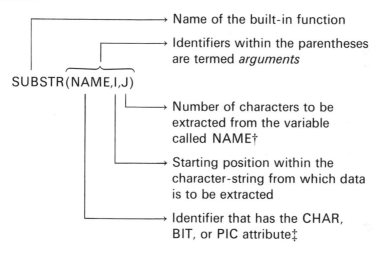

Name of the built-in function

Identifiers within the parentheses are termed *arguments*

SUBSTR(NAME,I,J)

Number of characters to be extracted from the variable called NAME†

Starting position within the character-string from which data is to be extracted

Identifier that has the CHAR, BIT, or PIC attribute‡

Recall that the DATE built-in function returns the date in the form of YYMMDD. However, we would like to have the date printed in the form of MM/DD/YY. Thus, it is necessary to extract substrings "YY," "MM," and "DD," not only for purposes of concatenating the slashes, but also to rearrange the subfields within the date character-string. For example:

```
DCL EDIT_DATE CHAR(8), TODAY CHAR(6), DATE BUILTIN;
TODAY=DATE;  /* INVOKE THE DATE FUNCTION */
EDIT_DATE=SUBSTR(TODAY,3,2) || '/' || SUBSTR(TODAY,5,2)
   || '/' || SUBSTR(TODAY,1,2);
/* THUS, EDIT_DATE=MM/DD/YY */
```

Notice that DATE was declared to have the BUILTIN attribute. Usually, it is not necessary to declare built-in functions as having the BUILTIN attribute, because most functions are assumed to have this attribute. However, for built-in functions that do not have an *argument*, the BUILTIN attribute should be declared.

---

†In the subset language, the third argument may only be a decimal constant. In the full language, it may be a constant, a variable, or an expression.

‡In the full language, SUBSTR can be directly used with other data types (which will be automatically converted to character-strings).

Pseudo-Variables

A pseudo-variable is a built-in function name (and arguments) that may appear on the left side of an assignment symbol. SUBSTR may also be used as a *pseudo-variable*.

Using SUBSTR as a pseudo-variable will provide an efficient means of preparing the final total line on the output report shown in Figure 8.7. After all detail lines are printed, this final total line should show the amount due for books delivered. Editing of the detail lines can be done by assigning the calculated variables (e.g., AMT and BACK) to identifiers in the structure, OUTPUT_AREA. Editing of the final total line can be handled in the following manner:

DCL TOTAL_LINE CHAR(60) DEFINED OUTPUT_AREA;

In the above statement, a character-string of length 60 has been overlay defined on the structure from which data is to be written on the line printer. Now, we have two ways of "looking at" one area—as a structure, and as a single character-string. The next statement would be

TOTAL_LINE = '-';

The above statement causes a (-) to be assigned to the first position (i.e., the carriage control position) of the character-string called TOTAL_LINE. Blanks are padded to the right of the (-) character. The (-) is the carriage control character to cause spacing of three lines before printing. Now, to move the literal FINAL TOTAL into print positions 22–32 of the OUTPUT_AREA, we could write the following:

SUBSTR(TOTAL_LINE,23,11) = 'FINAL TOTAL';

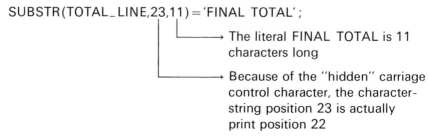

→ The literal FINAL TOTAL is 11 characters long

→ Because of the "hidden" carriage control character, the character-string position 23 is actually print position 22

The next step is to edit the total amount. Recall the layout of the OUTPUT_AREA structure:

```
DCL 1 OUTPUT_AREA,
      2 CARRIAGE_CONTROL CHAR(3),
      2 CATALOG_# PIC '(5)9(7)B',
      2 BOOK_TITLE CHAR(24),
      2 BACK_ORDERED PIC '(3)Z9(6)B',
      2 AMT_DUE PIC '$$$,$$$V.99B';
```

The first four elementary items in the above structure have been cleared to blanks and the literal FINAL TOTAL has been placed in the twenty-third position of the structure and will appear in the twenty-second print position on printer page. Assume the total amount is called TOTAL_AMT. To edit this field, the following assignment statement may be written:

$$AMT\_DUE = TOTAL\_AMT;$$

Recall that TOTAL_LINE was a character-string that was overlay defined on OUTPUT_AREA. We have been moving data for output to TOTAL_LINE. However, for purposes of editing, TOTAL_AMT was assigned to a subfield in OUTPUT_AREA. Keep in mind that OUTPUT_AREA and TOTAL_LINE represent the same area of storage. To print the TOTAL_LINE we will code the following:

$$WRITE\ FILE(PRINTR)FROM(OUTPUT\_AREA);$$

Because TOTAL_LINE and OUTPUT_AREA actually occupy the same storage area, the data assigned to TOTAL_LINE is in OUTPUT_AREA. In record I/O, you may not specify I/O areas that have the DEFINED attribute. Hence, it would have been invalid to have written

WRITE FILE(PRINTR)FROM(TOTAL_LINE);   /* INVALID */

because TOTAL_LINE has the attribute DEFINED.

Figure 8.8 shows the book status report program in its entirety.

Explanation of the Program in Figure 8.8

Statement 2.   Both files are declared in this one statement. Notice that a blank followed the CTLASA option. Options in the ENVIRONMENT section must be separated by a blank if there are no delimiters (e.g., parentheses) separating the options. Thus, no blank was needed between the F(60) option and the MEDIUM option because the right parenthesis following the value 60 served as a delimiter. Note that commas may *not* be used to separate options in the ENVIRONMENT section.

Statement 3.   This structure describes the card data the program will be reading. Recall from the card layout in Figure 8.6 that this program did not use the author or publisher fields; thus, the length of these fields plus the remaining unused card columns have been grouped into one field called REST_OF_RECORD in the structure.

Statement 4.   A character-string of length 60 is declared. Later, character constants in the heading will be assigned to this variable.

```
 1    BOOK: PROC OPTIONS(MAIN);
 2          DCL CARDIN FILE INPUT RECORD ENV(F(80)MEDIUM(SYSIPT,2540)),
            PRINTR FILE OUTPUT RECORD ENV(CTLASA F(60)MEDIUM(SYSLST,1403));
 3          DCL 1 CARD_AREA,
                2 CATALOG_NO PIC'(5)9',
                2 AUTHOR_NO CHAR(4),
                2 QTY_ORDERED PIC'9999',
                2 QTY_DELIVERED PIC'9999',
                2 USUSED CHAR(6),
                2 PRICE PIC'99V99',
                2 TITLE CHAR(20),
                2 REST_OF_RECORD  CHAR(33);
 4          DCL HEADING CHAR(60);
 5          DCL 1 OUTPUT_AREA,
                2 CARRIAGE_CONTROL CHAR(3) INIT(' '),
                2 CATALOG_# PIC'(5)9(7)B',
                2 BOOK_TITLE CHAR(24),
                2 BACK_ORDERED PIC '(3)Z9(6)B',
                2 AMT_DUE PIC'$$$,$$$V.99B';
 6          DCL BACK FIXED(5), AMT FIXED(7,2),TOTAL_AMT FIXED(7,2) INIT(0);
 7          ON ENDFILE(CARDIN) GO TO EOJ;
 8          OPEN FILE(CARDIN), FILE(PRINTR);
 9          LINE_CT = 46;
10    LOOP: READ FILE(CARDIN)INTO(CARD_AREA);
11          BACK = QTY_ORDERED - QTY_DELIVERED; AMT = PRICE * QTY_DELIVERED;
13          TOTAL_AMT = TOTAL_AMT + AMT;
14          IF LINE_CT > 45 THEN DO; LINE_CT = 0;
16                          HEADING='1CATALOG NO.'||(11)' '||'TITLE'||(9)
                           ' '||'BACK ORD.   AMT.DUE FOR';
17                          WRITE FILE(PRINTR)FROM(HEADING);
18                          HEADING =(48)' '||'BOOKS DELV''D';
19                          WRITE FILE(PRINTR) FROM(HEADING);
20                          END;
21          CATALOG_# = CATALOG_NO;     BOOK_TITLE = TITLE;
23          BACK_ORDERED = BACK; AMT_DUE = AMT;
25          WRITE FILE(PRINTR) FROM (OUTPUT_AREA);
26          LINE_CT  = LINE_CT + 1;
27          GO TO LOOP;
28          DCL TOTAL_LINE CHAR(60) DEFINED OUTPUT_AREA;
29    EOJ:  TOTAL_LINE = '-';
30          SUBSTR(TOTAL_LINE,23,11) = 'FINAL TOTAL';
31          AMT_DUE = TOTAL_AMT;
32          WRITE FILE(PRINTR) FROM(OUTPUT_AREA);
33          DCL TODAY CHAR(6), TODAY_EDITED CHAR(8);
34          DCL DATE BUILTIN; TODAY = DATE;
36          TODAY_EDITED=SUBSTR(TODAY,3,2)||'/'||SUBSTR(TODAY,5,2)||'/'||
                          SUBSTR(TODAY,1,2);
37          TOTAL_LINE='-END OF JOB -- '||TODAY_EDITED;
38          WRITE FILE(PRINTR)FROM(OUTPUT_AREA);
39          END;
```

FIGURE 8.8   Book status report program.

Statement 5. The output area is described. How data is edited into these fields was discussed previously in this chapter. Notice how INIT was used to initialize the carriage control character. A blank simply means to space up one line before print. Two things to remember about pictures: to specify leading blanks on a numeric field (e.g., BACK_ORDERED), use the PICTURE character Z; to specify trailing blanks in a numeric field, use the PICTURE character B. Also, note that a PICTURE was specified for AMT_DUE that was large enough to contain the AMT figure for the detail line as well as FINAL_TOTAL in the total line.

Statement 6.   The program's calculated variables are declared. It is more efficient to declare these values in the FIXED DECIMAL form than to specify PICTURE for them. While the input data fields do have the PICTURE attribute, when they are used in a calculation, they will be automatically converted to a FIXED DECIMAL data format; hence, assigning the results of these calculations to FIXED DECIMAL fields is the most efficient method for calculating and accumulating results.

Statement 7.   This statement tells the system where to go when the end-of-file condition is raised. Notice that this statement is *outside* of the repetitive operation (i.e., loop) of reading cards and printing on the printer.

Statement 8.   For the subset language, record I/O files must be explicitly opened. This statement would be optional for the full language.

Statement 9.   It has been established that 45 lines, excluding headings, are to be printed per page of output. Setting the line counter to a value one greater than 45 at the beginning of the program will force headings to be printed before the first detail line is printed. Statement 14 tests the line counter for being greater than 45. If it is greater than 45, then it is time to skip to a new page and print headings. Note that another method in Statement 14 could have been to test line counter for being *equal* to 46. Either approach accomplishes the same thing.

Statement 10.   The label LOOP marks the beginning of the repetitive operation of reading cards, calculating results, and printing detail lines.

Statements 11–12.   The back ordered quantity and the amount due for books delivered are calculated.

Statement 13.   The detail line AMT is accumulated into the variable TOTAL_AMT. Notice, from statement 6, that TOTAL_AMT had to be initialized with the value of zero. If this initialization had not been specified, this program would probably *blow up* at this point, because TOTAL_AMT would already contain whatever was left in main storage from the program executed just prior to the execution of this program.

Statements 14–20.   A test is made to determine if it is time to skip to a new page and print headings.

Statements 21–22.   The catalog number and book title in the CARD_

AREA are moved (through the use of the assignment statement) to the OUTPUT_AREA.

Statements 23—24. The calculated variables AMT and BACK are edited through their assignment to PICTURES in the OUTPUT_AREA.

Statement 25. A detail line is printed. Notice that this statement is identical with the statements 32 and 38.

Statements 26—27. The line counter is incremented by one, indicating that a line of output has just been printed; then there is a branch back to LOOP to read the next input card.

Statement 28. A character-string is overlay defined on the OUTPUT_AREA structure. This is because we want to look at the output area as a single character-string for purposes of clearing the structure to blanks and assigning the literal FINAL TOTAL to that area. Note that DECLARE statements may appear anywhere in your PL/I program.

Statement 29. This is the label and location to which the system will branch when the ENDFILE condition is raised. TOTAL_LINE is set to a minus sign in the first position and blanks in all remaining positions of the character-string.

Statement 30. Through the use of SUBSTR as a pseudo-variable, the literal FINAL TOTAL is moved into the output area.

Statement 31. The accumulated figure for total amount (TOTAL_AMT) due for books delivered is edited into the output area.

Statement 32. The final total line is printed. Notice also, from the sample output shown in Figure 8.9, that there are two spaces between the last detail line in the report and the final total line. It was previously stated that a carriage control character of minus specifies to space three lines before printing. Thus, there will be *two* blank lines on the report, and the output will be printed on the *third* line.

Statement 33. Character-strings for the date are declared.

Statements 34—35. The DATE built-in function is declared with the BUILTIN attribute, and the function is invoked.

Statement 36. The "YY," "MM," and "DD" characters are rearranged and concatenated with slashes to form the string value of MM/DD/YY.

CATALOG NO.	TITLE	BACK ORD.	AMT.DUE FOR BOOKS DELV'D
05001	THE AMBASSADORS	2	$10.00
05002	THE AMERICAN	0	$12.50
05003	THE BEAR	20	$.00
05004	BRIGHTON ROCK	1	$7.80
05005	THE BROTHERS KARAM	5	$7.50
05006	CANDY	97	$3.00
05007	THE CAPTIVE WITCH	2	$.00
05008	THE CORRUPTERS	16	$1.50
05009	CRIME AND PUNISH.	9	$.95
05011	DAISY MILLER	2	$.00
05013	DEVOTIONS	1	$.00
05014	DIAMOND HEAD	28	$1.50
05015	DR. ZHIVAGO	38	$1.90
05016	FAIROAKS	18	$1.50
05017	THE FIXER	48	$10.00
05020	GOLDFINGER	182	$13.50
05027	LADY CHATTERLEYS	28	$3.00
05028	LOLITA	37	$2.85
06040	THE SEA AROUND US	9	$.75
06042	SONS AND LOVERS	12	$.00
06043	STORIES OF ARTISTS	1	$.00
06044	THE STRANGER	10	$.00
06045	THE SUBTERRANEANS	1	$.00
06046	THE SUN ALSO RISES	37	$7.50
07047	SWAN'S WAY	4	$.00
07048	THOSE WHO LOVE	11	$4.00
07049	TOM JONES	12	$.00
08050	TURN OF THE SCREW	10	$.00
08051	VICTORY	14	$.00
08052	WAR AND PEACE	5	$.00
20001	ADVANCE CALCULUS	1	$.00
20002	COLLEGE ALGEBRA	5	$.00
20003	DIFFENTIAL EQUATIONS	9	$4.00
20004	ELEMENTS OF ALGEBRA	10	$.00
20006	LIMITS	19	$.25
20007	MEN OF MATHEMATICS	2	$.00
20008	WHAT IS MATHEMATICS	10	$.00
25002	HUMAN PHYSIOLOGY	2	$.00
25003	PRIN. OF GENETICS	9	$5.00
30001	ELEM. OF QUANT.ANALY	11	$8.00
30002	ORGANIC CHEMISTRY	6	$.00
30003	PRIN. OF PHYS.CHEM	12	$.00
30004	QUANTITATIVE ANALYS	12	$.00

| | FINAL TOTAL | | $107.00 |

END OF JOB -- 07/07/77

FIGURE 8.9   Sample output from book status report program.

Statement 37. Next, the literal '-END OF JOB--' is concatenated with the edited date and assigned to the output area. Note the minus carriage control character in front of the word END.

Statements 38–39. The last line of the report is printed, and the program is logically terminated.

Record I/O and Arrays

In a READ or WRITE statement, the data area may be a single variable (e.g., a character-string), a structure, or an array. Here is an example of reading data into an array using the READ statement:

```
DCL AREA(20) PIC'9999';
READ FILE(CARD)INTO(AREA);
```

└───────→ May be an array *but* must be *unsubscripted* when specified here

In the above example, columns 1–4 will be placed into AREA(1), columns 5–8 into AREA(2), and so on until columns 77–80 are placed into AREA(20).

Structures

A *structure* is a collection of data items requiring storage for each item to be in a particular order and having a logical relationship to one another. For example, in a payroll application, there are a number of data items about one employee that could be logically grouped together. These items might be the following:

Names used in the program	Data
LAST	DOE
FIRST	JOHN
MIDDLE	J
MAN_NO	72535
REGULAR	40
OVERTIME	4
REG_PAY	4.00
OT_PAY	6.00

Declaring these items as a *structure* allows us to give a name to the whole collection. SALARY_RECORD, for example, could be the name given to the above list of variables.

It is often more convenient, however, to subdivide the entire structure into smaller logical groups so as to be able to refer collectively to more than one, but not all of the variables in the structure. The above example might be subdivided as follows:

Names used in the program			Data
		LAST	DOE
	NAME	FIRST	JOHN
		MIDDLE	J
SALARY_RECORD	MAN_NO		72535
	HOURS	REGULAR	40
		OVERTIME	6
	WAGES	REG_PAY	8.00
		OT_PAY	12.00

It would now be possible to refer to NAME in your PL/I program; the implication is that you are actually referring to the items LAST, FIRST, and MIDDLE. Thus, if the statement

PUT LIST(NAME);

were specified, the items LAST, FIRST, and MIDDLE would be printed. Structuring allows you the additional flexibility of being able to reference the individual item as well as the substructure NAME. For example, in the statement,

PUT LIST(LAST);

only the last name will be printed.

The hierarchy of items shown above can be considered to have different *levels*. At the highest level is the *major structure* name, SALARY_RECORD; at an intermediate level are substructure names called *minor structures* (NAME, HOURS, WAGES); and at the lowest level are *elementary* items (LAST, MAN_NO, REGULAR, etc.). MAN_NO is considered to be an elementary item because there is no further division of the item.

When a structure is declared, the level of each name is indicated by a *level number*. The major structure name (at the highest level) must be numbered 1. Each name at a deeper level is given a greater number to indicate the level depth. Note that the level number must be followed by a blank. The maximum level number that may be specified is 255. This is the sequence to follow in declaring structures:

1. The major structure name is declared first.
2. The elementary items in each minor structure are completely declared before the next minor structure is declared.
3. The elementary items contained in a minor structure must be declared with a greater level number than that of the minor structure.

```
DECLARE 1 SALARY_RECORD,      /* MAJOR STRUCTURE */
          2 NAME,             /* MINOR STRUCTURE */
            3 LAST,           /* ELEMENTARY ITEM */
            3 FIRST,          /* ELEMENTARY ITEM */
            3 MIDDLE,         /* ELEMENTARY ITEM */
          2 MAN_NO,           /* ELEMENTARY ITEM */
          2 HOURS,            /* MINOR STRUCTURE */
            3 REGULAR,        /* ELEMENTARY ITEM */
            3 OVERTIME,       /* ELEMENTARY ITEM */
          2 WAGES,            /* MINOR STRUCTURE */
            3 REG_PAY,        /* ELEMENTARY ITEM */
            3 OT_PAY;         /* ELEMENTARY ITEM */
```

The topical outline pattern of indentation is used only to improve readability of the PL/I structure. The statement could be written in a continuous string, such as:

```
DECLARE 1 SALARY_RECORD, 2 NAME, 3 LAST, 3 FIRST,
   3 MIDDLE, 2 MAN_NO, 2 HOURS, 3 REGULAR,
   3 OVERTIME, 2 WAGES, 3 REG_PAY, 3 OT_PAY;
```

In references to the structure or its elements, no level numbers are used.
   A single declared variable is not preceded by a level number when coded, because it is assumed to be a "level 1" identifier. For example, in the statement

```
DCL 1 SINGLE_VALUE FIXED;
```

the "1" specification is redundant and is an invalid use of the level number in the subset language.

If attributes are to be explicitly declared in a structure, they may only be specified for elementary items. For example:

```
DECLARE 1 SALARY_RECORD,
         3 NAME,
              5 LAST CHAR(12),
              5 FIRST CHAR(8),
              5 MIDDLE CHAR(1),
         3 MAN_NO CHAR(5),
         3 HOURS,
              5 REGULAR PICTURE '99',
              5 OVERTIME PICTURE '99',
         3 WAGES,
              5 REG_PAY PIC '99V99',
              5 OT_PAY PIC '99V99';
```

Notice from the example above that the level numbers do not have to be successive; however, each item must have a higher number than that of the level it is subdividing.

Factored Attributes in Structures

Factoring in PL/I is the grouping together of identifiers for the purpose of giving them a common attribute. The elementary names under HOURS and WAGES in the above example could have been factored as follows:

```
2 HOURS,
     3 (REGULAR,OVERTIME) PIC'99',
2 WAGES,
     3 (REG_PAY, OT_PAY) PIC'99V99';
```

Here is another example of factoring within a structure showing how the level numbers may be factored out of the list of identifiers:

```
DECLARE 1 SYMPTOM,
          (2 COLD,
           2 HEADACHE,
           2 FEVER,
           2 DIZZINESS,
           2 RINGING,
           2 BACKACHE) BIT(1);
```

The INITIAL Attribute in Structures

Elementary items in structures may be initialized using the INITIAL attribute, providing the structure is not overlay defined on another structure, character-string, or other data item. As long as the structure is the *base identifier* (the structure onto which other identifiers are being overlayed), it may contain the INITIAL attribute. For example,

```
DECLARE 1 A,                        /* BASE IDENTIFIER */
          2 B,
             3 C CHAR(9) INIT('TOM JONES'),
             3 D PIC'999V99' INIT(123.45),
          2 E CHAR(25);
DECLARE AA CHAR(39) DEFINED A;   /* OVERLAY DEFINING */
```

Qualified Names

All names within a single procedure must be unique. But within structures, it is often desirable to be able to use the same identifier for related names and yet retain the uniqueness. In the SALARY_RECORD structure, for example, the last portion of the structure might have been declared:

```
          2 HOURS,
             3 REGULAR,
             3 OVERTIME,
          2 WAGES,
             3 REGULAR,
             3 OVERTIME;
```

Notice that we now have two REGULARs and two OVERTIMEs. The use of a *qualified name* in referring to the individual data item avoids ambiguity. A qualified name is a substructure or element name that is made unique by qualifying it with one or more names of a higher level. The individual names within a qualified name are connected by a period. If, for example, you wanted to process the data items that were read into the structure declared above, the following arithmetic operations might be specified:

```
REGULAR_PAY = HOURS.REGULAR*WAGES.REGULAR;
OVERTIME_PAY = HOURS.OVERTIME*WAGES.OVERTIME;
```

The qualified name HOURS.REGULAR refers to REGULAR in the substructure HOURS; the qualified name WAGES.REGULAR refers to

REGULAR in the substructure WAGES, etc. Qualified names are merely used for reference to avoid ambiguity; they are not declared in a structure. A qualified name may not contain comments. In some compilers, blanks may appear on either side of the period (e.g., A . B). Qualification need go only as far as necessary to make the name unique. Intermediate qualifying of names can be omitted. Consider the following structure:

```
DECLARE 1 A,
          2 B,
               3 C,
               3 D,
          2 BB,
               3 C,
               3 E;
```

In this example, to refer to the first C in the structure, you could write

A.B.C

or simply,

B.C

Do you see the ambiguity that would arise if you wrote

A.C

Suppose E is a name used in another structure in the same procedure; then to qualify E in this structure, you may write

A.E

or

BB.E

or

A.BB.E

The maximum length allowed for qualified names varies slightly in the different PL/I compilers. Generally, if you keep the maximum length under 140 characters, including the decimal points, you will be within the limit of the various compilers' restrictions.

Arrays in Structures

Like a structure, an array is a collection of data. Unlike a structure, all elements in an array have identical attributes. It is possible to include an array within a structure:

```
DECLARE 1 INVENTORY_ITEM,
          2 PART_NO CHAR(8),
          2 QTY_ON_HAND PIC'9999',
          2 MINIMUM_NO PIC'9999',
          2 SALES_HISTORY(12) PIC'99999';
```

In the above example of an inventory record, each record would contain the part number, the present quantity on hand, a minimum quantity to be kept on hand at all times, and finally a *sales history*. SALES_HISTORY is an array of 12 elements. Each element represents a month in the year. For example, SALES_HISTORY(1) contains the number of items sold in January; SALES_HISTORY(2) contains the number of items sold in February; SALES_HISTORY(3) in March; and so on. If the product is a seasonal one, this kind of historical information might be valuable in a program for determining varying reorder quantities at different times of the year.

Arrays of Structures

An array of structures is an array whose elements are structures having identical names, levels, and elements. For example, if a structure, WEATHER, were used to process meteorological information for each month of a year, it might be declared as follows:

```
DECLARE 1 WEATHER(12),
          2 TEMPERATURE,
               3 HIGH DECIMAL FIXED(4, 1),
               3 LOW DECIMAL FIXED(3, 1),
          2 WIND_VELOCITY,
               3 HIGH DECIMAL FIXED(3),
               3 LOW DECIMAL FIXED(2),
          2 PRECIPITATION,
               3 TOTAL DECIMAL FIXED(3, 1),
               3 AVERAGE DECIMAL FIXED(3, 1);
```

Thus, a programmer could refer to the weather data for the month of July by specifying WEATHER(7). Portions of the July weather could be referred to by TEMPERATURE(7), WIND_VELOCITY(7), and/or PRECIPITATION(7). TOTAL(7) would refer to the total precipitation during the month of July. TEMPERATURE.HIGH(3), which would refer to the high temperature in March, is called a *subscripted qualified name*.

	Arrays of structures
Subset language	No
Full language	Yes

The LIKE Attribute

The LIKE attribute is used to indicate that the name being declared is to be given the same structuring as the major structure or minor structure name following the attribute LIKE. For example:

```
DECLARE 1 BUDGET,
      2 RENT FIXED(5,2),
      2 FOOD,
            3 MEAT FIXED(4,2),
            3 DAIRY FIXED(4,2),
            3 PRODUCE FIXED(4,2),
      2 TRANSPORTATION,
            3 WORK FIXED(5,2),
            3 OTHER FIXED(4,2),
      2 ENTERTAINMENT FIXED(5,2);
      DECLARE 1 COST_OF_LIVING LIKE BUDGET;
```

This declaration for COST_OF_LIVING is the same as if it had been declared:

```
            DECLARE 1 COST_OF_LIVING,
                  2 RENT FIXED(5,2),
                  2 FOOD,
                        3 MEAT FIXED(4,2),
                        3 DAIRY FIXED(4,2),
                        3 PRODUCE FIXED(4,2),
                  2 TRANSPORTATION,
                        3 WORK FIXED(5,2),
                        3 OTHER FIXED(4,2),
                  2 ENTERTAINMENT FIXED(5,2);
```

The LIKE attribute copies structuring, names, and attributes of

the structure below the level of the specified name only. No dimensionality of the specified name is copied. For example, if BUDGET were
declared as 1 BUDGET(12), the declaration of COST_OF_LIVING
LIKE BUDGET would not give the dimension attribute to COST_OF_
LIVING. To achieve dimensionality of COST_OF_LIVING, the declaration would have to be DECLARE 1 COST_OF_LIVING(12) LIKE
BUDGET.

A minor structure name can be declared LIKE a major structure
or LIKE another minor structure. A major structure name can be
declared LIKE a minor structure or LIKE another major structure.

	LIKE attribute
Subset language	No
Full language	Yes

Structure Assignment: Structure-to-Structure

Structures may be moved (that is, assigned) to other structures
or parts of structures. The structure name to the right of the assignment symbol must have the same relative structuring as the structure
name to the left. Relative structuring means that the structures must
have the same minor structuring, the same number of elementary items
within each minor and/or major structure, and, if arrays are contained
in structures, the same number of bounds. You may assign major
structures to major structures, minor structures to major structures,
and vice versa, as long as the relative structuring is the same. For
example:

```
DECLARE 1 CARD_REC,
          2 KEY_FIELD CHAR(16),
          2 OTHER CHAR(64);
DECLARE 1 DISK_REC,
          2 FLAG CHAR(1),
          2 RECORD,
             3 KEY CHAR(16),
             3 OTHER CHAR(64);
RECORD=CARD_REC;   /* STRUCTURE ASSIGNMENT */
```

In the above example, the major structure CARD_REC is assigned to the minor structure RECORD. After the assignment, KEY will contain the value in KEY_FIELD, and RECORD.OTHER will contain the value in CARD_REC.OTHER. As you can see from this example, the level numbers need not be identical when a structure or part of a structure is being assigned to another structure. The important thing is to have the same number of elementary items contained within each structure or minor structure name as well as the same relative structuring.

The attributes of the corresponding elementary items in the structure assignments do not have to be the same. If the elementary items have different attributes, the variables will be converted according to the arithmetic rules explained in previous chapters. Let us look at an example in which conversions would take place when structure AA is assigned to structure A.

```
DECLARE 1 A,
            2 B FIXED(5),
            2 C FIXED BINARY(31),
            2 D CHAR(20),
            2 E PIC'S99V99',
            2 F FLOAT(16) ;
DECLARE 1 AA,
            2 BB PIC'99999',
            2 CC FIXED DECIMAL,
            2 DD CHAR(10),
            2 EE FIXED(4,2),
            2 FF FIXED(6) ;
      A = AA ;
```

There are a number of things to observe in the above example :

1. In a structure move, elementary items are moved to the corresponding elementary items. In other words, the first item in AA is assigned to the first item in A; the second item in AA is assigned to the second item in A, etc.
2. When the elementary items of one structure are moved to their corresponding variables in another structure through a structure assignment statement, arithmetic conversion occurs, if necessary. In the above example, FF is a FIXED DECIMAL value that will be converted to FLOAT DECIMAL when it is assigned to F.

3. The receiving field does not have to be the same length as the sending field: D in structure A is 20 characters long; DD is only 10 characters long. When DD is assigned to D, it will be placed in the 10 leftmost positions of D, and then D will be padded on the right with blanks. Of course, care must be taken not to assign a longer arithmetic field to a shorter field, for you will lose significance in your resulting value. And, you may not specify illegal combinations. For example, in the subset language, a variable whose attribute is CHARACTER may not be assigned to a coded arithmetic field or a PICTURE data item.

4. When the structure assignment statement

$$A = AA;$$

is given, in essence, five assignment statements are generated:

$$B = BB; \quad C = CC; \quad D = DD; \quad E = EE; \quad F = FF;$$

Structure Assignment BY NAME

One exception to the rule that structures assigned to other structures must have the same relative structuring is the case in which the structure expression appears in an assignment statement with the BY NAME option. For example, consider the following INPUT and OUTPUT structures:

```
DCL 1 INPUT,
          2 EMP_NAME CHAR(20),
          2 MAN_NO CHAR(6),
          2 HOURS,
                    3 REG PIC'99',
                    3 OT PIC'99',
          2 GROSS_PAY PIC'999V99',
     1 OUTPUT,
          2 CC CHAR(1),
          2 MAN_NO CHAR(12),
          2 EMP_NAME CHAR(25),
          2 GROSS_PAY PIC'$$$$V.99BBBB';
```

To move those elements of INPUT whose names are identical to elements of OUTPUT, simply write

$$OUTPUT = INPUT, \ BY \ NAME;$$

The BY NAME option may only appear in an assignment statement, and it must always be preceded by a comma.

	BY NAME option
Subset language	No
Full language	Yes

Structure Assignment: Scalar-to-Structure

A *scalar* is simply a single data element, and it is sometimes called an elementary item. You may assign a scalar to a structure. For example:

```
DECLARE 1 CUSTOMER,
            2 NAME CHAR(20),
            2 ADDRESS,
                        3 STREET CHAR(25),
                        3 CITY CHAR(20),
                        3 STATE CHAR(2),
                        3 ZIP_CODE CHAR(5),
            2 ACCOUNT_# CHAR(7);
CUSTOMER = ' '; /* CLEAR CUSTOMER STRUCTURE TO BLANKS */
```

The blank character constant is a scalar. Because we are assigning character-to-character, the assignment is valid. Six assignment statements are effectively generated from the statement

$$CUSTOMER = ' ';$$

The six statements are

```
NAME = '  '; STREET = '  '; CITY = '  '; STATE = '  ';
ZIP_CODE = '  '; ACCOUNT_# = '  ';
```

Recall that when a smaller field, in this case a single blank, is assigned to a larger character field, there is padding on the right of the larger field with blanks.

Overlay Defining: Scalar Variable on a Structure

There is actually a more efficient way to clear the CUSTOMER structure and that is through the use of the DEFINED attribute. The

DEFINED attribute allows us to refer to the same area of storage by different names, and perhaps different attributes. Assume the following statement is added to the structure example above:

DECLARE CUST CHAR(79) DEFINED CUSTOMER;

If you will count the character lengths of each elementary item in the CUSTOMER structure, you will find there are a total of 79 characters. Therefore, a character-string called CUST with a length attribute of 79 was overlay defined on the CUSTOMER structure, setting aside one area of storage, but providing two ways of looking at it: first, as a structure, and second, as a *single* character-string. When the statement

CUST=' ';

is given, only *one* assignment statement is generated: that of moving a blank to the first position of CUST, and then padding on the right with 78 more blanks. Thus, through the technique of overlay defining a scalar variable on the structure, we were able to save five assignment statements from being generated for clearing our structure to blanks.

Aside from facilitating more efficient coding, there is another case in which overlay defining is needed: when you want to clear a structure containing decimal PICTURE attributes to blanks. For example, consider the following structure:

DCL 1 INVENTORY_ITEM,
      2 PART_NUMBER CHAR(8),
      2 QUANTITY_ON_HAND PICTURE'ZZZZ9',
      2 PRICE PICTURE'$ZZV.99';

Suppose it is desired to clear the above structure to blanks before assigning any values to the elementary items. It would be invalid to code

INVENTORY_ITEM = ' ';

because the structure contains one or more elementary items having a PICTURE of 9's. A field described with 9's may have assigned to it *only* digits from 0 to 9. A CONVERSION error would result if a blank character were moved into this field, because a blank is not a numeric digit. The following coding, however, can be written to clear the INVENTORY_ITEM structure to blanks:

DCL INVENTORY CHAR(19) DEFINED INVENTORY_ITEM;
INVENTORY=' ';

In the above example, not only did we get around the problem of assigning blanks directly to a PICTURE with 9's, but also we used a more efficient method for clearing a structure to blanks. Normally, you would not have the need to clear structures to blanks, because any data assigned to a structure destroys its previous contents. Certainly, it would be superfluous to clear a structure to blanks and then immediately assign meaningful data to that structure. However, here is an example illustrating when the need for clearing structures to blanks might arise.

Assume we have the following structure from which data is output to a printer:

```
DCL 1 PRINT_OUT,
      2 DESCRIPTION CHAR(25),
      2 QUANTITY PIC'9999BBB',
      2 PRICE PIC'$ZZZV.99BB',
      2 EXTENSION PIC'$ZZ,ZZZV.99';
```

Quantity is multiplied by price to give the EXTENSION. Then a line is printed for the item. Assume that a total of the EXTENSION for each item is to be accumulated. This could be accomplished with the following statements:

```
DCL TOTAL FIXED(6,2) INIT(0);
TOTAL=TOTAL+EXTENSION;
```

After the last detail line is printed, it is then necessary to print the total of all EXTENSIONs. It is possible to use the structure PRINT_OUT for the printing of the final total. The advantage is that main storage is saved, because it is not necessary to reserve a separate area for the final total line. EXTENSION is a picture large enough to contain the final total. All that is necessary is to move TOTAL to EXTENSION:

```
EXTENSION=TOTAL;
```

However, if the PRINT_OUT structure were output without the other fields being cleared, the DESCRIPTION, QUANTITY, and PRICE from the last detail line of print will appear on the output line along with the final total assigned to the EXTENSION field. The solution to the problem is to use the DEFINED attribute for the purpose of clearing the DESCRIPTION, QUANTITY, and PRICE field to blanks. These three fields add up to 41 characters. Thus, we may code

```
DCL P_O CHAR(41) DEFINED PRINT_OUT;
```

Note that P_O did not have to be as long as the structure. When the program is ready to print the final total line, it will not only edit TOTAL into the EXTENSION field, but it will also clear the other fields to blanks by the statement

$$P\_O = '\quad';$$

Now, when the WRITE statement from the PRINT_OUT structure is executed, only the EXTENSION, which represents the final total, will be printed.

Overlay Defining: A Structure on a Structure

It is also possible to overlay define a major structure on a major structure. The need for overlay defining one structure on another arises when you are working with two or more different input data formats for records being read from the same device. For example, assume a program is to process data cards containing either information on items *received* into a company's inventory or items *issued* from inventory. The card records are formatted as follows:

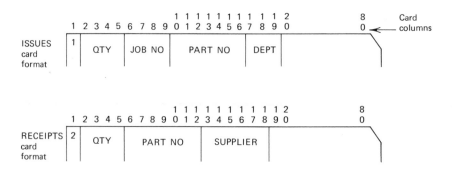

The cards will have been sorted into sequence by part number. However, the program can only differentiate between issues and receipts by the "transaction code" punched in column one of each card: a "1" punch will represent an issue and a "2" punch, a receipt. The structures, which are overlay defined, and the READ statement follow:

```
DECLARE 1 ISSUES,
         2 CODE CHAR(1),
         2 QTY PIC'9999',
         2 JOB_NO CHAR(4),
         2 PART_NO CHAR(7),
         2 DEPT CHAR(3),
         2 REST_OF_RECORD CHAR(61);

DECLARE 1 RECEIPTS DEFINED ISSUES,
         2 CODE CHAR(1),
         2 QTY PIC'9999',
         2 PART_NO CHAR(7),
         2 SUPPLIER CHAR(6);

READ FILE(INPUT)INTO (ISSUES);
IF ISSUES.CODE = '1' THEN GO TO PROCESS_ISSUES;
IF ISSUES.CODE = '2' THEN GO TO PROCESS_RECEIPTS;
    ELSE GO TO ERROR;
```

Notice how the IF statement tests column one of the input card for the transaction code. If the code is a '1', then a branch is made to the routine in our program that processes the issues card. If the code in column one is not a '1', we might logically assume that it must be a '2' and that the program will branch to PROCESS_RECEIPTS. It is good programming practice, however, to test for the other code, because there might be a keypunch error.

Record I/O operations may take place only from the base identifier. Thus, in the above example, the data area named in the READ statement is ISSUES, because ISSUES does not have the DEFINED attribute.

	Overlay defining
Subset language	You may code an overlay define at the major structure level only (level 1 name overlay defined on a level 1 name)
Full language	You may code an overlay define at the major structure, minor structure, elementary item in a structure as well as a major structure

When May Structures Contain Only CHARACTER and PICTURE Data?

Recall that in record I/O, there is no conversion of the external characters to an internal format, or vice versa. Thus, when you issue a READ statement for the card reader or a WRITE statement for the card punch, or line printer, the structures on which you are doing input or output would normally have either CHARACTER or PICTURE attributes. The exception is if you wish to punch *binary* data into cards or read this binary data from cards.

This would not be true, however, for tape or DASD files. The data would probably still be read from punched cards into structures that contained only CHARACTER and PICTURE attributes. But then the data in these structures could be moved (assigned) to other structures that contained such attributes as FIXED DECIMAL or FIXED BINARY. These structures would now be written onto a tape or direct access device. Representing data in coded arithmetic form rather than CHARACTER or PICTURE has the advantage of minimizing the amount of storage required for data. For example:

```
DCL A PIC'999V99';   /* 5 BYTES OF STORAGE USED */
DCL B FIXED(5,2);    /* 3 BYTES OF STORAGE USED */
```

Structures in Stream I/O

Names of structures may also be specified in edit-directed and list-directed I/O statements. The names may be major level or intermediate level structure names. Of course, elementary names in a structure may also be specified. Here is an example of specifying a major structure name in a GET EDIT:

```
DCL 1 INVENTORY,
      2 PART_NUM CHAR(6),
      2 QTY_ON_HAND FIXED(5),
      2 PRICE FIXED(5,2);
GET EDIT(INVENTORY) (A(6),F(5),F(5,2));
```

Notice that three format items were specified. You must specify as many format items as data items. Of course, if there are not as many format items as elementary items in the structure specified in the data list, then there is a return to the beginning of the format list and the format items are used again in describing the remaining elements of the structure.

Here is an example of specifying an intermediate structure name in a PUT EDIT statement:

```
DCL 1 INVEN,
       2 PART#,
          3 TYPE CHAR(2),
          3 CODE CHAR(3),
       2 REORDER_QTY PIC'(4)9';
PUT EDIT(PART#, REORDER_QTY) (A(2),A(3),F(9)) ;
```

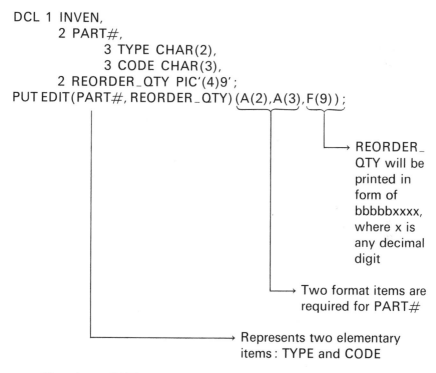

→ REORDER_QTY will be printed in form of bbbbbxxxx, where x is any decimal digit

→ Two format items are required for PART#

→ Represents two elementary items: TYPE and CODE

The above PUT statement is equivalent to

```
PUT EDIT(TYPE,CODE,REORDER_QTY) (A(2),A(3),F(9)) ;
```

Notice how the format specification for REORDER_QTY has a *width* larger than the internal specification. The precision of REORDER_QTY is 4. The F(9) specification will cause the four decimal digits to be printed right-justified in the output field; to the left of the value will be five blanks. Thus, spacing between the PART# and REORDER_QTY is achieved.

If a data list element is a structure variable, the elements of the structure are transmitted in the order specified in the structure declaration. For example, if a declaration is

```
DECLARE 1 A,2 B(10), 2 C(10) ;
```

then the statement

PUT EDIT (A) (F(12)) ;

would result in the output being ordered as follows:

A.B(1) A.B(2) A.B(3)...A.B(10) A.C(1) A.C(2) A.C(3)...A.C(10)

In the case of data-directed I/O in the full language implementations, if the data list includes the names of structure elements, then
fully qualified names must appear in the stream, although full qualification is not required in the data list. Consider the following structures:

```
DCL 1 INPUT,
      2 PARTNO CHAR(6),
      2 DESC CHAR(20),
      2 PRICE
              3 RETAIL FIXED(7,2),
              3 WHSL FIXED(7,2) ;
DCL 1 OUTPUT,
      2 PARTNO CHAR(10),
      2 DESC CHAR(25),
      2 PRICE,

              3 RETAIL PIC'(8)$V.99',
              3 WHSL PIC'(8)$V.99' ;
```

If it is desired to read a value for INPUT. PRICE. RETAIL, the data
specification could be

GET DATA(INPUT.RETAIL) ;

but the input data stream must have the following form:

INPUT. PRICE. RETAIL=4.75 ;

The maximum number of elements permitted in a list for data-directed
input is 320. Each element of a structure counts as a separate list
element.

Case Study: Sequence Checking

In commercial applications, input or output data records are usually
arranged into some numeric or alphabetic sequence. In the case of
input, if it is desired that records be in ascending sequence, the program

reading these records verifies this sequence. In the case we are going to examine, it is *imperative* that the input records be in ascending sequence in order to obtain the correct results. Our study will be of a department store. Sales are to be totaled, by department, at the end of each day's business. For each sales receipt issued to the customer, a card will be punched containing the department number and sales amount. The cards are in department number sequence and the department numbers are in ascending sequence. We are to accumulate the total amount of sales for each department and print that total along with its associated department number. If the department numbers are out of sequence, we want to print an error message and terminate the job. Figure 8.10 shows the printer layout for the desired output and Figure 8.11 shows a flowchart. An explanation of the program in Figure 8.12 follows.

Statement 2.   Both card and printer files are declared in this statement. This program was compiled and executed under the DOS/TOS operating system. It is not necessary to modify the program in any way in order to compile and execute it under the OS operating system. However, in OS versions of PL/I, the MEDIUM option is ignored in the file declaration statement. Thus, for OS, the following file declarations would suffice:

```
/* OS PL/I OPTIMIZING COMPILER */
DCL CARDIN FILE RECORD INPUT ENV(F BLKSIZE(80));
DCL PRINTR FILE RECORD OUTPUT ENV(F BLKSIZE(33)
    CTLASA);
/* PL/I F COMPILER */
DCL CARDIN FILE RECORD INPUT ENV (F(80));
DCL PRINTR FILE RECORD OUTPUT ENV(F(33)CTLASA);
```

Statement 3.   The variable LBL is given the LABEL attribute and initialized to a place in the program called LOOP1. As you will see

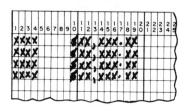

FIGURE 8.10   Desired
printer layout for case study.

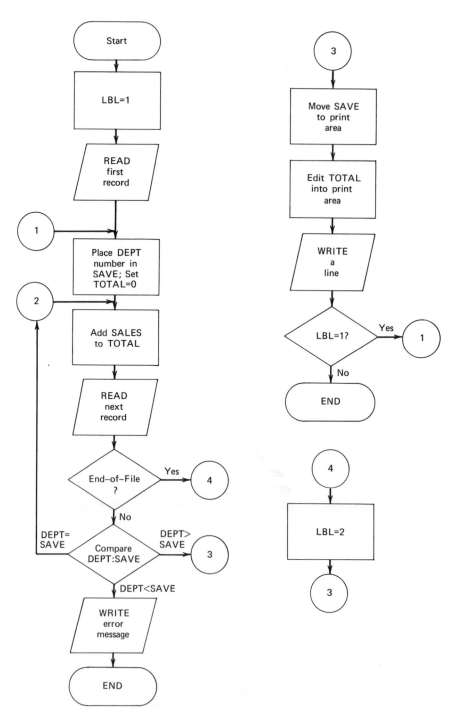

FIGURE 8.11 Case study flowchart for sequence checking.

```
 1   CASE:    PROC OPTIONS(MAIN);
 2            DCL CARDIN FILE RECORD INPUT ENV(F(80)MEDIUM(SYSIPT,2540)),
              PRINTR FILE RECORD OUTPUT ENV(F(33)CTLASA MEDIUM(SYSLST,1403));
 3            DCL LBL LABEL INIT(LOOP1);
 4            DCL 1 CARD_AREA,
                    2 DEPT CHAR(4),
                    2 SALES PIC'(4)9V99',
                    2 REST_OF_RECORD CHAR(70);
 5            DCL PRT CHAR(33) DEFINED PRINT_AREA;
 6            DCL 1 PRINT_AREA,
                    2 CC CHAR(1) INIT('1'),
                    2 DEPT CHAR(9),
                    2 SALES_AMT PIC'$$$,$$$V.99',
                    2 REST CHAR(13) INIT(' ');
 7            DCL SAVE_DEPT CHAR(4), TOTAL FIXED(8,2);
 8            ON ENDFILE(CARDIN) GO TO EOJ;
 9            OPEN FILE(CARDIN), FILE(PRINTR);
10            READ FILE(CARDIN) INTO(CARD_AREA);
11   LOOP1:   SAVE_DEPT = CARD_AREA.DEPT;
12            TOTAL = 0;
13   LOOP2:   TOTAL = TOTAL+ SALES;
14            READ FILE(CARDIN) INTO(CARD_AREA);
15            IF CARD_AREA.DEPT = SAVE_DEPT THEN GO TO LOOP2;
16            IF CARD_AREA.DEPT < SAVE_DEPT THEN DO;
17                    PRT = '-DEPARTMENT CARDS OUT OF SEQUENCE';
18                    WRITE FILE(PRINTR)FROM(PRINT_AREA);
19                    GO TO FINI;
20                    END;
              /* CARD_AREA.DEPT > SAVE_DEPT */
21   PRINT:   PRINT_AREA.DEPT = SAVE_DEPT;
22            SALES_AMT = TOTAL; /* EDIT DEPARTMENT TOTAL */
23            WRITE FILE(PRINTR) FROM(PRINT_AREA);
24            CC = ' ';
25            GO TO LBL;
26   EOJ:     LBL = FINI;
27            GO TO PRINT;
28   FINI:    END;
```

FIGURE 8.12 **Case study program illustrating sequence checking.**

later in the program, we use the variable LBL to affect the order in which statements are executed.

Statement 4. The card input structure is declared. In record input of cards, you may not read less than 80 columns; thus, the elementary item REST_OF_RECORD was necessary to make the structure size the same as the declared length—F(80)—in the ENVIRONMENT section of the DECLARE statement for CARDIN.

Statement 5. A character-string called PRT is declared as having a length of 33. In selecting the length of the output area, you must consider the length of the longest record that will be output to a given data set. That length becomes the record length in the file declaration [e.g., F(33)]. Also, that length must be the size of all output areas from which data will be written. The longest message (i.e., record) in this program is the error message (see statement 17). It is 33 characters long. Thus, all output areas in this program that are referenced with respect to the PRT file must be this length. PRT is also overlay defined on PRINT_AREA. This technique will facilitate more efficient utilization, because PRINT_AREA (which holds detail line output) and PRT (which holds the error message if a sequence error is found) now occupy the same area of core storage. Overlay defining is possible here because, logically, the declared area is used for either the detail line of output or the error message, *but not both* at the same time.

Statement 6. The print area is declared. In this structure, CC is for the carriage control character. The elementary item arbitrarily called REST was necessary to make the structure size 33 characters in length, as PRT (the overlay defined item) is 33 characters long.

Statement 7. Because we are going to check the department numbers of the input cards for ascending sequence, it is necessary to declare a variable (i.e., SAVE_DEPT) for the purpose of *saving* the first department number read. When the next department number is read, we can compare this with the previous department number.

Statement 11. The department number from the first card is assigned to the variable SAVE_DEPT. Note that the use of a qualified name was necessary here because the PRINT_AREA and CARD_AREA structures both contain elementary items called DEPT. This is also the statement to which we will return each time we are to begin accumulating totals for a *new* department.

Statement 13. The sales amount is accumulated into TOTAL. This is the statement to which we will return each time a new card is read for the *same* department.

Statements 15–16. These statements test for ascending sequence of the department numbers. If there is a sequence error, PRT is assigned the error message.

Statement 17. The minus sign (−) preceding the character constant is the carriage control character. It will not show up on the printout; it simply indicates to space up three lines before printing the data. In the case study, PRT is overlay defined on the structure PRINT_AREA. PRT is used for the purpose of assigning to it the error message character-string. You may have wondered why we could not have written

PRINT_AREA='-DEPARTMENT CARDS OUT OF SEQUENCE';

Some strange output would result if we coded this statement, because of the elementary item-for-elementary item nature of structure moves.

Earlier in this chapter, it was shown how there are as many assignment statements generated as elementary items in the structure when that structure is involved in a move operation. Thus, the following coding would have been generated for the above assignment statement:

```
CC='-DEPARTMENT CARDS OUT OF SEQUENCE';
DEPT='-DEPARTMENT CARDS OUT OF SEQUENCE';
SALES_AMT='-DEPARTMENT CARDS OUT OF SEQUENCE',
     /* INVALID */
REST='-DEPARTMENT CARDS OUT OF SEQUENCE';
```

In all of the above cases, the *receiving* fields are shorter than the *sending* fields. In character-strings, we assign data from left to right and truncate on the right, if necessary. Thus, we would end up with the following values in PRINT_AREA's elementary items:

```
CC='-';
DEPT='-DEPARTM';
REST='-DEPARTMENT C';
```

It is not possible to assign alphabetic characters to SALES_AMT, because this field contains numeric data and editing characters. The compiler will flag this error.

Statement 18. The error message is printed. Notice that we must WRITE from the PRINT_AREA structure, not from PRT. PRT and PRINT_AREA represent the same area of storage known by two names. Thus, when we write from PRINT_AREA, we are printing the data assigned to PRT (see statement 17). The reason we output from PRINT_AREA is that we may not WRITE from a variable that has the DEFINED attribute, which is the case with PRT.

Statements 21–23. At this point in the program, it is time to print the department total. The "old" department number is assigned to the print area. TOTAL is moved and edited into the SALES_AMT field in the PRINT_AREA. The department total is printed.

Statement 24. The carriage control character is reset to a blank, which is the code to space one line before printing. Notice from the declared PRINT_AREA structure that CC was initialized to a '1', which causes a skip to a new page for the *first* WRITE statement. Thereafter, we simply space one line. Approximately 60 lines may be printed on standard printer paper. Assume for this problem that there are less than 60 departments for which sales are to be totaled. Because the entire report will fit on one page, it is not necessary to program for page overflow.

Statement 25. In statement 3, LBL was initialized to LOOP1. Thus, when the statement

GO TO LBL;

is executed, we transfer to the location LBL, in which the address LOOP1 is found. Thus, in effect, a branch to LOOP1 is accomplished. This will be true in all cases except that in which the last card has been read and the ENDFILE condition has been raised. In that case, when

GO TO LBL;

is executed, transfer will actually be to the statement labeled EOJ.

Statements 26–27. When there are no sequence errors and the ENDFILE condition has been raised, program control transfers to statement 26. It is still necessary to print the accumulated sales total for the last department. The *brute force* method of programming would be to repeat at this point the output statements necessary to print the last line of the report, which would mean a total of three statements identical to those in statements 21 – 23. Instead of inserting duplicate coding in the program, a *program switch* was used. This programming technique is similar in concept to that of a station master who must throw a switch to determine on which set of tracks a particular train is to travel. In this case study, the *program switch* is LBL. In statement 26, LBL which had been assigned to the label LOOP1 is now assigned the label FINI. Statement 27 specifies

GO TO PRINT;

We return to statement 21 and edit and print the last department's total sales figure. When statement 25,

GO TO LBL;

is executed, we now transfer to FINI.

SUMMARY

Record I/O Programming Steps: *Declare files:* A PL/I file is represented in the program by the file name which is declared to have the FILE attribute. It is through the use of this name that we will access or create the data records which are stored on an external device such as a disk or tape or cards. The collection of records is called a data set. The ENVIRONMENT attribute of the DECLARE statement describes the physical environment of the data set. To accomplish carriage control for record I/O, the keyword CTLASA or CTL360 must be added to the ENVIRONMENT section of the file declaration to notify PL/I that these carriage control characters are being used in the program and that the I/O routines are to interpret the first character of each record to indicate the action we want performed. It is the programmer's responsibility to place a meaningful control character in the first position of the output area if either CTL option is specified.

Reserve I/O areas: For card and printer record I/O operations, declare either character-strings, structures, or arrays. In record I/O, there is no conversion of the external characters to an internal format, or vice versa. Thus, when you issue a READ statement for the card reader or a WRITE statement for the card punch or line printer, the structures on which you are doing input or output would normally have either CHARACTER or PICTURE attributes. The I/O area must be equal to the length of the record declared in the ENVIRONMENT options list; e.g.,

ENV(F(80));

└──────────────→ I/O area must also be length 80

Open files: Files must be opened before a READ or WRITE to these files is executed. A file is automatically opened the first time a READ or WRITE to that file is issued. However, in the subset language, record files must be explicitly opened. The opening of files causes attributes to be merged, labels to be checked, and device readiness to be established.

Specify action for ENDFILE condition: When an end-of-file condition is raised, signifying that there is no more data in the accessed data set, one of two courses of action may be taken:

1. *System action:* The system immediately terminates the job with an abnormal ending error message, unless this is overridden by programmer-defined action.
2. *Programmer-defined action:* This is done with the ON ENDFILE statement. This statement need be executed only once in your program, because once you have specified what action is to be taken when the

end-of-file is detected, that information is "remembered." The ENDFILE statement may be executed either before or after the OPEN statement is specified.

Read data: This is accomplished by

READ FILE(file name) INTO(variable);

> └─────→ Must be a level 1 structure name or an unsubscripted variable not contained in a structure; it cannot be a label variable or a parameter, and it cannot have the DEFINED attribute

Following each READ, the system checks for an end-of-file condition and takes the action specified in the ON ENDFILE statement if the last record has been read.

Write a record: When a WRITE statement is executed, a carriage control operation will take place first, if the CTLASA option is specified; then the data will be printed. The rules and syntax for the WRITE statement are the same as for the READ statement. After a record is written, loop back to read the next record.

Wrap-up program: When the ENDFILE condition is raised, program wrap-up might include closing files, printing total accumulations, and/or an end-of-job message.

Structures: A structure is a collection of data items whose locations relative to one another are critical. Usually, the data items which appear in a structure have a logical relationship to each other. Structure names always have a level number of 1. Any number greater than 1 may be used for subdivisions of the structure. At the highest level is the major structure name, at an intermediate level are substructure names called minor structures, and at the lowest level are elementary items. The major structure name must be numbered 1. Each name at a deeper level is given a greater number to indicate the level depth. Level numbers must be followed by a blank.

The INITIAL Attribute in Structures: Elementary items in structures may be initialized using the INITIAL attribute, providing the structure is not overlay defined on another data item.

Qualified Names: A qualified name is a substructure or element name that is made unique by qualifying it with one or more names of a higher level. The individual names within a qualified name are connected by a period; e.g., the qualified name HOURS.REGULAR refers to REGULAR in the substructure HOURS. A qualified name also may not contain blanks or comments. Qualification need go only as far as necessary to make the name unique. Intermediate qualifying of names can be omitted.

Arrays in Structures: An array may be thought of as a table of data elements. Structures may contain arrays; e.g.,

```
DCL 1 A,
       2 B(5),
       2 C(10);
```

Here, the "A" structure contains two arrays: the "B" array of five elements and the "C" array of ten elements.

Arrays of Structures: An array of structures is an array whose elements are structures having identical names, levels, and elements; e.g.,

```
DCL 1 A(10),
       2 B,
       2 C,
       2 D;
```

Here, there are ten "A" structures consisting of three elementary items: B, C, and D.

The LIKE Attribute: The LIKE attribute is used to indicate that the name being declared is to be given the same structuring as the major structure or minor structure name following the attribute LIKE.

Structure Assignment: There are several types of structure assignments:

1. *Structure-to-structure:*   Structures may be moved (i.e., assigned) to other structures or parts of structures. The structure name to the right of the assignment symbol must have the same relative structuring as the structure name to the left. You may assign major structures to major structures, minor structures to major structures, and vice versa, as long as the relative structuring is the same.

2. *BY NAME:*   One exception to the rule that structures assigned to other structures must have the same relative structuring is the case in which the structure expression appears in an assignment statement with the BY NAME option; e.g.,

```
OUTPUT=INPUT, BY NAME;
```

3. *Scalar-to-structure:*   A scalar is simply a single data element. When a scalar is assigned to a structure, it results in being assigned to each elementary item of the structure.

Overlay Defining: The DEFINED attribute is often useful in manipulating data in a structure. Two types of define overlays are possible:

1. *Scalar variable on a structure:*   The DEFINED attribute allows us to refer to the same area of storage by different names; e.g.,

```
DECLARE S CHAR(79) DEFINED STRUCTURE;
```

2. *Structure on a structure* : Example :

```
DCL 1 A,
        2 B CHAR(20),
        2 C CHAR(40),
        2 D CHAR(20) ;

DCL 1 AA DEF A,
        2 B CHAR(40),
        2 C CHAR(40) ;
```

CHECKPOINT QUESTIONS

1. What are the merits of selecting record I/O over stream I/O?

2. If you use record I/O to punch cards, read cards or print, then what attribute(s) must the data area named in the READ or WRITE statements have?

3. What form (coded arithmetic or decimal) would data stored on a tape or direct access device most likely take?

4. What is the programming error in the following coding segment?

```
DCL PRT FILE OUTPUT RECORD ENV(F(121)CTLASA
    MEDIUM(SYSLST,1403)) ;
DCL PRINT_AREA CHAR(8) INIT('1HEADING') ;
WRITE FILE(PRT)FROM(PRINT_AREA) ;
```

5. Which segment of coding is preferred assuming the coding is part of a larger program that accomplishes an 80/80 list?

```
(a)   LOOP:   READ FILE(CARD)INTO(AREA) ;
              ON ENDFILE(CARD)GO TO EOJ;
              WRITE FILE(PRINT)FROM(AREA) ;
              GO TO LOOP;

(b)           ON ENDFILE(CARD)GO TO EOJ;
      LOOP:   READ FILE(CARD)INTO(AREA) ;
              WRITE FILE(PRINT)FROM(AREA) ;
              GO TO LOOP;
```

6. What actions take place when files are opened?

7. What is the difference between CTLASA and CTL360?

8. Under what circumstances may structures contain only CHARACTER or PICTURE attributes?

	BY NAME option	LIKE attribute	POSITION attribute	Arrays of structures	Maximum number of nested levels allowed
Subset language	No	No	No	No	8
Full language	Yes	Yes	Yes	Yes	15

FIGURE 8.13 Language implementations for structures.

9. What will YY, MM, and DD contain after the DATE function is invoked assuming the date is July 7, 1977? (Be careful, this is a "trick" question.)

```
DCL DATE BUILTIN;
DCL 1 TODAY,
        2 YY CHAR(2),
        2 MM CHAR(2);
        2 DD CHAR(2);
    TODAY=DATE;
```

10. In programming, what is sequence checking?

11. Write the structure given in question 9 above, but *factor* the attributes.

12. When may elementary items in a structure not be initialized using the INITIAL attribute?

13. Which of the following is a valid qualified name?
    (a) HOURS_REGULAR
    (b) HOURS-REGULAR
    (c) HOURS.REGULAR
    (d) HOURS REGULAR

14. What is the purpose of the LIKE attribute?

15. Is this a valid example of a structure move?

```
DCL 1 CAT,
        2 A,
          3 B,
          3 C,
        2 D;
DCL 1 DOG,
        2 A,
        2 B,
        2 C,
        2 D;
    DOG=CAT;
```

16. Under what circumstances may a structure be assigned to another structure that does not have the same relative structuring?

17. Given the following structure, write the most efficient coding to clear the structure to blanks.

```
DCL 1 A,
        2 B CHAR(20),
        2 C CHAR(10),
        2 D,
          3 E CHAR(5),
          3 F CHAR(7);
```

18. Why would one structure be overlay defined on another structure?

TERMS TO STUDY

base identifier
carriage control character
data set labels
elementary item
factoring (as used in PL/I)
level number

major structure
minor structure
qualified name
scalar variable
structure
80/80 list

PRACTICE PROBLEMS

1. Accounts Receivable Report

Problem Statement: List an accounts receivable file of cards. Print headings and 45 detail lines per page. Accumulate a final total of the invoice amounts.

Purpose of the Problem: To gain experience in declaring structures, using record I/O, using the SUBSTR built-in function and pseudo-variable.

Card Input
Columns 1–5   Customer number
Columns 6–25   Customer name
Columns 26–30   Invoice number
Columns 31–36   Invoice date (e.g., 09/17/82 will be punched 091782)
Columns 37–42   Invoice amount (e.g., $1,705.98 will be punched as 170598)

Suggested Test Data: See Figure 8.14.

Printer Layout: See Figure 8.15.

Sample Output Using Suggested Test Data: See Figure 8.16.

```
12810AMERICAN CAN        11223112381157468
12810AMERICAN CAN        12336123081040902
21654APPLEBEE MFG.       09852010582033000
22873BAKER TOOL          12453112681057690
24251C.F.B. FREIGHT      13342010682130076
```

FIGURE 8.14   Suggested test data for Problem 1.

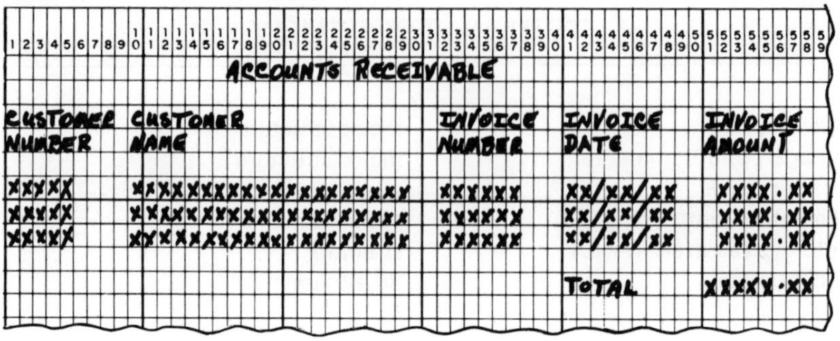

FIGURE 8.15   Printer layout for Problem 1.

2.   Preparation of Partial Invoice

Problem Statement: Each time a customer places an order with the Humphrey Hardware Co., an invoice is prepared manually and sent along with the shipment of goods to the customer. In addition, a sales card is punched for each item listed on the invoice. For example:

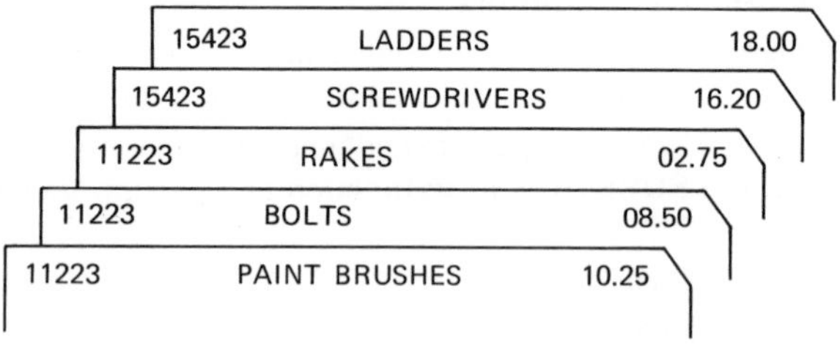

Obviously, there may be several sales cards per invoice. When these sales cards are processed by a computer program, they should be in ascending sequence by invoice number. Write a program to read these cards and list each invoice on a separate page. Check for ascending sequence of the invoice numbers. If a sequence error is detected, print a message to that effect and terminate the job. Otherwise, accumulate the total sales amount for each invoice and print this total at the end of the invoice. Also, accumulate a final total of all invoices, and print this total on a separate page at the end of the job. Note that this is only a partial invoicing application, because that part of the program that would print customer billing and shipping addresses is eliminated. You may wish to draw a flowchart before coding this problem.

Purpose of the Problem: To write a record I/O program which incorporates several basic, but important, programming techniques: use of program switches to facilitate logic and minimize coding; manipulation of data to provide two levels of totals (invoice total and final total); use of structure moves for data; the DATE built-in function; and the SUBSTR pseudo-variable.

```
                    ACCOUNTS RECEIVABLE
CUSTOMER  CUSTOMER                INVOICE   INVOICE    INVOICE
NUMBER    NAME                    NUMBER    DATE       AMOUNT


 12810    AMERICAN CAN            11223     11/23/81   1574.68
 12810    AMERICAN CAN            12336     12/30/81    409.02
 21654    APPLEBEE MFG.           09852     01/05/82    330.00
 22873    BAKER TOOL              12453     11/26/81    576.90
 24251    C.F.B. FREIGHT          13342     01/06/82   1300.76


                                           TOTAL      4191.36
```

FIGURE 8.16   Sample output for Problem 1 using suggested test data.

Card Input

Columns 1–5	Invoice number
Columns 6–25	Item description
Columns 26–31	Sales amount (e.g., $1050.40 will be punched as 105040)

Suggested Test Data: See Figure 8.17.

Printer Layout: See Figure 8.18.

Sample Output Using Suggested Test Data: See Figure 8.19. Notice that the invoice number is to be printed on the first line of output for each invoice. However, output of the invoice number is to be suppressed for the subsequent detail lines of print. No headings are required, and the number of detail lines of output will not exceed one page in length.

After you have checked out your program, rearrange the data card input so as to force a sequence error when the program is run again. This will verify the sequence checking logic of your program.

3.   Weekly Payroll Proof Totals

Problem Statement: A "proof total" is to be printed after a file of payroll earnings cards has been processed. There are four kinds of earnings cards in the

```
        ┌──── Column 1           ┌──── Column 26
        ▼                        ▼
    11223NUTS                002500
    11223BOLTS               003250
    11223HAMMERS             001475
    11224SHOVELS             003700
    11224RAKES               004050
    11225SCREWDRIVERS        001620
    11225CHISELS             002450
    11225HINGES              000850
    11225PAINT BRUSHES       001025
```

FIGURE 8.17   Suggested test data for Problem 2.

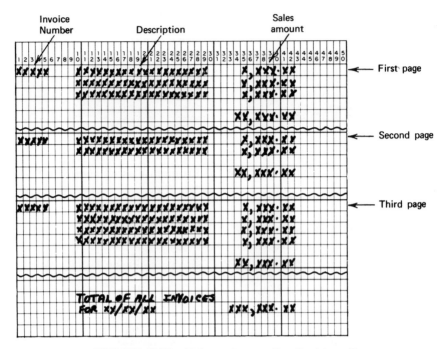

FIGURE 8.18   Printer layout for Problem 2.

file: regular, overtime, bonus, and other. Count each type of record and compute the total earnings for each type.

Purpose of the Problem: To use record I/O and the DEFINED attribute.

Card Input

Column 1	CARD TYPE:
	=1 REGULAR
	=2 OVERTIME
	=3 BONUS
	=4 OTHER
Columns 2–6	EMPLOYEE NUMBER
Columns 7–11	EARNINGS (150.75 will be punched as 15075)

Suggested Test Data: See Figure 8.20.

Desired Printer Layout: See Figure 8.21.

Sample Output Using Suggested Test Data: See Figure 8.22.

4.   Calculating Reorder Quantities in an Inventory Application

Problem Statement: A file of inventory records on punched cards contains the usage for each item for this month, last month, and two months ago. If the expected usage for next month causes an out-of-stock condition (that is, the expected usage exceeds the on-hand quantity), an order card is to be

```
11223     NUTS                    25.00
          BOLTS                   32.50
          HAMMERS                 14.75

                                  72.25


11224     SHOVELS                 37.00
          RAKES                   40.50

                                  77.50


11225     SCREWDRIVERS            16.20
          CHISELS                 24.50
          HINGES                   8.50
          PAINT BRUSHES           10.25

                                  59.45


          TOTAL FOR ALL INVOICES
          FOR 07/07/77           209.20
```

FIGURE 8.19   Sample output using suggested test data for
Problem 2.

punched; also, the order information is to be printed, with headings, on a
report. Expected usage for next month is equal to the average usage for the
preceding three-month period. Each record contains the item number and
description, as well as the number on hand, the usage for each of the last three
months, and the quantity to be ordered if an order is necessary.

Purpose of the Problem: To gain experience using arrays within structures
and the SUM built-in function.

INPUT: The following structure describes the card input record:

```
DCL 1 INVENTORY_RECORD,
      2 ITEM_# CHAR(5),
      2 DESC CHAR(20),
      2 QTY_ON_HAND PIC'9999',
      2 USAGE(3) PIC'9999',
      2 REORDER_QTY PIC'9999',
      2 REST_OF_RECORD CHAR(35);
```

```
11111108542
21111101465
21111101465
11111206765
11111206765
31111200535
31111230535
11111305530
11111305530
21111300510
21111300510
31111300600
31111300600
41111301000
41111301000
```

FIGURE 8.20   Suggested test data for Problem 3.

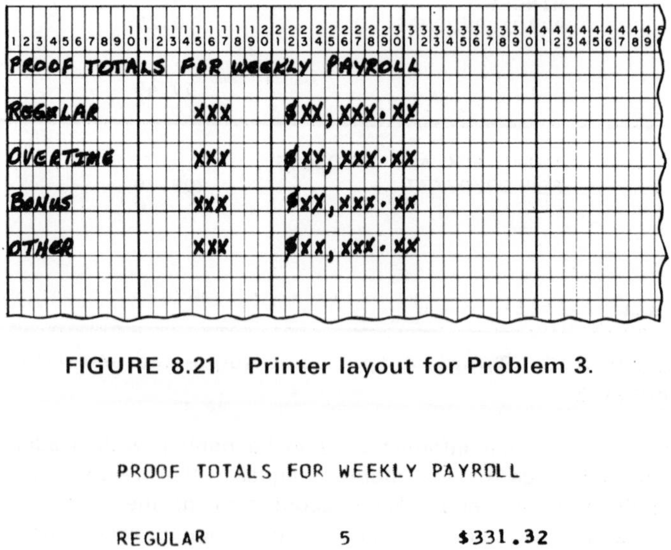

FIGURE 8.21   Printer layout for Problem 3.

```
       PROOF TOTALS FOR WEEKLY PAYROLL


       REGULAR           5        $331.32


       OVERTIME          4        $331.32


       BONUS             4         $22.70


       OTHER             2         $20.00
```

FIGURE 8.22   Sample output using suggested test data for Problem 3.

```
┌──── Column 1              ┌──── Column 26
▼                          ▼
14325BOLT                  01000100010201990400
15367HAMMER                00140050007500000160
16001NUT                   14631000C50015002500
19732PLIERS                00500080004800510075
24376LADDER                00000010001500250020
```

FIGURE 8.23 Suggested input data for Problem 4.

Suggested Input Data: See Figure 8.23.
Desired Printer Layout: See Figure 8.24.
Sample Output: See Figure 8.25.

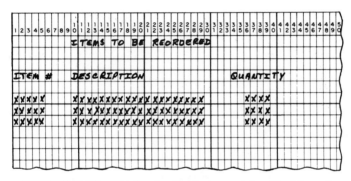

FIGURE 8.24 Desired printer layout for Problem 4.

5. Search Array

A structure contains 35 students' names and their corresponding grade-point averages received for History 101; e.g.,

```
DCL 1 HISTORY_101 EXTERNAL
      2 NAME(35) CHAR(20),
      2 GPA(35)FIXED (4,1);
```

It is desired to identify all students who have a grade-point average of 92.5 or better. Write a subroutine procedure to search the structure (which has the EXTERNAL attribute) for names of students who received a grade of 92.5 or better, and place those names into an array argument. The calling sequence is:

```
DCL HONOR_STUDENTS(35)CHAR(20)INIT('  ');
CALL FINDH(HONOR_STUDENTS);
```

⟶ Students' names are to be placed in this array

⟶ Subroutine to be coded

ITEMS TO BE REORDERED

ITEM #	DESCRIPTION	QUANTITY
14325	BOLT	400
15367	HAMMER	160
19732	PLIERS	75
24376	LADDER	20

FIGURE 8.25   Problem 4 sample output
using suggested test data.

chapter 9

Programming
Consecutive
Files

A *file* is a PL/I symbolic representation, within the program, of a *data set*, which is an organized collection of data external to a program. A file declaration can be associated with more than one data set at different times during execution of the program, or one data set can be represented by different file declarations. In a less strict sense, however, *file* and *data set* are terms used interchangeably to mean "a collection of data records."

In this chapter, we are going to examine the programming aspects and applications of data sets organized in a consecutive manner. In a consecutive data set, records are organized on the basis of their successive physical positions as, for example, on magnetic tape or in punched cards. Records having this type of organization can be processed or retrieved in sequential order only. Input/output devices permitted for use with consecutive data sets include magnetic tape drives, card readers and punches, line printers, printer—keyboards, and direct access storage devices.

Data in a tape or direct access file are arranged into physical groupings called *blocks*. A block is also called a *physical record*, because it is the unit of data that is physically transferred to and from the external storage medium. For processing purposes, each block or physical record consists of one or more logical parts called *logical records*, each of which can in turn contain one or more data items.

Logical versus Physical Records

To illustrate the need for both physical and logical records, let us take the example of the recording of data on magnetic tape. The recording density of IBM magnetic tapes is typically either 800 bytes per inch (bpi) or 1600 bpi. If all 80 columns of a card record are to be stored as a tape record, simple arithmetic indicates that we may store either ten or twenty cards worth of data in an inch of magnetic tape, depending on the density. However, this is not quite the case, because, between any two physical records stored on magnetic tape, there is a *gap*.

456

The reading of tape data is from gap to gap. Because the tape physically stops between records, the gap is necessary for the *slow-down* and *start-up* of the tape. This gap to which we have been referring is 6/10 inch in length and is known as the *interblock gap* (IBG). In an 800 bpi tape, 80 characters would occupy only 1/10 inch. Thus, we could have the following tape layout:

8 0 B Y T E S	IBG	8 0 B Y T E S	IBG	8 0 B Y T E S	IBG	8 0 B Y T E S
1/10 inch	6/10 inch	1/10 inch	6/10 inch	1/10 inch	6/10 inch	1/10 inch

In this example, there is considerably more space taken up by the gaps between records than is used for the recording of actual data. The solution to this problem is to group a number of records together into a block. The grouping of records is commonly referred to as "the blocking of records." For example, suppose ten card records are blocked together on an 800 bpi tape; now the block becomes the physical record and each 80-character record in the block becomes the logical record. We would also say that the *blocksize* is 800 characters and the *recordsize* is 80 characters.

By blocking records, greater efficiency is realized, because more data can be stored in the same amount of space. For example, in the above tape layout, only 320 bytes of data could be stored in 2.2 inches. If ten 80-byte records are grouped to form a blocksize of 800 bytes, note from the following diagram how 1280 bytes of data may be stored in 2.2 inches:

800 BYTES	IBG	480 BYTES
1 inch	6/10 inch	6/10 inch

It is also desirable to have records blocked in any DASD data set. Throughput time is also improved because larger quantities of data may be read or written at one time. For example, it is far more efficient to issue one WRITE command for the output of an entire 500-byte record than to issue five WRITE commands for the output of five 100-byte records. If you do not block with DASD, it can be slower than tape.

Thus, we have seen an advantage to the blocking of records— that of conserving space on the external storage medium. From what has been presented so far it might seem desirable to make blocks as large as possible, like 100,000 bytes. This, however, would not be the case. When data records are input or output, the records pass through a *buffer* which is actually a reserved area of main storage. For example:

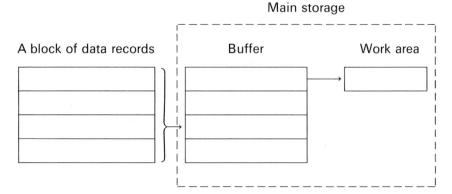

Main storage

A block of data records   Buffer   Work area

Notice from the above diagram that the size of the buffer is the length of the physical record. (On the other hand, the work area is the size of the logical record. Records are moved one at a time to the work area; this is called the *unblocking* or *deblocking* of records.) Larger physical records require larger buffers. Thus, it is not desirable to make blocks as large as possible, because a corresponding amount of main storage must be reserved for the buffer.

Logical Record Formats

Logical records can exist in one of three general formats: fixed length (format F), variable length (format V), and undefined length (format U). In declaring a file and its attributes, one of these formats must be specified. These different formats provide flexibility in the design of files and allow the programmer to take advantage of the characteristics of specific input or output devices.

Fixed-Length Records

Fixed-length records may be either blocked or unblocked, and may reside on either direct access or magnetic tape devices. Figure 9.1 illustrates how unblocked and blocked records would appear on tape. As has been noted, the concept of blocking also applies to any DASD data set, except that there are no "large" interblock gaps between physical records.

Variable-Length Records

Magnetic tapes and disks, drums, etc., because of their physical features, have the flexibility for storing data sets having variable-length records. Figure 9.2 shows the format of variable-length records as recorded on magnetic tape. This concept also applies to DASD variable-length records.

In a data set having variable-length records, it is implied that each record may be of a different length. For example, one record may be 84 bytes long; another, 104 bytes long; another, 124 bytes, etc.

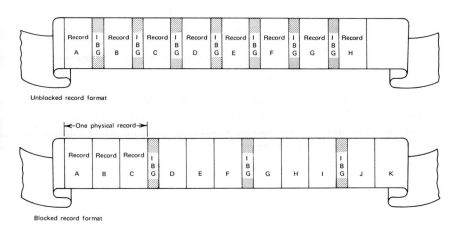

Unblocked record format

Blocked record format

FIGURE 9.1   Example of fixed-length records on magnetic tape.

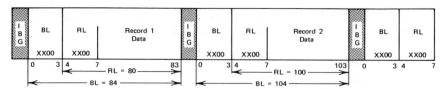

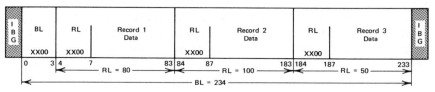

FIGURE 9.2 Example of variable-length records on magnetic tape. (KEY: BL, blocklength; RL, record length.)

The format of variable-length, unblocked records is:

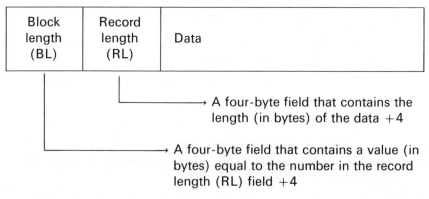

To apply these formulas, let us assume that we have a data record for output to a 132 position line printer. To represent this data record in the variable format, we would establish the following values for block length and record length:

BL = 141	RL = 137	DATA = 133†

In variable-length *blocked* records, record length is still computed as being equal to the size of the data area plus 4 bytes. The block length,

†Includes one byte for carriage control character.

however, is computed as being equal to the sum of the values in each record length field in the block plus 4 bytes. For example, for blocked records, we might have the following figures:

I B G	BL 0234	RL 0080	RECORD 1 DATA 76 bytes	RL 0100	RECORD 2 DATA 96 bytes	RL 0050	RECORD 3 DATA 46 bytes	I B G

The insertion of the block length (BL) and record length (RL) values is done automatically by the system when the file is created. Variable-length records are automatically blocked if their lengths are such that two or more records can be placed into a block. In writing a PL/I file declaration for this type of data set, the programmer simply specifies the *maximum* number of bytes for a block. In selecting a maximum blocksize, one must take into account the bytes required for block and record lengths. For example, assume that the largest record in a variable-length record file will *not* exceed 250 bytes and that we wish to assign up to three records to a block. The maximum blocksize we would specify is 766 bytes [V(766)], which is computed as follows:

$$750 \quad (3 \times 250\text{-byte records})$$
$$12 \quad (3 \times 4\text{-byte record length fields})$$
$$4 \quad (1 \times 4\text{-byte block length field})$$
$$\overline{766} \quad \text{bytes}$$

When variable-length records are processed, neither the block length nor the record length values are transferred to any declared structures, arrays, or scalar variables.

Undefined-Length Records

In this format, each block consists of only one record, though the blocks (i.e., records) may be of varying lengths. Only the maximum length of the largest record in the file is specified in the file declaration. If you desire a length specification in the record, you must, through programming, insert and retrieve it yourself; whereas, in the variable-length record format, the record length information is automatically manipulated by the system.

Allowable Block Lengths

Block length is the size of the *physical record*. For most types of records, the *minimum* block length must be at least one byte. For IBM magnetic tape data sets, block length must be at least 18 bytes. For card input, using record I/O, record length must be 80 bytes. Some device types and corresponding *maximum* block lengths are shown in Figure 9.3.

Characteristics of Consecutive Data Sets

The programming activities involving data sets may be divided into three functions: file creation, retrieval, and update.

When a consecutive data set is *created*, records are written in contiguous locations. Case Study One in this chapter will illustrate the programming steps required to create such a data set.

Retrieval of records in a consecutive data set consists of reading every record up to and including the last desired record. While it is possible that some of the records in a consecutive data set are not to be processed, those records must still be input. For example, to read and process the fifth record in a tape file, it is necessary to read (but not process) the records that precede it.

Updating of records consists of either modifying existing records, deleting records, or adding new records to a file. If new records are to be added to a consecutive data set, then the entire file with changes is, typically, copied onto another storage medium. For example, the diagram below shows how a magnetic tape file might be updated.

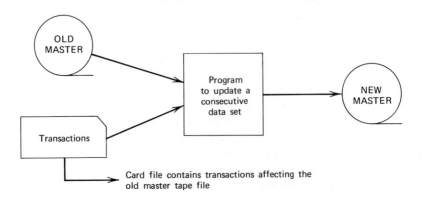

IBM device	Maximum blocksize for F or V but not VS or VBS
2540	80
2540 (CTLASA, CTL360)	81
1442	80
1442 (CTLASA, CTL360)	81
2520	80
2520 (CTLASA, CTL360)	81
2501	80
1403 (PRINT attribute or CTLASA or CTL360)	133
1403 (no PRINT attribute)	132
1404 (PRINT attribute or CTLASA or CTL360)	133
1404 (no PRINT attribute)	132
1443 (PRINT attribute or CTLASA or CTL360)	145
1443 (no PRINT attribute)	144
1445 (PRINT attribute or CTLASA or CTL360)	114
1445 (no PRINT attribute)	113
2311 (no key)	3625
2311 (including key)	3605
2314 (no key)	7294
2314 (including key)	7249
2321 (no key)	2000
2321 (including key)	1984
3330 (no key)	13030
2305 Model 1 (no key)	14136
2305 Model 2 (no key)	14660
2301 (no key)	20483
3211 (no PRINT attribute)	132 or 150
3211 (PRINT attribute or CTLASA or CTL360)	133 or 151
2303 (no key)	4892

FIGURE 9.3   Allowable maximum block lengths for IBM I/O devices.

Obviously, now, the old master no longer contains current information. The next time the tape file is to be updated, the *new master* along with the *changes* file constitute input to the update program. At this point, then, the new master becomes the old master (#2) and yet another new master tape is produced. Typically, old master tapes are kept for a certain period of time before the data on these tapes is destroyed. The above diagram could illustrate the function of changing, deleting, or adding records to a tape file. The adding of records is often referred to as *merging*, which is the combining of records from two or more similarly sequenced files into one sequenced file. This is further illustrated in Case Study Two of this chapter.

In the case of DASD files, records may be modified without creating a new data set, as is necessary for tape files. However, if records are to be added, then the data set with additions is copied onto another area of the same direct access device or another external storage medium. In deleting records from a DASD data set, the record could be *flagged* as being inactive or not rewritten if the data set is being copied onto another storage medium.

Declaring Consecutive Files

There are a number of attributes and options that you may specify in the declaration of consecutive files. These are explained in the following paragraphs.

FILE Attribute

The FILE attribute, when used, denotes the identifier preceding FILE as a file name. For example, MASTER is declared to be a file name in the following statement:

DECLARE MASTER FILE . . .

For documentation purposes, the FILE attribute should be declared. However, the word FILE does not have to be specified if the compiler can determine from the other attributes (INPUT, OUTPUT, etc.) that the name declared could only be referring to a file.

The break character should not be used in file names. This is because the character set of job control language does not contain the break character, and it is through job control that a file name is related to a specific data set. In the subset language, file names may be from one to six alphameric characters; in the full language, file names may be from one to seven alphameric characters.

EXTERNAL/INTERNAL Attributes

EXTERNAL is always the default attribute for file names. It means that a declared file may be known in other PL/I procedures, providing those blocks also contain an external declaration of the same file name. The INTERNAL attribute specifies that the file name be known only in the procedure block in which it was declared. INTERNAL may not be specified in the subset language implementations.

STREAM and RECORD Attributes

These attributes describe the characteristics of the data to be used in input and output file operations. The STREAM attribute causes the file associated with the file name to be treated as a continuous stream of data in character format. The STREAM attribute can be specified only for files of consecutive organization.

The RECORD attribute causes the file associated with the file name to be treated as a sequence of logical records, each record consisting of one or more data items recorded in any internal data format. If neither is specified, the default attribute is STREAM.

INPUT, OUTPUT, and UPDATE Attributes

These attributes determine the direction of data transfer. The INPUT attribute applies to files that are to be read only. The OUTPUT attribute applies to files that are to be created or extended, and hence are to be written only. The UPDATE attribute describes a file that can be used for both input and output; it allows records in an existing file to be altered, and it applies only to files located on a direct access device.

SEQUENTIAL, DIRECT, and TRANSIENT Attributes

These are *access* attributes and apply only to a file with the RECORD attribute. The access attributes describe how the records in a file are to be created or retrieved.

The SEQUENTIAL attribute specifies that records in a data set are to be accessed in physical sequence—that is, from the first record of the data set to the last.

The DIRECT attribute specifies that records in a data set are accessed in random order. The location of the record in the data set is determined by a *key*. A key is a unique character-string identifying each record in a data set. For example, it could be a part number in an inventory file or an employee man number in a payroll file. Keys and the DIRECT attribute will be more fully discussed in the next chapter, which deals with INDEXED and REGIONAL files.

The TRANSIENT attribute applies to files used for teleprocessing applications.

BUFFERED and UNBUFFERED Attributes

The buffering attributes apply to a file that has the SEQUENTIAL and RECORD attributes. The BUFFERED attribute indicates that logical records transferred to and from a file must pass through an intermediate storage area. The size of the buffer corresponds to the size of the physical records in the data set associated with the file. The use of buffers may help speed up processing by allowing overlap of I/O and computing time.

The UNBUFFERED attribute indicates that a logical record in a data set need not pass through a buffer, but can be transferred directly to and from the internal storage associated with a variable name. Records may not be blocked in a data set having the UNBUFFERED attribute. Generally, there are no advantages to specifying the UN-BUFFERED attribute.

A *buffer* is an area of main storage that is automatically reserved by PL/I for files having the BUFFERED attribute.† In this case, when data is to be input, the input characters are first read into the buffer and then transferred to your named structure or other data area.

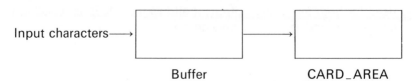

Input characters Buffer   CARD_AREA

While a program is processing data in the CARD_AREA, it is possible for the system input routines to be reading the next record into the buffer. The reading of another record while concurrently processing the previous record is referred to as *overlapping*. In the case of blocked records, it would be necessary to have at least two buffers reserved to overlap input and processing from the same file, or processing and output to the same file. To indicate the number of buffers reserved,

†The size of the buffer is the size of the physical record; e.g., if F(800,80) is declared, buffer size will be 800 bytes.

the BUFFERS option is specified in the ENVIRONMENT section of a file declaration. Generally, the use of buffers improves the throughput of data to or from a program. The BUFFERED attribute applies to both input and output files.

BACKWARDS Attribute

This attribute applies to files stored on magnetic tape when reverse processing (i.e., from last record to first) is desired.

KEYED Attribute

This attribute indicates that records in the file can be accessed by means of a key. The stream attribute cannot be applied to a file that has the KEYED attribute. The nature and use of keys is discussed in Chapter 10.

ENVIRONMENT Attribute

The ENVIRONMENT attribute specifies the physical character- istics of the file and the type of device on which the file is now stored or will be stored. These characteristics are indicated in a parenthesized *option list* following the ENVIRONMENT attribute specification. They are not a part of the PL/I language; they are keywords having to do with the capabilities or limitations of specific PL/I implementatiqns. Following is a list of some of the PL/I keywords that may appear in the ENVIRONMENT option list. These keywords will be defined either on the following pages of this chapter or in the next chapter dealing with *indexed sequential* and *direct* files :

```
F | FB
V | VB | VS | VBS
U
BUFFERS(n)
CTLASA | CTL360
LEAVE | REWIND
NOTAPEMK
NOLABEL
CONSECUTIVE | INDEXED | REGIONAL(1) | REGIONAL(2) |
    REGIONAL(3)
VERIFY
MEDIUM
```

F (blocksize). The F designates that records in this data set are fixed length. The blocksize refers to the size of the physical record. For example, F (80) means that each record in a data set is 80 characters (or bytes) long.

F (blocksize, recsize). Records in this data set are fixed length and blocked on tape or DASD files. All blocks contain the same number of records except, perhaps, the last block in the file. The *blocksize* is the total number of bytes in the physical record, whereas the *recsize* is the number of bytes in one logical record contained within the block. For example:

F (500, 100)

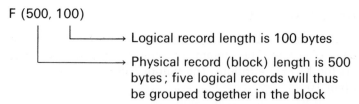

→ Logical record length is 100 bytes

→ Physical record (block) length is 500 bytes; five logical records will thus be grouped together in the block

V (maxblocksize). Figure 9.2 illustrates the format of this type of record. As shown in that figure, the first four bytes of each block are the block length. In DOS, as many records as will evenly fit are placed in the block. Each record in the block is also preceded by a four-byte record control field. In this ENVIRONMENT option, the maximum blocksize must include the number of bytes required for the data as well as the control fields. For example:

V (250)

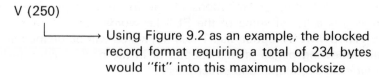

→ Using Figure 9.2 as an example, the blocked record format requiring a total of 234 bytes would "fit" into this maximum blocksize

	Allows V format records for a printer
Subset language	No
Full language	Yes

V (maxblocksize, maxrecsize). In this format type, the programmer may specify the maximum blocksize and the maximum record size. Again, four bytes must be provided for the block as well as four bytes for each record. The record size must never exceed the blocksize.

[For example, if the maximum data length anticipated is 120 bytes, a blocksize of not less than 128 bytes must be specified, whether the records are blocked or not, inasmuch as unblocked records are considered to be in blocks of one record each; if the records are blocked, the record size must not be more than 124 bytes (assuming 128-byte block).] This format applies to OS.

U (maxblocksize). Each block on tape or DASD consists of one record. The blocks (records) are of varying lengths. No system control bytes appear in the block. For example:

U (500)

→ Maximum record length is 500 bytes, though some may be smaller

Record Format Options for the Optimizing Compilers. Record formats in the DOS or OS PL/I Optimizing Compilers may be specified in one of the following formats:

F	Fixed-length, unblocked
FB	Fixed-length, blocked
V	Variable-length, unblocked
VB	Variable-length, blocked
U	Undefined-length, cannot be blocked

Following one of the above record format designations (i.e., F, FB, etc.) the keyword BLKSIZE(n) and/or RECSIZE(n) is to be specified, where n may be a decimal integer constant or a variable with the attributes FIXED BINARY(31) STATIC. Here are some examples:

```
F  BLKSIZE(80)      or     F  RECSIZE(80)
FB BLKSIZE(800) RECSIZE(80)
V  BLKSIZE(400)      or     V  RECSIZE(400)
VB BLKSIZE(256) RECSIZE(126)
U  BLKSIZE(500)
```

Here is an example in which the record length specified is a variable:

```
DCL SIZE FIXED BINARY(31) STATIC;
DCL ALPHA FILE RECORD OUTPUT ENV(F BLKSIZE(SIZE));
```

Spanned Records. This record type is available through OS. There are several record formats that may be specified:

VS	Variable-length, spanned
VBS	Variable-length, blocked, spanned

These record formats are known as *spanned records*, because they can start in one block and be continued in the next. But the programmer is concerned only with complete records; segmentation and reassembly are handled automatically. The use of spanned records allows the programmer to select a blocksize, independently of record size, that will combine optimum usage of external storage space with maximum efficiency of transmission. The general forms of these record types are listed here.

PL/I F	OS PL/I Optimizing Compiler
VS(maxblocksize)	VS BLKSIZE(m)
VS(maxblocksize,maxrecsize)	VS BLKSIZE(m) RECSIZE(n)
VBS(maxblocksize)	VBS BLKSIZE(m)
VBS(maxblocksize,maxrecsize)	VBS BLKSIZE(m) RECSIZE(n)

The record size specified for VS format records can exceed the blocksize; if necessary, the records are segmented, and the segments are placed in consecutive blocks. Each block can contain only one record or segment of a record, and each contains two four-byte fields, one to specify the block length and the other the record or segment length. For example, if the record format is specified as VS(80, 200), a record that includes 180 bytes of data will appear in the data set as two blocks of 80 bytes (8 control bytes and 72 data bytes) and one block of 44 bytes (8 control bytes and 36 data bytes).

VBS format differs from VS format only in that each block contains as many records or segments as it can accommodate; each block is, therefore, substantially the same size (although there can be a variation of up to four bytes, inasmuch as each segment must contain at least one byte of data). For example, a block might contain the last segment of one record, or more complete records and the first segment of another record.

BUFFERS(n) Option. The BUFFERS(n) option is used to specify the number of buffers to be used in files having the BUFFERED attribute. In the subset language, BUFFERS(2) is the maximum that may be specified.

CTLASA | CTL360 Options. The CTLASA and the CTL360 options are two mutually exclusive options of the ENVIRONMENT attribute which are used for record printer and punch files; they specify whether the first character of the record is to be interpreted as an ASA or System/360 control character. It is the programmer's responsibility to provide a correct control character as the first character of the record variable.

The character codes that can be used with CTLASA are listed with their interpretations in Figure 8.3. The 8-bit codes that can be used with CTL360 are given in Figure 8.4. Unpredictable results will occur if the control character is not one of those listed.

LEAVE Option. The LEAVE option is used to specify that no rewind operation is to be performed at file open or close time. It should be used for files having the BACKWARDS attribute to ensure proper positioning of the file.

REWIND Option. This option specifies the action to be taken when the end of a magnetic tape volume is reached, or when a data set on a magnetic tape volume is closed. The *disposition* of the data set determines the action taken. For example, if the file is to be kept (DISP= KEEP or DISP=CATLG in OS job control statement), then the tape is rewound to the beginning of the volume and unloaded. On the other hand, if the file is to be deleted in this job step (DISP=DELETE), then the tape is rewound to the beginning of the volume but not unloaded. Finally, if the file is to be passed on to another job step (DISP=PASS), the tape is wound on to the end of the data set or repositioned at the beginning for a data set that does not have the BACKWARDS attribute. REWIND is not available in DOS/TOS.

NOTAPEMK Option. Available only in DOS/TOS, the NOTAPEMK option for tape files enables the programmer to prevent the writing of a leading tapemark ahead of the data records on unlabeled tape files. NOTAPEMK may be used for tape OUTPUT files with NOLABEL specified. This option is not allowed for UNBUFFERED files.

NOLABEL Option. Available in DOS/TOS only, the NOLABEL option is used to specify that no file labels are to be processed for a magnetic tape file. This option would be used for *scratch* tapes; that is, tapes onto which data is to be temporarily written during the execution of the program. Permanent tapes should always have labels as a protection against inadvertent destruction of the tape's data through programming errors.

CONSECUTIVE Option. This is the type of data set organization in which records are organized on the basis of their successive physical positions in the data set. Records in this type of file organization can only be processed in sequential order. Input/output devices permitted for consecutive files include magnetic tape drives, card readers and punches, line printers, disks, and drums.

VERIFY Option. Available in DOS/TOS only, the VERIFY option is used to specify that a *read* and *check* data is to be performed after every write operation. This option is permitted only with a direct access device.

MEDIUM Option. Available only in DOS/TOS, this option is used to connect or relate a *logical unit name* and the *physical device* with which you wish to communicate in your PL/I program. Logical unit names always begin with the letters SYS, followed by either three letters that have a special meaning or by three numeric digits of your choice. The logical unit name has the form SYSxxx; the following list defines the possible designations that xxx may take:

IPT	System input device (e.g., card reader)
LST	System output device (e.g., printer)
PCH	System output device (e.g., card punch)
000–244	Logical units SYS000 through SYS244

The physical device is simply referred to by its number. For example, the IBM 1442 Card Read/Punch would be designated

. . .MEDIUM (SYSIPT, 1442). . .

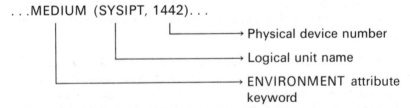

→ Physical device number

→ Logical unit name

→ ENVIRONMENT attribute keyword

The physical device numbers specified would depend on the I/O devices available with the computer on which your PL/I program is to be run.

OPEN Statement Attributes and Options

The OPEN statement for a stream or record file associates a file name with a data set. It can also be used to specify additional attributes for a file if a complete set of attributes has not been previously declared. The general format is

OPEN FILE (filename) additional attributes;

	Attributes that may be specified in OPEN statement
DOS/TOS	PAGESIZE INPUT and OUTPUT if file has UNBUFFERED attribute
OS	BUFFERED or UNBUFFERED STREAM or RECORD INPUT, OUTPUT, or UPDATE PRINT, LINESIZE, PAGESIZE DIRECT or SEQUENTIAL BACKWARDS KEYED, EXCLUSIVE TITLE

If attributes are specified in the OPEN statement, then those attributes must not be specified in the file declaration statement. If several files are to be opened at one time, it is more efficient in some operating systems to open them with one OPEN statement, e.g.,

OPEN FILE(CARDIN),FILE(PRINTR),FILE(TAPE) ;

than to code three separate OPEN statements :

OPEN FILE(CARDIN) ;
OPEN FILE(PRINTR) ;
OPEN FILE(TAPE) ;

The options LINESIZE and PAGESIZE were described in Chapter 5, which covered stream I/O, as these options may only be specified for stream files. The TITLE option, which is available in OS, allows a programmer to choose dynamically—at open time—one among several data sets to be associated with a particular file name. Consult the appropriate PL/I reference manual (i.e., PL/I F or OS PL/I optimizing compiler) for a detailed description of this option and its related job control statements.

The REWRITE Statement

The REWRITE statement is a record output statement that transfers a record from a variable in internal storage to an UPDATE file. The general format is

REWRITE FILE(filename)FROM(variable) ;

The syntax rules for this statement are the same as for the READ and WRITE statements. The REWRITE statement would be used in consecutive file programming when it is desired *to modify* an existing record in that file, whereas a WRITE statement is issued when it is desired *to create* a consecutive file.

Two case studies are presented in this chapter. The first case study will create a master payroll tape and the second case study will process that tape.

Case Study One

A master payroll tape file is to be created. The tape records are in sequence by Social Security number and contain the following fields:

1. Employee name
2. Social Security number
3. Year-to-date gross earnings
4. Year-to-date tax withheld
5. Year-to-date FICA (Social Security Insurance) withheld

Figure 9.4 is a program flowchart for creating this master payroll tape. The program is to read cards punched with the employee payroll information and write these records on magnetic tape. A count of the number of records written on tape is to be accumulated and printed at the end of the job. In addition, the records are to be listed on the line printer as they are being written on tape. Because the tape records must be in Social Security number order, the program should also sequence check the input cards. Should a card be out of sequence, an error message is to be printed, the remaining input cards are to be read but not processed, and the job is to be terminated.

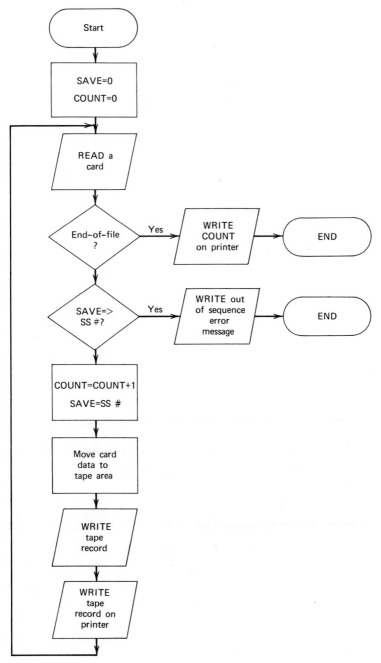

FIGURE 9.4   Flowchart for Case Study One.

Description of the Data

Following is the structure that describes the card input data:

```
DCL 1 CARD_AREA,
       2 NAME CHAR(20),
       2 SOCIAL_SECURITY_# PIC'(9)9',
       2 GROSS PIC'99999V99',
       2 TAX PIC '9999V99',
       2 FICA PIC'999V99',
       2 REST_OF_RECORD CHAR(33);
```

All of the items in the above structure, with the exception of REST_OF_RECORD, require a total of 47 characters. However, the corresponding tape record will require fewer bytes because some of the data fields may be stored in a more compact fashion on tape (i.e., packed decimal). Here is the structure that describes the tape record:

```
DCL 1 TAPE_AREA,
       2 NAME CHAR(20),                     /* 20 BYTES */
       2 SOCIAL_SECURITY_# PIC'(9)9',       /*  9 BYTES */
       2 GROSS FIXED(7,2),                  /*  4 BYTES */
       2 TAX FIXED(6,2),                    /*  4 BYTES */
       2 FICA FIXED(5,2):                   /*  3 BYTES */
```

Because GROSS, TAX, and FICA may be represented in FIXED DECIMAL, the number of bytes required for those fields on tape is less than the number of columns (characters) required for those fields in a punched card. The card record data requires 47 characters of storage, whereas the tape record data will require only 40 characters.

In Case Study Two, the data from this master tape will be read. It is imperative that identical attributes be declared for the structure into which the tape records are to be input. Of course, the elementary item names do not have to be the same.

Creation of a Consecutive File

Figure 9.5 shows the program that creates the master payroll tape. Several statements to study in this program are discussed below.

Statement 3. The master tape file is declared in this statement. Notice that the records are blocked, ten records to the block. This affords us greater efficiency in the use of space on the tape. For OS PL/I compilers, the MEDIUM option would not appear in the declaration. The symbolic unit name, SYS005, is arbitrarily selected. Through

```
       /* CREATE MASTER TAPE FILE */
 1     CASE1:  PROC OPTIONS(MAIN);
 2             DCL CARDIN FILE INPUT RECORD ENV(F(80)MEDIUM(SYSIPT,2540));
 3             DCL TAPE FILE OUTPUT RECORD ENV(F(400,40)MEDIUM(SYS005,2400));
 4             DCL COUNT FIXED BINARY INIT(0), SAVE PIC'(9)9' INIT(0);
 5             ON ENDFILE(CARDIN) GO TO EOJ;
 6             OPEN FILE(TAPE),FILE(CARDIN);
 7             DCL 1 CARD_AREA,
                 2 NAME CHAR(20),
                 2 SOCIAL_SECURITY_# PIC'(9)9',
                 2 GROSS PIC'99999V99',
                 2 TAX PIC '9999V99',
                 2 FICA PIC'999V99',
                 2 REST_OF_RECORD CHAR(33);
 8             DCL 1 TAPE_AREA,
                 2 NAME CHAR(20),              /* 20 BYTES */
                 2 SOCIAL_SECURITY_# PIC'(9)9', /*  9 BYTES */
                 2 GROSS FIXED(7,2),           /*  4 BYTES */
                 2 TAX FIXED(6,2),             /*  4 BYTES */
                 2 FICA FIXED(5,2);            /*  3 BYTES */
 9     LOOP:   READ FILE(CARDIN)INTO(CARD_AREA);
10             IF SAVE >= CARD_AREA.SOCIAL_SECURITY_# THEN DO;
11             ON ENDFILE(CARDIN) GO TO FINI;
12             PUT PAGE LIST('PAYROLL RECORDS OUT OF SEQUENCE');
13     CANCEL: READ FILE(CARDIN)INTO(CARD_AREA);
14             GO TO CANCEL;
15             END;
16             COUNT = COUNT + 1;
17             SAVE = CARD_AREA.SOCIAL_SECURITY_#;
18             TAPE_AREA.NAME = CARD_AREA.NAME;
19             TAPE_AREA.SOCIAL_SECURITY_# = CARD_AREA.SOCIAL_SECURITY_#;
20             TAPE_AREA.GROSS = CARD_AREA.GROSS;
21             TAPE_AREA.TAX = CARD_AREA.TAX;
22             TAPE_AREA.FICA = CARD_AREA.FICA;
23             WRITE FILE(TAPE) FROM(TAPE_AREA);
               /* THE FOLLOWING STATEMENT PROVIDES A LISTING OF TAPE RECORDS*/
24             PUT SKIP LIST(TAPE_AREA);
25             GO TO LOOP;
26     EOJ:    PUT SKIP(3)LIST('NO. OF RECORDS ON TAPE IS',COUNT);
27     FINI:   END;
```

FIGURE 9.5 Program to create master tape file.

job control statements, the SYS005 is related to the physical drive on which the tape is mounted. Consult the appropriate PL/I programmer's guide for job control statements needed.†

Statements 18–22. These statements move the CARD_AREA elements to the TAPE_AREA structure. In full language implementations, these five statements could be replaced with the following statement:

TAPE_AREA=CARD_AREA,BY NAME;

This is possible because the elementary item names in both structures are identical for those fields that appear in both structures.

†Appendix B provides a bibliography of these programmer's guides.

Statement 24.   This PUT LIST statement prints the data previously written on tape. Notice how only the structure name, TAPE_AREA, is specified. However, each field within this structure is output separately, one field per tab position. Figure 9.6 shows a small sampling of the output listing.

It should be noted that in this case study there would be no difference in the programming approach had we wished to create a consecutive file on a disk or other DASD. The only program modification would be to change the MEDIUM option in a DOS/TOS program from

. . .MEDIUM(SYS005,2400). . .

                                   └────────────────→ IBM tape drive

to

. . .MEDIUM(SYS005,2314). . .

                                   └────────────────→ IBM disk drive

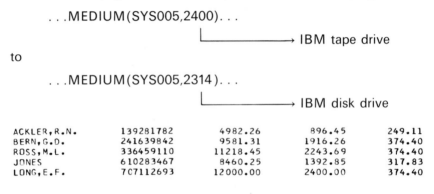

```
ACKLER,R.N.         139281782         4982.26         896.45         249.11
BERN,G.D.           241639842         9581.31        1916.26         374.40
ROSS,M.L.           336459110        11218.45        2243.69         374.40
JONES               610283467         8460.25        1392.85         317.83
LONG,E.F.           707112693        12000.00        2400.00         374.40

NO. OF RECORDS ON TAPE IS                5
```

FIGURE 9.6   **Sample output of data written from tape.**

Case Study Two

The Purpose of this case study is to illustrate the usefulness of consecutive files and to provide examples of their file declarations.

This problem illustrates the *merging* of two files. One of these is the tape master file created in Case Study One; the other is a card file containing new records to be added to the tape master file. The records in each file are in Social Security number sequence. As the new master tape is being created, all records are to be listed on the line printer and the input cards are to be checked for ascending sequence of Social Security number. In addition, an *exception report* is to be printed if the tape file already contains a payroll master record equivalent to the one being added in the card file. The diagram illustrates the flow of data in this case study. As you can see, two reports are to be output: the listing of all regular records in the new master payroll tape and the

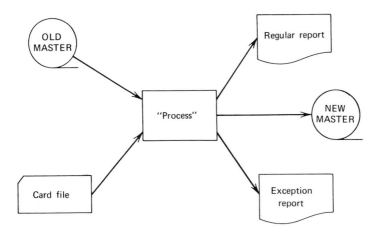

exception listing for duplicate records found. Assuming there is only one line printer available for this program, the problem becomes one of how to print two reports when the information for those reports is determined only at the time the tape and card records are read. The records in the *regular report* are to be listed as all records are written on the *new master* tape. However, because the line printer is being used for the regular report, it will be necessary to store the data for the *exception report* elsewhere. A consecutive disk file will meet our needs. Thus, as the output for the exception report is determined, that information will be written on a disk file. At the conclusion of the program, the contents of the file will be printed.†

File and Data Area Declarations

As mentioned before, the tape input will be the newly created master file from Case Study One, which, when processed as input to the Case Study Two program, becomes the old master called OLDTP. The following are the file and tape input area declarations:

```
DCL OLDTP  FILE INPUT RECORD ENV(F(400,40)MEDIUM(SYS006,2400)));
DCL 1 TAPE,
        2 NAME CHAR(20),
        2 SS_# PIC'(9)9',
        2 YTD_GROSS FIXED(7,2),
        2 YTD_TAX FIXED(6,2),
        2 YTD_FICA FIXED(5,2);
```

†In the OS operating system for S/360 or S/370, the programming step of writing the exception report to the disk would not be necessary because of the Output Writer feature of OS.

480 PL/I Programming

Note that the blocking factor in the OLDTP declaration must be identical to that in the program which created this tape. Also, the elements of the data area structure must have attributes identical to those of the structure from which the data was written initially.

The new master tape will also have the same specifications as the old master. The following are the file and tape output area declarations:

```
DCL NEWTP FILE OUTPUT RECORD ENV(F(400,40)MEDIUM(SYS005,2400));
DCL 1 TAPE_OUT,
      2 NAME CHAR(20),
      2 SS_# PIC'(9)9',
      2 YTD_GROSS FIXED(7,2),
      2 YTD_TAX FIXED(6,2),
      2 YTD_FICA FIXED(5,2);
```

In the full language implementations, it would be possible to use the LIKE attribute in the structure declaration for TAPE_OUT, because the elementary items are identical to those declared in the TAPE structure. Thus, this statement could have been coded:

DCL 1 TAPE_OUT LIKE TAPE;

The card input file contains the records to be merged with the old master tape records. Here are the file declaration and corresponding card input area declaration:

```
DCL CARDIN FILE INPUT RECORD ENV(F(80)MEDIUM(SYSIPT,2540));
DCL 1 CARD,
      2 CARD_RECORD,
        3 NAME CHAR(20),
        3 SS_# PIC'(9)9',
        3 GROSS PIC'(5)9V99',
        3 TAX PIC'(4)9V99',
        3 FICA PIC'(3)9V99',
      2 REST CHAR(33);
```

Figure 9.7 shows the desired output for the regular report. Notice that print positions are required. In addition to detail lines, headings are to

FIGURE 9.7   Regular report printer layout.

be printed. For purposes of simplicity, this case study will not consider page overflow programming; the method has been covered in previous chapters. Here are the printer file and print output area declarations:

```
DCL PRINTR FILE OUTPUT RECORD
        ENV(F(75)CTLASA MEDIUM(SYSLST,1403));
DCL HDNG CHAR(75) DEF PRINT_OUT;
DCL 1 PRINT_OUT,
      2 CC CHAR(1),
      2 AREA,
        3 NAME CHAR(25),
        3 SS_# CHAR(15),
        3 GROSS PIC'ZZ,ZZZV.99(5)B',
        3 TAX PIC'ZZ,ZZZV.99(5)B',
        3 FICA PIC'ZZZV.99';
```

While 74 positions are needed for printing, we can see that 75 positions are actually specified because of the CTLASA option in the file declaration. This option, you will recall, requires that the first character of the output area be set aside for carriage control. Although page overflow will not be used, for the purpose of printing headings the initial skipping to a new page will be incorporated in the program. Notice that HDNG is declared as a character-string and that it is overlay defined on PRINT_OUT. HDNG will be the receiving field for the character-string constants that make up the page headings. The overlay defining technique was selected because it saves storage.

Figure 9.8 shows the desired output for the exception report. Notice that the layout of the detail lines in this report is identical to that of the regular report. Thus, the PRINT_OUT area declared above will also suffice for the handling of the exception data. If a duplicate record is found during the creation of the new master tape, the exception record will be moved to the PRINT_OUT structure and that structure's contents will be written into a sequential disk file. This physical file is both *output* and *input*. It is an *output* file while records are being written onto it. At the termination of the case study program, it is time to print the contents of this file. It then becomes an *input* file inasmuch as the records previously written must be read into main

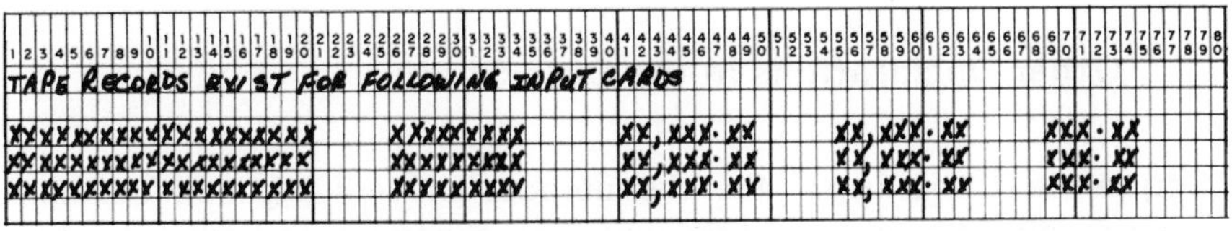

FIGURE 9.8 Exception report printer layout.

storage before printing can take place. Because the attributes INPUT and OUTPUT would constitute *conflicting attributes* if they both appeared in one file, it will be necessary to declare the following two files:

```
DCL DKOUT FILE OUTPUT RECORD ENV(F(750,75)MEDIUM(SYS007,2311));
DCL DKIN  FILE INPUT  RECORD ENV(F(750,75)MEDIUM(SYS007,2311));
```

Two names, DKIN and DKOUT, are given to the same physical file. Through job control statements in the various operating systems, the file names DKIN and DKOUT are designated as referring to the same physical file.

Notice that the record length in both file declarations is 75 and the block length is 750. When records are blocked and the record length is not divisible by eight, in some compilers you will get a warning diagnostic during compilation. Such would be the situation with this program. Thus, we would receive the following message:

```
          DECLARE STATEMENT DIAGNOSTICS.

W RECORDSIZE OF RECORD NOT DIVISIBLE BY 8 IN FILE DKOUT
W RECORDSIZE OF RECORD NOT DIVISIBLE BY 8 IN FILE DKIN
```

⎣⎯⎯⎯⎯⎯⎯⟶ W for "warning"

Because this is only a warning, it does not interfere with the correct execution of this program. However, should a structure contain data items that require boundary alignment (e.g., FIXED BINARY must be on a fullword boundary), then you must take corrective action regarding the above diagnostic. The action would consist of declaring in the structure a variable with a character length attribute long enough to bring the record size up to a value that *is* divisible by eight. Inasmuch as our PRINT_OUT structure contains the data to be written into the DKOUT file, and because there are no boundary alignment requirements for the PICTURE and CHARACTER data contained in that structure, the warning message may be ignored.

Other Declarations in the Case Study

Sequence Checking. For the purpose of verifying that the card input records are in ascending sequence according to Social Security number, a variable must be declared and initialized to zero. For example :

DCL PREV_SS_# PIC'(9)9'INIT(0) ;

Then, when each card is read, the Social Security number must be ascertained to be greater than the previous Social Security number. If the new number is greater than the value in PREV_SS_#, then the new number is moved into PREV_SS_#.

This sequence checking is done in the source statements 25–29 (see Figure 9.10). Notice from these statements that if the new Social Security number is not greater than the value in PREV_SS_#, then a sequence error exists. In this case, the program prints an error message and terminates the program with a RETURN statement.

Program Switches. A *switch* is a condition-remembering "device," and the device, in turn, is actually an identifier or variable. When set to a value of "zero," for example, it may indicate that a certain condition does not exist; when set to a value of "one," it may indicate that the condition does exist. In this case study program, three program switches are needed :

DCL (TP_ENDED,CD_ENDED,EXCPTN)BIT(1) INIT('0'B) ;

The first two switches, TP_ENDED and CD_ENDED, will be set to a value of '1'B whenever an end-of-file condition arises on either the OLDTP or the CARDIN file, respectively. Initially, both switches are set to '0'B. Likewise, the switch named EXCPTN will be set to '1'B whenever an exception record is written onto the disk file. If, at the end of the program, EXCPTN = '0'B, as it was initially, we know that no duplicate records were encountered and that exception report needs to be written. If EXCPTN is '1'B, there is at least one record on the disk file that must be printed.

Altering Program Flow. This can be accomplished through the use of another form of switch declared to have the LABEL attribute. For example :

DCL NEXT_OPER LABEL ;

The identifier NEXT_OPER will be set to one of two labels in the program. After a record has been written onto the new master tape, NEXT_OPER will contain the label of the point to which the program is to transfer.

484 PL/I Programming

Handling Two End-of-File Conditions

Because there are two input files to this program, CARDIN and OLDTP, two end-of-file conditions will be raised: one for the card reader and one for the old master tape. Here are the ON statements for this program:

ON ENDFILE(OLDTP) GO TO END_TP;
ON ENDFILE(CARDIN) GO TO END_CD;

When the statement labeled END_TP is reached, and before it is executed, a check must be made to see if CARDIN has actually encountered end-of-file. If so, the program is concluded by printing the exception report. If CARDIN has not reached end-of-file, we must remember the fact that OLDTP has ended by setting the TP_ENDED switch to '1'B. Moreover, in case the card file contains a record with a Social Security number greater than the last record on OLDTP, we must ensure that all the remaining cards are merged into the NEWTP file. We can do this by placing a very high SS_# in the tape input area (e.g., all 9's). It will be this high SS_# which will be compared against the remainder of the card file. The same kind of action must be taken whenever the CARDIN file is exhausted.

Opening of Files

All files, except DKIN, may be opened at the beginning of the program. For example:

```
OPEN FILE(CARDIN), FILE(OLDTP),FILE(NEWTP),
     FILE(PRINTR), FILE(DKOUT);
```

Recall that DKIN and DKOUT are physically the same file. Thus, when DKOUT is open and we are communicating with that file, it is as though DKIN does not exist. However, when DKOUT is closed, we may then open DKIN and read records from the beginning of that file.

Writing Headings

The following are the statements that output the two heading lines for the regular report:

```
HDNG='1Y E A R - T O - D A T E    P A Y R O L L   '
||'T O T A L S';
WRITE FILE(PRINTR) FROM(PRINT_OUT);
HDNG='-NAME'||(21)' '||'SOC.SEC.#'||(8)' '||'GROSS'||(9)' '||
'TAX'||(9)' '||'FICA';
WRITE FILE(PRINTR) FROM(PRINT_OUT);
```

The flowchart in Figure 9.9 diagrams the logic for the merging of the card and tape files. Figure 9.10 shows the entire program that accomplishes the problem defined in this case study. The coding utilized should be familiar to you at this point in the book; hence, it will not be discussed in any more detail. You should study the coding, however, in preparation for tackling Practice Problem 2 at the end of this chapter.

Figure 9.11 shows the sample output from Case Study Two. A comparison of this output with the output from Case Study One (Figure 9.6) shows that three new records were added to the master file and that the records were added in the proper sequence.

SUMMARY

Consecutive Files: In a consecutive file, records are organized on the basis of their successive physical positions as on magnetic tape or in punched cards. Records having this type of file organization can be processed or retrieved in sequential order only.

Physical and Logical Records: A physical record is the unit of data that is physically transferred to and from an external storage medium. Each physical record consists of one or more logical records. The grouping of logical records is commonly referred to as "the blocking of records."

Logical Record Formats

1. *Fixed-length records:* Fixed-length records may be either blocked or unblocked and may reside on any device.

2. *Variable-length records:* Magnetic tapes, disks, drums, etc., because of their physical features, have the flexibility for storing data sets having variable-length records. In a data set having variable-length records, each record may be of a different length, and records may be blocked or unblocked. In writing a PL/I file declaration for this type of file, the programmer simply specifies the maximum number of bytes for a block. For example, the variable length specification for a line printer with 132 positions would be V(141) [carriage control character included].

3. *Undefined-length records.* In this format, each block consists of only one record, though the blocks may be of varying lengths. Only the maximum length of the largest record in the file is specified.

Characteristics of Consecutive Files: When a consecutive file is created, records are written in contiguous locations. Retrieval of records in a consecutive

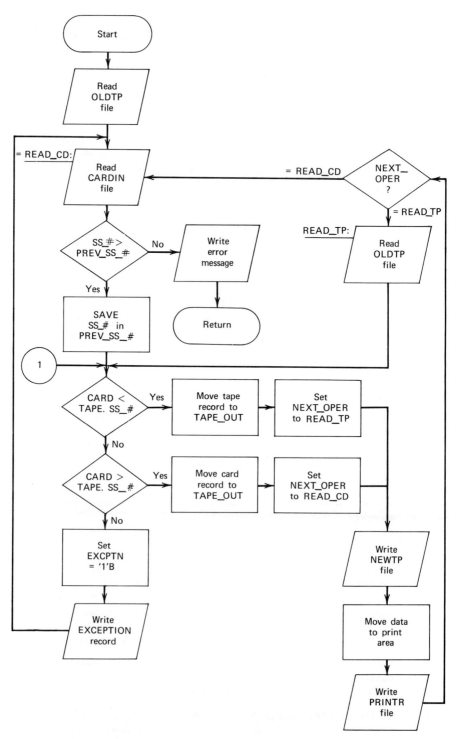

FIGURE 9.9   Flowchart for Case Study Two.

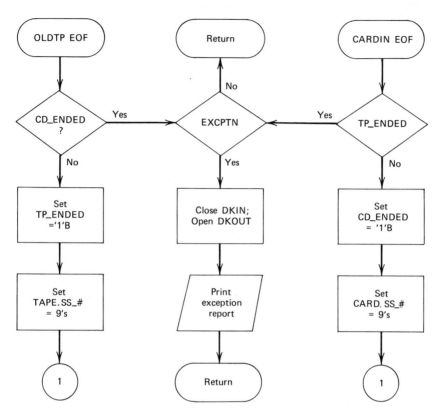

FIGURE 9.9 *Continued*

file consists of reading every record up to and including the last desired record. Updating of records in a file consists of either modifying existing records, deleting records, or adding new records to a file. If new records are to be added to a consecutive file, then the entire file with changes is copied onto another storage medium. The adding of records to a file is often referred to as merging, where a merging is the combining of records from two or more similarly sequenced files into one sequenced file.

Attributes for File Declarations

1. *FILE attribute:* Denotes that the identifier preceding FILE is a file name.
2. *EXTERNAL/INTERNAL attributes:* External means that a declared file may be known in other PL/I procedures. The INTERNAL attribute specifies that the file name be known only in the PROCEDURE block in which it was declared.
3. *STREAM and RECORD attributes:* The STREAM attribute causes the file associated with the file name to be treated as a continuous stream of

```
 1   CASE2:   PROC OPTIONS(MAIN);
 2            DCL OLDTP  FILE INPUT RECORD ENV(F(400,40)MEDIUM(SYS006,2400));
 3            DCL 1 TAPE,
                    2 NAME CHAR(20),
                    2 SS_# PIC'(9)9',
                    2 YTD_GROSS FIXED(7,2),
                    2 YTD_TAX FIXED(6,2),
                    2 YTD_FICA FIXED(5,2);
 4            DCL NEWTP FILE OUTPUT RECORD ENV(F(400,40)MEDIUM(SYS005,2400));
 5            DCL 1 TAPE_OUT,
                    2 NAME CHAR(20),
                    2 SS_# PIC'(9)9',
                    2 YTD_GROSS FIXED(7,2),
                    2 YTD_TAX FIXED(6,2),
                    2 YTD_FICA FIXED(5,2);
 6            DCL CARDIN FILE INPUT RECORD ENV(F(80)MEDIUM(SYSIPT,2540));
 7            DCL 1 CARD,
                    2 CARD_RECORD,
                      3 NAME CHAR(20),
                      3 SS_# PIC'(9)9',
                      3 GROSS PIC'(5)9V99',
                      3 TAX PIC'(4)9V99',
                      3 FICA PIC'(3)9V99',
                    2 REST CHAR(33);
 8            DCL PRINTR FILE OUTPUT RECORD
                   ENV(F(75)CTLASA MEDIUM(SYSLST,1403));
 9            DCL HDNG CHAR(75) DEF PRINT_OUT;
10            DCL 1 PRINT_OUT,
                    2 CC CHAR(1),
                    2 AREA,
                      3 NAME CHAR(25),
                      3 SS_# CHAR(15),
                      3 GROSS PIC'ZZ,ZZZV.99(5)B',
                      3 TAX PIC'ZZ,ZZZV.99(5)B',
                      3 FICA PIC'ZZZV.99';
11            DCL DKOUT FILE OUTPUT RECORD ENV(F(750,75)MEDIUM(SYS007,2311));
12            DCL DKIN  FILE INPUT  RECORD ENV(F(750,75)MEDIUM(SYS007,2311));
13            DCL PREV_SS_# PIC'(9)9' INIT (0);
14            DCL NEXT_OPER LABEL;
15            DCL (TP_ENDED,CD_ENDED,EXCPTN) BIT (1) INIT ('0'B);
16            ON ENDFILE (OLDTP) GO TO END_TP;
17            ON ENDFILE (CARDIN) GO TO END_CD;
18            OPEN FILE(CARDIN), FILE(OLDTP),FILE(NEWTP),
                   FILE(PRINTR), FILE(DKOUT);
19            HDNG='1Y E A R - T O - D A T E      P A Y R O L L    '
                   ||'T O T A L S';
20            WRITE FILE(PRINTR) FROM(PRINT_OUT);
21            HDNG='-NAME'||(21)' '||'SOC.SEC.#'||(8)' '||'GROSS'||(9)' '||
                   'TAX'||(9)' '||'FICA';
22            WRITE FILE(PRINTR) FROM(PRINT_OUT);
```

FIGURE 9.10   Case Study Two program.

data items recorded in character format. The STREAM attribute can be specified only for files of consecutive organization. The RECORD attribute causes the file associated with the file name to be treated as a sequence of logical records, each record consisting of one or more data items recorded in any format.

4. *INPUT, OUTPUT, and UPDATE attributes:* These attributes determine the direction of data transfer. The INPUT attribute applies to files that are to be read only. The OUTPUT attribute applies to files that are

```
23                    READ FILE (OLDTP) INTO (TAPE); /*FIRST TIME ONLY*/
24        READ_CD:READ FILE (CARDIN) INTO (CARD);
25        SEQ_CK: IF CARD.SS_# <= PREV_SS_# THEN DO; /*SEQ ERROR*/
26                    HDNG = '1INPUT CARDS OUT OF SEQUENCE';
27                    WRITE FILE (PRINTR) FROM (PRINT_OUT);
28                    RETURN;
29                    END;
30                PREV_SS_# = CARD.SS_#;
31                GO TO  COMPARE;
32        READ_TP:READ FILE (OLDTP) INTO (TAPE);
33        COMPARE:IF CARD.SS_# > TAPE.SS_# THEN DO;
34                    TAPE_OUT = TAPE;
35                    NEXT_OPER = READ_TP;
36                    END;
37                ELSE IF CARD.SS_# < TAPE.SS_# THEN DO;
38                    TAPE_OUT = CARD_RECORD;
39                    NEXT_OPER = READ_CD;
40                    END;
41                ELSE /* CARD.SS_# = TAPE.SS_# */ DO;
42                    AREA = CARD_RECORD;
43                    WRITE FILE (DKOUT) FROM (PRINT_OUT);
44                    GO TO READ_CD;
45                    END;
46        WRIT_TP:WRITE FILE (NEWTP) FROM (TAPE_OUT);
47                AREA = TAPE_OUT;
48                WRITE FILE (PRINTR) FROM (PRINT_OUT);
49                GO TO NEXT_OPER;
50        END_CD: IF TP_ENDED THEN GO TO PRINT_EXCPTN;
51                CD_ENDED = '1'B;
52                CARD.SS_# = 999999999;
53                GO TO COMPARE;
54        END_TP: IF CD_ENDED THEN GO TO PRINT_EXCPTN;
55                TP_ENDED = '1'B;
56                TAPE.SS_# = 999999999;
57                GO TO COMPARE;
58        PRINT_EXCPTN:
                      IF ¬EXCPTN THEN GO TO FINI;
59                CLOSE FILE(DKOUT); OPEN FILE(DKIN);
61                HDNG ='1TAPE RECORDS EXIST FOR FOLLOWING INPUT CARDS';
62                WRITE FILE(PRINTR)FROM(PRINT_OUT);
63                ON ENDFILE(DKIN) GO TO FINI;
64        LOOP2:    READ FILE(DKIN)INTO(PRINT_OUT);
65                CC='-';
66                WRITE FILE(PRINTR)FROM(PRINT_OUT);
67                GO TO LOOP2;
68        FINI:   END;
```

FIGURE 9.10 *Continued*

to be created or extended. The UPDATE attribute describes a file that
can be used for both input and output; it allows records in an existing
file to be altered or added, and it applies only to files located on a direct
access device.

5. *SEQUENTIAL, DIRECT, and TRANSIENT attributes:* These attributes
    may be used only for record files. They describe how records in a file
    are to be created or retrieved. In SEQUENTIAL files, records are
    accessed in physical sequence. In DIRECT files, records may be

Y E A R – T O – D A T E   P A Y R O L L   T O T A L S

NAME	SOC.SEC.#	GROSS	TAX	FICA
BROWN,D.A.	132242596	6,473.18	1,294.63	323.65
ACKLER,R.N.	139281782	4,982.26	896.45	249.11
BERN,G.D.	241639842	9,581.31	1,916.26	374.40
ROSS,M.L.	336459110	11,218.45	2,243.69	374.40
MILLS,G.L.	384910401	7,421.18	1,484.24	371.06
KING,M.K.	510174239	7,459.30	1,491.86	327.96
JONES	610283467	8,460.25	1,392.85	317.83
LONG,E.F.	707112693	12,000.00	2,400.00	374.40

FIGURE 9.11   Sample output from Case Study Two.

accessed in random order according to a *key* which is a unique character-string identifying each record. TRANSIENT applies to teleprocessing files.

6. *BUFFERED and UNBUFFERED attributes:*   The BUFFERED attribute indicates that logical records transferred to and from a file must pass through an intermediate storage area. The UNBUFFERED attribute indicates that a logical record in a data set neet not pass through a buffer, but can be transferred directly to and from the internal storage associated with a variable name. The following items are DOS/TOS restrictions :

   (a)   UNBUFFERED is not permitted with card, printer, and IBM 2321 data cell files.

   (b)   Tape files with the UNBUFFERED attribute must also have the NOLABEL option specified in the ENVIRONMENT attribute.

   (c)   Disk files with UNBUFFERED attribute are considered work files. Thus, the file will be deleted from the disk when the file is closed.

7. *PRINT attribute:*   This attribute causes the first byte of each record to be reserved for a printer control character. PRINT applies only to STREAM, OUTPUT files.

8. *BACKWARDS attribute:*   This attribute applies to magnetic tape files when reverse processing is desired.

9. *KEYED attribute:*   This attribute applies to records that may be accessed by means of a key.

10. *ENVIRONMENT attribute:* This attribute specifies the physical characteristics of the file and the type of device on which the file is now stored or will be stored. The characteristics are not so much a part of the PL/I language as they are keywords having to do with the capabilities or limitations of specific PL/I implementations under a given operating system.

   (a) *Record types:* Following is a summary of some of the record types available :

	Subset	Full
F(blocksize)	y	y
F(blocksize, recsize)	y	y
V(maxblocksize)	y	y
V(maxblocksize, maxrecsize)	n	y
U(maxblocksize)	y	y
VS(maxblocksize)	n	y
VS(maxblocksize, recsize)	n	y
VBS(maxblocksize)	n	y
VBS(maxblocksize, recsize)	n	y

   (b) *BUFFERS (n) option:* The BUFFERS(n) option is used to specify the number of buffers to be used in files having the BUFFERED attribute.

	Default number of buffers used	Maximum number of buffers that may be specified for one file
DOS/TOS	1	2
OS	2 (if any)	255

A buffer is an area of main storage that is automatically reserved by PL/I for files having the BUFFERED attribute. Input data is first read into the buffer and then transferred to your named structure or other data area. The size of the buffer is the size of the declared physical record.

   (c) *CTLASA | CTL360 options:* Used for record printer and punch files, these options specify whether the first character of the record is to be interpreted as an ASA or S/360 control character. It is the programmer's responsibility to provide a correct control character as the first character of the record variable.

(d)   *LEAVE option:*   The LEAVE option is used to specify that no rewind operation is to be performed at file open or close time.

(e)   *NOTAPEMK option:*   Available only in DOS/TOS, the NOTA-PEMK option for tape files enables the programmer to prevent the writing of a leading tapemark ahead of the data records on unlabeled tape files.

(f)   *NOLABEL option:*   Specifies that no file labels are to be processed for a magnetic tape file. This option would be used for scratch tapes.

(g)   *CONSECUTIVE option:*   The type of data set organization in which records are organized on the basis of their successive physical positions in the data set.

(h)   *VERIFY option:*   Checks data after every DASD write operation.

(i)   *MEDIUM option:*   This option is used to connect or relate a logical unit name and the physical device with which you wish to communicate in your PL/I program. The logical unit name has the form SYSxxx and is only used in DOS.

OPEN Statement: The OPEN statement for a stream or record file associates a file name with a data set. It can also be used to specify additional attributes for a file if a complete set of attributes has not been previously declared.

REWRITE Statement: This is a record output statement that transfers a record from a variable in internal storage to an UPDATE file. This statement would be used in consecutive file programming when it is desired to modify a record or add a record to an existing file.

CHECKPOINT QUESTIONS

1.   What types of I/O devices are permitted for use with consecutive files?
2.   Why are records blocked?
3.   The programming activities involving files may be divided into three basic functions. What are they?
4.   If records in a DASD file are to be modified, is it necessary to create a new file as it is with tape files?
5.   What is the essential difference between variable-length and undefined-length records?

TERMS TO STUDY

buffer (noun)
DASD
data set
file
file label
interblock gap
logical record
merge
new master

old master
overlap
physical record
retrieve
spanned records
tape mark
transactions
update

PRACTICE PROBLEMS

1. Year-to-Date Payroll Proof Totals

Problem Statement: A payroll proof listing is to be run using both year-to-date and current earnings cards which are in one file in ascending numeric sequence by man number. Sequence checking and headings are not required for this problem. Print one line of information for each employee. Normally, both a year-to-date card (code Y) and a current earnings card (code C) will be present for each employee, but it is possible that because of sickness or vacation there may be no current earnings card; also, because of new hires, there may be no year-to-date card. Punch a year-to-date card for each new hire. For an employee who has both kinds of cards, the current earnings will follow the year-to-date.

Purpose of the Problem: To DECLARE files for several devices (i.e., card reader, card punch, line printer).

Card Input

Column 1	CODE:
	Y = Year-to-date card
	C = Current earnings card
Columns 2–5	EMPLOYEE NUMBER
Columns 6–12	EARNINGS (XXXXX.XX)

Suggested Test Data: See Figure 9.12.
Desired Printer Layout: See Figure 9.13.

┌───── Column 1

Y10110300000
C10110015000
C13020020000
Y14030450000
Y14040500000
C16050030000
Y16160350000
C16160017500

FIGURE 9.12   Suggested test data.

Program Flowchart: You may wish to draw a flowchart before coding this problem.

Sample Output Using Suggested Test Data: See Figure 9.14.

2.   Update Master Payroll File

Introduction: This is a tape update problem. It assumes that a master tape has been created containing records to be modified. If you wish to code and execute this practice problem, it will be necessary for you (or your instructor) to create this master tape. This may be accomplished by simply punching into cards the information as illustrated in Figure 9.6. Compile and execute this program using the suggested data shown in Figure 9.15.

Problem Statement: A master payroll tape file is to be updated using information from a card file (time cards). Both the tape file and the card file are in Social Security number sequence. The processing is to include a sequence check of the card input records and calculations of year-to-date gross, year-to-date withholding tax, and year-to-date FICA. As old master records are modified with the current information, they are to be written on a new master tape along with any unaffected master records. In addition, the modified records only are to be listed on the line printer. Excess FICA, that amount which is

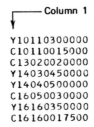

FIGURE 9.13   Desired printer layout.

```
Y13020020000
Y16050030000
```

Printed output

EMPLOYEE NUMBER	YEAR-TO-DATE EARNINGS	CURRENT EARNINGS
1011	$ 3,000.00	$150.00
1302		$200.00
1403	$ 4,500.00	
1404	$ 5,000.00	
1605		$300.00
1616	$ 3,500.00	$175.00

FIGURE 9.14 Sample output using suggested test data.

```
      ┌──── Column 1              ┌──── Column 21
      ▼                           ▼
BROWN, D. A.       1322425960647318129463 32365
ACKLER, R.N.       1392817820498226089645 24911
BERN, G.D.         2416398420958131191626 37440
ROSS, M.L.         3364591101121845224369 37440
MILLS, G.L.        3849104010742118148424 37106
KING, M.K.         5101742390745930149186 32796
JONES              6102834670846025139285 31783
LONG, E.F.         7071126931200000240000 37440
```

FIGURE 9.15 Suggested data for creating master tape.

over the limit set by law ($468.00 in 1972), is to be printed on an exception list, showing the employee name, his Social Security number, and the amount of excess FICA.

Assume that this exception list will be used later for purposes of making a refund to the employee. (Another method for refunding excess FICA to an employee is to simply add the amount of excess FICA to net pay for that period. However, the purpose of this problem is to have you program as many consecutive files as possible.) If an excess FICA amount occurs, the amount to be recorded in the new master tape record for that employee is the legal limit. Inasmuch as a regular report is being produced on the line printer simultaneously with update, it will be necessary to write any entries to this exception report temporarily onto a consecutive disk file. At the end of the program, we must test a *program switch* to determine if there are any such records to be printed. If there are, the disk output file should be closed, the disk input file opened, and its records listed on the line printer.

Purpose of the Problem: To write a program to manipulate numerous consecutive files; to provide experience in working with sequential disk I/O, sequential tape I/O, and card and printer I/O.

Card Input: The following structure describes the card data:

```
DCL 1 CARD,
      2 NAME CHAR(20),
      2 SS_# PIC'(9)9',
      2 GROSS PIC'99999V99',
      2 TAX PIC'9999V99',
      2 FICA PIC'999V99',
      2 REST CHAR(33) ;
```

Tape Input: The following structure describes the *old master* tape data:

```
DCL 1 TAPE,
      2 NAME CHAR(20),
      2 SS_# PIC'(9)9',
      2 YTD,
        3 YTD_GROSS FIXED(7,2),
        3 YTD_TAX FIXED(6,2),
        3 YTD_FICA FIXED(5,2) ;
```

┌── Column 1	┌── Column 21
BROWN,D.A.	1322425960026972005394013 51
ACKLER,R.W.	1392817820020759004152010 39
ROSS,M.L.	3364591100046744009348023 37
MILLS,G.L.	3849104010030921006184015 46
KING,M.K.	5101742390031080006216015 54
LONG,E.F.	7071126930046744009348000 00

FIGURE 9.16 Suggested test data for Problem 2.

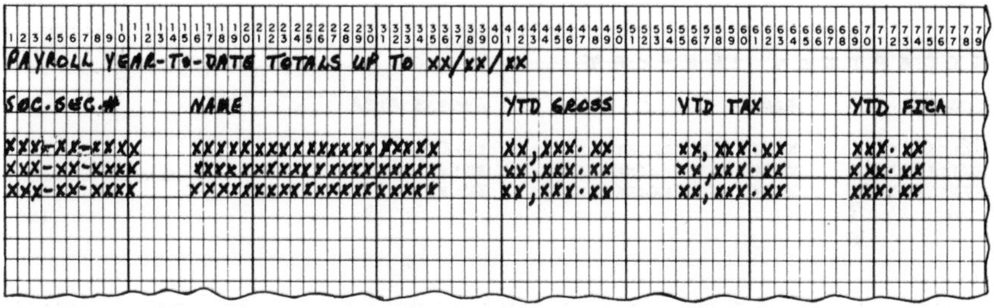

FIGURE 9.17   Desired printer layout for Problem 2.

Suggested Test Data for Input Cards: See Figure 9.16.

Desired Printer Layouts: The following structure describes the printer layout shown in Figure 9.17:

```
DCL HDNG CHAR(77) DEF REGULAR;
DCL 1 REGULAR,
      2 CC CHAR(1) INIT('1'),
      2 SS_# CHAR(15),
      2 NAME CHAR(25),
      2 PRINT_AREA,
         3 YTD_GROSS PIC'ZZ,ZZ9V.99(5)B',
         3 YTD_TAX PIC'ZZ,ZZ9V.99(5)B',
         3 YTD_FICA PIC'ZZ9V.99BB';
```

The HDNG character-string is overlay defined on REGULAR as a storage saving

EMPLOYEE NUMBER	YEAR-TO-DATE EARNINGS	CURRENT EARNINGS
1011	$ 3,000.00	$150.00
1302		$200.00
1403	$ 4,500.00	
1404	$ 5,000.00	
1605		$300.00
1616	$ 3,500.00	$175.00

FIGURE 9.18   Sample output from Problem 2.

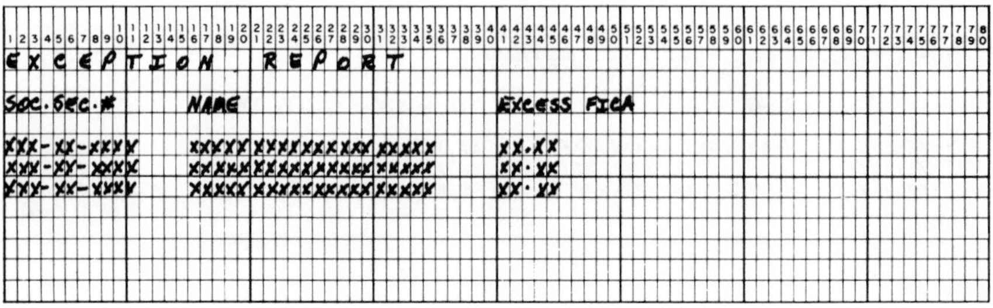

498 PL/I Programming

FIGURE 9.19   Exception report.

technique. HDNG will be assigned the literal data that constitutes the headings or subheadings. Figure 9.18 shows sample output using the suggested test data.

The following structure describes the output format of the exception report illustrated in Figure 9.19:

```
DCL 1 EXCEPTION,
      2 CC CHAR(1) INIT('−'),
      2 SS_# CHAR(15),
      2 NAME CHAR(25),
      2 EXCESS_FICA PIC'99V.99',
      2 REST CHAR(31) INIT('     ');
```

The exception report is to be output to a sequential disk file similar to the handling of exception reporting in Case Study Two.

File Declarations: In this program, six files will need to be declared:

OLDTP	Old master tape
NEWTP	New master tape
DKOUT	Disk file for exception report†
DKIN	Same file, only input†
CARDIN	Card reader
PRINTR	Printer

Program Flowchart: It is recommended that you draw a program flowchart before coding this problem.

Sample Output Using Suggested Test Data: See Figures 9.20 and 9.21.

†In OS, just define *one* disk file but do not include the INPUT or OUTPUT attributes. Use the OPEN statement to supply these attributes. After the file has been opened as an Output file and the file is created, it should be closed and reopened with the INPUT attribute.

PAYROLL YEAR-TO-DATE TOTALS UP TO 07/07/77

SOC.SEC.#	NAME	YTD GROSS	YTD TAX	YTD FICA
132-24-2596	BROWN,D.A.	6,742.90	1,348.57	337.16
139-28-1782	ACKLER,R.N.	5,189.85	937.97	259.50
336-45-9110	ROSS,M.L.	11,685.89	2,337.17	374.40
384-91-0401	MILLS,G.L.	7,730.39	1,546.08	374.40
510-17-4239	KING,M.K.	7,770.10	1,554.02	343.50
707-11-2693	LONG,E.F.	12,467.44	2,493.48	374.40

FIGURE 9.20   Sample output using suggested test data for Problem 2.

E X C E P T I O N   R E P O R T

SOC.SEC.#	NAME	EXCESS FICA
336-45-9110	ROSS,M.L.	23.37
384-91-0401	MILLS,G.L.	12.12

FIGURE 9.21   Sample output (exception report) using suggested test data for Problem 2.

chapter 10

Indexed and
Regional File
Programming
Concepts

Introduction

In Chapter 9, we learned how to communicate with records in a consecutive file. In this type of file organization, records are organized on the basis of their successive physical positions, as for example, on magnetic tape or in punched cards or on a disk. Records in consecutive files can be processed or retrieved in sequential order only. There are times, however, when sequential processing is impractical. For example, assume a consecutive disk file has been created that contains payroll information on 2500 employees. If it is desired to locate information on a given employee, a program would have to be written that began reading the records from the beginning of the file and check the employee number within each record until the desired record is found. It is quite possible that a large number of records would have to be read and employee numbers tested before the desired record is located. This, of course, takes time, and could be impractical if it is desired to repeat the search operation several times in looking for a given number of random records. A method other than a *sequential* search must be employed. This method would be the *direct* method. We can see that, because of the physical characteristics of punched cards or magnetic tape as storage mediums, it is impossible to think of *directly* accessing a record—say, in the middle of a card or tape file, because the records preceding the desired record must first be processed. With a file stored on a disk or other direct access device, however, we have the capability of being able to access information in the middle of a file without reading or processing the records that precede the desired record. (As an analogy, consider the "direct access capability" of a long-playing record versus stereo tape when it is desired to hear the fourth selection on either of these recording mediums.) To *directly* access a record is to call for that record by means of a *key*. A *key* is any numeric or alphameric combination of characters that makes a record unique from all other records in a given file. Thus, the employee number in a payroll file could be a key, because each number will be different from all other numbers in the file. In a consecutive file, records may have a key associated with them; however, you may not reference or retrieve records by that key. Two other file organizations are provided where records may be accessed by means of keys: INDEXED and REGIONAL. With these two types of file organizations, there are a great many differences between the various PL/I compilers due to the operating systems under which these compilers run. The objective of this chapter is to introduce you to the concepts of INDEXED and REGIONAL file organizations so that you may be prepared to read the appropriate PL/I reference manual for the programming details.

This chapter assumes that you have an understanding of the physical characteristics (e.g., cylinder, track, disk pack) of a disk. You may wish to consult an IBM manual, *Introduction to IBM System/360 Direct Access Storage Devices and Organization Methods*, C20–1649, for a discussion of the functional characteristics of direct access devices.

Figure 10.1 illustrates one type of disk—the IBM 2311—so that you may review some of the hardware terms. There are a number of direct access devices besides the IBM 2311. These devices vary in

1. physical appearance
2. capacity
3. speed
4. price

However, DASD's are alike in

1. data recording
2. checking
3. formatting
4. program control

Thus, the PL/I programming considerations are the same regardless of the DASD model. For purposes of illustration in this chapter, the IBM 2311—with ten tracks per cylinder—will be used. However, all concepts and principles of programming apply to any other DASD.

A Word About Terminology

There are a number of terms unique to DASD file programming. For example, *file* and *data set* are synonyms. A file or data set is any group of related records. You will probably use the word *file* if you are working with a medium-sized computer using DOS. If you are working with OS, the term *data set* is preferred.

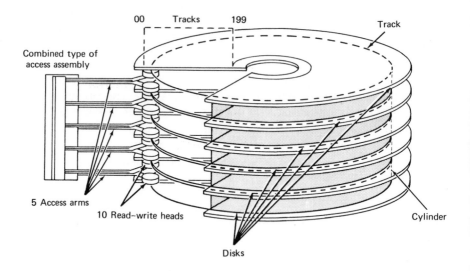

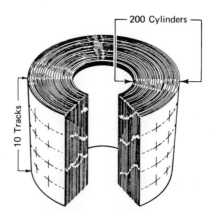

FIGURE 10.1 Disk hardware concepts. Records may be organized on a disk in different ways. For example, the disk pack shown at the top of the figure has 10 recording surfaces of 200 tracks each. Each track of a recording surface is read by a separate position of the access mechanism. It is clear, however, that each position of the access mechanism can actually access ten tracks, one on each physical recording surface. From an access point of view, therefore, the disk pack can be considered to consist of 200 vertical cylinders of 10 tracks each, as shown in the lower part of the figure. The representation of the disk pack as concentric cylinders is important to the programmer in the creation and use of INDEXED data sets. (Chart courtesy of IBM.)

The term *data management* is used when talking about the three basic types of file organizations which in general usage are called

1. sequential
2. indexed sequential
3. direct

These three general terms for file organizations may be confused with the two general terms for file access methods:

1. sequential
2. random (referred to as *direct* in the introduction)

In PL/I, however, an attempt has been made to use terminology that distinguishes between file organizations and access methods without using duplicate terms. Figure 10.2 shows a comparison of these terms.

Indexed Data Sets

Indexed File Organization Concepts

This type of file organization gets its name because records are organized in much the same way as we might file letters, documents, memos, etc., as illustrated in Figure 10.3. In an indexed file, each record has a unique key. In addition, records are organized according to a scheme:

1. Numeric keys are in ascending sequence (1234, 1237, 1254, 1281, etc.).

	General	PL/I
File organizations	Sequential Indexed sequential Direct	CONSECUTIVE INDEXED REGIONAL
Access methods	Sequential Random	SEQUENTIAL DIRECT

FIGURE 10.2   Terminology compared.

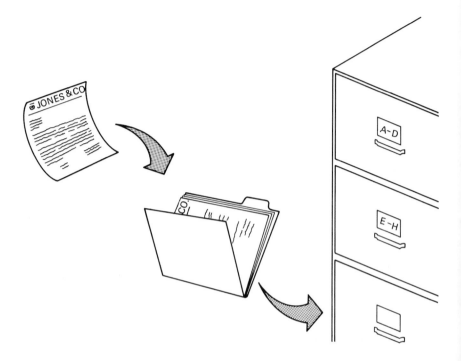

FIGURE 10.3   An indexed filing system.

2. Alphabetic keys are in alphabetic order (ABCD, ABDE, ACDB, etc.).
3. Alphameric keys are in collating sequence† (ABCD, AB15, AC12, BZ10, 1B23, 2CD4, 9FGH, . . .).

Note, then, *numbers* collate higher than alphabetic characters. Records in an indexed file are in *sequential* order.

When an indexed file is created, a series of *indexes* is automatically established by the system from the keys presented. These indexes provide the capability to read and write records from anywhere in the file. There are always at least two indexes: a *cylinder index* for the whole file and a *track index* for each cylinder. Optionally, there may be a *master index*. Figure 10.4 illustrates these terms by an analogy to a dictionary.

---

†See the EBCDIC Code Chart in Appendix D.

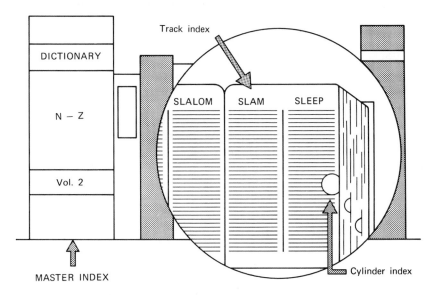

FIGURE 10.4 **Indexed organization concept.**

Prime Data Area

An indexed data set could occupy any number of cylinders and tracks. The track index is always placed in track 0 of every cylinder. The remaining tracks in the cylinder may contain data records. The track index and the associated data records in a cylinder make up the *prime data area*.

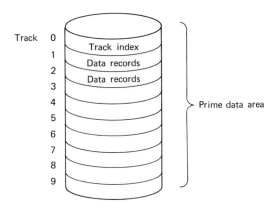

The track index contains the highest keys from each track in the cylinder, as illustrated in Figure 10.5. In the pictured disk, there are ten tracks per cylinder. Other disks may have more tracks per cylinder. An *extent* is a consecutive area of a DASD. In indexed files, there are always at least two extents: (a) the prime data area and (b) a cylinder index.

Sequential processing of an indexed file may be slower than that of a corresponding consecutive file, because the records it contains are not necessarily arranged in physical sequence, but are logically chained in order of ascending key values. In comparing indexed to consecutive files, we see that it would take more time to create an indexed data set than it would to create a consecutive data set, because of the indexes that must be constructed by system routines at file create time. A disadvantage of indexed files might be the extra time it takes to search indexes to locate a given record. However, if you are trying to locate a specific record—as in the employee payroll records example in this chapter's introduction—searching indexes would, in all probability, reduce the overall amount of time required to select a given record. Thus, an advantage of indexed over consecutive files stored on a DASD is that records in an indexed data set may be retrieved either by the *sequential* or the *direct* access method—thereby taking full advantage of the physical properties of a DASD.

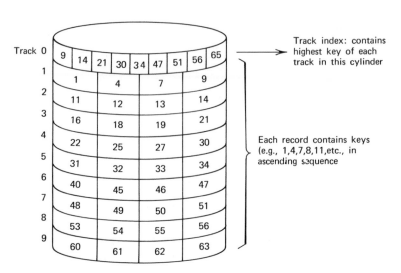

FIGURE 10.5   Prime data area of an indexed data set.

Cylinder/Master Indexes

The *cylinder index* contains the highest key of each track index. For example, assume a data set will require three cylinders:

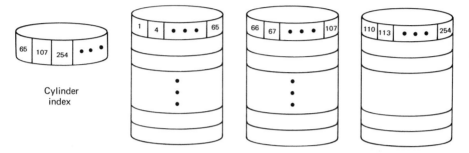

Cylinder index

The system locates a given record by its key after a search of, first, the cylinder index, and then, the track index within that cylinder. Thus, in locating a record by the direct access method, it will be necessary for the system to first scan the cylinder index. As will be seen later, it is possible to specify that the cylinder index reside in main storage during the execution of a program. If this option is exercised, the time required to search the cylinder index is greatly reduced at the cost of needing more main storage for the problem program.

If the cylinder index—which may or may not be stored on the same direct access storage device as the prime data area—exceeds four tracks in size, then it is desirable to use a third index to reduce the amount of time required to search indexes in locating specific records. This third index is called a *master index*, and each entry in this index points to a track in the cylinder index. A master index is optional, but, if specified, it will be contiguous to the cylinder index. For example:

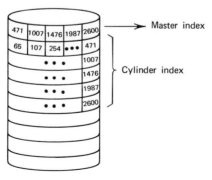

Thus, to directly access a record in an indexed data set that has three levels of indexes, the following operations are performed by the system:

1. Scan master index to locate appropriate cylinder index.
2. Scan cylinder index to locate appropriate cylinder.
3. Scan track index to locate appropriate track.
4. Scan the track until comparison key and recorded key match.

If there is room in main storage for the cylinder index (or a part of the cylinder index), then it would not be necessary to have a master index. In summary, when you create an indexed file, all you have to do is present the records with keys in ascending sequence. All indexes are automatically constructed for you. Two indexes are required: the cylinder index and the track index. The master index is optional. If a master index is specified, it will be contiguous to the cylinder index on the specified direct access storage device.

Because indexed data sets are stored only on direct access storage devices, they are capable of being processed sequentially or directly. When records are read in sequence, they are presented in the order of ascending key sequence. Or, a record in an indexed data set may be directly accessed; that is, a given record may be selected without having to process all records that precede the desired record.

Overflow Areas

The keys in an indexed file are in ascending sequence. In some cases, there are keys missing (e.g., 2, 3, 5, 6, etc.) from the data set; however, it is not necessary to leave room in the prime data area should these records be added later. Instead, future additions will be placed into a DASD area called an *overflow area*. One or more tracks may be reserved in the prime data area as *overflow tracks*. For example:

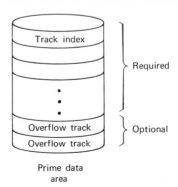

Prime data
area

Or, another type of overflow area may also be used—an *independent overflow area*. For example:

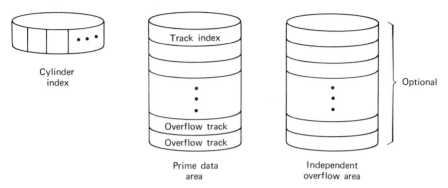

Cylinder index

Track index

Overflow track
Overflow track

Prime data area

Independent overflow area

Optional

The independent overflow area may be used in conjunction with track overflow areas, or instead of track overflow areas. Generally, it would be used in conjunction with track overflow areas.

Records placed in the overflow areas (after the indexed data set has been created) are not in strict physical sequence. For example, in Figure 10.6, two records whose keys are 15 and 10 have been added to the overflow track area. It is still possible, however, to retrieve the records in ascending key sequence, because *pointers* automatically

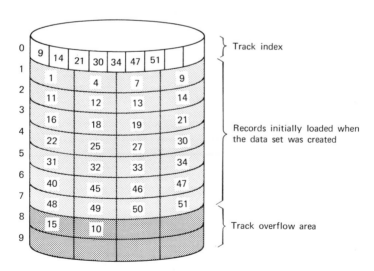

FIGURE 10.6 Prime data area with two additions in overflow area.

developed by the system indicate where the next key in sequence is located. Thus, in a sequential read of the indexed file, the keys are always presented in order, regardless of their physical appearance in the data set.

Location of Keys in Indexed Records

When you write a program to create an indexed file, all you have to do is present a record to the system routine records on a DASD. This is accomplished by means of a WRITE statement. For example:

```
WRITE FILE(PAYRL)FROM(EMP_REC)
    KEYFROM(EMP_#);
```

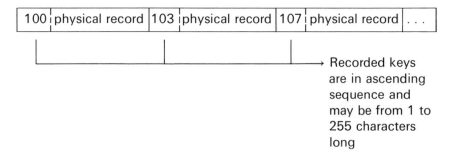

└─────────────────→ Called the *source key*

The output routine, as commanded by the above statement, will write into a file called PAYRL the information contained in the structure called EMP_REC. In addition, the source key found in the identifier called EMP_# will be recorded on the DASD immediately preceding each record or block of records. For example:

| 100 | physical record | 103 | physical record | 107 | physical record | . . . |

└────────────────────────┴────────────────────────┴────────────────→ Recorded keys are in ascending sequence and may be from 1 to 255 characters long

A source key is the character-string that appears in the KEY or KEYFROM option of an I/O statement. For example:

```
    READ FILE(PAYRL)INTO(EMP_REC)KEY(EMP_#);
    WRITE FILE(PAYRL)FROM(EMP_REC)KEYFROM(EMP_#);
```

If the length of a source key differs from the specified length of the recorded keys, the source key is truncated on the right or padded with blanks on the right to the specified length.

If records are unblocked in an indexed data set, the key need only precede the physical record in the file. The key in this case does

UNBLOCKED RECORDS

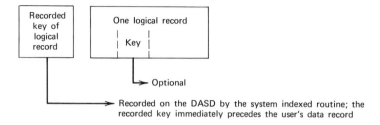

BLOCKED RECORDS

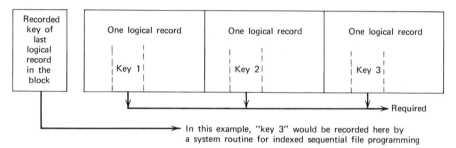

FIGURE 10.7 Unblocked and blocked records in an indexed data set.

not have to be part of the structure containing related information for a given record. On the other hand, if records are blocked, then the key must be stored within each record; that is, the key must be part of the structure that defines the record's information. The key of the last logical record in the block is stored automatically preceding the physical block. Figure 10.7 illustrates the difference between blocked and unblocked records in an indexed data set. In some operating systems, only fixed-length records are allowed in indexed files. In other systems, fixed-length or variable-length (but not undefined-length) records may be specified.

I/O Statements

To read records *sequentially* from an indexed data set, the standard READ statement is used:

```
READ FILE(PAYRL)INTO(EMP_REC);
```

Here is another form of a sequential READ statement:

READ FILE(PAYRL)INTO(EMP_REC)KEYTO(EMP_#);

L──→ This option causes the recorded key to be retrieved and placed into the identifier specified within parentheses following the KEYTO option

The KEYTO option is useful when you are sequentially reading unblocked records without an embedded key. (Refer to Figure 10.7.) If the key is not embedded within the record, it will not appear in the data area called EMP_REC in the example above. Typically, a program would need the recorded key, say, for the printing of pay checks or various weekly or quarterly reports. The KEYTO option will supply the recorded key to the program, thereby eliminating the need for the key to be embedded within the unblocked record should the program need the actual key.

To read records *directly* from an indexed file, this form of the READ statement would be used:

READ FILE(PAYRL)INTO(EMP_REC)KEY(EMP_#);

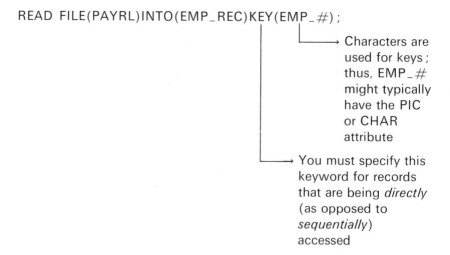

L──→ Characters are used for keys; thus, EMP_# might typically have the PIC or CHAR attribute

L──→ You must specify this keyword for records that are being *directly* (as opposed to *sequentially*) accessed

To write records *sequentially* into an indexed file, the standard WRITE statement may be used:

WRITE FILE(PAYRL)FROM(EMP_REC);

This statement would be used when you wish to *create* an indexed data set.

If it is desired to *add* a new record to an existing indexed data set, the WRITE statement could take this form:

WRITE FILE(PAYRL)FROM(EMP_REC)KEYFROM(EMP_#);

└─────→ Indicates *direct*
access of records

If it is desired to *update* records in an indexed file, that is, modify existing records, then the REWRITE statement would be used:

REWRITE FILE(PAYRL)FROM(EMP_REC)KEY(EMP_#);

└─────→ Indicates *direct*
access

Usually the occasion does not arise where it is necessary to update all records in an existing indexed file. However, it is possible to do so by this statement:

REWRITE FILE(PAYRL)FROM(EMP_REC);

In the full language implementations of PL/I, if it is desired to delete a record from an indexed file, the DELETE statement may be used. For example:

DELETE FILE(PAYRL)KEY(EMP_#);

The DELETE statement causes the first byte of a record to be loaded with the value (8)'1'B. The code (8)'1'B indicates that the record is a *dummy* record—that is, a null or a voided record. Typically, then, the first byte of a record in an indexed data set is set aside as a "flag" byte; the remaining bytes would contain the key and other data. For example:

```
DECLARE 1 EMP_REC,
          2 FLAG CHAR(1) INIT(' '),
          2 EMP_# CHAR(8),   /* KEY */
          2 HOURLY_RATE PIC'99V99',
          2 NO_OF_DEDUCTIONS PIC'99',
          2 REST_OF_RECORD CHAR(50);
```

In the subset language, where the DELETE statement is not provided, it is a simple matter for your program to set a reserved "flag" byte to (8)'1'B. Through a program test later, your program will be able to determine the dummy or deleted records and ignore or bypass these no longer needed records.

Declaring Indexed File Attributes

The following attributes may be declared for indexed files:

> INPUT, OUTPUT, or UPDATE
> DIRECT or SEQUENTIAL
> KEYED
> RECORD
> ENVIRONMENT (INDEXED. . .)

There are a number of options that may appear in the ENVIRONMENT attribute, depending on the PL/I compiler you are using. These options are defined in the following paragraphs. Figure 10.8 identifies the compilers for which these options are available, and reference is made to the subparameters of OS job control language statements that accomplish the equivalent ENV options.

INDEXED.   This option describes an indexed sequential data set that consists of keyed records, any one of which can be located by several levels of indexes.

KEYLENGTH(n).   This option is used to specify the length of the key.

EXTENTNUMBER(n).   This option is used to specify the number of extents used for indexed files. (An extent is a consecutive area of a DASD.) For indexed files in DOS, EXTENTNUMBER(n) must be specified. The value for n must include all data area extents, the master index and cylinder index extents (which must be adjacent to one another), and all independent overflow extents. Master and cylinder index extents count as one extent. Thus, the minimum number that can be specified is two: one extent for one prime data area and one for the cylinder index or the master/cylinder indexes. The maximum number of extents is 255.

INDEXMULTIPLE.   This option is used to specify that a master index will be or has been built for this file.

HIGHINDEX(device number).   This option is used for indexed files to specify the type of device (e.g., 2311, 2314) on which the high-level index or indexes reside(s) in case the device type differs from the one specified in the MEDIUM option. For example, in the declaration,

```
DCL ISFILE FILE OUTPUT RECORD SEQUENTIAL KEYED ENV
    (INDEXED F(100)MEDIUM(SYS001,2311) HIGHINDEX(2314)
    KEYLENGTH(16) EXTENTNUMBER(2));
```

	DOS PL/I D	DOS PL/I Optimizing	OS PL/I F		OS PL/I Optimizing	
	ENV options	ENV options	ENV options	JCL options	ENV options	JCL options
Record description	F(blksize [,recsize])	F(blksize [,recsize]) or F|FB BLKSIZE(n) RECSIZE(n)	F(blksize [,recsize]) V(blksize [,recsize])	RECFM=F|FB V|VB BLKSIZE=n LRECL=n	F(blksize [,recsize]) V(blksize [,recsize]) or F|FB|VB BLKSIZE(n) RECSIZE(n)	RECFM=F|FB V|VB BLKSIZE=n LRECL=n
Index control	INDEXMULTIPLE HIGHINDEX(2311|2314)	INDEXMULTIPLE HIGHINDEX (2311|2314|2321)		OPTCD=M UNIT=device type		OPTCD=M UNIT=device type
Space control	EXTENTNUMBER(n) OFLTRACKS(n)	EXTENTNUMBER(n) OFLTRACKS(n)		DD card CYLOFL=n OPTCD=Y		DD card CYLOFL=n OPTCD=Y
Key control	KEYLOC(n) KEYLENGTH(n)	KEYLOC(n) KEYLENGTH(n)	KEYLOC(n) KEYLENGTH(n) GENKEY	RKP=n KEYLEN=n	KEYLOC(n) KEYLENGTH(n) GENKEY	RKP=n KEYLEN=n
Write validation	VERIFY	VERIFY		OPTCD=W		OPTCD=W
Optimization	BUFFERS(n) ADDBUFF(n) INDEXAREA(n) NOWRITE	BUFFERS(n) ADDBUFF(n) INDEXAREA(n) NOWRITE	BUFFERS(n) INDEXAREA(n) NOWRITE	BUFNO=n	BUFFERS(n) ADDBUFF(n) INDEXAREA(n) NOWRITE	BUFNO=n

FIGURE 10.8 Options for indexed sequential file organization.

the prime data area will be on the IBM 2311 disk and the cylinder index will be stored on the IBM 2314 disk.

OFLTRACKS(n). This option is used for indexed OUTPUT and UPDATE files to specify the number of tracks to be reserved on each cylinder for adding records. The number specified must be within the following limits:

$$0 \leq n \leq 8 \quad \text{for} \quad \text{2311 files}$$
$$0 \leq n \leq 18 \quad \text{for} \quad \text{all other files}$$

For INPUT files, this option is meaningless and is therefore ignored.

KEYLOC(n). This option is used to specify the high-order position (leftmost position) of the key field within the data record. For unblocked records, this keyword is optional; for blocked records, KEYLOC must be specified. For DOS implementations, the leftmost position in the record is numbered 1; in OS, this position is numbered 0. Thus, N is relative to 0 or 1, depending on the operating system you are using. The default for N (blocked records only) is 1.

INDEXAREA(n). This option is used to specify that the cylinder index in main storage option is used for INDEXED DIRECT files. The value for n must be within the following limits:

$$3 \times (\text{keylength} + 6) \leq n < 32\text{K}$$

The number (N) of cylinder index entries that can be in main storage at one time may be calculated as follows:

$$N = n/(\text{keylength} + 6) - 2$$

ADDBUFF(n). This option is used when it is desired to add new records to an indexed data set. For example, assume that it is desired to add a record whose key is "5" to the BEFORE data set in Figure 10.9. In this case, the record will be placed into the first track in sequence and the last record in that track will be moved down to the overflow area. Note also that key "7" has to be moved over.

The shifting of records on a disk requires more time than if the records on a given track could be rearranged in main storage. The ADDBUFF option specifies the amount of main storage to be reserved for the movement of records within a track when new records are being added to a DIRECT UPDATE data set. The value of n is generally the number of bytes on a track of a given DASD.

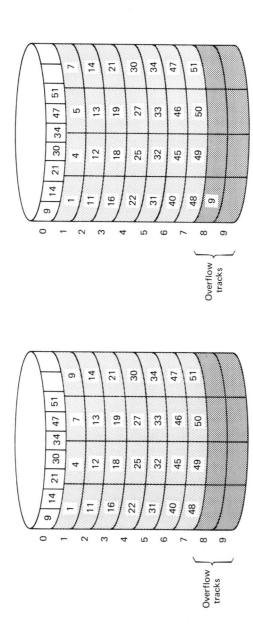

FIGURE 10.9 Shifting of records in an indexed data set.

Creating an Indexed Data Set

Before data is loaded into this type of data set, it must be pre-sorted by key into ascending sequence. This is a job step separate from PL/I programming. If there is an error in the key sequence, the KEY condition will be raised. (The KEY condition and several other on-units will be discussed in the next section of this chapter.) When an indexed data set is being created, the associated file is generally to be opened for SEQUENTIAL OUTPUT. (In OS, DIRECT OUTPUT could be used, but the keys must still be in ascending sequence.)

Retrieving Records from an Indexed Data Set

Either the SEQUENTIAL or DIRECT access method may be used. Sequential access is in order of ascending recorded-key values; records are retrieved in this order, and not necessarily in the order in which they were added to the data set. In sequential access, the I/O statements need not include source keys nor does the file need the KEYED attribute.

During SEQUENTIAL access of an indexed data set, it is possible to reposition the data set to a particular record by supplying a source key in the KEY option of a READ statement, and to continue sequential reading from that record. (The associated file must have the KEYED attribute.) Repositioning can occur in either a forward or a backward direction. Thus, a READ statement that includes the KEY option will cause the record whose key is supplied to be read; a subsequent READ statement without the KEY option will cause the record with the next higher recorded key to be read. This facility is sketched out in Figure 10.10, which shows a general flowchart and corresponding PL/I file declaration and I/O statements.

Modifying or Adding Records to an Indexed Data Set

Indexed data sets that have the UPDATE attribute may have records added to them or existing records modified. These two file activities may be done either by the SEQUENTIAL access method or the DIRECT method.

Deleting Records from an Indexed Data Set

In the full language, records can be effectively deleted from the data set; a DELETE statement marks a record as a dummy by putting (8)'1'B in the first byte of the record. The DELETE statement should not

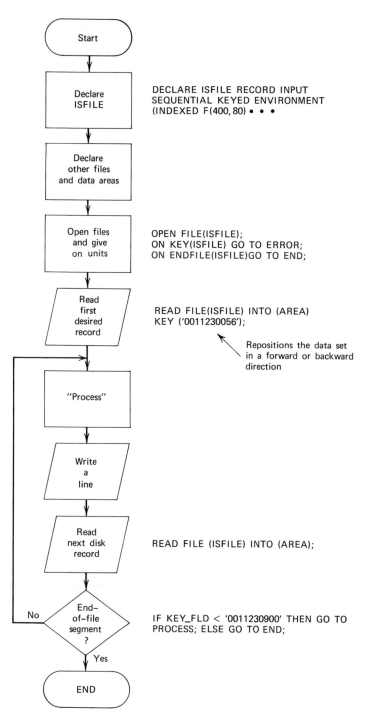

FIGURE 10.10   Processing part of an indexed data set.

File attribute	Access method	Purpose	I/O statement for an indexed data set	Sample file declaration (note, shaded attributes would be specified in PL/I D and DOS PL/I Optimizing compilers)
OUTPUT	SEQUENTIAL	To create a new indexed-sequential data set	WRITE FILE(IS) FROM(AREA) KEYFROM(KEY_FLD);	DCL IS FILE OUTPUT RECORD SEQUENTIAL KEYED ENV (INDEXED F(800,80) KEYLENGTH(16) KEYLOC(2) EXTENTNUMBER(2) OFLTRACKS(2) MEDIUM(SYS001,2311));
INPUT	SEQUENTIAL	To process *all* records	READ FILE(IS) INTO(AREA); /* OR */ READ FILE(IS) INTO(AREA) KEYTO(EMP_NO);	DCL IS FILE INPUT RECORD SEQUENTIAL KEYED ENV (INDEXED F(800,40) KEYLOC(5) KEYLENGTH(20) EXTENTNUMBER(3) MEDIUM(SYS002,2311));
	DIRECT	To process *selected* records	READ FILE(IS) INTO(AREA) KEY(PART_NO);	DCL IS FILE INPUT RECORD DIRECT KEYED ENV (INDEXED F(500,100) KEYLENGTH(16) EXTENTNUMBER(3) MEDIUM(SYS005,2311));

UPDATE	SEQUENTIAL	To modify *all* records	REWRITE FILE(IS) ; /* OR */ REWRITE FILE(IS) FROM(AREA) ;	DCL IS FILE UPDATE RECORD SEQUENTIAL ENV (INDEXED F(600,40) KEYLENGTH(8) EXTENTNUMBER(3) MEDIUM(SYS006,2314)) ;
	DIRECT	To modify *selected* records	REWRITE FILE(IS) FROM(AREA) KEY(PART_NO) ;	DCL IS FILE UPDATE RECORD DIRECT KEYED ENV (INDEXED F(200,100) KEYLENGTH(12) EXTENTNUMBER(3) INDEXMULTIPLE VERIFY MEDIUM(SYS007,2314)) ;
	DIRECT	To *add* new records to an existing data set	WRITE FILE(IS) FROM(AREA) KEY(PART_NO) ;	DCL IS FILE UPDATE RECORD DIRECT KEYED ENV (INDEXED F(560,80) KEYLENGTH(7) KEYLOC(2) EXTENTNUMBER(3) OFLTRACKS(2) ADDBUFF(3500) MEDIUM(SYS008,2314)) ;

FIGURE 10.11 Sample file declarations and I/O statements for indexed data sets.

be used to process a data set with blocked records whose keys begin at the first byte of the record.

Figure 10.11 summarizes the various I/O statements and corresponding sample file declarations for the various activities related to indexed data sets.

The Direct Data Set Organization

There are three basic types of data set organizations: sequential, indexed sequential, and direct. This section presents some general information on the *direct* organization. The term *direct* will be used in the following paragraphs because of the general nature of the material. The PL/I term for *direct* files is *regional*. Thus, in subsequent sections of this chapter, the PL/I term will be used. You should be aware that with regard to data set organization, regional and direct are synonyms.

Track Format. Information is recorded on all direct-access volumes in a standard format. In addition to device-dependent data (home address), each track contains a track descriptor record (also called a "capacity record") and one or more data records. The user's data is placed in the data records. The system maintains the track descriptor record on each track.

There are only two data record formats—Count-Data and Count-Key-Data, one of which can be used for a particular data set. The following illustrates the two possible data record formats:

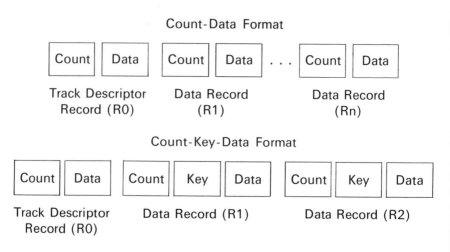

Count-Data Format

| Count | Data | Count | Data | ... | Count | Data |

Track Descriptor   Data Record   Data Record
Record (R0)   (R1)   (Rn)

Count-Key-Data Format

| Count | Data | Count | Key | Data | Count | Key | Data |

Track Descriptor   Data Record (R1)   Data Record (R2)
Record (R0)

The Count Area of each record contains ten bytes that identify the location of the record in terms of the cylinder, head, and record numbers; its key length (0 if no keys are used); and its data length.

If records are written with keys, the Key Area (1–255 bytes) contains a record key that identifies the following Data Area. This identifying information might be a part number, account number, or sequence number. The hardware is capable of searching the Key Area of each record on each track for a particular key. The keys do not have to be in any particular sequence.

The Data Area contains the user's data records. Its length can be up to 32,760 bytes, but realistically it is determined by the particular device's track capacity. Each Data Area contains a block. Each block can consist of one or more logical records. However, you must perform any blocking or deblocking if in fact there is more than one logical record per block. Thus, the terms *block* and *record* are used interchangeably. They both refer to the contents of the Data Area on a direct-access track.

Formatting the Data Set.   Before records can be placed in a direct data set, the DASD space allocated must be *formatted.* Formatting the data set is the process of initializing each track, one after another in a sequential fashion. For fixed-length records, formatting is essentially the process of creating *buckets,* which act as place holders for actual records to be added at a later time. For variable-length and undefined-length records, formatting is the process of initializing the Track Descriptor Record (there is one on the front of every track). Each will reflect the fact that there are no records written on the track and that the entire track space is available.

Keys.   Each record in a data set is comprised of one or more related data fields. One or more of these data fields may serve as an identifier or key field which uniquely distinguishes that record from others in the same data set. Typical keys are: names, part numbers, or chronologically assigned serial numbers such as employee number, invoice number, etc. The key is the means of selecting and retrieving a desired record from the data set.

Every record in a directly organized data set also has a unique address. This address identifies the location within the data set where the record should be found. The format of the record address will be discussed in the next section dealing with regional data sets.

In a direct data set, there is a definite relationship between the record key and the record address or location. It is this relationship which allows you to directly retrieve any record in the data set without a sequential or index search. This relationship is completely determined by each user; it might be a *direct* or an *indirect* relationship.

Direct Addressing. It is entirely possible to have keys which identify the location of the record in the data set. This is a direct addressing scheme, thus obviating the need for a transformation or mathematical manipulation of the key. One of the characteristics of a direct addressing scheme is that there is a unique DASD address for each record key.

The ideal situation would be to use the record's key as its DASD address, because there is a strict relationship between the record's key and its address in the data set. An example of this type of direct addressing would be a data set of personnel records where the four-digit employee number is the key and also serves as the location of the record, i.e., the record for employee number 6545 would be the 6545th record within the data set. This technique assumes that there is an addressable location or "bucket" available for each employee number, regardless of whether or not there is an employee with that number. For example, if we have employee numbers which range from 0001 to 9999, then we must have 9999 buckets, even though we may have only a few hundred employees.

The use of direct address using a strict relationship is usually limited to data sets with small numerical keys. Additionally, in all direct addressing schemes the data records must be fixed-length.

Cross-Reference Table (Index Searching). There is no unique and simple way of transforming a long key to a shorter unique address. One technique of handling records with a cumbersome key is to build a cross-reference table (index). When a record is written in the data set, you note the physical location and store this, along with its key, in the table. Finding the address of a particular key is achieved by programming a *table lookup* of the cross-reference table. For example, assume a key of SMITH serves as the argument in a programmed table lookup:

```
┌─────────────────────────────┐
│      Cross-reference         │
│           table              │
│      ─────────      ───      │
│                              │
│      ─────────      ───      │
│                              │
│      SMITH          623      │
│      ─────────      ───      │
└─────────────────────────────┘
```

When the argument is found in the table, the corresponding value (623 in this example) will be the address of SMITH's record in the direct data set.

This technique of direct addressing allows DASD space to be allocated on the basis of the number of records in the data set rather than on the range of keys. New records can be added sequentially to the end of the data set space and their location noted and placed in the cross-reference table.

The obvious disadvantages are that cross-referencing requires the user to maintain the table, and main storage and processing time are required to search and update the table.

Indirect Addressing. A more common technique for organizing the data set involves the use of indirect addressing. In indirect addressing, the address of each record in the data set is determined by a mathematical manipulation of the key. This manipulation of the key is referred to as randomizing. There are many different techniques of transforming a record key (external identification) into the corresponding record address (internal location). One technique is the *division/remainder* method. This technique may be used for numeric or alphabetic or alphameric keys. The bytes in the key are treated as a binary value. The key is divided by a prime number† that is closest to the number of records in the data set. The remainder is the address. For example, assume a 1000 record file:

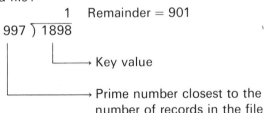

$$997 \overline{)\ 1898} \quad \begin{array}{l} 1 \quad \text{Remainder} = 901 \end{array}$$

→ Key value

→ Prime number closest to the number of records in the file

Thus, the number 901 would be the record's address or location.

An inevitable result of this calculation technique is the occurrence of synonyms—two or more stored records whose keys result in the same storage address. For example, if the calculation is performed for key value 5886 and 1898, the relative addresses derived are the same:

$$997 \overline{)\ 5886} \quad \begin{array}{l} 5 \quad \text{Remainder} = 901 \end{array}$$

The record that is written where it belongs is called the *home record*. The second and subsequent records with keys which convert to the

---

†A *prime number* is a number evenly divisible only by itself and by one.

same address are called *overflow records*. A procedure must be provided for storing elsewhere those overflow records whose keys convert to an address that is already occupied. There are many different techniques used to handle overflow records. One method is called *progressive overflow*. Progressive overflow assumes that the entire data set space is not 100% used; that is, there are buckets that are not yet filled and the overflow record may be stored in one of them. The search for an empty bucket starts at the address produced by the randomizing scheme and continues through consecutive addresses.

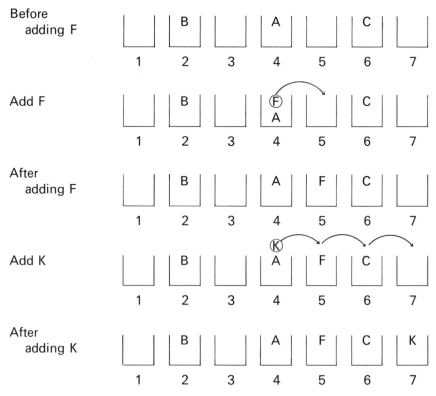

In the above example, a data set contains seven buckets presently having three records. Let's suppose we add a record with a key of F and that our randomizing scheme assigns F to bucket 4. Since bucket 4 is already occupied, a search is made for an empty bucket. Bucket 5 is empty, and F is placed in it. Next we add a record with a key of K, and once again let's suppose our randomizing scheme assigns K to bucket 4. When we attempt to put K in bucket 4, we find it is occupied, so we attempt to put it in bucket 5. But bucket 5 is also occupied, so we attempt to put it in bucket 6. This process continues until an empty bucket is found, which in this example is bucket 7.

In searching for an empty bucket in which to store an overflow record, the system must have some way of knowing when it encounters an empty or available record. This is done by initially loading the data set with *system dummy records*. The format of these records will be described later. In order for the system to handle the placement of overflow records, the data set must be recorded in the Count-Key-Data format. How far will the system search for an empty bucket? This is a function of the operating system you are using. In DOS, the search is to the end of the cylinder. In OS, the LIMCT parameter in the DD statement specifies the number of additional tracks to be searched.

Synonyms should be kept to a minimum because of the additional time required to locate overflow records. A way to minimize synonyms is to allot more space for the file than is actually required to hold all the records. The term "packing factor" means the percentage of allotted locations that are actually used. For an indirectly addressed file, an initial packing factor of 80–85% is suggested. For example, a 10,000 record file packed 83% would be allotted space for 12,000 records.

The basic objectives of the calculation technique described here are:

1. To derive a valid address for every key in the data set.
2. To distribute the addresses or region numbers as evenly as possible across the key range to minimize the number of synonyms.

A sought-after goal is to have no more than 20% synonyms. The division/remainder method automatically achieves the first objective mentioned—that is, to have all keys convert to addresses within the allotted range. Whether it achieves the second objective for a particular file—that is, to have a few synonyms—can be determined only by trying it.

REGIONAL Data Sets

Introduction

REGIONAL organization of a data set permits the programmer to control the physical placement of records in the data set and enables him to optimize the access time for a particular application. Such optimization is not available with consecutive or indexed organizations.

REGIONAL organization is applicable only to direct access storage devices.

The term *region* was selected to describe a type of data set that is divided into regions (rather than records). As will be seen, one or more records may be stored in each region. There are three types of REGIONAL data sets: REGIONAL(1), REGIONAL(2), REGIONAL(3).

Relative Record versus Relative Track

A REGIONAL data set is divided into *relative* regions, each of which is identified by a region number and each of which may contain one or more records. The regions are numbered in succession, beginning with zero, and a record is accessed by specifying its region number in a record-oriented I/O statement.

Two kinds of regional specifications are used: relative record and relative track. A *relative record* is a region in a data set; it is referenced by a number relative to the first record in the data set, which is number zero. The disk on the left in Figure 10.12 illustrates the organization on a disk of a REGIONAL file where each region contains one record. The concentric circles in this figure represent the tracks into which a disk is divided—one circle represents one track. As can be seen, a number of regions may appear in one track. REGIONAL(1) and REGIONAL(2) have this type of data set organization.

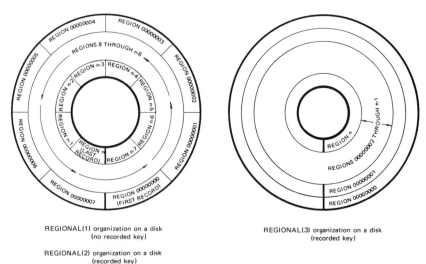

REGIONAL(1) organization on a disk
(no recorded key)

REGIONAL(2) organization on a disk
(recorded key)

REGIONAL(3) organization on a disk
(recorded key)

FIGURE 10.12   Relative record versus relative track.

A *relative track* specification refers to a region of the data set by specifying the number of a particular track relative to the first track of the data set, which is track zero. The disk on the right in Figure 10.12 illustrates this type of disk arrangement which is used in REGIONAL(3) data sets. As can be seen, each region is a track. REGIONAL(3) organization allows *more than one* record to be stored in each region. By contrast, REGIONAL(1) and REGIONAL(2) allow only *one* record per region. A relative track or relative record specification always refers uniquely to one region in a data set.

Size of REGIONAL Data Sets

The size of a data set or the number of records that may be stored in a data set depends upon how much space on a disk (or other DASD) you reserve for a data set. The allocating of external storage for a data set is handled through the job control language statements, not PL/I.

Source and Recorded Keys

A *source key* is the character-string value specified in the record-oriented I/O statements following the KEY or KEYFROM options. In REGIONAL(1), the source key is a region number that serves as the sole identification of a particular record. For example:

READ FILE(REG1)INTO(AREA)KEY(REGION#) ;

> The region number consisting of an eight-position character-string containing the digits 0–9; if more than eight characters appear in the key, only the rightmost eight are used as the region number

The largest region number that may be specified is 16777215 ($2^{24} - 1$).

	REGIONAL source key specification
Subset language	Leading blanks not allowed
Full language	Leading blanks will be treated as zeros

The character-string value of the source key for REGIONAL(2) and REGIONAL(3) files can be thought of as having two logical parts: the *region number* and the *comparison key*. For example:

```
WRITE FILE(REG2)FROM(AREA)KEYFROM
    (PART#||REGION#);
```

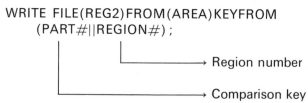

→ Region number

→ Comparison key

The source key need not be specified as an expression with concatenation as shown above, but may be written as one character-string. For example:

```
WRITE FILE(REG2) FROM
    (AREA)KEYFROM('AB123400000057');
```

Source key

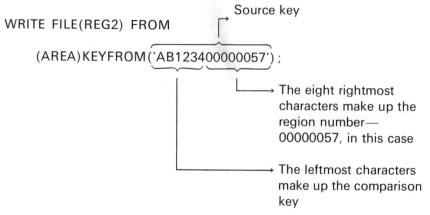

→ The eight rightmost characters make up the region number— 00000057, in this case

→ The leftmost characters make up the comparison key

A *recorded key* is a character-string that immediately precedes each record in the data set to identify that record. Here is a REGIONAL(2) example:

Region 0		Region 1		Region 2		
Recorded key	Logical record	Recorded key	Logical record	Recorded key	Logical record	. . .

In REGIONAL(3), because more than one record could appear in a region, we might have the following arrangement:

Region 0						Region 1				
Recorded key	Logical record	Recorded key	Logical record	Recorded key	Logical record	Recorded key	Logical record	Recorded key	Logical record	...

The recorded key may be from 1 to 255 characters long. This length is specified either through job control statements or through the KEYLENGTH option of the ENVIRONMENT attribute in a file declaration statement. The KEYLENGTH option is provided in all compilers except PL/I F. Thus, with PL/I F, use the DD job control statement, subparameter KEYLEN=n, to indicate the number of characters in the key.

The KEYLENGTH option (or KEYLEN in the DD statement) specifies the number of characters in the comparison key. *On output, the comparison key is written as the recorded key.* For example, assume the ENVIRONMENT attribute specifies KEYLENGTH(6). Then, in the statement,

WRITE FILE(REG2)FROM(AREA)KEYFROM('AB123400000057');

the recorded key would be the character-string value:

'AB1234'

If KEYLENGTH(14) were specified, then the recorded key would be the character-string value:

'AB123400000057'

As can be seen, then, the comparison key can actually include the region number, in which case, the source key and the comparison key are identical; alternatively, part of the source key may be unused. For example, if KEYLENGTH(4) is specified, the comparison key consists of the leftmost four characters:

'AB12'

The characters between the comparison key and the region number ('34' in this case) are ignored.

On input, the comparison key is compared with the recorded key. For example, assume KEYLENGTH(8) is specified, and the following WRITE statement creates a record:

WRITE FILE(REG2)FROM(AREA)KEYFROM('AB123400000057');

The recorded key in this case is

'AB123400'

because the keylength is eight characters. Thus, when it is desired to read the above record, the following READ statement might be coded:

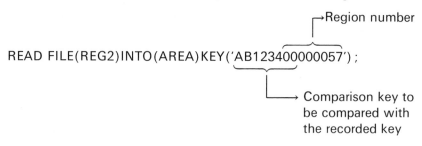

	Recorded key for REGIONAL(2) and REGIONAL(3)
Subset language	The recorded key must consist of the comparison key and the region number; this means that the KEYLENGTH specification must always be 9 or greater: 8 for the region specification plus at least 1 for the comparison key
Full language	It is optional to include the region number in the recorded key

Why Three Types of REGIONAL Data Sets?

So far, we have talked about relative records and relative tracks in REGIONAL data sets, and comparison keys (found in the READ or WRITE statement) and recorded keys [precede records in REGIONAL (2) and REGIONAL(3) files]. At this point, we need to put the three types of REGIONAL data sets into perspective and consider under what conditions each type could be useful. To do this, you must have an understanding of the three common methods previously discussed for accessing stored records in REGIONAL data sets: *direct addressing, index searching,* and *indirect addressing.*

Direct Addressing. In this type of addressing, every possible key in the data set corresponds to a unique storage address on the disk. In this case, the key could only be numeric. A location must be reserved in the data set for every key in the range. For example, if the complete text of, perhaps, a reference book were to be stored, each page of the text could be kept in a region. Thus, region 5 could correspond to page 5, region 6 to page 6, and so on. (In this case, region 0 probably would not be used.) When it is desired to update or correct a given page in the reference manual, it is a simple matter to retrieve the corresponding data set record. For example:

.

.

.

```
DCL PAGE PIC'(8)9';
GET LIST(PAGE);
READ FILE(BOOK)INTO(AREA)KEY(PAGE);
```

.

.

.

As another example, if a company that markets a product has divided its sales area into territories, each territory could be given a number (i.e., 0, 1, 2, 3, etc.). Then, information regarding sales in each of the territories could be stored, where each logical record corresponds to a sales territory. Thus, region 0 would contain sales information on territory 0, region 1 on territory 1, etc. In the area of scientific computation, tables of data to be reduced could be stored—one table per region. Or, historical information on power plant equipment could be stored where, perhaps, region 1 contains the performance record of generator number 1, region 2 of generator number 2, etc.

Using the key of a record as its address is called *direct addressing* (as opposed to *indirect addressing*). In the examples cited above, direct addressing was suggested as the means for identifying records. The method of direct addressing not only allows minimum disk time when processing at random, but is also ideal for sequential processing, because the records are written in key sequence. A possible disadvantage of this type of approach is that there may be a large amount of unused storage. For example, in an inventory file, assume the part numbers are used as the keys and that the numbers range from 10000 to 99999. Out of this range, however, there are only 3000 inventory items. Thus, if the part number is the key, there will be a large amount of *unused* direct access storage, because a location must be reserved for every key in the file's range even though many of them are not used.

Index Searching.   This method alleviates some of the shortcomings of direct addressing. In this method, an index is maintained consisting of keys and assigned hardware (e.g., region number) addresses. For example, when a REGIONAL data set is created, the programmer also constructs an index table which is typically another data set:

Key	Region number
012	001
035	002
020	003
435	004
250	005
176	006
551	007
043	008

Notice that the keys are not in sequence. They are simply assigned a region number within the data set. The index table would be saved on a DASD along with the REGIONAL data set. When a stored record is to be retrieved from the REGIONAL data set, the index table would be first read by your program into main storage and then searched to locate the required key value. When the corresponding region number is obtained, that number is used to access the given stored record. The *index search* method allows data sets to be allocated space based only on the actual space requirements of the stored records and not on all possible key values within a range. Thus, in the previous inventory example in which the key values ranged from 10000 to 99999 but there were only 3000 actual inventory items, a considerable saving of DASD space can be effected by using the index search technique. Also, keys do not have to be numeric values, as in direct addressing. Unique addresses are assured and any record can be accessed with only one seek to the DASD once the address is obtained from the index. However, time is required to look up the address in the index— which may be a serious disadvantage when it contains many entries. The index also requires additional storage in excess of that required by the stored records in the REGIONAL file. For sequential retrieval, the index can be sorted into key sequence.

Indirect Addressing.   This method may be used for nonnumeric keys, or when the range of keys for a file contains so many unused values that direct addressing is impractical, or when the number of records is so large that using an index table is cumbersome. The purpose of indirect addressing is to manipulate keys in a data set by some algorithm to compress the range of key values to a smaller range of stored addresses (region numbers). There are a number of techniques used to calculate region numbers from a given set of key values. For example, assume we have a file of 1000 records and that there is enough room on each track of the direct access storage device to store 15 records. Thus, if we divide the number of records by the number of records per track, we see that this file will require 67 tracks:

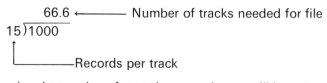

$$\frac{66.6}{15 \overline{)1000}} \longleftarrow \text{Number of tracks needed for file}$$

Records per track

(To determine the number of records per track, you will have to reference the hardware specifications for the particular DASD you are using. The number of bytes per track vary between DASD's.)

To determine a region number for a given key in this 1000-record data set, divide any key in the file by the prime number closest to 1000—in this case 997. For example, assume they key is 1898:

$$\frac{1}{997 \overline{)1898}} \qquad \text{Remainder} = 901$$

The remainder, 901, could be the relative region number in RE-GIONAL(1) or REGIONAL(2) data sets. Recall that in REGIONAL(2), the key—1898 in the above example—would be recorded with the record. The key would not, however, be recorded in the REGIONAL(1) data set record. (It could be embedded in your record, however.)

In REGIONAL (3), the region number is a relative track number. To determine a relative track address, divide the key by the prime number closest to the number of tracks (67 in this example) required for the file:

$$61 \overline{)1898} \qquad \frac{31}{} \qquad \text{Remainder} = 7$$

Relative track 7 is a valid reference that could be used in REGIONAL (3).

Opening REGIONAL Files

The OPEN statement opens a file by associating a file expression with a data set. It can also complete the specification of attributes for the file if a complete set of attributes has not been declared for the file being opened. Some of the attributes related to REGIONAL files that may appear in an OPEN statement are summarized below.

	REGIONAL file attributes that may appear in the OPEN statement
Subset language	None allowed
Full language	DIRECT or SEQUENTIAL INPUT or OUTPUT or UPDATE RECORD KEYED

Typically, however, you will probably find that specifying all file attributes in the DECLARE statement will meet your programming requirements. Recall that in the subset languages, a record I/O file must be explicitly opened, whereas in the full languages, if a file is not explicitly opened, it will be opened automatically when the first READ, WRITE, or REWRITE statement is issued to that file.

Preformatting REGIONAL Files

Preformatting consists of writing *dummy records* into a data set. A dummy record does not contain meaningful data, but rather some constant that is unlikely to appear in meaningful data records. This constant, then, identifies the record as being a dummy record—one that is available in which to store new and meaningful information.

	Preformatting REGIONAL files
Subset language	Must be explicitly specified through job control language statements and a DOS utility program called CLRDSK (see "Preformatting REGIONAL Files" in the index of the DOS PL/I Programmer's Guide)
Full language	If a REGIONAL file has the OUTPUT attribute, the data set will automatically be written with dummy records when the file is opened; the nature of dummy records depends on the type of REGIONAL organization

Declaring REGIONAL File Attributes

There are a number of attributes that may be specified in the DECLARE statement for a file. Most of the attributes have been explained in the previous two chapters; thus, these will be mentioned only briefly here.

INPUT, OUTPUT, or UPDATE.   The attributes INPUT and OUTPUT specify the direction of data transmission. The UPDATE attribute specifies that a record is to be either retrieved, added, replaced, or deleted from a file.

DIRECT or SEQUENTIAL.   These attributes specify the manner in which the records in a data set are to be accessed. DIRECT specifies that records are to be accessed by use of a key; thus, each record has a key associated with it. SEQUENTIAL implies that the records are to be accessed according to their sequence in the data set. These two attributes specify only the current usage (method of access) of the file; they do not indicate any physical properties of the data set associated with the file.

	Method of access for REGIONAL data sets
Subset language	DIRECT
Full language	DIRECT or SEQUENTIAL

KEYED. This attribute specifies that each record has a key associated with it. In the case of REGIONAL(1), there is a key associated with the record, although it is not recorded with the record. In REGIONAL(2) and REGIONAL(3), the keys associated with records in these data sets are actually recorded immediately preceding the logical records. KEYED must be specified if the method of access is DIRECT; KEYED is optional if the method of access is SEQUENTIAL and the I/O statements do not contain the options KEY, KEYTO, or KEYFROM.

RECORD. Regional data sets are intended to be accessed by record-oriented data transmission statements (READ, WRITE, etc.); thus, this attribute should be declared.

ENVIRONMENT. The options specified in the ENVIRONMENT attribute vary with the operating system and the PL/I compiler you are using. The options for REGIONAL files include:

1. *REGIONAL (1), REGIONAL (2), REGIONAL (3):* One of these options must be specified for REGIONAL data sets.
2. *Format type:* Only unblocked records are allowed in REGIONAL data sets.

	Format type of records allowed in REGIONAL data sets
Subset language	F format [REGIONAL(1), (2), and (3)]
Full language	F format [REGIONAL(1), (2), and (3)] V format [REGIONAL(3) only] U format [REGIONAL(3) only]

3. *KEYLENGTH:* The option specifies the length of the recorded key for KEYED files. (*Note:* The KEYLENGTH option is provided in all compilers except PL/I F. Thus, with PL/I F, use the DD

job control statement, subparameter KEYLEN = n, to indicate the number of characters in the key.)

4. *MEDIUM* (*symbolic unit, symbolic device*): This option is used in those compilers that run under DOS. If specified for programs running under OS, the MEDIUM option is ignored. An example is

MEDIUM(SYS006,2311)

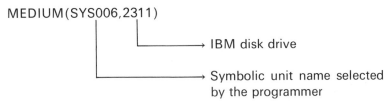

IBM disk drive

Symbolic unit name selected by the programmer

REGIONAL(1) Data Sets

What Each Region Contains. Each region contains one un-blocked F format record that does not have a recorded key. For example:

Region 0	Region 1	Region 2	
Logical record 1	Logical record 2	Logical record 3	. . .

Region Number. Each region number represents the position of one logical record within the data set. The relative position of the first record is zero.

Source Key. The region number serves as the sole identification of a particular logical record. The source key must be expressed as an eight-position character-string consisting of the digits 0–9. One good way of doing this is to declare all source keys as decimal character variables by using the PICTURE '(8)9' attribute. For example, to read the first 25 records in a REGIONAL(1) data set, we could code the following:

```
            DCL LRN PIC'(8)9';
LOOP:       DO LRN=1 TO 25;
            READ FILE (REG1)INTO(AREA)KEY(LRN);
            .
            .
            .
            END LOOP;
```

The value of the source key must represent an unsigned decimal integer that does not exceed 16777215 ($2^{24} - 1$).

Dummy Records. In the full language, a dummy record in a REGIONAL(1) data set is identified by the constant (8)'1'B in its first byte. Although such dummy records are automatically inserted in the data set, either when it is created or when a record is deleted, they are *not* ignored when the data set is read; the PL/I program must be prepared to recognize them. Dummy records can be replaced by valid data.

Creating a REGIONAL(1) Data Set. A REGIONAL(1) data set can be created by the DIRECT method. Following is an example of a file declaration and I/O statement:

```
/* CREATE REGIONAL(1) DATA SET */
DCL REG1 FILE RECORD OUTPUT DIRECT KEYED
   ENV(REGIONAL(1)F(500) MEDIUM(SYS006,2311));
DCL KEY_FIELD PIC'(8)9', DATA(125);
OPEN FILE (REG1);
DO K=1 TO 35;
GET LIST (KEY_FIELD,DATA);
WRITE FILE(REG1)FROM(DATA)KEYFROM(KEY_FIELD);
END;
```

	Creating a REGIONAL(1) data set
Subset language	DASD area must be preformatted before PL/I program attempts to create the data set
Full language	The space allocated to the data set is filled with dummy records when the file is opened

In the full language, a REGIONAL(1) data set may also be created sequentially. For example:

```
DCL REG1 FILE RECORD OUTPUT SEQUENTIAL KEYED
   ENV(REGIONAL(1) F(248));
DCL K PIC'(8)9', DATA(62)FIXED(7,2);
DO K=1 TO 35;
GET EDIT(DATA) (COL(1), F(7,2));
WRITE FILE(REG1)FROM(DATA)KEYFROM(K);
END;
```

When a SEQUENTIAL OUTPUT file is used to create the data set, records must be presented in ascending order of region numbers; any region that is omitted from the sequence is filled with a dummy record. If there is an error in the sequence, or if a duplicate key is presented, the KEY condition will be raised. When the file is closed, any space remaining at the end of the data set is filled with dummy records.

	Creating a REGIONAL data set
Subset language	Via the DIRECT attribute only
Full language	Via the DIRECT or SEQUENTIAL attribute

Retrieving Records from a REGIONAL(1) Data Set.   To retrieve records from a REGIONAL(1) data set, the file may have the attributes INPUT and DIRECT. For example:

```
DCL REG1 FILE RECORD INPUT DIRECT KEYED
   ENV(REGIONAL(1)F(100) MEDIUM(SYS003,2314)) ;
DCL LRN PIC'(8)9', DATA(25)CHAR(4) ;
OPEN FILE(REG1) ;
GET LIST(LRN) ;
READ FILE(REG1)INTO(DATA)KEY(LRN) ;
   .
   .
   .
```

In the full language, SEQUENTIAL (rather than DIRECT) may be specified. For example:

```
        DCL REG1 FILE ENV(REGIONAL(1)) ;
        DCL LRN PIC'(8)9', DATA(25)CHAR(4) ;
        OPEN FILE(REG1) INPUT SEQUENTIAL;
LOOP:   DO LRN=0 to 99;
        READ FILE(REG1)INTO(DATA) ;
           .
           .
           .
        END LOOP;
```

Even though a key is associated with a REGIONAL(1) data set, the KEYED attribute is not needed, because the sequential access method is being used and the READ statement does not contain the

KEY option. However, if the KEYTO option appears, in the READ statement, e.g.,

READ FILE(REG1)INTO(DATA)KEYTO(LRN);

⎣———→ The region number of the record just read will be placed into this variable

then the file declaration must contain the KEYED attribute.

Records may also be retrieved from a file that has the DIRECT UPDATE attributes. The UPDATE attribute is used when it is desired to retrieve, add, modify, or replace records in a data set. If you wish to retrieve only, then the INPUT attribute would logically be specified; if you wish to retrieve a record for the purpose of modifying it, then the UPDATE attribute would be specified. Here is an example in which part of a given record is to be changed:

```
DCL REG1 FILE UPDATE DIRECT KEYED ENV(REGIONAL(1)F(350)
   MEDIUM(SYS004,2314));
DCL LRN PIC'(8)9', DATA(10) CHAR(35);
OPEN FILE (REG1);
/* GET THE SOURCE KEY */
GET LIST (LRN);
/* READ SPECIFIED RECORD */
READ FILE(REG1)INTO(DATA)KEY(LRN);
/* GET NEW DATA AND MODIFY THE RECORD */
GET LIST(K,DATA(K));
/* OUTPUT MODIFIED RECORD */
REWRITE FILE(REG1)FROM(DATA)KEY(LRN);
```

In the full language, if all records in a REGIONAL(1) data set are to be retrieved and modified, then the file attributes could be SEQUENTIAL UPDATE.

In a REGIONAL(1) data set, both dummy† and actual records may be retrieved. For example, if a READ statement specifies the key

†Dummy records are not provided in the subset languages. The programmer may flag records within a data set to signify that a given region does not contain meaningful data; however, to the system, the flagged record is just like a valid record.

(region number) of a dummy record, that data will be placed into the variable indicated. In the full language implementations, dummy records are indicated by a '(8)1'B in the first byte of the REGIONAL(1) record. The program must be prepared to recognize dummy records. For example:

```
      /* FULL LANGUAGE EXAMPLE */
      DCL REG1 FILE SEQUENTIAL UPDATE
         ENV(REGIONAL(1)F(100));
      DCL DATA CHAR(100);
      ON ENDFILE(REG1) GO TO END;
LOOP:  READ FILE(REG1)INTO(DATA);
      /* TEST FIRST BYTE OF THE INPUT RECORD */
      IF SUBSTR(DATA,1,1) = '(8)1'B THEN GO TO LOOP;
      .
      .
      .
      GO TO LOOP;
END:  /* CONTINUE */
```

Deleting Records from a REGIONAL(1) Data Set.   In the full language, if it is desired to delete a record from a REGIONAL file, then a dummy record is written over the existing record as indicated by the DELETE statement. For example:

```
      DELETE FILE(REG1)KEY(PART#);
```

In the subset language, the deletion of records must be simulated, because the DELETE statement is not available. Thus, a "dummy" record of a format selected by the programmer would have to be written over an existing record using the REWRITE statement. For example:

```
      DCL AREA CHAR(124),FIRST BIT(8) DEF AREA;
      BIT = '(8)1'B;
      REWRITE FILE(REG1)FROM(AREA)KEY(PART#);
```

REGIONAL(2) Data Sets

This type of data set is available in those PL/I compilers that will run under OS (e.g., PL/I F and OS PL/I optimizing compilers).

What Each Region Contains.   Each region contains one unblocked F format record that is identified by a recorded key preceding each record. For example:

Region 0		Region 1		Region 2		
Recorded key	Logical record	Recorded key	Logical record	Recorded key	Logical record	. . .

Significance of the Region Numbers. The actual position of a record in the data set relative to other records is determined not by its recorded key, but by the *region number* that is supplied in the source key of the WRITE statement that adds a record to the data set. For example, assume we have a data set containing four records and that two of those four records have meaningful data, while the other two contain dummy records. To illustrate:

Region 0		Region 1		Region 2		Region 3	
100	Data	Dummy		107	Data	Dummy	

└──────────────────────┴────────────────→ Recorded keys

Recall the layout of regions in the physical tracks of a direct access storage device as shown in Figure 10.12. When a record is added to a REGIONAL(2) data set, it is written with its recorded key in the first available space after the beginning of the track that contains the region specified. Given the file declaration,

DCL REG2 FILE RECORD UPDATE DIRECT KEYED
ENV(REGIONAL(2)F(100) KEYLENGTH(3));

and the WRITE statement,

WRITE FILE(REG2)FROM(AREA)KEYFROM('10900000000');

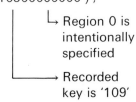

└→ Region 0 is intentionally specified

└→ Recorded key is '109'

the added record will be placed into region 1, which is the first available space after the beginning of the track that contains the region specified.

Now, with the added record, we have the following configuration:

Region 0	Region 1	Region 2	Region 3
100 ¦ Data	109 ¦ Data	107 ¦ Data	Dummy ¦

Thus, in the above example, region 0 was specified in the WRITE statement, but the record and its recorded key were actually written in region 1.

When a record is read, the search for a record with the appropriate recorded key begins at the start of the track that contains the region specified. Unless it is limited by the LIMCT subparameter of the DD statement that defines the data set in OS, the search for a record or for space to add a record continues right through to the end of the data set and then from the beginning until the whole of the data set has been covered. The closer a record is to the specified region, the more quickly it can be accessed.

Dummy Records. A REGIONAL(2) data set can contain dummy records which are recognizable by their keys: the key of a dummy record has the constant (8)'1'B in its first byte. The first *data* byte of a dummy record contains the sequence number of the record on the track. Dummy records can be replaced by valid data. They are inserted automatically either when the data set is created or when a record is deleted, and they are ignored when the data set is read.

REGIONAL(3) Data Sets

What Each Region Contains. Each region may contain one or more unblocked records. For example:

Region 0

Recorded key	Logical record	Recorded key	Logical record	Recorded key	Logical record

Region 1

Recorded key	Logical record	Recorded key	Logical record	. . .

	Record formats allowed in REGIONAL(3)
Subset language	F format
Full language	F format V format U format

Significance of the Region Number. Each region number identifies a *track* (see Figure 10.12) on the direct access storage device that contains the data set; the region number may not exceed 32767 ($2^{16} - 1$). The addition of records to a REGIONAL(3) data set is the same as described for REGIONAL(2) data sets.

	Searching REGIONAL(3) data sets
Subset language	Search for a record begins at the track specified and, if the record is not found in that cylinder, the search stops and the KEY condition is raised
Full language	Search for a record begins at the track specified and, if the record is not found, continues on to the next track; if specified, there is a search to the end of the data set; if record is not found, the KEY condition is raised

Dummy Records

Dummy records are not automatically provided in the subset language. In the full language, dummy records for REGIONAL(3) data sets with F format records are identical with those for REGIONAL(2) data sets. Dummy records cannot be inserted when a data set is created with V format or U format records, because their lengths cannot be known before they are written; however, the operating system maintains a *capacity record* at the beginning of each track, in which it records the amount of space available on that track.

V Format and U format dummy records are identified by the fact that they have dummy recorded keys [(8)'1'B in the first byte]. The four control bytes in each V format dummy record are retained, but otherwise the contents of V format and U format dummy records are undefined. V Format and U format dummy records are inserted in a data set only when a record is deleted; the space they occupy cannot be used again.

Some On-Units and Built-in Functions

On-Units

On-units that applied to computational and stream I/O conditions were initially covered in Chapter 3. The remaining on-units are described here because of their applicability to record I/O data transmission for DASD data sets.

KEY Condition. The KEY condition can be raised during operations on keyed records. It is raised in any of the following cases:

1. The keyed record cannot be found for a READ or REWRITE statement. In this case, the contents of the variable into which data is to be read is unpredictable.
2. An attempt is made to add a duplicate key by a WRITE statement for a REGIONAL(1) or INDEXED data set.
3. The key has not been correctly specified.
4. No space is available to add the keyed record.

In the absence of an on-unit, the system prints a message and raises the ERROR condition. KEY is always enabled; it cannot be disabled and a null on-unit cannot be specified. Here is a sample statement:

ON KEY(FILE1) GO TO ERROR_RT;

UNDEFINEDFILE Condition. The UNDEFINEDFILE condition is raised whenever an attempt to open a file is unsuccessful. Some causes for the condition occurring are as follows:

1. A conflict in attributes exists (e.g., opening a CONSECUTIVE data set with DIRECT or KEYED attributes).
2. Attributes are incomplete (e.g., no blocksize specified, no key-length specified for creation of indexed data sets).

In the absence of an on-unit, the system prints a message and raises the ERROR condition. The UNDEFINEDFILE condition is always enabled and cannot be disabled. Upon normal completion of the on-unit, control is given to the statement immediately following the statement that causes the condition to be raised.

RECORD Condition. The RECORD condition can be raised during a READ, WRITE or REWRITE operation. It is raised by either of the following:

1. The size of the record is greater than the size of the variable (for F, V, U formats).
2. The size of the record is less than the size of the variable (for F format).

If the size of the record is greater than the size of the variable, the excess data in the record is lost on input and is unpredictable on output. If the size of the record is less than the size of the variable, the excess data in the variable is not transmitted on output and is unaltered on input. (In the case of fixed blocked records, the record condition is raised as many times as there are records in the block.) In the absence of an on-unit, the system prints a message and raises the ERROR condition. RECORD is always enabled; it cannot be disabled. Upon execution of a null on-unit, execution continues with the statement immediately following the one for which RECORD occurred:

ON RECORD(FILE2)CALL PRTMSG;

TRANSMIT Condition. The TRANSMIT condition can be raised during any I/O operation. It is raised because of a hardware failure. Any data transmitted is potentially incorrect. In the absence of an on-unit, the system prints a message and raises the ERROR condition. TRANSMIT is always enabled; it cannot be disabled. Upon the normal completion of the on-unit, processing continues as though no error had occurred. If the TRANSMIT error is a recurring condition, the customer engineer or maintenance engineer should be called to fix the hardware failure.

Built-in Functions

Following are descriptions of two built-in functions available only in the full language implementations. These functions would be useful in responding to errors detected by the system during the execution of PL/I statements that communicate with data sets.

ONKEY Condition Built-in Function. ONKEY extracts the value of the key for the record that caused an I/O condition to be raised. This function can be used in the on-unit for an I/O condition or a CONVERSION condition; it can also be used in an on-unit for an ERROR condition. The value returned by this function is a varying-length character-string giving the value of the key for the record that caused an I/O condition to be raised. For example:

```
DCL ONKEY BUILTIN;
DCL KEY_IN_ERROR CHAR(20)VARYING;
/* ON-UNIT FOR THE KEY CONDITION */
ON KEY(ISFILE)BEGIN;
    /* INVOKE BUILTIN FUNCTION */
    KEY_IN_ERROR=ONKEY;
    .
    .
    .
END;
```

If the interrupt is not associated with a keyed record, the returned value is the null string.

ONFILE Condition Built-in Function. ONFILE determines the name of the file for which an I/O or conversion condition was raised and returns that name to the point of invocation. This function can be used in the on-unit for any I/O or conversion condition; it also can be used in an on-unit for an ERROR condition. The value returned by this function is a varying-length character-string, of 31-character maximum length, consisting of the name of the file for which an I/O or conversion condition was raised. For example, this built-in function is needed in the KEY on-unit if there is more than one keyed data set for which the KEY condition could be raised:

```
DCL ONFILE BUILTIN;
DCL NAME CHAR(31) VARYING;
ON KEY BEGIN;
    /* INVOKE BUILTIN FUNCTION */
    NAME=ONFILE;
    .
    .
    .
END;
```

552   PL/I Programming

In the case of a conversion condition, if that condition is not associated with a file, the returned value is the null string.

Case Study

Two programs are illustrated in this case study:

1. File create program
2. File update program

The File Create Program

This program is illustrated in Figure 10.13. It creates a REGIONAL(1) data set from a sequential data set called INPUT. (The name of the REGIONAL(1) data set is REG1.) Records that contain an 'L' in the first position of records stored in the INPUT data set are to be loaded into the REG1 data set. At the same time records are being loaded into the REG1 file, an indexed data set called ISAM is also to be created. Records in the ISAM file will contain the key and the region number of each record loaded into REG1. The ISAM file is being created so that the *index search* method can be used to locate records in the REGIONAL file. (This technique was described in this chapter under the heading "Why Three Types of REGIONAL Data Sets?") Here are the record layouts:

1. INPUT_RECORD

Position	1	CODE
	2–5	Not used
	6–10	RECORD_ID (Keyfield in character form)
	11–20	F1
	21–30	F2
	31–40	F3
	41–50	F4 Seven fields of 10 characters each
	51–60	F5
	61–70	F6
	71–80	F7

2. ISAM_RECORD

Position	1	Delete byte
	2–6	RECORD_ID
	7–14	Relative pointer (REL_PTR) in picture 9's form

```
CREATE: PROC OPTIONS(MAIN);
  /********************************/
  /*  FILE DECLARATIONS           */
  /********************************/
        DCL INPUT FILE RECORD INPUT ENV(CONSECUTIVE);
        DCL ISAM FILE RECORD KEYED ENV(INDEXED);
        DCL REG1 FILE RECORD KEYED ENV(REGIONAL(1));
  /********************************/
  /*  RECORD DEFINITIONS          */
  /********************************/
        DCL 1 INPUT_REC,
              2 CODE CHAR(1),
              2 FILL1 CHAR(4),
              2 IN_KEY PIC '(5)9',
              2 FIELDS,
                3 (F1,F2,F3,F4,F5,F6,F7)CHAR(10);
        DCL 1 ISAM_REC,
              2 DELETE CHAR(1),
              2 ISAM_KEY PIC '(5)9',
              2 REL_PTR PIC'(8)9' INIT(1);
        DCL 1 REG1_REC,
              2 REG1_KEY PIC '(5)9',
              2 FILL2 CHAR(5) INIT(' '),
              2 FIELDS,
                3 (F4,F1,F5,F2,F6,F7,F3)CHAR(10);
  /********************************/
  /*  ON-UNITS SPECIFIED          */
  /********************************/
        ON ENDFILE(INPUT) BEGIN;
          REG1_KEY = REL_PTR;
          WRITE FILE(REG1)FROM(REG1_REC)KEYFROM('0');
          GO TO PRINT_RT;
          END;
        ON KEY(ISAM)BEGIN;
          PUT SKIP LIST(ONFILE,ONKEY,ONCODE);
          GO TO READ_INPUT;
          END;
  /********************************/
  /*  OPEN FILES                  */
  /********************************/
        OPEN FILE(ISAM) SEQL OUTPUT,
             FILE(REG1) DIRECT OUTPUT;
READ_INPUT:
        READ FILE(INPUT)INTO(INPUT_REC);
        IF CODE ¬= 'L' THEN GO TO READ_INPUT;
        ISAM_KEY,REG1_KEY=IN_KEY;
        REG1_REC = INPUT_REC, BY NAME;
        WRITE FILE(ISAM)FROM(ISAM_REC)KEYFROM(ISAM_KEY);
        WRITE FILE(REG1)FROM(REG1_REC)KEYFROM(REL_PTR);
        REL_PTR = REL_PTR + 1;
        GO TO READ_INPUT;
PRINT_RT:
        CLOSE FILE(ISAM),FILE(REG1);
        OPEN FILE(ISAM) INPUT SEQL,
             FILE(REG1) INPUT DIRECT;
        ON ENDFILE(ISAM) GO TO EOJ;
READ_ISAM:
        READ FILE(ISAM)INTO(ISAM_REC);
        READ FILE(REG1)INTO(REG1_REC)KEY(REL_PTR);
        PUT EDIT(REG1_REC.FIELDS)(SKIP,COL(10),(7)A(10));
        GO TO READ_ISAM;
EOJ:    END CREATE;
```

FIGURE 10.13 File create program (full language version).

3. REG1_RECORD

Position		
1–5	RECORD_ID	
6–10	Not used	
11–20	F4	
21–30	F1	
31–40	F5	*Note:* These fields are in a different
41–50	F2	sequence from the fields in the
51–60	F6	INPUT_RECORD
61–70	F7	
71–80	F3	

As a further illustration, then, records in the REG1 data set would look like this:

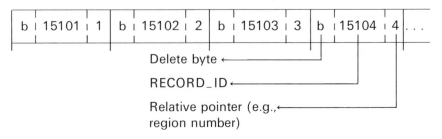

→ The region 0 record contains the region number of the next available region into which a new record could be added; thus, the last processing step that your file create program will perform is to load this value into region 0

Records in the ISAM data set would look like this:

There are some things to observe in the program in Figure 10.13:

1. Notice how the first byte of ISAM_REC is reserved as the "delete" byte. As will be seen in the file update program, there is provision for the possible deletion of records from the REG1 file. The deletion is done in the ISAM file by simply setting the first byte of the appropriate ISAM record to (8)'1'B.

2. The ENDFILE on-unit consists of a begin block (available in full language only) that causes a pointer to be written in region

0. This pointer points to the next available record in the REG1 file. Then, there is an exit to a print routine in which the contents of the REG1 data set will be listed on the printer.

3. The KEY on-unit is a begin block in which three full language built-in functions are invoked: ONFILE, ONKEY, and ONCODE. The ONFILE function causes the file name in which the KEY condition was raised to be printed. The ONKEY function returns the key value that caused the KEY condition to be raised. The key value is printed because of the appearance of ONKEY in the PUT LIST statement. Finally, ONCODE returns a value indicating additional information about the nature of the error. The meaning of this code should be looked up in the appropriate PL/I reference manual.

4. The opening of files in this program is unique to full language PL/I implementations. Notice that ISAM is assigned the attributes SEQUENTIAL and OUTPUT at OPEN time. In the print routine portion of this program, ISAM will be closed—thereby dissociating all attributes with the file. Then ISAM will be immediately opened again—this time with the added attributes SEQUENTIAL INPUT. Assigning the attributes INPUT or OUTPUT at open time gives us the flexibility of being able to read and write the same file in a single program. (This is not possible in the subset language. There, two files must be declared, one for INPUT and one for OUTPUT.)

The File Update Program

This program is illustrated in Figure 10.14. It updates the REG1 file created in the previous program. The update records are in a sequential file called INPUT. The records have an 'A' in position one for addition, a 'U' for update, and a 'D' for delete. Any other code in this position is to be ignored by the program. The data set record layouts are the same as those described in the first program.

SUMMARY

In this summary, a number of charts are presented that compare the various data set organizations. The charts are full language implementation-oriented. The subset restrictions are listed in the captions of these charts. Figure 10.15

```
UPDATE: PROC OPTIONS(MAIN);
   /********************************/
   /*  FILE DECLARATIONS           */
   /********************************/
         DCL INPUT FILE RECORD INPUT ENV(CONSECUTIVE);
         DCL ISAM FILE RECORD KEYED ENV(INDEXED);
         DCL REG1 FILE RECORD KEYED ENV(REGIONAL(1));
   /********************************/
   /*  RECORD DEFINITIONS          */
   /********************************/
         DCL 1 INPUT_REC,
               2 CODE CHAR(1),
               2 FILL1 CHAR(4),
               2 IN_KEY PIC '(5)9',
               2 FIELDS,
               3 (F1,F2,F3,F4,F5,F6,F7)CHAR(10);
         DCL 1 ISAM_REC,
               2 DELETE CHAR(1),
               2 ISAM_KEY PIC '(5)9',
               2 REL_PTR PIC'(8)9';
         DCL 1 REG1_REC,
               2 REG1_KEY PIC '(5)9',
               2 FILL2 CHAR(5) INIT(' '),
               2 FIELDS,
               3 (F4,F1,F5,F2,F6,F7,F3)CHAR(10);
   /********************************/
   /*  ON-UNITS SPECIFIED          */
   /********************************/
         ON KEY(ISAM)BEGIN;
           PUT SKIP LIST(ONFILE,ONKEY,ONCODE);
           GO TO READ_INPUT;
           END;

         ON ENDFILE(INPUT) BEGIN;
           REG1_KEY = REL_PTR;
           WRITE FILE(REG1)FROM(REG1_REC)KEYFROM('0');
           GO TO PRINT_RT;
           END;
   /********************************/
   /*  OPEN FILES                  */
   /********************************/
         OPEN FILE(ISAM) UPDATE DIRECT,
              FILE(REG1) UPDATE DIRECT;
```

FIGURE 10.14   File update program (full language version).

compares record-oriented data set organizations; Figure 10.16 shows the various file activities for each organization; and Figure 10.17 identifies the three additional on-units covered in this chapter.

A SEQUENTIAL file specifies that the accessing, creation, or modification of the data set records is performed from the first record of the data set to the last record of the data set.

A DIRECT file specifies that the accessing, creation, or modification of

```
                DCL NEXT_AVAILABLE PIC'(5)9';
                READ FILE(REG1)INTO(REG1_REC)KEY('0');
                NEXT_AVAILABLE= REG1_KEY;
READ_INPUT:
                READ FILE(INPUT)INTO(INPUT_REC);
CHECK:
                IF CODE ='A' THEN GO TO ADD_ROUTINE;
                IF CODE ='U' THEN GO TO UPDATE_ROUTINE;
                IF CODE ='D' THEN GO TO DELETE_ROUTINE;

                GO TO READ_INPUT;
ADD_ROUTINE:
                ISAM_KEY,REG1_KEY = IN_KEY;
                REL_PTR = NEXT_AVAILABLE;
                WRITE FILE(ISAM)FROM(ISAM_REC)KEYFROM(ISAM_KEY);
                REG1_REC = INPUT_REC, BY NAME;
                WRITE FILE(REG1)FROM(REG1_REC)KEYFROM(REL_PTR);
                NEXT_AVAILABLE = NEXT_AVAILABLE +1;
                GO TO READ_INPUT;
UPDATE_ROUTINE:
                READ FILE(ISAM) INTO(ISAM_REC)KEY(IN_KEY);
                READ FILE(REG1)INTO(REG1_REC)KEY(REL_PTR);
                REG1_REC = INPUT_REC, BY NAME;
                REWRITE FILE(REG1)FROM(REG1_REC)KEY(REL_PTR);
                GO TO READ_INPUT;
DELETE_ROUTINE:
                READ FILE (ISAM) INTO(ISAM_REC)KEY(IN_KEY);
                DELETE FILE(ISAM)KEY(IN_KEY);
                DELETE FILE(REG1)KEY(REL_PTR);
                GO TO READ_INPUT;
PRINT_RT:
                CLOSE FILE(ISAM),FILE(REG1);
                OPEN FILE(ISAM) INPUT SEQL,
                     FILE(REG1) INPUT DIRECT;
                ON ENDFILE(ISAM) GO TO EOJ;
READ_ISAM:
                READ FILE(ISAM)INTO(ISAM_REC);
                READ FILE(REG1)INTO(REG1_REC)KEY(REL_PTR);
                PUT EDIT(REG1_REC.FIELDS)(SKIP,COL(10),(7)A(10));
                GO TO READ_ISAM;
EOJ:            END UPDATE;
```

FIGURE 10.14 *Continued*

the data set records may be performed in random order. The particular record of the data set to be operated upon is identified by a specified key.

A data set that is accessed, created, or modified in the SEQUENTIAL access method may or may not have recorded keys. If it does, the keys may be ignored while accessing sequentially, or they may be extracted from the data set or placed into the data set by the KEYTO and KEYFROM options.

Existing records of a data set in a SEQUENTIAL UPDATE file can be rewritten, modified, or ignored, but the number of records cannot be increased

Organization	Devices	Record formats	Recorded keys	Key specification	Dummies
CONSECUTIVE	Any	F, U, V, blocked or unblocked	No	Not applicable	Not applicable
INDEXED	DASD	F blocked or unblocked	Yes	1–255 byte character-string	First character of record contains (8)'1'B
REGIONAL(1)	DASD	F unblocked	No	8 characters representing region (relative record) are character representation of unsigned decimal integer 16777216	First character of record contains (8)'1'B
REGIONAL(2)	DASD	F unblocked	Yes	Low-order 8 bytes as in REGIONAL(1); high-order bytes (1–255) are recorded key	First character of key contains (8)'1'B; first character of record contains record number
REGIONAL(3)	DASD	F, U, V unblocked	Yes	As in REGIONAL(2) except maximum region is 32767 and region is a relative track	F: same as in REGIONAL(2); U or V: first byte of key contains (8)'1'B; record control bytes are valid

FIGURE 10.15 Record-oriented data set organizations. [Subset restrictions: No REGIONAL(2) organization; no U or V record formats in REGIONAL(3); no dummy records.]

Organization	Creation		Retrieval		Addition		Update	
	SEQUENTIAL	DIRECT	SEQUENTIAL	DIRECT	SEQUENTIAL	DIRECT	SEQUENTIAL	DIRECT
CONSECUTIVE	No keys	Not applicable	Can read tape backwards with fixed-length records	Not applicable	Can extend if DISP=MOD in OS/360 JCL	Not applicable	REWRITE after READ on DASD	Not applicable
INDEXED	Values of keys in ascending order	Values of keys in ascending order	Can start at other than first record	Indices direct search to prime track or overflow	Not applicable	Usually causes a record to go into overflow	REWRITE after READ if blocked	REWRITE after READ if blocked
REGIONAL(1)	Keys in sequential order: get dummies for missing keys and remaining tracks	Tracks initialized with dummies; then records added	Real and dummy records retrieved in sequence	Record retrieved whether real or dummy	Not applicable	Overwrite existing record whether real or dummy	READ then REWRITE; delete overwrites with dummy; updates whether real or dummy	DELETE writes a dummy record; updates whether real or dummy
REGIONAL(2)	Keys in sequential order: get dummies for missing keys and remaining tracks	Tracks initialized with dummies; then records added	Retrieved in order written; dummies not available	Searches for matching key starting at track containing specified region and going LIMCT records	Not applicable	Record put in next available location starting at track containing specified region and going LIMCT records	READ then REWRITE; delete overwrites with dummy	DELETE writes a dummy record; record with specified key must exist
REGIONAL(3)	Records in region number order; system writes dummies (F) or initializes capacity records (V or U) for portions of tracks skipped	F: tracks initialized with dummies and records added; V or U: capacity records initialized; then add records	Retrieved in order written; dummies not available	Searches for matching key starting at specified track and going LIMCT tracks	Not applicable	Record put in next available location starting at specified track and going LIMCT tracks	READ then REWRITE; DELETE—F: writes a dummy record; U or V space is not reused	DELETE—F: writes a dummy record; U or V space is not reused

FIGURE 10.16 Comparison of data set activities. [Subset restrictions: No SEQUENTIAL attribute allowed for REGIONAL data sets; only search to end of the track for a record in REGIONAL(3); no DELETE; no dummy records.]

On-condition and abbreviation	Normally Enabled/disabled	Cause	What the programmer should do	Normal return to:	Standard system action	Condition Built-in functions useful in on-unit
KEY (file name)	Enabled (cannot be disabled)	1. Keyed record cannot be found 2. Attempt to add a duplicate key 3. No space available to add keyed record 4. Key is out of sequence 5. Error occurred in the conversion of the key 6. Key has not been specified correctly	Dependent upon requirements of installation	The statement immediately following the statement that caused the condition to be raised	ERROR condition	ONCODE ONCOUNT ONFILE ONKEY ONLOC
RECORD (file name)	Enabled (cannot be disabled)	READ, WRITE, or REWRITE statement because: 1. Size of record greater than size of variable 2. Size of record less than size of variable 3. Record of zero length has been read or 4. Attempt made to write a record of zero length	What is necessary to assure that the size of the variable and the record it is being read into or out of are the same and the length is not zero	The statement immediately following the statement that caused the condition to be raised	ERROR condition	ONCODE ONCOUNT ONFILE ONKEY ONLOC
TRANSMIT (file name)	Enabled (cannot be disabled)	Permanent transmission error	Dependent upon requirements of installation	Continuation of execution as though no transmission error had occurred	ERROR condition	ONCODE ONCOUNT ONFILE ONKEY ONLOC

FIGURE 10.17 Input/output conditions.

or decreased. An existing record in an UPDATE file can be replaced through use of a REWRITE statement.

A WRITE statement adds a record to a data set, while a REWRITE statement replaces a record. Thus, a WRITE statement may be used with OUTPUT files and DIRECT UPDATE files, but a REWRITE statement may be used with UPDATE files only. Moreover, for DIRECT files, a REWRITE statement uses the KEY option to identify the existing record to be replaced; a WRITE statement uses the KEYFROM option, which not only specifies where the record is to be written in the data set, but also specifies, except for REGIONAL(1), an identifying key to be recorded in the data set.

CHECKPOINT QUESTIONS

1. DCL FILE FILE RECORD OUTPUT DIRECT ENV (INDEXED F(400,80)
   MEDIUM (SYS011,2311) EXTENTNUMBER(2)
   KEYLENGTH(16)OFLTRACKS(2));
   In the above DECLARE statement, which omitted attribute is mandatory?
   (a) ADDBUFF
   (b) KEYLOC
   (c) KEYED
   (d) SEQUENTIAL
2. DCL KEYED FILE RECORD INPUT KEYED DIRECT ENV
   (MEDIUM (SYS011,2311) F(1024)EXTENTNUMBER(2)
   REGIONAL(1));
   In the above DECLARE statement, which of the following attributes must also be specified?
   (a) KEYLOC
   (b) KEYLENGTH
   (c) Both A and B
   (d) Neither A nor B
3. DCL INDEX FILE RECORD INPUT DIRECT KEYED ENV
   (MEDIUM (SYS011,2311) F(400)REGIONAL(3));
   In the above DECLARE statement, which omitted option is mandatory?
   (a) BUFFERS(2)
   (b) KEYLENGTH
   (c) INDEXED
   (d) KEYLOC

4. Write the PL/I OUTPUT statement to transmit a record from the variable AREA_1 to XFILE, a REGIONAL(1) output file. The record is to be transmitted to region 293. (Record size is 100.)

5. Which types of organization use recorded keys on the external media?
   - (a) CONSECUTIVE
   - (b) INDEXED
   - (c) REGIONAL(1)
   - (d) REGIONAL(2)
   - (e) REGIONAL(3)

6. Write the PL/I OUTPUT statement to replace the record specified by the comparison key EMP# and relative region number called TRACK# in DFILE, a REGIONAL(3) update file, with the record in the variable named CARD_REC.

7. Write the file declarations for the following files:
   INDISK, a REGIONAL(1) input file; disk unit blocksize is 600
   DISKOT, a REGIONAL(3) output file; blocksize is 800; keylength is 25
   UPREC, a REGIONAL(3) update file; the character-string key identification is 10 characters long; blocksize is 480

8. What would happen if you issued a READ to an indexed data set, supplying a key, processing DIRECT, and there was no record with the specification key in the data set?

TERMS TO STUDY

comparison key
cylinder index
data set
direct addressing (with respect to data sets)
direct search
dummy record
extent
indexed sequential
indirect addressing
master index
overflow area
packing factor
preformatting (DASD area)

prime data area
prime number
recorded key
region
region number
relative record
relative track
sequential search
source key
synonym
track index
update

PRACTICE PROBLEMS

1.   Create a REGIONAL(3) Data Set

Problem Statement: Write a PL/I program to create a REGIONAL(3) data set from the following card data:

Columns 1–5	Catalog number; an alphameric field (columns 1–2 category number within catalog number, columns 3–5 order number within catalog number)
Columns 6–9	Author number; an alphameric field
Columns 10–13	Quantity ordered; four digits
Columns 14–17	Quantity delivered; four digits
Columns 18–21	Quantity-on-hand; four digits
Columns 22–23	Minimum number to be kept on hand; two digits
Columns 24–27	Unit price; a four-digit number with an assumed decimal point between the second and third digits
Columns 28–46	Title; an alphameric description
Columns 47–57	Author; an alphameric description
Columns 58–67	Publisher; an alphameric description
Columns 68–80	Blank—unused at this time

Input: See Figure 10.18 for suggested input data.

Processing: Count the number of records loaded into the disk file. In developing the key for this data set, let the first two digits of the catalog number (columns 1 and 2) be the *relative track number;* the last three digits of the catalog number (columns 3–5) can make up the comparison key.

Output: List each record loaded into the file. Each field should be separated by three or more spaces on the printed output. Also, print the record count at the end of the record listing.

2.   Retrieving Records from a REGIONAL(3) Data Set

Problem Statement: Using the REGIONAL(3) data set created in Problem 1, write a program to read data cards for specific keys. Use these keys to locate the corresponding disk records. Print a report which shows the catalog number, title, number of books back-ordered (if any), and the amount due for books delivered.

Input: Read card records in the following format:

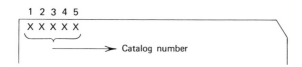

```
050020110000500050005050250THE AMERICAN
050030500002000000025150075THE BEAR
050040080000500040004010195BRIGHTON ROCK
050050040001500100012050075THE BROTHERS KARAM
050060122010000030122100100CANDY
050070045002000000000010100THE CAPTIVE WITCH
050080185001700015020050150THE CORRUPTERS
050090040001000010010050095CRIME AND PUNISH.
050110110000200000000010100DAISY MILLER
050130035000100001001010300DEVOTIONS
050140070003000028040050075DIAMOND HEAD
050150150004000020020050095DR. ZHIVAGO
050160195002000020020050075FAIROAKS
050170130005000020030050500THE FIXER
050200060020000183212250075GOLDFINGER
050270125003000027027200150LADY CHATTERLEYS
050280140004000030039100095LOLITA
060400020001000010012100075THE SEA AROUND US
060420125001200008008100125SONS AND LOVERS
060430110000100001001010150STORIES OF ARTISTS
060440015001000007008050125THE STRANGER
060450120001000000000010150THE SUBTERRANEANS
060460090004000037051100250THE SUN ALSO RISES
070470163000400002002010300SWAN'S WAY
070480180001200012012050400THOSE WHO LOVE
070490055001200006006100150TOM JONES
080500110001000002002050100TURN OF THE SCREW
080510025001400003005050100VICTORY
080520190000500000001051500WAR AND PEACE
200010061000100001001010500ADVANCE CALCULUS
200020133000500004007010300COLLEGE ALGEBRA
200030103001000010013010400DIFFENTIAL EQUATION
200040127001000009011010250ELEMENTS OF ALGEBRA
200060187002000012050010025LIMITS
200070009000200002002010600MEN OF MATHEMATICS
200080032001000003003010450WHAT IS MATHEMATICS
250020100002000020020118600HUMAN PHYSIOLOGY
250030034001000010010010500PRIN. OF GENETICS
300010062001200012012010800CELEM. OF QUANT.ANAL
300020011000600000000011000ORGANIC CHEMISTRY
300030012001200009009010650PRIN. OF PHYS.CHEM
300040057001200008007010700QUANTITATIVE ANALYS
```

FIGURE 10.18 Sample input data for Problems 1 and 3.

where the first two digits of the catalog number may be the *relative track number*, and the last three digits are the *key*.† The REGIONAL(3) file that has been created contains 80-byte records in the format described for card input in Problem 1.

Processing: After a data card is read, read the corresponding disk record. Compute the number back-ordered (BACK = Quantity ordered − Quantity delivered). Compute the amount to be paid (AMT = Quantity delivered * unit

†Or use the division/remainder randomizing technique to derive a relative track number from the catalog number.

price). After all the data cards have been read, print final totals for number of books back-ordered (BACKF) and for amount to pay (AMTF).

Output: Print results in format shown in Figure 10.19.

3. Create an Indexed Data Set

Problem Statement: Write a program to create an indexed data set from the data described in Problem 1.

Input: Suggested input is shown in Figure 10.18.

Processing: Same as for Problem 1, except that the key should be the entire catalog number (columns 1–5).

Output: Same as for Problem 1.

4. Sequential Access of an Indexed Data Set

Problem Statement: Using the indexed data set created in Problem 3, write a program to retrieve all records by the SEQUENTIAL method and print a report as defined in Problem 2.

Input: There is no card input—only disk record input.

Processing: See Problem 2.

Output: See Figure 10.19.

5. Direct Access of an Indexed Data Set

Problem Statement: Using the data set created in Problem 3, write a program to read data cards for specific keys. Use these keys to locate the corresponding disk records. Print a report as defined in Problem 2.

Input: Selected catalog numbers should be punched in columns 1–5.

Processing: See Problem 2.

Output: Print results in format shown in Figure 10.19.

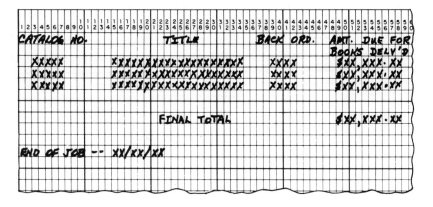

FIGURE 10.19   Sample output for Problems 2 and 4.

chapter 11

Storage Classes and Scope of Identifiers

This chapter discusses how statements can be organized into blocks to form a PL/I program, how control flows within a program from one block of statements to another, and how storage may be allocated for data within a block of statements. In addition, PL/I storage classes are defined.

Procedure Blocks

A *block* is a sequence of statements that constitute a section of a program. There are two types of blocks: procedure blocks and begin blocks. A PL/I program consists of one or more procedures, each of which may contain other procedure or begin blocks. If a procedure is nested within another procedure, it is called an *internal procedure*. If a procedure is compiled separately, it is called an *external procedure*. In the coding shown here, then,

```
P1:    PROC OPTIONS(MAIN);  /* EXTERNAL PROCEDURE */
       .
       .
       .
       IF ISW=2 THEN CALL P2;
       IF ISW=3 THEN CALL P3;
P2:    PROC;   /* INTERNAL PROCEDURE */
       .
       .
       .
       END P2;
P3:    PROC;   /* INTERNAL PROCEDURE */
       .
       .
       .
       END P3;
       END P1;
```

568

P1 is an external procedure; P2 and P3 are internal procedures because they are nested within P1. We can tell they are nested because of the position of the END statements. Notice that P2 and P3 contain only the keyword PROC; the keywords OPTIONS(MAIN) do not appear with these statements. An external procedure consists of *one* OPTIONS(MAIN) statement and nested procedure blocks *without* the OPTIONS(MAIN). Thus, the internal procedures are like subroutines or functions that you learned to code in Chapter 7. In a PL/I program, the MAIN procedure will be the first executed block. The nested or internal procedures will be executed by a CALL or function reference. Notice, then, from the above coding that the way in which P2 and P3 are executed is by a CALL. Had the IF statement

IF ISW = 2 THEN CALL P2;

been eliminated from the P1 program, then the P2 procedure would never be executed—even though the coding is nested within the main program.

Storage Classes

Data names (i.e., variables) actually represent locations in main storage where the data items are recorded. When a location in main storage has been associated with a data name, the storage is said to be *allocated*. In PL/I, we have the facility to allocate main storage at different times. The time at which storage is to be allocated depends on the *storage class* of the data. There are four storage classes: AUTO-MATIC, STATIC, BASED, and CONTROLLED.

AUTOMATIC Storage

Unless declared to have another storage class, all variables will have the AUTOMATIC attribute. As an illustration of what this attribute means in a PL/I program, three procedures are shown in Figure 11.1. SUBRT and FUNCT are internal procedures; that is, they are nested within the MAIN procedure. This is the same configuration as the P1, P2, and P3 example, except that the procedure names have been changed.

Data names, such as STRUCTURE, TABLE, and LIST in the above example, actually represent locations in main storage where the data

```
MAIN:     PROC OPTIONS(MAIN);
          DCL 1 STRUCTURE,
                2 (A, B, C)
                2 D FIXED;
          CALL SUBRT;
          Y=FUNCT(A);
          .
          .
          .

SUBRT:    PROC;
          DCL TABLE(100) CHAR(1);
          .
          .
          .
          END SUBRT;

FUNCT:    PROC(A);
          DCL LIST(50) FIXED;
          .
          .
          .
          END FUNCT;

          END MAIN;
```

FIGURE 11.1   A program consisting of three procedures.

items are recorded. When a location in main storage has been associated with a data name, the storage is said to be *allocated*. The fact that certain variables, such as TABLE, are used in one procedure of a program and not in others makes it possible to allocate the same storage space at different times to different variables.

For example, SUBRT manipulates the data in TABLE. When SUBRT is finished and FUNCT begins execution, it is possible (and desirable from a main storage utilization standpoint) to allocate LIST to the storage area previously occupied by TABLE. If the value of TABLE is not needed when the procedure is invoked again, there is no need to keep the space reserved after execution of the procedure is completed. The storage area can be freed and then used for other purposes. Such use of main storage is called *dynamic storage allocation.*

When storage is allocated dynamically, it is allocated during the execution of a procedure. Storage remains allocated as long as the procedure in which it was allocated remains active. To illustrate this concept, when the MAIN procedure in Figure 11.1 is activated, i.e., "called," the storage for STRUCTURE will be allocated, giving the following main storage configuration:

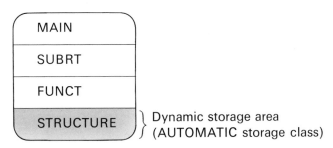

Even though SUBRT and FUNCT are nested within MAIN, these blocks of coding will be extracted by the compiler and placed below the coding for the MAIN procedure. Following the PL/I procedure blocks will be the dynamic storage area.

To see how more dynamic storage (that is, AUTOMATIC storage) is allocated, assume the MAIN procedure calls SUBRT. MAIN remains an active procedure; hence, storage for STRUCTURE stays allocated. The only way in which MAIN may be deactivated is to terminate this procedure with a STOP, END, EXIT, or RETURN.

When SUBRT is activated (by a CALL), storage is allocated for the data area called TABLE. The program in main storage now has this configuration:

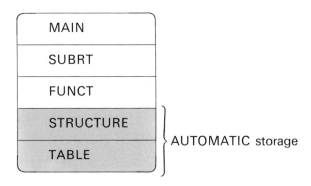

(In some operating systems, AUTOMATIC storage may not be contiguous to the program area. What is being illustrated here is a *concept* of the dynamic allocation of storage. Its actual position in main storage is not of importance to the programmer—unless he is trying to read a *core dump.*)

When SUBRT is terminated, it is "deactivated;" hence, storage for TABLE is released to give the following configuration:

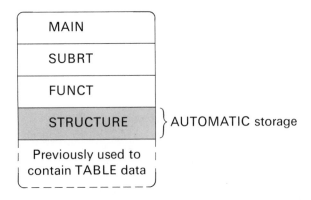

Next, the MAIN procedure invokes FUNCT. The activation of FUNCT causes storage to be allocated for the data area called LIST in Figure 11.1. Main storage would now look like this:

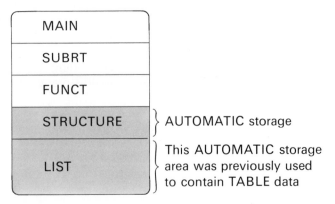

This example illustrates an important point: When a procedure (such as SUBRT) is activated and deactivated, the contents of its data areas may be lost. Thus, if SUBRT is called a second time from MAIN, data recorded in TABLE the first time SUBRT was executed will not be there the second time. As illustrated before, this is because an intervening procedure, FUNCT, was executed and its data area (LIST) was allocated to the area where TABLE once resided. The dynamic allocation of storage applies to *begin* blocks as well as procedure blocks.

This dynamic allocation of main storage is one of the outstanding features of PL/I, because it provides for efficient use of main storage. Total storage requirements of a program may be reduced because of this automatic data overlay feature. The programmer does not have to code extra instructions or steps to cause this allocation to take place. It is done for him *automatically*. All the programmer needs to do is be aware of how and when storage is allocated. All variables that have not been explicitly declared with a storage class attribute are assumed to have the AUTOMATIC attribute.

Prologue.   The allocation of dynamic storage, that is, for variables that have the AUTOMATIC attribute, is performed by a routine called a *prologue.* This routine is set up by the compiler and attached to the beginning of each block. It is always executed as the first step of a block. One of the prologue's functions is to allocate dynamic storage for variables declared within the block to which it is attached. In addition, it allocates storage for *dummy arguments* (discussed in Chapter 7) and "saves" the status of on-units.

Epilogue.   The release of main storage that has been allocated to AUTOMATIC variables is handled by a routine called an *epilogue*. In addition, it reestablishes the on-units to the status that existed before the block was activated. The epilogue routine is logically appended to the end of each block and is executed as the final step before the termination of the block. Prologues and epilogues are set up by the compiler, not the programmer. They are discussed here because knowledge of them may assist you in improving the performance of your programs.

STATIC Storage

We saw earlier that if MAIN calls SUBRT and then FUNCT, SUBRT's data area (TABLE) was overlayed by FUNCT's data area (LIST). In some cases, we may not want LIST to overlay TABLE. Whenever the value of a variable must be saved between different invocations of the same procedures, storage for that variable has to be allocated statically. In this case, storage is allocated before execution of the program and remains allocated throughout the entire execution of the program.

Data areas have the AUTOMATIC attribute by default. However, had the procedures declared STRUCTURE, TABLE, and LIST to have the STATIC attribute, e.g.,

```
DCL 1 STRUCTURE STATIC,
      2 (A, B, C),
      2 D FIXED;
DCL TABLE(100) CHAR(1) STATIC;
DCL LIST(50) STATIC FIXED;
```

then main storage would typically appear as follows:

MAIN procedure
SUBRT procedure
FUNCT procedure
STATIC storage
AUTOMATIC storage

Thus, STATIC storage follows the external procedure MAIN, which is then followed by AUTOMATIC storage for that external procedure. Had MAIN, SUBRT, FUNCT each been a separately compiled procedure such as

```
MAIN:   PROC OPTIONS(MAIN);
           .
           .
           .
        END MAIN;
SUBRT:  PROC;
           .
           .
           .
        END SUBRT;
FUNCT:  PROC(A);
           .
           .
           .
        END FUNCT;
```

then main storage would typically appear like this:

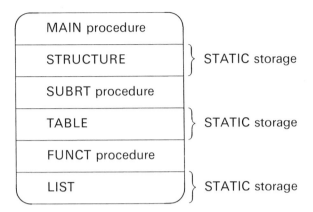

In this example, then, there is no AUTOMATIC storage. Typically, however, a program will have both STATIC and AUTOMATIC storage areas. Program constants and variables declared with the EXTERNAL attribute have the STATIC storage class attribute.

Initializing STATIC versus AUTOMATIC Variables. Variables, whether main storage space is allocated to them dynamically or statically, may be given *initial values* at the time of storage allocation. You can save program overhead by declaring variables that are to be initialized to have the STATIC attribute. For example:

```
DCL A FIXED(5,2) INIT(0) STATIC;
DCL CTR FIXED(3) INIT(100) STATIC;
```

STATIC variables are initialized only once—before execution of a program begins. AUTOMATIC variables are reinitialized at each activation of the declaring block.

Scope of Identifiers

In PL/I, an identifier may have only one meaning at any point in time. For example, the same name cannot be used for both a file and a floating-point variable. It is not necessary, however, for a name to have the same meaning throughout a program. Because it is possible for a name to have more than one meaning, it is important to define which part of the program a particular meaning applies to. In PL/I, a name is given attributes and a meaning by a declaration (not necessarily explicit). The part of the program for which the meaning applies is called the *scope of the declaration* of that name. Generally, the scope of a name is determined entirely by the position at which the name is declared within the program (or assumed to be declared if the declaration is not explicit).

Consider the following nested blocks:

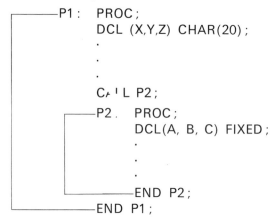

```
P1 :   PROC;
       DCL (X,Y,Z) CHAR(20);
       .
       .
       .
       CALL P2;
P2.    PROC;
       DCL(A, B, C) FIXED;
       .
       .
       .
            END P2;
       END P1;
```

Because of the way in which dynamic storage is allocated, a name declared within a block has a meaning only within that block or to blocks nested within it. In the above example, here is how the scope of identifiers is affected:

Activate P1:	Storage is allocated for X, Y, and Z. At this point, the variables A, B, and C are not known to P1 because storage has not yet been allocated.
Activate P2:	Storage is allocated for A, B, and C. P2 can manipulate not only A, B, and C but also X, Y, and Z, because the P1 procedure is still active.
Deactivate P2:	When there is an exit from P2, the storage for A, B, and C is released. Do you see how A, B, and C can be known only within the P2 block?

Here is an example of how the scope of an identifier may be limited to a given block. Had the nested blocks been specified, A, B, and C in the outer block would refer to different data items than do A, B, or C in the inner block. In some instances, the use of nested blocks to limit or redefine the scope of a variable provides an ease of programming not usually available in other computer languages. For example, assume a programmer has coded a problem in which he has used the variable name DATE to represent a FIXED DECIMAL value.

```
          ┌──────────P1 :   PROC ;
          │                 DCL(A, B, C) CHAR(20) ;
          │                 .
          │                 .
          │                 .
          │                 CALL P2 ;
          │         ┌───────P2 :   PROC ;
          │         │             DCL(A, B, C) FIXED ;
          │         │             .
          │         │             .
          │         │             .
          │         └──────────END P2 ;
          └─────────────────END  P1 ;
```

This data name has been used a number of times in his program. Later, it is decided to have the date printed with the output from this program. The appropriate coding that invokes the DATE built-in function and prints the date edited with slashes can be easily inserted. However, there is one problem : The programmer has already used the identifier DATE to mean something else, so it cannot be used to refer to the DATE built-in function at the same time. The solution to this problem would be to create a nested block that can be used to *limit the scope* of a variable. For example :

```
P1 :   PROC OPTIONS(MAIN) ;
       .
       .
       .
       DCL DATE FIXED(3),TODAY CHAR(6) ;
       DATE = 302 ;
       CALL P2 ;
P2 :   PROC ;
       DCL DATE BUILTIN ;
       TODAY = DATE ;   /* INVOKE DATE FUNCTION */
       END ;
       .
       .
       .
       END  P1 ;
```

In this example, DATE is declared in the outer block to be FIXED DECIMAL(3) and is initialized to the value 302. Also, TODAY is declared to be a character-string of length six. When it is desired to invoke the DATE function, a nested block is created. Within this block, DATE is declared to have the BUILTIN attribute; thus, the scope of the identifier, DATE, is being redefined—actually, its scope is being *limited* to the internal block. The value returned from the DATE function is a character-string that is assigned to TODAY. Notice that TODAY is declared outside the nested block, but may be referenced by statements within the nested block. An analogy that might be drawn regarding the scope of identifiers is to think of the declaration as a "one-way looking glass." Inner blocks can "see out," but the outer blocks cannot "see in." In other words, within the begin block, any variable declared inside of it is known only to that block or any other block nested within it. However, identifiers declared outside the block are known to the inner block providing that a "redefinition" of the variable name has not been specified in the nested block. This, of course, was the case with the identifier DATE.

Scope of an Explicit Declaration

The scope of an explicit declaration of a name is that block to which the declaration is internal. This includes all nested blocks *except* those blocks (and any blocks contained within them) to which another explicit declaration of the same identifier is internal. For example:

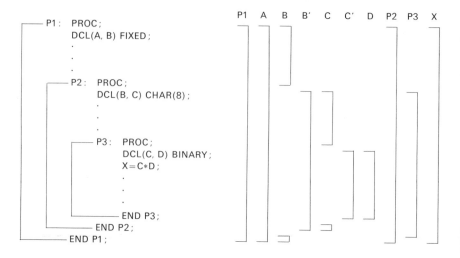

The lines to the right indicate the scope of the names : B and B' indicate the two distinct uses of the name B ; C and C' indicate the two uses of the name C.

Scope of Contextual Declaration

The scope of a contextual declaration is determined as if the declaration were made in a DECLARE statement immediately following the PROCEDURE statement of the *external* procedure in which the name appears.

It is important to understand that contextual declaration has the same effect as if the name were declared in the *external* procedure. This is the case even if the statement that causes the contextual declaration is internal to a block (called P3, for example) that is contained in the external procedure. Consequently, the name is known throughout the entire external procedure, except for any blocks in which the name is explicitly declared. It is as if block P3 has inherited the declaration from the containing external procedure.

Begin Blocks

We saw earlier how we could use a nested procedure block to limit the scope of a variable in the case of the DATE built-in function and the FIXED(3) variable also called DATE. A disadvantage to using the nested procedure is that it must be called in order to execute that block of coding; hence, extra statements are added to our program. Using a begin block would be more convenient, because this type of block is executed in the normal flow of a program. It does not have to be called or invoked as does a procedure block. We have seen, in the full language implementations of PL/I, how a begin block may follow an on-unit. For example :

```
ON ENDPAGE(SYSPRINT)BEGIN ;
                    PUT PAGE LIST('HEADING') ;
                    END ;
```

However, the real reason for using begin blocks is to limit the scope of a variable and to effect storage allocation. (In the above on-unit's begin block, dynamic storage will be allocated in the same manner as

AUTOMATIC storage for procedure blocks.) Figure 11.2 shows the segment of coding that limits the scope of the variable DATE—this time with a begin block. Notice that there is no CALL to the begin block, for it will automatically be executed in the normal flow of the program.

In the subset language, begin blocks may be nested within other procedure or begin blocks; however, begin blocks may not follow an on-unit.

A label may be prefixed to a BEGIN statement; it serves to identify the starting point of the block, but is not required. Begin blocks may only be nested within other begin blocks or other procedures; they may never be separately compiled as may a procedure block. Here is an example of nested begin blocks:

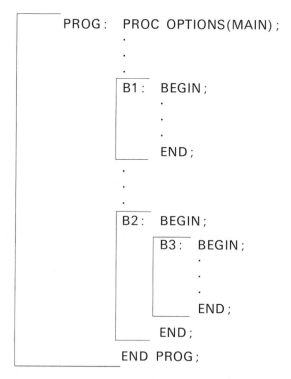

```
PROG:    PROC OPTIONS(MAIN) ;
             .
             .
             .
    B1 :   BEGIN ;
             .
             .
             .
           END ;
             .
             .
             .
    B2 :   BEGIN ;
        B3 :   BEGIN ;
                 .
                 .
                 .
               END ;
           END ;
         END PROG ;
```

A begin block is executed to the normal flow of a program just as a DO-group is executed in the normal flow of a program. Normally, control is passed to a begin block without reference to the name of that block. However, control can be transferred to a labeled BEGIN statement by

```
P1:      PROC OPTIONS(MAIN);
         DCL DATE FIXED(3), TODAY CHAR(6);
         DATE = 302;
            BEGIN;
            DCL DATE BUILTIN;
            TODAY = DATE; /* INVOKE DATE FUNCTION */
            END;
         JDATE = DATE; /* JDATE = 302 */
         PUT EDIT(SUBSTR(TODAY,3,2),'/',
                  SUBSTR(TODAY,5,2),'/',
                  SUBSTR(TODAY,1,2))(SKIP,5A);
                  /* OUTPUT IS MM/DD/YY */
         /* ... */
         /* ... */
         /* ... */
         END P1;
```

FIGURE 11.2   Limiting the scope of an identifier.

the execution of a GO TO. For example:

```
        .
        .
        .
   GO TO B2;
        .
        .
        .

        B2:   BEGIN;
              .
              .
              .
              END B2;
        .
        .
        .
```

Of course, begin blocks that follow on-units will be executed only when the on-unit condition is raised. Begin blocks are not essential to the construction of a PL/I program; however, there are times when it is advantageous to use begin blocks. These advantages include:

1. To limit the scope of an identifier
2. To effect storage allocation

The above two advantages also apply to procedure blocks; thus, the only other small advantage of begin blocks would be the elimination of the CALL or function reference that is required for procedure blocks.

Flow of Control

Figure 11.3 illustrates a logical flow of control for a procedure and a begin block. *Flow of control* refers to the sequence or path in which blocks may be executed. In this example, the B procedure is never executed because there is no CALL or function reference to it. Figure 11.4 illustrates how B may be executed by a CALL that appears within the begin block labeled C. The flow of control is depicted by the "arrowed" lines in this figure. Note that if a block is nested, it may be called or referenced only from the next outer block. Thus,

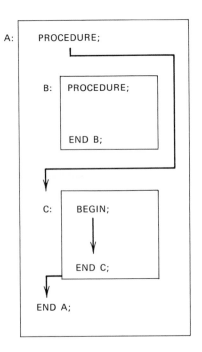

FIGURE 11.3   Simple flow of control.

the statement *CALL C*; in

```
A:   PROC;
     .
     .
     .
     CALL C;  /* ERROR */
        B:   BEGIN;
             .
             .
             .
             C:   PROC;
                  .
                  .
                  .
                  END C;
             END B;
     .
     .
     .
     END A;
```

is incorrectly placed, because C is not being invoked from the next outer block. To correct the above error, the CALL statement to invoke C should be placed within the begin block.

BASED Storage Class

The storage class of a variable determines the way in which the address of that variable is obtained. In STATIC storage, we saw that the address of an identifier is determined when the program is loaded into main storage for execution. For a variable of the AUTOMATIC storage class, the address is determined upon entry to a block. With

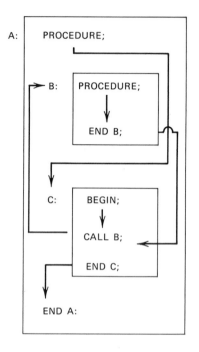

FIGURE 11.4 More complex flow of control.

BASED storage, the address is contained in a *pointer variable*. For example:

```
DCL P POINTER;
DCL A(100) FIXED BASED(P);
```

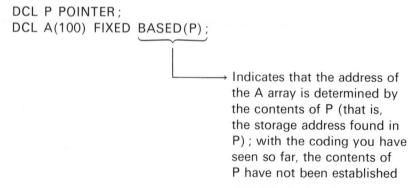

Indicates that the address of the A array is determined by the contents of P (that is, the storage address found in P); with the coding you have seen so far, the contents of P have not been established

The identifier P has been given the POINTER attribute, a new attribute, and one that has not been mentioned before in this book. A pointer variable is a special type of variable which you can use to locate data in storage; that is, to "point" to data in storage. Consequently, a pointer variable can be thought of as an *address*. Before a reference can be made to a based variable (the A array in the above example), a value must be given to the pointer (P, in this case) associated with it. This can be done in any of five ways:

1. By assignment of the value returned by the ADDR built-in function.
2. By assignment of the value of another pointer.
3. With the SET option of a READ statement.
4. With the SET option of a LOCATE statement.
5. By an ALLOCATE statement (not available in subset PL/I).

These five methods will be explained as the applications and advantages of BASED storage are illustrated.

Using BASED Variables Instead of the DEFINED Attribute

The DEFINED attribute allows you to overlay one storage area on another. For example:

        DCL A(100) FIXED BINARY(15);
        DCL B(50) FIXED BINARY(15) DEFINED A;

Both A and B reference the same storage area; thus, two different identifiers may be used to refer to the space in main storage. A restriction of the DEFINED attribute is that only identifiers of the same base, scale, and precision may be overlay defined. For example, if we would like to have a storage area contain a FIXED BINARY array at one time during the execution of our program and then contain a structure of various attributes at another time, this may not be accomplished through overlay defining. However, BASED storage will provide this flexibility. A *based variable* is a *description of data*—that is, a pattern for which no storage space is reserved but that will be overlaid on data in storage *pointed* to by an associated pointer variable. For example, let us declare a 100-element array with the following attributes:

        DCL A(100) FIXED BINARY;

Next, assume it is desired to "overlay define" on A an array of a different base, scale, and precision. The array is declared:

        DCL B(50) FLOAT DECIMAL BASED(P);

The address for the B array will be established by the pointer variable P.

Thus, it will be necessary to declare P as a pointer variable:

DCL P POINTER;

If B is to be in effect, "overlay defined" on A, we must set P equal to the address of the A array. This is done by a built-in function called ADDR.

P = ADDR(A);

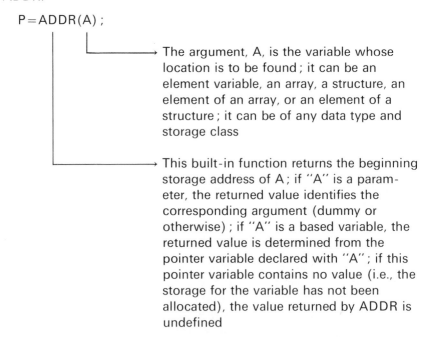

The argument, A, is the variable whose location is to be found; it can be an element variable, an array, a structure, an element of an array, or an element of a structure; it can be of any data type and storage class

This built-in function returns the beginning storage address of A; if "A" is a parameter, the returned value identifies the corresponding argument (dummy or otherwise); if "A" is a based variable, the returned value is determined from the pointer variable declared with "A"; if this pointer variable contains no value (i.e., the storage for the variable has not been allocated), the value returned by ADDR is undefined

The program in Figure 11.5 illustrates how a based variable may be used to simulate overlay defining. The purpose of this program is

```
1    BASED:  PROC OPTIONS(MAIN);
2            DCL (SUM1,A(100)) FIXED BINARY(31);
3            DCL B(50) FLOAT DECIMAL(6)BASED(P);
4            DCL P POINTER;
5            GET LIST(A);
6            SUM1 = SUM(A);
7            P = ADDR(A);
8            GET LIST(B);
9            SUM2 = SUM(B);
10           PUT LIST(SUM1,SUM2);
11           END;
```

FIGURE 11.5   Using based variables to simulate overlay defining

simply to find the sums of two arrays: one array has the attributes FIXED BINARY(31) and the other array has the attributes FLOAT DECIMAL(6). The larger of the two arrays is declared in statement 2. Statement 3 declares the smaller array and *bases* the address of the array on the larger array. Statement 4 declares P to have the POINTER attribute. Next, the data for the A array is read using list-directed input and the sum of the input data is found using the SUM built-in function. In statement 7, the address of A is assigned to the pointer variable, P. Now that the pointer address has been established, it is possible to read data into the B array. The B array occupies the same area of storage as the A array did; hence, as data is being input into B, the previous contents of A are being destroyed. Statement 9 finds the sum of the floating-point data in B, and statement 10 prints results.

Another method for establishing a pointer variable value is by assignment of the value of another pointer. For example:

```
DCL ARRAY(25);
DCL (P,Q) POINTER;  /* BOTH P AND Q ARE POINTERS */
P=ADDR(ARRAY); /* P CONTAINS THE ADDRESS OF ARRAY */
Q=P;  /* Q NOW CONTAINS THE ADDRESS OF ARRAY */
```

It is also possible to have more than one variable based on another variable. For example:

```
DCL PTR POINTER;
DCL 1 A,
      2 B PIC'9999',
      2 C FIXED(13,2),
      2 D CHAR(21);
DCL 1 W BASED(PTR),
      2 X FIXED BINARY,
      2 Y FLOAT DECIMAL,
      2 Z BIT(7);
DCL 1 I BASED(PTR),
      2 J,
      2 K;
PTR=ADDR(A);
```

Any reference to the W structure or the I structure elements points to the storage area occupied by A.

Using BASED Variables to Process Data in Buffers

When data values are input, the general flow is this:

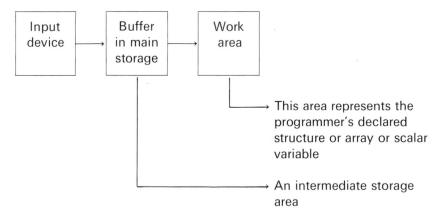

This area represents the programmer's declared structure or array or scalar variable

An intermediate storage area

This flow of data is termed *move mode,* because data is moved into program storage via a buffer. In the move mode, a READ statement causes a record to be transferred from external storage to the variable named in the INTO option (via an input buffer if a BUFFERED file is used); a WRITE or REWRITE statement causes a record to be transferred from the variable named in the FROM option to external storage (perhaps via an output buffer). The variables named in the INTO and FROM options can be of any storage class.

Figure 11.6 illustrates data flow for blocked records. Assume the following statements cause the reading and writing of these blocked records:

```
LOOP:   READ FILE(DISKIN) INTO(AREA);
          .
          .
          .
        WRITE FILE(DKOUT)FROM(AREA);
        GO TO LOOP;
```

The first time the READ statement is executed, a block is transmitted from the data set. DISKIN to an input buffer, and the first record in the block is assigned to the variable AREA; further executions of the READ statement assign successive records from the buffer to AREA. When the buffer is empty, the next READ statement causes a new block to be transmitted from the data set. The WRITE statement is

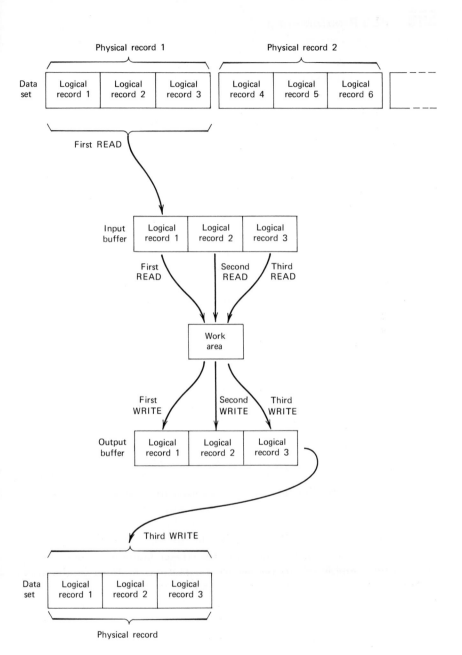

FIGURE 11.6 Input and output; move mode.

executed in a similar manner, building physical records in an output buffer and transmitting them to the data set associated with the file DKOUT each time the buffer is filled.

There is another processing mode which allows the programmer to process his data while it remains in a buffer (that is, without moving it into the storage area allocated to his program); this is termed the *locate mode*, because the execution of a data transmission statement merely identifies the location of the storage allocated to a record in the buffer. The locate mode is applicable only to BUFFERED SEQUENTIAL files. Which mode is used (locate or move) is determined by the data transmission statements and options coded by the programmer.

The processing of data in buffers slightly reduces execution time by avoiding an additional move of the record to another place in main storage (referred to above as *work area*).

Here is an example of how to declare a based variable and set the corresponding pointer to process data directly into the input buffer:

```
DCL P POINTER
DCL 1 IN_REC BASED(P),
      2 A PIC'99',
      2 B CHAR(8),
      2 C FIXED(7,2),
      2 REST_OF_RECORD CHAR(66) ;
READ FILE(TAPEIN) SET(P) ;
```

The READ statement causes a block of data to be read from the file named TAPEIN to an input buffer, if necessary, and then sets the pointer variable named in the SET option to point to the location in the buffer of the next record; the data in the record can then be processed by reference to the based variable (the structure called IN_REC) associated with the pointer variable. The record is available only until the execution of the next READ statement that refers to the same file.

Thus, it is the SET option of the READ statement that causes the pointer variable, P, to be *set* to the starting address of the next record in the internal buffer. When data is to be processed in an input buffer, improved throughput of data results if two input buffers are reserved. This is done in the file declaration statement. For example:

```
DCL TAPEIN FILE INPUT RECORD ENVIRONMENT
            (F(80)BUFFERS(2)MEDIUM(SYSIPT,2540)) ;
```

The use of based variables and pointers also allows you to read more than one type of record into the same buffer by using a different based variable to define each record format. For example:

```
DCL P POINTER;
DCL TAPE FILE INPUT RECORD ENVIRONMENT
    F(240,24)BUFFERS(2)MEDIUM(SYS005,2400));
DCL 1 ISSUES BASED(P),
      2 CODE CHAR(1),
      2 QTY PIC'(4)9',
      2 JOB_# PIC'(4)9',
      2 PART_# PIC'(7)9',
      2 DEPT PIC'99';
DCL 1 RECEIPTS BASED(P),
      2 CODE CHAR(1),
      2 QTY PIC'(4)9',
      2 UNUSED CHAR(6),
      2 PART_#'(7)9',
      2 SUPPLIER PIC'(6)9';
READ FILE(TAPE) SET(P);
IF ISSUES.CODE='1' THEN GO TO PROCESS_ISSUES;
IF ISSUES.CODE='2' THEN GO TO PROCESS_RECEIPTS;
```

Figure 11.7 illustrates locate mode input and move mode output for blocked records. In studying this figure, assume the following statements are coded:

```
             DCL AREA CHAR(104)BASED(P);
    LOOP:    READ FILE(TAPE) SET(P);
             .
             .
             .
             WRITE FILE(OUT) FROM(AREA);
             GO TO LOOP;
```

The first time the READ statement is executed, a block is read from the data set associated with the file TAPE to an input buffer, and the pointer variable P is set to point to the first record in the buffer; any reference to the variable AREA or to any other based variable qualified by the pointer P will then in effect be a reference to this first record. Further executions of the READ statement set the pointer variable P to point to succeeding records in the buffer. When the buffer is empty, the next READ statement causes a new block to be read from the data set.

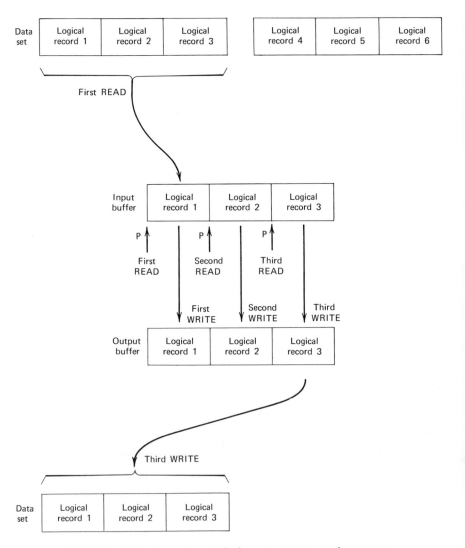

FIGURE 11.7   Locate mode input; move mode output.

Locate mode may be specified for output operations as well as input operations. Locate mode for output requires the use of based variables, the same as it does for input.

When writing from based variables in buffers, the WRITE statement is replaced with the LOCATE statement. In the following example, the pointer variable Q is set by the LOCATE statement :

LOCATE OUT FILE(TAPOUT)SET(Q) ;

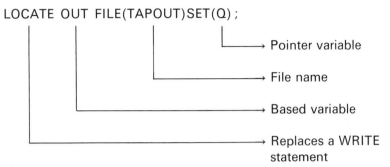

         → Pointer variable

         → File name

         → Based variable

         → Replaces a WRITE
statement

    By means of the LOCATE statement with the SET option, the structure of the based variable is superimposed on the data in the output buffer so that any reference to that allocation of the based variable is a reference to that data.

    In locate mode output, the following statements might be coded :

```
             DCL AREA CHAR(106) BASED(Q) ;
    LOOP:    READ FILE(TAPE) INTO (AREA) ;
             LOCATE AREA FILE(OUT) SET(Q) ;
                 .
                 .
                 .
             GO TO LOOP ;
```

In this example, each record is read into an input buffer and then moved to AREA (automatically by the READ statement). AREA represents the output buffer ; that is, it is a based variable that is effec-tively overlaid on the data in the output buffer.

    Each execution of the LOCATE statement reserves storage in an output buffer for a new allocation of the based variable AREA and sets the pointer variable Q to point to this storage. The first execution of the READ statement causes a block to be transmitted from the data set associated with the file TAPE to an input buffer, and the first record in the block to be assigned to the first allocation of AREA ; subsequent executions of the READ statement assign successive logical records to the current allocation of AREA. When the input buffer is empty, the next READ statement causes a new block to be transmitted from the data set. Each record is available for processing during the period between the execution of the READ statement and the next execution of the LOCATE statement. When no further space is available in the output buffer, the next execution of the LOCATE statement causes a block to be transmitted to the data set associated with the file OUT and a new buffer to be allocated.

It is doubtful whether the use of locate mode for both input and output would result in increased efficiency. Typically, the method would be to use move mode for input and locate mode for output or locate mode for input and move mode for output. Even though the LOCATE statement replaces a WRITE statement, the LOCATE statement will not appear in the same place as a WRITE statement might appear in a program. Figure 11.8 illustrates the placement of the LOCATE statement with respect to the READ statement and processing steps.

Locate mode frequently provides faster execution than move mode, because there is less movement of data. To illustrate the number of moves required for each of the four combinations of I/O operations illustrated in Figure 11.8, assume it is desired to perform a *copy* operation (that is, records in one file are to be copied onto another data set). This is one of the simplest forms of programming, because there is no processing of data.

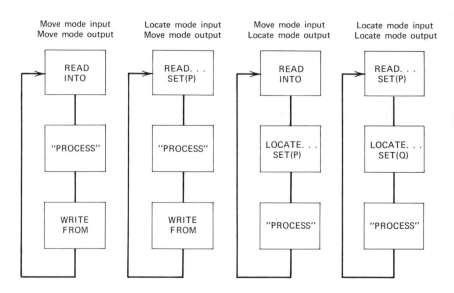

FIGURE 11.8   Move versus locate mode.

Move versus Locate Mode for Unblocked Records

In the case of unblocked records, a READ statement will cause the input of a physical record which consists of one logical record. Each subsequent READ statement causes the input of a new block or physical record. With unblocked records, this is also true for the WRITE and LOCATE statements.

A. Move Mode Input; Move Mode Output.   Given the program segment,

```
              DCL AREA CHAR(80) ;
     LOOP:    READ FILE(CARDIN)INTO(AREA) ;
              WRITE FILE(PRINTR)FROM(AREA) ;
              GO TO LOOP;
```

the operations would be as follows:

1. Read data into input buffer.
2. Move input buffer data to AREA.
3. Move data from AREA to the output buffer.
4. Write data from output buffer.

B. Locate Mode Input; Move Mode Output.   Given the program segment,

```
              DCL AREA CHAR(80) BASED(P) ;
     LOOP:    READ FILE(CARDIN)SET(P) ;
              WRITE FILE(PRINTR)FROM(AREA) ;
              GO TO LOOP;
```

the steps taken would be as follows:

1. Read data into input buffer.
2. Move data from the input buffer to the output buffer associated with the PRINTR file.
3. Write data from the output buffer.

C. Move Mode Input; Locate Mode Output.   Given the program segment,

```
              DCL A1 CHAR(80), A2 CHAR(80)BASED(P) ;
     LOOP:    READ FILE(CARDIN) INTO(A1) ;
              LOCATE A2 FILE(PRINTR)SET(P) ;
              A2=A1 ;
              GO TO LOOP;
```

the steps taken include:

1. Read data into input buffer.
2. Move data from input buffer to A1.
3. Move data from A1 to output buffer (via the assignment statement).
4. Write data from the output buffer.

D. Locate Mode Input; Locate Mode Output. Given the program segment,

```
        DCL A1 CHAR(80)BASED(P);
        DCL A2 CHAR(80)BASED(Q);
LOOP:   READ FILE(CARDIN)SET(P);
        LOCATE A2 FILE(PRINTR)SET(Q);
        A2=A1;
        GO TO LOOP;
```

the steps taken would include:

1. Read data into the input buffer.
2. Move input buffer to the output buffer (A1 → A2).
3. Write data from the output buffer.

Thus, we see that items B and D above require the least amount of move operations. Note that in item D, however, the programmer must include the assignment statement that specifies the move from one buffer to another, whereas in item B, there is no move *explicitly* coded by the programmer.

There is no way in PL/I to read and write from the same buffer, because a separate buffer is automatically reserved for each default or explicitly declared file.

Move versus Locate Mode for Blocked Records

In the case of blocked records, a READ statement will cause the input of a physical record which will consist of two or more logical records. Thus, the execution of subsequent READ statements will not cause the input of a new physical record as long as there are logical records in the block to be processed. With blocked records this is also true for the WRITE and LOCATE statements.

A.   **Move Mode Input ; Move Mode Output.**   Given the program

```
            DCL AREA CHAR(80) ;
LOOP:   READ FILE(INPUT)INTO(AREA) ;
            WRITE FILE(OUTPUT)FROM(AREA) ;
            GO TO LOOP;
```

the execution of the READ statement would cause a logical record to be moved from the input buffer to the work area named AREA. If this logical record were the last one in the input buffer, a request would be made to fill the buffer with a new block of logical records. The execution of the WRITE statement would cause the data in the work area named AREA to be moved into the next position of the output buffer. If this data causes the output buffer to be filled, then a request will be made to write the physical block and to provide a new empty output buffer.

B.   **Locate Mode Input; Move Mode Output.**   Given the program segment,

```
            DCL AREA CHAR(80) BASED(P) ;
LOOP:   READ FILE(INPUT)SET(P) ;
            WRITE FILE(OUTPUT)FROM(AREA) ;
            GO TO LOOP;
```

the execution of the READ statement will cause the *address* of the next logical record in the input buffer area to be stored in the pointer variable, P. No move of data takes place, but the data in the logical record can be referenced by the variable AREA which is based on P. The execution of the WRITE statement will cause the data in AREA to be moved into the next position of the output buffer. Because AREA is based on the pointer P and P currently contains the address of a logical record within the input buffer for file INPUT, the effect of this WRITE statement is to move data directly from the input buffer to the output buffer without passing through an intermediate work area.

C.   **Move Mode Input; Locate Mode Output.**   Given the program segment,

```
            DCL A1 CHAR(80), A2 CHAR(80)BASED(P) ;
LOOP:   READ FILE(INPUT)INTO(A1) ;
            LOCATE A2 FILE(OUTPUT)SET(P) ;
            A2=A1 ;
            GO TO LOOP;
```

the execution of the READ statement would cause a logical record to be moved from the input buffer to the work area named A1. The execution of the LOCATE statement causes the pointer variable P to be set to the next position of the output buffer associated with file OUTPUT. Because A2 is based on the pointer P and P currently contains the address of a logical record in the output buffer, the assignment statement

$$A2 = A1 ;$$

causes data to be moved from the work area (A1) to the output buffer. When the output buffer is full or the OUTPUT file is closed, there is a request to write the physical block and provide a new empty output buffer.

D. Locate Mode Input; Locate Mode Output.   Given the program segment,

```
         DCL A1 CHAR(80)BASED(P) ;
         DCL A2 CHAR(80)BASED(Q) ;
LOOP:    READ FILE(INPUT)SET(P) ;
         LOCATE A2 FILE(OUTPUT)SET(Q) ;
         A2 = A1 ;
         GO TO LOOP;
```

the execution of the READ statement will cause the *address* of the next logical record within the input buffer area to be stored in the pointer variable P. No move of data takes place, but the data in the logical record can be referenced by the variable A1, which is based on P. The execution of the LOCATE statement causes the pointer Q to be set to the next position of the output buffer associated with file OUTPUT. Because A2 is based on the pointer Q and Q currently contains the address of a logical record in the output buffer, the assignment statement

$$A2 = A1 ;$$

causes data to be moved from the input buffer to the output buffer. When the output buffer is full or the file is closed, the physical block is written.

Locate mode can provide faster execution than move mode, because there is less movement of data. Less storage may be required, because work areas are eliminated. But locate mode must be used carefully; in particular, the programmer must be aware of how his data will be aligned in the buffer and how structured data will be mapped. (You may wish to consult the appropriate PL/I programmer's guide for a discussion of structure mapping.) You should be aware that boundary alignment problems could arise (hence, your program "blows up") with blocked records that contain FIXED BINARY, FLOAT BINARY, or FLOAT DECIMAL data where the record size is not divisible by 4 (or 8 if long-form floating-point is being used). Move mode may be simpler to use than locate mode, because there are no buffer alignment problems in move mode. Furthermore, move mode can result in faster execution where there are numerous references to the contents of the same record, because of the overhead incurred by the indirect addressing technique used in locate mode.

BASED storage is the most powerful of the PL/I storage classes, but it must be used carefully; many of the safeguards against error that are provided for other storage classes cannot be provided for in BASED storage.

Figure 11.9 shows a file copy program using locate mode I/O.

In the subset language, the LOCATE statement must always be coded with the SET option. However, in the full language implementations, it is optional to explicitly specify the SET option. For example, the statement

LOCATE OUT FILE(TAPOUT) ;

when executed, causes the pointer associated with the data area called OUT to be set. In other words, because a pointer variable appears in a

```
      /***** A FILE COPY PROGRAM USING LOCATE MODE RECORD I/O *****/
 1    LOCATE: PROC OPTIONS (MAIN);
 2         DCL INFILE FILE RECORD INPUT SEQUENTIAL BUFFERED
                  ENV(F(80) CONSECUTIVE BUFFERS(2) MEDIUM(SYS004,2400)),
              OTFILE FILE RECORD OUTPUT SEQUENTIAL BUFFERED
                  ENV(F(80) CONSECUTIVE BUFFERS(2) MEDIUM(SYS005,2400)),
              (IN_POINTER,OUT_POINTER) POINTER,
              1 IN_RECORD BASED (IN_POINTER),
                2 FIELD_1 CHAR (10),
                2 FIELD_2 CHAR (70),
              1 OUT_RECORD BASED (OUT_POINTER),
                2 FIELD_1 CHAR (10),
                2 FIELD_2 CHAR (70);
 3        ON ENDFILE (INFILE) GO TO END_OF_PROGRAM;
 4        OPEN FILE (INFILE), FILE (OTFILE);
 5    READ_A_RECORD:
          READ FILE (INFILE) SET (IN_POINTER);
 6        LOCATE OUT_RECORD FILE (OTFILE)  SET (OUT_POINTER);
 7        OUT_RECORD = IN_RECORD;
 8        GO TO READ_A_RECORD;
 9    END_OF_PROGRAM:
          CLOSE FILE (INFILE), FILE (OTFILE);
10        END LOCATE;
```

FIGURE 11.9   Locate mode I/O program example.

DECLARE statement, i.e.,

DCL OUT BASED(Q);

the pointer Q will be *set* when the LOCATE statement without the SET option is executed.

Also, it is a restriction in the subset language that all pointer variables must be explicitly declared. For example:

DCL Q POINTER;

However, in the full language, it is not necessary to explicitly declare pointer variables to have the POINTER attribute. This is because they will be recognized contextually by the compiler. For example:

DCL OUT BASED(Q);

⎣───────→ By context, Q could only be a
pointer variable

	Locate mode allowed for indexed data sets
Subset language	No
Full language	Yes

CONTROLLED Storage

This is the fourth storage class in PL/I. It is not available in the subset language. CONTROLLED storage is similar to BASED storage in that the programmer has a greater degree of control in the allocation of storage than he does for STATIC or AUTOMATIC storage classes. In the full language implementations of PL/I, variables may be declared to have the CONTROLLED attribute in the following manner:

DCL A(100)INIT((100)0) CONTROLLED;

The storage for A in the above example will be allocated by the ALLOCATE statement and freed by the FREE statement. For example:

```
DCL A(100)INIT((100)0) CONTROLLED;
DCL B(100);
.
.
.

ALLOCATE A;
B=A;
FREE A;
.
.
.
```

A variable that has the CONTROLLED attribute is allocated upon the execution of an ALLOCATE statement specifying that variable. This allocation remains in effect even after termination of the block in which it is allocated. Storage remains allocated for a controlled variable until the execution of a FREE statement in which the variable is specified.

There are several built-in functions that are useful when working with controlled storage. These functions, which are available in the full language implementations of PL/I, are explained below, and their applications are illustrated.

ALLOCATION Built-in Function

This function determines whether or not storage is allocated for a given controlled variable and returns an appropriate indication to the point of invocation. For example:

J=ALLOCATION(X);

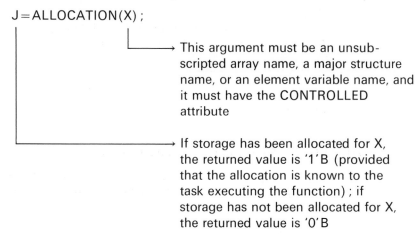

This argument must be an unsubscripted array name, a major structure name, or an element variable name, and it must have the CONTROLLED attribute

If storage has been allocated for X, the returned value is '1'B (provided that the allocation is known to the task executing the function); if storage has not been allocated for X, the returned value is '0'B

The following example shows two procedures, P1 and P2, nested within P; P1 allocates the controlled variable called D, and P2 frees D. Assume that another external procedure, Q, is part of the main program along with P. In P1, storage is allocated for D. Because Q may be entered without P1 having been executed first, Q must determine if it is necessary to allocate D before referencing the variable. The ALLO-CATION built-in function is invoked in the IF statement to determine the status of the controlled variable, B.

```
P:     PROC;
       DCL A EXTERNAL;
       CALL P1;
       CALL P2;
P1:    PROC;
       DCL D EXTERNAL CONTROLLED;
       ALLOCATE D;
         .
         .
         .
       END P1;
P2:    PROC;
       DCL D EXTERNAL CONTROLLED;
         .
         .
         .
       FREE D;
       END P2;
       END P;
Q:     PROC;
       DCL A EXTERNAL, D EXTERNAL CONTROLLED;
       IF ALLOCATION(D) = '0'B THEN ALLOCATE D;
         .
         .
         .
       END Q;
```

LBOUND Array Manipulation Built-in Function

This function finds the current lower bound for a specified dimension of a given array and returns it to the point of invocation. For example :

I = LBOUND(X,N) ;

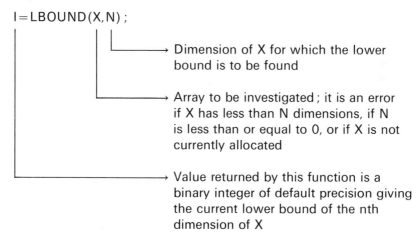

→ Dimension of X for which the lower bound is to be found

→ Array to be investigated ; it is an error if X has less than N dimensions, if N is less than or equal to 0, or if X is not currently allocated

→ Value returned by this function is a binary integer of default precision giving the current lower bound of the nth dimension of X

This function is available only in the full language implementations of PL/I.

HBOUND Array Manipulation Built-in Function

This function finds the current upper bound for a specified dimension of a given array and returns it to the point of invocation. For example :

I = HBOUND(X,N) ;

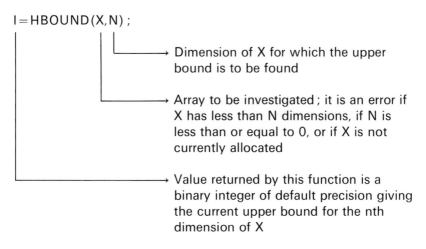

→ Dimension of X for which the upper bound is to be found

→ Array to be investigated ; it is an error if X has less than N dimensions, if N is less than or equal to 0, or if X is not currently allocated

→ Value returned by this function is a binary integer of default precision giving the current upper bound for the nth dimension of X

This function is only available in the full language implementations of PL/I.

The two external procedures shown in Figure 11.10 illustrate a use for LBOUND and HBOUND functions. Following is an explanation of the CONTR procedure.

Statement 2. In this statement, A, B, and C are declared to be CONTROLLED arrays whose bounds will be specified later in the ALLOCATE statement. This statement illustrates one more use of the asterisk notation. The asterisks for bounds indicate that the bounds that are specified by the ALLOCATE statement should be used. Here, A and B are two-dimensional arrays, and C is a one-dimensional array.

Statement 3. The variables I and J are assigned values through this input statement.

Statement 4. The A and B arrays are allocated with the bounds just read in.

Statement 5. The data for A and B are input. The array bounds are, of course, known now so that the correct number of elements can be read into each array.

```
1    CONTR:   PROC OPTIONS(MAIN);
2             DCL (A(*,*),B(*,*),C(*))CONTROLLED;
3             GET LIST(I,J);
4             ALLOCATE A(I,J),B(I,J);
5             GET LIST(A,B);
6             CALL ADDAR(A,B,C);
7             PUT LIST(C);
8             END;


1    ADDAR:   PROC(R,S,T);
2             DCL (R(*,*),S(*,*),T(*)) CONTROLLED;
3             ALLOCATE T(LBOUND(R,1):HBOUND(R,1));
4    L1:      DO K = LBOUND(R,1) TO HBOUND(R,1);
5             T(K)=0;
6    L2:      DO J = LBOUND(R,2) TO HBOUND(R,2);
7             T(K) =R(K,J) + S(K,J) +T(K);
8             END L2;
9             END L1;
10            FREE R,S;
11            END;
```

FIGURE 11.10 CONTROLLED storage with array bounds determined dynamically.

Statement 6. The ADDAR procedure is invoked; C will contain the sum of elements of corresponding rows of A and B. For example:

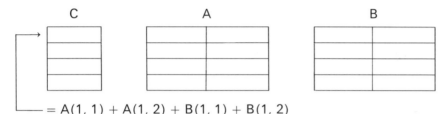

$$= A(1, 1) + A(1, 2) + B(1, 1) + B(1, 2)$$

Note that C can be passed as an argument, although it has not yet been allocated.

Statement 7. Here, C is written out, element-by-element.

Following is an explanation of the ADDAR procedure also shown in Figure 11.10.

Statement 1. In this statement, R, S, and T are the parameters of ADDAR.

Statement 2. The asterisks for bounds indicate that the bounds these arguments have at the time the procedure is called should be used. For T, still not allocated, bound specification is being delayed until allocation in this procedure.

Statement 3. Here T is finally allocated; T is a one-dimensional array whose bounds are the same as R. The LBOUND and HBOUND functions are invoked in the ALLOCATE statement as a means of determining the lower and upper bounds of T.

Statement 4. The outer DO is set up; it establishes the beginning and ending rows of the arrays to be summed.

Statement 6. The inner DO is written to find the sum of the elements of the columns of a given row in a two-dimensional array.

Statement 7. The sum is calculated.

Statements 8–9. The DO-groups are ended.

Statement 10. Because the R and S arrays are no longer needed by the program, their storage areas may be freed.

Statement 11. This statement causes a return to the calling program —in this case, CONTR.

DIM Array Manipulation Built-in Function

This function finds the current extent for a specified dimension of a given array and returns it to the point of invocation. For example:

$I = DIM(X, N)$;

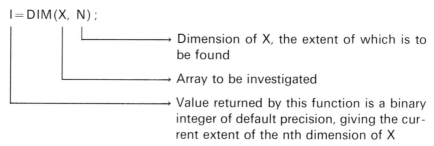

→ Dimension of X, the extent of which is to be found

→ Array to be investigated

→ Value returned by this function is a binary integer of default precision, giving the current extent of the nth dimension of X

This function is available only in the full language implementations of PL/I.

Case Study

This chapter has dealt with a number of important topics—storage classes, flow of control, scope of identifiers, and PL/I block structure. The programs in Figures 11.11 and 11.12 illustrate all of these topics,

```
 1    A:      PROC OPTIONS(MAIN);
 2            DCL E ENTRY;
 3            DCL DATA CHAR(5) EXTERNAL;
 4            DATA = 'ALPHA';
 5            PUT EDIT('A:',DATA)(A,COLUMN(5),A);
 6    B:        PROCEDURE;
 7              DCL DATA BIT(8);
 8              DATA = '11000001'B;
 9              PUT EDIT('B:',DATA)(SKIP,A,COLUMN(5),B);
10              CALL C;
11    C:          PROCEDURE;
12                PUT EDIT('C:',DATA)(SKIP,A,COLUMN(5),B);
13                END C;
14            END B;
15            CALL B;
16    D:      BEGIN;
17              PUT EDIT('D:',DATA)(SKIP,A,COLUMN(5),A);
18            END D;
19            CALL E;
20            END A;
```

FIGURE 11.11   Case study: An external procedure with nested blocks to illustrate scope of an identifier.

```
1    F:        PROCEDURE;
2              DCL DATA CHAR(5) EXTERNAL;
3              PUT EDIT('E:',DATA)(SKIP,A,COLUMN(5),A);
4              END E;
```

FIGURE 11.12   Case study: An external procedure to be
linked to external procedure A in Figute 11.11.

although BASED and CONTROLLED storage classes are not employed.
The programs together consist of five blocks named A, B, C, D, and E:
A and E are external procedures; B and C are internal procedure
blocks with B nested within A, and C nested within B; D is a begin
block internal to A. The problem is coded such that the blocks will be
activated in the sequence A, B, C, D, and E. Because one of the purposes
of using nested blocks is to limit the scope of identifiers, this function
is illustrated in the following way:

1. In procedure A, an EXTERNAL variable called DATA is declared
    to be a character-string initialized to the constant 'ALPHA'. The
    procedure's name and the value of DATA is then printed using a
    PUT EDIT statement. DATA, because it has the EXTERNAL
    attribute, will be of the STATIC storage class.
2. In procedure B, a variable named DATA is declared to be a bit-
    string. Thus, DATA in this procedure is different from DATA in
    the A procedure. The scope of the identifier, DATA, is being
    limited to the B and C procedures. This identifier is of the
    AUTOMATIC storage class.
3. In procedure C, there are no data declarations. However, the
    variable called DATA—which was declared in procedure B—
    will be printed. The output value will be the bit-string declared
    in B. Notice that for C to be called, only the B procedure could
    contain the CALL statement. It would be invalid to call a nested
    procedure from any block except the most immediate block in
    which the nested procedure is contained.
4. The begin block, D, is on the same *block level* as the B procedure.
    Thus, the reference to DATA in the begin block is a reference
    to the DATA that was declared in the A procedure.
5. The E procedure is a separate compilation (see Figure 11.12).
    This procedure picks up the value of DATA from the A procedure,
    because DATA was declared to have the EXTERNAL attribute in
    both procedures.

Figure 11.13 shows the output from this program.

```
A:   ALPHA
B:   11000001
C:   11000001
D:   AL PHA
E:   AL P HA
```

**FIGURE 11.13
Output from
case study
program.**

SUMMARY

Procedure Blocks: A PL/I program consists of one or more procedures, each of which may contain other procedures and/or begin blocks. If a procedure is nested within another procedure or begin block, then it is called an internal procedure. If a procedure is compiled separately, it is called an external procedure. Procedures are not executed in the normal flow of a program as are begin blocks, but rather, they are executed by a subroutine CALL or function reference.

Begin Blocks: In the full language implementations of PL/I, begin blocks may follow an on-unit. In either implementation, they may be nested within a procedure block or other begin block. A begin block is executed in the normal flow of a program. Normally, control is passed to a begin block without reference to the name of that block. Begin blocks are not essential to the construction of a PL/I program; however, they are useful in limiting the scope of an identifier and facilitate programming responses to on-unit conditions that may be raised. Begin blocks are always internal blocks.

Storage Classes: When a location in main storage has been associated with a data name, the storage is said to be allocated. In PL/I, we have the facility to allocate main storage at different times. The time at which storage is to be allocated depends on the storage class of the data. There are four storage classes:

1. *AUTOMATIC storage:* Unless declared to have another storage class, all variables will have the AUTOMATIC attribute. The fact that certain variables are used in one procedure of a program and not in others makes it possible to allocate the same storage space at different times to different variables. When storage is allocated dynamically, it is allocated during the execution of a procedure. Storage remains allocated as long as the block in which it was allocated remains active. When a block is

activated and deactivated, the contents of its data areas may be lost. This is because an intervening block may be executed and its data area will be allocated to the area where the first block's data once resided. The dynamic allocation of storage applies to begin blocks as well as procedure blocks. This dynamic allocation of main storage is one of the outstanding features of PL/I, because it provides for efficient use of main storage. Total storage requirements of a program may be reduced because of this automatic data overlay feature. The programmer does not have to code extra instructions or steps to cause this allocation to take place. It is done for him automatically. All the programmer needs to do is to be aware of how and when storage is allocated.

(a) *Prologue:* The allocation of dynamic storage is performed by a routine called a prologue. This routine is set up by the compiler and attached to the beginning of each block. It is always executed as the first step of a block.

(b) *Epilogue:* The release of main storage that has been allocated to AUTOMATIC variables is handled by a routine called an epilogue. The epilogue routine is logically appended to the end of each block and is executed as the final step before the termination of the block.

2. *STATIC storage:* Whenever the value of a variable must be saved between different invocations of the same procedures, storage for that variable has to be allocated statically. In this case, storage is allocated before execution of the program and remains allocated throughout the entire duration of the program. Typically, a program will have both STATIC and AUTOMATIC storage areas. Program constants and variables declared with the EXTERNAL attribute have the STATIC storage class attribute. Variables, whether main storage space is allocated to them dynamically or statically, may be given initial values at the time of storage allocation. You can save program overhead by declaring variables that are to be initialized to have the STATIC attribute. STATIC variables are initialized only once before execution of a program begins. AUTOMATIC variables are reinitialized at each activation of the declaring block.

3. *BASED storage:* The storage class of a variable determines the way in which the address of that variable is obtained. With BASED storage, the address is contained in a pointer variable. A pointer variable can be thought of as an address. Before a reference can be made to a based variable, a value must be given to the pointer associated with it. This can be done in any of five ways:

(a) By assignment of the value returned by the ADDR built-in function.

(b) By assignment of the value of another pointer.

(c) With the SET option of a READ statement.

(d) With the SET option of a LOCATE statement.

(e) By an ALLOCATE statement (not available in subset PL/I).

A based variable is a description of data—that is, a pattern for which no storage is reserved but which will be overlaid on data in storage pointed to by an associated pointer variable. Thus, based storage may be used to simulate overlay defining. Based variables may also be used to process data in buffers. This processing of data while it remains in a buffer is termed the locate mode. The processing of data in buffers slightly reduces execution time by avoiding an additional move of the record to a work area. It is the SET option of the READ statement that causes the pointer variable, P, to be set to the starting address of the next record in the internal buffer. When data is to be processed in an input buffer, improved throughput of data results if two input buffers are reserved. The use of based variables and pointers allows you to read more than one type of record into the same buffer by using a different based variable to define each record format.

4. *CONTROLLED storage:* A variable that has the CONTROLLED attribute is allocated upon the execution of an ALLOCATE statement specifying that variable. Storage remains allocated for that variable until the execution of a FREE statement in which the variable is specified. There are several built-in functions that are useful when working with CONTROLLED storage.

(a) *ALLOCATION built-in function:* This function determines whether or not storage is allocated for a given controlled variable and returns an appropriate indication to the point of invocation.

(b) *LBOUND array manipulation built-in function:* This function finds the current lower bound for a specified dimension of a given array and returns it to the point of invocation.

(c) *HBOUND array manipulation built-in function:* This function finds the current upper bound for a specified dimension of a given array and returns it to the point of invocation.

(d) *DIM array manipulation built-in function:* This function finds the current extent for a specified dimension of a given array and returns it to the point of invocation.

CONTROLLED storage is not available in the subset language.

Scope of Identifiers: An identifier may have only one meaning at any point in time; e.g., the same name cannot be used for both a file and a floating-point variable. It is not necessary, however, for a name to have the same meaning throughout a program. In some instances, the use of nested blocks to limit or redefine the scope of a variable provides an ease of programming not usually available in other computer languages.

1. *Scope of an explicit declaration:* The scope of an explicit declaration of a name is that block to which the declaration is internal, including all nested blocks except those blocks to which another explicit declaration of the same identifier is internal.

2. *Scope of a contextual declaration:* The scope of a contextual declaration is determined as if the declaration were made in a DECLARE statement immediately following the PROCEDURE statement of the external procedure in which the name appears.

Groups and Blocks Contrasted: Groups and blocks are terms used to refer to sets of statements in a program. Sets of statements are grouped together to provide flexibility and to facilitate control of storage allocation. Their features are summarized in Figure 11.14.

	Block nesting	Maximum number blocks in compilation
Subset language	3	63
Full language	50	255

CHECKPOINT QUESTIONS

1. What is a *block* in PL/I? What are the two types?
2. In the subset implementations, may begin blocks follow an on-unit?
3. How is a begin block executed?
4. Distinguish between *external* and *internal* procedure blocks.
5. What is *flow of control*?
6. Why are there different *storage classes* in PL/I?
7. Unless declared to have another storage class, what storage class will variables have?
8. What is *dynamic storage allocation*?
9. What functions do the *prologue* and *epilogue* routines perform?
10. Storage that is allocated before execution of the program and remains allocated throughout the entire execution of the program is called

    _____.
11. Why use BASED storage?
12. How may a value be assigned to a pointer used to reference a based variable?

	DO ... END	BEGIN ... END	PROCEDURE ... END
Activation	A DO-group is activated by normal sequential program flow	A begin block is activated by normal sequential program flow	A procedure block is activated remotely by CALL statements or function references
Scope (area in which an identifier is known)	Does not limit the scope of identifiers	Limits the scope of identifiers	Limits the scope of identifiers
Labels	The label(s) on DO statements is optional	The label(s) on begin blocks is optional	The PROCEDURE statement must have label(s) for referencing the primary entry point
Argument handling	The DO statement does not have the mechanism for argument handling or return	The begin block does not have the mechanism for argument handling or return	The PROCEDURE statement has the facilities of argument handling and return
Logical ending	Every DO-group *logically* ends with an END statement	Every begin block *can* *logically* end with an END statement	Every PROCEDURE must logically end with either a RETURN, STOP, EXIT, GO TO, or END statement
Physical ending	Must *physically* end with END	Must physically end with END	Must physically end with END
Prologue	No	Yes	Yes

FIGURE 11.14 Groups and blocks compared.

13. In programming, what is a *buffer*?
14. What does the term *work area* refer to?
15. What is *locate mode*?
16. When is a variable that has the CONTROLLED attribute allocated?
17. What does the ALLOCATION built-in function accomplish?
18. What is the *scope* of an identifier that is *explicitly* declared?
    What is the *scope* of an identifier that is *contextually* declared?
19. (True or False)   Based variables direct the compiler to reserve storage for them.

TERMS TO STUDY

activate	internal procedure
allocate	locate mode
block	move mode
dynamic storage allocation	prologue
epilogue	scope of the declaration work area
external procedure	
flow of control	

PRACTICE PROBLEMS

1. Modify Existing Program to Implement Locate Mode

Problem Statement: Take any program you have coded using record I/O (e.g., any practice problem at the end of Chapter 8) and modify it so that it will execute using locate mode input and move mode output. Compare main storage requirements and execution time between the modified and the unmodified record I/O program.

2. Modifying Existing Program to Implement STATIC Attribute

Problem Statement: Take Problem 1 of Chapter 2, and modify the declared variables so that they will have the STATIC attribute rather than the AUTOMATIC attribute. Run the program and compare main storage requirements between the modified and unmodified programs.

3. Nested Procedures

Problem Statement: Take Case Study Two in Chapter 9, and modify it in the following ways:

(a)   Implement locate mode I/O for the tape files.

(b)   Make the "exception routine" (labeled PRINT_EXCPTN) a nested procedure block.

(c)   Declare all variables that are to have initial values (e.g., HDNG, PREV_SS_#, TP_ENDED, CD_ENDED, EXCPTN) to have the STATIC attribute.

Appendices

appendix A

Keywords Available in
Various PL/I Compilers

Keyword	Abbreviation	PL/C	Model 20	PL/I D	PL/I F	DOS PL/I optimizer	OS PL/I optimizer	PL/I checkout
A(w)		x	x	x	x	x	x	x
ABS(x)		x	x	x	x	x	x	x
ACOS(x)						x	x	x
%ACTIVATE	%ACT					x	x	x	x
ADD(x,y,p[,q])		x		x	x	x	x	x
ADDBUFF(n)				x		x	x	x
ADDR(x)			x	x	x	x	x	x
ALIGNED		x		x	x	x	x	x
ALL(x)		x		x	x	x	x	x
ALL		x					x	x
ALLOCATE		*			x	x	x	x

618

Use of keyword	Examples and other information
Format item	DCL STR CHAR(20); PUT EDIT(STR) (A(22)); Places the contents of STR in a field of length 22 in output stream
Built-in function	X = ABS (5 − Y/2); Calculates the absolute value of 5 − Y/2 and places it in X
Built-in function	A = ACOS (Z**F); Returns the angle in radians whose cosine is Z ** F
Preprocessor statement	%LOOK : ACTIVATE X,Y; Makes explicitly deactivated compile-time identifiers replaceable
Built-in function	SUM = ADD (A,B,7,3); Equivalent to A + B in a field of seven digits, three of which are fractional
Option of ENVIRONMENT attribute	DCL F FILE ENV(ADDBUFF(3000)); Used to allocate additional workspace for DIRECT indexed files
Built-in function	P = ADDR(A); Returns a pointer which identifies the location of the named variable
Attribute	DCL 1 BOY ALIGNED, . . . Specifies that each variable to start at implementation boundary
Built-in function	B = ALL(TABLE); Each item in TABLE is converted to bit-string and logically ANDed bit-by-bit
Option of PUT statement	PUT ALL; Debugging facility; places values of all variables on SYSPRINT file
Option of DEFAULT statement	DEFAULT ALL SYSTEM; All variables are subject to DEFAULT specifications
Statement	ALLOCATE A,B,C; Allocates storage for controlled or based variables

Note: x = feature available; * = feature planned but not implemented at time of publication of this text; blank = feature not available.

Keyword	Abbreviation	PL/C	Model 20	PL/I D	PL/I F	DOS PL/I optimizer	OS PL/I optimizer	PL/I checkout
ALLOCATION(x)					x	x	x	x
ALTTAPE			x					
ANY(x)		x		x	x	x	x	x
AREA					x	x	x	x
AREA[(size)]		*			x	x	x	x
ARGn						x	x	x
ASIN(x)						x	x	x
ATAN(x[,y])		x	x	x	x	x	x	x
ATAND(x[,y])		x		x	x	x	x	x
ATANH(x)		x		x	x	x	x	x

Use of keyword	Examples and other information
Built-in function	PL/I F Returns '1'B if CTL argument is allocated, '0'B if not; IF ALLOCATION(X) THEN . . . Optimizers Return the number of generations of CTL variables allocated
Option of ENVIRONMENT attribute	DCL F FILE ENV(ALTTAPE); Indicates that an alternate tape drive can be assigned for multivolume tape files
Built-in function	D = ANY(TABLE); Each item in TABLE is converted to bit-string and logically ORd bit-by-bit
Condition	ON AREA BEGIN; Specifies on-unit when the request for allocation in an area exceeds available storage
Attribute	DCL A AREA(1000); Specifies that A is to be an area of storage 1000 bytes in length available for allocation of based variables
Option of NOMAP, NOMAPIN, and NOMAPOUT options of the OPTIONS attribute	DCL COBA OPTIONS(COBOL NOMAP(ARG1)); Used in interlanguage communication to specify which arguments are to be transformed
Built-in function	A = ASIN(Z**F); Returns the angle in radians whose sine is $Z ** F$
Built-in function	A = ATAN(Z**F); Returns the angle in radians whose tangent is $Z ** F$ A = ATAN(Z, F); Returns ATAN(Z/F)
Built-in function	A = ATAND(Z**F); Returns the angle in degrees whose tangent is $Z ** F$ A = ATAND(Z, F); Returns ATAND(Z/F)
Built-in function	A = ATANH(Z**Q); Returns hyperbolic arctangent of $Z ** Q$; if $ABS(x) > 1$ error will result

Note: x = feature available; * = feature planned but not implemented at time of publication
of this text; blank = feature not available.

Keyword	Abbreviation	PL/C	Model 20	PL/I D	PL/I F	DOS PL/I optimizer	OS PL/I optimizer	PL/I checkout
AUTOMATIC	AUTO (not allowed in subset)	x	x	x	x	x	x	x
B[(x)]		x		x	x	x	x	x
BACKWARDS			x	x	x	x	x	x
BASED[(locator-expression)]		*	x	x	x	x	x	x
BEGIN		x		x	x	x	x	x
BINARY	BIN (not allowed in subset)	x		x	x	x	x	x
BINARY(x[,p[,q]])	BIN	x		x	x	x	x	x
BIT[(length)]		x		x	x	x	x	x
BIT(expression[size])		x		x	x	x	x	x
BLKSIZE(expression)						x	x	x
BOOL(x, y, z)		x		x	x	x	x	x

Use of keyword	Examples and other information
Attribute	DCL VAR AUTOMATIC; Specifies that storage for VAR is to be allocated upon entry to the block and released upon leaving the block
Format item	PUT EDIT(A)(B(10)); Specifies that A is to be placed in the output stream in a field 10 characters wide as at bit value
Attribute	DCL F FILE BACKWARDS; Specifies that file F is to be read backwards; valid for magnetic tape files only
Attribute	DCL A BASED, B BASED(P); Specifies that A and B are to be used in list processing or locate mode I/O; the pointer P will be associated with B
Statement	BEGIN; ... END; Delimits the start at a begin block; block must be terminated with an END statement
Attribute	DCL A FIXED BINARY; Specifies that A is to have a binary base
Built-in function	A = BINARY(B,7,2); Converts B to a binary base with precision (7,2); assigns the result to A
Attribute	DCL B BIT(10); Specifies that B is to occupy 10 bit positions of main storage
Built-in function	A = BIT(C + D, 10); Converts the result of C + D to a bit-string length 10; assigns the result to A
Option of ENVIRONMENT attribute	DCL F FILE ENV(BLKSIZE(K)); Specifies the size in bytes for each record in file F; K must have a valid value when file is opened
Built-in function	A = BOOL (B, C, '0110'B); Performs one of 16 possible logical operations between corresponding bits of B and C; places results in A

Note: x = feature available; * = feature planned but not implemented at time of publication of this text; blank = feature not available.

Keyword	Abbreviation	PL/C	Model 20	PL/I D	PL/I F	DOS PL/I optimizer	OS PL/I optimizer	PL/I checkout
BUFFERED	BUF (not allowed in subset)	*		x	x	x	x	x
BUFFERS(n)			x	x	x	x	x	x
BUILTIN		x	x	x	x	x	x	x
BY		x	x	x	x	x	x	x
BY NAME		x			x	x	x	x
C(x[,y])		x			x	x	x	x
CALL		x	x	x	x	x	x	x
CALL		x			x	x	x	x
CEIL(x)		x	x	x	x	x	x	x
CHAR(expression[size])		x	x	x	x	x	x	x
CHARACTER[(length)]	CHAR	x	x	x	x	x	x	x
CHECK[(name list)]		x			x	x	x	x

624

Use of keyword	Examples and other information
Attribute	DCL F FILE BUFFERED; Records from F must pass through intermediate storage; valid only for SEQUENTIAL RECORD files
Option of ENVIRONMENT attribute	DCL F FILE ENV(BUFFERS(5)); Specifies that file F is to have 5 buffers allocated when it is opened
Attribute	DCL DATE BUILTIN; Specifies that appearance of the identifier DATE is to be a reference to the PL/I function
Option of DO statement	DO I=1 BY 2; Specifies the increment amount in an iterative DO statement
Option of assignment statement	ST1 = ST2, BY NAME; Assigns to elements of structure ST1 those elements of structure ST2 whose names are identical
Format item	PUT EDIT (CMPLX)(C(F(7, 2), F(7, 2))); Specifies complex number format; x and y are any two real, format items to which the two parts of the complex number CMPLX are to be transmitted
Statement	CALL SUBRT; Specifies that control is to be passed to the entry point SUBRT
Option of INITIAL attribute	DCL A INIT CALL SUB; Specifies that the subroutine SUB is to be invoked to initialize A
Built-in function	A = CEIL(B); Returns the smallest integer not exceeded by B
Built-in function	A = CHAR(B, 10); Causes B to be converted to a character-string of length 10 and assigned to A
Attribute	DCL A CHAR(10); Specifies that A is to occupy 10 bytes of storage and represent a character-string variable
Condition	ON CHECK(A, B) SYSTEM; Causes new values of A or B to be output to SYSPRINT

Note: x = feature available; * = feature planned but not implemented at time of publication of this text; blank = feature not available.

Keyword	Abbreviation	PL/C	Model 20	PL/I D	PL/I F	DOS PL/I optimizer	OS PL/I optimizer	PL/I checkout
CHKPT			x					
CLOSE		x	x	x	x	x	x	x
COBOL					x	x	x	x
COBOL						x	x	x
COLUMN(w)	COL(w) (not allowed in subset)	x		x	x	x	x	x
COMPLETION(event)					x	x	x	x
COMPLEX	CPLX	x			x	x	x	x
COMPLEX(a, b)	CPLX(a,b)	x			x	x	x	x
CONDITION(name)		x			x	x	x	x
CONDITION					x	x	x	x
CONJG(x)		x			x	x	x	x
CONNECTED	CONN					x	x	x

626

Use of keyword	Examples and other information
Option of ENVIRONMENT attribute	DCL F FILE ENV(CHKPT); Specifies that a tape input file contains checkpoint records within data records
Statement	CLOSE FILE(F); Closes file F and releases the resources assigned to it
Option of ENVIRONMENT attribute	DCL F FILE ENV(COBOL); Specifies that records from file F are to be mapped according to the COBOL algorithm
Option of OPTIONS attribute/option	DCL E ENTRY OPTIONS(COBOL); Specifies that E is a COBOL program
Format item	PUT EDIT(A)(COL(10), F(10)); Specifies absolute horizontal spacing for PRINT file
Built-in function, pseudo-variable	IF COMPLETION (EV) THEN . . .; Returns a '1'B if event has completed, otherwise '0'B
Attribute	DCL A COMPLEX; Specifies that A is to be stored in the form $a + bi$, a real part and an imaginary part
Built-in function, pseudo-variable	C=CPLX(A, B); Combines A and B into the complex form $A + B$; A and B must be real
Condition	SIGNAL CONDITION(PRIVATE); Defined by the programmer; SIGNAL causes interrupt and specified action
Attribute	DCL UNDERFLOW CONDITION; Specifies that UNDERFLOW is to be interpreted as a condition; used when name has been used for other purposes
Built-in function	A=CONJG(B+4I); Returns the conjugate of a complex number; the conjugate of $a + bi$ is $a - bi$
Attribute	DCL A(*) CONNECTED; Specifies that A is an array which occupies contiguous storage locations; thus, can be used in record I/O, overlay defining

Note: x = feature available; * = feature planned but not implemented at time of publication of this text; blank = feature not available.

Keyword	Abbreviation	PL/C	Model 20	PL/I D	PL/I F	DOS PL/I optimizer	OS PL/I optimizer	PL/I checkout
CONSECUTIVE		*	x	x	x	x	x	x
CONTROLLED	CTL	*			x	x	x	x
CONVERSION	CONV (not allowed in subset)	x	x	x	x	x	x	x
COPY		x			x	x	x	x
COS(x)		x	x	x	x	x	x	x
COSD(x)		x		x	x	x	x	x
COSH(x)		x		x	x	x	x	x
COUNT(filename)		x			x	x	x	x
CTLASA		*	x	x	x	x	x	x
CTL360				x	x	x	x	x
DATA		x			x	x	x	x
DATAFIELD		x			x		x	x
DATE		x	x	x	x	x	x	x

Use of keyword	Examples and other information
Option of ENVIRONMENT attribute	DCL F FILE ENV(CONSECUTIVE); Specifies that the organization of data records is tapelike
Attribute	DCL A CTL; ALLOCATE A; Specifies that A is of the CONTROLLED storage class; A must be allocated before use, later freed by FREE
Condition	ON CONVERSION GO TO ERROR; Raised by illegal conversion from character- or bit-string; standard system action: comment + ERROR
Option of GET statement	GET LIST(A, B, C)COPY; Places a copy of input file on SYSPRINT
Built-in function	A=COS(B); Returns the cosine of B; B expressed in radians
Built-in function	A=COSD(B); Returns the cosine of B; B expressed in degrees
Built-in function	A=COSH(B); Returns hyperbolic cosine of B; B expressed in radians
Built-in function	I=COUNT(PAYROLL); Returns the number of data items transmitted during last GET or PUT on the file PAYROLL
Option of ENVIRONMENT attribute	DCL OUT FILE ENV(CTLASA); Specifies that each record transmitted will be preceded by an ASA carriage control character
Option of ENVIRONMENT attribute	DCL OUT FILE ENV(CTL360); Specifies that each record transmitted will be preceded by a machine carriage control character
Stream I/O transmission mode	GET DATA; PUT DATA(A, B, C); Specifies that data values and names are to be transmitted
Built-in function	C = DATAFIELD; Extracts contents of data field that caused the NAME condition to be raised
Built-in function	TODAY=DATE; Returns YYMMDD character-string

Note: x = feature available; * = feature planned but not implemented at time of publication of this text; blank = feature not available.

Keyword	Abbreviation	PL/C	Model 20	PL/I D	PL/I F	DOS PL/I optimizer	OS PL/I optimizer	PL/I checkout
%DEACTIVATE	%DEACT					x	x	x	x
DECIMAL	DEC	x	x	x	x	x	x	x
DECIMAL(a[,p[,q]])	DEC	x	x	x	x	x	x	x
DECLARE	DCL	x	x	x	x	x	x	x
%DECLARE	%DCL					x	x	x	x
DEFAULT						x	x	x
DEFINED	DEF		x	x	x	x	x	x
DELAY(n)					x	x	x	x
DELETE					x	x	x	x
DESCRIPTORS						x	x	x
DIM(x,n)		x			x	x	x	x
DIRECT		*	x	x	x	x	x	x
DISPLAY			x	x	x	x	x	x

Use of keyword	Examples and other information
Preprocessor statement	%DEACTIVATE A, B, C; Suspends compile-time action on variables listed
Attribute	DCL A DECIMAL; Specifies that A is to have a decimal arithmetic base
Built-in function	A = DECIMAL(B, 5, 2); B is to be converted to decimal base precision (5, 2)
Statement	DCL A; Used to state attributes for programmer-defined identifiers
Preprocessor statement	% DECLARE A,B; Specifies that A and B are to be compile-time variables; attributes are also specified with %DCL
Statement	DEFAULT ALL STATIC; Allows programmer control over default rules
Attribute	DCL A(10, 10), B(100) DEFINED A; Allows multiple names to refer to the same storage location; e.g., B(11) is same as A(2, 1)
Statement	DELAY(1000); Delays execution of the program for 1000 milliseconds of real time
Statement	DELETE FILE(F)KEY(K); Deletes the record whose key is K from F file; only record files with indexed or REGIONAL options
Option of DEFAULT statement	DEFAULT DESCRIPTORS(FIXED); Describes default attributes for parameters
Built-in function	I = DIM(TABLE, 2); Returns the current extent of the second dimension of TABLE
Attribute	DCL F FILE DIRECT; Specifies that records will be transmitted by key directly to or from file; record files only
Statement	DISPLAY ('THIS IS A MESSAGE'); Displays the string on operator's console; in M−20, displays one character in T−R register

Note: x = feature available; * = feature planned but not implemented at time of publication of this text; blank = feature not available.

Keyword	Abbreviation	PL/C	Model 20	PL/I D	PL/I F	DOS PL/I optimizer	OS PL/I optimizer	PL/I checkout
DIVIDE(x,y,p[,q])		x		x	x	x	x	x
DO		x	x	x	x	x	x	x
%DO						x	x	x	x
E(w,d[,s])		x	x	x	x	x	x	x
EDIT		x	x	x	x	x	x	x
ELSE		x	x	x	x	x	x	x
%ELSE						x	x	x	x
EMPTY						x	x	x	x
END		x	x	x	x	x	x	x
%END						x	x	x	x
ENDFILE(file expression)		x	x	x	x	x	x	x
ENDPAGE(file expression)		x	x	x	x	x	x	x
ENTRY		x	x	x	x	x	x	x

632

Use of keyword	Examples and other information
Built-in function	A = DIVIDE(B,C,8,2) ; Divides B by C in a field of 8 digits with 2 fractional places
Statement	DO ; . . . END ; DO I=1 TO 10 ; . . . END ; DO WHILE (x=0) ; . . . END ; Forms a DO-group
Preprocessor statement	%DO ; . . . %END ; %DO I=1 TO 10 ; . . . %END ; Forms a preprocessor DO-group
Format item	PUT EDIT (A)(E(10, 3, 4)) ; Specifies that values in the I/O stream are in floating-point form ; i.e., x.xxxE±nn
Stream I/O transmission mode	PUT EDIT(A)(F(3)) ; Specifies that data is to be transmitted according to the specifications in the accompanying format list
Clause of IF statement	IF A=B THEN . . .; ELSE . . .; The ELSE clause is executed if the test is false
Clause of %IF statement	%IF A=B %THEN . . .; %ELSE . . .; The %ELSE clause is executed if the test is false
Built-in function	AREA = EMPTY ; Resets the contents of an AREA variable to empty status
Statement	A :PROC ; . . . END ; BEGIN ; . . . END ; DO ; . . . END ; Terminates blocks and groups
Preprocessor statement	%A : PROC ; . . . %END ; %DO ; . . . %END ; Terminates compile-time functions and groups
Condition	ON ENDFILE(PAYROL)GO TO EOJ ; Raised by attempt to read past end-of-file during GET or READ ; standard system action : ERROR
Condition	ON ENDPAGE(PRNT)GO TO HDNG ; Raised by attempt to print past page size ; PRINT files only ; standard system action : start new page, continue
Attribute, statement	DCL E ENTRY ; F : ENTRY ; Attribute specifies that identifier is an EXTERNAL entry point ; statement specifies secondary entry point

Note: x = feature available ; ∗ = feature planned but not implemented at time of publication of this text ; blank = feature not available.

Keyword	Abbreviation	PL/C	Model 20	PL/I D	PL/I F	DOS PL/I optimizer	OS PL/I optimizer	PL/I checkout
ENVIRONMENT	ENV	*	x	x	x	x	x	x
ERF(x)		x		x	x	x	x	x
ERFC(x)		x		x	x	x	x	x
ERROR		x	x	x	x	x	x	x
EVENT					x	x	x	x
EXCLUSIVE	EXCL				x		x	x
EXIT		x			x		x	x
EXP(x)		x	x	x	x	x	x	x
EXTENTNUMBER(n)			x	x		x		
EXTERNAL	EXT	x	x	x	x	x	x	x
F		*	x	x	x	x	x	x
F(x[,y[,z]])		x	x	x	x	x	x	x

Use of keyword	Examples and other information
Attribute	DCL F FILE ENV(options) ; List of options is implementation-defined, specifies file options not included in PL/I language
Built-in function	SUMX=ERF(3) ; Returns the value of the error function
Built-in function	SUMX=ERFC(3) ; Returns $1 - ERF(x)$, the complement of the error function
Condition	ON ERROR PUT LIST('OUCH') ; Raised by an error forcing termination ; standard system action : raise FINISH condition
Attribute, option of CALL, DELETE, DISPLAY, READ, REWRITE, WRITE statements	DCL EV EVENT; CALL X EVENT(EV) ; WAIT (EV) ; Specifies that an asynchronous I/O is to be performed, or multitasking
Attribute	DCL F FILE EXCLUSIVE ; Prevents other tasks from accessing the file F simultaneously
Statement	EXIT ; Causes termination of the task executing EXIT and all dependent tasks
Built-in function	A=EXP(B) ; Returns e^x
Option of ENVIRONMENT attribute	DCL F FILE ENV(EXTENTNUMBER(3)) ; Specifies the number of disk extents for indexed and REGIONAL files
Attribute	DCL A EXTERNAL ; Specifies that the same storage location is to be used for any variable name A with EXT attribute in other blocks
Option of ENVIRONMENT attribute	DCL A FILE ENV(F(80)) ; Specifies record form and length
Format item	PUT EDIT(A)(F(7, 2)) ; Specifies that value is to be displayed in a field of 7 characters, two of which are to the right of decimal point

Note: x = feature available ; ∗ = feature planned but not implemented at time of publication of this text; blank = feature not available.

Keyword	Abbreviation	PL/C	Model 20	PL/I D	PL/I F	DOS PL/I optimizer	OS PL/I optimizer	PL/I checkout
FB		*				x	x	x
FBS							x	x
FILE		x	x	x	x	x	x	x
FINISH		x			x	x	x	x
FIXED		x	x	x	x	x	x	x
FIXED(x[,p[,q]])		x		x	x	x	x	x
FIXEDOVERFLOW	FOFL (not allowed in subset)	x	x	x	x	x	x	x
FLOAT		x	x	x	x	x	x	x
FLOAT(x[,p])		x		x	x	x	x	x
FLOOR(x)		x	x	x	x	x	x	x
FORMAT(list)		x	x	x	x	x	x	x
FORTRAN						x	x	x

Use of keyword	Examples and other information
Option of ENVIRONMENT attribute	DCL F FILE ENV(FB) ; Specifies fixed-length blocked records
Option of ENVIRONMENT attribute	DCL F FILE ENV(FBS) ; Specifies fixed-length blocked standard records
Attribute, option of OPEN, READ, WRITE, DELETE, GET, PUT, CLOSE statements	OPEN FILE(IN) ; READ FILE(IN)INTO(A) ; Specifies the name of a PL/I file, either stream- or record-oriented
Condition	ON FINISH PUT LIST('EOJ') ; Raised before termination of program by execution of any statement causing end ; i.e., STOP, RETURN
Attribute	DCL A FIXED ; Specifies that variable is to have arithmetic fixed-scale values
Built-in function	FX = FIXED(FL, 5, 2) ; Returns a fixed-scale value of precision (5, 2) ; base is the same as base of first argument
Condition	ON FOFL GO TO OVF_ER ; Raise when result of arithmetic operation on fixed-scale data exceeds implementation maximum
Attribute	DCL FL FLOAT ; Specifies that variable is to have floating scale
Built-in function	FL = FLOAT(FX,6) ; Specifies that scale of first argument to be converted to float with precision 6
Built-in function	I = FLOOR(A) ; Returns largest integer not exceeding A
Statement	FR : FORMAT(SKIP,A) ; PUT EDIT(X)(R(FR)) ; Specification of remote format list, referred to with R format item ; must be labeled
Option of OPTIONS attribute/option	DCL FRTRN ENTRY OPTIONS(FORTRAN) ; Specifies that associated entry point is a program compiled by a FORTRAN compiler

Note: x = feature available ; * = feature planned but not implemented at time of publication of this text ; blank = feature not available.

Keyword	Abbreviation	PL/C	Model 20	PL/I D	PL/I F	DOS PL/I optimizer	OS PL/I optimizer	PL/I checkout
FREE		*			x	x	x	x
FROM		x	x	x	x	x	x	x
G(max-msg-size)					x			
GENERIC					x			
GENERIC						x	x	x
GENKEY					x		x	x
GET		x	x	x	x	x	x	x
GO TO	GOTO	x	x	x	x	x	x	x
%GOTO	%GOTO				x	x	x	x
HALT							x	x
HBOUND(x,n)		x			x	x	x	x
HIGH(i)		x	x	x	x	x	x	x

Use of keyword	Examples and other information
Statement	FREE A; Specifies that storage previously allocated for a BASED or CTL variable is to be released
Option of READ and REWRITE statements	WRITE FILE(F) FROM(A); Specifies the variable from which data is to be transmitted to a record I/O file
Option of ENVIRONMENT attribute	DCL TP FILE TRANSIENT ENV(G(200)); Specifies the maximum record size for a teleprocessing file
Attribute	DCL E GENERIC (A ENTRY(FIXED), B ENTRY (FLOAT)); Specifies a family of entry points, one to be chosen on basis of attributes of arguments
Attribute	DCL E GENERIC(A WHEN(FIXED), B WHEN(FLOAT)); Specifies a family of entry points; one to be chosen on basis of attributes of arguments
Option of ENVIRONMENT attribute	DCL F FILE ENV(GENKEY); Specifies for indexed files that records are to be read using only high-order portion of the key
Statement	GET LIST(A, B, C); Specifies an input operation on a stream file
Statement	GO TO ST#10; Specific transfer of control to named statement
Preprocessor statement	%GO TO LBL; Transfers control of preprocessor scan to LBL
Statement	HALT; Causes conversational mode program to be interrupted and control passed to the terminal
Built-in function	I = HBOUND(TBL, 2); Returns the high bound of the nth-dimension of the first argument
Built-in function	KEY = HIGH(5); Returns a string, i characters long, of the high collating value; in S/360 implementations, hex FF

Note: x = feature available; * = feature planned but not implemented at time of publication of this text; blank = feature not available.

Keyword	Abbreviation	PL/C	Model 20	PL/I D	PL/I F	DOS PL/I optimizer	OS PL/I optimizer	PL/I checkout
HIGHINDEX					x		x	
IF		x	x	x	x	x	x	x
%IF						x	x	x	x
IGNORE(n)		x				x	x	x	x
IMAG(x)		x				x	x	x	x
IN (area-variable)						x	x	x	x
%INCLUDE		x				x	x	x	x
INDEX (string,config)		x		x	x	x	x	x
INDEXAREA [(size)]					x	x	x	x	x
INDEXED			x	x	x	x	x	x
INDEXMULTIPLE					x		x	
INITIAL	INIT	x	x	x	x	x	x	x

Use of keyword	Examples and other information
Option of ENVIRONMENT attribute	DCL F FILE ENV (HIGHINDEX(2314)) ; Specifies device type on which high-level index of indexed file resides
Statement	IF A=B THEN . . .; ELSE . . .; Specifies that the logical expression is to be evaluated; if true THEN, if false ELSE
Preprocessor statement	%IF A=B %THEN . . .; %ELSE . . .; Specifies that the logical expression is to be evaluated; if true THEN . . .; if false ELSE . . .;
Option of READ statement	READ FILE(F) IGNORE (10); Indicates that 10 records are to be skipped
Built-in function, pseudo-variable	R = IMAG(CPX); Extracts the imaginary part of a complex number
Option of ALLOCATE and FREE statements	ALLOCATE X IN (AR); Specifies the AREA in which a based variable is to be ALLOCATED or FREED
Preprocessor statement	%INCLUDE PAYROLL; Requests that text from an external file is to be included during preprocessor scan
Built-in function	I = INDEX(STR, 'ABC'); Returns the position within first argument at which first occurrence of second argument begins
Option of ENVIRONMENT attribute	DCL F FILE ENV(INDEXAREA(10000)); Requests high-level index of indexed file be made resident in main storage
Option of ENVIRONMENT attribute	DCL F FILE ENV(INDEXED); Specifies that the organization of the file is indexed sequential
Option of ENVIRONMENT attribute	DCL F FILE ENV(INDEXMULTIPLE); Specifies that a multiple-level index is to be created for an indexed file
Attribute	DCL A INITIAL(123.4); Specifies an initial value for a variable

Note: x = feature available; * = feature planned but not implemented at time of publication of this text; blank = feature not available.

Keyword	Abbreviation	PL/C	Model 20	PL/I D	PL/I F	DOS PL/I optimizer	OS PL/I optimizer	PL/I checkout
INPUT		x	x	x	x	x	x	x
INTER						x	x	x
INTERNAL	INT (not allowed in subset)	x	x	x	x	x	x	x
INTO (variable)		x	x	x	x	x	x	x
IRREDUCIBLE	IRRED				x	x	x	x
KEY (file expression)		*	x	x	x	x	x	x
KEY(x)		*	x	x	x	x	x	x
KEYED		*	x	x	x	x	x	x
KEYFROM(x)		*	x	x	x	x	x	x
KEYLENGTH(n)			x	x		x	x	x
KEYLOC(n)			x	x		x	x	x
KEYTO(x)		*		x	x	x	x	x

Use of keyword	Examples and other information
Attribute	DCL F FILE INPUT; Specifies that a file is to be input with GET or READ statements
Option of OPTIONS attribute	DCL E ENTRY OPTIONS (INTER); Specifies that PL/I is not to handle interrupts in called entry point
Attribute	DCL A INTERNAL; Limits the scope of the name to procedure containing declaration and internal procedures
Option of READ statement	READ FILE(F) INTO(AR); Specifies location to which record is to be transmitted
Attribute	DCL E ENTRY IRREDUCIBLE; An optimization specification; different values will be returned by E each time it is invoked
Condition	ON KEY(FILEX)BEGIN; . . . Raised by improper presence or absence of key in KEYED record file
Option of READ, DELETE, and REWRITE statements	READ FILE(X)INTO(Y)KEY(K); Identifies the record to be read from named file
Attribute	DCL F FILE KEYED; Specifies that each record in the file has a key; record files only
Option of WRITE and LOCATE statements	LOCATE X KEYFROM(K); Specifies the key of the record to be written; record files only
Option of ENVIRONMENT attribute	DCL F FILE KEYED ENV(KEYLENGTH(10)); Specifies the length of the key field of a record file
Option of ENVIRONMENT attribute	DCL F FILE KEYED ENV(KEYLOC(5)); Specifies location of key field within each record, starting with 1
Option of READ statement	READ FILE(F)INTO(A)KEYTO(K); Specifies location to which key value of record is to be assigned

Note: x = feature available; * = feature planned but not implemented at time of publication of this text; blank = feature not available.

Keyword	Abbreviation	PL/C	Model 20	PL/I D	PL/I F	DOS PL/I optimizer	OS PL/I optimizer	PL/I checkout
LABEL		x	x	x	x	x	x	x
LBOUND(x,n)		x			x	x	x	x
LEAVE					x	x	x	x
LENGTH(string)		x			x	x	x	x
LIKE		*			x	x	x	x
LINE(n)		x		x	x	x	x	x
LINENO (file expression)		x			x	x	x	x
LINESIZE(w)		x			x	x	x	x
LIST		x		x	x	x	x	x
LOCATE			x	x	x	x	x	x
LOG(x)		x	x	x	x	x	x	x
LOG2(x)		x		x	x	x	x	x

Use of keyword	Examples and other information
Attribute	DCL L LABEL; L=ST#10; GO TO L; Specifies that L is to take on as values the address of statement labels
Built-in function	I=LBOUND(TABLE,3); Returns the current lower bound of the third dimension of TABLE
Option of ENVIRONMENT attribute	DCL F FILE ENV(LEAVE); Requests that tape is to remain at end of data after reading for quick reread BACKWARDS
Built-in function	I=LENGTH(STR); Returns the current length of the string argument
Attribute	DCL 1 ST2 LIKE ST1; Specifies that the elements of ST2 are to be identical to those in ST1
Format item; option of PUT statement	PUT EDIT(A)(LINE(3), F(5)); Specifies absolute vertical spacing for a PRINT file
Built-in function	IF LINENO(PRT)>50 THEN . . .; Returns the current line number of the named PRINT file
Option of OPEN statement	OPEN FILE(F) LINESIZE(120); Specifies the number of character positions in a line of print on file F
Stream I/O transmission mode	PUT LIST(A, B, C); Specifies list-directed stream I/O
Statement	LOCATE AREA FILE(F)SET(P); Allocates a record buffer and transmits previously *located* record to the file; for full language, SET option need not be coded
Built-in function	A=LOG(B); Returns the logarithm of x to the base e; error if $x <= 0$
Built-in function	A=LOG2(B); Returns the logarithm of x to the base 2; error if $x <= 0$

Note: x = feature available; * = feature planned but not implemented at time of publication of this text; blank = feature not available.

Keyword	Abbreviation	PL/C	Model 20	PL/I D	PL/I F	DOS PL/I optimizer	OS PL/I optimizer	PL/I checkout
LOG10(x)		x		x	x	x	x	x
LOW(i)		x	x	x	x	x	x	x
MAIN		x	x	x	x	x	x	x
MAX$(x_1, y_2, \ldots, x_n)$		x	x	x	x	x	x	x
MEDIUM (device name, device type)			x	x		x		
MIN$(x_1, x_2, \ldots, x_n)$		x	x	x	x	x	x	x
MOD(x, x_2)		x		x	x	x	x	x
MULTIPLY$(x,y,p[q])$		x		x	x	x	x	x
NAME (file expression)		x			x	x	x	x
NCP(n)					x		x	x
NOCHECK[(name list)]		x			x	x	x	x
NOCONVERSION	NOCONV (not allowed in subset)	x	x	x	x	x	x	x

Use of keyword	Examples and other information
Built-in function	A = LOG10(B) ; Returns the logarithm of x to the base 10; error if x < = 0
Built-in function	S = LOW(5) ; Returns the low collating value in a string of length i; for S/360 implementations hex 00
Option of the OPTIONS attribute/option	A : PROC OPTIONS(MAIN) ; Specifies this procedure to be primary entry point for program execution
Built-in function	A = MAX (B, C, D, E) ; Returns value of the greatest of the arguments
Option of ENVIRONMENT attribute	DCL F FILE ENV(MEDIUM(SYS005, 2314)) ; Specifies device-dependent type, logical unit name
Built-in function	A = MIN (B, C, D, E) ; Returns the value of least of the arguments
Built-in function	A = MOD(B, C) ; Returns the positive remainder after division of B by C
Built-in function	A = MULTIPLY(B, C, 10, 5) ; Equivalent to B * C in a field of 10 digits, 5 of which are fractional
Condition	ON. NAME(INPT)BEGIN ; Raised when unrecognizable name encountered during GET DATA; standard system action: comment and continue
Option of ENVIRONMENT attribute	DCL F FILE ENV(NCP(5)) ; Specifies the number of outstanding I/O requests maximum for asynchronous I/O
Condition prefix	(NOCHECK(A, B, C)) : X : GO TO Y ; Specifies that CHECK condition to be disabled for scope of statement
Condition prefix	(NOCONVERSION) : A = B + C ; Disables conversion condition for scope of statement

Note: x = feature available; * = feature planned but not implemented at time of publication of this text; blank = feature not available.

Keyword	Abbreviation	PL/C	Model 20	PL/I D	PL/I F	DOS PL/I optimizer	OS PL/I optimizer	PL/I checkout
NOFIXEDOVERFLOW	NOFOFL (not allowed in subset)	x	x	x	x	x	x	x
NOLABEL			x	x		x		
NOLOCK					x		x	
NOMAP						x	x	x
NOMAPIN						x	x	x
NOMAPOUT						x	x	x
NOOVERFLOW	NOOFL (not allowed in subset)	x	x	x	x	x	x	x
NORESCAN						x	x	x
NOSIZE		x	x	x	x	x	x	x
NOSTRINGRANGE	NOSTRG	x			x	x	x	x
NOSTRINGSIZE	NOSTRZ					x	x	x

648

Use of keyword	Examples and other information
Condition prefix	(NOFOFL) : A = B∗C ; Disables FIXEDOVERFLOW condition for scope of statement
Option of ENVIRONMENT attribute	DCL F FILE ENV(NOLABEL) ; Specifies that tape data set has no labels
Option of READ statement	READ FILE(F) INTO(A)KEY(K) NOLOCK ; Specifies that exclusive use of record with key K is not required
Option of OPTIONS attribute/option	DCL E ENTRY OPTIONS(COBOL NOMAP) ; Prevents the manipulation of data aggregates in the interface between a PL/I and COBOL program
Option of OPTIONS attribute/option	DCL E ENTRY OPTIONS(FORTRAN NOMAPIN) ; Prevents the manipulation of data aggregates in the interface between a PL/I and FORTRAN program
Option of OPTIONS attribute/option	DCL E ENTRY OPTIONS(FORTRAN NOMAPOUT) ; Prevents the manipulation of data aggregates in the interface between a PL/I and FORTRAN program
Condition prefix	(NOOVERFLOW) : A = B∗C ; Disables the OVERFLOW condition for the scope of the statement
Option of %ACTIVATE statement	%ACTIVATE A NORESCAN ; Specifies that after replacement of A, text is not to be rescanned for further replacement
Condition prefix	(NOSIZE) : BEGIN ; . . . ; Disables the SIZE condition for the scope of the statement
Condition prefix	(NOSTRINGRANGE) : A = SUBSTR(B, 10, N) ; Disables the STRINGRANGE condition for the scope of the statement
Condition prefix	(NOSTRINGSIZE) : ST = SUBSTR(B, 3) ; Disables the STRINGSIZE condition for the scope of the statement

Note: x = feature available ; ∗ = feature planned but not implemented at time of publication of this text ; blank = feature not available.

Keyword	Abbreviation	PL/C	Model 20	PL/I D	PL/I F	DOS PL/I optimizer	OS PL/I optimizer	PL/I checkout
NOSUBSCRIPTRANGE	NOSUBRG	x			x	x	x	x
NOTAPEMK			x	x		x		
NOUNDERFLOW	NOUFL (not allowed in subset)	x	x	x	x	x	x	x
NOWRITE					x	x	x	x
NOZERODIVIDE	NOZDIV (not allowed in subset)	x	x	x	x	x	x	x
NULL				x	x	x	x	x
OFFSET (area name)					x	x	x	x
OFFSET(p, a)						x	x	x
OFLTRACKS(n)			x	x		x		
ON		x	x	x	x	x	x	x
ONCHAR		x			x	x	x	x

Use of keyword	Examples and other information
Condition prefix	(NOSUBRG) : A = B(I + 10) ; Disables the SUBSCRIPTRANGE condition for the scope of the statement
Option of ENVIRONMENT attribute	DCL F FILE ENV (NOTAPEMK) ; Specifies that file located on magnetic tape is not preceded by a tape mark
Condition prefix	(NOUNDERFLOW) : A = B/C ; Disables the UNDERFLOW condition for the scope of the statement
Option of ENVIRONMENT attribute	DCL F FILE ENV(NOWRITE) ; Requests space optimization when no records will be added to an indexed file
Condition prefix	(NOZERODIVIDE) : A = B/C ; Disables the ZERODIVIDE condition for the scope of the statement
Built-in function	P = NULL ; Returns a null locator value
Attribute	DCL R OFFSET(AR) ; Specifies that R will contain the address of a location within AR, relative to the beginning of AR
Built-in function	R = OFFSET(P, AR) ; Converts a pointer to an offset value from beginning of second argument AREA variable
Option of ENVIRONMENT attribute	DCL F FILE ENV(OFLTRACKS(2)) ; Specifies that n tracks per cylinder are to be reserved for new records
Statement	ON ENDPAGE(F) . . . ; Specifies the on-unit to be executed when condition named is raised
Built-in function, pseudo-variable	ER_CHAR = ONCHAR ; Returns character which caused conversion condition to be raised; the ONCHAR may only appear in the conversion on-unit

Note: x = feature available;* = feature planned but not implemented at time of publication of this text; blank = feature not available.

Keyword	Abbreviation	PL/C	Model 20	PL/I D	PL/I F	DOS PL/I optimizer	OS PL/I optimizer	PL/I checkout
ONCODE		x			x	x	x	x
ONCOUNT		x			x	x	x	x
ONFILE		x			x	x	x	x
ONKEY					x	x	x	x
ONLOC		x			x	x	x	x
ONSOURCE		x			x	x	x	x
ONSYSLOG				x				
OPEN		x	x	x	x	x	x	x
OPTIONS (list)		x	x	x	x	x	x	x
OPTIONS (list)						x	x	x
ORDER		x			x	x	x	x
OUTPUT		x	x	x	x	x	x	x

Use of keyword	Examples and other information
Built-in function	I = ONCODE; Returns an implementation-defined value which uniquely designates the error encountered; valid only in an on-unit
Built-in function	I = ONCOUNT; Returns the number of interrupts pending
Built- in function	C = ONFILE; Returns the name of the file which encountered an error; valid only in an on-unit
Built-in function	C = ONKEY; Returns the value of the key, causing the KEY condition to be raised
Built-in function	C = ONLOC; Returns the name of the entry point containing the statement whose execution caused an interrupt
Built-in function, pseudo-variable	C = ONSOURCE; Returns the value of the field containing the character causing the conversion condition to be raised
Option of OPTIONS option of PROCEDURE statement	A: PROC OPTIONS(ONSYSLOG); Specifies that error messages are to be produced on the operator's console
Statement	OPEN FILE(F); Prepares a file for processing
Option of PROCEDURE statement	A: PROC OPTIONS(MAIN); Specifies implementation-defined information
Option of ENTRY statement, attribute	DCL E ENTRY OPTIONS(COBOL); Specifies interlanguage communication between PL/I and COBOL or FORTRAN modules
Option of PROCEDURE and BEGIN statements	BEGIN ORDER; Optimization specification requesting strict sequencing of computation be maintained
Attribute	DCL F FILE OUTPUT; Specifies that data is to be transmitted to file using GET, WRITE, or LOCATE statements

Note: x = feature available; * = feature planned but not implemented at time of publication of this text; blank = feature not available.

Keyword	Abbreviation	PL/C	Model 20	PL/I D	PL/I F	DOS PL/I optimizer	OS PL/I optimizer	PL/I checkout
OVERFLOW	OFL (not allowed in subset)	x	x	x	x	x	x	x
P'picture specification'		*			x	x	x	x
PAGE		x	x	x	x	x	x	x
PAGESIZE(w)		x	x	x	x	x	x	x
PENDING (file expression					x		x	x
PICTURE	PIC	*	x	x	x	x	x	x
POINTER	PTR		x	x	x	x	x	x
POINTER(n,a)						x	x	x
POLY(a,x)					x	x	x	x
POSITION(expression)	POS				x	x	x	x

654

Use of keyword	Examples and other information
Condition	ON OVERFLOW . . .; Raised when exponent of floating-scale variable exceeds limit
Format item	PUT EDIT(A)(P'ZZ,ZZZ'); Allows editing of output or input variables using picture specification characters
Format item, option of PUT statement	PUT PAGE; Specifies positioning of PRINT file at the beginning of a new page
Option of OPEN statement	OPEN FILE(F) PAGESIZE(50); Specifies the number of lines to be printed before ENDPAGE condition raised; may only be specified for STREAM PRINT files
Condition	ON PENDING BEGIN:. . .; Raised when a READ on a TRANSIENT file finds that no records are currently in the file
Attribute	DCL A PIC'999V99', B PIC'(5)ZV.99'; Specifies base, mode, scale, and precision of numeric data items; also editing characters
Attribute	DCL A POINTER; Specifies that A will take on as values the location addresses of other variables; used in list processing and locate mode I/O
Built-in function	P = POINTER(OFST,AR); Returns a pointer value representing the sum of the address of the area AR and the value of the OFFSET variable OFST
Built-in function	A = POLY(B,X); If B and X are vectors, then POLY returns the polynomial value formed by using the B_i as coefficients and the πx as independent variables
Attribute	DCL A CHAR(10), B CHAR(5) DEF C POSITION(6); Specifies that B is to occupy the same location as the last half of A

Note: x = feature available; * = feature planned but not implemented at time of publication of this text; blank = feature not available.

Keyword	Abbreviation	PL/C	Model 20	PL/I D	PL/I F	DOS PL/I optimizer	OS PL/I optimizer	PL/I checkout
PRECISION (x,p [q])	PREC (not allowed in subset)	x		x	x	x	x	x
PRINT		x	x	x	x	x	x	x
PRIORITY(x)					x		x	x
PRIORITY(task name)					x		x	x
PROCEDURE	PROC	x	x	x	x	x	x	x
%PROCEDURE	%PROC				x	x	x	x
PROD(x)		x		x	x	x	x	x
PUT		x	x	x	x	x	x	x
R(x)		x	x	x	x	x	x	x
R (max-rec-size)					x			
RANGE						x	x	x
READ		x	x	x	x	x	x	x

656

Use of keyword	Examples and other information
Built-in function	A = PRECISION(B, 7, 5) ; Returns the value of B with precision (7, 5) ; same base, scale, mode
Attribute	DCL F FILE PRINT; Specifies that the final destination of the file will be the printed page
Option of CALL statement	CALL T PRIORITY(−2) ; Assigns a priority to a task relative to calling task
Built-in function, pseudo-variable	A = PRIORITY(T) ; Returns priority of task T relative to invoking task
Statement	A : PROCEDURE; Specifies beginning of a procedure block, defines primary entry point
Preprocessor statement	%A : PROC; Specifies beginning of compile-time procedure; must be invoked via compile-time function reference
Built-in function	A = PROD(B) ; B is an array; returns the product of all elements of B
Statement	PUT DATA(X, Y, Z) ; Stream output statement; specifies transmission of data elements contained in data list
Format item	PUT EDIT(A, B, C)(R(FMT)) ; Specifies that format list is remote (R) ; name in parentheses must be label of FORMAT statement
Option of ENVIRONMENT attribute	DCL TP FILE TRANSIENT(R(100)) ; Specifies for teleprocessing files that logical records of max-rec-size maximum are to be transmitted
Option of DEFAULT statement	DEFAULT RANGE(A:H) SYSTEM; Specifies the range of identifiers to be affected by the DEFAULT specification
Statement	READ FILE(F)INTO(A) Transfers a record from a record file into main storage

Note: x = feature available; * = feature planned but not implemented at time of publication of this text; blank = feature not available.

Keyword	Abbreviation	PL/C	Model 20	PL/I D	PL/I F	DOS PL/I optimizer	OS PL/I optimizer	PL/I checkout
REAL		x			x	x	x	x
REAL(x)		x			x	x	x	x
RECORD		x	x	x	x	x	x	x
RECORD(file name)		x	x	x	x	x	x	x
RECSIZE(expression)						x	x	x
RECURSIVE		x			x	x	x	x
REDUCIBLE	RED				x	x	x	x
REENTRANT					x		x	x
REFER					x	x	x	x
REGIONAL(1)			x	x	x	x	x	x
REGIONAL(2)					x	x	x	x
REGIONAL(3)				x	x	x	x	x

658

Use of keyword	Examples and other information
Attribute	DCL A REAL; Specifies that the variable will contain only real arithmetic values, *not* complex
Built-in function, pseudo-variable	A = REAL(C) ; REAL(C) = B ; Returns or accepts the real portion of the complex argument
Attribute	DCL F FILE RECORD; Specifies that the file will consist of discrete records to be transmitted with READ or WRITE statements
Condition	ON RECORD(F) BEGIN; . . . Raised size of record variable is not compatible with actual record size
Option of ENVIRONMENT attribute	DCL F FILE ENV (RECSIZE(100)); Specifies logical record length
Option of PROCEDURE statement	A : PROC RECURSIVE; Specifies that the procedure may invoke itself
Attribute	DCL E ENTRY REDUCIBLE; Specifies that the compiler is allowed to optimize by reducing the number of references to the entry point
Option of OPTIONS option of PROCEDURE statement	A : PROC OPTIONS(REENTRANT); Specifies that the procedure may be invoked for asynchronous execution with previous invocations
Option of BASED attribute	DCL 1 A BASED, 2 B, 2 C (D REFER (B)); Used to declare varying-length arrays or strings in a BASED structure
Option of ENVIRONMENT attribute	DCL F FILE ENV(REGIONAL(1)); Specifies data set organization; records are to be transmitted via relative record number
Option of ENVIRONMENT attribute	DCL F FILE ENV(REGIONAL(2)); Specifies data set organization; records are to be transmitted via relative record plus a recorded key
Option of ENVIRONMENT attribute	DCL F FILE ENV(REGIONAL(3)); Specifies data set organization; records are to be transmitted via relative track plus a recorded key

Note: x = feature available; * = feature planned but not implemented at time of publication of this text; blank = feature not available.

Keyword	Abbreviation	PL/C	Model 20	PL/I D	PL/I F	DOS PL/I optimizer	OS PL/I optimizer	PL/I checkout
REORDER						x	x	x	x
REPEAT(string,i)		x		x	x	x	x	x
REPLY(c)			x	x	x	x	x	x
REREAD						x	x	x
RESCAN						x	x	x
RETURN		x	x	x	x	x	x	x
RETURNS		x	x	x	x	x	x	x
REVERT		x		x	x	x	x	x
REWRITE		*	x	x	x	x	x	x
ROUND(x,n)		x	x	x	x	x	x	x
SCALARVARYING						x	x	x

660

Use of keyword	Examples and other information
Option of PROCEDURE and BEGIN statements	A: PROC REORDER; Optimization specification; allows compiler to reorder the evaluation of expressions for optimum speed
Built-in function	A = REPEAT(B, 7); Specifies that B is to be concatenated to itself 6 times (7 B's altogether) and returned to the point of invocation
Option of DISPLAY statement	DISPLAY(A)REPLY(B); Specifies variable to which operator response is to be assigned
Option of ENVIRONMENT attribute and CLOSE statement	DCL F FILE ENV(REREAD); Specifies that tape file is to be rewound in preparation for reading again
Option %ACTIVATE statement	%ACTIVATE A RESCAN; Specifies that the value of A is to be rescanned by the preprocessor for further replacement
Statement	RETURN; Returns control to the point of invocation
Attribute, option of PROCEDURE and %PROCEDURE statements	A: PROC RETURNS(CHAR); Specifies the attributes of the value to be returned by the entry point after function reference DCL FUNCT RETURNS FIXED; Specifies the attributes of the function to be invoked
Statement	REVERT ZERODIVIDE; Causes the action specified for stated condition in the encompassing block to be activated
Statement	REWRITE FILE(F) FROM(A); Specifies that a record is to be returned to the file; valid for RECORD UPDATE files only
Built-in function	A = ROUND(B, 2); Returns the value of B rounded at the second place to the right (+2) of decimal point
Option of ENVIRONMENT attribute	DCL F FILE ENV(SCALARVARYING); Specifies the inclusion of a length field with record indicating length of varying string

Note: x = feature available; * = feature planned but not implemented at time of publication of this text; blank = feature not available.

Keyword	Abbreviation	PL/C	Model 20	PL/I D	PL/I F	DOS PL/I optimizer	OS PL/I optimizer	PL/I checkout
SEQUENTIAL	SEQL (not allowed in subset)	x	x	x	x	x	x	x
SET (pointer)		*	x	x	x	x	x	x
SIGN(x)		x		x	x	x	x	x
SIGNAL		x		x	x	x	x	x
SIN(x)		x	x	x	x	x	x	x
SIND(x)		x		x	x	x	x	x
SINH(x)		x		x	x	x	x	x
SIZE		x	x	x	x	x	x	x
SKIP[(n)]		x	x	x	x	x	x	x
SNAP		x			x	x	x	x
SQRT(x)		x	x	x	x	x	x	x
STATIC		x	x	x	x	x	x	x
STATUS [(event-name)]						x	x	x	x

662

Use of keyword	Examples and other information
Attribute	DCL F FILE SEQUENTIAL; Specifies that data is to be transmitted according to physical order of data set
Option of ALLOCATE, LOCATE, and READ statements	READ FILE(F)SET(P); Sets pointer value to indicate start of area allocated or record in buffer
Built-in function	I=SIGN(X); Returns -1 if $X < 0$, 0 if $X = 0$, and $+1$ if $X > 0$
Statement	SIGNAL ENDPAGE (PRT); Simulates the occurrence of the stated condition
Built-in function	A=SIN(B); Returns the sine of B radians
Built-in function	X=SIND(Y); Returns the sine of Y where Y is expressed in degrees
Built-in function	X=SINH(Y); Returns the hyperbolic sine of Y radians
Condition	ON SIZE BEGIN; . . .; Raised by assignment of data which causes truncation of high-order significance
Format item, option of GET and PUT statements	PUT LIST(A, B, C) SKIP(2); Specifies relative vertical spacing or beginning of next logical record; assumed 1 if (n) omitted; for M–20 and PL/I D, (n) maximum is 3
Option of ON statement	ON CONVERSION SNAP; A calling trace is printed on SYSPRINT when condition occurs
Built-in function	X=SQRT(Y); Returns positive square root; error if argument is less than 0
Attribute	DCL A STATIC; Specifies that storage is to be allocated before program execution and remain until termination
Built-in function, pseudo-variable	I=STATUS(EV); Returns the status value of an EVENT variable

Note: x = feature available; * = feature planned but not implemented at time of publication of this text; blank = feature not available.

Keyword	Abbreviation	PL/C	Model 20	PL/I D	PL/I F	DOS PL/I optimizer	OS PL/I optimizer	PL/I checkout
STOP		x		x	x	x	x	x
STREAM		x	x	x	x	x	x	x
STRING(x)		x		x	x	x	x	x
STRING (string name)		x	x	x	x	x	x	x
STRINGRANGE	STRG	x			x	x	x	x
STRINGSIZE	STRZ					x	x	x
iSUB						x	x	x	x
SUBSCRIPTRANGE	SUBRG	x			x	x	x	x
SUBSTR(string,i[,j])		x	x	x	x	x	x	x
SUM(x)		x	x	x	x	x	x	x
SYSIPT			x	x		x		
SYSIN		x			x	x	x	x

664

Use of keyword	Examples and other information
Statement	STOP; Causes immediate termination of the main task and all subtasks
Attribute	DCL F FILE STREAM; Specifies that the data on the external medium is to be considered a continuous stream of characters
Built-in function, pseudo-variable	X = STRING(Y); Returns a string representing the concatenation of all elements of a structure or array
Option of GET and PUT statements	GET STRING(X) EDIT (A, B, C) (3F(3)); Data is to be transmitted from string X to the variables A, B, and C
Condition	(STRINGRANGE): X = SUBSTR(Y, 1, I); Raised when arguments of SUBSTR specify substring beyond the range of the first argument
Condition	(STRINGSIZE): X = SUBSTR(Y, I, J); Raised when longer string assigned to shorter string requiring truncation
Dummy variable of DEFINED attribute	DCL A(10, 10), B(10)DEF A(1SUB, 1SUB); Specifies that B(i) is the same element as A(i, i)
Condition	(SUBRG): A = B(I*J); Raised when subscript exceeds upper bound or lower bound of array dimension
Built-in function, pseudo-variable	A = SUBSTR(B, 1, 5); Returns the portion of the first string argument starting at the ith position for j characters
Built-in function	X = SUM(Y); Returns the sum of all elements of an array argument
Standard DOS system input logical unit name	DCL C FILE INPUT RECORD ENV(F(80)MEDIUM(SYSIPT,2540)); Data will be transmitted from the device which is assigned to SYSIPT
Standard PL/I input file name	GET LIST(A, B, C); Exactly equivalent to GET FILE (SYSIN) LIST(A, B, C):

Note: x = feature available; * = feature planned but not implemented at time of publication of this text; blank = feature not available.

Keyword	Abbreviation	PL/C	Model 20	PL/I D	PL/I F	DOS PL/I optimizer	OS PL/I optimizer	PL/I checkout
SYSLST			x	x		x		
SYSPRINT		x			x	x	x	x
SYSTEM		x	x	x	x	x	x	x
SYSTEM						x	x	x
TAN(x)		x	x	x	x	x	x	x
TAND(x)		x		x	x	x	x	x
TANH(x)		x	x	x	x	x	x	x
TASK					x		x	x
TASK(task name)					x		x	x
THEN		x	x	x	x	x	x	x
%THEN					x	x	x	x

Use of keyword	Examples and other information
Standard DOS system output logical name unit	DCL F FILE OUTPUT PRINT ENV(F(121)MEDIUM(SYSLST, 1403)); Data will be transmitted to the device which is assigned to SYSLST
Standard PL/I output file name	PUT LIST(A, B, C); Exactly equivalent to PUT FILE(SYSPRINT) LIST (A, B, C);
Option of ON statement	ON FOFL SYSTEM; Specifies that standard system action is to take place when condition is raised
Option of DEFAULT statement	DEFAULT RANGE(*) SYSTEM; Specifies that standard PL/I default rules are to be in effect
Built-in function	X=TAN(Y); Returns the tangent of the argument expressed in radians
Built-in function	X=TAN(Y); Returns the tangent of the argument expressed in in degrees
Built-in function	X=TANH(Y); Returns the hyperbolic tangent of argument expressed in radians
Attribute, option of PROCEDURE statement	DCL T TASK; Specifies that the associated identifier is the name of a task
Option of CALL statement	CALL X TASK(T); Specifies that a task named T is to be created by invoking the entry point X
Clause of the IF statement	IF A=B THEN . . .; Specifies the action to be taken if the logical expression is true
Clause of the %IF statement	%IF A=B %THEN . . .; Specifies the action to be taken if the logical expression is true

Note: x = feature available; * = feature planned but not implemented at time of publication of this text; blank = feature not available.

Keyword	Abbreviation	PL/C	Model 20	PL/I D	PL/I F	DOS PL/I optimizer	OS PL/I optimizer	PL/I checkout
TIME		x		x	x	x	x	x
TITLE(x)		x			x		x	x
TO		x	x	x	x	x	x	x
TP(M | R)							x	x
TRANSIENT					x		x	x
TRANSLATE(s,r,p)		x			x	x	x	x
TRANSMIT(file name)			x	x	x	x	x	x
TRKOFL					x		x	x
TRUNC(x)		x	x	x	x	x	x	x
U			x	x	x	x	x	x
UNALIGNED	UNAL (not allowed in subset)	x		x	x	x	x	x
UNBUFFERED	UNBUF (not allowed in subset			x	x	x	x	x

668

Use of keyword	Examples and other information
Built-in function	T=TIME; Returns the time of day in the form HHMMSSTTT, where HH is the hour, MM is the minute, SS is the second, and TTT are milliseconds
Option of OPEN statement	OPEN FILE(F)TITLE('FILE1'); Specifies the DD name to be used to locate and define the data set
Clause of DO statement	DO I=1 TO 100; Specifies the limit value of the control variable
Option of ENVIRONMENT attribute	DCL F FILE TRANSIENT(TP(M) RECSIZE(200)); Specifies that teleprocessing data is to be transmitted in record (R) or message (M) form
Attribute	DCL F FILE TRANSIENT; Specifies a teleprocessing file
Built-in function	A=TRANSLATE(B,',.', '.,'); Returns B with all periods replaced with commas and all commas replaced by periods
Condition	ON TRANSMIT(F)BEGIN; . . .; Raised by a permanent I/O error on named file
Option of ENVIRONMENT attribute	DCL F FILE ENV(TRKOFL); Specifies that records may overflow the end of a track on a direct access device
Built-in function	X=TRUNC(Y); Returns an integer; FLOOR(Y) if $Y > = 0$; CEIL(Y) if $Y < 0$
Option of ENVIRONMENT attribute	DCL F FILE ENV(U); Specifies that records in file are of undetermined length
Attribute	DCL X UNAL; Specifies that data item need not be mapped on an integral word boundary
Attribute	DCL F FILE UNBUF; Specifies that records need not pass through intermediate storage

Note: x = feature available; * = feature planned but not implemented at time of publication of this text; blank = feature not available.

Keyword	Abbreviation	PL/C	Model 20	PL/I D	PL/I F	DOS PL/I optimizer	OS PL/I optimizer	PL/I checkout
UNDEFINEDFILE(file name)	UNDF	x			x	x	x	x
UNDERFLOW	UFL (not allowed in subset)	x	x	x	x	x	x	x
UNLOAD			x					
UNLOCK					x		x	x
UNSPEC(x)		x		x	x	x	x	x
UPDATE		*	x	x	x	x	x	x
V			x	x	x	x	x	x
VALUE						x	x	x
VARIABLE						x	x	x
VARYING	VAR	x			x	x	x	x
VB					x	x	x	x
VBS					x		x	x

Use of keyword	Examples and other information
Condition	ON UNDEFINEDFILE(F)BEGIN; . . . ; Raised if named file cannot be opened
Condition	ON UNDERFLOW BEGIN; . . . ; Raised if exponent of floating scale variable becomes too small
Option of ENVIRONMENT attribute	DCL F FILE ENV(UNLOAD); Causes a tape file to be rewound and unloaded at EOF, EOV, or CLOSE
Statement	UNLOCK FILE(F); Releases exclusive control of a file
Built-in function, pseudo-variable	X=UNSPEC(Y); Returns bit-string which is the internal representation of argument
Attribute	DCL F FILE UPDATE; Specifies that the file is to be used for both INPUT and OUTPUT
Option of ENVIRONMENT attribute	DCL F FILE ENV(V(100)); Specifies that file contains variable-length records
Option of DEFAULT statement	DEFAULT RANGE(*)VALUE(CHAR(10)); Establishes default rules for string length, area size, and precision
Attribute	DCL (E ENTRY, F FILE) VARIABLE; Specifies that the associated ENTRY, FILE, or LABEL is to be a variable rather than a constant
Attribute	DCL C CHAR(100) VARYING; Specifies that the string is to varying length; length causes maximum required space to be allocated
Option of ENVIRONMENT attribute	DCL F FILE ENV(VB); Specifies record format to be variable-length blocked
Option of ENVIRONMENT attribute	DCL F FILE ENV(VBS); Specifies that the record format is variable blocked spanned

Note: x = feature available; * = feature planned but not implemented at time of publication of this text; blank = feature not available.

Keyword	Abbreviation	PL/C	Model 20	PL/I D	PL/I F	DOS PL/I optimizer	OS PL/I optimizer	PL/I checkout
VERIFY			x	x		x	x	
VERIFY(string$_1$,string$_2$)		x			x	x	x	x
VS					x		x	x
WAIT					x	x	x	x
WHEN						x	x	x
WHILE		x		x	x	x	x	x
WRITE		x	x	x	x	x	x	x
ZERODIVIDE	ZDIV (not allowed in subset)	x	x	x	x	x	x	x

672

Use of keyword	Examples and other information
Option of ENVIRONMENT attribute	DCL F FILE ENV(VERIFY); Specifies that write disk check be performed by reading and comparing
Built-in function	IF VERIFY(S, '0123456789')=0 THEN ...; Returns the position within the first string argument in which a character appears which is not present in the second argument
Option of ENVIRONMENT attribute	DCL F FILE ENV(VS); Specifies that the record format is variable spanned
Statement	WAIT (EV1,EV2,EV3)(1); The task will wait until one of the list of events has completed
Used with GENERIC attribute	DCL E GENERIC(E1 WHEN(FIXED), E2 WHEN (FLOAT)); Specifies the selection criteria for entry point selection
Option of DO statement	DO WHILE(P¬=NULL); Specifies iterative processing as long as WHILE clause is true
Statement	WRITE FILE(F) FROM (A); Specifies output data transmission for record files
Condition	ON ZERODIVIDE BEGIN; Raised when an attempt to divide by zero is made

Note: x = feature available; * = feature planned but not implemented at time of publication of this text; blank = feature not available.

Some Debugging Tools for the PL/C Compiler

Following is a chart depicting a number of useful debugging features of PL/C. These features, in many cases, have a counterpart in IBM's PL/I Checkout Compiler. The examples provided here are applicable to PL/C. Consult the programmer's guide for the Checkout Compiler for the equivalent features which are requested via the *PROCESS statement.

PL/C keyword	Use of keyword	Examples and other information
ALL	Diagnostic option of PUT statement	PUT ALL; Debugging facility; places value of all *scalar* variables on SYS-PRINT file (note distinction from PUT ALL of the optimizer and checkout compilers)
ARRAY	Diagnostic option of PUT statement	PUT ARRAY; Debugging facility; places value of all scalar *and array* variables on SYSPRINT file
CHECK[(a[,b])]	Statement	CHECK(10,20); Enables printing for the next 10 changes of value for CHECKed variables in the current block, and the first 20 in any block entered from this one
DEPTH(exp)	Diagnostic option of PUT statement	PUT SNAP DEPTH(3); Debugging facility; limits traceback to 3 levels
FLOW	Condition	ON FLOW BEGIN; Specifies on-unit whenever sequential execution is interrupted by a GO TO, CALL, IF ... THEN ... ELSE, DO, END, RETURN, or other such statement

FLOW	Diagnostic option of PUT statement	PUT FLOW; Debugging facility; places on SYSPRINT the current history of nonsequential execution (i.e., execution which raised the FLOW condition)
FLOW[(a[,b])]	Statement	FLOW(10,20); Invokes automatic printing for the next 10 instances of non-sequential execution in the current block, and the first 20 in any block entered from this one
NOCHECK	Statement	NOCHECK: Cancels printing of value changes of CHECKed variables
NOFLOW	Condition prefix	(NOFLOW): CALL SUB1(X); Disables the FLOW condition for scope of statement
NOFLOW	Statement	NOFLOW; Cancels automatic printing for instances of nonsequential execution
NOSOURCE	Statement	NOSOURCE; Cancels source program listing from this point
OFF	Diagnostic option of PUT statement	PUT OFF; Debugging facility; cancels subsequent output on SYSPRINT
ON	Diagnostic option of PUT statement	PUT ON; Debugging facility, restores printing on SYSPRINT

(Continued)

PL/C keyword	Use of keyword	Examples and other information
ONDEST	Built-in function	I=ONDEST; Returns the statement number of the statement which was the destination of the nonsequential execution causing the FLOW condition to be raised
ONORIG	Built-in function	I=ONORIG; Returns the statement number of the statement which was the origin of the nonsequential execution causing the FLOW condition to be raised
SNAP	Diagnostic option of PUT statement	PUT SNAP; Debugging facility; causes a traceback of currently active blocks to be placed on SYSPRINT
SOURCE	Statement	SOURCE; Restores source program listing from this point
STMTNO (label)	Built-in function	I=STMTNO(L); Returns the statement number of the statement labeled L

appendix B

Bibliography

PL/I Programmer's Guides

Model 20 Disk Programming System PL/I User's Guide, GC33–6007
PL/I (D) Programmer's Guide, C24–9005
PL/I (F) Programmer's Guide, C28–6594
OS PL/I Optimizing Compiler Programmer's Guide, SC33–0006
OS PL/I Checkout Compiler Programmer's Guide, SC33–0007
DOS Optimizing Compiler Programmer's Guide, SC33–0008

Language Reference Manuals

Disk and Tape Operating Systems PL/I Subset Reference Manual, C28–8202
PL/I (F) Language Reference Manual, GC28–8201
DOS PL/I Optimizing Compiler Language Reference Manual, SC33–0005
OS PL/I Optimizing Compiler Language Reference Manual, SC33–0009

appendix C

Data Conversion Rules

This appendix gives the rules for arithmetic conversion and for conversion of problem data types. This appendix has been directly taken from the IBM PL/I F Reference Manual (GC28-8201-3). Due to the importance of the topic, it was felt that this material should be included in this text in the event that the reader does not have access to an appropriate reference manual. Rules for arithmetic conversion may change or vary from PL/I implementation to PL/I implementation. A current reference manual should always be the final authority.

For an example of how to use and interpret these charts, you may wish to refer to Chapter 6, pp. 319–322. Following is an explanation of the symbols used in these charts:

p = Resulting precision
q = Resulting number of fractional digits
p_1 = Precision of the first operand
p_2 = Precision of the second operand
q_1 = Number of fractional digits in the first operand
q_2 = Number of fractional digits in the second operand
r = The meaning of this symbol is defined where needed in the appropriate boxes
s = The meaning of this symbol is defined where needed in the appropriate boxes

SECOND OPERAND	First Operand			
	DECIMAL FIXED(p_1,q_1)	DECIMAL FLOAT(p_1)	BINARY FIXED(p_1,q_1)	BINARY FLOAT(p_1)
DECIMAL FIXED (p_2,q_2)	DECIMAL FIXED(p,q) $p=1+MAX(p_1-q_1,p_2-q_2)+MAX(q_1,q_2)$ $q=MAX(q_1,q_2)$	DECIMAL FLOAT(p) $p=MAX(p_1,p_2)$	BINARY FIXED(p,q) $p=1+MAX(p_1-q_1,r-s)+MAX(q_1,s)$ $q=MAX(q_1,s)$ where: $r=1+p_2*3.32$ $s=q_2*3.32$	BINARY FLOAT(p) $p=MAX(p_1,r)$ where: $r=p_2*3.32$
DECIMAL FLOAT (p_2)	DECIMAL FLOAT(p) $p=MAX(p_1,p_2)$	DECIMAL FLOAT(p) $p=MAX(p_1,p_2)$	BINARY FLOAT(p) $p=MAX(p_1,r)$ where: $r=p_2*3.32$	BINARY FLOAT(p) $p=MAX(p_1,r)$ where: $r=p_2*3.32$
BINARY FIXED (p_2,q_2)	BINARY FIXED(p,q) $p=1+MAX(r-s,p_2-q_2)+MAX(s,q_2)$ $q=MAX(s,q_2)$ where: $r=1+p_1*3.32$ $s=q_1*3.32$	BINARY FLOAT(p) $p=MAX(r,p_2)$ where: $r=p_1*3.32$	BINARY FIXED(p,q) $p=1+MAX(p_1-q_1,p_2-q_2)+MAX(q_1,q_2)$ $q=MAX(q_1,q_2)$	BINARY FLOAT(p) $p=MAX(p_1,p_2)$
BINARY FLOAT (p_2)	BINARY FLOAT(p) $p=MAX(r,p_2)$ where: $r=p_1*3.32$	BINARY FLOAT(p) $p=MAX(r,p_2)$ where: $r=p_1*3.32$	BINARY FLOAT(p) $p=MAX(p_1,p_2)$	BINARY FLOAT(p) $p=MAX(p_1,p_2)$

FIGURE C.1 Attributes of result in addition and subtraction operations.

SECOND OPERAND	First Operand			
	DECIMAL FIXED(p_1,q_1)	DECIMAL FLOAT(p_1)	BINARY FIXED(p_1,q_1)	BINARY FLOAT(p_1)
DECIMAL FIXED (p_2,q_2)	DECIMAL FIXED(p,q) $p=p_1+p_2+1$ $q=q_1+q_2$	DECIMAL FLOAT(p) $p=MAX(p_1,p_2)$	BINARY FIXED(p,q) $p=p_1+r+1$ $q=q_1+s$ where: $r=1+p_2*3.32$ $s=q_2*3.32$	BINARY FLOAT(p) $p=MAX(p_1,r)$ where: $r=p_2*3.32$
DECIMAL FLOAT (p_2)	DECIMAL FLOAT(p) $p=MAX(p_1,p_2)$	DECIMAL FLOAT(p) $p=MAX(p_1,p_2)$	BINARY FLOAT(p) $p=MAX(p_1,r)$ where: $r=p_2*3.32$	BINARY FLOAT(p) $p=MAX(p_1,r)$ where: $r=p_2*3.32$
BINARY FIXED (p_2,q_2)	BINARY FIXED(p,q) $p=r+p_2+1$ $q=s+q_2$ where: $r=1+p_1*3.32$ $s=q_1*3.32$	BINARY FLOAT(p) $p=MAX(r,p_2)$ where: $r=p_1*3.32$	BINARY FIXED(p,q) $p=p_1+p_2+1$ $q=q_1+q_2$	BINARY FLOAT(p) $p=MAX(p_1,p_2)$
BINARY FLOAT (p_2)	BINARY FLOAT(p) $p=MAX(r,p_2)$ where: $r=p_1*3.32$	BINARY FLOAT(p) $p=MAX(r,p_2)$ where: $r=p_1*3.32$	BINARY FLOAT(p) $p=MAX(p_1,p_2)$	BINARY FLOAT(p) $p=MAX(p_1,p_2)$

FIGURE C.2 Attributes of result in multiplication operations.

FIGURE C.3 Attributes of result in division operations.

SECOND OPERAND	First Operand			
	DECIMAL FIXED(p_1,q_1)	DECIMAL FLOAT(p_1)	BINARY FIXED(p_1,q_1)	BINARY FLOAT(p_1)

DECIMAL FIXED (p_2,q_2)	DECIMAL FIXED(p,q)
	$p=15$
	$q=15-((p_1-q_1)+q_2)$
		DECIMAL FLOAT(p)
		$p=MAX(p_1,p_2)$
			BINARY FIXED(p,q)
			$p=31$
			$q=31-((p_1-q_1)+s)$
			where:
			    $s=q_2*3.32$
				BINARY FLOAT(p)
				$p=MAX(p_1,r)$
				where:
				    $r=p_2*3.32$

DECIMAL FLOAT (p_2)	DECIMAL FLOAT(p)
	$p=MAX(p_1,p_2)$
		DECIMAL FLOAT(p)
		$p=MAX(p_1,p_2)$
			BINARY FLOAT(p)
			$p=MAX(p_1,r)$
			where:
			    $r=p_2*3.32$
				BINARY FLOAT(p)
				$p=MAX(p_1,r)$
				where:
				    $r=p_2*3.32$

BINARY FIXED (p_2,q_2)	BINARY FIXED(p)
	$p=31$
	$q=31-((r-s)+q_2)$
	where:
	    $r=1+p_1*3.32$
	    $s=q_1*3.32$
		BINARY FLOAT(p)
		$p=MAX(r,p_2)$
		where:
		    $r=p_1*3.32$
			BINARY FIXED(p,q)
			$p=31$
			$q=31-((p_1-q_1)+q_2)$
				BINARY FLOAT(p)
				$p=MAX(p_1,p_2)$

BINARY FLOAT (p_2)	BINARY FLOAT(p)
	$p=MAX(r,p_2)$
	where:
	    $r=p_1*3.32$
		BINARY FLOAT(p)
		$p=MAX(r,p_2)$
		where:
		    $r=p_1*3.32$
			BINARY FLOAT(p)
			$p=MAX(p_1,p_2)$
				BINARY FLOAT(p)
				$p=MAX(p_1,p_2)$

FIGURE C.4 Attributes of result in exponentiation operations.

Case	First Operand	Second Operand (Exponent)	Target Attributes of Result
(1)	FIXED DECIMAL(p_1,q_1)	Unsigned integer constant with value n	FIXED DECIMAL(p,q) [provided $p\leq15$] $p=(p_1+1)*n-1$ $q=q_1*n$
(2)	FIXED BINARY(p_1,q_1)	Unsigned integer constant with value n	FIXED BINARY(p,q) [provided $p\leq31$] $p=(p_1+1)*n-1$ $q=q_1*n$
(3)	FIXED DECIMAL(p_1,q_1) or FLOAT DECIMAL(p_1)	FIXED DECIMAL(p_2,q_2) or FLOAT DECIMAL(p_2)	FLOAT DECIMAL(p) [unless case (1) or (7) is applicable] $p=MAX(p_1,p_2)$
(4)	FIXED BINARY(p_1,q_1) or FLOAT BINARY(p_1)	FIXED DECIMAL(p_2,q_2) or FLOAT DECIMAL(p_2)	FLOAT BINARY(p) [unless case (2) or (7) is applicable] $p=MAX(p_1,CEIL(3.32*p_2))$
(5)	FIXED DECIMAL(p_1,q_1) or FLOAT DECIMAL(p_1)	FIXED BINARY(p_2,q_2) or FLOAT BINARY(p_2)	FLOAT BINARY(p) [unless case (1) or (7) is applicable] $p=MAX(CEIL(3.32*p_1),p_2)$
(6)	FIXED BINARY(p_1,q_1) or FLOAT BINARY(p_1)	FIXED BINARY(p_2,q_2) or FLOAT BINARY(p_2)	FLOAT BINARY(p) [unless case (2) or (7) is applicable] $p=MAX(p_1,p_2)$
(7)	FLOAT DECIMAL(p_1) or FLOAT BINARY(p_1)	FIXED DECIMAL$(p_2,0)$ or FIXED BINARY$(p_2,0)$	FLOAT(p_1) [with base of first operand]

appendix D

Data Formats and
Number Systems

As long as man has had the need to count, number systems have existed. The decimal (*base 10*) number system is the one most widely used in the western world, undoubtedly because man has ten fingers. Other number systems have been used by man. The Babylonians and Sumerians used a *base 60* (time), the Mayans a *base 20* (fingers and toes?), and some North American Indian tribes a *base 5* (one hand?). You not only use the base 10 system today, but also several other number systems: *base 12* for the measurement of inches and feet, and *base 16* for the measurement of ounces and pounds.

Most number systems have these things in common:

1. There are as many unique symbols as the base. There are ten symbols, 0 through 9, in the base 10 system. The binary system—base 2— requires only two symbols, 0 and 1.
2. The place value of the least significant digit always begins with 1.
3. Each subsequent place value is n times greater than the previous place value, where n is the number of the base. Thus, in the decimal number system, each place value is ten times greater than the previous place value. In the binary number system, each place value is two times greater than the previous place value.

Decimal Number System Reviewed

Following is an illustration of the significance of *place values* in the decimal numbering system. Using the decimal number 2435, we have:

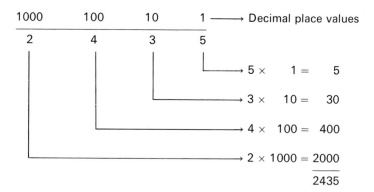

Note, for example, that the digit "4" has a value of "400" because it appears in the "100's position."

Binary Number System Explained

The digits used to express binary quantities are 0 and 1. A binary digit is called a *bit*, a contraction of the words *bi*nary and di*git*. In the base 2 or binary system, each place value is two times greater than the previous place value. For example:

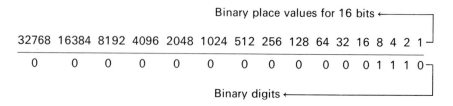

In the above example, the decimal value 14 is represented in binary as 1110. One process of converting binary numbers to their decimal equivalents is to add together the place values for each binary position where a "1" appears.

Let us try another example :

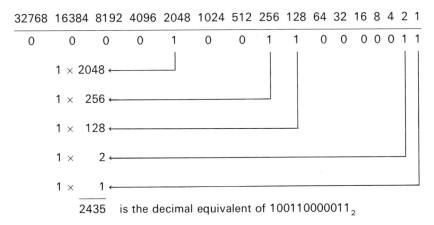

32768 16384 8192 4096 2048 1024 512 256 128 64 32 16 8 4 2 1

| 0 | 0 | 0 | 0 | 1 | 0 | 0 | 1 | 1 | 0 | 0 | 0 | 0 | 0 | 1 | 1 |

1×2048 ←

$1 \times \quad 256$ ←

$1 \times \quad 128$ ←

$1 \times \quad\quad 2$ ←

$\underline{1 \times \quad\quad 1}$ ←

2435 is the decimal equivalent of 100110000011_2

Seldom does a programmer have to be concerned with converting decimal numbers to binary or vice versa. However, as pointed out in Chapter 1, the use of binary data in a PL/I program can result in faster execution time and more efficient use of storage in the representation of data.

Hexadecimal Number System Explained

There are occasions when it may be necessary to print the contents of main storage so that a programmer can peruse the storage "dump" in an effort to locate errors in his programming logic or data formats. There are utility programs designed to dump the contents of main storage in a data format called hexadecimal or *base 16*. Hexadecimal is a shorthand notation used to express binary data in a more concise form on printout. Let us see how base 16 meets the requirements for number systems.

1.   "There are as many unique symbols as the base." The 16 symbols used in the hexadecimal number system are: 0, 1, 2, 3, 4, 5, 6, 7, 8, 9, A, B, C, D, E, and F. As can be seen in Figure D.1, the letter A corresponds to the decimal value of 10, the letter B is equal to a decimal value of 11, C is used to represent a decimal 12, D for 13, E for 14, and F for 15.
2.   "The place value of the least significant digit is always 1."
3.   "Each place value is n times greater than the previous place value, where n is the number of the base." Thus, in base 16, each place value is 16 times greater than the previous place value.

Here are the hexadecimal place values:

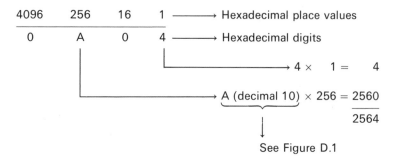

See Figure D.1

Thus, in the above example, $(A04)_{16} = (2564)_{10}$. Here is an example of how the hexadecimal value 3EAF is equal to a decimal value of 16,047:

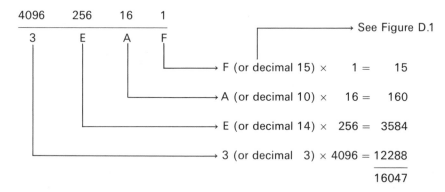

There is a relationship between hexadecimal and binary number systems. Every four bits of a 16-bit binary number can be expressed as a hexadecimal digit. For example:

```
1 1 1 1   0 0 0 1   0 0 0 0   1 0 0 1 → Binary value

   F         1         0         9     → Hexadecimal equivalent
```

Figure D.1 shows the binary and hexadecimal equivalents for the decimal values 1 to 15. Here is how the conversion from binary to hexadecimal numbers works: To convert binary to hexadecimal, divide the 16-bit binary number into groups of four bits each; mentally place the decimal values 8 4 2 1 above each group of four bits; and convert each group of four bits to a hexadecimal number.

Decimal	Binary	Hexadecimal
0	0000	0
1	0001	1
2	0010	2
3	0011	3
4	0100	4
5	0101	5
6	0110	6
7	0111	7
8	1000	8
9	1001	9
10	1010	A
11	1011	B
12	1100	C
13	1101	D
14	1110	E
15	1111	F

FIGURE D.1 Binary and hexadecimal equivalents for the decimal values 1 to 15.

For example:

```
8 4 2 1   8 4 2 1   8 4 2 1   8 4 2 1 ← Binary place values for
                                        each group of 4 bits
1 1 1 1   0 0 0 1   0 0 0 0   1 0 0 1 ← Binary value

   F         1         0         9    ← Hexadecimal equivalent
```

Compare the binary place values with the hexadecimal place values. Notice that every *fourth* binary place value (starting with the first place value) is

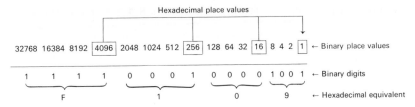

equal to a place value in the hexadecimal number system. Because every fourth binary place value is a place value in the hexadecimal number system, there is a relationship between binary and hexadecimal. Let us take another example

686 PL/I Programming

Positive Binary Values Bit Positions 11 1111 1111 2222 2222 2233 / 0123 4567 8901 2345 6789 0123 4567 8901	Powers of 2	Absolute Values Decimal Notation Base – 10	Absolute Values Hexadecimal Notation Base – 16	Negative Binary Values Bit Positions 11 1111 1111 2222 2222 2233 / 0123 4567 8901 2345 6789 0123 4567 8901
0000 0000 0000 0000 0000 0000 0000 0000	–	0	0	No negative zero
0000 0000 0000 0000 0000 0000 0000 0001	0	1	1	1111 1111 1111 1111 1111 1111 1111 1111
0000 0000 0000 0000 0000 0000 0000 0010	1	2	2	1111 1111 1111 1111 1111 1111 1111 1110
0000 0000 0000 0000 0000 0000 0000 0100	2	4	4	1111 1111 1111 1111 1111 1111 1111 1100
0000 0000 0000 0000 0000 0000 0000 1000	3	8	8	1111 1111 1111 1111 1111 1111 1111 1000
0000 0000 0000 0000 0000 0000 0001 0000	4	16	10	1111 1111 1111 1111 1111 1111 1111 0000
0000 0000 0000 0000 0000 0000 0010 0000	5	32	20	1111 1111 1111 1111 1111 1111 1110 0000
0000 0000 0000 0000 0000 0000 0100 0000	6	64	40	1111 1111 1111 1111 1111 1111 1100 0000
0000 0000 0000 0000 0000 0000 1000 0000	7	128	80	1111 1111 1111 1111 1111 1111 1000 0000
0000 0000 0000 0000 0000 0001 0000 0000	8	256	100	1111 1111 1111 1111 1111 1111 0000 0000
0000 0000 0000 0000 0000 0010 0000 0000	9	512	200	1111 1111 1111 1111 1111 1110 0000 0000
0000 0000 0000 0000 0000 0100 0000 0000	10	1,024	400	1111 1111 1111 1111 1111 1100 0000 0000
0000 0000 0000 0000 0000 1000 0000 0000	11	2,048	800	1111 1111 1111 1111 1111 1000 0000 0000
0000 0000 0000 0000 0001 0000 0000 0000	12	4,096	1,000	1111 1111 1111 1111 1111 0000 0000 0000
0000 0000 0000 0000 0010 0000 0000 0000	13	8,192	2,000	1111 1111 1111 1111 1110 0000 0000 0000
0000 0000 0000 0000 0100 0000 0000 0000	14	16,384	4,000	1111 1111 1111 1111 1100 0000 0000 0000
0000 0000 0000 0000 1000 0000 0000 0000	15	32,768	8,000	1111 1111 1111 1111 1000 0000 0000 0000
0000 0000 0000 0001 0000 0000 0000 0000	16	65,536	10,000	1111 1111 1111 1111 0000 0000 0000 0000
0000 0000 0000 0010 0000 0000 0000 0000	17	131,072	20,000	1111 1111 1111 1110 0000 0000 0000 0000
0000 0000 0000 0100 0000 0000 0000 0000	18	262,144	40,000	1111 1111 1111 1100 0000 0000 0000 0000
0000 0000 0000 1000 0000 0000 0000 0000	19	524,288	80,000	1111 1111 1111 1000 0000 0000 0000 0000
0000 0000 0001 0000 0000 0000 0000 0000	20	1,048,576	100,000	1111 1111 1111 0000 0000 0000 0000 0000
0000 0000 0010 0000 0000 0000 0000 0000	21	2,097,152	200,000	1111 1111 1110 0000 0000 0000 0000 0000
0000 0000 0100 0000 0000 0000 0000 0000	22	4,194,304	400,000	1111 1111 1100 0000 0000 0000 0000 0000
0000 0000 1000 0000 0000 0000 0000 0000	23	8,388,608	800,000	1111 1111 1000 0000 0000 0000 0000 0000
0000 0001 0000 0000 0000 0000 0000 0000	24	16,777,216	1,000,000	1111 1111 0000 0000 0000 0000 0000 0000
0000 0010 0000 0000 0000 0000 0000 0000	25	33,554,432	2,000,000	1111 1110 0000 0000 0000 0000 0000 0000
0000 0100 0000 0000 0000 0000 0000 0000	26	67,108,864	4,000,000	1111 1100 0000 0000 0000 0000 0000 0000
0000 1000 0000 0000 0000 0000 0000 0000	27	134,217,728	8,000,000	1111 1000 0000 0000 0000 0000 0000 0000
0001 0000 0000 0000 0000 0000 0000 0000	28	268,435,456	10,000,000	1111 0000 0000 0000 0000 0000 0000 0000
0010 0000 0000 0000 0000 0000 0000 0000	29	536,870,912	20,000,000	1110 0000 0000 0000 0000 0000 0000 0000
0100 0000 0000 0000 0000 0000 0000 0000	30	1,073,741,824	40,000,000	1100 0000 0000 0000 0000 0000 0000 0000
0111 1111 1111 1111 1111 1111 1111 1111	–	2,147,483,647	7F,FFF,FFF	1000 0000 0000 0000 0000 0000 0000 0001
No positive equivalent	31	2,147,483,648	80,000,000	1000 0000 0000 0000 0000 0000 0000 0000

FIGURE D.2   Powers of two table.

in converting binary to hexadecimal:

```
0 0 0 1   0 0 1 0   0 0 1 1   0 1 0 0 → Binary number
   1          2         3         4    → Hexadecimal equivalent
```

Again, to arrive at the hexadecimal equivalents, you must mentally place over each group of four bits the decimal place values 8 4 2 1. For example:

```
8 4 2 1   8 4 2 1   8 4 2 1   8 4 2 1 → Place values for each
                                         group of 4 bits
0 0 0 1   0 0 1 0   0 0 1 1   0 1 0 0 → Binary number
   1          2         3         4    → Hexadecimal equivalent
```

Hexadecimal and Decimal Conversion

To find the decimal number, locate the hexadecimal number and its decimal equivalent for each position. Add these to obtain the decimal number.

To find the hexadecimal number, locate the next lower decimal number and its hexadecimal equivalent. Each difference is used to obtain the next hexadecimal number until the entire number is developed.

Figure D.2 shows a powers of two table that should be helpful in converting decimal to binary or vice versa. Figure D.3 should be helpful in converting hexadecimal to decimal values.

BYTE		BYTE		BYTE	
0123	4567	0123	4567	0123	4567
HEX DEC	HEX DEC	HEX DEC	HEX DEC	HEX DEC	HEX DEC
0 0	0 0	0 0	0 0	0 0	0 0
1 1,048,576	1 65,536	1 4,096	1 256	1 16	1 1
2 2,097,152	2 131,072	2 8,192	2 512	2 32	2 2
3 3,145,728	3 196,608	3 12,288	3 768	3 48	3 3
4 4,194,304	4 262,144	4 16,384	4 1,024	4 64	4 4
5 5,242,880	5 327,680	5 20,480	5 1,280	5 80	5 5
6 6,291,456	6 393,216	6 24,576	6 1,536	6 96	6 6
7 7,340,032	7 458,752	7 28,672	7 1,792	7 112	7 7
8 8,388,608	8 524,288	8 32,768	8 2,048	8 128	8 8
9 9,437,184	9 589,824	9 36,864	9 2,304	9 144	9 9
A 10,485,760	A 655,360	A 40,960	A 2,560	A 160	A 10
B 11,534,336	B 720,896	B 45,056	B 2,816	B 176	B 11
C 12,582,912	C 786,432	C 49,152	C 3,072	C 192	C 12
D 13,631,488	D 851,968	D 53,248	D 3,328	D 208	D 13
E 14,680,064	E 917,504	E 57,344	E 3,584	E 224	E 14
F 15,728,640	F 983,040	F 61,440	F 3,840	F 240	F 15
6	5	4	3	2	1

FIGURE D.3 Hexadecimal conversion chart.

S/360 and S/370 Data Formats

Packed Decimal

From one to 16 bytes may be used to store a sequence of decimal digits representing an arithmetic value. A pattern of four bits is defined for each decimal digit. Since a byte consists of eight bits, up to two decimal digits may be *packed* into one byte. In addition, one half of a byte is reserved for the algebraic sign (+ or −) of the number. For example, to represent +5, one byte is needed:

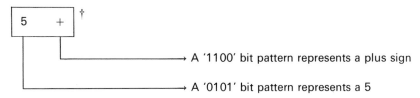

A '1100' bit pattern represents a plus sign

A '0101' bit pattern represents a 5

†Each rectangle represents one byte which is the basic unit of main storage in S/360 and S/370. A byte (for BinarY TErm) consists of eight bits. A byte or combination of contiguous bytes may be used to store data.

To represent −12, two bytes are used:

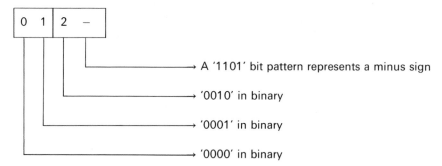

Notice how the sign of the number always appears in the rightmost four bits of the right-hand byte. Also notice, in the above example, how a leading zero was filled in on the left when an even number (e.g., 2, 4, 6, 8, etc.) of digits are to be represented in the packed decimal data format. In the following example, notice that only two bytes are needed to represent a three-digit number:

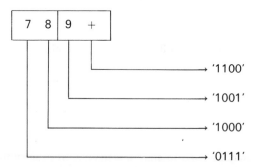

Although S/360 or S/370 provides for a maximum of 16 bytes (or 31 decimal digits) for the packed decimal data format, a maximum of eight bytes, which can contain 15 decimal digits, are allowed in most PL/I compilers.

Fixed-Point

Two or four contiguous bytes may be used to represent this type of data. When two bytes are combined to represent fixed-point binary data, the result is said to be *halfword binary*. Four contiguous bytes constitute a *word*, but the word's address must begin on a "fullword" boundary. This simply means that the starting core address of the four contiguous bytes must be evenly divisible by four. (Halfwords of binary data must have even-numbered core addresses.) The PL/I programmer generally does not have to be concerned that this type of data will be properly placed in main storage (i.e., on a fullword boundary), since the assigning of data to proper storage addresses is automatically done for him by the PL/I compiler.

Here is an example of the value $+65$ as it would appear in fixed-point binary format:

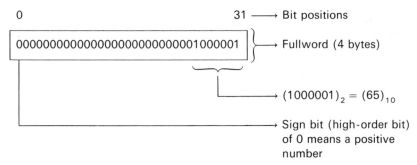

Although it is not important that you understand how negative numbers are represented in fixed-point binary, an example of -5 is shown below. (Fixed-point binary numbers are represented in two's complement form.)

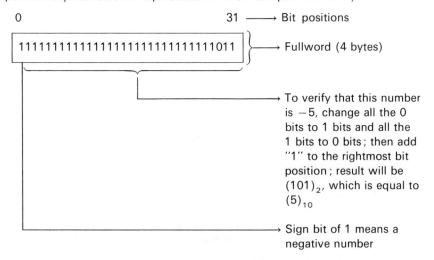

Floating-Point

A floating-point format of ten represents data in a more compact form than does a fixed-point format. This is generally the case when a large number of zeros is required to fix the location of the decimal or binary point in a fixed-point format. For example, the fixed-point decimal fraction .000000009 requires eight zeros to establish the location of the decimal point. In floating-point format the zeros are not needed, because the location of the decimal point is specified by an integer exponent appearing within the floating-point data item.

There are three forms of floating-point data: short form, long form, and extended form:

	1 byte	← 3 bytes →
Short form 4 bytes (fullword)	Exponent	Value

	1 byte	←——— 7 bytes ———→
Long form 8 bytes (double word)	Exponent	Value

	1 byte	←——— 7 bytes ———→
Extended form 16 bytes (two double words)	Exponent	High-order value
	Unused	Low-order value

The primary difference between each form lies in the longer form being able to contain more digits of significance. For example, the number 742682.1130 could not be contained in the short-form floating-point number. The closest that we could come would be 742682, truncating the fraction because of too few bits in the value field. In order to provide a more precise representation of the above number, we must choose a form supplying longer precision (either long or extended).

The *values* of the numbers we can represent in the various forms are, for all practical purposes, the same, because the exponent field determines the magnitude of the number stored in the value field. But the precision maintained in each type is different: for short form, up to six decimal digits; for long form, up to 16 decimal digits; and for extended form, up to 33 decimal digits. Not all PL/I compilers implement all forms of floating-point data. Check the specifications of the compiler you are using for the maximum precision allowed.

As an example of how a decimal number would look in floating-point format inside the computer, consider the decimal value 22.5, which would be written in binary as follows:

16	8	4	2	1	.	1/2	1/4	1/8	→ Binary place values
1	0	1	1	0	.	1	0	0	→ Binary equivalent of 22.5

In terms of S/360 and S/370, floating-point data values are represented in hexadecimal. Thus, the binary value 10110.1 would be represented as follows:

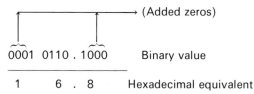

0001 0110 . 1000   Binary value

1   6 . 8   Hexadecimal equivalent

Notice how it was necessary to "pad" with zeros both to the right and to the left of the straight binary value to yield the hexadecimal equivalent. Inside the computer, there is no way to physically record the position of the hexidecimal (or decimal or binary, for that matter) point. The position of the *point* is recorded in the form of an exponent. To relate this back to decimal, we know that

$$22.5 \quad \text{is equivalent to} \quad .225 \times 10^{+2}$$

where 10^{+2} is the exponent. It follows, then, that the hexadecimal value

$$16.8 \quad \text{is equivalent to} \quad .168 \times 16^{+2}$$

Recall the short-form floating-point format:

Exponent	Value
1 byte	←————— 3 bytes —————→

To show how the hexadecimal value would be represented in this format, we begin with the following:

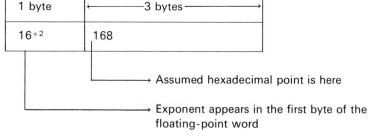

Actually, the first byte of the floating-point data item is called a *characteristic*. Characteristic is the preferred term, because it is made up of the exponent plus another factor which is a constant. The constant value is a hexadecimal 40. For example, if the characteristic is $40)_{16}$, then it is assumed that the fractional value (which is called the *mantissa*) is scaled at 16^0; for a characteristic of $41)_{16}$, the mantissa is scaled at 16^1; for a characteristic of 39, the mantissa is scaled at 16^{-1}. As a further illustration, then, we would have the following:

Hexadecimal characteristic	Equivalent exponent
.	.
.	.
.	.
43	16^3
42	16^2
41	16^1
40	16^0
39	16^{-1}
38	16^{-2}
37	16^{-3}
.	.
.	.
.	.

Thus, the decimal value 22.5 is represented in its hexadecimal equivalent, which is 16.8. Because floating-point values are assumed to be fractions, we will say that the value is $.168 \times 16^2$. The exponent "2" will be added to the hexadecimal constant "40" to give us the characteristic. All of this may be depicted in the following bit structure:

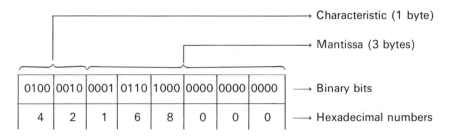

Character

One or more bytes of storage is used to represent a string of characters. One byte of storage is used to represent each alphameric character in a string. In PL/I, the characters may be any of those allowable on a particular computer. For S/360 or S/370 they may be any of the 256 EBCDIC† character set. As an example, to represent KENT, WASH. 98031, 16 bytes are needed:

K	E	N	T	,		W	A	S	H	.	9	8	0	3	1

†Extended Binary Coded Decimal Interchange Code.

Figure D.4 is a chart showing the character codes used in S/360 and S/370 computers. About half of these characters will be familiar to you (e.g., A,a,B,b,C,...). These symbols and other graphics appear in the third column in Figure D.4. The familiar characters may be entered into the computer via a punched card or typewriter or other special input device and are entered in single-character form (i.e., one card column or one typewriter character). There are a number of *control symbols* (e.g., NUL, DEL, ENQ) that are defined on p. 700. These symbols require multiple punches in a card column because the character is not represented on a standard keypunch. Some of these control characters are represented on a typewriter (e.g., EOT) but have no corresponding graphic output. Many of the 256 characters would not be applicable to all I/O devices.

Decimal	Hexadecimal	Graphic and control symbols	Punched card code	S/360, S/370 8-bit code
0	00	NUL	12-0-1-8-9	0000 0000
1	01	SOH	12-1-9	0000 0001
2	02	STX	12-2-9	0000 0010
3	03	ETX	12-3-9	0000 0011
4	04	PF	12-4-9	0000 0100
5	05	HT	12-5-9	0000 0101
6	06	LC	12-6-9	0000 0110
7	07	DEL	12-7-9	0000 0111
8	08		12-8-9	0000 1000
9	09		12-1-8-9	0000 1001
10	0A	SMM	12-2-8-9	0000 1010
11	0B	VT	12-3-8-9	0000 1011
12	0C	FF	12-4-8-9	0000 1100
13	0D	CR	12-5-8-9	0000 1101
14	0E	SO	12-6-8-9	0000 1110
15	0F	SI	12-7-8-9	0000 1111
16	10	DLE	12-11-1-8-9	0001 0000
17	11	DC1	11-1-9	0001 0001
18	12	DC2	11-2-9	0001 0010
19	13	TM	11-3-9	0001 0011
20	14	RES	11-4-9	0001 0100
21	15	NL	11-5-9	0001 0101
22	16	BS	11-6-9	0001 0110
23	17	IL	11-7-9	0001 0111
24	18	CAN	11-8-9	0001 1000
25	19	EM	11-1-8-9	0001 1001

FIGURE D.4 System/360 and System/370 character code chart.

Decimal	Hexadecimal	Graphic and control symbols	Punched card code	S/360, S/370 8-bit code
26	1A	CC	11-2-8-9	0001 1010
27	1B	CU1	11-3-8-9	0001 1011
28	1C	IFS	11-4-8-9	0001 1100
29	1D	IGS	11-5-8-9	0001 1101
30	1E	IRS	11-6-8-9	0001 1110
31	1F	IUS	11-7-8-9	0001 1111
32	20	DS	11-0-1-8-9	0010 0000
33	21	SOS	0-1-9	0010 0001
34	22	FS	0-2-9	0010 0010
35	23		0-3-9	0010 0011
36	24	BYP	0-4-9	0010 0100
37	25	LF	0-5-9	0010 0101
38	26	ETB	0-6-9	0010 0110
39	27	ESC	0-7-9	0010 0111
40	28		0-8-9	0010 1000
41	29		0-1-8-9	0010 1001
42	2A	SM	0-2-8-9	0010 1010
43	2B	CU2	0-3-8-9	0010 1011
44	2C		0-4-8-9	0010 1100
45	2D	ENQ	0-5-8-9	0010 1101
46	2E	ACK	0-6-8-9	0010 1110
47	2F	BEL	0-7-8-9	0010 1111
48	30		12-11-0-1-8-9	0011 0000
49	31		1-9	0011 0001
50	32	SYN	2-9	0011 0010
51	33		3-9	0011 0011
52	34	PN	4-9	0011 0100
53	35	RS	5-9	0011 0101
54	36	UC	6-9	0011 0110
55	37	EOT	7-9	0011 0111
56	38		8-9	0011 1000
57	39		1-8-9	0011 1001
58	3A		2-8-9	0011 1010
59	3B	CU3	3-8-9	0011 1011
60	3C	DC4	4-8-9	0011 1100
61	3D	NAK	5-8-9	0011 1101
62	3E		6-8-9	0011 1110
63	3F	SUB	7-8-9	0011 1111

FIGURE D.4 *Continued*

Decimal	Hexadecimal	Graphic and control symbols	Punched card code	S/360, S/370 8-bit code
64	40	SP	no punches	0100 0000
65	41		12-0-1-9	0100 0001
66	42		12-0-2-9	0100 0010
67	43		12-0-3-9	0100 0011
68	44		12-0-4-9	0100 0100
69	45		12-0-5-9	0100 0101
70	46		12-0-6-9	0100 0110
71	47		12-0-7-9	0100 0111
72	48		12-0-8-9	0110 1000
73	49		12-1-8	0100 1001
74	4A	¢	12-2-8	0100 1010
75	4B	.	12-3-8	0100 1011
76	4C	<	12-4-8	0100 1100
77	4D	(	12-5-8	0100 1101
78	4E	+	12-6-8	0100 1110
79	4F	|	12-7-8	0100 1111
80	50	&	12	0101 0000
81	51		12-11-1-9	0101 0001
82	52		12-11-2-9	0101 0010
83	53		12-11-3-9	0101 0011
84	54		12-11-4-9	0101 0100
85	55		12-11-5-9	0101 0101
86	56		12-11-6-9	0101 0110
87	57		12-11-7-9	0101 0111
88	58		12-11-8-9	0101 1000
89	59		11-1-8	0101 1001
90	5A	!	11-2-8	0101 1010
91	5B	$	11-3-8	0101 1011
92	5C	*	11-4-8	0101 1100
93	5D	)	11-5-8	0101 1101
94	5E	;	11-6-8	0101 1110
95	5F	¬	11-7-8	0101 1111
96	60		11	0110 0000
97	61	/	0-1	0110 0001
98	62		11-0-2-9	0110 0010
99	63		11-0-3-9	0110 0011
100	64		11-0-4-9	0110 0100
101	65		11-0-5-9	0110 0101

Decimal	Hexadécimal	Graphic and control symbols	Punched card code	S/360, S/370 8-bit code
102	66		11-0-6-9	0110 0110
103	67		11-0-7-9	0110 0111
104	68		11-0-8-9	0110 1000
105	69		0-1-8	0110 1001
106	6A		12-11	0110 1010
107	6B	,	0-3-8	0110 1011
108	6C	%	0-4-8	0110 1100
109	6D	—	0-5-8	0110 1101
110	6E	>	0-6-8	0110 1110
111	6F	?	0-7-8	0110 1111
112	70		12-11-0	0111 0000
113	71		12-11-0-1-9	0111 0001
114	72		12-11-0-2-9	0111 0010
115	73		12-11-0-3-9	0111 0011
116	74		12-11-0-4-9	0111 0100
117	75		12-11-0-5-9	0111 0101
118	76		12-11-0-6-9	0111 0110
119	77		12-11-0-7-9	0111 0111
120	78		12-11-0-8-9	0111 1000
121	79		1-8	0111 1001
122	7A	:	2-8	0111 1010
123	7B	#	3-8	0111 1011
124	7C	@	4-8	0111 1100
125	7D	'	5-8	0111 1101
126	7E	=	6-8	0111 1110
127	7F	' '	7-8	0111 1111
128	80		12-0-1-8	1000 0000
129	81	a	12-0-1	1000 0001
130	82	b	12-0-2	1000 0010
131	83	c	12-0-3	1000 0011
132	84	d	12-0-4	1000 0100
133	85	e	12-0-5	1000 0101
134	86	f	12-0-6	1000 0110
135	87	g	12-0-7	1000 0111
136	88	h	12-0-8	1000 1000
137,	89	i	12-0-9	1000 1001
138	8A		12-0-2-8	1000 1010
139	8B		12-0-3-8	1000 1011

FIGURE D.4 *Continued*

Decimal	Hexadecimal	Graphic and control symbols	Punched card code	S/360, S/370 8-bit code
140	8C		12-0-4-8	1000 1100
141	8D		12-0-5-8	1000 1101
142	8E		12-0-6-8	1000 1110
143	8F		12-0-7-8	1000 1111
144	90		12-11-1-8	1001 0000
145	91	j	12-11-1	1001 0001
146	92	k	12-11-2	1001 0010
147	93	l	12-11-3	1001 0011
148	94	m	12-11-4	1001 0100
149	95	n	12-11-5	1001 0101
150	96	o	12-11-6	1001 0110
151	97	p	12-11-7	1001 0111
152	98	q	12-11-8	1001 1000
153	99	r	12-11-9	1001 1001
154	9A		12-11-2-8	1001 1010
155	9B		12-11-3-8	1001 1011
156	9C		12-11-4-8	1001 1100
157	9D		12-11-5-8	1001 1101
158	9E		12-11-6-8	1001 1110
159	9F		12-11-7-8	1001 1111
160	A0		11-0-1-8	1010 0000
161	A1		11-0-1	1010 0001
162	A2	s	11-0-2	1010 0010
163	A3	t	11-0-3	1010 0011
164	A4	u	11-0-4	1010 0100
165	A5	v	11-0-5	1010 0101
166	A6	w	11-0-6	1010 0110
167	A7	x	11-0-7	1010 0111
168	A8	y	11-0-8	1010 1000
169	A9	z	11-0-9	1010 1001
170	AA		11-0-2-8	1010 1010
171	AB		11-0-3-8	1010 1011
172	AC		11-0-4-8	1010 1100
173	AD		11-0-5-8	1010 1101
174	AE		11-0-6-8	1010 1110
175	AF		11-0-7-8	1010 1111
176	B0		12-11-0-1-8	1011 0000
177	B1		12-11-0-1	1011 0001

Decimal	Hexadecimal	Graphic and control symbols	Punched card code	S/360, S/370 8-bit code
178	B2		12-11-0-2	1011 0010
179	B3		12-11-0-3	1011 0011
180	B4		12-11-0-4	1011 0100
181	B5		12-11-0-5	1011 0101
182	B6		12-11-0-6	1011 0110
183	B7		12-11-0-7	1011 0111
184	B8		12-11-0-8	1011 1000
185	B9		12-11-0-9	1011 1001
186	BA		12-11-0-2-8	1011 1010
187	BB		12-11-0-3-8	1011 1011
188	BC		12-11-0-4-8	1011 1100
189	BD		12-11-0-5-8	1011 1101
190	BE		12-11-0-6-8	1011 1110
191	BF		12-11-0-7-8	1011 1111
192	C0		12-0	1100 0000
193	C1	A	12-1	1100 0001
194	C2	B	12-2	1100 0010
195	C3	C	12-3	1100 0011
196	C4	D	12-4	1100 0100
197	C5	E	12-5	1100 0101
198	C6	F	12-6	1100 0110
199	C7	G	12-7	1100 0111
200	C8	H	12-8	1100 1000
201	C9	I	12-9	1100 1001
202	CA		12-0-2-8-9	1100 1010
203	CB		12-0-3-8-9	1100 1011
204	CC		12-0-4-8-9	1100 1100
205	CD		12-0-5-8-9	1100 1101
206	CE		12-0-6-8-9	1100 1110
207	CF		12-0-7-8-9	1100 1111
208	D0		11-0	1101 0000
209	D1	J	11-1	1101 0001
210	D2	K	11-2	1101 0010
211	D3	L	11-3	1101 0011
212	D4	M	11-4	1101 0100
213	D5	N	11-5	1101 0101
214	D6	O	11-6	1101 0110
215	D7	P	11-7	1101 0111
216	D8	Q	11-8	1101 1000

FIGURE D.4 *Continued*

Decimal	Hexadecimal	Graphic and control symbols	Punched card code	S/360, S/370 8-bit code
217	D9	R	11-9	1101 1001
218	DA		12-11-2-8-9	1101 1010
219	DB		12-11-3-8-9	1101 1011
220	DC		12-11-4-8-9	1101 1100
221	DD		12-11-5-8-9	1101 1101
222	DE		12-11-6-8-9	1101 1110
223	DF		12-11-7-8-9	1101 1111
224	E0		0-2-8	1110 0000
225	E1		11-0-1-9	1110 0001
226	E2	S	0-2	1110 0010
227	E3	T	0-3	1110 0011
228	E4	U	0-4	1110 0100
229	E5	V	0-5	1110 0101
230	E6	W	0-6	1110 0110
231	E7	X	0-7	1110 0111
232	E8	Y	0-8	1110 1000
233	E9	Z	0-9	1110 1001
234	EA		11-0-2-8-9	1110 1010
235	EB		11-0-3-8-9	1110 1011
236	EC		11-0-4-8-9	1110 1100
237	ED		11-0-5-8-9	1110 1101
238	EE		11-0-6-8-9	1110 1110
239	EF		11-0-7-8-9	1110 1111
240	F0	0	0	1111 0000
241	F1	1	1	1111 0001
242	F2	2	2	1111 0010
243	F3	3	3	1111 0011
244	F4	4	4	1111 0100
245	F5	5	5	1111 0101
246	F6	6	6	1111 0110
247	F7	7	7	1111 0111
248	F8	8	8	1111 1000
249	F9	9	9	1111 1001
250	FA		12-11-0-2-8-9	1111 1010
251	FB		12-11-0-3-8-9	1111 1011
252	FC		12-11-0-4-8-9	1111 1100
253	FD		12-11-0-5-8-9	1111 1101
254	FE		12-11-0-6-8-9	1111 1110
255	FF		12-11-0-7-8-9	1111 1111

700 PL/I Programming

The various symbols in Figure D.4 are defined as follows:

Control character representations

ACK	Acknowledge	IGS	Interchange group separator
BEL	Bell	IL	Idle
BS	Backspace	IRS	Interchange record separator
BYP	Bypass	IUS	Interchange unit separator
CAN	Cancel	LC	Lower case
CC	Cursor control	LF	Line feed
CR	Carriage return	NAK	Negative acknowledge
CU1	Customer use 1	NL	New line
CU2	Customer use 2	NUL	Null
CU3	Customer use 3	PF	Punch off
DC1	Device control 1	PN	Punch on
DC2	Device control 2	RES	Restore
DC4	Device control 4	RS	Reader stop
DEL	Delete	SI	Shift in
DLE	Data link escape	SM	Set mode
DS	Digit select	SMM	Start of manual message
EM	End of medium	SO	Shift out
ENQ	Enquiry	SOH	Start of heading
EOT	End of transmission	SOS	Start of significance
ESC	Escape	SP	Space
ETB	End of transmission block	STX	Start of text
ETX	End of text	SUB	Substitute
FF	Form feed	SYN	Synchronous idle
FS	Field separator	TM	Tape mark
HT	Horizontal tab	UC	Uppercase
IFS	Interchange file separator	VT	Vertical tab

Special graphic characters

¢	Cent sign	−	Minus sign, hyphen
.	Period, decimal point	/	Slash
<	Less Than sign	,	Comma
(	Left parenthesis	%	Percent
+	Plus sign	_	Underscore
|	Logical OR	>	Greater Than sign
&	Ampersand	?	Question mark
!	Exclamation point	:	Colon
$	Dollar sign	#	Number sign
*	Asterisk	@	At sign
)	Right parenthesis	'	Prime, apostrophe
;	Semicolon	=	Equal sign
¬	Logical NOT	"	Quotation mark

Bit

From one to eight bits require one byte of storage. A "bit" is not a data type per se. With S/360 or S/370, bit-strings are stored eight bits to a byte. For example, the bit-string 101110011 (nine bits) would require two bytes of storage:

First byte	Second byte
10111001	10000000

Notice that the bit-string is left-justified and that zeros are padded to the right of the string to fill out the second byte

appendix E

PL/C: The Cornell University Compiler for PL/I

PL/C is a compiler for PL/I that is compatible with the IBM OS F-level compiler. Programs developed and tested under PL/C may be run without change under the IBM compiler. PL/C has been designed to provide very high compilation speeds and extraordinary diagnostic assistance. Depending somewhat on the type of operating system, the type of program, and the options specified, compilation speeds four to ten times that of the IBM compiler are provided. (Compilation speed ranges from 7000 to 12,000 statements per minute on Cornell's 360/65.) The object code generated by PL/C is not optimized and contains diagnostic monitoring code, so that execution time ranges from "equal to" to several times slower than the same program under an IBM compiler. However, PL/C is a compiler, and execution does not suffer the severe penalty usually associated with interpretive execution. Both compilation and execution speed are roughly comparable to that of the best fast FORTRAN compilers, in spite of the greater complexity of the PL/I language. Efficiency is further enhanced by the ability to do internal batching, so that any number of independent source programs appear to be a single job to the operating system.

PL/C provides diagnostic assistance. Where most compilers detect errors, PL/C also attempts to repair errors. An error message is produced and PL/C displays the source statement that results from the repair. A significant fraction of trivial errors of punctuation, spelling, and syntax are correctly repaired. The repairs of substantive and semantic errors rarely reconstruct what the programmer intended, but they do prolong the life of a faulty program and greatly increase the amount of diagnostic information that can be obtained from each run. PL/C exercises a degree of control over execution usually found only in interpretive systems, but it does so without suffering the slow execution of interpretation. PL/C also includes several diagnostic statements that provide a convenient trace and dump capability, and enhance the utility of the CHECK

702

condition. Although these statements are not found in PL/I F, they can be enclosed in "PL/C pseudo-comments" so that complete compatibility with PL/I F can be preserved.

PL/C has been in classroom and production use for more than a year and has been installed at more than one hundred computing centers. These are primarily educational institutions where PL/C characteristics are particularly advantageous for large numbers of relatively short programs produced by relatively inexperienced programmers. However, several installations are in industrial centers where PL/C is used for inhouse training, open-shop programming, and production program check-out. Installation is simple and well-documented; the system is compatible with IBM PL/I, so that programmers can readily shift back and forth between PL/C and PL/I.

The PL/C project is a long-term development project of the systems programming group of the Department of Computer Science at Cornell University. Future releases will add additional language features, as well as improve performance and diagnostic assistance.

Documentation

The *PL/C User's Guide* precisely defines PL/C by direct comparison with the IBM F-level implementation of PL/I. The guide gives PL/C restrictions (relative to PL/I), error messages, and control cards and options. The guide is intended for use as a supplement to standard PL/I texts and references. A document provides installation and systems programmer instructions.

The *Technical Report* series of the Department of Computer Science includes several reports on the internal structure of the compiler. The compiler itself (written in assembly language with extensive use of special macros) is also well-documented.

Configuration and Operating System

PL/C is usually run in an automatic overlay mode. In this form, very small programs can be run in a partition of approximately 90K, but 100K is more typical and useful and will accommodate programs of 200–250 statements. PL/C uses whatever region is made available. (Many student programs of over 1000 statements in 130–150K are run at Cornell.) PL/C can be run without overlaying, but approximately 140K is required for a 200 statement program, and in a multiprogramming environment, the improvement in performance is modest.

PL/C is being run on S/360's ranging from Model 40 to Model 91. The OS version is used with MVT, MFT, and PCP, and under HASP, LASP, and CP-67. The interface with the operating system is particularly clean and localized, and PL/C has already been converted to DOS, MTS, and RAX systems for the S/360, as well as systems for RCA and ICL computers.

Further information may be obtained by contacting Professor Richard W. Conway, Department of Computer Science, Cornell University, Ithaca, N.Y. 14850. The current features implemented in PL/C at the time of publication of this book are included in the comparison charts in Appendix A.

appendix F

File Declaration Charts

In the following pages are charts taken from IBM reference manuals that may be of value to you in selecting attributes and options in the declarations of files. The information in these charts is subject to change, so the current reference manual should always be the final authority.

FILE ATTRIBUTES AND OPTIONS / TYPE OF FILE	STREAM INPUT CARD	STREAM INPUT TAPE	STREAM INPUT DASD	STREAM OUTPUT NOT PRINT CARD/PRINTER	STREAM OUTPUT NOT PRINT TAPE	STREAM OUTPUT NOT PRINT DASD	STREAM OUTPUT PRINT PRINTER	STREAM OUTPUT PRINT TAPE	STREAM OUTPUT PRINT DASD	RECORD CONSECUTIVE BUFFERED INPUT CARD	RECORD CONSECUTIVE BUFFERED INPUT TAPE FORWARDS	RECORD CONSECUTIVE BUFFERED INPUT TAPE BACKWARDS	RECORD CONSECUTIVE BUFFERED INPUT DASD	RECORD CONSECUTIVE BUFFERED OUTPUT CARD/PRINTER	RECORD CONSECUTIVE BUFFERED OUTPUT TAPE	RECORD CONSECUTIVE BUFFERED OUTPUT DASD	RECORD CONSECUTIVE BUFFERED UPD. DASD UPDATE	RECORD CONSECUTIVE UNBUFFERED TAPE INPUT/OUTPUT	RECORD CONSECUTIVE UNBUFFERED DASD INPUT/OUTPUT	RECORD CONSECUTIVE UNBUFFERED DASD UPDATE	RECORD REGIONAL (1) DASD ONLY INPUT	RECORD REGIONAL (1) DASD ONLY OUTPUT	RECORD REGIONAL (1) DASD ONLY UPDATE	RECORD REGIONAL (3) DASD ONLY INPUT	RECORD REGIONAL (3) DASD ONLY OUTPUT	RECORD REGIONAL (3) DASD ONLY UPDATE	RECORD INDEXED SEQUENTIAL DASD ONLY INPUT	RECORD INDEXED SEQUENTIAL DASD ONLY OUTPUT	RECORD INDEXED SEQUENTIAL DASD ONLY UPDATE	RECORD INDEXED DIRECT DASD ONLY INPUT	RECORD INDEXED DIRECT DASD ONLY UPDATE
filename [1–6 characters]	S	S	S	S	S	S	S	S	S	S	S	S	S	S	S	S	S	S	S	S	S	S	S	S	S	S	S	S	S	S	S
FILE	S	S	S	S	S	S	S	S	S	S	S	S	S	S	S	S	S	S	S	S	S	S	S	S	S	S	S	S	S	S	S
RECORD										S	S	S	S	S	S	S	S	S	S	S	S	S	S	S	S	S	S	S	S	S	S
STREAM	D	D	D	D	D	D	D	D	D																						
INPUT	S	S	S							S	S	S	S					E	E		S			S			S			S	
OUTPUT				S	S	S	D	D	D					S	S	S		E	E			S			S			S			
UPDATE																	S			S			S			S			S		S
SEQUENTIAL										D	D	D	D	D	D	D	D	D	D	D							D	D	D		
DIRECT																					S	S	S	S	S	S				S	S
KEYED																					S	S	S	S	S	S	S	S	S	S	S
BACKWARDS												S						O													
PRINT							S	S	S																						
BUFFERED										D	D	D	D	D	D	D	D										D	D	D		
UNBUFFERED																		S	S	S											
ENVIRONMENT (	S	S	S	S	S	S	S	S	S	S	S	S	S	S	S	S	S	S	S	S	S	S	S	S	S	S	S	S	S	S	S
MEDIUM (	S	S	S	S	S	S	S	S	S	S	S	S	S	S	S	S	S	S	S	S	S	S	S	S	S	S	S	S	S	S	S
SYSIPT,	C	C	C							C	C		C																		
SYSPCH,				C	C	C								C	C	C															
SYSLST,				C	C	C	C	C	C					C	C	C															
SYSnnn, [nnn = 000–222]	C	C	C	C	C	C	C	C	C	C	C	S	C	C	C	C	S	S	S	S	S	S	S	S	S	S	S	S	S	S	S
2501 | 2520 | 2540 | 1442)	S			C						S				C																	
1403 | 1404 | 1443 | 1445)				C			S							C																	

FIGURE F.1 File attributes and options for PL/I D and DOS PL/I optimizing compilers.

| | 2400) |
| 2311 | 2314 | 2321) |
| U (maxblocksize) |
| F (blocksize) |
| F (blocksize, recsize) |
| V (maxblocksize) |
| BUFFERS (1) |
| BUFFERS (2) |
| CTLASA | CTL 360 |
| LEAVE |
| NOLABEL |
| NOTAPEMK |
| VERIFY |
| CONSECUTIVE |
| REGIONAL (1) |
| REGIONAL (3) |
| INDEXED |
| KEYLENGTH (n) [n = 9 - 255 for REGIONAL (3)] [n = 1 - 255 for INDEXED] |
| EXTENTNUMBER (n)** |
| INDEXMULTIPLE |
| HIGHINDEX ((2311|2314)) |
| OFLTRACKS (n) [n = 0 - 8 for 2311] [n = 0 - 18 for all other DASDs] |
| KEYLOC (n) [1≤n≤recsize-keylength+1] |
| INDEXAREA (n)[n<32K] |
| ADDBUFF (n)[(64+blocksize+keylength≤n<32K] |
|) |
| EXTERNAL |

S = Attribute or option must be specified
D = Default attribute or option if not specified
O = Optional attribute or option; Specify if applicable
C = Choice must be made between these options
E = Must be specified here or in the OPEN statement (but not in both places)
B = Optional for unblocked files; The default value for blocked files is n = 1

No entry is permitted where a blank appears.
* UNBUFFERED is not permitted for files residing on a 2321 Data Cell Drive.
**For INDEXED files, EXTENTNUMBER (n) must be specified [2 ≤ n < 256].
For REGIONAL files, EXTENTNUMBER (n) is optional [0 ≤ n < 256].

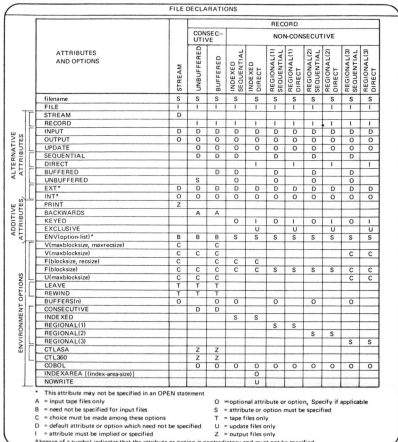

FILE DECLARATIONS											
		CONSEC-UTIVE		NON-CONSECUTIVE							
ATTRIBUTES AND OPTIONS	STREAM	UNBUFFERED	BUFFERED	INDEXED SEQUENTIAL	INDEXED DIRECT	REGIONAL(1) SEQUENTIAL	REGIONAL(1) DIRECT	REGIONAL(2) SEQUENTIAL	REGIONAL(2) DIRECT	REGIONAL(3) SEQUENTIAL	REGIONAL(3) DIRECT
filename	S	S	S	S	S	S	S	S	S	S	S
FILE	I	I	I	I	I	I	I	I	I	I	I
STREAM	D										
RECORD		I	I	I	I	I	I	I	I	I	I
INPUT	D	D	D	D	D	D	D	D	D	D	D
OUTPUT	O	O	O	O	O	O	O	O	O	O	O
UPDATE		O	O	O	O	O	O	O	O	O	O
SEQUENTIAL		D	D	D		D		D		D	
DIRECT					I		I		I		I
BUFFERED			D	D		D		D		D	
UNBUFFERED		S		O		O		O		O	
EXT*	D	D	D	D	D	D	D	D	D	D	D
INT*	O	O	O	O	O	O	O	O	O	O	O
PRINT	Z										
BACKWARDS		A	A								
KEYED				O	I	O	I	O	I	O	I
EXCLUSIVE					U		U		U		U
ENV(option-list)*	B	B	B	S	S	S	S	S	S	S	S
V(maxblocksize, maxrecsize)	C		C								
V(maxblocksize)	C	C	C							C	C
F(blocksize, recsize)	C		C	C	C						
F(blocksize)	C	C	C	C	C	S	S	S	S	C	C
U(maxblocksize)	C	C	C							C	C
LEAVE	T	T	T								
REWIND	T	T	T								
BUFFERS(n)	O		O	O		O		O		O	
CONSECUTIVE		D	D								
INDEXED				S	S						
REGIONAL(1)						S	S				
REGIONAL(2)								S	S		
REGIONAL(3)										S	S
CTLASA		Z	Z								
CTL360		Z	Z								
COBOL		O	O	O	O	O	O	O	O	O	O
INDEXAREA [(index-area-size)]					O						
NOWRITE					U						

Leftmost groupings: ALTERNATIVE ATTRIBUTES / ADDITIVE ATTRIBUTES / ENVIRONMENT OPTIONS

* This attribute may not be specified in an OPEN statement

A = input tape files only
B = need not be specified for input files
C = choice must be made among these options
D = default attribute or option which need not be specified
I = attribute must be implied or specified
Absence of a symbol indicates that the attribute or option is contradictory and must not be specified.

O = optional attribute or option, Specify if applicable
S = attribute or option must be specified
T = tape files only
U = update files only
Z = output files only

FIGURE F.2   File attributes and options for PL/I F and OS PL/I optimizing compilers.

appendix G

Glossary of PL/I Terms

Following are definitions of a number of PL/I terms as well as general terms used in data processing. The author wishes to thank IBM for permission to use the PL/I definitions as supplied by the PL/I Mission Publications group, IBM United Kingdom Laboratories Limited, Hursley Park, England. The terms marked with an asterisk are the IBM definitions. The standards bodies, ANSI and ECMA, are currently in the process of standardizing PL/I. Hence, some of the IBM definitions in this glossary are subject to change. Those terms marked with double asterisks are USASI proposed definitions.

access: to reference or retrieve data

*activate (a block): to initiate the execution of a block; a procedure block is activated when it is invoked at any of its entry points; a begin block is activated when it is encountered in normal flow of control, including a branch

*activation (of a block): (1) the process of activating a block; (2) the execu- of a block

*additive attributes: attributes for which there are no defaults and which, if required, must always be added to the list of specified attributes or be implied (i.e., they have to be added to the set of attributes, if they are required)

address: an identification for a register, location in storage, or other data source or destination; the identification may be a name, label or number

algorithm: a prescribed set of rules for the solution of a problem in a finite number of steps

aggregate: *see* data aggregate

*aggregate expression: an array expression or a structure expression

*alignment: the storing of data items in relation to certain machine-dependent boundaries

allocate: to grant a resource to, or reserve it for, a job or task; e.g., to grant main storage to a PL/I program when there is a request for the storage (usually during object program execution)

709

*allocated variables: a variable with which internal storage has been associated and not freed

*allocation: (1) the reservation of internal storage for a variable; (2) a generation of an allocated variable

*alphabetic character: any of the characters A through Z of the English alphabet and the alphabetic extenders #, $, and @ (which may have different graphic representation in different countries)

*alphameric character: an alphabetic character or a digit

*alternative attribute: an attribute that may be chosen from a group of two or more alternatives; if none is specified, a default is assumed

*ambiguous reference: a reference that is not sufficiently qualified to identify one and only one name known at the point of reference

*argument: an expression in an argument list as part of a procedure reference

*argument list: a parenthesized list of one or more arguments, separated by commas, following an entry name constant, an entry name variable, a generic name, or a built-in function name; the list is passed to the parameters of the entry point

*arithmetic constant: a fixed-point constant or a floating-point constant; although most arithmetic constants can be signed, the sign is not part of the constant

*arithmetic conversion: the transformation of a value from one arithmetic representation to another

*arithmetic data: data that has the characteristics of base, scale, mode, and precision; it includes coded arithmetic data, pictured numeric character data, and pictured numeric bit data

*arithmetic operators: either of the prefix operators + and −, or any of the following infix operators: +, −, *, /, **

*arithmetic picture data: decimal picture data or binary picture data

*array: a named, ordered collection of data elements, all of which have identical attributes; an array has dimensions specified by the dimension attribute, and its individual elements are referred to by subscripts; an array can also be an ordered collection of identical structures

*array expression: an expression whose evaluation yields an array value

*array of structures: an ordered collection of identical structures specified by giving the dimension attribute to a structure name

*assignment: the process of giving a value to a variable

*asynchronous operation: the overlap of an input/output operation with the execution of statements, or the concurrent execution of procedures using multiple flows of control for different tasks

*attribute: (1) a descriptive property associated with a name to describe a characteristic of items that the name may represent; (2) a descriptive property used to describe a characteristic of the result of evaluation of an expression

*automatic storage allocation: the allocation of storage for automatic variables

*automatic variable: a variable that is allocated automatically at the activation of a block and released automatically at the termination of that block

auxiliary (peripheral) equipment: equipment not actively involved during the processing of data, such as input/output equipment and auxiliary storage utilizing punched cards, magnetic tapes, disks, or drums

base: the number system in which an arithmetic value is represented: decimal or binary in PL/I

*base element: the name of a structure member that is not a minor structure

*base item: the automatic, controlled, or static variable or the parameter upon which a defined variable is defined. The name may be qualified and/or subscripted

*based storage allocation: the allocation of storage for based variables

*based variable: a variable whose generations are identified by locator variables; a based variable can be used to refer to values of variables of any storage class; it can also be allocated and freed explicitly by use of the ALLOCATE and FREE statements

batch processing: a system approach to processing where similar input items are grouped for processing during the same machine run

*begin block: a collection of statements headed by a BEGIN statement and ended by an END statement that is a part of a program that delimits the scope of names and that is activated by normal sequential flow of control, including any branch resulting from a GO TO statement

binary: (1) the number system based on the number 2; (2) pertaining to a choice or condition where there are two possibilities

*bit: a binary digit (0 and 1); a contraction of the term *bi*nary digi*t*

*bit-string: a string composed of zero or more bits

*bit-string operators: the logical operators ¬ (not), & (and), and | (or)

blank: a code character to denote the presence of no information rather than the absence of information

block: (1) a begin block or procedure block; (2) a physical record consisting of more than one logical record, i.e., a group of records handled as one unit

blocking: the grouping of records to form one physical record to be stored on a DASD or tape device

block length: physical record length as contrasted with logical record length *block heading statement: the PROCEDURE or BEGIN statement that heads a block of statements

Boolean algebra: an algebra named for George Boole (1815–1864); Boolean algebra is similar in form to ordinary algebra, but it deals with logical relationships rather than quantifiable relationships

*bounds: the upper and lower limits of an array dimension

branch: (1) a sequence of instructions executed as a result of a decision instruction; (2) to depart from the usual sequence of executing instructions in a computer; synonymous with jump or transfer

*buffer: intermediate storage, used in input/output operations, into which a record is read during input and from which a record is written during output

*built-in function: a function that is supplied by the language

byte: a contiguous set of eight binary digits operated upon as a unit

*call: (1) (verb) to invoke a subroutine by means of the CALL statement or CALL option; (2) (noun) such an invocation

card code: the combinations of punched holes which represent characters (letters, digits, special characters) in a punched card

card column: one of the vertical lines of punching positions on a punched card

card punch: a device to record information in cards by punching holes in the cards to represent letters, digits, and special characters

card reader: a device which senses and translates into internal form the holes in punched cards

carriage control: the process of directing the movement of paper through a line printer from a program

carriage control characters: standard characters (CTLASA or CTLASA or CTL360) used by a program to affect the movement of paper through a line printer

carriage tape: a special, 12-channel tape, usually made of Mylar ®, with punches which direct the movement of paper through a line printer

central processing unit (CPU): the unit of a computing system that contains the circuits that calculate and perform logic decisions based on a man-made program of operating instructions

character: an element of a character set

characteristic: in S/360 and S/370 data, that part of a floating-point number that contains the exponent

*character set: a defined collection of characters; See data character set and language character set

character-string: a string composed of zero or more characters from the complete set of characters whose bit configuration is recognized by the computer system in use; for S/360 and S/370 implementations, any of the 256 EBCDIC characters can be used

*character-string picture data: data described by a picture specification which must have at least one A or X picture specification character

checkout: the process of locating errors in a program by testing the program with sample data

clear: to put a storage or memory device into a state denoting zero or blank

closing (of a file): the dissociation of a file definition from a data set

COBOL: COmmon Business Oriented Language; a data processing language that resembles business English

coded arithmetic data: arithmetic data stored in a form that is acceptable, without conversion, for arithmetic calculations (i.e., FIXED BINARY, FIXED DECIMAL, FLOAT BINARY, FLOAT DECIMAL)

coding: (1) (verb) process or act of writing program statements or instructions; (2) (noun) program language statements or instructions

coding form: a preprinted page onto which program statements or instructions are written

collating sequence: the sequence in which letters, number, and special characters are ranked; the ranking of the alphameric data is taken into account when data is to be sorted

comment: an expression which explains or identifies a step in a program, but has no effect on the execution of the program; a string of characters, used for documentation, which is preceded by /* and terminated by */

*commercial character: the following picture specification characters: (1) CR (credit); (2) DB (debit); (3) T, I, and R, the overpunched-sign characters, which indicate that the associated position in the data item contains, or may contain, a digit with an overpunched sign, and that this overpunched sign is to be considered in the character-string value of the data item

comparison: the examination of the relationship between two similar items of data; usually followed by a decision

*comparison operators: infix operators used in comparison expressions; they are $\neg <$ (not less than), $<$ (less than), $< =$ (less than or equal to), $\neg =$ (not equal to), $=$ (equal to), $> =$ (greater than or equal to), $>$ (greater than), and $\neg >$ (not greater than)

compile: to convert a source-language program such as PL/I to a machine-language program

compiler: a program that translates source statements to object form

compile-time: the time during which a source program is translated into an object module; in PL/I, it is the time during which a source program can be altered (preprocessed), if desired, and then translated into an object program

compile-time statements: *see* preprocessor statement

*complex data: arithmetic data, each item of which consists of a real part and an imaginary part

*composite operators: an operator composed of two operator symbols, e.g., ¬ >

*compound statement: a statement whose statement body contains one or more other statements

*concatenation: the operation that joins two strings in the order specified, thus forming one string whose length is equal to the sum of the lengths of the two strings; it is specified by the operator ||

*condition: *see* on-condition

*condition list: a list of one or more condition prefixes

*condition name: a language keyword (or condition followed by a parenthesized programmer-defined name) that denotes an on-condition that might arise within a task

*condition prefix: a parenthesized list of one or more language condition names, prefixed to a statement; it specifies whether the named on-conditions are to be enabled

console: the unit of equipment used for communication between the operator or service engineer and the computer

*constant: an arithmetic or string data item that does not have a name and whose value cannot change; an unsubscripted label prefix or a file name or an entry name

*contained text: all text in a procedure (including nested procedures) except its entry names and condition prefixes of the PROCEDURE statement; all text in a begin block except labels and condition prefixes of the BEGIN statement that heads the block; internal blocks are contained in the external procedure

*contextual declaration: the appearance of an identifier that has not been explicitly declared, in a context that allows the association of specific attributes with the identifier

*control format item: a specification used in edit-directed transmission to specify positioning of a data item within the stream or printed page

*controlled parameter: a parameter for which the CONTROLLED attribute is specified in a DECLARE statement; it can be associated only with arguments that have the CONTROLLED attribute

controlled storage allocation: the dynamic allocation of storage for variables that have the CONTROLLED attribute

*controlled variable: a variable whose allocation and release are controlled by the ALLOCATE and FREE statements, with access to the current generation only

*control variable: a variable used to control the iterative execution of a group; see iterative DO-group

*conversion: the transformation of a value from one representation to another to conform to a given set of attributes

core storage: a form of magnetic storage that permits high-speed access to information within the computer; see magnetic core

*cross section of an array: the elements represented by the extent of at least one dimension (but not all dimensions) of an array; an asterisk in the place of a subscript in an array reference indicates the entire extent of that dimension

DASD: Direct Access Storage Device, such as a disk, drum, or data cell

*data: representation of information or of value in a form suitable for processing (also see problem data)

*data aggregate: a logical collection of two or more data items that can be referred to either collectively or individually; an array or structure

*data character set: all of those characters whose representation is recognized by the computer in use

data conversion: the process of changing data from one form of representation to another

*data-directed transmission: the type of stream-oriented transmission in which data is transmitted as a group, ended by a semicolon, where each item is of the form

name = constant

*data format item: a specification used in edit-directed transmission to describe the representation of a data item in the stream

data item: a single unit of data; it is synonomous with *element*

*data list: a parenthesized list of expressions or repetitive specifications, separated by commas, used in a stream-oriented input or output specification that represents storage locations to which data items are to be assigned during input or values which are to be obtained for output

data management: a general term that collectively describes those functions of the control program that provide access to data sets, enforce data storage conventions, and regulate the use of input/output devices

*data set: a collection of data external to the program that can be accessed by the program by reference to a single file name

*data specification: the portion of a stream-oriented data transmission statement that specifies the mode of transmission (DATA, LIST, or EDIT) and includes the data list (or lists) and, for edit-directed mode, the format list (or lists)

716   PL/I Programming

***data stream**: data being transferred from or to a data set by stream-oriented transmission, as a continuous stream of data elements in character form

***data transmission**: the transfer of data from a data set to the program, or vice versa

debug: *see* checkout

***decimal digit character**: the picture specification character 9

***decimal picture data**: arithmetic picture data specified by picture specifications containing the following types of picture specification characters: (1) decimal digit characters; (2) the virtual point picture character; (3) zero-suppression characters; (4) sign and currency symbol characters; (5) insertion characters; (6) commercial characters; (7) exponent characters

decimal point alignment: *see* point alignment

decision: the computer operation (directed by programming) of determining if a certain relationship exists between data

***declaration**: (1) the establishment of an identifier as a name and the construction of a set of attributes (partial or complete) for it; (2) a source of attributes of a particular name

***default**: the alternative attribute or option assumed, or specified for assumption by the DEFAULT statement, when none has been specified

***defined item**: a variable declared to represent part or all of the same storage as that assigned to another variable known as the base item

***delimiter**: all operators, comments, and the following characters; percent, parentheses, comma, period, semicolon, colon, assignment symbol, and blank; they define the limits of identifiers, constants, picture specifications, and keywords

descriptor: *see* parameter descriptor

device independence: the ability to request input/output operations without regard to the characteristics of the input/output devices

diagnostic routine: a programming routine designed to locate and explain errors in a computer routine or hardware components

digit: one of the characters 0 through 9

digital data: information expressed in discrete symbols

***dimensionality**: the number of bounds specifications in an array declaration

diode: an electronic device used to permit current flow in one direction and to inhibit current flow in the opposite direction

direct access: *see* random access

***disabled**: the state in which a particular on-condition will not result in an interrupt

disk storage: a storage device which uses magnetic recording on flat rotating disks

documentation: written description, program listings, flowcharts, operator's guide, explaining the way in which a computer application is solved

*DO-group: a sequence of statements headed by a DO statement and ended by its corresponding END statement, used for control purposes

DO-loop: *see* iterative DO-group

DOS: Disk Operating System

downtime: the elapsed time when a computer is not operating correctly because of machine or program malfunction

*drifting characters: *see* sign and currency symbol characters

drum storage: a method of storing information in code, magnetically, on the surface of a rotating cylinder

*dummy argument: temporary storage that is created automatically to hold the value of an argument that is (1) a constant, (2) an operational expression, (3) a variable whose attributes differ from those specified for the corresponding parameter in a known declaration, or (4) an argument enclosed in parentheses

dump: to copy the contents of all or part of a storage, usually from a central processing unit into an external storage device

dynamic storage variable: *see* automatic variable

dynamic storage: storage that is allocated during the execution of an object program

EBCDIC: Extended Binary Coded Decimal Interchange Code, an 8-bit code used to represent a maximum of 256 unique letters, numbers, or special characters

edit: to arrange information for machine input or output; may involve the deleting of unwanted data (truncation), the insertion of decimal points for printed output, or the suppression of leading zeros on printed or punched values

*edit-directed transmission: the type of stream-oriented transmission in which data appears as a continuous stream of characters and for which a format list is required to specify the editing desired for the associated data list

*element: a single item of data as opposed to a collection of data items such as an array; a scalar item

*element expression: an expression whose evaluation yields an element value

*element variable: a variable that represents an element; a scalar variable

*enabled: that state in which a particular on-condition will result in a program interrupt

718 PL/I Programming

**end-of-file mark: a code which signals that the last record of a file has been read

**end-of-tape marker: a marker on a magnetic tape used to indicate the end of the permissible recording area; for example, a photoreflective strip; a transparent section of tape, or a particular bit pattern

*entry name: an identifier that is explicitly or contextually declared to have the ENTRY attribute or has an implied ENTRY attribute

*entry point: a point in a procedure at which it may be invoked; *see* primary entry point and secondary entry point

*epilogue: those processes that occur automatically at the termination of a block

evaluation: reduction of an expression to a single value (which may be an array or structure value)

event: an activity in a program whose status and completion can be determined from an associated event variable

event variable: a variable with the EVENT attribute, which may be associated with an event; its value indicates whether the action has been completed and the status of the completion

exceptional condition: an occurrence, which can cause a program interrupt of an unexpected situation; such as, an overflow error, or an occurrence of an expected situation; such as, an end-of-file, that occurs at an unpredictable time

execute: to carry out an instruction or a program

*explicit declaration: the appearance of an identifier in a DECLARE statement, as a label prefix, or in a parameter list

exponent: (1) a number placed at the right and just above a symbol in typography to indicate the number of times that symbol is a factor; i.e., 10 to the fourth power (10^4) equals $10 \times 10 \times 10 \times 10$ or 10,000; (2) in a floating-point constant, a decimal integer constant specifying the power to which the base of the floating-point number is to be raised

*expression: a notation, within a program, that represents a value; a constant or a reference appearing alone, or combinations of constants and/or variables with operators

*extent: the range indicated by the bounds of an array dimension, the range indicated by the length of a string, or the range indicated by the size of an area

external declaration: an explicit or implicit declaration of the EXTERNAL attribute for an identifier; such an identifier is known in all other procedures for which such a declaration exists

external name: a name (with the EXTERNAL attribute) whose scope is not necessarily confined only to one block and its contained blocks

external procedure: a procedure that is not contained in any other procedure

external storage: a storage device outside the computer which can store information in a form acceptable to the computer

factoring (of attributes): enclosing of names (in a DECLARE statement) having the same attributes in parentheses; following the parenthesized list is the set of attributes that apply, in order to eliminate repeated specification of the same attributes for more than one name

*__field (in the data stream)__: that portion of the data stream whose width, in number of characters, is defined by a single data or spacing format item

*__field (of a picture specification)__: any character-string picture specification or that portion (or all) of a numeric character or numeric bit picture specification that describes a fixed-point number

*__file__: a named representation, within a program, of a data set; a file is associated with a single data set for each opening

file declaration: the association of attributes with a file name in a program

*__file attribute__: any of the attributes that describe the characteristics of a file

*__file constant__: a name declared for a file and for which a complete set of file attributes exists during the time that the file is open

file maintenance: the processing of information in a file to keep it up to date

*__file name__: a name declared for a file

fixed-point constant: *see* arithmetic constant

flip-flop: a circuit or device containing active elements capable of assuming either one of two stable states at a given time

floating-point constant: *see* arithmetic constant

flow of control: sequence of execution of PL/I blocks

flowchart: (1) system flowchart depicts flow of data from outside the computer to the computer; explains or illustrates various job steps; (2) program flowchart diagrams the sequence in which the computer is to carry out instructions

*__format item__: a specification used in edit-directed transmission to describe the representation of a data item in the stream (data format item) or to specify positioning of a data item within the stream (control format item)

*__format list__: a parenthesized list of format items required for an edit-directed data specification

FORTRAN: stands for FORmula TRANslation; a data processing language that closely resembles algebraic notation

*__fully qualified name__: a qualified name that includes all names in the hierarchical sequence above the structure member to which the name refers, as well as the name of the member itself

*__function__: a function procedure (programmer-specified or built-in); a procedure that is invoked by the appearance of one of its entry names in a function reference and which returns a value to the point of reference

*__function reference__: the appearance of an entry name or built-in function name (or an entry variable) in an expression

__generic key__: character-string that identifies a class of keys—all keys that begin with the string are members of that class; for example, the recorded keys 'ABCD,' 'ABCE,' and 'ABDF' are all members of the classes identified by the generic keys 'A' and 'AB,' and the first two are also members of the class 'ABC'; and the three recorded keys can be considered to be unique members of the classes 'ABCD,' 'ABCE,' and 'ABDF,' respectively

*__group__: a DO-group; it can be used wherever a single statement can appear, except as an on-unit

__hard copy__: a printed copy of machine output, e.g., printed reports, listings, documents, etc.

__hardware__: the physical computer equipment; such as, the card reader, console printer, and CPU; any data processing equipment

__heading__: an alphameric message that precedes an output report

__hexadecimal__: base 16 number system

__hexadecimal digits__: 0, 1, 2, 3, 4, 5, 6, 7, 8, 9, A, B, C, D, E, F

__high-level language__: a programming language that is not restricted by the computer on which it will be used; a language that is not machine-dependent and more closely resembles our own language, allowing the programmer to concentrate on how to solve a problem and not how to solve a problem within the framework of a specific computer; e.g., PL/I

__Hollerith card code__: punch card code named after its developer, Herman Hollerith

__housekeeping__: operations in a routine which do not contribute directly to the solution of a problem but do contribute directly to the execution of a program by the computer

*__identifier__: a string of alphameric and, possibly, break characters, not contained in a comment or constant and which is preceded and followed by a delimiter; the initial character must be alphabetic

__imaginary number__: a number whose factors include the square root of -1

*__implicit declaration__: the establishment of an identifier, which has no explicit or contextual declaration, as a name; a default set of attributes is assumed for the identifier

*__implicit opening__: the opening of a file as the result of an input or output statement other than the OPEN statement

__inactive block__: a procedure or begin block that has not been activated or that has been terminated

__inclusive OR__: a logical operation specified by the stroke symbol (|) in PL/I *infix operator: an operator that appears between two operands

initial value: value assigned to a variable at the time storage is allocated to it

initialize: to set program counters or program switches to a predetermined value, usually at the beginning of a program

*input/output (I/O): the transfer of data between an external medium and internal storage

*insertion picture character: a picture specification character that is, on assignment of the associated data to a character-string, inserted in the indicated position; When used in a P format item for input, an insertion character serves as a checking picture character

instruction: a statement that calls for a specific computer operation

*internal block: a block that is contained in another block

*internal name: a name that is not known outside the block in which it is declared

*internal procedure: a procedure that is contained within another block

*internal text: all of the text contained in a block except that text that is contained in another block; thus, the text of an internal block (except its entry names) is *not* internal to the containing block

*interrupt: the redirection of flow of control of the program (possibly temporary) as the result of the raising of an enabled on-condition or attention

*invocation: the activation of a procedure

*invoke: to activate a procedure at one of its entry points

*invoked procedure; a procedure that has been activated at one of its entry points

*invoking block: a block containing a statement that activates a procedure

iterate: to repeat, automatically, under program control, the same series of processing steps until a predetermined stop or branch condition is reached; to loop

*iteration factor: an expression that specifies: (1) in an INITIAL attribute specification, the number of consecutive elements of an array that are to be initialized with a given constant; (2) in a format list, the number of times a given format item or list of items is to be used in succession (*also see* repetition factor)

*iterative DO-group: a DO-group whose DO statement specifies a control variable and/or a WHILE option

job: a group of one or more tasks (subjobs) that are to be performed by the computer under the direction of the operating system

K: see kilo

*key: data that identifies a record within a direct access data set; *see* recorded key and source key

keyfield: generally, a numeric alphanumeric field within a record that makes that record unique from all other records in a given file; it is the identifying field by which a given record or records are located

keypunch: (1) (verb) to manually punch holes in cards or paper tape as contrasted with output from a computer program causing holes to be punched in cards or tape; (2) (noun) a key-driven device

*keyword: an identifier that, when used in the proper context, has either a language-defined or an implementation-defined meaning in the program

kilo (K): a prefix meaning one thousand; e.g., 16K means 16,000, although, on a binary machine it also means the power of two that is closest to 16,000; e.g., 16,384

*label: a name used to identify a statement other than a PROCEDURE or ENTRY statement; a statement label

*label constant: an unsubscripted name that appears prefixed to any statement other than a PROCEDURE or ENTRY statement

*label prefix: a label prefixed to a statement

*label variable: a variable declared with the LABEL attribute and thus able to assume as its value a label constant

*language character set: a character set which has been defined to represent program elements in the source language (in this context, character-string constants and comments are not considered as program elements)

*leading zeros: zeros that have no significance in the value of an arithmetic integer; all zeros to the left of the first significant integer digit of a number

*level number: an unsigned decimal integer constant in a DECLARE or ALLOCATE statement that specifies the position of a name in the hierarchy of a structure; it precedes the name to which it refers and is separated from that name only by one or more blanks

*level one variable: a major structure name; any unsubscripted variable not contained within a structure

library routine: a special-purpose program which may be maintained in storage for use when needed

line printer: an output unit that is capable of printing an entire line at a time, as contrasted with a typewriter that prints a character at a time

list-directed transmission: the type of stream-oriented transmission in which data in the stream appears as constants separated by blanks or commas and for which formatting is provided automatically

list items: single variable names, array names or structure names listed in a GET or PUT statement (also called *data list items*)

*locator variable: a variable whose value identifies the location in internal storage of a variable or a buffer *logical level (of a structure member): the depth indicated by a level number when all level numbers are in direct sequence, that is, when the increment between successive level numbers is one

*logical operators: the bit-string operators ¬ (not), & (and), and | (or)

loop: the repeated execution of a series of instructions for a fixed number of times or a sequence of instructions that is repeated until a terminal condition exists

*lower bound: the lower limit of an array dimension

machine instruction: an instruction that the particular computer can recognize and execute

machine language: a language that is used directly by a given computer

machine operator: the person who manually controls a computer

macro instruction: a single instruction that causes the computer to execute a predetermined sequence of machine instructions

magnetic core (main storage): a configuration of tiny doughnut-shaped magnetic elements in which information can be stored for use at extremely high speed by the central processing unit

magnetic tape: a plastic tape with a magnetic surface on which data can be stored in a code of magnetized spots

main storage: the internal storage area of the central processing unit (CPU)

*major structure: a structure whose name is declared with level number one

*major task: the task that has control at the outset of execution of a program; it exists throughout execution of the program; e.g., an OPTIONS(MAIN) procedure

mantissa: the fractional portion of a floating-point number

microsecond (μsec): a millionth of a second

millisecond (ms): a thousandth of a second

*minor structure: a structure that is contained within another structure; the name of a minor structure is declared with a level number greater than one

*mode (or arithmetic data): a characteristic of arithmetic data: real or complex

*multiple declaration: two or more declarations of the same identifier internal to the same block without different qualifications, or two or more external declarations of the same identifier with different attributes in the same program

*multiprogramming: the use of a computing system to execute more than one program concurrently, using a single processing unit

*name: an identifier appearing in a context where it is not a keyword

*nesting: the occurrence of (1) a block within another block; (2) a group within another group; (3) an IF statement in a THEN clause or an ELSE clause; (4) a function reference as an argument of a function reference; (5) a remote format item in the format list of a FORMAT statement; (6) a parameter description list in another parameter descriptor list; (7) an attribute specification within a parenthesized name list for which one or more attributes are being factored

null statement: represented by a semicolon; indicates that no action is to be taken

*null string: a string data item of zero length

number system: a system of counting; e.g., decimal (base 10) number system, hexadecimal (base 16) number system, or binary (base 2) number system

numeric character data: *see* decimal picture data

object program: the output from a compiler

*on-condition: an occurrence, within a PL/I task, that could cause a program interrupt; it may be the detection of an unexpected error or of an occurrence that is expected, but at an unpredictable time

*on-unit: the specified action to be executed upon detection of the on-condition named in the containing ON statement

*opening (of a file): the association of a file with a data set and the completion of a full set of attributes for the file name

operand: an expression to whose value an operator is applied

operating system: an organized collection of techniques and procedures combined into programs that direct a computer's operations

operation expression: an expression containing one or more operators

operator: a symbol specifying an operation to be performed; *see* arithmetic operators, bit-string operators, comparison operators, and concatenation

optimist: a programmer who codes in ink

option: a specification in a statement that may be used to influence the execution or interpretation of the statement

OR: *see* inclusive OR

output: (1) (verb) to print or punch data from a computer program or to write data onto tape or DASD; (2) (noun) results from a computer program

overflow: in PL/I, occurs when the characteristic in a floating-point value exceeds (as a result of algebraic computation) 10^{+75}

packed decimal: the S/360 and S/370 internal representation of a fixed-point decimal data item

padding: one or more characters or bits concatenated to the right of a string

to extend the string to a required length; for character-strings, padding is with blanks; for bit-strings, with zeros

*parameter: a name in a procedure that is used to refer to an argument passed to that procedure

parameter descriptor: the set of attributes specified for a single parameter in an ENTRY attribute specification

*parameter descriptor list: the list of all parameter descriptors in an ENTRY attribute specification

*partially qualified name: a qualified name that is incomplete, i.e., that includes one or more, but not all, names in the hierarchical sequence above the structure member to which the partially qualified name refers, as well as the name of the member itself

picture specification: a character-by-character description of the composition and characteristics of binary picture data, decimal picture data, and character-string picture data

*picture specification character: any of the characters that can be used in a picture specification; *see* binary picture data, character-string picture data, and decimal picture data

*point alignment: alignment of arithmetic data in a variable depending upon the location of the decimal point as specified by the precision attributes

point of invocation: the point in the invoking block at which the procedure reference to the invoked procedure appears

*pointer variable: a locator variable with the POINTER attribute, whose value identifies an absolute location in internal storage

*precision: the value range of an arithmetic variable expressed as a total number of digits and, for fixed-point variables, the number of those digits assumed to appear to the right of the decimal or binary point

prefix: a label or a parenthesized list of one or more condition names connected by a colon to the beginning of a statement

*prefix operator: an operator that precedes an operand and applies only to that operand; the prefix operators and + (plus), − (minus), and − (not)

preprocessed text: the output from the first stage of compile-time activity; this output is a sequence of characters that is altered source program text and which serves as input to the processor stage in which the actual compilation is performed

*preprocessor: a program that examines the source program for preprocessor statements which are then executed, resulting in the alteration of the source program

*preprocessor statement: a special statement appearing in the source program that specifies how the source program text is to be altered; identified by a leading percent sign and executed as it is encountered by the

preprocessor (appears without the percent sign in preprocessor procedures, which are invoked by a preprocessor function reference)

*primary entry point: the entry point identified by any of the names in the label list of the PROCEDURE statement

*problem data: string or arithmetic data that is processed by a PL/I program

*procedure: a collection of statements, headed by a PROCEDURE statement and ended by an END statement, that is a part of a program, that delimits the scope of names, and that is activated by a reference to one of its entry names

*procedure reference: an entry constant or variable or a built-in function name followed by none or more argument lists; it may appear in a CALL statement or CALL option or as a function reference

*processor: a program that prepares source program text (possibly preprocessed text) for execution

*program: a set of one or more external procedures

*program control data: data used in a PL/I program to affect the execution of the program; that is, any data that is not string or arithmetic data

programming: the art of reducing the plan for the solution of a problem to machine-sensible instructions

*prologue: the processes that occur automatically on block activation

*pseudo-variable: any of the built-in function names that can be used to specify a target variable

punched card: (1) a card punched with a pattern of holes to represent data; (2) a card as in 1, before being punched (slang)

*qualified name: a hierarchical sequence of names of structure members, connected by periods, used to identify a component of a structure; any of the names may be subscripted

quote mark: see single quote mark

random access: a technique for storing and retrieving data which does not require a strict sequential storage of the data nor a sequential search of the data nor a sequential search of an entire file to find a specific record; a record can be addressed and accessed directly at its location in the file

*range (of a default specification): a set of identifiers, constants, and/or parameter descriptors to which the attributes in a default specification of a DEFAULT statement apply

read: (1) to transcribe information from an input device to internal storage; (2) to acquire data from a source

receiving field: any field to which a value may be assigned

record: (1) a group of related facts or fields of information treated as a unit;

contains information to describe an item; (2) the unit of transmission in a record I/O operation in the internal form of a level-one variable

record I/O: the transmission of collections of data, called records, one record at a time; the external representation of the data is an exact copy of the internal representation, and vice versa; there is no arithmetic or character conversion in record I/O

*recorded key: a key recorded in a direct access volume to identify an associated data record

*recursion: the reactivation of an active procedure

*reference: the appearance of a name, except in a context that causes explicit declaration

register: a high-speed device used in a central processing unit for temporary storage of small amounts of data or intermittent results during processing

*remote format item: the letter R specified in a format list together with the label of a separate FORMAT statement

*repetition factor: a parenthesized unsigned decimal integer constant that specifies: (1) the number of occurrences of a string configuration that make up a string constant; (2) the number of occurrences of a picture specification character in a picture specification

*repetitive specification: an element of a data list (of GET or PUT statements) that specifies controlled iteration to transmit one or more data items, generally used in conjunction with arrays

*returned value: the value returned by a function procedure to the point of invocation

round: (1) to adjust the least significant digits retained in truncation to partially reflect the dropped portion (*see* truncation) (2) a built-in function in PL/I

routine: a sequence of instructions which carry out a specific processing function

run: (1) (noun) a single, continuous performance of a computer or device; (2) (verb) to execute an object program

*scalar item: a single item of data; an element

*scalar variable: a variable that can represent only a single data item; an element variable

*scale: a system of mathematical notation: fixed-point or floating-point

*scale factor: a specification of the number of fractional digits in a fixed-point number

*scope (of a condition prefix): the portion of a program throughout which a particular condition prefix applies

*scope (of a declaration): the portion of a program throughout which a particular declaration is a source of attributes for a particular name

*scope (of a name): the portion of a program throughout which the meaning of a particular name does not change

*secondary entry point: an entry point identified by any of the names in the label list of an ENTRY statement

*separator: *see* delimiter

*sign and currency symbol characters: the picture specification characters S, +, −, and $; these can be used (1) as static characters, in which case they are specified only once in a picture specification and appear in the associated data item in the position in which they have been specified; (2) as drifting characters, in which case they are specified more than once (as a string in a picture specification) but appear in the associated data item at most once, immediately to the left of the significant portion of the data item

single quote mark: alternative term for apostrophe; surrounds string data

simulate: to represent the functioning of a system or process by a symbolic (usually mathematical) analogous representation of it

software: a program or set of programs written for a computer

sort: to arrange data fields or records in either ascending or descending sequence

source document: contains original data; e.g., an employee's time card

source key: a character-string referred to in a record transmission statement that identifies a particular record within a direct access data set; the source key may or may not also contain, as its first part, a substring to be compared with, or written as, a recorded key to positively identify the record (*note:* the source key can be identical to the recorded key)

source language: a language nearest to the user's usual business or professional language which enables him to instruct a computer more easily; FORTRAN, COBOL, ALGOL, BASIC, PL/I are a few examples

source program: the program that serves as input to the compiler; the source program may contain preprocessor statements

space: (1) refers to a blank on a printed line; (2) also used to refer to "line spacing" on a printer, which is the advancement of the paper in a printer moving up one horizontal line

stacker: on a card reader, the place into which cards that have been processed are fed

*standard file: a file assumed by the processor in the absence of a FILE or STRING option in a GET or PUT statement; SYSIN is the standard input file and SYSPRINT is the standard output file

*standard system action: action specified by the language to be taken in the absence of an on-unit for an on-condition

*statement: a basic element of a PL/I program that is used to delimit a portion of the program, to describe names used in the program, or to specify action

to be taken; a statement can consist of a condition list, a label list, a statement identifier, and a statement body that is terminated by a semicolon

*__statement body__: that part of a statement that follows the statement identifier, if any, and is terminated by the semicolon; it includes the statement options

*__statement identifier__: the PL/I keyword that indicates the purpose of the statement

__statement-label constant__: *see* label constant

__statement-label variable__: *see* label variable

*__static storage allocation__: the allocation of storage for static variables

*__static variable__: a variable that is allocated before execution of the program begins and that remains allocated for the duration of execution of the program

__storage allocation__: association of a storage area with a variable

__stream__: data being transferred from or to an external medium represented as a continuous string of data items in character form

__stream-oriented I/O__: transmission of data items as a continuous stream of characters that are, on input, automatically converted to conform to the attribute of the variables to which they are assigned and, on output, are automatically converted to character representation

*__string__: a connected sequence of characters or bits that is treated as a single data item

__string operator__: the string operator is ||, denoting concatenation of character- or bit-strings

*__string variable__: a variable declared with the BIT or CHARACTER attribute, whose values can be either bit-strings or character-strings

*__structure__: a hierarchical set of names that refers to an aggregate of data items that may have different attributes

*__structure expression__: an expression whose evaluation yields a structure value

*__structure member__: any of the minor structures or elementary names in a structure

*__structure of arrays__: a structure containing arrays specified by declaring individual members' names with the dimension attribute

*__structuring__: the makeup of a structure, in terms of the number of members, the order in which they appear, their attributes, and their logical level (but not necessarily their names or declared level numbers)

*__subfield (of a picture specification)__: that portion of a picture specification field that appears before or after a V picture specification character

*__subroutine__: a procedure that is invoked by a CALL statement or CALL option; A subroutine cannot return a value to the invoking block, but it can alter the value of variables

*subscript: an element expression that specifies a position within a dimension of an array; a subscript can also be an asterisk, in which case it specifies the entire extent of the dimension

substructure: structure declared one or more levels below the major structure level

*synchronous: using a single flow of control for serial execution of a program

syntax: the rules governing sentence structure in a language or statement structure in a programming language

table: a collection of data in a form suitable for ready reference; it is frequently stored in contiguous machine locations or written in the form of an array of n dimensions

*target variable: a variable to which a value is assigned

*task: the execution of one or more procedures by a single flow of control

*termination (of a block): cessation of execution of a block, and the return of control to the activating block by means of a RETURN or END statement, or the transfer of control to the activating block or to some other active block by means of a GO TO statement

*termination (of a task): cessation of the flow of control for a task

time-share: to interleave the use of a computer to serve many problem-solvers during the same time span

truncation: the removal of one or more digits, characters, or bits from one end of an item of data when a string length or precision of a target variable has been exceeded (e.g., the reduction of precision by dropping one or several of the least significant digits in contrast to round-off; e.g., the value 3.14159265 truncated to five digits is 3.1415, whereas one may round off to five digits giving the value 3.1416)

two's complement: the way in which negative fixed-point numbers are represented in binary; to find the two's complement of a positive binary value, change all the ones to zeros and all the zeros to ones, and add one

underflow: occurs in floating-point arithmetic operations when the algebraic result would cause the exponent to be less than 10^{-78}

unformatted: no editing of data before an I/O operation is to take place

update: to modify a file record with current information according to a specified procedure

*upper bound: the upper limit of an array dimension

V: *see* virtual point picture character

*variable: a named entity that is used to refer to data and to which values can be assigned; its attributes remain constant, but it can refer to different values at different times; variables fall into three categories, applicable to any data type: element, array, and structure; variables may be subscripted and/or qualified or pointer qualified *__variable name__: an alphameric name selected by the programmer to represent data; an identifier

*__virtual point picture character__: the picture specification character V, which is used in picture specifications to indicate the position of an assumed decimal or binary point

__word__: a set of characters which has one addressable location and is treated as one unit

*__zero-suppression characters__: the picture specification characters Z, Y, and *, which are used to suppress zeros in the corresponding digit positions

Index

The "G" next to some entries indicates that the word is defined in the Glossary (Appendix G). Not all Glossary words are entered here, so you may wish to check the Glossary in addition to the Index. Some key entries that you may find particularly useful are

Attributes (keywords)
Commercial programming techniques
Debugging techniques
PL/I statements
Scientific programming techniques

Appreciation is extended to Marcia Rhoades for her capable assistance in the preparation of this index.

733

About the Author

Joan K. Hughes has ten years of data processing experience that spans three generations of computing equipment. She began her career as a programmer for the Bunker-Ramo Corporation in Woodland Hills, California. Later she became an instructor for the IBM Corporation at its Los Angeles Education Center. There she has taught PL/I extensively as well as a variety of other programming languages and computer concepts courses. She was selected by IBM to serve as one of two technical advisors for the IBM publication of a FORTRAN IV programmed instruction text. In addition, she has developed educational materials including video tapes for television that are used by IBM on a nationwide basis. Mrs. Hughes, who was graduated from the University of California, Los Angeles, with a BA degree in English, is the author of *Programming the IBM 1130*, New York: John Wiley & Sons, Inc., 1969. She and her husband, Bill, have one son and live in Van Nuys, California.